A TRAVEL GUIDE TO
JEWISH EUROPE

A TRAVEL GUIDE TO
JEWISH EUROPE
SECOND EDITION

By Ben G. Frank

PELICAN PUBLISHING COMPANY
Gretna 1999

First edition, April 1992
Second edition, January 1996
Second edition, Second printing, November 1999

Library of Congress Cataloging-in-Publication Data

Frank, Ben G.
    A travel guide to Jewish Europe / by Ben G. Frank. — 2nd ed.
      p. cm.
    Includes bibliographical references and index.
    ISBN 1-56554-037-9 (pbk.)
    1. Jews—Europe—History. 2. Kosher restaurants—Europe-
-Directories. 3. Synagogues—Europe—Directories. 4. Jews—Europe-
-Societies, etc.—Directories. 5. Europe—Guidebooks. I. Title.
DS135.E8F7 1995
940'.04924—dc20   94-34689
                                                             CIP

Maps and cover art by Joseph Honig

Information in this guidebook is based on authoritative data available at the time of printing. Prices and hours of operation of businesses are subject to change without notice. Readers are asked to take this into account when consulting this guide.

Manufactured in the United States of America

Published by Pelican Publishing Company, Inc.
1000 Burmaster Street, Gretna, Louisiana 70053

To my wife, Riva,
and my children,
Martin and Jodi
and
Monte and Leah,
for their
love and devotion

Contents

Acknowledgments   9

Introduction   13

France: The Fourth Largest Jewish Community
in the World   21

England: Cromwell, Disraeli, and the Rothschilds   117

Ireland: Dublin Has Had Jewish Mayors   151

Italy: Jews Sell Cameos in St. Peter's Square   159

Spain: Columbus, a Jew?   191

Portugal: Saying the Mourner's Prayer in Rossio Square   227

Austria: Where Jews Have Memories   241

Switzerland: Home of the First World Zionist Congress   263

Belgium: Diamonds, Rubies, and the Most Luxurious Ghetto
in the World   279

Holland: The European Jewish Grandees and
Anne Frank   295

Germany: Jews Do Live There   319

Greece: Grandeur at the Jewish Museum   357

Turkey: Jewish History from Constantinople to Istanbul   369

Scandinavia: Something for Everyone   377

The Czech Republic: The Spotlight Shines on Prague   413

Hungary: The Largest Jewish Community in
Eastern Europe   457

Slovakia: Jews Are Here to Stay   483

Poland: Someplace Along the Polish Road,
You Will Shed a Tear   497

Index   579

Acknowledgments

It is one thing to write a first travel book; it is another to write a second one in order to bring the first volume up-to-date and to add new chapters. Patience and skill are not enough. One needs the encouragement, advice, and help of friends, colleagues, and fellow writers, as well as many wonderful individuals and groups. It could not have been done without them.

My thanks go again to Doris Gold, advisor and editor; Françoise Bartlett, editorial advisor and consultant who read and edited my new chapters; my son Martin Frank, journalist, who made suggestions and edited my chapter on Poland; Joseph Honig, designer and graphic artist who designed and added maps this time around as well; Maxwell J. Lillienstein, Esq., who believed in my idea from the beginning; my brother and sister-in-law, Dr. Ivan and Malke Frank, who helped me on the chapters on Spain, Portugal, and Poland; Deborah Kahn Cunningham, a very patient word processing consultant; and, of course, Elizabeth Ackley, who word-processed my updated and new chapters.

Gathering information and historical background was obviously a task and I am forever grateful to the entire staff of the Chappaqua Library: Mark Hasskarl, director; and the reference librarians, Martha Alcott, Carolyn Jones, Paula Peyraud, Mary Platt, Carolyn Reznick, Bertha Cheatham, Susan Farber, and Linda Morgese; as well as staff members, Marilyn Coleman, Lois Siwicki, Sheila Rosenkranz, and Mary McGrath.

I also wish to thank my traveling colleagues and friends who on their return to home base briefed me with the latest tourist information: Howard Green for photos and information on

Germany; Jessica Spitalnic for information on England; Eva and Robert Fischer for my chapter on Italy; Joshua Fogelman for his help on England and Germany; Ed Robin for his knowledge of Eastern Europe; Aaron Meyer for his help on Hungary; friends Vivian and Joseph Goldreich, Sheila and Jerry Rosenkranz, Ronnie and Larry Ackman, Elysia and Stephen Wolnek, Elliott and Ruth Bier, and Haya and Sam Urman, for their help on the Czech Republic, Hungary, and other countries.

Of necessity, this travel guide, with its detailed information, could not have been written without the expertise and professionalism of the tourist office and airlines of France, Great Britain, Ireland, Germany, Holland, Belgium, Switzerland, Portugal, Spain, Greece, and Turkey, as well as Italy, Norway, Denmark, Sweden, the Czech Republic, Slovakia, Hungary, and Poland.

I especially want to cite for their cooperation the French Government Tourist Office, George Hern, public relations director; and Jackie Schaff and Marian Fourestier. Special thanks also go to Air France; Bruce C. Haxthausen, media relations manager, Corporate Communications, USA; Rosario Mariani, a manager for Alitalia Airlines; Allen Stolz, chief executive officer of Jet Vacations; Hedy Wuerz, director of public relations for the German National Tourist Office; Dagobert Scher, executive vice-president of marketing, and Bonnie Bancroft, of Rail Europe; Erika Lieben, manager, public relations, and Evelyne Mock of the Swiss National Tourist Office; Gerhard F. M. Markus, director of communications, and Gabriele Wolf, of the Austrian National Tourist Office; Vladimir Hulpach of CEDOK, Central Europe travel service; Miroslav Ehl, general manager, North America, of Czech Airlines, CSA; and Rina Allalouf of Czech Airlines, CSA; Peter Gomori of Ibusz Hungarian Travel; Stefan Adamec, Slovakia Travel Service and representative of SATUR; and Joram Kagan, director, special projects, LOT Polish Airlines.

Many Jewish community leaders in Europe were very helpful and sent me information, but deep gratitude goes to my friend, Leon Masliah, executive director of the Consistoire Central in

Paris, and Tomas Kraus, executive director of the Federation of Jewish Communities in the Czech Republic; L. Orlikova and Susan Pultrova of the Federation of Jewish Communities in the Czech Republic; Dr. Leon Zelman of Vienna; and to three wonderful Jewish leaders in Bratislava: university professor Dr. Pavel Traubner, M.D., Ph.D.; assistant professor Juraj Stern, Ph.D., and Tomas Stern; Ms. Maya Ehrenberg of the Consistoire in Brussels; Dr. Peter Schiffer and Ms. Judith Poray, both of Budapest; as well as Dr. Frank Reiss, consultant, of New York, for his help on the Czech Republic and Slovakia; Rabbi Andor Weiss, executive director of The Emanuel Foundation of New York and Budapest, who helped me understand the Jewish community of Hungary.

In Poland, I must thank the following, all of whom helped me chart "unknown waters": Rabbi Haskel Besser, chairman for Poland of the Ronald S. Lauder Foundation; Basia Jakubowska, assistant to Rabbi Besser; Rabbi Michael Schudrich, director of the Ronald S. Lauder Foundation in Poland; Yale J. Reisner, director of Research and Archives of the Ronald S. Lauder Foundation in Warsaw; Grazyna S. Pawlak, Ph.D., executive director of the Jewish Historical Institute of Poland; Henryk Halkowski, historian, writer, guide, and community leader in Cracow; Joachim S. Russek, director of the Jagiellonian University Research Center on Jewish History and Culture in Poland and the Center for Jewish Culture in Kazimierz, Cracow; Stanislaw Krajewski, Jewish community leader in Warsaw; and Dr. Yehuda Nir, author, lecturer, and professor.

I can only hope that I am not omitting any name. If I am, I apologize. I am especially indebted to the unnamed helpful residents of many countries who pointed me in the right direction.

I offer praise and appreciation to Dr. Milburn Calhoun, publisher and president of Pelican Publishing Company, and the entire staff at Pelican who immediately saw the need for this travel book as well as a second edition. I owe a special debt of gratitude to my editors at Pelican, Nina Kooij, who realized the demanding pressure on an author once again to meet deadlines, and who helped make this edition the book that it is, and Christine L. Benson, for her constant interest and hard work in editing the updated and new chapters.

My deepest thanks, of course, go to my family—to my wife, Riva, for her understanding, her help, her faith in me, and her patience; to our children, Martin and Jodi and Monte and Leah, for their support and encouragement; to my wife's parents, the late Rabbi Solomon and Jeanette Spitz, survivors of the Holocaust, who inspired me to learn more and to keep alive the traditions of the Jewish people; and my mother, Sonya, and my late father, Nathan M. Frank, who gave me the inner strength to keep at it and who taught me to believe that "the journey is the reward."

Introduction

This is a unique travel guide. It is a practical, anecdotal, and adventurous journey through historic Jewish Europe, including kosher restaurants, cafes, synagogues, and museums, plus cultural and heritage sites.

The reader will visit more than fifty cities: including some of the most fascinating capitals on the European continent: Paris, London, Madrid, and Lisbon. He or she will saunter along the "Italian honeymoon trail" of Venice, Florence, and Rome. The traveler who peruses this guide will inhale the fresh air of Central Europe's "Golden Triangle": Prague, Budapest, and Vienna.

The tourist can also use it as a full resource to search for his or her roots in the rich past that was Polish Jewry, as well as for those who stand silently in the death camps and recall loved ones and those who perished in the Holocaust. With this volume, the traveler can join in an activity of the struggling but still amazingly alive Polish Jewish community in Warsaw, Cracow, and Lublin. It is all here!

This is also a second sojourn to Jewish Europe. This writer still identifies himself as Benjamin of New York, who like his twelfth-century namesake, Benjamin of Tudela, travels the Jewish world in Europe, Asia, and Africa and writes chronicles about Jews. Like Benjamin of Tudela, this author records the Jewish population, describes the people, tells their history, comments on their rulers, and defines the Jewish community structure.

Since 1960, the cities of Europe have served as my grazing grounds, so to speak, much of that time, west of the old "Iron Curtain." Indeed, the first edition of *A Travel Guide to Jewish Europe* did not fully discuss the Jewish sites or institutions of

Eastern Europe that after World War II struggled to survive "forty years of Communist darkness."

But in 1989, communism crumbled. The Cold War ended. New destinations beckoned. The traveler, tourist, and business person refocused and came up with a new mind-set that propelled them to push away the past anxiety and fear of visiting a Communist country and to return to nations breathing freedom for the first time in four decades.

This author, too, followed the "yellow brick road" to such "refreshed" cities as Prague, Budapest, Bratislava, Warsaw, Cracow, and East Berlin. The result is this second edition of *A Travel Guide to Jewish Europe.*

Prague is in. Budapest is in. Cracow is in. When I visited these cities, I carried on my tradition of seeing not only places of interest but also visiting with Jews, learning how they live or exchange ideas, and attending Sabbath services, bar mitzvahs, and social functions.

Now besides having danced at parties in Marseilles, dined with Rothschilds in Paris, had lunch with the Abouaziz family in Cannes, chatted with Israelis in Rome, or met Jews in Granada, I have spent a Sabbath afternoon around a table with the Jews of Prague. We shared food at a *shalosh s'udot,* (a gathering to share the third meal of the Sabbath). As we studied and talked, the Sabbath drew to a close and we sang *zmiros* (Sabbath songs). Then we recited the evening prayers—all this in the oldest standing synagogue in Europe, the Altneuschul, where you can almost feel the spirit of the famous Rabbi Judah Loew ben Bezalel, known as the *Maharal* (the Hebrew acronym for "most venerated teacher and rabbi"), and the *golem,* a robot figure serving the rabbi for his good works.

Near the Ukrainian-Slovak border, I talked with American Jewish builders and developers and who were helping the new nation of Slovakia. I visited the concentration camp at Terezin in the Czech Republic and said, *"zachor"* ("remember") and "never again." I listened to hypnotic gypsy music in Budapest, "the queen of the Danube." I strolled the streets of Bratislava, where once Yeshiva students walked in the shadow of buildings that housed the greatest Talmudic schools of learning in

Europe. I walked the streets of the Warsaw Ghetto, shed a tear in Auschwitz, and sang Hebrew songs with young Polish Jews in Kazimierz, the still-preserved old Jewish town section of Cracow.

Major differences in culture, history, religion, customs, and tradition, of course, mark Eastern Europe from Western Europe. Every state sports a different shape today than it did seventy-five years ago. The complexities of Eastern Europe, the suspicions, the mistrust, the hatreds are still there. And Eastern Europe, including Russia, certainly bore the greatest burden of World War II. Whereas in France there are 700,000 Jews and England has 300,000 Jews, the Czech Republic has only 13,000 Jews. And Hungary, the largest Jewish community in Eastern Europe, counts 80,000 to 100,000 Jewish citizens. Poland, once the second largest Jewish community in the Diaspora, with about 3.5 million Jews, now contains perhaps 5,000 to 6,000 Jews. Yet Jewish leaders say there could be additional thousands of Jews and that many now openly declare, "We are Jews." While anti-Semitism exists throughout the world, it is amazing that anti-Semitism flourishes in Eastern Europe, which contains very few Jews. I label it "anti-Semitism without Jews."

In Western Europe, the Jewish community is struggling with assimilation. In Eastern Europe, the Jewish community is being revived. It is seeking to educate, locate, and greet Jews who voluntarily or involuntarily have hidden and may even still hide their Jewishness. These Jewish communities are doing this with one hand while with the other hand they are attempting to survive in hard-pressed economies changing over from government management to free-market economies. Still, despite all, we now see rapidly growing, stronger, and new Jewish communities in Central and Eastern Europe. Moreover, American Jews want to meet their co-religionists. I have discovered that American Jews today not only want to travel to Eastern Europe, to find their roots, but they want to do it with their parents and grandparents or their sons and daughters. This guide to Jewish Europe will help them.

While this is a travel book, it is more than that. I have attempted to answer some of the questions that will enable us to learn how a people, forced to disperse throughout the world almost two thousand years ago, continue to share a sense of identity.

This volume is an attempt to provide some of the information necessary to answer these questions. It contains my experiences and observations as a Jewish journalist who has traveled to Jewish communities in Europe. It explores the customs, mores, and politics of Jews in societies as diverse as Dusseldorf, Madrid, Budapest, Prague, Warsaw, Lublin, Cracow, and Istanbul.

Each chapter contains a description of Jews within a specific society and institutions, customs, places of interest—even restaurants within the Jewish community. Each chapter explores the relationships among Jews and between Jews and non-Jews. Cited, too, are Jewish contributions to the countries of their origin.

Travel stimulates the mind and the love of travel is inherent in the Jewish consciousness. Jews have been traveling for centuries. Obviously, expulsion has a lot to do with it. Some of the journeys were extremely unpleasant, to say the least: wandering through the desert to the Promised Land, the brutal and oppressive expulsions, the flight from the Spanish and Portuguese inquisitions, the pogroms, fleeing from Nazi terror, and running the British naval blockade to reach the shores of Palestine. All this bitter uprooting taught the Jews how to move about, and quickly; how to seek a comfortable and tranquil home; how to long for the Holy Land and finally regain it as a nation of their own. *A Travel Guide to Jewish Europe* will help you understand the significance of those events as they relate to the present and soon-to-be twenty-first century.

On May 14, 1948, when the State of Israel was established, the pace of Jewish travel was increased. Only this time, they were driven to see the new nation.

On their way to and from Israel, Jews and non-Jews would stop off in other lands. I discovered an interesting phenomenon. People who rarely would visit a synagogue or church in their own town or city, now not only toured shrines throughout Europe, but prayed in the houses of worship of their religion.

Moreover, those of the Jewish faith, who back home might not even keep Jewish traditional dietary laws, would hasten to unearth a kosher restaurant in Paris, London, or Nice, and upon their return to America, would immediately tell their friends of the tasty and spicy pastrami sandwiches they devoured near the Champs-Elysées or dumplings in the kosher restaurant in Prague.

I recall observing American businessmen who for a whole week savored the best "Michelin Guide" cuisine, but who one night stole away to Goldenberg's kosher-style restaurant in the Jewish section of Paris. They would go there even after the establishment was shot up by terrorists: it was "an act of faith" to stop at Goldenberg's.

Besides insights into Jewish life, I provide lists of synagogues, kosher restaurants, hotels, and Jewish sites, along with travel descriptions of the wonderful cities I have visited today.

It is now a half-century since the end of a war in which evil came close to winning. Jews and humanity have yet to recover fully from that conflagration and the Holocaust.

But this book dispels the myth that after World War II, Jewish life ceased to exist on the Continent. Today, there are thriving Jewish communities throughout Europe. In fact, France contains the fourth largest Jewish community in the world and the third largest outside of Israel; and with Russian Jewry emigrating in such large numbers, France someday may be designated the second largest Jewish community outside of Israel.

Europe has taken giants steps and slowly moves to greater integration as embodied in the 1991 Maastrict Treaty. It is more united and strong. More countries are joining the European Union. Even the future membership of Poland, Hungary, Slovakia, and the Czech Republic into that Union and NATO is being discussed.

So join me on a second trip in this second edition of *A Travel Guide to Jewish Europe*. Jewish and non-Jewish travelers will find the basic ingredients of a travel guide in this book. It will also help the business person plan his or her journey.

Yet, as noted, this volume differs from other texts. I believe you, the traveler, want to know something about the background and history of what you are about to see. "You cannot tell the players without a scorecard," as they say, and you cannot truly appreciate a site without fully knowing its origin.

So let us fly away and visit Prague, now called "the left bank of the 1990s." Or let us take a trip to Budapest, often called "Europe's most seductive capital." Neither city has reason to feel inferior to any other. We can still stop and stroll along the rue de la Paix of Paris, or the Bahnhofstrasse in Zurich, or Regent Street in London.

Yes, let us begin our new journey. As the Chinese say, the journey of a 1,000 li begins with the first step.

A TRAVEL GUIDE TO
JEWISH EUROPE

FRANCE

Rouen • Reims •
☆ PARIS
Strasbourg •

Rennes •

Angers • Dijon •

FRANCE

Lyon •

Bordeaux •

Avignon • Monte Carlo
Nice •
Cannes •
Marseilles •

France

The Fourth Largest Jewish Community in the World

France is the home of the largest Jewish community in Europe, the third largest in the Diaspora, and the fourth largest in the world.

France is the home of 700,000 Jews, more than 300 Jewish organizations and associations, several hundred synagogues, about 30 day schools, 180 Talmud Torahs (Jewish schools), many kosher butcher shops, as well as B'nai B'rith lodges, a Jewish art museum, and a Jewish library of more than 160,000 volumes.

France is the home of families whose names are Rothschild, Abitbol, Cohen, Goldenberg, and Kahn.

France is the home of Jewish men and women who have contributed much to art, literature, music, science, and government.

France today is the home of 300,000 Jews from North Africa, who, in the 1960s, settled in towns and villages where at the time there were no Jews.

France, which has a diverse Jewish population, is one of the few countries outside of Israel where Sephardic Jews now outnumber the Ashkenazic.

("Sepharad" is the Hebrew word for Spain. Sephardim are those Jews who trace their origins to Spain or Portugal before the 1492 expulsion, and include Jews from the Mediterranean basin who share a common cultural legacy, as well as those Jews who follow the traditions, customs, rituals, and culture of the Jews of Spain and Portugal.)

Ashkenazic Jews are those whose religious rites and customs
stem from Germany and Eastern Europe and whose household
language at home was Yiddish.)

A Brief History

Jewish history in France probably begins with the Roman
period after the conquest of Jerusalem, and certainly by the
fourth century, when Jews pitched their tents along the great
trade routes. Jews migrated to the French Mediterranean
coast, in and around Marseilles. Soon they settled in the south
of Gaul, near Bordeaux and Avignon.

By the fourth and fifth centuries, Jews lived in Metz, Poitiers,
Avignon, Arles, Brittany, Clermont-Ferrand, and Narbonne. By
524, they settled in Valence. A synagogue was founded in Paris
in 582. Jews served as merchants, physicians, and sailors.
Although restricted by Christianity, they lived comfortably.
They fared well under Charlemagne and his successors in the
eighth and ninth centuries.

The days of the intellectual glory of French Jewry did not
occur until the eleventh and twelfth centuries. This Golden
Age of French Jewry was sparked by such luminaries as
Rabbenu Gershom, the Light of Exile (960–1030), and Rashi
(1040–1105), the great commentator on the Bible who lit up
the sky of Jewish religious thought. By the mid-eleventh century, Joseph B. Samuel Bonfils taught in Limoges, and Moses
haDarshan in Narbonne.

The first significant act of anti-Semitism in the form of a
blood libel charge occurred in 1171 in the Loire town of Blois.
Thirty-two Jews were burned at the stake. A similar event had
already taken place in Norwich, England, in 1144.

Many times since, the Jews of France and Europe were to
suffer from the false charge of murdering Christians and
draining their blood for Passover. Thus began a period of
expulsions and murder. In 1182, King Philip Augustus
expelled the Jews—only to recall them sixteen years later.

In the next century, severe anti-Jewish persecutions erupted. In 1242, at the instigation of the Catholic church, copies of the Talmud were seized from French Jewish homes, libraries, and synagogues and hurled into town squares where they were burned.

On July 22, 1306, Philip IV, known as the "Fair," seized Jewish property and banished the Jews from France. More than 100,000 Jews fled. They found refuge in Belgium, Italy, and Spain. Several decades later those Jews who had remained in France would again be victimized. Now they would be charged with poisoning the wells during the Black Plague.

The great creativity of medieval French Jewry soon ended, even though they were readmitted to France in 1315. We know that Jewish communities thrived in Bayonne, Bordeaux, Toulouse, Marseilles, Limoges, Poitiers, Nantes, Angers, Dijon, Le Havre, Rouen, Verdun, Valence, and, of course, in Alsace and Lorraine in such cities as Mulhouse, Colmar, and Strasbourg. While some were purveyors to the Imperial Court, most were engaged in finance.

In 1394, Charles VI expelled the Jews once again. For two hundred years, only a handful of Jews remained on French soil—in Alsace-Lorraine and Avignon, the latter called the "Pope's Jews" because they were protected by the pope. Much has been written about these Jews of Avignon who, with their brothers and sisters of Carpentras, Cavaillon, and L'Isle-sur-la-Sorges, comprised the four communities of the Comtat Venaissin (lands of the pope). Here Jews established centers and historical sites, one of which is the Synagogue in the Round in Avignon. Large concentrations of Jews had settled there in the fifth and sixth centuries.

After 1394, Jews in France did not practice their religion openly. Yet, following the Spanish Inquisition and expulsion in 1492, Marranos (secret Jews) began to arrive in the southwest corner of the country. Called members of the "Portuguese Nation" or "Portuguese merchants," they crossed the border near the Pyrenees. It was safer to be Portuguese than to be known as a Jew. Starting in 1550, under the guise of being "New Christians," these Marranos were granted letters of protection by Henry II, who permitted them to live in France wherever they desired. Other Marranos and Jews settled in Bayonne and Bordeaux and in numerous small cities in this Atlantic-coast corner of France. Some went north to La Rochelle, Nantes, and Rouen.

The 1648 Chmielnicki massacres in the Ukraine caused Jews to flee to France from Poland and Russia and to settle in Alsace-Lorraine. By 1657, there were 96 Jewish families in Metz. After the Treaty of Westphalia in 1648, Jews were allowed to remain in Lorraine. For the first time since 1394, Jews were legally permitted to live in France.

Later Cardinal Richelieu invited Marranos to settle in French port cities for the purpose of expanding French overseas trade.

By the close of the seventeenth century, Jews were welcome in France because of the policies of Jean-Baptiste Colbert, finance minister to Louis XIV. Colbert believed in mercantilism, that the purpose of the state was to increase its wealth. Colbert figured Jews would bring business skills to France. This they certainly did, including chocolate making in Bayonne. They enhanced shipping and trading in the port of Bordeaux.

By the beginning of the eighteenth century, Jews began to return to Paris. They were peddlers who sold secondhand clothes and rags. Because of occupational restrictions, Jews were forced to become moneylenders, military purveyors, and petty traders.

Two groups existed side by side in France: Sephardic Jews in Bordeaux, Avignon, and Comtat Venaissin, and Ashkenazim in Alsace-Lorraine and other provinces.

In 1732, Sephardic Jews were formally recognized by royal decrees and permitted to practice Judaism. In 1787, on the eve of the French Revolution, 40,000 Jews lived in France, 20 times more than in the fledgling Jewish community in that new land across the ocean, the United States.

Notable French Jews

By the end of the nineteenth century, the Jewish population increased to 90,000, of which 50,000 lived in Paris, the center of European capitalism. It was then that Jews achieved fame in

France, which until World War I was certainly the cultural center of the world. Before World War I, Jewish painters and sculptors helped make the so-called "Paris School" famous: Pissarro, Soutine, Pascin, Modigliani, Chagall, Mane Katz, as well as Benn. (They also used Jewish subjects in their works.)

The names of Jacques Offenbach, Claude Kahn, Darius Milhaud, Paul Dukas—all Jews—are well known in French music; and Jews in French literature are legion both past and contemporary.

France boasts two Jewish Nobel laureates, Henri Bergson in literature and Rene Cassin, winner of the World Peace Prize in 1968. Writers include Marcel Proust, Andre Maurois, Edmond Fleg, Eugene Ionesco, Armand Lurel, Albert Memmi, Clara Malraux, and Joseph Kessel of the Académie Française. Goncourt Prize winners include Roger Ikor, Romain Gary, Andre Schwarz-Bart, and Anna Longfus. Philosophers and writers Bernard-Henri Levy, Alain Finkelkraut, Victor Malka, Roland Goetschel, and novelists Andre Schwarz-Bart and Marek Halter have achieved world acclaim. The writer Elie Wiesel, who received the Nobel Peace Prize in 1986, is well known in France. He lived there after his release from the Nazi death camps and wrote distinguished literary works in French.

Jews in academic life include Raymond Aron, Robert Aron, George Steiner, Claude Levi-Strauss, Georges Friedman, and Bernhard Blumenkranz.

French Jews have starred in the theater, film, and television: Rachel, Sarah Bernhardt, Jules Dassin, Simone Signoret, Marcel Marceau, Anouk Aimee, Jean-Pierre Aumont, Claude Lelouch, Claude Berri, Regine, and Claude Lanzmann. The latter won a "Cesar," France's equivalent of the Oscar, for his epic *Shoah,* the film on the Holocaust.

French Jews who excelled in science include: Henri Moissan, Andre Lwoff, Gabriel Lippman, François Jacob (all Nobel Prize winners from France), Henri-Marc Baruk, Bernard Halpern, and Eugene Minkoski.

In industry, Max Hymans and Bernard Attali each served as the director general of Air France. Andre Citroen founded the famous French automobile company.

The Concorde of Air France. (Photo courtesy Air France)

Finally, Jews played a role in government and politics. Leon Blum, Rene Mayer, and Pierre Mendes-France were prime ministers. Daniel Mayer, Jules Moch, Pierre Masse, Georges Mandel, Jean Pierre-Bloch, Simone Veil, Lionel Stoleru, and former Minister of Justice Robert Badinter, who now serves as president of the Constitutional Council, all achieved prominence in government. Jack Lang, a minister of culture, is Jewish. Laurent Fabius, who served as prime minister in the 1980s, was a member of an old French Jewish family that converted to Catholicism after World War II. His wife, the former Françoise Castro, is Jewish and Jewish community sources, according to the Jewish Telegraphic Agency, stated that their children "are Jewish according to any halachic interpretation." Isaac-Adolphe Cremieux was a foreign minister. He gave French citizenship to Algerian Jews. Nearly a hundred years later, his act enabled the Jews of Algeria to leave and resettle in France as full citizens of the Republic.

Jewish Life in Twentieth-Century France

Apart from a few wealthy capitalists, the great majority of French Jews were middle class—peddlers, merchants, craftsmen, painters, hat makers, tailors, and shoemakers.

By 1914, the Jewish population of France included 20,000 Eastern European Jews. Their brothers and sisters migrated to Paris during the upheaval caused by the Russian Revolution. In 1935, 260,000 Jews lived in France.

Between World War I and World War II, Eastern European Jews continued to flee to France, which had become a land of refuge. By 1939, there were about 300,000 Jews in France, half of whom were not French citizens.

In the late 1930s, as in all of Europe, a wave of anti-Semitism enveloped France. It culminated in the capitulation of the Vichy French government and its subsequent Vichy collaboration with the Nazis. Despite the roundups and the terror, more than two-thirds of the estimated 350,000 Jews who were living in France in 1940 were saved. After the war, Jews from Eastern Europe flocked to France, many on their way to the future

Jewish state in Palestine. For a decade, the old-time French Jewish community was weak. On the one hand it tried to aid the Jewish displaced persons and on the other it sought to revitalize itself. Only the arrival of the Sephardim from North Africa actually rejuvenated the community, and in France today, Jews are vocal and visible.

The one "burning issue" uniting all French Jews is the survival of the State of Israel and the activism that is needed to ensure that survival. This ideal and goal has been enhanced by the influx of North African Jews.

In the 1970s, activism on behalf of Israel found its expression in *Renouveau Juif,* Jewish Renewal. This group galvanized the community and encouraged Jews to be more vociferous in espousing the cause of Israel and the Jewish people. They felt that, to reach French public opinion, they had to hold rallies and demonstrations against the policy of the French government toward Israel, a policy that from time to time has tilted towards the Arabs.

The Jews from Algeria, Morocco, and Tunisia were also more observant than their Ashkenazic co-religionists.

Major publishing houses began printing well-known Jewish authors, Hebrew classics, and contemporary books on French history, theology, Israel, and Jewish tradition.

At the universities, Hebrew studies programs leading to advanced degrees have been established. The purpose of "Jewish Renewal" was "to create a sense of renewal in the Jewish community, to unify the community through political activism and to integrate French Jews into Jewish life."

Enrollment in Jewish schools today is higher than ever, consisting of 10 percent of school-age children. About 16,000 students are enrolled full-time in France's more than 30 Jewish schools. An equal number attend Sunday School. The new economic prosperity of the Sephardim fuels a revival of religious education. They realize that only Jewish education can save them from rampant assimilation.

Jews around France can tune into any of 13 radio stations playing Hebrew and Yiddish songs and broadcasting cultural programs and news commentaries. The three Paris stations alone claim a daily audience of 37,000 Jews. *Judeotel,* a video magazine, has introduced programs that consist of Jewish news and culture and is sent via computer over sophisticated telephone lines.

Jewish publications have more readers than ever. Numerous weeklies are distributed free of charge in Jewish Centers and shops. The monthly *L'Arche,* aimed at France's educated middle class, reaches about 10,000 subscribers. Every year, an international festival of Jewish films is held.

Many Jews, including Michel Boujenah, a Jewish actor of Tunisian origin, are involved in the film industry. In June of each year a Yiddish festival takes place.

There has been a "continued blossoming of Jewish culture by the French public." Nelly Hansson noted in the 1988 edition of the *American Jewish Yearbook* that "even as many Jews were becoming personally de-Judaized, French society was becoming culturally Judaized."

The French rightist politician LePen and his brand of anti-Semitism probably do not constitute a crisis for French Jews today, though these extremists are always a danger if there is no "eternal vigilance." By the mid-1990s, LePen's appeal seems to be waning in "multicultural" France. Today's Jewish problems consist of assimilation and mixed marriages.

France is changing. With the new united Europe, the French are accepting minorities and are less nationalistic, it is said. But Marek Halter was probably right when he said, "Jews never lived so freely as they do today in France," and they stand by Israel. In 1991, during the Gulf War, when the Jewish State was being bombarded by SCUD missiles, about 1,500 French Jewish men, women, and children, in a show of solidarity, visited Israel. They were the largest solidarity group to arrive from the Diaspora. Also, once every two years, more than 40,000 Jews gather at Le Bourget Airport for a "Yom Ha-Torah," a day of Torah study.

Jewish Paris

For nearly everyone, there is the Paris of art, culture, and romance, the banks of the River Seine, the galleries, the

The Eiffel Tower. (Photo courtesy French Government Tourist Office)

museums, the cathedrals, the Champs-Elysées, the Eiffel Tower, the parks, the superb restaurants, and thousands of sidewalk cafes and bistros. To arrive in the City of Light for the first time or the tenth time is to be "touched by beauty." As William L. Shirer said, Paris is "as near to paradise on this earth as any man could ever get." The writer John Galsworthy said, "Paris pets the senses." Observe the cafes; sail on the Bateau Mouche; walk along the boulevard St-Michel; inhale the "Paris of the common man, the Paris born of the French Revolution."

For Jews, there is another Paris. It can be found on the Left Bank and on the Right Bank, on the avenue de Wagram, in the student quarter on the boulevard St-Michel, in the rue Richer and the rue des Rosiers.

Before there was France, even before there were a people called the French, there was Paris. And Jews have lived in Paris since the year 582.

The capital of France is the center of French Jewish activities. Half of the 700,000 French Jews live in and around Paris. You meet them everywhere: on the Champs-Elysées, in the fashionable sixteenth Arrondissement, in the attractive suburb of Neuilly, in the elite shops of the exquisite rue Faubourg de St-Honore, in the restaurants on the rue Richer, on the "bateaux mouches" that cruise up and down the Seine River, and in the immaculate and superb gardens and parks of this beautiful metropolis. Indeed, Jewish travelers to Paris are increasing five to ten percent each year.

Jewish Paris is alive and full of contrasts. One can see a Chassidic Jew on a bicycle delivering kosher take-out Chinese food.

In the elegant Place des Vosges, probably the most beautiful square in Europe, just outside the Temple des Vosges at No. 14, I saw a bride and groom leave the synagogue after a Jewish wedding where the *shamash* was dressed in the "bicorne" (cocked hat of the Napoleonic era), knee-length black coats, and silver chains of office.

JEWISH SITES IN PARIS

Visit the **"Pletzel."** This neighborhood, this still visible center of Jewish life in Paris, is located in the Marais/St. Paul section of the city.

As you walk through the maze of those tight alleys and winding streets with walls of quaint old buildings forming odd angles at the narrow streets below, you quickly sense that you are taking a sentimental journey. Depending on the world situation, you can always spot the Jewish synagogue, center, or museum from several blocks away, simply because there are armed security forces standing in front of these institutions. Fear, however, does not appear to linger in the air in the Pletzel. People bustle about this old-world neighborhood, which has and always will exude a Jewish atmosphere. Some head home; some saunter along with their children. Some fathers hold the hands of their tots; some children play tag in the streets. Some do last-minute shopping; some take home the long, fresh hot French bread from the kosher bakery. Some pick up a Hebrew or Yiddish paper.

Usually when I go to these old neighborhoods, it is just as if I am meandering along the Lower East Side of New York. I romanticize: "This is the way it must have been 75 years ago when the Jews started settling here in large numbers—bearded Orthodox men with long black coats and fur *shtreimels,* all engaged in deep conversation."

To this day in the Pletzel, on the rue des Rosiers, rue des Hospitalieres-St-Gervais, rue des Ecouffes (meaning pawnbrokers), rue Ferdinand Duval, rue Geoffroy l'Asnier, and rue Vieille du Temple, you will find a Jewish atmosphere of small synagogues, shops, apartments, restaurants, delicatessens, and monuments; in short, the old neighborhood. To start, here are some art and book stores in the Pletzel:

Bibliophane, 26, rue des Rosiers, 75004, Paris. Tel: 48-87-82-20.
Diasporama, 20, rue des Rosiers, 75004, Paris. Tel: 42-78-30-50. FAX: 42-74-38-76. Open Sunday to Friday, 10-7:30, except

Photo courtesy French Government Tourist Office

Kosher restaurants along the rue Richer. (Photo courtesy French Government Tourist Office)

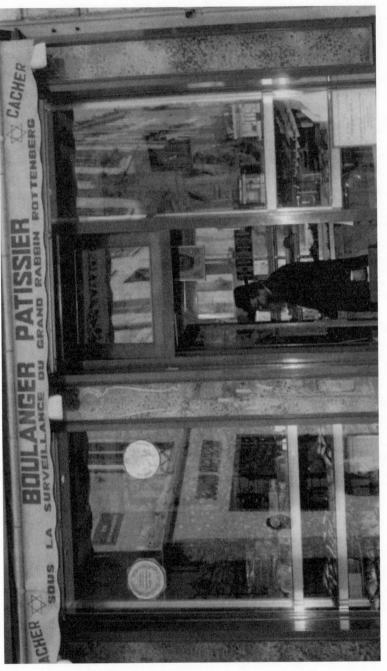

A Jewish bakery in Paris. (Photo by Gerard Halary)

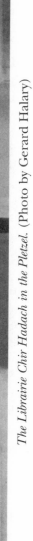

The Librairie Chir Hadach in the Pletzel. (Photo by Gerard Halary)

Friday when it closes before the Sabbath. It stays closed on the Sabbath. Diasporama is a fine Judaica and Jewish gift store featuring menorahs, silver and pewter items, kiddush cups and seder plates, original paintings, video tapes, cassette tapes, and Limoges plates. Chana and Patrick Hagistare are proprietors.

Librairie Chir Hadach, 52, rue des Rosiers, 75004, Paris. Tel: 42-72-38-00. Fine selection of scholarly "learning" books.

Librairie du Marais, 7, rue des Rosiers, 75004, Paris. Books, religious items, tapes.

Librairie Hebraica, Judaica, 12, rue des Hopitalieres-St-Gervais, 75004, Paris.

The Pletzel is located on the site of the thirteenth-century ghetto of Paris known as the **Juiverie.** When the Jewish people were permitted to return to the Kingdom of France in 1198, they settled on what is now the rue Ferdinand Duval, then called "street of the Jews." Once it was in the neighborhood of the rich, but after the storming of the Bastille on July 14, 1789, the poor moved in. When those first Jewish immigrants settled in this section in the twelfth century, they called it "little square," or in Yiddish, the "Pletzel."

Today, several thousand Jews, many of them religious, live in the Pletzel. On Friday afternoons, one can observe Chassidim dressed in long black coats with their round *shtreimels* (fur hats), scurrying home to prepare for the Sabbath Queen.

Seen in shop windows in the Pletzel are religious goods, such as *yarmulkes* and *talesim* (skullcaps and prayer shawls); Israeli and Yiddish newspapers; and Israeli food products, including humus and felafel and matzot for Passover. Jewelry and gift shops display necklaces and bracelets, many of which are made in Israel. Record albums and tapes by Israeli stars are available.

JEWISH RESTAURANTS IN PARIS

In Paris, one place to meet Jews is in restaurants and cafes. Meeting people in a cafe is typically French, for the Parisians include the surrounding eating establishments in their definition of home.

A Jewish bookstore in Paris. (Photo courtesy French Government Tourist Office)

A store selling religious goods in the rue des Rosiers, Paris. (Photo courtesy French Government Tourist Office)

The Librairie du Marais is a religious bookstore in the Jewish quarter of Paris known as the Pletzel. (Photo by Gerard Halary)

Paris is the gastronomic capital of the world. This city loves a carefully prepared meal that is appreciatively savored. According to Parisians, a meal is a very special experience, a pleasure of life. The French do not eat; they dine. The traveler seeking **kosher** cuisine does not have to be wary about finding it in Paris, where there may be more kosher facilities than in New York, Chicago, and Los Angeles combined. One can certainly enjoy a wide variety of French, Eastern European, and North African specialties.

Kosher restaurants are usually open from noon to about 3 and from 6 until 11, except for Friday and Saturday. Some open Saturday night depending on the season. Addresses and hours change, so it is best to telephone ahead to confirm hours and make reservations. Nearly 100 kosher restaurants in Paris will certainly meet the traveler's needs. Most kosher restaurants carry the sign of the Beth Din of Paris certifying "kosher here," but some also have the approval sign of Lubavitch.

Jewish restaurants are institutions where people are ready to extend a warm welcome to the visitor. Ironically one of the best-known Jewish tourist spots in Paris is a Jewish restaurant that is *not* kosher, but kosher-style. I like to call it "Chez Goldenberg."

Goldenberg's, 7, rue des Rosiers, 75004, Paris. Tel: 48-87-20-16 or 48-87-70-39. A mainstay eatery in the Marais. It remains open everyday from 8 A.M. to 2 A.M.

Jo Goldenberg likes to say his meals are for the *"kleine or groysse fresser."* Gastronomes will enjoy Goldenberg's pastrami and corned beef, although it is spicier than that in the United States. Also available are pickled fleish, borscht, schmaltz herring, pickled flanken, chopped liver, smoked salmon, herring, matjes herring, and, of course, Eastern European specialties such as *zakuski, pojarski,* and Hungarian goulash. A lively lunch atmosphere also percolates from the take-out deli in front, the counter and table areas in the front, and the red leather sofa chairs in the back, during the long midday meal. And you never know who is going to drop in from government, business, and the professions during that time. This restaurant is an "in" place to eat and be seen.

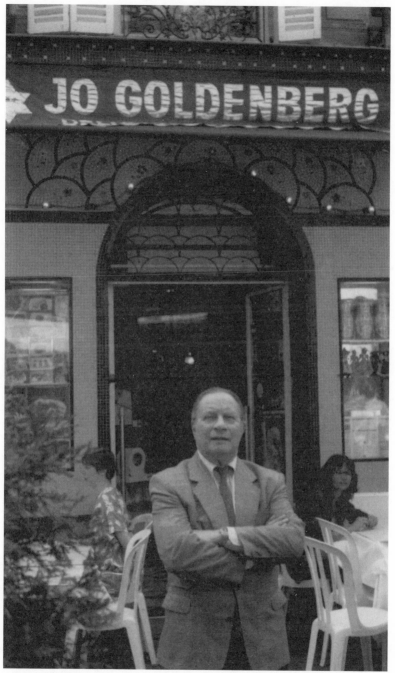

Jo Goldenberg and his restaurant in Paris. (Photo by Gerard Halary)

At night, there is singing and dancing and music fills the air. Call for reservations and plan to arrive at about 9. That's the best time for the gaiety.

Everyone comes to Goldenberg's. Jo Goldenberg tells customers about his famous guests, such as former President of the Republic François Mitterrand and former Prime Minister Michel Rocard, who have dined here often, Abba Eban, Charlie Chaplin, Barbra Streisand, Charles Aznavour, and Simone Veil, who has served as president of the European Parliament.

Jo is a delightful man. He is an engaging host. He still hops from table to table. He embraces guests. He tastes everything. He munches bread. He samples the strudel. He sips a glass of tea.

One of Jo Goldenberg's hobbies is to collect samovars. He has them lined up on the staircase of his two-story establishment. He is a child of the Marais. He speaks French, Yiddish, Hebrew, and some English. He points proudly to a photo on the second floor of the restaurant. There is a picture of his father, who opened a deli restaurant in the 1920s just down the street from the present Goldenberg's.

Jo circles the bullet holes. That the restaurant functions to this day is a victory over a terrorist attack on the place in 1982.

Well, a decade later, they still come. Only now, besides American Jewish tourists, I often find young Germans who, every time they come to Paris, make their pilgrimage to Goldenberg's, too. Jo believes they feel guilty about the actions of their fathers and grandfathers, so they come to a Jewish atmosphere, and Goldenberg's at night, for sure, is certainly it.

Kosher Restaurants

Boulangerie Patisserie Murciano, 14-16, rue des Rosiers, 75004, Paris. Tel: 48-87-48-88.

Kosher Pizza, 11, rue de Rosiers, 75004, Paris. Tel: 48-87-17-83. Delicious, strictly kosher pizza.

La Petite Famille, 32, rue des Rosiers, 75004, Paris. Tel: 42-77-00-50.

Le Mazel-Tov, 25, rue des Rosiers, 75004, Paris. Tel: 40-27-87-40.

Kosher Pizza, in the Jewish quarter. (Photo by Gerard Halary)

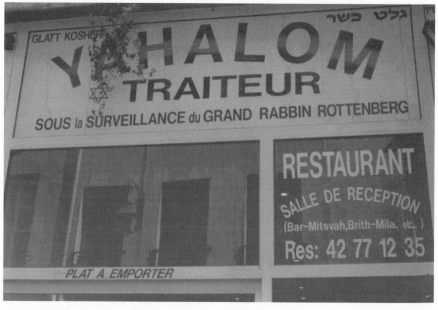

Yahalom, a Jewish kosher restaurant in Paris in the Pletzel. (Photo by Gerard Halary)

Micky's Deli, 23 bis, rue des Rosiers, 75004, Paris. Offers Glatt kosher meat sandwiches. The small counter and good takeout service make this a nice stop on a sojourn in the Marais.

Pita Burger, 23, rue des Rosiers, 75004, Paris. Tel: 42-77-59-41.

Tutti Frutti, 38, rue des Rosiers, 75004, Paris. Tel: 42-76-04-75. This is a very popular takeout place with a small counter. It is especially known for "panini sandwiches" (tuna and cheese on grilled French bread). It also serves yogurt. English and Hebrew are spoken here. (Tutti Frutti is strictly kosher, "Halav Yisrael.")

Yahalom, 24, rue des Rosiers, 75004, Paris. Tel: 42-77-12-35. This place is strictly glatt kosher. They offer you felafel, humus, tehina, and eggplant. Full-course meals include Israeli dishes as well as meat dishes. You will find that snacks are also available.

Chinese Kosher

Le Lotus de Nissan, 39, rue Amelot, 75011, Paris. Tel: 43-55-80-42. For a change of pace, excellent kosher Chinese food awaits the tourist in Paris. This charming kosher Chinese restaurant presents a menu that includes fried wonton, chop suey, spring rolls, duck, and beef. It's all here! Reservations advised.

Lotus de Nissan has a kosher take-out that will deliver right to your hotel for lunch or dinner. The take-out facility is located at 53, rue Amelot, 75011, Paris. Tel: 43-57-44-05.

Other Kosher Restaurants

Adolphe, 14, rue Richer, 75009, Paris. Tel: 47-70-91-25.

Aux Iles Philippines, 17, rue La Place, Paris.

Aux Surprises, 40 bis, rue du Faubourg-Poissonniere, 75010, Paris. Tel: 47-70-55-96. Milk bar.

Azar et Fils, 6, rue Geoffroy-Marie, 75009, Paris. Tel: 47-70-08-38.

Blue Bird, 91, avenue Secretan, 75019, Paris. Tel: 42-39-50-41.

Centre Edmond Fleg, 8 bis, rue de l'Eperon, 75006, Paris. Tel: 46-33-43-31.

Centre Rachi, 30, boulevard Port-Royal, 75005, Paris. Tel: 43-31-98-20.

Chez Gabin, 92, boulevard de Belleville, 75020, Paris. Tel: 43-58-78-14.

Fradji, 42, rue Poncelet, 75017, Paris. Tel: 47-54-91-40. Highly recommended.

Gagou, 8, rue de la Grange-Bateliere, 75009, Paris. Tel: 47-70-05-02.

Juliette, 14, rue Duphot, 75001, Paris. Tel: 42-60-18-05 or 42-60-18-10.

King Salomon, 46, rue Richer, 75009, Paris. Tel: 42-46-31-22.

La Grillade, 42, rue Richer, 75009, Paris. Tel: 47-70-24-64.

La Rose Blanche, 10 bis, rue Geoffroy-Marie, 75009, Paris. Tel: 45-23-37-70.

Le Castel, 4, rue Saulnier, 75009, Paris. Tel: 47-70-44-08. Excellent cuisine and highly recommended.

Le Renaissance, 4, rue Biscornet, 75012, Paris. Tel: 43-43-17-06.

Le Roll's Pizzeria, 126, boulevard Voltaire, 75011, Paris. Tel: 48-06-53-46.

Le Roll's Pizzeria, 56, avenue de la Republique, 75011, Paris. Tel: 43-38-63-18.

Les Jardins du Belvedere, 111, avenue de Villiers, 75017, Paris. Tel: 42-27-16-91. Highly recommended.

Les Relais, 69, boulevard de Belleville, 75020, Paris. Tel: 43-57-83-91.

Les Tables de la Loi, 15, rue St-Gilles, 75003, Paris. Tel: 48-04-38-02.

Nini, 24, rue Saussier-Leroy, 75017, Paris. Tel: 46-22-28-93. Excellent food and highly recommended. Nini is very popular with American Jews. It has been called a "Tunisian-chic restaurant." Served here are steaks, veal, lamb chops, mixed grill, and couscous.

Paris Texas, 101, avenue Jean Jaures, 75019, Paris. Tel: 42-45-48-61. Good kosher pizza.

Restaurant "Les Ailes," 34, rue Richer, 75009, Paris. Tel: 47-70-62-53. Grill and Tunisian specialties. Also high on the list of kosher diners.

Tibi, 128, boulevard de Clichy, 75018, Paris. Tel: 45-22-80-26.

Zazou, 19, rue du Faubourg-Montmartre, 75009, Paris. Tel: 40-22-08-33.

LODGING

Lebron, 4, rue Lamartine, 75009, Paris. Tel: 48-78-75-52. FAX: 49-95-94-64. Besides fine hotel rooms with TVs, this kosher facility maintains a glatt kosher restaurant, dining room, and conference room. One can order meals ahead of time for the Sabbath. The hotel is near numerous synagogues and not far from Temple Victoire, as well as the synagogue on rue Buffault. Lubavitch is several doors down, at 8, rue Lamartine. Moreover, the hotel is near fine kosher restaurants in rue Richer and the surrounding area.

The quarter around rue Richer is another Parisian section where one can meet Jews. Throughout the world, No. 32 rue Richer is known as the Folies Bergeres. This is one of the most dynamic streets of Paris.

Walk along the rue Richer, between rue du Faubourg-Poissonniere and rue Faubourg-Montmartre. Explore the side streets. Lunch or dine in one of the many kosher restaurants and snack bars.

Browse in one of the largest Jewish bookstores, the **Colbo,** at No. 3, rue Richer. Tel: 47-70-21-81.

SYNAGOGUES IN PARIS

The Jewish tourist in France has no difficulty finding a synagogue to visit, whether in Paris or the countryside. Several hundred exist in France. There are more than 50 Jewish houses of worship in Paris alone. And many of the Parisian suburbs contain synagogues. To check times of services, please contact the **Consistoire Central,** 19, rue St-Georges, 75009, Paris. Tel: 49-70-88-00.

Temple Victoire, 44, rue de la Victoire, 75009, Paris. Tel: 45-26-95-36. A must for American visitors. This beautiful, austere building is frequently referred to as the Rothschild Synagogue because members of the renowned family attend services here. Built in 1874, it was constructed in neo-Romanesque style,

An interior view of the Temple Victoire. (Photo courtesy French Government Tourist Office)

lavishly decorated with marble and stained glass, and is dominated by opulent candelabras. It is often called the "Cathedral Synagogue."

The synagogue is on a relatively narrow street. Jewish officials had hoped to have the facade on the somewhat more conspicuous rue St-Georges, from which one now enters the community offices, but the empress of France's confessor, reportedly a converted Jew, did not want the building to be visible on a heavily traversed thoroughfare. So the congregation had to put up with the resulting incorrect orientation of the Holy Ark, writes Carol Herselle Krinsky in *Synagogues in Europe*. The interior is impressive.

Because the Rothschilds pray here, let us reflect on this family of financiers and philanthropists, who have contributed greatly to Jewish causes. The head of the Rothschild family was Mayer Amschel Rothschild of Frankfurt (1744–1812), who had five sons. They were Amschel Mayer (1773–1836), who stayed in Frankfurt; Solomon Mayer (1774–1855), who went to Vienna; Nathan Mayer (1777–1855), to London; Karl Mayer (1788–1855), to Naples; and James Jacob (1792–1868), to Paris.

The French branch of the family was founded when James, the youngest of the sons, settled in Paris in 1812. As an agent of his brother Nathan, James established the firm of Rothschild Freres. Financially, he aided the Bourbon and Orleans families, the kings of France, and Napoleon III. From then on, apart from its banking activities, the Rothschild family was active in the French Jewish community.

James de Rothschild built the Rothschild Hospital, which still stands today in Paris. An early railroad entrepreneur, James helped set up many government railroad lines. The Rothschilds financed the main rail networks in France, including the Chemin de Fer du Nord.

The Rothschild family assumed positions of responsibility in the French Jewish leadership, holding respected posts. Baron Guy de Rothschild was president of Fonds Social Juif Unifié (FSJU). He was succeeded by his son, David Rothschild. The late Baron Alain de Rothschild was president of the Consistoire and headed the Representative Council of Jewish Organizations in

The front of Agoudas Hakehilos Orthodox synagogue in the rue Pavée. It was designed in 1913 by the famous art nouveau architect of the Metro, Hector Guimard. (Photo by Gerard Halary)

France (CRIF). Baron Elie de Rothschild is active in the French United Jewish Appeal.
Synagogue services: Friday nights at 6:30, Saturday mornings at 9:30. (Metro: Le Peletier.) There is also a Tunisian and an Egyptian congregation on the premises.

Agoudas Hakehilos, 10, rue Pavee, 75004, Paris. Tel: 48-87-21-54. A school is located here. Austere on the outside, but beautiful inside, this Orthodox synagogue in the Pletzel was designed in 1913 by Hector Guimard, the famous art nouveau architect of the Metro, who fled to the United States in 1942 and whose wife was Jewish. The building itself is neo-Gothic in feeling. There are two lateral aisles, each having two rows of overhead galleries for the women's section, supported by four massive pillars, plus wooden benches. Orthodox Ashkenazic services every day. Sabbath morning services at 9:20. (Metro: St-Paul.)

A second synagogue, located at 23, rue Petion, 75011, Paris, opened in March 1991. Services are held Friday evenings at 6:30 and Saturday mornings at 10. (Metro: Voltaire-Leon Blum.)

Ohel Avraham, 31, rue Montevideo, 75016, Paris. Tel: 45-04-66-73.

Oratoire, 223, rue Vercingetorix, 75014, Paris. Tel: 45-45-50-51. (Metro: Daumesnil.)

Oratoire, 42, rue des Saules, 75018, Paris. Tel: 46-06-71-39. (Metro: Jules Joffrin.)

Oratoire, 120, boulevard de Belleville, 75020, Paris. Tel: 47-97-46-96.

Oratoire, 13, rue Fondary, 75015, Paris. Tel: 45-04-66-73. (Metro: Grenelle.)

Synagogue, 15, rue Notre-Dame de Nazareth, 75003, Paris. Tel: 42-78-00-30. (Metro: Republique.)

Synagogue, 21 bis, rue des Tournelles, 75004, Paris. Tel: 42-74-32-80. This is a Sephardic synagogue known for its wrought-ironwork interior. It is situated back-to-back with the Ashkenazic synagogue known as **Temple des Vosges,** which fronts on the Place des Vosges, 14, Place des Vosges, 75004, Paris. Tel: 48-87-79-45. A must for the visitor, the Place des Vosges, located in the heart of the Marais, is probably one of

the most beautiful squares in all of Paris. Victor Hugo lived at No. 6; the house is now a museum. (Metro: Bastille.)
Synagogue (Rabbinical Seminary), 9, rue Vauquelin, 75005, Paris. Tel: 47-07-21-22. FAX: 43-37-75-92. (Metro: Monge.)
Synagogue, 28, rue Buffault, 75009, Paris. Tel: 45-26-80-87. (Metro: Cadet.)
Synagogue Kahal Yreim, 10, rue Cadet, 75009, Paris. Tel: 42-46-36-47. (Metro: Cadet.)
Synagogue Berith Shalom, 18, rue St-Lazare, 75009, Paris. Tel: 48-78-45-32 and 48-78-38-80.
Synagogue Rachi, 6, rue Ambroise-Thomas, 75009, Paris. Tel: 48-24-86-94. This synagogue is named after Rashi, who is considered the leading commentator on the Bible and the Talmud. Born in Troyes in 1040, he learned a great deal about viticulture and husbandry. In Rashi's time, Jews lived in Champagne and other wine districts of northern France. He himself studied in Worms and Mainz. About 1070, he founded a school in Troyes that made French Judaism renowned for its scholarship. But not all was tranquil. During the First Crusade, Rashi had to flee anti-Jewish riots in and around Troyes. Once he established himself in Worms, Germany, he lived and studied there. Rashi died in 1105. His burial place is not known. (Metro: Cadet.)
Synagogue, 130, rue du Faubourg-St Martin, 75010, Paris. (Metro: Gare de l'Est.)
Synagogue Don Isaac Abravanel, 84-86, rue de la Roquette, 75011, Paris. Tel: 47-00-75-95. (Metro: Bastille.)
Synagogue, 14, rue Chasseloup-Laubat, 75015, Paris. Tel: 42-73-36-29. (Metro: Segur.)
Synagogue de Montmartre, 12, rue Ste-Isaure, 75018, Paris. Tel: 42-64-48-34. (Metro: Jules Joffrin.)
Synagogue de Neuilly, 12, rue Ancelle, Neuilly Sur-Seine. (Metro: Las Sablons.) Tel: 46-24-49-15.
Synagogue Or Torah, 15, rue Riquet, 75019, Paris.
The Liberal Synagogue, 22-24, rue Copernic, 75116, Paris. Tel: 47-04-37-27. On Friday night and Saturday, many American visitors and residents pray at the Union Liberale Israelite de France (The Liberal Synagogue). Services at 6 on Friday evenings and at 10:30 A.M. Saturdays. Holiday services at

Inside the synagogue at 28, rue Buffault. (Photo courtesy French Government Tourist Office)

10 A.M. On Passover, there is an attempt to have part of the traditional seder in English. An English-speaking secretary is available all week long to help weary travelers. (Metro: Victor Hugo. Bus: 22, 82, 30, 52.)

Movement Juif Liberal de France, 11, rue Gaston de Cailavet, 75015, Paris. Tel: 45-75-38-01. Spiritual leaders are Rabbi Daniel Farhi and Pauline Bebe. Services at 6:15 on Friday evenings and 10:30 Saturday mornings. Telephone first for directions. (Metro: Charles Michels.)

Masorati (Conservative Movement of Judaism)

Synagogue Adath Shalom, 22 bis rue des Belles-Feuilles, 75016, Paris. Tel: 45-53-57-47.

Synagogue, 218-220, rue Faubourg Saint-Honore, 75008, Paris. Tel: 45-61-20-25.

OFFICIALS AND ORGANIZATIONS

Chief Rabbi Joseph Sitruk serves as chief rabbi of France. His office is at 19, rue St-Georges, 75009, Paris. Tel: 49-70-88-00. FAX: 42-81-03-66.

Rabbi Alain Goldmann is the grand rabbi of Paris. His office is at Consistoire de Paris, 17, rue St-Georges, 75009, Paris. Tel: 40-82-26-26. FAX: 42-81-92-46.

Note: For American travelers, questions regarding synagogue services, religious matters, and tickets for high holidays should be directed to Consistoire Central, 19, rue St-Georges, 75009, Paris. Tel: 49-70-88-00. FAX: 42-81-03-66. Many officials here also speak English and Hebrew. Contact Leon Masliah, executive director.

Paris is the center of Jewish activities in France, as all major institutions have their headquarters there.

Conseil Representatif des Institutions Juives de France (CRIF), 19, rue de Teheran, 75008, Paris. Tel: 49-77-88-00. CRIF, the representative council of Jewish organizations, was founded in 1944 to protect the rights of Jews in the Republic. Today, more than 35 groups belong to CRIF, which speaks and acts on behalf of the organized Jewish community in representations to the government.

Consistoire Central, Union des Communautés Juives de France, 19, rue St-Georges, 75009, Paris. Tel: 49-77-88-00. FAX: 42-87-03-66. The Consistoire is a major force in French Jewish organizational life. The Consistoire Central recently moved its headquarters next door to 19 rue St-Georges. The building contains an assembly hall for lectures and ceremonies and special offices.

Fonds Social Juif Unifie (FSJU), 19, rue de Teheran, 75008, Paris. Tel: 45-63-17-28. FAX: 45-63-34-62. The words on the banner at the entrance of this important institution tell the story of the goals of the revitalized Jewish community of France:

> For a strong community.
> To help Israel.
> For your active participation in Jewish life.

These words define the goals of the Fonds Social Juif Unifie, translated as the United Jewish Social Fund, similar to a federation and welfare fund in the United States.

The FSJU coordinates, supervises, and plans major social, educational, and cultural activities and enterprises of the French Jewish community. This building also houses the offices of L'Appel Unifie Juif de France (the French UJA) and the Conseil Representatif des Institutions Juives de France (CRIF), which is a council of Jewish organizations.

The "Appel" has introduced American fund-raising techniques in soliciting funds.

Lubavitch is very active and maintains more than 40 Chabad Centers in France, as well as many synagogues. The main **Synagogue and Center** is located at Beth Loubavitch, 8, rue Lamartine, 75009, Paris. Tel: 45-26-87-60. Orthodox Shabbat service is at 10:30 A.M. on Saturdays. Call for a list of group activities and services. You will be welcome.

In addition to the above, there are hundreds of distinguished groups, international and local, which are active. A partial list includes the World Jewish Congress, ORT, B'nai B'rith, a number of Sephardic and Zionist groups, the American

Jewish Joint Distribution Committee, the Jewish Agency for Israel, the Weizmann Institute, the France-Israel Alliance, and WIZO (Women's International Zionist Organization).

Anti-Defamation League, 4 bis, rue de Lota, 75016, Paris. Tel: 45-53-03-22.

B'nai B'rith, 38, rue de Clichy, 75009, Paris. Tel: 40-82-91-11. FAX: 40-82-91-05.

Embassy of Israel, 3, rue Rabelais, 75008, Paris. Tel: 40-76-55-00. FAX: 45-25-53-56.

Embassy of the United States of America, 2, avenue Gabriel, 75008, Paris. Tel: 42-96-12-02.

European Council of Jewish Community Services, 4 bis, rue de Lota, 75016, Paris. Tel: 45-53-31-26.

Jewish Agency, 17, rue Fortuny, 75017, Paris. Tel: 44-15-23-23.

Joint Distribution Committee, 33, rue de Miromesnil, 75008, Paris. Tel: 42-68-05-68.

ORT-France—Organisation Reconstruction, Travail Association, 10, Villa d'Eylau, 75116, Paris. Tel: 4500-74-22. ORT, as it is known throughout the world, operates vocational and technical schools.

World Jewish Congress, 78, avenue des Champs-Elysées, 75008, Paris. Tel: 43-59-94-63. FAX: 42-25-45-28.

Youth Organizations

B'nai B'rith Youth Organization, 38, rue de Clichy, 75009, Paris. Tel: 40-82-91-00.

Lubavitch, 8, rue Lamartine, 75009, Paris. Tel: 45-26-87-60. There is also a synagogue here.

Scout Eclaireurs Israelites de France, 27, avenue de Segur, 75007, Paris. Tel: 47-83-60-33.

Jewish Community Activity Centers

Centre Bernard Lazare, 10, rue Saint-Claude, 75003, Paris.

Centre Communautaire Maison des Jeunes, 5, rue de Rochechouart, 75009, Paris. Tel: 49-95-95-92. FAX: 42-80-10-66. Located here are many activities, such as sports, lectures, theater programs, and an ulpan to study Hebrew. A kosher cafeteria serves lunch from 12 noon to 2 P.M. and dinner from 6 to 8 P.M. There are services on Friday nights and at 8:45 A.M. on Saturdays.

Centre Edmond Fleg, 8 bis, rue de l'Eperon, 75006, Paris. Tel: 46-33-43-31. This is a university student center, sponsored by the Consistoire de Paris and named after a French Jewish writer. Young visitors should inquire about activities. A cafeteria serves hot kosher lunches.

Centre Israel Jeffroykin, 68, rue de la Flie Maricourt, 75011, Paris. Located near the Bastille. (Metro: Oberkampf.)

Centre Rachi, 30, boulevard Port-Royal, 75005, Paris. Tel: 43-31-98-20 or 43-31-75-47. Open from 9 A.M. to 11 P.M. A good spot, especially for university students and adults interested in intellectual activities. Seminars, lectures, and films. A kosher cafeteria and circular coffee bar make it a fine gathering place. Services are at 8 Friday night and 8 Saturday morning in the summer; 4:30 P.M. Friday and 9 A.M. Saturday in the winter.

Centre Rambam, 19-21, rue Galvani, 75017, Paris. Tel: 45-74-52-80 or 45-74-51-81. Located in a growing Jewish neighborhood, this Sephardic center contains a beautiful Moroccan-style synagogue, library, meeting rooms, reception, and catering area. Sabbath services. This is a good site to reflect upon the impact of the arrival in the 1960s of the Sephardim to France.

During the thirty years since their departure from North Africa, Sephardic Jews from Morocco have established this Sephardic center in Paris. The center, which was named Rambam, hosts study groups devoted to Spanish Jewish traditions as well as organizes lectures. Rambam is the acronym of Rabbi Moses ben Maimon (1135–1204), or as he is more widely known, Maimonides, one of the most illustrious figures of the post-Talmudic era.

The massive flux in the 1950s and 1960s of Sephardic Jews from North Africa to France was one of the most exciting movements of immigration in contemporary European history. Nearly 300,000 Sephardic Jews came to France in the early 1960s. They revitalized and revolutionized French Jewry to such an extent that some have called the present community the Second French Jewry.

The Sephardim brought activity and momentum, an infusion of new blood. They set up community institutions, synagogues, and Talmud Torahs. They were proud of their Jewishness. Although half settled in and around Paris, many moved into towns such as Avignon, Arles, Aix-en-Provence—towns that had heretofore contained few Jews.

This was one of the few times in Jewish history when the Jewish community changed from Ashkenazic to Sephardic. Not only was their arrival welcome, their integration into Jewish and French society was also very successful. They launched themselves into key positions in French government, education, art, and science.

Maison France-Israel. Located only a few short blocks from the Arc de Triomphe is the Maison France-Israel, at 64, avenue Marceau, 75008, Paris. Tel: 44-43-36-00. FAX: 44-43-35-20. This can be a home away from home for American tourists. First of all, this new institution contains three strictly kosher restaurants as well as meeting rooms. Established and led by former government minister Lionel Stoleru, the officers and staff want visitors to feel at home. In the courtyard stands the superb statue, *La Fontaine de Rachi,* named after the great French Talmudist, Rashi, and dedicated to the enhancement of two cultures: France and Israel. Here in this building are halls named after Chagall and Rothschild. Dedicated by former French President François Mitterrand and former Israeli President Chaim Herzog, the mansion houses the Simon Wiesenthal Center, Friends of the Israel Museum in Jerusalem, L'Alliance France-Israel, the France-Israel Chamber of Commerce, and other organizations. Kosher restaurants include a gastronomic restaurant called Le Table de David, and Le Sabra, which specializes in Israeli food. Several Jewish radio stations, including Radio Shalom, broadcast from this building, Tel: 44-43-36-03.

Rabbinical School of Paris, 9, rue Vauquelin, 75005, Paris. Tel: 47-07-21-22. American students may want to contact this Orthodox, rabbinic seminary for a schedule of activities, classes, and religious services.

MUSEUMS

The Jewish artists Soutine, Pascin, Chagall, Pissarro, Modigliani, Mane-Katz, Benn, and Lipchitz worked and created masterpieces in France. Many of their works are exhibited in various Parisian museums.

Centre National d'Art et de Culture Georges Pompidou, better known as Beaubourg, on rue Beaubourg, 75004, Paris. Tel: 42-77-12-33. Paintings by Jewish artists, such as Chagall, Soutine, and Modigliani. Hebrew and Yiddish language lessons available on taped cassettes. Numerous books on Jewish history, Judaica, Israel, and Jewish literature. The Pompidou Centre, which is visited by about 25,000 persons daily, is not far from the Pletzel in the Marais section.

Jewish Art Museum (Le Musée d'Art Juif de Paris), 42, rue des Saules, 75018, Paris. Tel: 42-57-84-15. Created in 1948, this museum is located in the shadow of the Sacré-Coeur. It is open Sunday, Tuesday, and Thursday, from 3 to 6. Enhancing the museum is a collection of religious items, sculptures, mosaics, drawings, engravings, and paintings by well-known artists, such as Chagall, Mane-Katz, Benn, and Lipchitz. Rare exhibits of beautifully detailed models of Eastern European wooden synagogues of the sixteenth, seventeenth, and eighteenth centuries are highlights. Exhibitions are presented and special visits planned for groups. The projected new Museum of Jewish Art and Culture will be housed in the Hotel de St-Aignan, one of the finest seventeenth-century mansions in the Marais. Sponsored by the French Jewish community, the mayor of Paris, and the French Ministry of Culture, the museum is scheduled to open in several years. (Metro: Lamarck-Caulaincourt.)

Library of the Alliance Israelite Universelle, 45, rue la Bruyere, 75009, Paris. Tel: 42-80-35-00 or 47-44-75-84. More than 100,000 books of Judaic interest, including manuscripts. Permission to visit needed.

Musée Carnavalet, 23, rue de Sevigne, 75003, Paris. Tel: 42-72-21-13. Open 10 to 5:40 every day except Monday. The aim of the museum is to illustrate the history of Paris from its origins to the present day. The building and mansion display a number of personal souvenirs and artifacts of Rachel, one of France's most famous Jewish actresses.

The building also houses the Museum of the History of Paris, which covers the sixteenth to the nineteenth centuries. The museum has branched out into a new addition next door, the Hotel le Peletier-St-Farglau, which includes the bedroom of the famous Jewish writer Marcel Proust. Open 10 to 5:40 every day except Monday.

A wonderful exhibit entitled "The French Revolution" enhances this inspiring structure and is well worth seeing. At the time of the French Revolution, about five hundred Jews resided in Paris. Many had bribed the chief of police for permission to settle there. Looking back to the days of the French Revolution, we learn that the Jews of that time were indebted to liberal Count Mirabeau and a liberal Catholic cleric named Abbe Gregoire, who supported Jewish equality. The Declaration of Human Rights was passed in the summer of 1789. The Jewish question did not come up for debate until December 24, 1789. The revolutionary Count Mirabeau simply did not possess the votes. The matter was tabled until the next month. On January 28, 1790, Talleyrand brought in a report by the Committee of the Constitution in favor of "equality."

On that day, however, only the Sephardic Jews, those "who were known in France by the names of the Portuguese, Spanish, and Avignonnais Jews," would henceforth enjoy the rights of active citizens. Twenty months would pass until equal rights were given to the Ashkenazic Jews. On September 27, 1791, after much debate and many delays, the Ashkenazim who lived in Alsace and the surrounding area were emancipated.

Regarding the impact of the French Revolution on the Jews, "for the first time in the modern history of the West, all the Jews within the borders of a European state were united with all its other citizens, as equals before the law," writes Arthur Hertzberg in *The French Enlightenment and the Jews*. A new era in Jewish history was born.

Robespierre himself was one of the first to demand citizenship for the Jews. True, some synagogues were closed during the Revolution because of the anti-religious policy which the

Jacobins directed against the powerful Catholic church. But the Jacobins fought against all religious symbols. Although there was anti-Jewish discrimination, neither during the Reign of Terror nor during the Thermidor was a Jew executed solely because he was a Jew.

Soza Szajkowski, author of *Jews and the French Revolution of 1789, 1830, 1848,* says that "the vast majority of Jews did favor the new regime, but because of their diverse economic and regional attachments, Jews were active in all factions of the Revolutionary regime."

A Jewish Jacobin Club sprung up in the "Jewish suburb" of St-Esprit in Bayonne. A synagogue still stands in that very section—at 35, rue Maubec in Bayonne.

The armies of the Revolution and, later, of Napoleon himself carried the banner and, more important, put into practice "Liberty, Equality and Fraternity." For Jews, the cry meant freedom. Napoleon was the liberator of the Jews of Europe.

While on the one hand the French gave Jews human rights, virulent anti-Semitism existed in the philosophical writings of such Frenchmen as Voltaire and Diderot. While the Enlightenment helped the Jews, these French thinkers were widely read and their anti-Semitic writings would in the end harm the Jewish people.

Still, the Republic attracted Jews from all over the world. Because of the country's liberal immigration policy, Jews from Eastern Europe poured into France. In the nineteenth century, this flow would increase.

One outcome of the Revolution of course was the Sanhedrin. In 1806, Napoleon convoked a Grand Sanhedrin which codified religious decisions. It met in 1807. Napoleon was determined to provide the Jews of France with a central organization supervised by the State and loyal to the government. He followed the example of the arrangements he had already introduced for other religions.

The emperor possessed an ulterior motive. He wanted Jews assimilated. He felt their emancipation had not produced the anticipated results. Jews, he said, were really a nation within a nation. But because of its group nature, the Sanhedrin was distorted by anti-Semites as an international conspiracy plotting ritual murder.

The Consistoire Central in France was established on July 17, 1808, along with the institution of the chief rabbinate. Following the Revolution of July 1830, the French government proposed that the Jewish religion have equal status with the Catholic church and Protestantism. One year later it was done.

Musée Cluny, 6, Place Paul-Painleve, 75005, Paris. Tel: 43-25-62-00. Contains furniture, Jewish engagement rings, sculpture, fragments representing kings of Judea. Displayed here are the famous Strauss-Rothschild collections of Jewish ritual objects.

Musée du Louvre, rue de Rivoli, 75001, Paris. Tel: 42-60-39-26. Spectacular is the new glass pyramid entrance to the Louvre, as well as the spiral staircases, designed by I. M. Pei and Partners, which lead from ground level down to the welcoming area. From below ground level, one proceeds to various pavilions, such as the Sully, Danton, or Richelieu Pavilions, or to the museum's cafeteria or bookstore. The Palais du Louvre contains many Jewish archeological items and antiques from Israel, such as a terra-cotta ossuary discovered in a funeral cave in Azor near Tel Aviv. The museum itself contains about six thousand paintings. In 1993, part of the collection was housed in the Richelieu Pavilion in the rue de Rivoli. Until now, this pavilion has been used for offices by the French Ministry of Finance. Open Thursday, Friday, Saturday, and Sunday, 9 to 6; Monday and Wednesday, 9 A.M. to 9:40 P.M. (Closed Tuesday.) The Pyramid is open every day except Tuesday. (Metro: Palais Royal Musée du Louvre.)

Musée d'Orsay, 62, rue de Bellechasse, 75007, Paris. Tel: 45-49-48-14. A former *belle époque* railroad station was renovated in 1986 to become a modern museum of nineteenth-century art, including the works of two well-known French Jewish artists, Pissarro and Modigliani. Contains impressionist paintings by Manet, Monet, Van Gogh, Degas, Sisley, Renoir, Cezanne, Seurat, Signac, and Gauguin. Open daily from 10 to 6 and until 9:45 on Thursday. Closed Monday.

Bibliothèque Nationale (The National Library), 58, rue de Richelieu, 75009, Paris. Tel: 47-03-81-26. Magnificent Hebrew manuscripts, Dead Sea Scroll fragments, Bibles, Haggadoth, ketubot. More than 30,000 volumes are in the Hebraic section. A regular exchange with Israel has ensured the acquisition of all books published there since 1953. One must write for permission to see the manuscripts or use the library.

MEMORIAL SITES

Memorial in Le Drancy, avenue Jean-Jaures, Le Drancy. Drancy is a town three miles from Paris, a short express ride on the RER train (suburban express subway). Located here is one of the most befitting memorials to the six million Jews who were murdered by the Nazis and to those Jews deported from France, often with the help of the collaborationist Vichy government. Drancy was the site of an internment camp that supplied the concentration camps with inmates.

Established in 1940, it was an unfinished housing project with apartment buildings on three sides of a rectangular court. Jews were quartered in the large, grim buildings that still stand today as part of a municipal housing project. The gathering camp was supervised by Alois Brunner, one of the last major Nazi war criminals still at large and believed to be living in Syria. He is still in the news, as Jewish groups are demanding his extradition from Syria.

The outdoor monument in the form of a statue was dedicated in 1976. It bears a quotation from Lamentations 1:12: "Behold, and see if there be any pain like unto my pain." Just behind the monument is an old railroad boxcar once used in the deportation process. Inside the railroad car is a pictorial exhibit showing the roundups of Jews, their boarding the railroad cars, and their crowded quarters in camps.

The monument is dedicated to the martyrs, victims of the barbaric Nazis. One poster reads, "Never Again a Camp at Drancy. Never Again Auschwitz."

The town of Drancy itself was a stronghold of the Resistance.

The key to the railroad car exhibit must be obtained in advance from the town hall, except on Saturday. However, travelers can visit the railroad boxcar from 2 P.M. to 4 P.M. every Saturday, except when Saturday falls on a bank holiday. On other days, one may be able to obtain the key from the Cultural Department of the Mayor's Office located in the town hall at Place Maurice Thorez, 93700, Le Drancy. Take the RER at Gare du Nord. At Drancy station, take bus number 148, direction Pantin, to the memorial. If it is not Saturday, ask to get off at City Hall to obtain the key to the boxcar. *Tip:* Arrangements should be made in advance.

If the collapse of France and the ultimate establishment of the Fascist state of Vichy under Pétain and Laval were painful to France, they were far more tragic for Jews. And yet fifty years after the war, France is coming to grips with the collaborationist Vichy regime role in deporting some 76,000 Jews. In 1994, at least one Frenchman, Paul Touvier, who was then 79, was brought to trial for crimes against humanity during the war— the first Frenchman brought to trial for crimes against humanity. He served in a pro-Nazi militia during the German occupation of France. Touvier was a key aide during World War II to Gestapo chief Klaus Barbie, who was tried in 1987 for war crimes and sentenced to life imprisonment. Barbie died in 1991.

Touvier picked at random seven Jewish prisoners and lined them up in front of the cemetery wall at Rillieux-la-Page, outside of Lyon. They were shot by a firing squad. In April 1994, a French court convicted him of the charge of crimes against humanity and he was sentenced to life imprisonment. Writing in *The New York Times,* on April 20, 1994, Alan Riding stated, "The trial assumed special significance because it was the first time a French court had examined any aspect of French persecution of Jews when the country was under German occupation between 1940 and 1944."

Another Vichy aide accused of war crimes, Rene Bousquet, had been shot dead by a lone gunman at his home in Paris in 1993, thus precluding a long-promised public trial.

A third accused of war crimes, Maurice Papon, still faces charges and may never be brought to face a court on charges of crimes against humanity.

To this day, the memory of Vichy remains a stain on the nation. All the trials force the French more and more to assign responsibility to Vichy France for its "complicity" with the

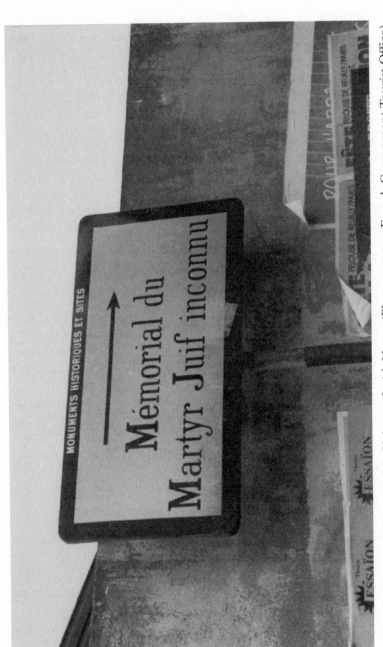

A sign leading to the Memorial of the Unknown Jewish Martyr. (Photo courtesy French Government Tourist Office)

Nazis in the deportation of Jews from France, a fact that many in France have known but have preferred to remain silent about. As Susan Zuccotti has shown in her book, *The Holocaust, the French, and the Jews*, Vichy was overtly and actively chauvinistic and anti-Semitic.

At first, Vichy, which was subservient to Germany, turned over only foreign Jews to the Nazis. Later, when the Germans seized all of France, Jews—French-born or not—were seized. Still, of the approximately 75,000 Jews deported to the concentration camps, only 15,000 were of French descent. The remaining 60,000 were either naturalized or immigrants. If we include all the other Jews who found themselves on French soil when the Armistice was declared, we find that 10 percent of French Jews died. This contrasts with the death of 40 percent of immigrant or recently arrived Jews. France lost about 25 percent of her Jews, including foreigners, in comparison to 55 percent for Belgium and 86 percent for Holland.

French Jews played an outstanding role in the Resistance. Some say that one-quarter of the Resistance was Jewish.

Today, a new organization, the Association of Conservatoire Camp de Drancy, reminds men and women everywhere of the camp, which was liberated on August 17, 1944. One of the apartments has been made over into a flat just as it was during the war. For further information on the former camp and the model apartment, contact the Association du Conservatoire Camp de Drancy, 15 Cite de la Muette, 93700 Le Drancy. Tel: 48-32-11-21 or 48-95-35-05.

A **synagogue** in Drancy is located at 15, boulevard St. Simon, Drancy. Tel: 48-32-54-82.

Memorial of the Unknown Jewish Martyr, 17, rue Geoffroy-l'Asnier, 75004, Paris. Tel: 42-27-44-72. FAX: 48-87-12-50. Metro: Pont-Marie or Saint-Paul. This four-story memorial is one of the most moving Jewish sites in Paris and a tribute to the six million Jews who perished in the Holocaust. The museum displays documents and photographs of Nazi camps and prisons and contains material devoted to the Archives of the Centre Documentation Juive Contemporaine. Before one enters the building, however, one passes through a massive courtyard that

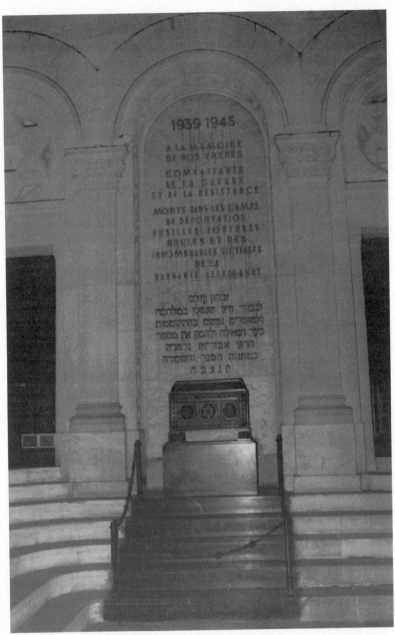

A synagogue memorial to those who died at the hands of the Nazis in World War II. (Photo courtesy French Government Tourist Office)

actually is the roof of an underground crypt. In the street-level courtyard is a large bronze cylinder shaped in the form of a burial urn. On it are engraved the names of some of the notorious concentration camps and the Warsaw Ghetto. Below the courtyard—two flights down—is a tomb of black marble in the form of a Star of David. An "eternal flame" flickers at its center. Erected in 1956, the memorial building contains archives, books, and a library reading room. Open Monday through Friday, 10 to noon and 2 to 5; open Sunday, 2 to 5.

Memorial to the Deported is located in a garden behind Notre Dame on the tip of the Ile de la Cité, not far from the Pletzel. This memorial is dedicated to the 200,000 French men and women of all races and religions who died in the Nazi death camps during World War II.

Vél' d'Hiv, located at 8, boulevard Grennelle, Paris, 15th Arrondissement (Metro: Bir Hakeim.). A plaque on this monument commemorates the imprisonment of Jews rounded up by the French police and placed in the Vélodrome d'Hiver Stadium on July 16, 1942. This was a huge indoor sports arena for winter bicycle races, eventually torn down in 1989. When a large-scale manhunt was conducted in Paris on July 16, 1942, about 13,000 Jews, including 4,000 children, were arrested and corralled at the sports facility. "The operation was poetically christened 'Spring Wind' by the French Police, who executed the German orders with almost excessive zeal," writes Annie Cohen-Solal in *Sartre: A Life.* Later they were moved to Drancy, a gathering camp, and sent to Auschwitz. More Jews were rounded up during the summer. The July and August transports included 25,000 French Jews. In the Holocaust, some 75,000 Jews were deported from France to death camps, and only 3,000 of those survived. A square located at the intersection of quai de Grenelle and boulevard de Grenelle, near the former stadium, has been named "Place des Martyrs Juifs du Vélodrome d'Hiver" (Square of Jewish Martyrs of the Winter Velodrome).

On July 16, 1995, French President Jacques Chirac's admission of national guilt for deporting Jews to Nazi death camps during World War II was received as a "significant historical step," and Jewish leaders throughout the world praised the French President's commentary on Vel d'Hiv. Chirac said in his speech, "Fifty-three years ago . . . 450 French police officers, acting under the authority of their chiefs, complied with the Nazis' demands." He added, "the criminal insanity of the occupier was assisted by the French people, by the French state." Until then, no French leader had acknowledged the state's role in collaborating with the Germans in deporting Jews.

OTHER SITES

Hotel de Castille, 37, rue Cambon. This is the building in which Theodor Herzl, the father of modern Zionism, wrote his famous tract, *The Jewish State*. The spark was the trial of Capt. Alfred Dreyfus. Nearly 100 years after emancipation, the Jews of the Republic and the world were shocked by the Dreyfus Affair. For most of the nineteenth century, anti-Semitism had been a weapon in the hands of the royalists, the clergy, the military. These forces also opposed successive Republican governments. The battle lines were being drawn. Usually, the conservative anti-Republican forces disliked the Jews.

Statue of Capt. Alfred Dreyfus, on the Boulevard Raspail in a small park near the intersection with Notre Dame de Champs. Captain Dreyfus, a Jew, was a member of the general staff of the French Army. The victim of a forgery, he was framed and unjustly court-martialed in a secret trial in 1894. There were many reasons to go after Dreyfus: "he was rich, he was snobbish and he was a Jew."

The charges, the trial, and the resultant riots tore France asunder. They unleashed a wave of anti-Semitism. Every family was affected. The French were split down the middle; you were either for, or against, Dreyfus. A crisis of conscience had penetrated France and the repercussions caused an upheaval in political life that translated into serious consequences for Jewish life. Shock waves rocked Europe. Found guilty of treason, Dreyfus was relegated to Devil's Island, where he spent almost five years. However, some citizens of France rallied to his side. Among them was the writer Emile Zola (1840–1902), who on January 13, 1898, published an open letter to the president of the Republic. It appeared on the front page of the newspaper *L'Aurore* and was entitled, "J'accuse." Proclaiming Dreyfus's innocence, it accused his attackers of libel. Zola is buried in the Pantheon.

Dreyfus was retried by a military court. But again, he was found guilty by army officers who just could not admit the army was guilty of conspiracy. Later, after he had been exonerated and pardoned, Dreyfus was reinstated in the army. On July 28, 1906, he received the Order of the Legion of Honor. In World War I, he served with dignity and honor. He died in the 1930s as a colonel in the French Army. He is buried in the Montparnasse Cemetery, Division 29.

As a result of the trumped-up charges against Dreyfus and the new anti-Semitism, Theodor Herzl, then a Viennese journalist in Paris, founded the Zionist movement, which brought about the State of Israel. In the cobblestone military courtyard, as Dreyfus was being marched around the square and drummed out of the army, Herzl heard the captain shout: "I am innocent." Stefan Zweig wrote that the incident "convulsed Herzl's soul." Herzl knew Dreyfus was innocent: "He [Dreyfus] had brought the horrible suspicion of treason on himself merely by being Jewish." Subsequently, Herzl wrote his famous pamphlet, *The Jewish State,* in the Hotel de Castille.

CEMETERIES

Père Lechaise, boulevard de Menilmontant, Paris. (Another entrance is at rue des Rondeaux and for this, take the Metro to the Gambretta stop.) This is Paris's most impressive cemetery and many famous Jews are buried here, including many of the Rothschild family (Division 7). Some of the more noted Jewish persons buried here are the actresses Rachel (Division 7) and Sarah Bernhardt (Division 44), the painter Rosa Bonheur (Division 44), and writers Marcel Proust and Gertrude Stein (Division 85). The cemetery was opened in 1803.

Sephardic Cemetery, 44, rue de Flandres. Many Sephardic Jews who lived in Paris before the Revolution are buried here. Apply at the office of the Consistoire Central of Paris for the key, 17, rue St-Georges, 75009, Paris. Tel: 40-82-26-26.

RECOMMENDED HOTELS

Recommended hotels in Paris include Hotel Inter-Continental, 3, rue de Castiglione, 75040, Paris, Tel: 44-77-11-11; and Le Grand Hotel at 2, rue Scribe, Paris, Tel: 40-07-32-32, FAX: 42-66-12-51. Both of these are fine, first-class hotels. The Inter-Continental offers a full range of services and facilities for business and vacation travelers. It has recaptured its past history and it still has old-time charm and comfort. The Grand Hotel has undergone a drastic restoration and renovation. This is a palace-type hotel and it has close proximity to the Opera.

Also recommended are the Le Warwick and Westminster hotels. The Warwick often has kosher catered events. The Warwick is located at 5, rue de Berri, 75008, Paris, just 50 meters from what many call the "most beautiful avenue in the world," the Champs-Elysées. That is important because today there is no hotel on the Champs-Elysées itself. This is a good and unique business person's hotel as it contains conference rooms, telex, FAX machines, and parking with direct access to the lobby. The hotel is a fully air-conditioned, modern deluxe hotel.

Hotel Westminster at 13, rue de la Paix, 75002, Paris. Tel: 42-61-57-46. This one is a favorite, as it is located between the historical Opera and Place Vendrome. Surrounded by world-famous jewelry shops, the Hotel Westminster offers 102 elegant rooms and suites decorated in classical French style. Antique furniture, marble bathrooms, and crystal chandeliers complete the luxurious interior of the hotel.

The French Countryside

Paris dominates the cultural, business, governmental, and entertainment life of France. But that certain French "sweetness of life" is also found in Angers and Avignon, Biarritz and Bordeaux, St-Tropez and St-Jean-de-Luz, Lyon and Limoges, Strasbourg and St-Malo, Nice and Cannes.

The Hotel Westminster, rue de la Paix. Paris. (Photo courtesy Hotel Westminster)

THE LOIRE IS HEARTLAND FRANCE

A good place to start is the fabled valley of Loire, the Garden of France, and its special section, Touraine, which encompasses the famous town of Tours.

Step back into a magnificent past. Visit the amazing chateaux at **Amboise** with its sumptuous setting and wonderful views, **Brissac** with its two round defensive towers on a building standing in a fine park, **Chambord** with its rich Renaissance decoration, **Chaumont-sur-Loire** with its beautiful site on the Loire, and **Chenonceaux** with its gardens and edifice astride the gentle river. It is indeed a horticultural delight.

Follow the majestic river Loire through the heart of France. Travel alongside it from Orleans westward to Angers and Nantes on to the Atlantic Ocean. Jews settled in Touraine at the time of the Romans. They lived along the river and were active in shipping, commerce, and boating.

Centers of Jewish life flourished in the Loire Valley in the towns of Orleans, Tours, Chinon, and Angers. Today a Jewish community thrives again because thousands of Sephardic Jews from North Africa have migrated here to give the area new energy.

Visit a few of these Loire towns.

Angers

Angers is a town to roam around. The counts and dukes of Anjou made it their cultural center. Throughout the ages, it has remained the gateway to the west of France and to Brittany.

Angers is a major hub of commerce, transportation, and culture. Its gastronomy and wine cellars, parks and gardens, proximity to the chateaux at Brissac and Saumur, as well as its galleries, museums, and modern new library, make it a wonderful stop.

This capital of the Maine et Loire boasts a very fine, hospitable Jewish community.

The Jewish traveler will probably have a rewarding experience attending a Friday night service. At the Orthodox synagogue, there is usually a small minyan (quorum of 10 men) on the Sabbath eve. The congregation welcomes you with warm informality; they are extremely friendly.

Synagogue and **Community Center,** 12, rue Valdemaine, 49100, Angers. Tel: 41-87-48-18 or 41-87-48-10. FAX: 41-37-11-79. Passover seder and holiday celebrations are held.

About 50 Jewish families live in Angers. Mr. Samuel Marciano conducts the services, but on special occasions, a rabbi from Nantes visits the community.

Today two town streets are named after two notable Jewish personalities: Place Pierre Mendes-France, one of France's prime ministers, and Place Anne Frank (formerly known as de la Juiverie).

Tourist information can be obtained at the **Office of Tourism,** Place Kennedy, B.P. 2397, 49023, Angers. Tel: 41-88-69-93.

Orleans

"Paris is the head of France, Orleans is its heart," they say. Once Orleans was the second most important city in France. On May 8, 1429, Joan of Arc entered the city as its deliverer from the English and persuaded Charles VII to claim his throne.

Jews lived in Orleans before the sixth century. During the Middle Ages, its Jewish community was an important center of Jewish learning. In the fourteenth century, the Jews were expelled, not to return until the beginning of the nineteenth century.

The **Synagogue** and **Community Center** are located at 14, rue Robert-de-Courtenay, 45000, Orleans. Tel: 38-62-16-62. The synagogue is the heart of the Jewish community. This house of study, meeting place, and sanctuary is not difficult to find. It is next door to the cathedral, which dates from the Middle Ages. For further information, visitors can call Mr. Cogos, Tel: 38-88-40-13 or Mrs. Klein, Tel: 38-53-16-47.

Tourist information can be obtained at the **Office of Tourism,** boulevard Aristide Briand, 45000, Orleans. Tel: 38-53-05-95.

Tours

This is the home of Rabelais, Descartes, and Balzac—the home of good books, fine food, and distinctive wine.

Tours is probably one of the best starting points from which to see the impressive chateaux of the Loire. It is a convenient place from which to make excursions. Tours possesses one of the oldest Jewish communities in France. The first Jews probably arrived here in 570. Later, in medieval times, a Jewish quarter and synagogue thrived in this market town and provincial capital. Today about 200 Jewish families live in Tours.

Well worth a visit is the **Musée des Beaux-Arts,** 18, Place François-Secord, 37000, Tours. Tel: 47-05-68-73.

Historial de Touraine, Musée Grevin, Chateau Royal, Quai D'Orleans, 37000, Tours. Tel: 47-61-02-95. Brought to life here is the history of Touraine from the Gallo-Roman period to the mid-twentieth century. In almost lifelike scenes, painters, doctors, writers, and politicians are all on view: in one scene, French Jewish Prime Minister Leon Blum, and in another, Nobel Prize-winner Henri Bergson, the French Jewish philosopher.

Synagogue, 37, rue Parmentier, 37000, Tours. Tel: 47-05-56-95. Services are held at 6:30 Friday evenings in the winter and 7 P.M. during the summer. Saturday morning services are at 9. A study class conducted by the rabbi takes place every Saturday evening at 7. The synagogue was founded in 1908.

For those needing to stock up on or replenish kosher food for their journey through France, go to the store at 38, rue Parmentier, which sells kosher items. Open five days a week. Call the synagogue first for more information as to exact hours.

A **Jewish Community Center** is located at 6, rue Chalmel, Tours. Tel: 47-05-59-97.

Tourist information can be obtained at the **Office of Tourism,** Place du Marechal Leclerc, 37000, Tours. Tel: 47-05-58-08.

REIMS

All the kings of France were crowned in Reims, now conveniently a less than two-hour drive from Paris. It was in the cathedral in 1429 that Joan of Arc, after a legendary ride, achieved her wish of seeing Charles VII crowned king of France.

Reims proudly possesses one of the most beautiful and unique synagogues in the northeast part of France. Built in 1879, its architecture is imposing indeed.

A synagogue functioned here in medieval times. After the expulsion of the Jews from France in the fourteenth century, they did not reside in Reims for about 500 years. In 1820, a small group settled in the city.

Fifty years later, Jews from Alsace-Lorraine began to arrive in Reims, which is famous for its champagne wineries, its historic cathedral, as well as the schoolhouse where Supreme Allied Commander Dwight D. Eisenhower accepted the German surrender in May 1945.

Today 150 Jewish families live in Reims.

The **synagogue** at 49, rue Clovis, Reims, also has a community center. Tel: 26-47-25-69.

Tourist information is available at the **Office of Tourism,** 1, rue Jadart, 51100, Reims. Tel: 26-47-68-47.

STRASBOURG

Known as the Jerusalem of France, Strasbourg is an active, highly organized, intellectual Jewish community of about 12,500 persons. Most of the chief rabbis of France have come from this center of Jewry, which has deep roots in the province of Alsace.

The large, beautiful **Synagogue de la Paix** with its community center is located on la rue du Grand-Rabbin-Rene-Hirschler (avenue de la Paix), 67000, Strasbourg. Tel: 88-35-61-35. FAX: 88-24-26-69. Dedicated in 1958, the synagogue features a bronze menorah and a bronze grill which grace the front of the structure. Visitors have included the late President of the Republic Charles de Gaulle, Moshe Dayan, and Golda Meir.

This new synagogue replaced the historic Synagogue Consistoriale du Quai Kleber, which was destroyed by the Nazis in the war. The city has yeshivot and Talmud Torahs.

Akiba, 9-10, quai Zorn, 67000, Strasbourg. Tel: 88-35-48-58. Seven hundred students are enrolled in this famous day school.

Alsatian Museum, 23, quai St-Nicolas, Strasbourg. This site has a rich collection of Jewish ritual objects in an exhibit entitled "History of the Jews of Alsace-Lorraine."

Worth visiting is Strasbourg's **"La Petite France,"** an ancient quarter of 400-year-old houses.

Visitors to Strasbourg can enjoy a kosher meal in the **Restaurant Chalom** in the **Commmunity Center of the Synagogue** at la rue du Grand-Rabbin-Rene-Hirschler, Strasbourg. Tel: 88-36-56-30.

Magen David, 28, rue Sellenick, Strasbourg. Tel: 88-35-15-04. Bakery.

Restaurant Universitaire, 11, rue Sellenick, Strasbourg. Tel: 88-25-67-97.

Struthof Concentration Camp. F 67130 Natzweiller. Located on Route D 130, 50 kilometers west of Strasbourg in Alsace. On this site stands the only concentration camp built by the Nazis in France. They called it the "Konzentrationlager Natzweiller Elsass." Set up on May 12, 1941, its victims were from throughout Europe and included, French, German, Dutch, and Russian prisoners of war. Horrible medical experiments were conducted on 87 Jewish victims, including 30 women, all of whom perished. The camp was liberated by the First French Army and the Sixth American Army Corps on November 23, 1944.

A **Memorial to the Deported** was inaugurated by President Charles de Gaulle on July 23, 1960. The 41.5-meter-high concrete shaft spirals. Designed by architect B. Monnet, it not only symbolizes the flame of the crematorium, but also infinite freedom. The emaciated silhouette sculpted on the memorial by Lucien Fennaux recalls the hunger that precedes death. An inscription honors an "unknown deported prisoner." Another commemorative tablet reads: "Aux heros et martyrs de la

Deportation, la France reconnaissante," (To the heroes and martyrs transported, The French Republic is grateful). A visitor to the camp sees barracks, memorial stones, a national cemetery, and the crematorium. The crematorium has been preserved as well as an ash pit located between two huts and down close to the forest where the ashes of the victims were spread. A commemorative tablet with the Star of David memorializes the 87 Jews who were killed in this camp's gas chamber, as well as the six million Jews who were murdered by the Nazis throughout Europe during World War II. A museum has been placed at the entrance of the camp. Located close to the camp is the sand quarry where camp inmates were forced to toil. Three kilometers down the road back towards Struthof, visitors can view the gas chamber where they were put to death. For further information on the Struthof Concentration Camp, contact the Historical Society of the Jews of Alsace and Lorraine, c/o Andre Marc Haarscher, Secretaire, 20 rue Erwin, F 67000 Strasbourg. Tel: 88-22-01-02. FAX: 88-75-67-64. Hours: 9 A.M. to noon and 2 P.M. to 5 P.M.. The site is closed from December 25 to February 28. Entrance fee: FF8 (8 French francs) per person or FF5 per person for groups of ten or more. Children under 16 are free. Information: Camp de Concentration du Struthof, F 67130 Natzweiller. Tel: 88-97-04-04 or Tel: 88-76-76-76, ext. 6383, for the Direction Departementale des Anciens Combattants, Service du Struthof. Directions: 56.5 kilometers west of Strasbourg. From Strasbourg, take Highway A 35 followed by N 420 in the direction of Schirmeck/St-Die. In Schirmeck, take direction Rothau, then direction Natzweiller (Route D 130). The camp is located in the mountains on Road D 130, next to the village of Natzweiller. Coming from Paris on Highway A 4, take the Saverne exit. Then take direction Molsheim on Road N 4. In Molsheim, take direction Schirmeck Road N 420, and follow as above.

Lubavitch Youth, 59, faubourg de Pierre, 67000, Strasbourg. Tel: 88-75-66-05.

Tourist information is available at the **Office of Tourism,** Place des Congres, avenue Schutzenberger, 67000, Strasbourg. Tel: 88-35-03-00.

DIJON

Visit Dijon, provincial capital of Burgundy, the home of the legendary dukes. Here are the palaces of the dukes who in 1196 placed the Jews under their protection. Here is a small Arc de Triomphe in a city that is an important rail link in one of Europe's technologically advanced train systems.

About 250 Jewish families live in this charming university town in central France, 200 miles southeast of Paris. This fifteenth-century city of clean, winding pedestrian streets, of quaint shops, cafes, and homes, is also the headquarters of famous Dijon mustard and cassis. No wonder Dijon is often called the gastronomical capital of France, and, of course, boasts rare wines to go with delicious cuisine. Dedicated in 1879, the **synagogue** in Dijon is the focal point of the Jewish community. It is located at 5, rue de la Synagogue 21000, Dijon. Services are held Friday evenings and Saturday mornings. Activities for young people are held in the synagogue on Sundays. For information about kosher food and services, contact synagogue officials at Tel: 80-66-46-47 or Rabbi Simon Siboney, Tel: 80-67-50-98.

Many Jewish tourists visit Dijon for wine tasting and begin week-long vacations on the popular barge waterway program on the Burgundy Canal and Saone River.

Tourist information can be obtained at the **Office of Tourism,** Place Darcy, 21000, Dijon. Tel: 80-43-56-05.

LYON

To inhale the quality of French life outside of Paris, visit Lyon. This 2,000-year-old city on two rivers should be a stop on any tour of France. All roads lead to Lyon, France's second largest metropolitan area. More than 35,000 Jews call Lyon home, a unique location along the banks of the Saone and Rhone rivers. They live in the Lyon area, including Villeurbanne. They support over 20 synagogues, 15 kosher butcher shops, several kosher restaurants and day schools, and 13 Talmud Torahs.

Happily, Lyon keeps the charm of a great provincial city. This city of bridges is noted for the manufacture of silk. Lyon

Lyon. (Photo courtesy French Government Tourist Office)

boasts pleasantly paced living with parks, an extraordinary rose garden, sweeping pedestrian malls, a giant shopping center, plus 24 major museums.

The city's **Gallo-Roman Art Museum** is a unique design by Israeli architect Bernard Zehrfuss.

I like Lyon even if, as Ted Morgan notes, it "has always been in the shadow of Paris." It sports the Palace Bellecour, one of the largest public squares in France. It stands as a prosperous trading center and, let us face it, Lyon means serious gastronomy; it is, after all, a city of "haute cuisine," with its superb restaurants.

Many consider Lyon the capital of the French Resistance in World War II. Significantly, Lyon broke into the news headlines in the 1980s as the city that hosted the trial of the Gestapo commander, the late Klaus Barbie, otherwise known as "The Butcher of Lyon." This city not only served as the base for the French Resistance, but as a center of French Jewry. Barbie was stationed in Lyon and was responsible for the sending of area Jews—including the homeless, orphaned children at Izieu—to the gas chambers, as well as the torture and killing of French Resistance leaders, including Jean Moulin. Twice condemned to death in absentia after the war, Barbie lived in Latin America for several decades until he was tracked down by Beate Klarsfield, who searches for Nazis, in Bolivia in 1972 and brought to France 11 years later. He was convicted in 1987 as the chief enforcer of a Nazi reign of terror. Sentenced to life imprisonment, he died a prisoner in a French hospital in Lyon in the fall of 1991.

Sites in Lyon

Fonds Social Juif Unifié, 145 Gde, rue de la Guillotiere, 69007, Lyon. Tel: 78-72-88-23.

Musée de la Résistance, 5, rue Boileau.

Kosher Restaurants

Le Grillon D'Or, 20, rue Terme, 69001, Lyon. Tel: 78-27-33-09.

Lippmann, 4, rue Tony-Tollet, 69002, Lyon. Tel: 78-42-49-82. Lyonnaise kosher cuisine.

Synagogues in Lyon

American visitors will find a warm welcome at the synagogue-office of the Grand Rabbinat de Lyon and Rabbi Richard Wertenschlag, at the historic **Grande Synagogue,** 13, quai Tilsitt, 69002, Lyon. Tel: 78-37-13-43. FAX: 78-42-49-86. Write in advance to the rabbi for information regarding services and kosher food. This synagogue was built in 1864. Many American Jewish tourists attend services here.

Charre Tzedek, 18, rue St-Mathieu, 69008, Lyon. Tel: 78-00-72-50.

Ecole Juive, 40, rue Alexandre Boutin, 69100, Villeurbanne. Tel: 78-24-38-91.

La Fraternité, 4, rue Malherbe, 69100, Villeurbanne. Tel: 78-24-38-91.

Lubavitch Youth. Tel: 78-89-08-32.

Neveh Chalom at Centre Communautaire, 317, rue Duguesclin, 69007, Lyon. Tel: 78-58-18-74. This is a beautiful new Sephardic synagogue and community center. Many activities are held here.

Oratoire Etz Hayim Yechouron, 60, rue Crillon, 69006, Lyon. Tel: 78-89-08-32.

Oratoire Lubavitch, 3, impasse Cazenove, 69006, Lyon. Tel: 33-78-89-08-32.

Tourist information is available at the **Office of Tourism,** Place Bellecour, 69000, Lyon. Tel: 33-78-89-08-32.

BORDEAUX

Bordeaux, France's fifth largest metropolitan area, has a special place in Jewish history. Bordeaux is important in Jewish history because many of the Marranos—secret Jews—escaped from Spain and Portugal to this port city.

There are many interesting individuals in the area who know much about the Sephardic Jews of Bordeaux. If you're not in a hurry and would like to learn about a rich Jewish past which dates back to the sixth century, Bordeaux is a prime place to begin. On the eve of the French Revolution, only a few thousand Jews lived in France. Most were Sephardic Jews in Bordeaux and Bayonne.

On January 28, 1790, the leaders of the French Revolution declared that all Jews in France who were known as "Portuguese, Spanish and Avignonnais Jews . . shall enjoy the rights of citizens." Twenty months later on September 27, 1791, after debate and delays, all the other Jews of France, including Ashkenazim, were emancipated. France became the first European state to grant its Jewish residents the rights of citizenship.

Today, this active city of about 650,000 boasts eighteenth-century architecture, with an elegant **Grand Theater** in the very center of town. Outside the city are the celebrated vineyards of Mouton Rothschild, Chateau Lafitte, Chateau Margaux, and many others.

More than 15 Jewish organizations meet at the **Jewish Community Center** at 15, Place Charles Gruet, 33000, Bordeaux. Tel: 56-52-62-69. There are active B'nai B'rith and B.B.Y.O. groups in the center.

The **synagogue,** built in 1882 in the Spanish-Portuguese style, is at 8, rue du Grand Rabbin-Joseph-Cohen, 33000, Bordeaux. Tel: 56-91-79-39.

Henry IV is a kosher restaurant located at 89, rue Henry IV, Bordeaux. Tel: 56-92-74-90. The **Consistoire** is located at 213, rue Ste-Catherine, 33000, Bordeaux. Tel: 56-91-79-39. Further information on services and kosher food can be obtained by calling Tel: 56-91-79-39, at the synagogue.

Tourist information is available at the **Office of Tourism,** 12, cours 30-Juillet, 33000, Bordeaux. Tel: 56-44-28-41.

THE SOUTHWEST

Three towns, Biarritz, Anglet, and Bayonne, located in the southwest, are known as the "BAB" towns. About 250 Jewish families live in these municipalities. Most of the Jews who came here after the Inquisition and expulsion from Spain and Portugal were Marranos. They were called the "Portuguese

Nation," for it was safer to be called Portuguese than Jew. They settled in the BAB town area, which is about 25 miles from the Spanish border. In 1619, there were 2,000 Jewish congregants here. They and their descendants flourished in the area. Today, these "Basque-Country" Jews continue to prosper. Let us go first to Biarritz.

Biarritz

Biarritz is a resort town made famous by the monarchs of Europe, including Napoleon III, who built what is now the luxurious **Hotel du Palais** for his wife, Eugenie. The aristocracy summered in this city of nineteenth-century charm, and it remains an attractive summer place.

Synagogue, at corner of rue de la Russie and rue Pellot, 64200, Biarritz. Services during summer and on holidays only. Kosher food is available through the synagogue in nearby Bayonne. Tel: 59-55-03-95.

Tourist information can be obtained at the **Office of Tourism,** Square d'Ixelles, 64200, Biarritz. Tel: 59-24-20-24.

Bayonne

During the early sixteenth century, the Marranos from Portugal and Spain, who practiced Judaism secretly, were fearful that the long arm of the Inquisition would reach across the border from Spain and snare them in Bayonne, if they revealed their identity. They had settled in Bayonne because it was a thriving port and the commercial capital of Gascony. But when they came here, they were forced to live in the St-Esprit section of the city. Today they still live there, voluntarily of course. The neighborhood of St-Esprit, which supports a synagogue, is called Little Jerusalem.

Synagogue, 35, rue Maubec, 64100, Bayonne. Tel: 59-55-03-95.

Musée Basque de Bayonne, 1, rue Marengo, 64100, Bayonne. Tel: 59-59-08-98. The museum, dedicated to Basque history, draws visitors from all over the world. A room is devoted to Jewish religious objects, mezuzoth, prayer books, lithographs, and candles. It is well worth a visit.

Tourist information can be obtained at the **Office of Tourism,** Place de la Liberté, 64100, Bayonne. Tel: 59-59-31-31.

St-Jean-de-Luz

Because the beach resort of St-Jean-de-Luz has a small Jewish population of less than 100, visiting it will be a delightful experience. The town harbored many Jews who fled from Spain in the sixteenth century.

During World War II, Jews escaping the Nazis crossed here into Spain. Today the small Jewish community in this fishing village resort attends services in nearby Bayonne.

Tourist information is available at the **Office of Tourism,** Place du Marechal Foch, 64500, St-Jean-de-Luz. Tel: 59-26-03-75.

Pau

Gateway to the Basque Country, this nineteenth-century resort, popular with the English, was made famous by Henry IV, a Protestant king of France. Here in southwest France, Pau (pronounced "Po"), with a population of about 150,000, beckons every visitor to begin a sojourn by walking along the attractive boulevard des Pyrenees and marveling at the imposing mountain range.

About 160 Jewish families live in Pau. They support an active synagogue and a kosher butcher shop. The **synagogue** is located at 8, rue Trois-Frères-de-Bernadec, 64000, Pau. Tel: 59-62-37-85. A community center and Talmud Torah are part of the synagogue building, which survived World War II.

Services are held Friday evenings, Saturday mornings, and Saturday evenings.

Tourist information can be obtained at the **Office of Tourism,** Place Royale, 64000, Pau. Tel: 59-27-27-08.

Montpellier

Montpellier is a city rich in architecture, with charming eighteenth-century houses, the famous neoclassical pavilion Chateau d'Eau, and the Musée Fabre, one of the best museums outside of Paris. Rabelais once studied medicine here in

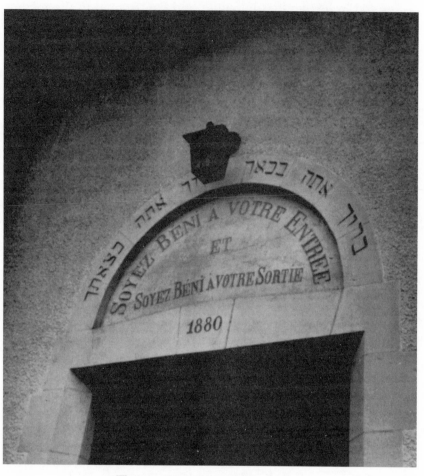

The entrance to the synagogue in Pau.

the city's fine medical facility, part of one of France's most famous universities. Many Jewish doctors and Talmudists resided in medieval Montpellier and contributed to the medical faculty. Today, Montpellier is considered a resort town with sandy beaches.

The **Musée Fabre,** at 37 boulevard Sarrail, is located in a district which boasts beautiful seventeenth- and eighteenth-century palaces.

Synagogue Ben-Zakai, 7, rue Général-Laffon, 34000, Montpellier. Tel: 67-92-02-07.

Synagogue, 18, rue Ferdinand-Fabre, 34000, Montpellier. Tel: 67-79-09-82.

Jewish Radio Station, 45, rue Proudhon.

Jewish Community Center, 27, rue Ferdinand Fabre, Montpellier, Tel: 67-79-68-93.

Beth Chabad, 10 Boulevard Berthelot, Montpellier, 34000, Tel: 33-67-92-86-93.

Toulouse

Toulouse is called *La Ville Rose,* "the pink city," and rightly so, for the sights, the gourmet restaurants, the architecture, the unhurried pace, the atmosphere of a university city (one-third of the population are students) spell out a cultural and intellectual city.

"If you are in Toulouse, you are safe." That is a saying that was not only heard during World War II, but also during the days of the Spanish Inquisition, especially in the fifteenth and sixteenth centuries.

During World War II, Toulouse was one of the principal centers for resistance to the Nazi invaders. Not only did Jews find refuge in this city steeped in history, but the Organisation Juive de Combat was founded in Toulouse and its leaders would often meet there.

One Jewish historian says Jews have resided in the area ever since the destruction of the second temple. Today, more than 28,000 Jewish residents call Toulouse their home. This is a city that has 30 to 40 active Jewish organizations; 6 kosher butcher shops; 3 day schools, including a technical school sponsored by

ORT; and 9 synagogues, with 3 functioning every day.

Only an hour's flight from Paris and located in the Midi-Pyrenees in the heart of France's Southwest, this region of open spaces, unique and prestigious, stands as an area where everything is possible. And it is right smack in the middle of the old trade routes between Montpellier and Bordeaux. For those interested in Jewish history, this is the road that makes its way from Beziers to Narbonne, to Carcassonne, to Toulouse, the principal cities of Languedoc, this delightful province bordering on the Mediterranean.

Centre Maimonide, 14, rue du Rempart-St-Etienne, 31000, Toulouse. Tel: 61-23-36-59. Located here is the synagogue, called the Old-New Synagogue because many of the Jews of Toulouse came from North Africa and brought from those lands, some of the synagogue's fixtures, such as the chandeliers. Beginning in 1995, plans were underway to build a new Jewish community center of 3,000 square meters, with 20 rooms, sports facilities, a restaurant and banquet area, and a mikveh.

Restaurant Le Kotel, 9, rue Clemence Isaure, 31000, Toulouse. Tel: 61-29-03-04. When in Toulouse, visit this excellent, strictly kosher restaurant. Hebrew, English, French, and Yiddish are spoken here. American visitors and business people involved with aerospace frequent this establishment. Served here are some favorite dishes such as gefilte fish, couscous, lamb, steak, chicken, and fish. The ownership is dedicated to keeping kosher ritual alive in this city. Hours are from 12 noon to 3 P.M. during the week and 8 to 11 P.M. Saturday night. The piano bar functions in a "cavelike" atmosphere. Closed on Friday night and the Sabbath.

Snack Pita Burger, 21, place Victor Hugo, Toulouse. Tel: 61-21-95-36. Kosher.

Synagogue Adath-Israel, 17, rue Alsace-Lorraine, 31000, Toulouse.

THE SOUTHEAST

Jewish communities dot the Southeast of France in Provence and the Alps. A comfortable way to reach such centers as Avignon, Nimes, and St-Etienne is the speedy and on-time

French National Railways, especially T.G.V., the world's fastest train, which averages 186 miles per hour.

Moving southward, a visitor sees and feels the warmth of Provence with its luminous sun, sleepy Roman towns, and striking antiquities. Its bright blue sky has inspired French artists, including Vincent van Gogh, Paul Cezanne, and Marc Chagall.

Provence is so named because it was the Province of Rome. Towns that attract the traveler are classic Aix-en-Provence, medieval Avignon, Carpentras, Cavaillon, and the great port of Marseilles.

Keep in mind that a mere two hours from Marseilles or Avignon are the celebrated ski slopes of the French Alps at the foot of Mont-Blanc, Europe's highest peak.

Provence was once an important European Jewish center—a place where Jews have lived continually in spite of persecutions and expulsions. The earliest evidence of Jews in Provence dates from the fifth century in Arles and the sixth century in Marseilles. Five centuries later, Jews lived in many towns of Provence.

While Rabbenu Gershom and Rashi were the products of Judaism of northern France during the tenth and eleventh centuries, Provence in the south was undergoing its own renaissance of learning. When Benjamin of Tudela visited Provence in 1160, he found renowned scholars teaching hundreds of students.

Much has been told about the Jews of Avignon, who with their fellow co-religionists of Carpentras, Cavaillon, and L'Isle-sur-la-Sorgue comprise the four communities of the Comtat Venaissin, where Jews established important centers of learning. These towns were the cities of the papal states. Here Jews were given protection by the popes and served as financiers and merchants. They were called the "Pope's Jews," and as will be noted in the chapter on Italy, the thinking of the church leaders often was to protect the Jews as a reminder to those who might reject the Catholic church that they would also be punished.

Nimes

Historically a major center of Jewish life in this part of France, Nimes is proud of two famous native sons, both French Jewish personalities.

Isaac-Adolphe Cremieux (1796–1880), French lawyer and statesman, was minister of justice in the Government of National Defense in 1870. He issued the Cremieux Decree by which the Jews of Algeria received French citizenship. This decree was very meaningful, as it enabled Jews of Algeria to settle in France as French citizens in the 1960s.

Bernard Lazare (1865–1903), liberal publicist, helped obtain the freedom of Capt. Alfred Dreyfus, who had been unjustly accused of espionage.

This handsome city has some of the most remarkable Roman structures outside of Italy—the **Roman Arena** and **Maison Carrée**—as well as magnificent gardens, fine museums, and a colorful medieval quarter.

Synagogue, 40, rue Roussy, 30000, Nimes. Tel: 66-29-51-81. Built in 1794, it is still used as a house of worship.

Community Center, 5, rue d'Angouleme, 30000, Nimes. Tel: 66-76-27-64.

Tourist information can be obtained at the **Office of Tourism,** 6, rue Auguste, 30000, Nimes. Tel: 66-67-29-11.

Avignon

Mention Avignon, and artists come to mind, as well as the medieval walls of the city and the children's song, "Sur le pont d'Avignon" ("On the Bridge at Avignon"). After 1309, Avignon became the residence of the popes. Joanna, countess of Provence, sold the city to Pope Clement VI and it belonged to the French states of the Holy See until the French Revolution. Thus, Jews were able to stay there even when they were excluded from the rest of France.

Discover the city's festive ambiance from the vantage point of a cafe along the **brue de la République** or on the **Place de L'Horloge.**

The famous bridge at Avignon. (Photo courtesy French Government Tourist Office)

Another major site is the **Petit Palais Museum** of medieval painting and sculpture. Savor art and music festivals staged in the municipal theater, or performances of choirs in the Palace.

From the nineteenth century onward, Jewish life almost ceased, until it was revived in the 1960s by Sephardic immigrants. There is a very narrow street called **rue de la Vieille Juiverie,** the old Jewish Quarter. Avignon has a small Jewish community of about 2,500.

The **synagogue** is located at 2, Place Jerusalem, 84000, Avignon. Tel: 90-85-21-24. Services are at 6 Friday night, at 7 in the summer, and on Saturday mornings at 9. This unusual circular synagogue was built in the Roman manner. It was erected on the site of the old Jewish quarter of the thirteenth century.

A **community center** is located at 18, rue Guillaume-Puy. Tel: 90-82-64-87.

Information can be obtained at the **Office of Tourism,** 41, cours Jean-Jaures, 84000, Avignon. Tel: 90-82-65-11.

Arles

According to a Jewish legend, one of three rudderless ships bearing Jewish exiles arrived in Arles, 27 miles south of Avignon, after the destruction of the Second Temple in 70 C.E. The first evidence of Jewish life here dates back to the fifth century. Rome made Arles famous. An ancient Roman theater and a vast arena still stand in the city.

Benjamin of Tudela, the famous Jewish traveler, notes in the twelfth century that a Jewish community of 200 existed in Arles. Jews were expelled in 1481. After the French Revolution, some Jews from the Comtat Venaissin settled in Arles, the city to which the famous artist van Gogh brought fame.

The **Musée Arlaten,** located in the Palais de Laval-Castellane at 42, rue de la République, founded by the famous Provençal poet Frederic Mistral, preserves the relics of Old Provence. It contains a collection of Jewish religious and cultural objects. **The Arles Museum** houses the Lunel collection.

Tourist information is available at the **Office of Tourism,** 35, Place de la République, 13200, Arles. Tel: 90-96-29-35.

Cavaillon

A short drive from Avignon is the wonderful, provincial town of Cavaillon, "known throughout France mainly for the succulence of its melons." A visit to this town is recommended for a look at the eighteenth-century synagogue and Jewish museum of the Comtat Venaissin at rue Hébraique, between rue Chabran and rue de la République.

There are 50 to 75 Jews in Cavaillon. The **Musée Judéo-Comtadin,** sponsored by the municipality and housed in an elegant rococo building, is certainly worth seeing. Open from 10 to noon and 2 to 5 every day except Tuesday, it includes an oven for the baking of matzot, prayer books, Torah scrolls, candelabra, and shofars. Many relics of the fourteenth and fifteenth centuries were kept in an earlier structure on the same site. Built in 1772, it is a national monument. There is a synagogue above the museum.

If the museum and synagogue are closed, contact Mr. Mathon at nearby 23, rue Chabran. Another contact is Maurice Palombo, Magasin Gigo, 36, rue Raspail. Tel: 90-78-02-46.

Tourist information can be obtained at the **Office of Tourism,** 79, rue Saunerie, 84200, Cavaillon. Tel: 90-71-32-01.

Carpentras

Here in this bustling, commercial town is a **synagogue** that may well be the oldest in France. Erected in 1367, it was repaired in 1677, 1730, and 1885 and has been restored several times in the twentieth century. The synagogue of 1367 contained a men's area and a separate women's section in a cellar. Two basement levels contained a matzoh bakery and ritual bath. The bimah is situated in the middle of the prayer hall. High above the congregation is a chair for the Prophet Elijah. And unusual today is that the rabbi's place from which he gave a sermon is also above the congregation. The synagogue is located at Place de la Synagogue, 84200, opposite the Town Hall, also known as Place de la Mairie. A national monument, the synagogue is open every day from 10 to noon and 3 to 5. But services are not usually held in the synagogue. In

Carpentras, the functioning synagogue and community center is at place Maurice Charretier, BP 19084206, Carpentras. Tel: 90-63-39-97. Call for information as to schedule of services.

Carpentras has about 100 Jewish families and sponsors special activities, such as holiday celebrations. Henry Kamm wrote in *The New York Times* on September 15, 1991, that "the two synagogues of Carpentras and Cavaillon . . . are reminders of the squalid, overcrowded ghettos in which Jews were forced to live from the mid-1400s until the French Revolution freed them and scattered their communities."

Tourist information is available at the **Office of Tourism,** 170, avenue Jean Jaures, 84200, Carpentras. Tel: 90-63-00-78.

COTE D'AZUR

Mention the names Cannes, Nice, Monte Carlo, Cap Ferat, Antibes, Juan-les-Pins, and St-Tropez and you picture beaches, villages, sun terraces on high-rise apartments, promenades, modern art museums, fireworks, flowers, and Mardi Gras carnivals. Mention the words delightful climate, clear sky, refreshing breezes, deep-blue waters, orange groves, and cassia plantations and you bring up before your eyes the French Riviera. Picasso, Matisse, and Renoir succumbed to this azure coast that now boasts film and folk festivals, as well as a vibrant landscape dotted with red tiled roofs and Mediterranean trees and gardens. It is one of the most beautiful areas in the world. The Riviera lies between the Maritime Alps and the Mediterranean Sea. Swathed in sunshine, a monument to leisure, its inviting hills are an open-air atelier for artists, with all the ripe pleasures of summer and sea.

More than 35,000 Jews live and work in this vacationland from Toulon to Menton, Cannes, Antibes, St-Tropez, Nice, and Juan-les-Pins. The area offers tourists an exciting visit in scenic luxury.

Monte Carlo

The Monte Carlo Jewish community has undergone some exciting moments recently. A group of Americans, Canadians, and English, many of them retired, have added vitality to the

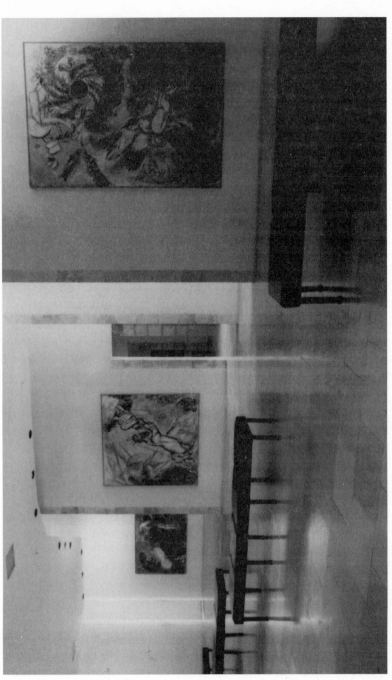

Inside the National Museum Biblical Message of Marc Chagall. (Photo courtesy French Government Tourist Office)

Sephardic Synagogue, which is located at 15, avenue de la Costa, 98000, Monaco. Tel: 93-30-16-46. FAX: 93-25-73-36. A community center is located there, too.

Half of the congregation is English-speaking and Ashkenazic. The Ashkenazim have joined with their Sephardic counterparts in attempting to improve the organization of the congregation.

In fact, one condominium on the boulevard des Moulins is the residence of a number of Anglo-Saxons, as they are called. Some of them are officers in the synagogue and leaders in the community. There are also a kosher butcher shop under the supervision of the Beth Din of Nice, a Talmud Torah, and several Jewish organizations.

Nice

Travel to Nice, the capital of the Riviera and of international tourism. Its festivals and jazz concerts are well known, as are its colorful old districts, casinos, markets, and fine hotels, such as the Negresco, the Hyatt Regency, Sofitel Splendid, the Meridien, and the Plaza. The museums of Nice contain fine collections of impressionist and contemporary art. Outstanding French artists such as Dufy, Matisse, and Picasso worked along this Mediterranean coast.

In Nice, which sits beside the beckoning blue waters of the Mediterranean, about 25,000 Jews support a dozen synagogues, about 20 kosher butcher shops, several Talmud Torahs, a yeshiva, and a headquarters for the Lubavitch movement including a youth hostel. In summer, of course, Nice flaunts its tourism. It is close to other resorts along the shore and is a few minutes' drive from the wonderful scenic mountain Corniche-drives to Monte Carlo.

Jewish tourists who seek information regarding synagogues and kosher food in Nice and the area should contact the office of the **Grand Rabbi,** 1, rue Voltaire. Tel: 93-85-82-06.

Nice likes to say that it remains one of the homes of the Jewish artist Marc Chagall in the form of **The National Museum Biblical Message of Marc Chagall,** located at avenue Docteur Menard and boulevard Cimiez. Tel: 93-81-75-75. It contains the most important permanent collection ever assembled that is devoted to Chagall, including large paintings, preparatory sketches, gouaches, and engravings. Chagall once said, "Perhaps in this abode, one will come and seek an ideal of fraternity and love such as my colors and my lines have dreamt." He commented on his famous Bible paintings hanging in the museum: "I want to leave them in this house so that people may find here a certain peace, a certain spirituality, a religious atmosphere, a feeling for life." Other media include stained-glass mosaics, lithographs, sculptures, and tapestries.

The Maeght Foundation, a major museum of contemporary paintings and sculpture, is set in a pine grove of St-Paul-de-Vence.

Synagogues and points of interest in Nice include:

Office of the Grand Rabbi, 1, rue Voltaire. Tel: 93-85-82-06. Rabbi Marc Bensoussan is Grand Rabbi.

Synagogue, 7, rue Gustave-Deloye, 06000, Nice. Tel: 93-92-11-38. Sephardic service. For those seeking an Ashkenazic service, attend **Synagogue Ezras Achim,** 1, rue Blacas.

Synagogue, 8, rue Marceau, 06000, Nice. Tel: 93-85-34-84.

Oratoire, Nice-Nord, 96, avenue St-Lambert.

Union Libérale Israelite de France, 24, rue de France, 06000, Nice. Tel: 93-82-26-15.

Organizations in Nice include:

Centre Michelet, 22, rue Michelet. Tel: 93-51-89-80. This new Jewish center contains a modern synagogue, library, mikveh (ritual bath), classrooms, and a hall for weddings and bar mitzvahs.

Fonds Social Juif Unifié, 15, rue d'Angleterre. Tel: 93-87-53-20.

Beth Lubavitch-Chabad, 22, rue Rossini, 06000, Nice. Tel: 93-82-46-86. Sponsored by the Lubavitch movement.

There are several kosher restaurants in Nice:

Au Roi David, 9, rue Clement-Roassal, 06100, Nice. Tel: 93-87-65-25.

Guez, 26, rue Pertinex. Tel: 93-62-30-77. Kosher foods and provisions and baked goods stock the store's shelves downstairs. Upstairs is a fine restaurant that features kosher Tunisian specialties.

La Tikva, 2, rue de Suisse. Tel: 93-87-61-21. Do call first to check hours, as well as to make reservations, if needed.

Tourist information can be obtained at the **Office of Tourism,** avenue Thiers, 06000, Nice. Tel: 93-87-07-07.

As noted, Nice is an excellent base from which to take day trips.

Cannes

If you are in Nice or Monte Carlo, certainly travel on to Cannes, the radiant city of the French Riviera with its sandy beaches, blue sky, and the beckoning Mediterranean, casinos, yacht harbors, palm trees, and the renowned **Palm Beach Club.** Cannes is the largest yachting center of the Riviera.

The luxury hotels of Carlton, Martinez, Grey Albion, and the Majestic dress up the city. But there are hotels for every budget.

Cannes has a major Jewish community of about 10,000. Many are involved in enhancing this city known for its film festivals and attractive boulevard La Croisette, as well as Old Port Quarter.

Synagogue, 20, boulevard d'Alsace, 06400, Cannes. Tel: 93-38-16-54.

Centre Communautaire, 3, rue de Bone. Tel: 93-99-24-95. The community center has a kosher restaurant, but check on hours.

Tourist information can be obtained at the **Office of Tourism,** Palais des Festivals et des Congrès, 1, La Croisette, 06400, Cannes. Tel: 93-39-24-53.

St-Tropez

Visit this wonderful resort town, a place of beaches, boutiques, cabarets, cafes, and countless yachts. St-Tropez has provided inspiration for so many artists, including Andre Lhote and Raoul Dufy. For those visiting St-Tropez, there is a **synagogue** at nearby **Frejus-St-Raphael,** in rue du Progrés, 83600, in Frejus-Plage. Tel: 94-52-06-87, 94-53-20-30, or 94-53-14-04.

Tourist information can be obtained at the **Office of Tourism,** Quai Jean-Jaures, 83990, St-Tropez. Tel: 94-97-45-21.

The harbor at Cannes, including the new convention center and festival center. (Photo courtesy French Government Tourist Office)

Antibes—Juan-les-Pins

Two towns, joined into one, sport a super night life, good shops, a fine beach, as well as a wonderful first-class, still-established family-style hotel, the **Hotel Juana,** avenue de Gallice, Juan les Pins. Nearby is the famous **Hotel du Cap** and its restaurant, **Eden-Roc**, in Cap d'Antibes. Both of these hotels are not to be missed on a trip to the Riviera. The Eden-Roc restaurant with its view of the bay is one of those never-to-be-forgotten sights.

Visit Antibes to see the famous castle of the Gromaldis, now the **Musée Picasso**. Juan-les-Pins, as the storybooks say, is a very popular international resort. It became famous after World War I, popularized by Jay Gould, the American railroad magnate who lived here.

In Juan-les-Pins, in July and August, there is a **kosher-deli restaurant** at 2, rue Roger Gallet.

Antibes—Juan-les-Pins Synagogue, 9, chemins des Sables Villa "La Monada," 06000, Antibes. Tel: 93-61-59-34. A Torah scroll is considered holy, sacred, venerable. To save a Torah scroll is a great mitzvah. The Antibes—Juan-les-Pins synagogue houses a famous Torah scroll, the story of which follows.

It is good to meet fellow co-religionists and exchange ideas and stories. Here is my experience on the Riviera, an experience that tells you much about the people—and one man in particular whom I interviewed, Leon Allouche—who make up French Jewry along this beautiful coast.

For the first 23 years of his life, Allouche lived in Algeria, that wonderful North African Jewish community, in the city of Bonne. As a result of the Cremieux Decree of the nineteenth century, Algerian Jews were French citizens. So when war clouds broke over Europe in 1939, Allouche was conscripted into the Army of the Republic of France and shipped off to Europe. When France capitulated to the Nazi onslaught in 1940, Allouche was taken prisoner. He escaped four months later and made his way back across the Mediterranean to Algeria, where he lived briefly until that hero of modern France, Gen. Charles de Gaulle, rallied the nation.

Allouche, like French Jewish men and women throughout the French Empire, immediately joined the ranks of General de Gaulle. Once again Allouche sailed across the Mediterranean.

As the Allied armies fought their way across eastern France, Allouche would stop and ask residents along the way, "Is there a synagogue here? Where is it?"

Nearly all Jewish houses of worship were gutted or completely destroyed. Many towns had no Jews. One day in 1944, in a small town in Alsace, Allouche asked several townspeople if there were a synagogue in the area. A civilian who had been jailed previously led him to a shattered building that was stripped bare and from which the Holy Ark had been ripped right out of the wall.

The Germans had transformed this house of worship into an army barracks and dumped all the religious items they could find into a garbage heap 100 yards away. Allouche then commandeered several German prisoners of war to locate the garbage site, and soon his group found it. There, sticking out of the refuse, were the two poles of a single Torah. The POW crew quickly cleared away the area and found three other Torah scrolls.

Because Allouche and his unit had to move out, he left three Torah scrolls at the liberated synagogue for the future Jewish community and took a small one with him on his journey across Nazi Germany. It protected him, he recalled 43 years later.

Discharged in 1945, Allouche carried the Torah back to his home in Bonne, Algeria. In 1962, when France pulled out of Algeria, the Jews departed with the French who lived in Algeria and were known as *pieds noirs* (black feet). About 100,000 Jews fled this North African country and came to France as part of a modern exodus. More than 10,000 went to Israel.

Allouche took the Torah with him to Antibes—Juan-les-Pins where, like his fellow Algerians, he could resume his life as a French citizen. (He would later become police chief of Antibes—Juan-les-Pins.) This beautiful municipality is described as "one of the flashiest places on the Riviera," such is the quality of night life and its beaches. Here rests the Torah now, in a town with a timeless Mediterranean charm.

Other synagogues along the Riviera near Antibes—Juan-les-Pins include:

Cagnes-sur-Mer, 5, Imp. Douce-France, 35.

Draguignan, 15, rue de l'Observance.

Grasse, place de la Buanderie.

Hyeres, Chemin de la Ritorte.

Menton, centre "Altyner," 106, cours du Centenaire.

St-Laurent-du-Var, Villa "Le Petit Clos," 35, avenue des Oliviers.

Marseilles

Is this how Jews live in North Africa? Is this Oran? Fez? Cairo? No, it is Marseilles.

Here are Arab men carrying long spits with roasted lamb. The guttural sounds of Arabic permeate the air as the bearers wail haunting Arabic melodies of the Sahara.

I must have attended several hundred bar mitzvah ceremonies in my life, opulent ones and frugal ones. Held in the summer house of a very successful professional, this one certainly belonged to the former category. Cocktails were served poolside, tables were set out on the veranda, champagne flowed, and food abounded—course after course of exotic Sephardic dishes. There even was the familiar bar mitzvah candle-lighting ceremony similar to the one in the United States, where the boy is joined by various relatives as they light each of the 13 candles to signify the boy's thirteenth birthday. Gathered here were many successful, educated North African Jews who would never go back to the continent across the Mediterranean. They were French. They mixed with French society. They were business persons and professionals: they lived well, dressed well in the latest Paris fashions, and belonged to clubs. Many had fashionable apartments on the affluent Avenue Parades and other upper middle-class thoroughfares.

Marseilles, it is said, is a mix of Catholics, Communists, socialists, free thinkers, Armenians, Corsicans, Africans, Arabs, Jews, and Gypsies. Many are newcomers, including repatriated *pieds noirs* from Algeria, Tunisia, and Morocco. Marseilles has one of France's largest concentrations of Arab immigrants. Lately the newest group are refugees from Vietnam. The city is an important center of France's extreme right political party, the National Front of Le Pen.

Marseilles remains bustling and cosmopolitan. The famous Canebière Boulevard is always full of sailors and crowds at cafes. The city boasts the **Longchamps Palace,** with its **Fine Arts Museum** and the **Natural History Museum.** Atop a hill, **Notre Dame de la Garde Basilica** offers a breathtaking panorama of Marseilles.

Walk around the old port at night. Visit the restaurants, which offer rich gastronomic rewards. The dining establishments, cafes, and fish houses are filled with tourists who come here for a meal that may include bouillabaisse, turbot, white wine, and Chianti. Just southwest of the port lie the islands of Rattonneau and Pomegues. Between them and the mainland is the isle of Chateau d'If, which was the scene of part of Alexandre Dumas's *Le Comte de Monte-Cristo.*

As an emporium, Marseilles trades with the Levant and the Near and Far East. The smell of the sea is everywhere. Called Europort of the South, City of Conventions, and Gateway to the Riviera, Marseilles has also been called a tough harbor city of smugglers, thieves, prostitutes, and undesirables.

Through this ancient harbor in the late 1940s passed thousands of Jews on their way to their homeland in Palestine. The former president of France, François Mitterrand, helped pave the way for Jewish ships to go to Israel. In the three years following the end of World War II in 1945, the French embarrassed the British in Palestine just as the British were trying to keep the French out of the Middle East. France lost Syria and Lebanon. Perhaps the British should lose Palestine, thought a few in the Quai d'Orsay, the French Foreign Office.

As one walks up and down the busy Canebière Boulevard or strolls around the Old Harbor (the *Vieux Port*), one cannot help but visualize those post-World War II days, when old, unseaworthy Staten-Island-ferry-type boats, their beams bursting from the overcrowding of humans literally stuffed on board, sailed out secretly at night into the blue Mediterranean to run the gauntlet of the British Navy in order to reach the Jewish homeland. The British and the world called them "illegals," these survivors of the Holocaust. They maintained they were neither displaced nor illegal.

Marseilles had been my stomping ground during the days of the recovery of France after World War II, as well as the days of the nightmare following the Algerian War. Some of my happiest and best travel experiences occurred in this thriving seaport. Algeria, they say, was France's Vietnam. In the late 1950s and early 1960s, Jews fled Algeria because they knew that the country would revert to Moslem rule, and they were not sure Moslems would allow them to live in peace.

During the Algerian War, Jews in France leaned toward the French view. After all, they were French citizens according to the 100-year-old Cremieux Decree. While some Jews fought on the Algerian side, they would never feel comfortable in an Arab society, even though, throughout history, the Arabs treated Jews relatively well compared with Christian Europe.

They were beginning a new life in a new land, and even though they knew the language, they struggled to settle in. But unlike other Jewish immigrants from the North African countries, Algerian Jews were French citizens. This instant citizenship granted them rights to health benefits, to the vote, and to hold political office.

The first stop of the North African Jews who came to Marseilles was the **Place de la Bourse,** a large downtown square, a place that has witnessed revolutions, demonstrations, financial crisis, peaceful gatherings, and celebrations. Now new activity began on the square: the welcoming of refugees, newcomers, people looking for jobs. When fighting in Algeria had ended, the OAS went underground in clandestine headquarters here.

Today, about 70,000 Jews live here, many from Morocco and Tunisia. They sponsor about 20 synagogues, day and vocational schools, and youth centers. Marseilles is now the second largest Jewish community in France and the third largest in Western Europe.

Marseilles is a city of Sephardic Jews with names like Chiche,

Dahan, Zana, Solal, Amsellem, and Zemmour. They are committed to Judaism. They are proud and active as they try to keep a community alive fighting assimilation and anti-Semitism.

Their community organizations are enough to boggle the mind: the Fonds Social Juif Unifié, the social welfare agency; community centers; WIZO; ORT; B'nai B'rith; Zionist groups; sports clubs. Many work under the umbrella organization known as CRIF, which makes representations to the government.

A Jewish radio station in Marseilles broadcasts cultural programs to the people of all religions. The radio serves an educational purpose; it brings Judaism into the home.

For the Jewish community in France, in the decade of the 1990s, whether it be Marseilles, Nice, Lyon, or Paris, where nearly two-thirds of the country's 700,000 Jews live, there is a new page in the annals of history. The French Jewish community can no longer be called a group of newcomers or of an immigrant generation.

Three decades after their arrival, Algerian Jews have entered various professions and have done well economically. Unlike their fellow Sephardic Jews in the United States, Sephardic Jews are in the majority in Marseilles and throughout France.

For information while in Marseilles, contact the following:

Appel Unifié Juif de France, 173, rue Paradis. Tel: 91-37-03-21. Similar to the American United Jewish Appeal, this organization is interested in meeting Americans and exchanging views.

B'nai B'rith, 41, cours d'Estienne-d'Orves, 13001, Marseilles. Tel: 91-33-80-50.

C.A.S.I.M., 61, rue de la Palud, 13006, Marseilles. Tel: 91-54-37-36.

Consistoire Israelite de Marseilles, 117, rue Breteuil, Marseilles. Tel: 91-37-49-64. *Note:* Visitors may call Mr. Rolland Drai, who will be particularly helpful with religious matters, synagogues, kosher food, services, and travel in Marseilles. Mr. Drai's telephone: 91-34-34-34, 91-37-71-84, or 91-37-42-83. He has indicated he can also arrange group tours of Jewish sites. It is advisable to contact him *before* you arrive.

Coopération Féminine, 67, rue Breteuil, 13006, Marseilles. Tel: 91-81-79-59.

Fonds Social Juif Unifié (FSJU), 67, rue Breteuil, 13006, Marseilles. Tel: 91-37-40-57.

K.K.L. (Jewish National Fund), 95, cours Pierre-Puget, 13006, Marseilles. Tel: 91-33-83-92.

Beth Chabad, 112, boulevard Bary, 13001, Marseilles. Tel: 91-06-00-61.

WIZO, 2, boulevard Theodore Thurner, 13006, Marseilles. Tel: 91-48-64-26.

Tourist information can be obtained at the **Office of Tourism,** 4, Canebière, 13001, Marseilles. Tel: 91-54-91-11.

For prayer service, American visitors can go to the **Temple Breteuil,** 117, rue Breteuil, 13006, Marseilles. Tel: 91-37-49-64. This main synagogue conducts a Sephardic service. The chief rabbi has his office at 119, rue Breteuil, 13006, Marseilles.

An Ashkenazic service is held in the **synagogue** at 8, impasse Dragon, 13006, Marseilles, just nearby.

Other synagogues include the following:

Chalom Rav, 8, impasse Dragon, 13006, Marseilles.

Chevet Ha'him, 18, rue Beaumont, Marseilles. Tel: 91-50-30-07.

Maguen David, 31, avenue des Olives, 13013, Marseilles (La Rose, a suburban area). Tel: 91-70-05-45.

Or Torah, 14, rue St-Dominique, 13001, Marseilles. Tel: 91-90-64-30.

Ozer Dalim, 8, impasse Dragon, 13006, Marseilles. Tel: 91-53-33-73.

Union Libérale Israelite de France, 24, rue Martigny, 13008, Marseilles. Tel: 91-71-97-46.

There are two community centers in Marseilles:

Centre Communautaire Edmond Fleg, 4, impasse Dragon, 13006, Marseilles. Tel: 91-37-42-01.

Centre Maguen David, 31, avenue des Olives, 13013, Marseilles (La Rose). Tel: 91-70-05-45. This center is located in the outskirts of Marseilles.

For kosher dining, try these restaurants:

Centre Communautaire Edmond Fleg, 4, impasse Dragon,

13006, Marseilles. Tel: 91-37-42-01 or 91-37-42-63. Sunday through Friday, 11 to 3, lunch only. Call for information.

Eden Up, 30, rue Tapis Vert. Tel: 91-91-47-59.

Hotel Frantel Centre, Bourse. Tel: 91-91-91-29. Groups can order kosher food. Call or write Mr. Rolland Drai, 119, rue Breteuil, 13006, Marseilles. Tel: 91-34-34-34, 91-37-71-84, or 91-37-42-83.

King Salomon, 11, rue du Di-Combalat. Tel: 91-37-89-04.

Lotus de Nissane, 94, cours Julien, 13006, Marseilles. Tel: 91-42-61-60. Chinese kosher food.

AIX-EN-PROVENCE

Just a half-hour from Marseilles—only 20 miles—rests the quiet but stimulating municipality of Aix-en-Provence. This delightful academic town is known as the town of spas and arts, of music and fountains. A scholastic center, it boasts three universities and many institutes and it hosts music and art events.

An American school where students from the United States study French language, history, and culture adds to the cultural impact of Aix as it is fondly called. Stroll along the Cours Mirabeau, the most celebrated avenue in France and called one of the "most beautiful main streets in the world." At the head of the avenue is a noted fountain, **La Rotonde,** a monument to nineteenth-century romanticism. Most travel writers advise that the best time to experience the life and sites of the Cours is early morning or late at night.

In spite of wars, construction, and other threats to the landscape, Aix has managed to hold on to its lively fountains along the middle of its lovely streets. It is this music of culture and scenic beauty that keeps many tourists in rapture.

Enjoy the cool, shady plane trees and the eighteenth-century facades of elegant manor houses. Stop at the cafes and watch the world go by. Paul Cezanne and Emile Zola did when they lived here.

Once the capital of Provence, the city has existed for more than 2,000 years. Jews have a long history in Aix. They have lived here since the fifteenth century. Darius Milhaud, the famous French Jewish composer, was born here. His great-grandfather helped establish a synagogue in Aix in 1840.

The Aix Jewish community of 600 families nearly ceased to exist after World War II. However, with the influx of North African Jews in the early 1960s, especially those from Algeria, the Jewish community was renewed.

A modern **synagogue** is located at 3 bis, rue de Jerusalem, 13100, Aix-en-Provence. The street may still be known as rue Montperrin since the new name, rue de Jerusalem, was designated only recently by the mayor of the town. Tel: 42-26-69-39. A community center, with classrooms, a library, and social hall, dates from the early 1970s.

Visitors are welcome to attend services each morning at 6:45. Evening services depend on sunset. On Saturday mornings, services are conducted at 8:30.

Tourist information is available at the **Office of Tourism,** Place du Général de Gaulle, 13100, Aix-en-Provence. Tel: 42-26-02-93.

NORMANDY

For centuries, Jews have lived in the serene and peaceful countryside of Normandy. Because of its scenery, splendid architecture, contrasting landscapes, rich agricultural lands, and historic past, it is one of the most attractive French provinces.

The towns of Normandy have retained their character despite wartime destruction and postwar building. In Normandy, too, are the D-day beaches that are part of American and French history: Utah, Omaha, Gold, Juno, and Sword. Farther east is Arromanches, where the British landed. And from the beautiful seaside town of Honfleur, Samuel de Champlain set sail to Quebec to explore the American Great Lakes.

Normandy is considered the home of the best cheese in the world, apple cider, strong Calvados, and tasty duck. It boasts lush, green fields, farmhouses, and estates. Today the Normans, active, friendly people, welcome tourists of all races and religions, just as they greeted the American GIs with glasses of cider following the D-day invasion.

This is the place that recalls the voice of our former president, then Gen. Dwight D. Eisenhower, who on June 6, 1944, declared, "Peoples of Western Europe, a landing was made today on your beaches. . . ."

Rouen

This municipality is one of the most interesting in Normandy; its main street is the River Seine. Devastated in World War II, the city was rebuilt in such a way that one is constantly reminded of its rich history, art, and architecture. It was at Rouen that the peasant girl, Jeanne d'Arc, (Joan of Arc) inspired France to oppose the invading English.

An archeological discovery was made beneath the parking lot of the **Palace of Justice.** Uncovered were the remains of a medieval Jewish building, appparently the only Jewish institution of higher learning in Europe whose walls have survived from either antiquity or the Middle Ages. This would account for the fact that the present Palace of Justice fronts on rue aux Juifs (Street of the Jews). Uncovered in the excavations dedicated that day were graffiti on the walls of the medieval academy. This discovery meant that Rouen was a most important medieval center in France for Jewish studies, overshadowing even Paris.

The Jewish school of learning dated back to about the year 1090. (Some believe the building was a synagogue.)

For Prof. Norman Golb of the University of Chicago, a specialist in Hebrew and Judaeo-Arabic studies, this find means that the Jewish presence in northern France was not only economic and commercial, but cultural as well. What makes the story even more exciting is that the location of the structure had been predicted by Golb, who reached his conclusion from a study of medieval manuscripts.

Months before the Romanesque building was discovered, the 52-year-old professor had published his hypothesis about the yeshiva in a book entitled *History and Culture of the Jews of Rouen.* It appeared in Hebrew in the spring of 1976.

He had researched 150 manuscripts which he studied in Jerusalem, the British Museum, the Bibliothèque Nationale in Paris, and libraries in Budapest, Amsterdam, and New York, as well as the Vatican Library.

His selection of the site of the yeshiva on Rouen's rue aux Juifs was based on the fact that references to the building stop with the sixteenth century. This was the point at which the highly ornamented Palais de Justice was built. "I surmised that they had razed the Jewish center to make way for the new construction," Golb told me in an interview.

Equally fascinating is the fact that Golb may have discovered why Rouen was overlooked as a center of Judaism during the Middle Ages. It may have been bypassed because Hebrew references to the city were misread by Latin scholars of the Middle Ages. Until the fourteenth century, Rouen was known as Rodom.

In surviving Hebrew manuscripts, the name *Rodom* is written like *Rhodoz,* a medieval city in southern France. What happened was that scholars, in recopying the manuscripts, often mistook the Hebrew letter *samech* for a final *mem.* Golb said he was fascinated by the possibility that the city they were really talking about and writing about as a "thriving Jewish community" was really Rodom or Rouen.

"I went back to the original manuscripts at the British Museum, and my suspicions were immediately confirmed," he said. Subsequent studies of manuscripts in Paris, Amsterdam, and Jerusalem revealed detailed maps, as well as descriptions of the Jewish quarter and of life in the city.

Today in Rouen, there are about 400 Jewish families engaged in professions and academic life, as well as industry and commerce. The Jews who came to Rouen in the 1960s from Algeria and Tunisia brought a Sephardic presence to the area.

With the archeological discovery, more people will be visiting Rouen. Since that day when the find was made, Rouen and the government of France have spent about $1 million on its restoration. It is a Jewish historic landmark in France not to be missed.

Appointments for group visits of no more than 20 persons should be made with the **Office of Tourism,** 25, Place de la Cathédrale, BP666, 76008, Rouen. Tel: 35-71-01-44.

Synagogue, 55, rue des Bons-Enfants, 76100, Rouen. Tel. 35-71-01-44.

St-Lô

Rabbi Edmond Beldreb is a circuit rabbi. St-Lô is one of the towns he covers. He drives through scenic Normandy on roads flanked by rows of high hedge forming a leafy canopy.

St-Lô was one of the towns that Gen. George Patton made famous. It was from here in June 1944 that his forces broke out of German encirclement, and the enemy front facing the West collapsed. (Behind the roads traveled on by the rabbi are the D-day beaches.)

True, there probably were no Jews here when Patton's Third Army moved out against the Germans. But a few Jewish families have now settled in this historic town.

Like the countryside around it, Normandy contains small Jewish communities tied together by joint activities and by visiting rabbis.

There are a few Jewish families in **Evreux,** about 10 families in **Lisieux,** 15 families in **Cherbourg,** 200 families in **Le Havre,** and 400 families in Rouen. And in **Caen,** almost entirely rebuilt after the war, there are about 100 Jewish families. After World War II, the Jews of Caen built their own **synagogue** at 46, avenue de la Libération. Tel: 31-43-60-54. Caen has a small but active Jewish community. Many arrived here from that cultural center of Jewish life in France, Strasbourg.

Memorial: A Museum for Peace, Esplanade Dwight Eisenhower, Caen, in Normandy. On April 26, 1992, a new and very moving exhibit citing the World War II deportations and acts of genocide was opened. The exhibit includes maps of the camps, items from deportations, a painting by Andre Roth, and a scenographic creation of shadows and vacillating lights dramatizing and highlighting the shameful place that the deportation occupies in the history of World War II. Museum hours: Open daily 9 A.M. to 7 P.M.; from July 11 to August 31, open until 9 P.M. Closed January 1 to 15, March 20, and December 25. Tel: 31-06-06-44.

The Jews of Normandy are a close-knit group. New superhighways and high-speed trains offer them the opportunity to go from Caen to Paris in two hours, from Rouen to Paris in a little more than an hour. But there are also intercity happenings. The Jews of Le Havre and Caen hold joint activities: seminars, lectures, and films.

During summer months, thousands of Jews also come to **Deauville,** which is the world-renowned resort of casinos, polo matches, and horse racing. In the summer, I was told, there is even a minyan in Deauville, whose summer population rises from about 10,000 persons to more than 100,000.

RENNES

Rennes is the capital of Brittany, the French province that is west of Paris and juts out into the Atlantic Ocean. Damaged in World War II and liberated by American GIs, the city boasts a beautiful town hall, with curved facades designed by Jacques Gabriel, as well as two important museums, **Musée de Bretagne** and **Musée des Beaux-Arts,** at 20 Quai Emile Zola. Artists such as Gaugin painted here, and writers such as Chateaubriand wrote here.

Rennes existed in the days of Gaul, the capital city of the Celtic tribe of the Redones. In the ninth century, Rennes became part of Brittany and gained prestige as a grand duchy.

There never have been many Jews in Brittany. Jews lived in nearby Nantes in the fifth century and were found in Brittany at the end of the twelfth century.

By an agreement of February 23, 1222, Pierre Mauclerc, Duke of Brittany, confirmed the jurisdiction of the bishop of Nantes over the Jews living in his area. In 1236, many Jews in Brittany were massacred by Crusaders. The remainder were expelled in April 1240 by Duke Jean le Roux, who declared a moratorium on all debts owed to Jews and ordered them to return all pledges of chattel or real estate. For several centuries, therefore, only converted Jews were found living in Brittany.

From the beginning of the seventeenth century, many Marranos settled in Brittany, mainly in Nantes, a little more than an hour from Rennes.

During the eighteenth century, Jewish traders from Bordeaux, as well as Alsace-Lorraine, began to visit area fairs and markets. But in 1780, Jews were expelled. After the French

Revolution, Jews returned to Brittany. In 1808, when Jewish community consistories were established in France, only 300 Jews lived in Rennes. Historically, one reason there may never have been many Jews here is that Brittany, unlike Paris, Strasbourg, Lyon, and Marseilles, is *not* a "gateway" or port city. The thinking goes: you needed a port city to attract Jews who were tradesmen.

What makes Rennes an interesting place to visit is its ancient ramparts with watchtowers and gates, narrow streets, little squares, and half-timbered houses.

Located in the heart of an agricultural region and sur-rounded by areas of beautiful beach coastline, Rennes main-tains a fine university and an excellent medical center. As a French Army administrative center, the city attracts many civil servants or, as the French call them, "fonctionnaires." The municipality is also the headquarters of the prefect, the official who supervises the whole region of Brittany.

There are usually jobs available here, and that is why many Jews settled in during the wave of the North African Jewish immigration in the 1960s.

What will possibly preserve the Jewish communities in the region is the T.G.V. high-speed train of the French National Railways, which makes the Paris-Rennes run in about two hours instead of three. French Railways schedules 14 trains daily to Nantes and Rennes from Paris. They run at about 186 mph.

The Jews in Brittany feel that their ties to Paris (where one-half of France's 700,000 Jews reside) will obviously be much stronger because the trip is now two hours instead of three. A one-day journey from Paris to attend a lecture on Jewish sub-jects or a visit to attend a Jewish program will help stimulate this small community.

When you visit Rennes, head towards the **Jewish Community Center,** 32, rue de la Marbaudais, 35000, Rennes. Tel: 99-63-57-18. The street is located within a large apartment complex. According to the plaque on the building wall, the synagogue is called "Centre Communautaire/Beith Hatikvah." The syna-gogue is part of a larger apartment-complex community center.

Jews must have lived here before World War II, although

people don't know too much about the old community. There is a monument in the synagogue reading, "Mortes en Déportation, 1942–1945." I counted more than 60 names on the memorial plaque, victims of the Holocaust.

Services are Friday at 7:15 P.M. They always have a minyan. One of the large community gatherings occurs on the Day of Remembrance, of the Holocaust. The municipal authorities of Rennes attend. According to Mary Elsy and Jill Norman in *Travels in Brittany,* Brittany contributed more men and women than any other province in France to the Free French Resistance movement. Some of World War II's fiercest fighting took place in Brittany, in such ports as Brest, Lorient, St-Nazare, and St-Malo.

Lecturers, such as writers Marek Halter, Victor Malka, and Rabbi Serat, the former chief rabbi, have visited the center.

On Yom Kippur, several hundred Jews pray in the synagogue's large room.

There are regional activities with Jewish communities in Nantes, Brest, and Lorient. One gets the impression they have many joint gatherings. The community is friendly and welcomes visitors.

Here in Rennes, this city of art and history, the second trial of Capt. Alfred Dreyfus took place at the turn of the century. Here again, Dreyfus was unjustly found guilty. But at his Rennes trial it was clear that this Jewish army officer had been framed and several of the judges wavered. The trial took place in the **red brick schoolhouse** that still stands. Later it was named after Emile Zola, the noted French writer who was instrumental in focusing world attention on the injustice to Dreyfus. It was his famous newspaper article that shouted out in a banner headline style, "I Accuse."

Obviously, Jews don't live in a vacuum. They are part of a city and a people with a rich history, and live in a land that should be explored. Brittany offers sandy seaside beaches, rivers, fishing, natural sites, and wildlife. You can live on a boat. You can play golf or ride a horse. You can camp out or stay in a fine hotel. And of course, you can visit a friendly Jewish community.

FRENCH SYNAGOGUES OUTSIDE OF PARIS

There are synagogues and community centers in more than 120 cities and towns in France. Further questions should be directed to the **Consistoire Central,** 19, rue St-Georges, 75009, Paris. Tel:49-70-88-00. FAX: 42-81-03-66.

Here is a partial listing:

Agen, 52, rue de Montesquieu.
Amiens, 90, rue St-Fuscien.
Annecy, 18, rue de Narvik.
Annemasse, 13, rue de la Paix.
Arcachon, 36, avenue Gambetta.
Bastia, 3, rue du Castagno.
Beauvais, rue Jules-Isaac.
Belfort, 6, rue de l'As-de-Carreau.
Besancon, 2, rue Mayence.
Beziers, 19, Place Pierre-Semard.
Brest, 40, rue de la République.
Chalons-sur-Marne, 21, rue Lochet.
Chalons-sur-Saone, 10, rue Germiny.
Chambery, 44, rue St-Real.
Clermont-Ferrand, 6, rue Blatin.
Colmar, 3, rue de la Cigogne.
Compiegne, 4, rue du Dr. Charles-Nicolle.
Creil, 1, Place de la Synagogue.
Dunkerque, 19, rue Jean-Bart.
Elbauf, 29, rue Grémont.
Epernay, 2, rue Placet.
Epinal, 7, rue Charlet.
Evian, avenue des Grottes.
Grenoble, 11, rue Andre-Maginot.
La Ciotat, 1, square de Verdun.
La Rochelle, 40, cours des Dames.
Le Havre, 40, rue Victor-Hugo.
Le Mans, 416, boulevard Paixhans.
Lille, 5, rue Auguste-Angellier.

Limoges, 25-27, rue Pierre-Leroux.

Luneville, 5, rue Castara.

Macon, 32, rue des Minimes

Melun, corner of rues Branly and Michelet.

Metz, 39, rue du Rabbin-Elie-Bloch.

Montauban, 12, rue Sainte Claire

Mulhouse, 19, rue de la Synagogue.

Nancy, 17, boulevard Joffre.

Nantes, 5, impasse Copernic.

Perigeux, 13, rue Paul-Louis-Courier.

Perpignan, 54, rue Arago.

Poitiers, 1, rue Guynemer.

Roanne, 9, rue Beaulieu.

St-Etienne, 34, rue d'Arcole.

St-Louis, rue du Temple.

Sedan-Charleville, 6, avenue de Verdun.

Sens, 14, rue de la Grande-Juiverie.

Sete, 136 chemin de l'Anglore.

Tarbes, 6, rue du Pradeau, Cite Rothschild.

Toulon, avenue Lazare-Carnot.

Troyes, 5, rue Brunneval.

Valence, 1, Place du Colombier.

Valenciennes, 36, rue de l'Intendance.

Verdun, impasse des Jacobins.

Versailles, 10, rue Albert-Joly.

Vichy, 2 bis, rue du Marechal-Foch.

Vitry-le-François, 29, rue du Mouton.

Vittel, rue Croix-Pierrot.

England, which we shall visit in the next chapter, is now closer to France, not only because of the European Union, but because in 1994, the Channel Tunnel linking the two countries and the Continent with the British Isles opened and no doubt the two large Jewish communities will forge new links between French and British Jewry. It takes about 2½ hours to go by train from London to Paris.

Suggested Reading

Adler, Jacques. *The Jews of Paris and the Final Solution.*

ben-Sasson, H. H., ed. *A History of the Jewish People.* Cambridge, Mass.: Harvard University Press, 1969.

Bernstein, Richard. *Fragile Glory: A Portrait of France and the French.* New York: Alfred A. Knopf, 1990.

Courthion, Pierre. *Paris in the Past.* Paris: Editions d'Art Albert Skira, 1957.

Culbertson, Judi, and Tom Randall. *Permanent Parisians: An Illustrated Guide to the Cemeteries of Paris.* Chelsea, Vt.: Chelsea Green Publishing, 1986.

Eban, Abba. *Heritage: Civilization and the Jews.* New York: Summit Books, 1984.

Halter, Marek. *The Book of Abraham.* New York: Henry Holt, 1983.

———. *The Jester and the King.* New York: Little, Brown, 1988.

Hertzberg, Arthur. *The French Enlightenment and the Jews.* New York: Columbia University Press, 1968.

Hyman, Paula. *From Dreyfus to Vichy: The Remaking of French Jewry, 1906–1939.* New York: Columbia University Press, 1979.

Johnson, Paul. *A History of the Jews,* New York: Harper & Row, 1987.

Jones, David Pryce. *Paris in the Third Reich.* New York: Holt, Rinehart and Winston, 1981.

Josephs, Jeremy. *Swastika Over Paris: The Fate of the Jews in France.* New York: Little, Brown, 1989.

Krinsky, Carol Herselle. *Synagogues of Europe: Architecture, History, Meaning.* Cambridge, Mass.: MIT Press, 1985.

Liebling, A. J. *Between Meals: An Appetite for Paris.* New York: Simon & Schuster, 1962.

Marrus, Michael R., and Robert O. Paxton. *Vichy France and the Jews.* New York: Basic Books, 1981.

Morgan, Ted. *An Uncertain Hour: The French, the Germans, the Jews, and the City of Lyon, 1940–1945.* New York: William and Morrow, 1990.

Posner, S. *Adolphe Cremieux: A Biography*. Philadelphia: Jewish Publication Society of America, 1940.

Roth, Cecil. *A History of the Jews: From Earliest Times through the Six Day War*. New York: Schocken Books, 1970.

Schnapper, Dominique. *Jewish Identities in France: An Analysis of Contemporary French Jewry*. Chicago: University of Chicago Press, 1983.

Szajkousky, Soza. *Jews and the French Revolution of 1789, 1830, 1848*. New York: Klav Publishing House, 1969.

Wilson, Derek. *Rothschild, the Wealth and Power of a Dynasty*. New York: Charles Scribner's Sons, 1988.

Zuccotti, Susan. *The Holocaust, the French, and the Jews*. New York: Basic Books, 1993.

England
Cromwell, Disraeli, and the Rothschilds

London casts a spell on the American visitor with its parks, museums, art galleries, and history. England was America's "mother country" and London, its capital. In our day, we recall World War II, when Great Britain stood alone against the Nazi tyranny. Bombed at night, the English still rose in the morning to meet the day. They never surrendered, either during or after Dunkirk and the blitz.

"Surrender?" a British sergeant asked his men when he heard of Belgium's 1940 collapse in World War II. "Let them all surrender; we never will!" And in modern times Britain has also stood up as America's ally.

A Brief History

The sites and sounds of London excite an American: the Houses of Parliament, Big Ben, the changing of the guard at Buckingham Palace, the British Museum, Her Majesty's Tower of London, the National Gallery, the National Portrait Gallery, Hyde Park, the Victoria and Albert Museum, Westminster Abbey, Whitehall, the Strand, Trafalgar Square, Madame Tussaud's Wax Museum, the royal parks, the pubs. Jews came to England with William the Conqueror (1027–87), who, in 1066, invaded England, which then was a Saxon-Scandinavian land. Those first Jews who arrived along with William were from France. Even in those days, one did not give up speaking

French easily; in fact, we are told, French continued to be the language of the Jews until they were expelled in 1290.

Jews counted themselves among the few Londoners to own stone houses. They lived in that square mile of central London called "the City" which ironically is located next to the East End. Centuries later it would again become the "old Jewish neighborhood," though by then a poorer area. A street called "Old Jewry" survives to this day in this section of central London; it is one of the area's most famous lanes, and contains much history. Located in EC3, it was once known as "Poor Jewry."

An English travel writer described the Jewish merchants of London long ago as having "the ageless eyes of the Jews." Others would translate "Jew" to mean "moneylender." The first impression of Jews in England was that of a peddler with a pack on his back.

As Jews were to become proprietors, and Christians could not float loans, Jews financed these non-Jews, offering capital with payment of interest. The church condemned moneylending as the "heinous sign of usury." Aaron of the town of Lincoln, a leading Jewish European financier in the twelfth century, became one of the wealthiest persons in England.

While Jewish tax collectors thought they were protected by royalty, they actually were "chattels of the King" and possessed few legal rights. Although the king and his associates were heavily in debt to the Jews, royalty soon discovered ways to renege on their payments by cancelling the debts or by killing or expelling the Jews.

Another way to wipe out debts was the fable of ritual murder, followed by blood libel. Jews were supposed to have murdered Christians, then to have used the blood of the victims to make matzoh on Passover.

In 1275, King Edward I prohibited Jews from collecting interest. That measure strangled the Jewish community. Later, on July 18, 1290, Edward I banished the Jews from England. By November 1, 1290, All Saints Day, most of the 16,000 Jewish refugees had made their way across the English Channel to France, Flanders, and Germany. Their descendants would not return for 400 years.

After four centuries, what finally would move England to readmit its Jews? British pounds and shillings would play a major role in bringing Jews back onto English soil. The return of Jews to England has its origin in Amsterdam. Working together would be the Puritan dictator Oliver Cromwell and a Dutch Jew named Manasseh Ben Israel (1604–57). As Winston Churchill wrote, "It was left to a Calvinist dictator [Cromwell] to remove the ban which a Catholic king had imposed."

Until 1616, a small colony of secret Jews, mostly Marranos who came to England about 1500, managed to keep Judaism alive. Toleration of the Jews' return to Britain was due in part to the fact that the English read the Old Testament. With Manasseh Ben Israel's pleading and Cromwell's "unwritten permission," Jews began arriving in England in 1656.

During the Revolution of 1688, William of Orange captured the throne of England and sparked the influx of additional Jews to England. The restored Stuarts protected the Jews, who could now earn a living among their Christian neighbors. But it would take 200 more years for them to obtain political rights.

The newcomers were Sephardim from Spain and Portugal. They had names like Pereira, de Castro, d'Oliveira, de Veifa, Mendes da Costa, Gimes, Nunes, Henriques, Alvares, and Lousades.

By the end of the seventeenth century, about 20,000 Jews lived in Great Britain. The majority settled in London. Besides the Bevis Marks Synagogue, three Ashkenazic synagogues were organized. Occupations ranged from peddlers and small traders to opticians, physicians, and teachers.

Indirect parliamentary recognition came in 1698. Later, with the Jew Bill of 1753, foreign-born Jews were permitted to acquire privileges enjoyed by native children. Still, despite commercial success, Jews were not permitted to hold political office; nor could they serve in Parliament, vote in municipal elections, or attend the universities. Finally, in 1826, Jews were at least able to become naturalized.

As in many countries, the Jews of England were expected to govern themselves. The Board of Deputies was established in

1760 as the representative house of British Jewry. To this day, it maintains de facto government recognition.

After the Napoleonic Wars, Jewish families, like the Goldsmiths and Rothschilds, played an important role in English finance and society.

By 1830, 30,000 Jews lived in England, two-thirds of them in London. But English Jews looked across the channel and saw that their French co-religionists were already emancipated. They wanted similar rights. By 1840, the last of the so-called disabilities for Jews in England had disappeared, with the exception of the right to sit in Parliament. At that time, the swearing-in ceremony for members of Parliament was taken "on the oath of the true faith, of a Christian," an oath a Jew obviously could not take.

In 1858, Lionel Nathan Rothschild became the first Jew to be admitted to the House of Commons. He was not forced to "take the oath of a Christian." Since then, one or more Jews have served in every Parliament.

In 1860, the Orthodox "United Synagogue" came under the jurisdiction of a chief rabbi. This group consisted of the vast majority of synagogues. Reform and Sephardic groups established their own units.

In the 1880s, Jews began to move from Eastern Europe to the west. A vast wave of immigrants from the east arrived in England. In 1880, 60,000 Jews lived in Great Britain. By 1905, there would be 150,000 Jews.

To Jews, London and the British Isles will always mean a land of temporary refuge. For many on the way to the United States in the nineteenth century, it was a stopping-off place. The first Jewish mayor of New York City, Abraham Beame, was born in England and came to New York City as a young child.

The new Jewish immigrants were Yiddish-speaking proletariat and middle-class Orthodox. They were tailors, boot and shoe manufacturers, and furniture suppliers. As immigrants, they set up their own life-style in the poor neighborhoods of British cities.

By the start of World War I, 300,000 Jews lived in Britain. About 50,000 Jews fought with the Allies during the war and

suffered 10,000 casualties. Approximately 1,500 Jews were decorated. Six persons were awarded the Victoria Cross, Britain's
highest order.

During World War II, about 90,000 Jews fled from Hitlerism
to the British Isles, of which 75,000 came from Germany and
Austria, Czechoslovakia, Poland, and Italy. Friction between
Britain's Jews and His Majesty's government would increase
over the country's League of Nations mandate in Palestine,
especially since Britain tightened Jewish immigration to the
future Jewish State.

In 1944, with the assassination of Lord Moyne and the
1947 hanging of two British Army sergeants, tension rose in
England, which had pursued a pro-Arab policy, to say the
least.

Ernest Bevin, the post-World War II British foreign secretary,
followed a Palestine policy that "virtually abrogated" the
Balfour Declaration. The latter called for a Jewish national
home in Palestine. He imposed severe restrictions on Jewish
immigration. Nothing moved Bevin, not even the thousands of
Jewish survivors still held in displaced persons (D.P.) camps.
His anti-Semitism blinded him.

Although they felt betrayed, English Jews rallied and, on
May 14, 1948, they too celebrated the establishment of the
State of Israel. After World War II, Jews moved to the suburbs,
mainly to the northwest to Wembley, Harrow, Stanmore,
Edgware, Finchley, Palmers Green, Ilford, Golders Green,
and Stamford Hill. Today, Jews are less than one percent of
the British population. About three-quarters of Great
Britain's estimated 300,000 Jews live in and around cosmopolitan London, which has 6.6 million people. One suburb, Golders Green, stands out as a comfortable middle-class
residential area of northern London. There—and in
Stamford Hill—you will find a Jewish neighborhood with
Jewish stores and synagogues. While probably not as high as
in the United States, intermarriage in England is about one
out of three. Intermarriage and assimilation are becoming
common in Jewish society here, for England, since World War
II, has become freer and less stratified.

Notable English Jews

The *Jewish Chronicle,* the first permanent Anglo-Jewish news-paper, was established in 1841. Located at 25 Furnival St., London EC4, it has the honor of being the oldest Jewish news-paper in the world in continuous publication. On its pages often appeared notices and reports on outstanding Jewish per-sonalities who contributed much to Great Britain and British Jewry.

Many times, of course, mention was made of Sir Moses Montefiore (1784–1885), a famous son of British Jewry. He was probably the outstanding figure in the Jewish community and the most celebrated Jew in England; he lived until the age of 101. Sir David Salomons became the first Jewish mayor of London in 1855; he was also the first Jewish sheriff in 1835, and the first Jewish alderman in 1847. Sir George Jessel was the first Jew to become a member of the government and was appointed solicitor in 1871.

Benjamin Disraeli (1804–81) was born a Jew, and he became one of the United Kingdom's greatest prime ministers.

Herbert Samuel, later viscount, became a British cabinet minister in 1909. He also was named as the first High Commissioner for Palestine in the 1920s. Solomon Schechter, rabbinic scholar and founder of Conservative Judaism, later took the post of president of the Jewish Theological Seminary in the United States, where he served from 1902 until his death in 1915. Siegfried Sassoon was a famous Jewish poet and author of *Memoirs of an Infantry Officer.*

Jewish London

THE EAST END

The first Jewish word that a Jewish traveler hears in the London of Disraeli, Rothschild, Adler, Schechter, and Balfour deals with Jewish food. The word is *heimisch,* "homey, informal, comfortable."

"Heimisch [homemade] mushroom barley soup," says a man between spiels in the weekly Sunday market in Petticoat

Lane. During the week, it is known as Wentworth Street. "Go over to Bloom's and have a bowl," he urges.

London's East End—with its flavor of New York's Lower East Side—deserves a stroll. This neighborhood has changed. Once it boasted many clubs, theaters, shelters, yeshivas, and schools. Today, there are few Jews, and fewer institutions, but the neighborhood is still exciting and vibrant, and it is good to begin a visit to London here in White Chapel and at such streets as Whitechapel High Street, Osborne Street, Brick Lane, Fournier Street, and Greatorex Street.

"The Asians are here now," says Mr. Meyers, the peddler in Petticoat Lane. "The newcomers want to succeed, so they go where the Jews began," he points out as he looks around at fellow hawkers who sell—from their stalls—leather bags, coats, umbrellas, jeans, mirrors, sweaters, and orange juice squeezers.

Or, put another way, "they're speaking Hindustani where *mamaloshen* [Yiddish] used to be spoken," according to Member of Parliament Grenville Janner.

The East End can be reached by Underground. Take the "tube" to Liverpool Street, Bethnal Green, Aldgate, Aldgate East, or Shoreditch. Several bus lines also serve the area—6, 8, 15, or 25 from Oxford Circus or the 6 or 15 from Charing Cross.

By the way, the area houses several streets and buildings of interest to Jewish travelers, including the home of Abe Saperstein, who founded the Harlem Globetrotters in the United States; the Jewish Working Men's Club on Alie Street where in 1896, Theodor Herzl launched the Zionist movement here.

A tour in the East End, the location of the original Jewish settlement, and elsewhere in London, is conducted by Londinium, 6 W. Heath Ave., London, NW11 7QL. Tel: (081) 458-2288 or FAX: 455-6612. Valeries Sussman and Sally Pitel conduct the Jewish tour by means of a private car. The tours can be tailor-made to the traveler's interests.

Several guided walking tours are available on Mondays, Wednesdays, and Fridays at 10:30 P.M. from Aldgate Underground Station. Contact them at 071-700-6931 for prices and further details.

One way to see the East End is to stroll along with Mr. or Mrs. Joseph, who conduct **walking tours** of the "Jewish East End." They point out all the nostalgic and historic sights of interest. The Josephs now take only groups around the area. Make sure you call ahead. Tel: 081-504-9159.

Historic Tours, 3 Florence Rd., South Croydon, CR2 0PQ. Tel: 081-668-4019. FAX: same as telephone. This is a historical walking tour tracing Jewish history in England from the time of William the Conqueror to World War II.

JEWISH SITES IN LONDON

Woburn House, Upper Woburn Place, London WC1. When sight-seeing in Jewish London, the traveler will discover that the East End does not have all the Jewish sites. Near B'nai B'rith Hillel House on Endsleigh Street is Woburn House, which is located at garden-filled Upper Woburn Place near the Euston subway station. The area surrounding Upper Woburn Place is serene and good for walking. Woburn House is the headquarters of British Jewry. The Board of Deputies, which is similar to a Jewish House of Representatives, meets here. More than 500 elected members representing some 250 congregations and organizations throughout the country gather together here to deal with the problems facing Jews in England.

The Jewish Museum is located in Woburn House in Upper Woburn Place, London WC1 HOEP. Tel: 071-388-4525. More than 10,000 visitors come here each year to see more than 1,000 items. Many displays, including some priceless ritual objects dating back to the Norman conquest of 1066, are packed into a single large room. Opened in 1932, it was the first permanent collection of Jewish items opened to the public. For example, you can see a thirteenth-century charter in Latin containing a restrictive covenant clause that forbids the transfer of real estate to monks or Jews.

A function of the Jewish Museum is to explain and teach Judaism. To illustrate current Jewish life, history, and religion, there are many visual aids and filmstrips for the numerous Jewish and non-Jewish religious classes who visit the museum.

In addition, eighteenth-century family portraits of Sephardic

Jews show us the life and times of days past. European circumcision sets, menorahs, Passover plates, and mezuzah cases abound. Another exhibit offers extensive Benjamin Disraeli memorabilia. A nearby case features exquisite miniatures. An English delftware soup plate probably dates back to 1770.

Browsing through the framed documents, visitors find a patent of arms granted to Levi Salomons, father of Sir David Salomons, the first Jewish lord mayor of London, who was elected to his post in 1855. This and other pieces are representative of British artifacts. Three major pieces of Anglo-Jewish silver include the Lord Mayors Silver and two cups, dating from 1702, 1745, and 1777 respectively. They were presentation pieces accompanying the annual gift of sweets conveyed from the Spanish and Portuguese Jews Congregation of the City to the lord mayor of London. The custom lasted from 1679 to 1779.

Dominating the exhibit is a massively rich sixteenth-century carved Holy Ark probably originating in a Venetian synagogue. Other items include an eighteenth-century Greek Torah cover and a silver gift breastplate from Augsburg from the mid-eighteenth century.

An etching of Manasseh Ben Israel by Rembrandt hangs in the museum. Manasseh Ben Israel led the fight for readmission to England. Born to Marrano parents in Madeira in 1604, he was baptized Manoel Dias Soeiro. His family moved to Amsterdam. Upon their arrival, they announced they were Jews. After studying with Rabbi Isaac Uziel, Manasseh was ordained a rabbi. He taught, wrote essays, and edited books, many of them for Christian audiences. He even corresponded with English religious leaders and intellectuals. Much of his motivation was mystical. You see, Manasseh had met a Jew named Antonio (Aaron) de Montezinos, who had told him that he had discovered Jews in America. Manasseh theorized that since Jews were now living in America, they were residents of every country on earth except one, that one of course being England. To make the dispersion cycle complete, and help the Messianic movement reach fulfillment, the Jews needed to reside in Britain. Then the Messiah would come and the Jews would return to their homeland—Palestine. During the conference to decide whether to admit Jews, Manasseh made a logical case for Jewish admission. He argued that wherever Jews live, they develop new branches of economy and trade flourishes. The meeting ended in a so-called compromise, with no official declaration, but it meant Jews were allowed to enter. However, Manasseh, who had fought so hard, took it as a personal defeat. He felt the compromise was a sham. He called for a formal recall of the Jewish people to England. When this did not happen, he returned to Amsterdam, where he died a broken man. He was buried in the cemetery at Ouderkerk, close to the Amstel River, not far from his father, Joseph Ben Israel, and near his teacher, Rabbi Isaac Uziel.

The Freud Museum, 20 Maresfield Gardens, Hampstead, London. Tel: 01-435-2002. This museum houses mementos of both Sigmund Freud, founder of psychoanalysis, and his daughter, Anna Freud, a leading authority on child psychoanalysis. In 1938, Sigmund Freud fled the Nazis in Vienna and settled in this house as a refugee. He brought with him his household furnishings, his books, and a collection of about 1,800 classical Egyptian and Oriental antiques. During his last days in 1939, he often asked that his bed be brought downstairs so he could enjoy the garden view. Anna Freud died in 1982. The museum is open Wednesday through Sunday, from noon until 5 P.M..

The Ben Uri Art Society at 21 Dean St., London W1, exhibits works by Jewish artists.

The J. F. S. Comprehensive School, 175 Camden Rd. This is a wonderful sight to see regarding Jewish life in Britain. I visited this excellent school and marveled at the sight of 1,500 Jewish boys and girls, ages 11 to 18, reciting the mincha (afternoon) service in the school's synagogue. The youths were dressed with blue-knit yarmulkes; blue blazers, grey slacks, and school ties for the boys; and blue blouses and grey skirts for the girls, the much-seen school clothes of British youth. The school is Orthodox and its subjects include Hebrew, Bible, laws, and Talmud, along with math, chemistry, history, tradition, and athletic events in fine facilities.

The Office of N. M. Rothschild & Sons is located at New Court, St. Swithins, in the heart of London. The headquarters of this remarkable Jewish family was responsible for many loans aiding the British government, including funds for the defeat of Napoleon, the relief of the Irish famine, the Crimean War, and, of course, the purchase of the shares of the Suez Canal owned by the khedive of Egypt. After the battle of Waterloo, the Rothschilds became bankers to the Holy Alliance of Christian Monarchs of Russia, Austria, Prussia, and Britain.

The Rothschild family moved to various European capitals to direct financial matters. James made Paris his base; Solomon moved to Vienna; Carl went to Naples; Mayer Amschel remained in Frankfurt. The main center of operations emerged at New Court, London, where the English branch was directed by Nathan Mayer Rothschild (1777–1836). He was the son of founder of the Rothschild dynasty, Mayer Amschel. The son, too, was a financial genius, a creative business person. Nathan Mayer Rothschild, "N.M.," as he was called, had been the first Rothschild to leave Frankfurt. He came to England, entered the textile importing business, and was an agent for his father. He became a British citizen in 1806 and married Hannah Cohen, whose sister married Moses Montefiore. The latter's brother married Nathan's sister, Henriette, and this liaison connected N.M. to the Salomons, Goldsmiths, and other prominent families. He helped establish the Jews' Free School. He was in the government loan business, especially since London was the financial center of the world. He transformed the Rothschilds into "the world's leading business house."

It took ten years of effort, but finally the son of "N.M." was the first Jew to sit in Parliament. You see, time after time, Lionel Nathan Rothschild had been elected by the City of London as its parliamentary representative. But the British Parliament refused to admit him to the House of Commons because, as a Jew, he refused to take the oath of office, which contained the words "on the true faith of a Christian." Ten years later, the House of Commons ended that oath. Even more time elapsed before a Jew could take his seat in the House of Lords. In 1885, Lionel's son, Nathaniel ("Natty")

Mayer Rothschild, became the first "professing" Jew to be raised to the peerage of a Lord and became a member of that august body. He was head of the British Jewish Community and president of the United Synagogue.

The Sternberg Centre for Judaism: The Manor House, 80 East End Rd., London N3 2SY. Tel: 081-346-2288 or 081-349-1143. Also known as The Manor House, this active institution is located on a seven-and-a-half-acre site in North London. Various organizations can be found here, including: The Manor House Society, which provides Jewish cultural and intellectual events and publishes a quarterly magazine, *Manna;* The Leo Baeck College, a rabbinical seminary for Britain's Progressive (Reform and Liberal) movements; Progressive Jewish Students and SATMAH, for college and university students; The Centre for Jewish Education; The Akiva Primary School; a synagogue; a biblical garden; and a number of other communal organizations.

Also at The Manor House, and well worth a visit, is **The London Museum of Jewish Life.** It is open Monday through Thursday, 10:30 to 5; Sunday, 10:30 to 4:40. This museum and research center is a new museum of Anglo-Jewish history. It contains displays, temporary exhibitions, educational programs, traveling displays, along with a large collection of objects, photos, and documents.

The Manor House Bookstore is open Monday through Thursday, 10 to 4; Sunday, 10 to 2. This well-stocked bookstore has a wide range of books of Jewish interest, educational materials, and Jewish artifacts.

KOSHER RESTAURANTS IN LONDON

Bloom's Restaurant, 90 Whitechapel High St., London E17RA. Tel: 071-247-6001/6835. The waiters, resplendent in their white jackets, are rather polite when they show you menus and suggest chopped liver, pickles, *kreplach,* turkey, Israeli wine, gefilte fish, *tzimmes,* cabbage, fish, and rye bread. And they speak Hebrew in Bloom's Restaurant, as well as Yiddish, English, Russian, and French. Bloom's also has another branch at 130 Golders Green Rd., London NW11, which is very similar to Bloom's establishment in the East End. Both are kosher. Bloom's is not the only kosher restaurant in the East End, however. Aldgate is the nearest Underground station.

Greenfeld's Deli and Snack Bar, 14 Stamford Hill, London N16.

The Jewish Vegetarian Society, 853-55 Finchley Rd., London NW11.

Kosher Luncheon Club, 9-11 Greatorex St., Morris Kasler Hall, London. Tel: 071-247-0039. Meet the Jews of England here from 9:30 A.M. to 3 P.M. Here one can find the kashrut authority of the Federation of Synagogues, as well as an Orthodox synagogue. The eating establishment, open from noon to 3 P.M. , Sunday to Friday, is described as the last of the old kosher eating halls, with its unique *heimisch* atmosphere. Try the kosher fish-and-chips; you will like them. The atmosphere is not fancy, but it is congenial. Tel: (01) 247-0039.

Kosherina, 8-9 Sentinel Square, Brent Street, London NW4.

Pizza Pitta, 119 Golders Green Rd., London NW11. Tel: 455-8921. Near the Bloom's of Golders Green.

Reubens, 20-A Baker St., London W1. Also has a snack bar and take-out.

The Sharon, 376-78 Cranbrook Rd., Grants Hill, Ilford.

Zakis, 634 Finchley Rd., London NW11.

Kosher Establishments under the Kashruth Division of the Court of the Chief Rabbi

Danny's, 4 Hallswelle Parade, Finchley Road, London NW11. Tel: 081-458-9090.

Eshel Hotel and Restaurant, Stamford Hill, London N16. Tel: 081-800-1445.

Marcus's, 146 Clapton Common, London E5. Tel: 081-458-4670.

Marcus's, 30-A Woodford Ave., Grants Hill, Ilford, Essex. Tel: 081-551-8002.

Rendezvous, 152-54 Golders Green Rd., Lincoln Gate, London NW11. Tel: 081-455-9001.

Sami's Restaurant, 85 Brent St., London NW4. Tel: 081-202-9247.

Woks, 148-150 Brent St., London NW4. Tel: 203-6779.

Kosher Establishments under
Kedassia Kosher Authority

Chopsticks, Sentinel Square, Brent St., Hendon, London NW4. Kosher Chinese.
King David, 293 Finchley Rd., London NW3.
The Plaza, 238 Stamford Hill, London N16.
Temptation, 9 Sentinel Square, Brent Street, Hendon NW4.

Kosher Establishments under
the London Kashrus Board

The board's headquarters are at 9-11 Greatorex St., London E1. Tel: 01-071-247-4471.
Aviv Restaurant, 87 High St., Edgware. Tel: 081-952-2484.

Kosher Establishments under the
Kashrut Division of the London Beth Din

Croft Court Hotel, 44 Ravenscroft Ave., London NW11 8AY. Tel: 081-458-3331. FAX: 081-455-9175.
Ha Mifgash, 8-10 Monkville Parade, London NW11 OAL. Tel: 458-8826.
Kadimah Hotel, 146 Clapton Common, London E5. Tel: 071-800-5960. FAX: 081-800-6237.
Morry's Milk Bar and Restaurant, 4 Windus Rd., London N16. Tel: 081-806-7796.

Kosher Take-Out Delis Licensed by the
Kashrut Division of the London Beth Din

B'nai B'rith Hillel Restaurant, ½ Endsleigh St., London WC1 H 0DS. Tel: 071-387-4644 or 071-380-0111. A fine place, it caters to university students in a marvelous college atmosphere in the area around Euston Station. Open Monday to Thursday, noon to 2:30 P.M. and 5:30 to 9 P.M., and on Friday, lunch only, from noon to 2. On Friday night, Shabbat meals are available. Advance booking, as the British say. Tel: 071-388-0801.
Carmel Delicatessen, 145 Clapton Common, London E5. Tel: 081-800-4033.

Goodies, 6 Hendon Lane, London N3. Tel: 071-349-1674. Also at 188 Kenton Rd., Kenton, Middlesex.

Steve's Delicatessen & Boucherie, 228-30 Station Rd., Edgware, Middlesex. Tel: 081-958-6715.

Steve's Kosher Kitchen, 5 Canons Corner, Stanmore, Middlesex. Tel: 081-958-9446.

Steve's on Broadway, 26 The Broadway, Stanmore, Middlesex. Tel: 081-954-6895.

SYNAGOGUES

British Jews, like their co-religionists in the United States, do not want to forget their heritage; hence their many synagogues.

Bevis Marks Synagogue, St. Mary Axe, London EC3. In the East End, this is the oldest Jewish synagogue in England. If you have only one day in London to see Jewish sites, you should make sure to visit this landmark. Services are held on Monday, Thursday, and Saturday morning.

Built in 1701, Bevis Marks is modeled after the Portuguese synagogue in Amsterdam, Holland. It is now a national monument worthy of preservation and located in St. Mary Axe (pronounced "Simmery Axe"). Here is a symbol of the resettlement of the Jews in England in 1656, after having been expelled for 400 years.

Dutch Jews brought the central chandelier from Amsterdam in the late 1600s. On the lectern in front of the Holy Ark are ten great brass candlesticks symbolizing the Ten Commandments. The 12 columns supporting the gallery in the three sides signify the 12 tribes of Israel. Worshippers can sit on the old, highly polished oak benches from the very first synagogue of the resettlement, which was then in Creechurch Lane, a short distance from the present site. The gates are often locked, so visitors wishing to see the Bevis Marks Synagogue should phone ahead. Telephone 624-1274 to check opening hours. Be sure to ask for directions and which entrance to use. The vestry office is at 4 Heneage Lane and the gates are on Houndstitch Street.

Interestingly, according to Carol Herselle Krinsky in *Synagogues of Europe: Architecture, History, Meaning,* Bevis Marks

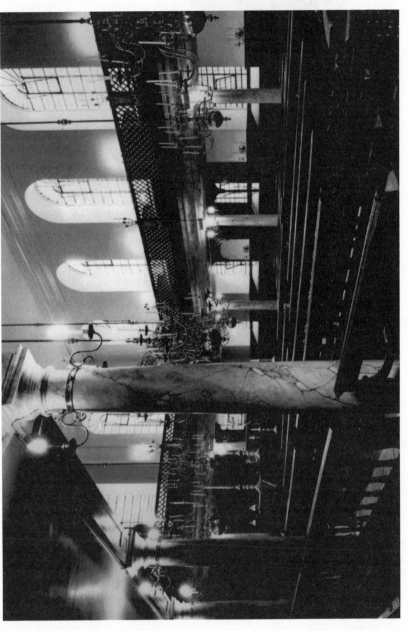

Bevis Marks Synagogue. (Photo courtesy British Tourist Office)

The Holy Ark of the Bevis Marks Synagogue. (Photo courtesy Library of the Spanish and Portuguese Synagogue)

Synagogue was built in a lane because Jews were not allowed to erect a synagogue on Bevis Marks Street. Joseph Avis, a Quaker, built the synagogue. When the building costs came to less than the estimate, he returned the difference. Finally, Queen Anne herself is said to have donated a wooden beam for the Bevis Marks Synagogue.

An **Ashkenazic synagogue** that stood in Duke's Place just next door to Bevis Marks was London's chief Ashkenazic place of worship. Called the Duke's Place Shul, it was considered the country's best-known synagogue, a popular choice for marriages, until it was destroyed in September 1941. The Rothschilds attended services here. A plaque is affixed to International House, which replaced the Duke's Place Shul.

Marble Arch Synagogue, 32 Great Cumberland Pl., West End, London W1. Tel: 723-7246. This synagogue is located in a beautifully designed area by a charming semicircular terrace of houses. Located near many hotels, it is difficult to tell that the building is a house of worship. This Orthodox synagogue took the place of the Great Synagogue on Duke's Place, which was destroyed by German bombers in 1941.

Sephardic Synagogue, Lauderdale Road, Maida Vale, London W9. This famous Spanish-Portuguese synagogue was established in the nineteenth century in a residential section near Paddington Station. A huge dome in the Arabesque style summons Jewish worshippers to prayer. During the service, rabbis and some congregants wear the traditional top hats.

Sephardic Synagogue, 8 St. James Gardens, London W11. Tel: 603-7961. Many of the congregation's members are from Greece and Turkey.

Central Synagogue, Great Portland Street, London W1. Tel: 580-1355. Here is another synagogue that was destroyed in the blitz of World War II. Today, a modern Orthodox building stands in its place.

Spanish and Portuguese Jews Congregation, 2 Ashworth Rd., London W9 1JY. Tel: 289-2573. This is also the headquarters of the Sephardic community and here the synagogue authorities showed me the registration of circumcision of Benjamin Disraeli, the great British prime minister who shortly before his bar mitzvah was converted by his father to the Church of England (see Statue of Disraeli in "Other Sites" section).

In Stamford Hill, many small Chassidic synagogues dot the area. Here are congregations whose members were born in Morocco, Iran, and India.

Synagogues of the United Synagogue (Orthodox)

The United Synagogue maintains its executive offices in Woburn House in Upper Woburn Place, London. It is the largest synagogue movement, with 40,000 members and 80 synagogues. The chief rabbinate and its Beth Din administer the religious life of large sections of provincial Jewry. One can also contact that office for more information on synagogue services. Tel: 071-387-4300.

Dollis Hill, Parkside, Dollis Hill Lane, London NW2.

Edgware, Edgware Way, Edgware, Middlesex.

Enfield and Winchmore Hill, 53 Wellington Rd., Bush Hill PR, Enfield.

Finchley, Kinloss Gardens, London N33DU.

Golders Green, 41 Dunstan Rd., London NW11 8AE.

Ilford, 24 Beehive Lane, Ilford, Essex.

New West End, St. Petersburgh Pl., London W2 4JT.

St. John's Wood, 37-41 Grove End Rd., London NW8 9WA. One of Britain's largest synagogues.

Synagogues of the Beth Din (Orthodox)

Finchley Central, Redbourne Ave., London N3.

Stamford Hill, Beth Hamidrash, 26 Lampard GR., London N16.

Yavneh, 25 Ainsworth Rd., London E9.

Yeshurun, Fernhurst Gardens, Edgware, Middlesex.

Independent, Liberal, Progressive, and Reform Synagogues

Liberal is equivalent to the American Reform Movement of Judaism and British Reform is similar to the American Conservative Movement of Judaism.

Barkingside Progressive Synagogue (Union of Liberal and Progressive Synagogues), 129 Perrymans Farm Rd., Barkingside, Ilford, Essex. Tel: 081-554-9682. Friday service, 8 P.M. Saturday, 11 A.M.

Belsize Square Synagogue (Ind), 51 Belsize Square, Hampstead, London NW3. Tel: 071-794-3949. Friday service, 6:30 P.M. Saturday, 11 A.M.

Edgware and District Reform Synagogue (Reform Synagogues of Great Britain), 118 Stonegrove, Edgware, Middlesex HA8 8AB. Tel: 081-958-978. Friday service, 8 P.M. Saturday, 11 A.M.

Finchley Progressive Synagogue (ULPS), Hutton Grove, Finchley, London N12. Tel: 071-446-4063.

Finchley Reform Synagogue (RSGB), Fallow Court Ave., Finchley, London N12 OBE. Tel: 071-446-3244.

Liberal Jewish Synagogue (ULPS), 28 St. John's Wood Rd., London NW8. Friday service, 8 P.M. Saturday, 11 A.M. Located near Regents Park, this is the chief liberal synagogue and probably has the largest seating capacity of any British synagogue. Similar to American Reform.

Mill Hill Reform Synagogue (RSGB), 366-A Stag Lane, Henry Harris Centre, Kingsbury, London NW9. Tel: 071-959-8317.

North London Progressive Synagogue (ULPS), 100 Amhurst Park, Stamford Hill, London N16. Tel: 800-8931. Friday service, 8:15 P.M. Saturday, 11 A.M.

North Western Reform Synagogue (RSGB), Alyth Gardens, Golders Green, London NW11 7EN. Tel: 455-6763. Friday service, 6:30 P.M. Saturday, 10:30 A.M.

The Settlement Synagogue (RSGB and ULPS), Stepney Jewish Settlement, Beaumont Grove, London E1. Tel: 071-790-6260. Friday service, 8 P.M. Saturday, 10:30 A.M. Located in London's East End, near Whitechapel; many senior citizens attend services here.

South London Liberal Synagogue (ULPS), Prentis Road, Streatham, London SW16. Tel: 769-4787. Friday service, 8:15 P.M. Saturday, 11 A.M.

Southgate Progressive Synagogue (ULPS), 75 Chase Rd., London N14. Tel: 886-0971. Friday service, 8:15 P.M. Saturday, 11 A.M.

West Central Liberal Synagogue (ULPS), 109-13 Whitfield St., London W1P 5RP. Tel: 071-636-7627. Saturday service, 3 P.M.

West London Synagogue of British Jews (RSGB), Upper Berkeley St., London W1N 6AT. Tel: 723-4404. Friday service, 6 P.M. Saturday, 11 A.M. Located near Hyde Park, this Reform synagogue for Ashkenazim and Sephardim is a fine example of Victorian architecture, and was founded by affluent West End London Jews. It celebrated its 150th anniversary in 1990. Having changed little, it remains one of the prime movers behind the Foundation of the Reform Synagogues of Great Britain, similar to the American Conservative Movement of Judaism. The Foundation consists of 30 other congregations in various parts of the country. The synagogue says its Holy Ark is famous for its open grillwork, which enables one to see the scrolls throughout the service. (Most synagogues cover their arks with a curtain.) In the main entrance hall to the synagogue, known as the Goldsmid Hall, there are Memorial Tablets dedicated to the memory of congregants who fell in the world wars.

Westminster Synagogue (Ind), Kent House, Rutland Gardens, London SW7 1BX. Tel: 071-584-3953. Friday service, 6:30 P.M. Saturday, 11 P.M. Housed here in the Czech Memorial Scrolls are 1,564 Torahs from the Jewish Museum in Prague, Czech Republic, in the Czech Memorial Scrolls Center, which is open to visitors on Tuesdays and Thursdays from 10 to 4 and at other times by appointment. Please let the center know you are planning a visit. Tel: 071-584-3953/3741.

Headquarters of Synagogue Governing Bodies

Adath Yisroel, 40 Queen Elizabeth's Walk, No. 16, London N16 OHH. Tel: 071-802-6226/7.

Chief Rabbinate Headquarters, Adler House, Tavistock, London WC1 H9HB. Tel: 071-387-1066. Next door to Woburn House, on Tavistock Square, is Adler House, the office of the chief rabbinate and the London Beth Din. The building is named after Dr. Herman Adler, chief rabbi of the Empire and son of Dr. Nathan Marcus Adler. British Chief Rabbi Dr. Nathan Marcus Adler (1803–90) established Jews' College in

1855 and the Jewish Board of Guardians in 1859. In 1866, he helped create the United Synagogue. Rabbi Lord Immanuel Jakobovits now serves as the chief rabbi and his office is in Adler House. He is the spokesperson for British Jewry. Some say that out of the 300,000 British Jews, the Orthodox number about 100,000, the Progressive Liberal (i.e., Reform and Conservative) about 60,000, and the rest—about 50 percent— are unaffiliated. Rabbi Lord Immanuel Jakobovits can sit in the House of Lords alongside the bishops of the established Church of England. He was inducted into the office as chief rabbi in April 1967. In 1988, he became a life peer. He is head of the United Hebrew Congregations of Britain and the Commonwealth.

Edgware Adath Yisroel, 261 Hale Lane, Edgware, Middlesex. This is a Union of Orthodox Hebrew Congregations synagogue.

Federation of Synagogues Headquarters, 9-11 Greatorex St., London E1. Tel: 071-247-4471. The second largest synagogue body in England is the Federation of Synagogues, boasting a membership of 17,000 in some 50 branches. As an Orthodox group, it set up independent courts of Jewish justice, as did the Union of Orthodox Hebrew Congregations and the Reform and Liberal movements of Judaism.

Lubavitch Foundation, Lubavitch House, 107-15 Stamford Hill, London N16. Tel: 081-800-0022 or 081-800-6432. This is the group's regional headquarters.

Reform Synagogues of Great Britain, The Manor House, 80 East End Rd., Finchley, London N3 2SY. Tel: 071-349-4731. Similar to American Conservative Movement of Judaism.

Spanish and Portuguese Synagogue, 2 Ashworth Rd., London W9 1JY. Tel: 289-2573. Located here is the Sephardic Kashrut Authority.

Union of Liberal and Progressive Synagogues, 109 Whitfield St., London W1P 5RP. Tel: 071-580-1663. This is also the headquarters of the World Union for Progressive Judaism (European Board). Tel: 071-637-7442.

United Synagogue (Orthodox), Woburn House, Upper Woburn Place, London WC1. Tel: 071-383-4300.

ORGANIZATIONS

Agudas Israel, Golders Green Road, London NW11. Tel: 081-458-8424.

Association for Jewish Youth, 50 Lindley St., London El 3AX. Tel: 071-790-6407. Information on youth groups can be obtained here.

B'nai B'rith Hillel House, ½ Endsleigh St., London WC1. Tel: 071-387-4644 or 071-380-0111.

Institute of Jewish Affairs, 11 Hertford St., London W1Y 7DX. Tel: 071-491-3517.

Jewish Agency, Balfour House, 741 High Rd., London N12 OB9. Tel: 01-446-1477.

Jewish Historical Society of England, 33 Seymour Pl., London W1H 5AP.

Jewish Memorial Council, Woburn House, Upper Woburn Place, London. Tel: 071-387-3081.

Maccabi World Union, North Ends Road, London NW11 7GY. Tel: 071-458-9488/9.

WIZO, 107 Gloucester Pl., London W1. Tel: 071-486-2691.

World Jewish Congress, 11 Hertford St., London W1Y 7DX. Tel: 081-491-3517.

MUSEUMS AND LIBRARIES

British Museum, Great Russell Street, Bloomsbury, London WC1. Tel: 071-636-1555. The Hebrew Library here contains about 50,000 volumes and 3,000 manuscripts including material from ancient Palestine. At times, letters from Benjamin Disraeli are shown. Also permanent exhibits contain archeological finds from the Middle East as well as a philatelic collection of early twentieth-century stamps, including pre-Israel Independence Palestine stamps. The British Museum contains the Balfour Declaration. On November 2, 1917, Foreign Secretary Arthur James Balfour wrote a letter to Lord Rothschild declaring, "His Majesty's Government view with favour the establishment in Palestine of a national home for the Jewish people."

Lord Balfour was interested in Zionism, perhaps as a result of a meeting with Dr. Chaim Weizmann in Manchester.

Weizmann had persuaded the British government and influenced Lord Arthur Balfour to favor the establishment of a Jewish state in Palestine. A distinguished scholar and scientist, Weizmann studied chemistry in Germany and Switzerland and as a British subject, he admired England and English ways. A leading British chemist, he had served as director of the laboratories of the British Admiralty and was instrumental in the "perfection of the most subtle and complex method of obtaining alcohol from wood, at a time when this material, absolutely vital for the production of explosives, was becoming impossible to obtain in sufficient quantities, because of the submarine campaign of the abnormal conditions of war!" After the Balfour Declaration, he became the leader of the World Zionist Movement and is considered a great Jewish statesman. He was named the first president of the State of Israel.

Beth Hamidrash, Adler House, Tavistock Square, London WC1. Tel: 071-203-6427/9.

Institute of Contemporary History and the Weiner Library, 4 Devonshire St., London W1. Tel: 071-636-7247. This library probably contains more than 50,000 books and periodicals and hundreds of thousands of newspaper clippings on Nazism and the Holocaust.

Jews' College, Albert Road, Hendon, London NW4 2SJ. Founded in 1855, coursework at this college leads to graduate degrees as well as rabbinical ordination. Includes a magnificent library of more than 80,000 volumes.

Leo Baeck College, Sternberg Centre for Judaism, The Manor House, 80 East End Rd., London N3 2SY. Tel: 081-349-4525.

Library of the Spanish and Portuguese Synagogue, Lauderdale Road, London W9.

Mocatta Library and Museum, University College, Gower Street, London WC1. Sponsored by the Jewish Historical Society, it contains a wonderful Hebraica and Judaica section in the Guild Hall Library. Abraham Mocatta was a leader of the Bevis Marks Synagogue. The family originally came from Spain and the Mediterranean area. The Mocattas were among the first Jews in England, as well as founders of the Bevis Marks congregation, West London Synagogue. They were active on the Jewish Board of Deputies.

Museum of the Jewish East End, Sternberg Centre for Judaism, The Manor House, 80 East End Rd., London N3 2SY.

OTHER SITES

Selfridge's Department Store, 400 Oxford St., London W1, maintains a Jewish book section, as well as a scrumptious kosher food department.

The Statue of Benjamin Disraeli in Westminster Abbey. One of the most popular tourist sites in England is Westminster Abbey, which is the burial site, as well as house of statues, of Great Britain's greatest heroes, scholars, and politicians. In the Statesmen's Corner of the Abbey, next to former Prime Ministers Peel and Gladstone, stands a statue of Benjamin Disraeli (1804–81). The guides usually tell you that Benjamin Disraeli was born a Jew, but he was converted by his father.

He was born at **No 22. Theobalds Rd.** There is also a statue of Benjamin Disraeli facing Parliament. He died at 19 Curzon St., London W1, in 1881. A plaque was erected on the building. Disraeli was a statesman, one of the greatest prime ministers of the United Kingdom, and a prolific writer and novelist. Among his books were *Vivian Grey, Alroy, Sybil,* and *Coningsby.* There are Jewish themes in many of his books. In the novel *Tancred,* Disraeli spoke out in favor of national independence of the Jews.

Just before his bar mitzvah, he was baptized by his writer-historian father, Isaac D'Israeli, after the latter had a quarrel with the Sephardic synagogue. The congregation had asked Isaac to serve on the board of trustees and Isaac refused. In those days, if you turned down your position, you had to pay a fine. Isaac refused again and left the congregation.

Even though Benjamin Disraeli was one of the most brilliant diplomats, and even though he was a regular church communicant, he never hid his Jewish origin and sympathies. As Disraeli liked to tell it, the family actually came from Italy, not Spain. "He believed that the Jews, by their virtue and their glorious past, were entitled to special esteem, and he devoted his tremendous audacity and imagination to securing it for them," writes Paul Johnson. Many say that, in Parliament, he spoke as if he were a Jew. He did much to improve the general social and political position of the Jews. As a young man, he had visited the Near East and Jerusalem.

Disraeli boasted of the "superiority of the Jewish race" as a storehouse of energy and vision. He believed Jews were the "aristocrats of mankind." He is quoted as saying, "The most inspiring singers, most graceful dancers and most delicate musicians are the sons and daughters of Israel." He once told Montefiore, "You and I belong to a race that can do everything but fail."

He was a great friend of the Rothschilds. With the financial help of the Rothschilds, he acquired the Egyptian khedive's shares in the Suez Canal to make sure England controlled the vital route to India. This action brought England right smack into the Middle East, next door to Palestine, which the British, under General Allenby, conquered in 1917 during World War I.

Perhaps Disraeli had indeed studied the map. Some historians say that in his bringing England into Egypt and closer to Palestine, perhaps he actually had in mind eventually to plant Britain in Palestine and thus be able to establish a Jewish state. Farfetched? Did not General Allenby invade Palestine from Egypt a half-century later?

His other great diplomatic victory was at the 1878 Congress of Berlin, when he prevented war in Eastern Europe.

Benjamin Disraeli presided at No. 10 Downing Street, the office of the Prime Minister, when it was the seat of the greatest empire the world had ever seen.

He got along splendidly with Queen Victoria, who laid a wreath upon his tomb. The marble tablet placed in the chancel of Hughenden Church after his death says, "To the Dear and Honored Memory of Benjamin, Earl of Beaconsfield. This memorial is placed by His Grateful Sovereign and Friend, Victoria, R.I. Kings love him that speaketh right."

The Statue of Cromwell. In Parliament Square stands the statue of Oliver Cromwell, the "Lord Protector" of England. He had a great deal to do with the Jewish return to England in 1656 after a 400-year absence. Indeed the *Standard Jewish Encyclopaedia* states that Manasseh Ben Israel's mission to England to petition for the readmission of Jews was probably undertaken at Cromwell's suggestion. Manasseh realized that Cromwell, a Puritan, viewed the Jews favorably and supported their readmission. To Cromwell it made good business sense. Cromwell had hoped to extend Britain's influence and its wealth, and to make England "number one" in Europe. He knew that Jews, as well as Marranos (secret Jews), had enriched other nations, including Holland, whose ships were out-trading the English. He hoped the Jews would do the same for England.

In December 1656, Cromwell convened the Whitehall Conference to consider the matter of the Jews. He himself presided over the opening session. He liked Manasseh Ben Israel, whose speech before the council was one of the most eloquent in Jewish history. It was called "Esperanca de Israel" ("The Hope of Israel"). But Cromwell later dissolved the conference when he realized the council's decision would be a resounding "no" to allowing Jewish immigration. Since he had the power, he could have rammed an admission bill through the meeting. Instead, he connived to allow the Jews to enter the country and stay, giving up attempts to permit their immigration on a formal basis—in short, a compromise.

Soon Jews were permitted to hold services in rented rooms. Later, they would be allowed to build their first synagogue in Creechurch Lane. In the spring of 1656, Cromwell received and granted a petition from the Marranos to establish a cemetery outside of London. Under Cromwell, Marranos obtained seats on the London Stock Exchange. From these trader families, the Jewish community created a network of other families who were prominent in banking, finance, and commerce.

The Statue of Winston Churchill. Near Parliament stands the statue of Winston Churchill. During World War II, Churchill was the voice of the free world. He uplifted men and women all over the globe. He was a leader. As you look at his statue, you cannot but admire this great man who rallied the people all over the world against Nazism. His patriotism, it is said, "was rooted in the very soil of the history of England."

Churchill was an ardent Zionist. His influence established the Jewish Brigade of Palestine in World War II. Churchill once wrote to Franklin D. Roosevelt, "I am strongly wedded to the Zionist policy, of which I was one of the authors." He was a bitter opponent of England's White Paper, which, in 1939, severely limited Jewish immigration and closed off Palestine as a refuge. But, as William Manchester notes, he was "unrepresentative of England's upper class, for even England was not free of anti-Semitism."

John Lukacs writes in his book, *The Duel,* that in 1938, when Churchill was in such debt that he was about to sell his beloved country house, Chartwell, Sir Henry Strakosch, a London financier of Jewish ancestry, "paid off his debts." Jewish groups would often cite Churchill for his "courageous defense of freedom and denunciation of Nazism." But even with Churchill's sympathy, it was always an uphill battle to establish the Zionist dream of a Jewish homeland. European Jews who were trapped during the war could not emigrate because most countries refused to admit Jews. And several ships, such as the *Patria,* were sunk because the English refused permission to dock in Palestine. Even after World War II, when Churchill was out of power, the British Labor Party resisted the establishment of a Jewish nation. It appeared that nothing could sway them, not even the death of the six million Jews.

Yet in the face of world opinion in favor of a Jewish state, the British finally relented. After the U.N. Partition Plan of November 1947, they left Palestine forever in 1948, bitter to the end. Almost five decades later, many Israelis say the British treated them not as colonial subjects but as human beings. Aspects of the Israeli parliament, judiciary, and bureaucracy are all patterned after the British, under whom the Jews developed self-government.

Wingate and Chindit Memorial. Victoria Embankment, outside the Ministry of Defence, London. This monument stands in honor of Maj. Gen. Orde Wingate and his Chindit forces of the Burma campaign during World War II. Wingate, friend of the Jews, some say "hero" of the Jews, helped train the

Palmach, the "shock troops," of Haganah, the self-defense army of Israel during the British Mandate in Palestine.

Brighton and Hove

Perhaps it is the Royal Pavilion, which houses a museum and art gallery; or the Dome area, which is used for concerts and conferences; or the Lanes and those famous antique shops that attract thousands. Maybe it is the boardwalk, the beaches, and the piers, but whatever it is, something lures tourists to this wonderful seaside resort on the English Channel, 51 miles south of London.

Many Jews from London retire to Brighton. A very active Jewish community exists here, one that for many years helped in the battle for freedom of Soviet Jewry. I remember back in the late 1970s when I visited Brighton, I was told about a Soviet Jew who was fortunate enough to leave the U.S.S.R. He stood before 200 synagogue women at a luncheon in the resort town and his accounts tugged at the heartstrings of these Jewish mothers.

Many Jews commute from here to London each day, and many come here in the summer and are active in the community, which has about 12,000 Jews.

In the middle of the eighteenth century, the town became famous as a resort and wealthy Jews settled here, including the Goldsmids and Sassoons. But the bulk of Jews probably did not settle here until about 1800.

SYNAGOGUES IN
BRIGHTON AND HOVE

Synagogue, 66 Middle St., Brighton. Tel: 27785. Brighton is also famous for this synagogue. It is a lovely, small synagogue consecrated in 1875, well known for its interior design.

Brighton & Hove Liberal Jewish Synagogue, 6 Landsdowne Rd., Hove. Tel: 737-223.

Orthodox Synagogue, Holland Road, Hove. Tel: 732-035.

Reform Synagogue, 65 Palmeira Ave., Hove. Tel: 735-343.

Synagogue, 29 New Church Rd., West Hove.

LODGING

The Hideaway Helmdon, 1 Furse Hill, Hove BN3 1PA. Tel: 772-038. This is a kosher boardinghouse in Hove.

Manchester

Manchester is often considered the prototypical city of the Industrial Revolution, and the first Jewish settlers arrived here from Liverpool in the eighteenth century. Nathan Mayer Rothschild's first residence in England was in Manchester, from where he exported cotton goods from 1798 to 1805. The large Jewish immigration came here between 1881 and 1914, generally tailors and capmakers. Lord Marks, founder of Marks and Spencer and one of the greatest leaders of the Zionist movement in Britain, was born in Manchester. In addition to the Manchester Jews who came to the city from Russia and Poland, a large number came here from the Middle East and established the important Sephardic congregations of South Manchester. From 1904 to 1916, Manchester was the home of Dr. Chaim Weizmann, the great Zionist leader and first president of Israel. Here he conducted his early scientific experiments and met the future leaders of the Zionist movement.

There probably are about thirty-five synagogues in Manchester, the second largest Jewish community in Great Britain.

The Manchester Jewish Museum is located on the premises of the former Spanish and Portuguese Synagogue at 190 Cheetham Hill Rd., Manchester, M88LW. Tel: 061-834-9879. The building, completed in 1874, is listed as being of historical importance. The ground floor of the structure has not been altered in any significant way, and is not used for worship services. A traveler can visit this remarkable synagogue. The former ladies' gallery now houses the permanent exhibition in which the history of Manchester's Jewish community, now more than 200 years old, is vividly brought to life. Homes, schools, and workshops of long ago have been recreated in detail to portray the lives of ordinary people. The museum opened in 1984. It is open Monday through Thursday,

10:30 A.M. to 4 P.M., and Sunday, 10:30 A.M. to 5 P.M.

The first Jewish school was founded in 1842.

An interesting site is the **library** in St. Peters Square, which has an excellent Jewish collection.

Fulda's Hotel is a kosher hotel located at 84 Bury Old Rd. in Sulford. Tel: 740-4551.

Lubavitch, Machon Levi Yitzchok, Bury Old Road. Tel: 795-4000.

Oxford

There is an old British expression that everyone journeys to Oxford sooner or later. Oxford is a city of all seasons, a city of learning and scholarship, and above all, a city built upon books, "books being read, books being written, books being published." This "sweet city with her dream spires" supports a labyrinth of libraries and dozens of bookstores.

The Oxford Center for Post-Graduate Hebrew Studies, 45 Giles St., Oxford OX1 3LP. Mix together a former British country estate, one of the world's greatest universities, nine cottages for Israeli and American Jewish writers, and a college junior-year-abroad program in Jewish studies, and you have an advanced research institute of Judaic studies. The university is Oxford, in the town of Oxford, 56 miles by road from London. The Jewish institute, located just four miles outside the City of Oxford, is the Oxford Center for Post-Graduate Hebrew Studies.

Yarnton Manor, a seventeenth-century manor house that once belonged to the Spencer family from whom Diana, Princess of Wales, is descended, is used for lectures, symposia, seminars, and conferences. At the manor are the Kressel Library and Archives. The library contains 35,000 volumes; the archives contain approximately one-half million newspaper clippings.

Oxford still remains one of the great centers of England. Historically, Jews came down here from London to sell hats, frocks, and shoes. And now, too, Jewish scholars and students of Judaism are coming to Oxford University, to the Oxford Center for Post-Graduate Hebrew Studies.

These scholars have produced more than 350 academic and

literary items, including 80 books, as a result of their stay. Such famous works of Hebrew literature as A. B. Yehoshua's *The Lover* and T. Carmi's *The Penguin Book of Hebrew Verse* were written, in whole or in part, at the center. Other writers who have worked here include Benyamin Tammuz, the Israeli novelist, who wrote *Minotaur* in the Apple Loft, one of the Yarnton Manor's estate cottages. In its English translation, *Minotaur* was chosen by the late Graham Greene as one of the three best novels of 1981.

Dr. David Patterson, founder and president of the center, Cowley Lecturer in Post-Biblical Hebrew, and fellow of St. Cross College in Oxford University, stresses that, during World War II, about 750 institutions of Jewish learning in Europe were lost forever. He recalls that when he started the center, he received the warm support of such leading scholars as Sir Isaiah Berlin and Professor David Daube, the former Regius Professor of Civil Law at Oxford University.

In an interview, Dr. Patterson told me that he knew that Oxford was exceptionally well qualified to serve the needs of an international center for Jewish learning. After all, the chair in Hebrew was established by Henry VIII, and Hebrew has been taught there in an unbroken tradition for more than 450 years since then.

Bodleian Library. Thousands of Hebrew books, handwritten Bibles, priceless Judaica, and manuscripts are located in the Bodleian Library, one of the outstanding libraries in the world. One estimate quotes that more than 30,000 Hebrew volumes are housed here.

Synagogue and Jewish Center, 21 Richmond Rd., Oxford OX1 2JL. Tel: 08-655-3042.

L'Chaim Society Center, 121 St. Aldate's, Carfax, Oxford. This is the Jewish student union, which sponsors speakers and other events.

Chabad House, 75 Cowley Rd., Oxford, OX11EH, Tel: 44-865-794-462.

B. H. Blackwell, Ltd., 48-51 Broad St., Oxford, OX1 3BQ. This impressive and large bookshop contains a Judaica section.

York

Clifford's Tower of York Castle. A tragic episode occurred in York on the Sabbath before Passover, March 16, 1190, the day preceding Palm Sunday. It took place at Clifford's Tower, located just across from the museum. The tragedy was described thusly: At Easter, villagers launched a whispering campaign that Jews were killing Christian children so they could use their blood for Passover rites. Frightened, the Jews of York, headed by Rabbi Yom To of Joigny, fled to the castle. Rather than surrender, they decided to kill each other. Given a so-called safe conduct, a few survivors left the castle. "Kill the Jews," yelled the villagers. After butchering the survivors, they quickly burned the financial debt notes owed to the Jewish moneylenders. York Jewry never recovered from the killings. Today, only about 45 Jews live in York. For an admission fee, one can climb to the top. Open March 15 to October 15, Monday through Friday, 9:30 to 6:30; Sundays, 2 to 4 in summer.

Suggested Reading

Bermant, Chaim. *The Cousinhood.* New York: Macmillan, 1971.

Blake, Robert. *Disraeli.* London: Methuen, 1969.

————. *Disraeli's Grand Tour: Benjamin Disraeli and the Holy Land, 1830–31.* New York: Oxford University Press, 1982.

Corbett, W. *Jews and the Jews of England.* Gordon, 1976.

Hyamson, Albert M. *A History of the Jews in England.* Chatto and Windus, 1908.

Litvinoff, Barnet. *The Burning Bush: Anti-Semitism and World History.* New York: Dutton, 1988.

Morris, James. *Oxford.* New York: Harcourt, Brace & World, 1965.

Morton, H. V. *In Search of London.* New York: Dodd, Mead, 1951.

Wasserstein, Bernard. *Britain and the Jews of Europe, 1939–1945.* New York: Oxford University Press, 1979.

Weintraub, Stanley. *Disraeli: A Biography.* New York: Truman Talley Blochs/Dutton, 1993.

Ireland
Dublin Has Had Jewish Mayors

They call it "Bloomsday" and it remains the major literary festival of Ireland. It celebrates the birthday of Leopold Bloom, the son of a Hungarian Jew and the hero in *Ulysses*, James Joyce's novel that depicts certain elements of Jewish life in Dublin at the beginning of the century. Joyce stands as Dublin's most famous writer and Dublin remains the center of the Jewish community of Ireland.

Less than 2,000 Jews inhabit Ireland, but they conduct a meaningful Jewish life with many activities. This Jewish community supports Orthodox synagogues, a large variety of religious, charitable, Zionist, and educational institutions, a religious school, and a museum. Relations between the Jewish community and the Catholic and Protestant populations are good.

A Brief History

The Irish love to link Ireland with biblical tradition, as well as the ancient Jews. "Legends that the Irish are the Ten Lost Tribes of Israel can prove very convincing when delivered in the midst of a peat bog and when shown the genuine Jacob's ladder to heaven in a secret cave near the Lakes of Killarney," writes Asher Benson, Dublin correspondent for the London *Jewish Chronicle*.

The earliest known reference to Jews in Ireland is in 613 when St. Columbanus penned an epistle to the pope of Rome, and smugly reported, "None of us has been a heretic, none of us a Jew. . . ." In the year 1079, five Jews came over the sea with gifts and were refused entry. Jews were forbidden to land in Ireland in the fifteenth and sixteenth centuries, although Marranos probably resided there.

After an absence of several hundred years, a number of Jewish families of Spanish and Portuguese descent and two or three of Polish or German origin settled in Dublin around 1660.

But Jews did not flock to Ireland in large numbers until after Cromwell permitted them to return to England in 1656. Marranos from London were the first Irish Jewish settlers. In the middle of the seventeenth century, more Marranos settled in the city. Thus, by the first quarter of the eighteenth century, Dublin was the only city in Ireland that had an organized Jewish community. And they came, according to Louis Hyman, because Dublin was the second city of the British Empire and the city was an excellent trading post, with a high society rivalling the heyday of Paris. Actually, eighteenth-century Dublin was a vital, innovative capital.

In 1717, a Jewish cemetery was set up and a synagogue was founded in 1746.

Throughout the eighteenth century, the Irish tried often to convert the Jews of Dublin. According to one convert, "the people of this Kingdom constantly rejoice when they see a Jew convert."

About 200 Jews lived in Dublin in 1750. But the failure of the Irish banks in 1727 and the famine of 1748 would hurt the city, including the Jews. Many Jews fled the severe famine, leaving only a few Jewish families in Dublin in the early nineteenth century. In 1816, the Irish Naturalization Act of 1783, from which the Jews had been excluded, was repealed: Jews could now be naturalized in Ireland. Dublin grew again in 1822 with the arrival of Polish and German Jews, most of whom had lived in England, writes Hyman. "In their struggle for political emancipation, the Jews of England found many a champion in Ireland," he adds.

But in the winter of 1845–46, Ireland again was stricken by a potato famine, which left a giant graveyard. One million persons fled to America. The relief measures taken by an unprepared government were almost useless, but there was outside aid in which British and American Jews were prominent. An Irish famine loan of 8 million British pounds was negotiated by Baron Lionel Rothschild of London, who waived all commission.

After 1882, the Russian Jews arrived and firmly established the Jewish community. They settled in Cork, Limerick, Londonderry, and Waterford. In 1881, there were 472 Jews. By 1901, that figure rose to 3,769.

While the Jewish community maintained neutrality during Ireland's fight for independence, Dublin Jews sheltered many Irish revolutionaries and individual Jews took a leading part in the rebellion. Robert Briscoe was among them. He later became lord mayor of Dublin.

In 1918, the office of the chief rabbi of Erie was established and Rabbi Isaac Herzog (1889–1959) was appointed. He later served as the first Ashkenazi chief rabbi of Israel. Rabbi Herzog was recognized as one of the great rabbinical scholars of his time. He was rabbi in Belfast from 1916 to 1919 and in Dublin until 1936, receiving the title of chief rabbi of the Irish Free State after 1921. He was a friend of Eamon deValera, the Irish leader and prime minister. His son, Chaim, was president of Israel May 1983 to May 1993.

Belfast-born Chaim Herzog also served Israel as a former intelligence officer, military commentator, military attache to Washington, and Israel's ambassador to the United Nations.

When Ireland became independent in 1921, the Jews set up their own community council. The 1937 Constitution of the Republic recognized Judaism as a minority faith and guaranteed Jews complete freedom from discrimination.

Israel's independence occurred on May 14, 1948. But, Ireland waited until February 12, 1949, to accord de facto recognition of Israel. In 1995 Ireland finally established diplomatic relations with Israel.

Today in the 1990s, there are about 1,900 Jews out of 3.5 million Irish men and women. Most Jews live in Dublin, except for some in Cork.

Jewish Dublin

Jews live in Dublin because it is a business center, vacation destination, and port city. It is a city of writers, revolutionaries, and talkers—a city of memories possessing a tragic and yet glorious history.

SITES IN DUBLIN

Birthplace of Leopold Bloom, 52 Upper Clanbrassil St., Dublin 8. This building is supposedly the birthplace of James Joyce's famous character in *Ulysses.*

Bloomfield House, Bloomfield Avenue, Dublin 8. This was formerly the Jewish Day School.

Clonyn Castle, Delvin, County Westmeath. More than 100 Jewish orphaned children from concentration camps had a temporary home here until 1948.

The Irish Jewish Museum, 3 and 4 Walworth Rd., Dublin 8. The Irish Jewish Museum officially was opened on June 20, 1985, by the then-president of Israel, Chaim Herzog. The building is located in the former Walworth Road Synagogue, which has been completely restored.

In planning the layout of the museum in the existing premises, a division was made between the secular and religious. The secular exhibition has been mounted downstairs in the reception hall of the former synagogue. The displays trace the history of the Jews in Ireland beginning with their arrival, their various commercial, business, and professional activities, the development of their institutions, and their integration to their present position and status.

Upstairs, at the rear of the synagogue in the Harold Smerling Gallery, a display of religious items has been set up.

This shows various ritual and religious objects, such as a large candelabrum.

Some of the exhibition topics are James Joyce and the Jewish characters and references in his novels; Jews in Irish provincial cities; anti-Semitism; the Holocaust; Irish Jews and families in public life, in the professions, and in business; the Jewish wedding; women in Judaism; and ritual objects.

Most people, when they think about Irish Jews, do not consider their artistic achievements. Perhaps the most unique aspect of a visit to this museum is to discover that Irish Jewry, which never numbered more than 6,000 persons, and now numbers less than 2,000, produced talented painters. Works by Harry Kernoff, David Eichenstein, Estella Solomons, Gerald Davis, and others are on display. A cabinet of books written by Irish Jews is a highlight of the exhibit.

The museum abounds in material regarding families and personalities. The lives of the chief rabbis are also portrayed. A favorite exhibit in the display cases is "Irish Jews in Public Life." One such personality, of course, is Robert Briscoe (1894–1969), the first Jewish member of the Irish Parliament and the first Jewish lord mayor of Dublin. He fought for Irish independence in the IRA from 1917 to 1924. One of the few Jews in the IRA, he was a member of Eamon deValera's party from 1927 to 1965. He supported Revisionist Zionism. Briscoe wrote a book, *For the Life of Me,* which was published in 1958, the year he was elected mayor of Dublin. "All the time I was growing up," he states, "I was being steeped in the dark, stormy, racked, light, short history of my country of Eire."

Through the Easter uprising, the terror, the Black and Tans, the controversial treaty with England, and the civil war, Briscoe—who claimed he was the only Jew in the IRA—fought for Irish independence. Some say he taught Vladimir Ze'ev Jabotinsky, Revisionist Zionist leader, guerrilla tactics he learned in fighting the British. He had listened to Jabotinsky address groups in Ireland. In his book, he tells how he pioneered and helped raise money for the famous "coffin ships" that smuggled thousands of Jews into Palestine. He said he regarded Zionism as a magnificent inspiration.

His son Benjamin Briscoe was Dublin's lord mayor from 1988 to 1989. He was then elected to Parliament from his father's constituency.

The Jewish Old Aged Home, Denmark Hill, Leinster Road West, Dublin 6. Tel: 972004. This home was founded in 1950. Services are held here; times vary according to season and needs of senior citizens.

Memorial to the Six Million Jews, in the synagogue grounds between 32 and 34 Rathfarnham Rd., Dublin 6. This monument remembers those Jews who perished in the Holocaust.

Office of the Chief Rabbi and Community Centre, Herzog House, 1 Zion Rd., Dublin 6. Tel: 923751.

Rabbi Herzog's Home, 33 Bloomfield Ave., Dublin 8. The first chief rabbi of Ireland resided here.

Stratford College and Dublin Talmud Torah, 1 Zion Rd., Dublin 6. Tel: 967351. This college incorporates kindergarten, primary school, and college secondary school.

SYNAGOGUES IN DUBLIN

The Dublin Hebrew Congregation, 36 Adelaide Rd., Dublin 2. Tel: 761734 or 766745. Dedicated in 1892. In a nearby structure, one finds the office of the chief rabbi of Ireland, the community center, a Talmud Torah and day school, as well as the headquarters of various Jewish organizations and Zionist groups. Services are Fridays at 8:30 P.M. in summer and at sunset in other seasons; every Saturday morning from 9:15 to 11:15.

Dublin Jewish Progressive Congregation, 7 Leicester Ave., Dublin 6. Tel: 973955 or 943947. Services are held Fridays at 8:15 P.M. and first Saturdays in every month at 10:30 A.M.

Machzikei Hadass, rear of 77 Terenure Rd. North, Dublin 6. Tel: 908413 or 906130. Services are held every Saturday at 9:30 A.M. Times for all other services vary according to season.

Terenure Hebrew Congregation, between 32 and 34 Rathfarnham Rd., Dublin 6. Tel: 908037, 905969, or 908544. Services are Fridays at 8:30 P.M. in summer and at sunset in other seasons; every Saturday morning from 9:15 to 11:15.

Suggested Reading

Briscoe, Robert, with Alden Hatch. *For the Life of Me.* Boston: Little, Brown, 1958.

Hyman, Louis. *The Jews of Ireland, from Earliest Times to the Year 1910.* Shannon, Ireland: Irish University Press, 1972.

Milan

Venice

ITALY

Florence

☆ ROME

Italy
Jews Sell Cameos
in St. Peter's Square

"All Italians look like Jews and all Jews look like Italians," said the Italian writer Luigi Barzini.

When I would stroll through St. Peter's Square in Rome, I would watch Italian men selling religious cameos. At least they looked Italian. I soon observed that if these salesmen thought you were Jewish, they might greet you in Yiddish with, "Hello, landsman." Considering that Jews have lived in Europe for hundreds of years, it is not strange to hear Yiddish on the Continent. However, it is uncommon to hear a Yiddish greeting from Jews in Italy who, by and large, are of Sephardic origin, or indigenous Italians who do not know Yiddish.

Anyway, what were Jews doing selling religious cameos in St. Peter's Square in the first place?

Believe it or not, the concession is said to be held by Jews, who knew that most American Jewish tourists are Ashkenazim. Like all good business persons, those Italian Jews also get attention by shouting out a Yiddish word in the Vatican, of all places. Incidentally, you will probably meet these Jewish super-salespersons at the Colosseum and the Pantheon, too.

A Brief History

Welcome to Italy, the home of about 30,000 Jews—Italy, the eternal, where beauty reigns supreme and where Jews have lived longer than in any other country in Europe. Italy probably was the first European country to which Jews migrated from the Holy Land. Ambassadors of Judah Maccabee set foot on Italian soil in 140 B.C. to seek alliances, and they found a warm welcome.

Italy, the only nation in Western Europe in which Jewish settlement has been continuous from the second century, is considered the oldest Jewish community in the Western world. Few towns or regions in Italy stand without a trace of Jewish presence: catacombs from first-century cemeteries, medieval and baroque synagogues, Jewish quarters and ghettos. Italy's museums and churches contain countless Jewish relics, and history's first Hebrew printing press was started here.

In A.D. 70, thousands of Jews were massacred in Palestine. Thousands more were deported to Rome. At one time, 1,500 Jews arrived in Rome in chains. Roman Jewish slaves worked on the Colosseum, that eternal symbol of the Eternal City, until they could buy their freedom. They would continue suffering at the hands of Tiberius, Claudius, and Nero.

When Rome fell and Christianity was accepted as the official religion, Jews were persecuted. The Church wanted Jews preserved, however, as "witnesses of ancient truths." Jews were seen as the enemies of Jesus, responsible for his death. They were second-class citizens, excluded from public offices and from various professions.

While Jews were persecuted by the Byzantines, conditions eased when Pope Gregory I (590–604) began his reign. He protected them and provided safety for Jews in Rome and other cities. After this, it becomes evident that Jewish history in Italy is linked with the pope. Some popes safeguarded Jews. They even hired Jewish financiers and doctors. On the other hand, many popes were bitterly anti-Semitic.

By the end of the eleventh century, Jews lived in northern Italy in such towns as Verona, Pavia, and Lucca. Talmudic academies existed in Rome. Hostility of the popes erupted in the twelfth century and culminated in the Fourth Lataran Council in 1215, which along with other discriminatory regulations forced Jews to wear a distinguishing badge on their clothes. In the thirteenth century and the beginning of the fourteenth,

Jews were allowed to become only moneylenders as the Church prohibited Christians from lending money for interest. After the Catholic monarchs of Spain expelled the Jewish people from Spanish soil in 1492, many Jews, as well as Marranos, found their way to Italy. But the Spaniards invaded the south late in the fifteenth century and forced the Jews to leave Sicily and the Italian south. In 1555, Pope Paul IV issued his infamous *Cum nimis absurdum,* banishing Jews to the ghetto. The document also prohibited them from engaging in any business except the sale of rags and other items.

During the Counter-Reformation, an Inquisition was instituted. Jews were burned at the stake. Many fled to the north, or out of Italy to North Africa, Greece, Turkey, and the Levant. Throughout the years, even as late as the eighteenth century, Jews, forced to listen to sermons, were often baptized against their will.

When Napoleon overran Italy in 1796, the Catholic church's political rule was taken away. Implementing the ideals of the Revolution, the French army freed the Jews. For the first time, Jews became Italian citizens. On July 9, 1798, the yellow badge that Jews had been forced to wear was abolished by an edict of the French general St. Cyr.

With Napoleon's abandonment of Italy and his downfall at Waterloo came reaction. Pope Pius VII returned to Rome in 1814 and introduced the Holy Inquisition again. Jews would have continued to suffer, except for the Risorgimento movement for freedom that started in the Piedmont in 1820–21 and culminated in the 1848–49 revolution in Milan, Rome, and Venice, the latter under the leadership of Daniele Manin, a Jew. In 1848–49, the walls of the ghetto of Rome came down. They had stood longer than any other in Western Europe. Yet again a wave of repression occurred. Finally, in 1870 when the united Italian kingdom was established, Jews received equal rights.

Cecil Roth points out in *The History of the Jews of Italy* that after 1870, there was no country in either hemisphere where Jewish conditions "were or could be better," . . . at least until the late 1930s. The 1938 racial laws against Jews restricted Jewish life and devastated the Jewish community.

As Germany's ally, Italy invaded France in 1940. Still, the Jews in Italian-occupied southern France, as well as in Italy itself, were reasonably safe. However, when Italy surrendered to the Allies on September 8, 1943, Jews immediately faced danger from the Germans, who rushed troops into central and northern Italy. Now Mussolini's puppet regime cooperated with the Nazis. The gestapo also quickly moved against the Jewish community. On September 24, 1943, they blackmailed the Jewish community: 50 kilos of gold within 36 hours, otherwise 200 Jews would be murdered. Four days later, they got their money. Pope Pius XII offered to provide as much as needed, but enough had been collected by the Jewish community. Nothing was taken from the Vatican. Contributions also came from non-Jews.

On October 16, 1943, "Black Saturday," a tragic day indeed, the Germans surrounded the Jewish quarter and arrested more than 1,000 Jews who were then shipped to Auschwitz, where all but 16 died. "Until that mass roundup, . . . the Jews of Rome believed themselves immune to crimes they heard were being committed by the Nazis against the Jews of other countries," writes Robert Katz.

The number of Italian Jews murdered in the Holocaust is estimated at 7,750 out of a total Jewish population of about 30,000 at the beginning of the German occupation, an 85 percent survival rate, second to Denmark.

According to Susan Zuccotti, in her book *The Italians and the Holocaust,* the Holocaust began late in Italy, in September 1943, when the Germans swooped south. Therefore, the danger period was shorter. The Italian Jews were one-tenth of 1 percent of the population. Financial resources as well as hard cash helped Jews survive. Physical appearances also mattered, for assimilated Jews could pass as non-Jews. Ordinary Italians, moreover, tried to help the Jews during the German occupation. Italy ranks with Denmark as one of the nations that rescued Jews during the dark years. After the war, Italy was the main "highway for Jewish refugees en route to Palestine," although some went to America. In 1945, the post-Holocaust era of Italian Jewry began with lives that had been disrupted.

"Those who remained began a slow and painful reconstruction," wrote Emily Braun in *Gardens and Ghettos*. But they were soon to be joined by Jews from Hungary and North Africa, especially Egypt, who lived in more than 200 Italian cities and towns.

By the 1990s the Jewish population was estimated at about 30,000, including about 2,000 Israeli students, out of a total Italian population of 62 million persons.

A high rate of assimilation and declining enrollment in Jewish schools, as well as an aging population, plagues Italian Jewry. According to the Institute of Jewish Affairs in London, 56 percent of Italian Jews have a diploma or university degree; 34 percent are engaged in trade or business; 13 percent are professionals; 5 percent are workers; and 4 percent are teachers.

Not only is Roman Jewry a community steeped in a unique history, but it is unique in temperament, too. Jews in Rome are more Mediterranean than Jews in the north. No matter where they are when they gather together, they obviously eat Italian food with a Jewish flavoring—pasta, pizza, Italian delicacies. Italy is a nation of food; people enjoy eating.

You will find that several streets contain Jewish-owned stores. One survey has reported that 70 percent of Rome's clothing shops are operated by Jews. The young people of Rome often go straight from school into their parents' businesses. However, Italy has in recent decades become a "heavily industrialized nation via American-style capitalism," and young Jews have moved more into industrial and technological professions.

In the 1980s there were some anti-Semitic incidents, a number of which were sparked by the war in Lebanon, but Chief Rabbi Elio Toaff spoke out and relations between Christians and Jews in Italy are still good. In 1965, the Second Vatican Council repudiated the notion that the Jews collectively were responsible for the death of Jesus and subsequently affirmed the enduring importance of Judaism. And late in 1993, the Vatican and Israel established diplomatic relations. Yet, with the elections of a Rightist Bloc in Italy's Parliament, Jewish concerns were raised, especially since a number of Rightists have been accused of anti-Semitism. Chances are that Jews will be in Rome for many centuries to come.

Notable Italian Jews

Within one or two generations, the Jews moved from crafts and small commerce to industry, the army, and government. Here are some examples. Luigi Luzzatti (1841–1927) was minister of finance and prime minister of Italy in 1910. Camillo Olivetti founded the famous typewriter company and Ernesto Nathan served as mayor of Rome in 1907.

The Italian cultural scene included such contributors as Primo Levi (1919–87), renowned Italian novelist and writer of books on the Holocaust. A chemist, a member of the anti-Fascist resistance, and a survivor of Auschwitz, Levi died in Turin in April 1987—an apparent suicide. Carlo Levi (1902–75) was a painter, doctor of medicine, political leader, and author of *Christ Stopped at Eboli*. Natalia Ginzburg (1917–91) was a novelist and playwright. She was a leader of the Italian Resistance, her husband, a victim of the Nazis. Giorgio Bassani (1916–), author of *The Garden of the Finzi-Continis*, wrote many stories dealing with the Holocaust. Novelist Alberto Moravia (1907–91), born Alberto Pincherle, was one of Italy's outstanding writers; he was estranged from Judaism. Amedeo Modigliani (1884–1920), the painter, was born in Leghorn and studied art in Florence and Venice. At 21 he went to Paris; his brother, Victor Emmanuel, was an active Socialist leader who fought Mussolini. Roberto Melli (1885–1958) was a sculptor forced into hiding during war; painter Mario Cavaglieri (1887–1969) was born in the Jewish quarter of Rovigo and lived in Padua.

Jewish Rome

JEWISH SITES IN ROME

The Ghetto of Rome. To find the ghetto in Rome, take buses 44, 56, 60, or 75 to Ponte Garibaldi near the Great Synagogue (see "Synagogues in Rome" section). Walk to the synagogue and then proceed to the area behind the temple.

Another way to reach the ghetto is to circle the Pantheon, going across the Via Botteghe Oscure and past the Caetani

Palace, until you reach the winding, narrow cobbled streets and alleyways. Small piazzas are the hallmark of the ghetto, which is on the left bank of the Tiber. The ghetto once was bounded by the Campo di Fiore, the Piazza di S. Croce, and the Piazza Guidea, ancient streets that still exist today.

A small group of Roman Jews still lives in the old ghetto adjacent to the main synagogue, but they live quietly and are reserved.

Before the ghetto was erected in 1555, and even as far back as the days of imperial Rome, Jews lived in the Trastevere section on the right bank of the Tiber. There may have been about 15 synagogues in that sector. A **medieval house of worship** can still be seen on Vicolo dell'Atleta, No. 13-14. It is located in a narrow alley behind the Cinema Esperia. That synagogue was founded by Rabbi Nathan ben Yehiel in the beginning of the twelfth century. He was the author of *Arukh,* the famous dictionary of the Talmud and the Midrash.

No Italian ghetto was to be as severe as the one in Rome. Wrote Jewish historian Cecil Roth, "The ghetto was situated in the fetid, low lying quarter on the left bank of the Tiber, frequently inundated by the overflowing of the river and heavily visited at the time of plagues."

The rules said Jews could have only one synagogue; they got around that stricture by maintaining five synagogues with different rites under a single roof. Needless to say, their whole life revolved around the ghetto. Today it even seems to be the "in" place to live. But if you really want to see what a ghetto street looked like, head for the **Via della Reginella**—it has survived. Gloomy and oppressive to this day, it is witness to the "misery that once dwelled here." This area of the Tiber at one time contained between 5,000 and 10,000 persons in one-third of a square mile. Another description says the enclosure was seven acres with 130 houses.

Today, Jews still live in the main street of the quarter, the **Via del Portico d'Ottavia.** The portico (gate), now in ruins, was built twelve years after the first Jews came to Rome from Palestine. Later this gate and others would be the only entrance and exit of the Jewish ghetto. On this street, you can see old buildings with stores, excellent restaurants that serve Jewish dishes alla Romana, kosher butcher shops, and bakeries.

Menorah, 1-A Via del Portico d'Ottavia. Tel: 687-9297. This Jewish bookstore contains an excellent collection, including some English books. Open on Sunday, too. Certainly worth a visit.

Marmertine Prison. This memorial near the Roman Forum contains the tablet of Gen. Simon Bar Giora, defender of the Jews against the Romans in Jerusalem (70 C.E.). Titus captured him and dragged him before the populace in Rome; he died in this prison.

A memorial **monument** of the massacres at the Ardeatine Caves is located just off the Porto San Paolo, a few yards from the main synagogue. This is an impressive memorial to the 335 persons, including 100 Jews, murdered by the Germans on March 23, 1944. The incident took place in the Ardeatine Caves just beyond the ancient walls of Rome. These lives were ended in retaliation for the killing of Nazis in the Via Rasella by Italian partisans. Thirty-three Germans were killed in that street near Rome's famous boulevard, the Via Veneto. Ten for one was the gestapo retribution. The 335 hostages, including Jews, were rounded up, taken to the Ardeatine Caves beyond the catacombs, and murdered by the S.S. The Germans tried to conceal the site, but it was soon discovered.

While the monument is here, the dead are buried nearby in **The Mausoleo delle Fosse Ardeatine Fine,** a mausoleum situated just off the Via Appia Antica between the Via Ardeatine and the Via delle Sette Chiese, a short distance from the catacombs of San Sebastian. Three huge figures are shown tied together. Dedicated in 1957, the mausoleum is in a courtyard. The caves are cut into the Ardeatine Hill. The Jewish graves are inscribed with a Star of David.

JEWISH RESTAURANTS IN ROME

Before dining in Rome, do check to see if the eating establishment is kosher and has rabbinic supervision. Below are some recommended spots.

Billo, Via S'ambiogio, No. 20, Rome. This eatery, located in the ghetto, is a take-out market. Tel: 687-7966.

Da Lisa, Via Ugo Foscolo, 16, Rome (not far from the main railroad station).

The Jewish Orphanage, Instituto Pitigliani, Via Arco de Tolomei 1. Tel: 580-0539. Open for kosher lunch every day. It is important to telephone first to make a reservation.

Tavola Calda, Via Livorno, 8, Rome. Tel: 442-92025. Take the B Metro from the Central Station and get off at the Piazza Bologne.

LODGING

Pensione Carmel, Via Gioffredo Mameli 11, Rome. Tel: 580-9921. Many Orthodox Jews stop at this hotel, as it is near the synagogue. Call for reservations. No meals are served here.

SYNAGOGUES IN ROME

The Great Temple (Tempio Maggiore), Lungotevere Cenci 9, on the banks of the Tiber. Tel: 687-5051. Built in 1901, the synagogue, which follows the Italian rite of worship, is Orthodox. There are daily services. A mikveh is located in this synagogue, which is situated between the Via Catalana and Lungotevere Cenci.

The synagogue itself was built on the ruins of the ancient Jewish quarter. Imposing in its Assyro-Babylonian style of architecture, it is set behind wrought-iron gates on the northern side of the Tiber River.

The synagogue interior possesses an Oriental motif. The visitor can see rows of varicolored glass in the top of the dome, stately marble columns and pillars that rise to form wide arcades, windows embellished with cornices, and walls richly painted with stylized floral motifs. Biblical inscriptions adorn the walls. In the synagogue, the Holy Ark comes from the destroyed Sicilian synagogue and bears the date 1586. The six Assyrian columns that surround it are admired for their volutes and elaborate gilded friezes. There are several annexes, such as the Spanish temple, where the Holy Ark was once part of the city's old synagogue.

Memorial tablets of Jews who fell in battle in World War I

The Great Temple of Rome.

and of Jews who were deported in World War II grace the walls. A third memorial recalls the Jews who, along with many Christians, were slaughtered by the Nazis in the Ardeatine Caves.

Sephardic services are held in a separate hall of the synagogue as the main service is in the "Italian rite."

The Jewish Museum is located in the same building as the Great Temple. It is open from Monday to Tuesday, 9:30 A.M. to 2 P.M. and 3 to 5 P.M.; Friday, 9:30 A.M to 1:30 P.M; Sunday, 9:30 A.M to 12:30 P.M. Sunday morning is a good time to visit. While tours are conducted, you may have to wait for an Italian-language tour to finish—that is, if you know only English.

The museum is proud of its exhibits dealing with "Two Thousand Years of Jewish History," as well as pages from the Talmud that refer to Italian Jewry. Rare prayer books, reprints of statements of the popes, maps and drawings of the Ghetto of Rome, Torah pointers, *rimmonim* (Torah ornaments), Hanukkah menorahs, Torah crowns, and candelabra round out the collection.

A guide gives a 20-minute tour of the museum and temple, in English or Italian, in which he describes the manuscripts and Jewish ceremonial objects. The collection includes Torah finials made by Roman goldsmiths in the eighteenth century, when Jews were not allowed to touch gold.

Official German records listing the names of some of the approximately 2,000 Jews who were deported from Rome during the Holocaust can be found here.

The history of the synagogue recalls that on October 1982, Palestinian terrorists attacked the building. A two-year-old child was killed and 37 were wounded. The Italian Jewish community was shocked that this terrorist murder could occur in Italy. At the time, the Jews accused the government of "flirting" with Arab terror groups.

One significant event was the visit of Pope John Paul II to the synagogue in April 1986. It was the first recorded pontifical visit to a Jewish house of worship in Rome in 800 years. Moreover, in 1994, the Vatican highlighted the Roman

Catholic church's commitment to the fight against renewed anti-Semitism. Pope John Paul II joined with Holocaust survivors at a concert in the Vatican commemorating the Holocaust. The concert marked the first time in the 50 years since the end of World War II that the Vatican had officially commemorated the Holocaust. Among the guests was Chief Rabbi Elio Toaff.

Synagogue, Via Balbo 33, Rome. Tel: 475-9881. There are two separate synagogues here. The Ashkenazic service is downstairs in this building where there is a daily minyan. On the main floor, Italian rite services are conducted, but only on Shabbat. This synagogue is near the Piazza Populle.

Synagogue for Young Adults, Tempio dei Giovianni isola, Tiberino.

ORGANIZATIONS

Communal Offices, Lungotevere Sanzio 9. Rome. Tel: 687-5051.

The Cultural Center, Via del Tempio 4. Tel: 687-5051. This center for the Jewish community of Rome is open from 9 A.M. to 1 P.M., but not on Saturdays.

The office of the Grand Rabbi is located here at Via Catalana 1, Rome. Tel: 687-5051. Also, **Spanish Synagogue,** Via Catalana 1, Rome. Nearby at Lungotevere Sanzio 14 and 12 are several schools, including a nursery, seminary, as well as the Italian Rabbinical College. Also at Lungotevere Sanzio 14 are the offices of Hashomer Hatzair and B'nai B'rith. Tel: 581-8346.

The Israeli Embassy, Via Michele Mercati 12. Tel: 322-1541/2/3/4.

The Jewish Agency, Keren Hayesod, and the **Zionist Federation,** Corso Vittorio Emanuele 173. Tel: 65-15-14.

The Jewish National Fund office, Via Gramsci 42-A.

Lubavitch, "Beth Chabad of Rome," Via Pancirole 7, Rome 00162. Tel: 39-6-8632-4176. Contact: Rabbi Yitzhak Hazan.

The Union of Italian Jewish Communities, Lungotevere Sanzio 9, Rome 00153. Tel: 580-3667. FAX: 589-9569.

MUSEUMS

See the "Synagogues in Rome" section above for a description of the **Jewish Museum.**

The Borghese Gallery displays the *David* of Bernini, and *David and Goliath* by Caravaggio.

The Doria Pamphili-Gallery exhibits the *Sacrifice of Isaac,* created by Van Dyck.

OTHER SITES

The Arch of Titus. This arch was erected in 81 C.E. by Emperor Domitian (81–91) to celebrate Titus's victory in 70 C.E. in Palestine. A triumphal arch, it symbolically recalls the destruction of the Temple in Jerusalem and shows the Jewish spoils swallowed up by the victors. For centuries, Jews did not walk under the arch. After all, it had been erected to praise Titus for destroying Jerusalem and the Temple. Titus, the son of Vespecian, deported thousands of Jews to Rome and its western provinces, including Sardinia. On one display on the arch, Jewish prisoners are portrayed carrying the booty of the seven-branched menorah, the candelabrum that was taken from the Temple in Jerusalem, as well as the Holy Ark and silver trumpets, the golden shewbread table—all part of the Temple rituals. According to H. V. Morton, "these are the only contemporary sculptured representatives of these objects in existence, and their ultimate fate is even now a mystery."

The prohibition of walking under the arch ended in World War II, when the Jewish Brigade from Palestine, a unit of the British Army, walked under the arch to signify the liberation of the Jewish people. Another report says the ban was broken when the United Nations declared a Jewish state in 1947 and again when Israel was declared a state on May 14, 1948.

On a visit in 1988, I saw scrawled in chalk the words, *"Am Yisrael Chai,"* "the Jewish people live." Today Jews are alive throughout the world. There is silence in the Roman Forum!

Piazza Navona. After you visit the Roman Forum, the Seven Hills, the monuments, the amphitheaters, the Colosseum, the Campo di Fiori, the Spanish Steps, the Trevi Fountain, and the

Pantheon, walk around the horseshoe-shaped Piazza Navona, where artists and crafts makers display their wares. But did you know that from the fifteenth to seventeenth centuries, it was a carnival sport and comic spectacle to beat and chase half-naked, half-starved Jews and force them to run around this square? Yes, the same Piazza Navona used for bullfights, tournaments, jugglers, tightrope walkers, and other entertainment was the scene of a degrading clownish show. Under Paul II in the fifteenth century, public sport was made of the Jews by forcing some to eat a heavy meal and then run in carnival races. As late as 1667, a guide to Rome noted that during the races "the asses ran first, then the Jews marched with only a band around the loins, then the buffalos, then the Barbary horses." Clement IX modified the custom the following year: "The victims were allowed to pay a heavy fine to avoid racing," writes E. R. Chamberlain in *Rome: The Great Cities.*

But it was the papacy again, especially during the years of the Holocaust, that aroused a great deal of controversy. Pope Pius XII was silent during all the years of mass murder. The Vatican argues that he said nothing in order to prevent even greater slaughter. Others claimed he did so to protect the Catholic church in Germany. The pope did not want to encourage communism by attacking the Nazis, says this argument. Robert Katz maintains in *Death in Rome* that the pope "interpreted the fall of Fascism as a victory for Communism." The church still could have saved thousands of Jewish lives. In *The Catholic Church and Nazi Germany,* Guenther Lewry writes, "Finally, one is inclined to conclude that the Pope and his advisors—influenced by the long tradition of moderate anti-Semitism so widely accepted in Vatican circles—did not view the plight of the Jews with a real sense of urgency and moral outrage." According to Rolf Hochhuth in *The Deputy,* Pope Pius failed to protest the roundup of Roman Jews for deportation to Auschwitz.

Moreover, evidence has since come to light that the Vatican aided and abetted the escape of "scores if not hundreds of S.S. and other Nazi genocidists . . . and it did nothing to bar their flight from justice," according to Charles R. Allen, in the magazine *Reform Judaism* (1983).

San Pietro in Vitcoli (Church of St. Peter in Chains). Here is the famous *Moses* of Michelangelo, sculpted in the early sixteenth century. This Moses has horns because of an error in the translation of the Book of Exodus where the Hebrew word *keren* was translated as *horn,* instead of *ray of light.*

The Vatican. In the Sistine Chapel of the Vatican are frescoes about the life of Moses in the Old Testament done by Pinturicchio, Botticelli, and Signorelli (wall frescoes), as well as the work of Michelangelo, the creator of the magnificent ceiling with its nine biblical scenes.

Ostia Antica. This town is the beach community close to the Italian capital, one hour from Rome. A Jewish community once thrived here in this ancient port of Rome. An ancient synagogue, one of the oldest in Europe, was discovered in 1961 by workmen building the Fiumicino Airport.

In the ruins of columns and pillars are the outlines of a prayer room, a study hall, an oven for unleavened bread, and a mikveh (ritual bath). In the building that has three entrance doors, go to the door in the center. A step leads down to the synagogue proper, a large hall divided into three aisles with marble columns. One of these sections may have been for women. The wall at the back is slightly curved. In the oldest hall, the seats were of stone, set against the walls.

In another building, the tabernacle for the Holy Ark rises behind the pulpit on the left side along its entire length, a few steps leading to it. Carved into the tabernacle are Jewish symbols that can also be found in other synagogues of that period: a seven-branched menorah, a shofar, a lulav, and an etrog. The floor is covered with mosaic. In recent years, many Soviet Jews found a temporary home in the town of Ostia, thus bringing Jews back to an ancient site. As Barbara G. Harrison wrote, "In Italy, history is never stale."

Milan

What a city! If ever there was a diverse city, indeed Milan is it. There are 37 ethnic origins alone just among the 9,000 Milanese Jews. Milan contains synagogues, kosher butcher shops, a day school, and several Talmud Torahs (Jewish schools). The Jewish community here boasts diverse Jewish elements, including many Ashkenazim who in the last century found their way to Milan as they moved down from northern Europe. They first concentrated in the wholesale and export business. Whereas the slower-paced southern Italian looks out to the calm Mediterranean, Jews in Milan scan both north and south in this commercial atmosphere.

One often hears men and women speaking Arabic, especially in the Galleria Vittorio Emanuele II, the galleria that inspired numerous North American imitations. The Arab speakers may be Jews, for there, one can often meet Jewish persons who emigrated from Libya and still speak Arabic. In 1948 and again in 1967, several thousand Libyan Jews came to Italy, although the majority went to Israel. They picked this land because they spoke Italian, for until the middle of World War II, Italy controlled Libya. Like Roman Jews, the Libyan Jews in Milan are by and large shopkeepers and traders. Their connections and linguistic knowledge help them develop trade between Italy and the Arab lands. Incidentally, the Galleria located near the Cathedral and La Scala Opera House is one of the world's first shopping centers, replete with outdoor cafes and famous shops. Located here is the notable establishment Biffi.

Part of the reason Jews settle in Milan is the cultural life of this metropolis. Many Milanese say their city begins in the Piazza della Scala, the location of La Scala Opera House. Since its inauguration more than two centuries ago, the legendary opera house, the home of Verdi and Puccini, has remained the pride of this Lombard capital.

Milan, the gateway to Italy, calls itself the money-maker of this republic, the industrial, commercial, and artisan capital of this nation. It is the most "city-like city in Italy," wrote the Sicilian author Giovanni Vergo a century ago.

Once called "muscular Milan," the city has been described as a city of go-getters and materialistic business persons. About 2 million people live in this bustling urban area located 300 miles northwest of Rome.

The Milanese claim their fashion industry ranks with Paris as a trend setter. Visit Via MonteNapoleone, the main shopping street, and see for yourself.

Because Milan is so close to the borders of Austria, Switzerland, and France, and because its two airports reach out to the rest of Europe, it always has focused its sights on its European neighbors. Many Jewish business persons fly in for the annual trade fair, one of the most important in the world.

"What do you do in Milan?" I asked a stranger. "You eat!" he exclaimed. Eating is synonymous with Milan, which is famous for its delicious cuisine.

And if you can spot Jewish salesmen in the Vatican, what would you expect to see in various Milanese neighborhoods, such as in the Via Spadari where one finds mouth-watering delicacies? Once a kosher butcher shop was located right next door to the Ambrosiana Museum, which is situated at Piazza Pio XI Square. Ironically, the museum contains Judaica and Hebrew books and manuscripts.

In Italy, the northern and the southern parts of the country vie for attention. This is often mirrored in the Jewish community, too. "Milan makes the money, Rome spends it," said one Jewish citizen of Milan.

Jews—professionals and business people—live and work in this trading center that boasts international fairs, a silk market, nearly 1,000 banks, more than 30,000 firms, and more than 26,000 manufacturers. Italian Jewry lives on because what it loses through assimilation and mixed marriages, it picks up in the immigration of new groups. In the 1980s, for instance, Russian Jews settled in Milan in addition to about 1,000 Iranian Jews. The latter maintain their own synagogue and club for young people. They are excellent business persons and are skilled in the diamond and carpet trades.

As a result of the immigration following the 1956 and 1967 Arab-Israel wars, many Egyptian Jews have settled here, too. The visitor observes streets such as Piazza Tel Aviv and Via Sally Mayer, the latter named for a noted industrialist and philanthropist. A small **synagogue** is located at Via Sally Mayer 4/6.

JEWISH RESTAURANTS IN MILAN

La Briut, Via Mose Bianchi 103. Tel: 481-4035.

Eshel Israel, Via Benvenuto Cellini 2, Milan. Tel: 545-9877.

Senior Citizens Home, Via Leone XIII 1. Kosher facility.

Jews hold kosher banquets, bar mitzvahs, and weddings in **Hotel Principe Savoia,** Piazza della Republica, and **Hotel Quark,** Via Lampedusa. Many Jewish business persons gather at the **Hotel Executive** on Viale Sturzo.

SYNAGOGUES AND DAY SCHOOLS IN MILAN

Beth Shelomo Synagogue, Corso di Porta Romana 63.

The Central Synagogue, Via Guastalla 19. Tel: 79-18-92. A Sephardic (Persian) synagogue and a mikveh are located here, as is the office of the chief rabbi. This house of worship was erected after World War II. The original was destroyed in an Allied bombing raid in 1943. The Holy Ark in the chapel originated in the ancient synagogue of Pesara.

Lebanese Synagogue, Via Dei Gracchi.

Ohel Jaakov Synagogue, Via Benvenuto Cellini 2. This synagogue follows the Ashkenazic rite. Service is led by Lubavitch.

Old Age Home, Via Leone XIII 1. A small synagogue is located here. This is a dignified, two-story building and was built in the late nineteenth century on the site of ancient buildings in which Jews had lived since 1516, when Europe's first ghetto was created.

Persian Synagogue, Via Monteculolo.

Synagogue, Via Eupili 8. Services are held on Sabbath and festivals. The B'nai B'rith organization also has its offices here.

ORGANIZATIONS

Jewish Community Center, Jewish National Fund, and Sally Mayer Hebrew School, Via Sally Mayer 4/6. At the Documentation Center, I saw young Jews studying the Holocaust period, as well as the history of pre-twentieth century Italian Jewish life.

WIZO, Piazza della Republica 6. Tel: 659-81-02.

Beth Chabad, Via F. Bronzetti 18, Milan 20129. Tel: 39-2-7010-0080.

Zionist Federation, Via DeAmicis 14. Tel: 83-57-558.

Venice

The tourist guide usually begins his or her talk to the large-ly American-Jewish audience thus: "The Jews arrived in Venice in the tenth century. They came from the Levant, Corfu, Greece, and Turkey. In the sixteenth century, the Venetians gave the Jews an area to live and work. They gave that desig-nated plot the Venetian name, the word 'ghetto.' The Jews had to wear a colorful cap so that they could be recognized as Jews. The five synagogues that exist in the ghetto today are the German, the Canton, the Italian, the Levantine, and the Spanish synagogues. . . ." There is so much history in that intro-ductory talk.

Visitors immediately realize that something memorable occurred in this city that was once called "la Serenissima," "the most serene one." For today, millions of people every year pour into this "dream city of lagoons," probably the most beautiful city in the world.

We must also remember that at one moment in the world's history, fifteenth-century Venice was rich and influential, the leader of the West. But just at the time when Venice was boom-ing, a "new India" was discovered to challenge the Venetians. We call that land "America." Trade patterns changed and the city's power faded.

Considered the most important Jewish community of north-ern Italy, Venice involved Jews in "banking, pawnbroking and second-hand dealing."

The Republic tolerated Jews because Jews were useful. They helped "ring the Venetian cash register." Indeed writer Jan Morris believes that Venice could not have gone on to great heights without Jews. They served as bankers, pawnbro-kers, suppliers, outfitters to diplomatic missions, agents, and scholars.

The Jews were usually safe under Venetian rule. But no Jew, not even a local resident, could stay in Venice without a permit, which cost a large sum of money. And it had to be renewed every five years. Jews were often segregated; in the thirteenth century, they were forced to dwell on the island of Spinalunga. We know it as the "Guidecca."

Before 1336, Jews could reside and work only in Mestre, a town just outside of Venice. Only that year did they receive permission to live in the "Lagoon City."

As a kabbalistic mystic center, learning and Hebrew printing thrived here.

Among the most distinguished of the new arrivals from Iberia after the expulsions and inquisitions was Don Isaac Abravanel. He belonged to Spanish diplomatic corps before he settled in Venice. We shall meet him later in the chapters on Spain and Portugal.

THE VENICE GHETTO

This is the city that gave the world the "ghetto." The Italians invented and set up the ghetto. A tourist spot today, it once contained several thousand Jews who were literally locked up at night.

The word *ghetto* comes from the Italian word *gettare*—to cast in metal. When the ghetto was established, it consisted of iron foundries, or *geto novo,* which means *new foundry* in the Venetian dialect.

Interestingly, some think the word *ghetto* comes from the Hebrew word *get* for divorce. These prison neighborhoods served as a way to separate Jews from Christians.

Generally, it is not easy to find Jewish sites in a European city, but not so in Venice. Everyone knows the location of the ghetto. Just ask! Say the word "ghetto." As we have seen, it is after all a Venetian word.

Located near the Venice railroad station, the ghetto can be reached by taking the vaporetti (motor bus-boats) via the Grand Canal. Get off at San Marcuolo landing. Walk away from the canal. Then walk toward Rio Terra San Leonardo. Follow the yellow signs. These signs are in Italian and Hebrew, and say *synagogue.* They will direct you to the ghetto, a lively area composed of Renaissance buildings, medieval houses and columns, and even some wonderful glassmaking shops. Another way to reach the ghetto is via Lake No. 1 Vaporetto, which passes under the Rialto Bridge. Walk a short distance to Calle Rabbia (Rabbi Street), turn right, and there you are.

While Rome's ghetto was crowded and unhealthy, Venice's remained larger. The ghetto district was located on an island cut off from Cannaregio by wide canals. It was also separated from its surroundings by a wall, gates, and drawbridges. Later in 1541, the "geto vecchio" ("the old foundry") was added to house more Jews. By 1663, the ghetto was so crowded that it was allowed to occupy the neighboring "Ghetto Nuovissimo," the site of the last remaining foundry in the district. In the fifteenth and sixteenth centuries, 5,000 people resided there. As street peddlers, rag pickers, dealers in secondhand merchandise, and pawnbrokers, they transformed the ghetto into a thriving beehive.

As a home for refugees, a medieval ghetto provided a certain amount of security. One felt safe from attack; sometimes its walls kept out the mob. On the other hand, when bigots wanted Jews killed, they knew where to find them. Established on April 10, 1516, the second day of Passover, the Venice Ghetto, as an institution, quickly spread throughout various cities of Italy. Unfortunately, it became accepted practice.

As you stand in the large square of the ghetto, remember that this was the meeting place of the community, and also the site of the well where water was obtained and gossip exchanged. A number of outstanding persons were born or lived in the Venetian ghetto. David Reuveni was one. He appeared in Italy in 1524. He asserted that his brother Joseph ruled over the tribes of Gad and Reuben and half the tribe of Manasseh. He claimed to have traveled, disguised as a Moslem, through Ethiopia, Egypt, and the Land of Israel. Reuveni said he came to Europe to obtain the military assistance of the Christian powers for the liberation of the Holy Land from the Turks. His "project" failed and he died in a Spanish prison.

When crowding became a problem, Jews always built upwards. Tall houses resembling skyscrapers were erected. Within the ghetto, there were several autonomous congregations. People worshiped in their own synagogues, according to their own rites, and as we shall see there were at least five different synagogues. The synagogue was the center of Jewish communal life in the ghetto.

When Napoleon's armies broke down the gates of the Venetian ghetto in 1797, it contained little more than a few old huts. The walls were torn down on July 10, 1797, the eve of the fast of the 17th of Tammuz. Emancipation came in 1866.

Although the Jews of Italy were guaranteed full civil equality by King Victor Emmanuel II in 1866, a large group of Jews voluntarily lived in the Venice ghetto until the days of Mussolini.

During World War II, more than 200 Jews, one-fourth of all Venetian Jews, were deported to concentration camps in Germany. They never returned. Today, a **monument** to the Holocaust, consisting of seven bronze tablets, stands on the western side of the Ghetto Nuovo, with the following message:

> Men, women, children,
> Masses for the gas chambers,
> Advancing toward horror,
> Beneath the whip of the executioners.
> Your sad Holocaust is
> Engraved in history.
> And nothing shall purge
> Your death from our memories
> For our memories are your only grave.
> The City of Venice remembers the Venetian Jews
> who were deported to the Nazi concentration camps
> on December 6, 1943 and August 7, 1944.

Jews still live in the ghetto. But today, most of the 650 to 700 Jews of Venice reside outside that neighborhood.

Jewish Rest Home, Ghetto Nuovo 2874. Tel: 71-60-02. It is possible for tourists to obtain kosher meals here, but do book early. Many stop here for meals, especially on the Sabbath. It is located in the ghetto's main square, the Campo Ghetto Nuovo.

The Jewish Community Center (Comunita Ebraica) and Rabbi's Study, Via Cannaregio 1188-A, Ghetto Vecchio. Tel: 71-50-12. The telephone of the rabbi of the community Rabbi Raphael Grassini is 71-51-18.

The Jewish community of Venice today is quite different

from those of the past. In an interview, Rabbi Grassini told me about his congregation. His flock of about 650 Venetian Jews meets in a synagogue about 400 years old. It is difficult to get a minyan (quorum, the 10 men required for a service). A Venetian, Rabbi Grassini studied at the Rabbinical Seminary in Rome. He says that there are small Talmud Torah classes, as well as courses in Torah and the Hebrew language. Interestingly, another course entitled "Bar Mitzvah for Adults" remains popular. While the religious observances and ceremonies are Orthodox, the community is not. Still, during the year, the congregation gathers together. People are not as busy in the winter as in the summer. The biggest problem, says Rabbi Grassini, is to save the Jewish population from assimilation. "It is not a problem of anti-Semitism; it is a problem for many to be a good Jew in Italy."

Jews and non-Jews are proud to live in Venice. It is said that people come here because it is unique. As long as Venice will be Venice, Jews will live and visit here.

Beth Chabad, Cannaregio 2884, Venice, 30121. Tel: 39-41-716-214.

Five Synagogues in the Venice Ghetto

Five synagogues rise within the ancient boundaries of the Venice ghetto. The five are the German, Italian, and Canton, situated in the Campo Ghetto Nuovo; the Levantine and Spanish, located in the Campello delle Scole.

They were erected by various Jewish groups that emigrated to Venice from other nations or other parts of Italy. (Sometimes, not all the synagogues are open to the public because of repairs.) Space in the ghetto was limited, so many of the prayer halls are located within a single room. In the synagogues, crystal chandeliers are in sharp contrast with the wooden benches of the worshippers. The *aron ha-kodesh* (Holy Ark) is usually at one end, the bimah at another.

In the summer in Venice, tourists may take one of the three synagogue tours in the morning at 10:30, 11:15, and noon; or three tours in the afternoon at 3:30, 4:15, and 5. The tours are offered from March 16 to November 15.

German Synagogue. The German synagogue, located in the Campo Ghetto Nuovo, is the popular one. This Ashkenazic house of worship is known as the Scola Tedesca Grande and is the oldest. Highlighting this temple are five interesting windows, three of which are walled up. The arches are in white stone. There is a beautiful gilded Holy Ark and a bimah. The women's gallery is an oval balcony. The synagogue was restored between 1890 and 1910.

The Jewish Museum, known as Museo della Comunita Ebraica, is located on the floor below the German synagogue, Scola Tedesca Grande, built in 1528 in the Campo Ghetto Nuovo. It features a collection of Jewish ritual silver articles and pieces of woven and embroidered materials, as well as a *hummash*—a Pentateuch—used by Maimonides.

The Italian Synagogue. The Italian Synagogue, Scola Italiana, was built in 1575. It is located in the Ghetto Nuovo. Crystal chandeliers are common here, and there are simple wooden benches. At one end stands the *aron ha-kodesh* (Holy Ark) dating from the early 1800s, a gift of Beniamino di Consiglio. This building is not in use, but is now being restored by the Italian Committee for Venice and the Committee for Jewish History of Venice.

The Canton Synagogue. Constructed in 1531, this synagogue is named after a German Ashkenazi banking family and is built into the corner of the piazza. Hebrew writing (names of donors) on the steps leading to the Holy Ark is an interesting sight. The synagogue is closed because of restoration being financed by the Venice Committee of St. Louis, Missouri.

The Levantine Synagogue. Located in the Campello delle Scole, this synagogue is used in the winter because it is heated. Founded in 1538, it is situated across the square from the Spanish synagogue. A plaque commemorates the visit of Sir Moses Montefiore, British Jewish philanthropist and leader, in 1875. Above the entrance to this synagogue is written: "Happy are they that dwell in thy House. They will ever praise thee" (Ps. 84:5).

Long benches fill the sanctuary. The men's pews have wooden stage cases inscribed with the names of members. Wood carvings decorate the ceiling, walls are covered alternately with wooded frames and damask panels, and four Corinthian columns surround the Holy Ark. The doors are inscribed with the Ten Commandments; the bimah features numerous carvings and wood sculptures. Surrounded by two wide curving stairways, the pulpit is framed by two decorated twisted columns resembling marble. This imitates Solomon's Temple. The women's gallery is above the long entrance side.

Spanish Synagogue. The Spanish synagogue (built in 1555 and restored in 1840), located in the Campello delle Scole, is called the Scola Spagnola. This Spanish-Portuguese synagogue was designed in classical baroque. Summer services are held here. The main sanctuary is an elongated space. The Holy Ark is in a classical-baroque style and is situated along the eastern wall; the bimah stands along the western wall. The bimah is composed of four Corinthian columns, two of them actually half-columns set against the west wall. The seating runs parallel along the north and the south walls. An oval gallery for women is an outstanding feature of the structure. The women used to sit upstairs, but now they are on the main level.

The building contains memorial plaques for Jews deported from Venice in World War II.

Florence

It is not difficult to find the Jewish community of Florence. Head for Via Luigi Carlo Farini 4, not far from San Marco Square, near St. Ambrose Church and off of Via dei Pilastri. Located in a large single compound, the Florence **synagogue** is one of the most beautiful in Europe. On the grounds of this large house of worship stand a Jewish day school, the offices of the Jewish community, as well as the headquarters of the B'nai B'rith and other organizations.

Italy often is pictured as a museum. Thousands of tourists visit Michelangelo's *David* in the Academy of Arts Museum in Florence in the province of Tuscany. The city stands as the great collector of Brunelleschi, Donatello, and Michelangelo. In one year alone, 1505, Michelangelo, Leonardo da Vinci, Machiavelli, and Raphael were working at the same time and within a few blocks of each other. The city contains more fine art per square mile than any other in Italy; be sure to visit the Uffizi Gallery, the Pitti Palace, the Accademia della Belle Arti, the Bargello, the Duomo, the Baptistery, and the Medici Chapels. Florence is also advertised as a shopping center where Ferragamo and Gucci have their headquarters.

If at one time on your trip you sit in Florence's town center in Florence in an outdoor cafe, you just might be at leisure in what once was the area of the ghetto.

We know that during the Renaissance, the Jews of Florence did not live in a ghetto. That enclosure would come later. The Jewish community of Florence was established in 1437, when some Jewish financiers were invited to open loan banks. During the time of Lorenzo de Medici (1449–92), Jewish intellectual life corresponded to the rich achievements of Florentine culture. The Medici in Florence were well disposed toward the Jews.

The heyday of the Florentine Jewish community was between the years 1437 and 1494, the most resplendent period in the history of Florence "or perhaps in any city in the world since recorded history began." Jewish literature, Jewish poetry, and Jewish learning flourished in fifteenth- and sixteenth-century Florence, even though the community did not number more than 100 families.

On October 3, 1570, Grand Duke Cosimo I, a Medici duke called "the Great," banished the Jews to a ghetto because they allegedly broke the law. He feared the Jews would fraternize with Christians, so he forced them to wear a yellow badge. The ghetto restricted Jewish culture in the city known as the "Athens of Italy" and the cradle of the Italian Renaissance.

In 1799, Napoleon and his army freed the Jews. But a year after the French emperor withdrew, a period of repression set in. In 1859, when Tuscany became part of the Kingdom of Italy, the Jews were recognized as citizens of the new kingdom. Free at last!

The Jewish population of Florence is about 1,200. About one-third are active in community programs to combat assimilationism. It is difficult to obtain a minyan, although one is scheduled.

JEWISH SITES IN FLORENCE

Beth Haknesset Firenze (The Synagogue of Florence), Via Farini 4. Tel: 245-252. One of the most beautiful synagogues in Europe, this structure is more than 100 years old. Whether seen from an airplane, from another tall structure in Florence, or from the popular tourist vista of Michelangelo Square, this landmark of Judaism in Italy stands out under the city's azure sky. Possessing a distinctive Moorish architectural style of three separate seaweed-green cupola domes and huge arched windows, this house of worship remains a tribute to Italian Jewry. What makes the synagogue so attractive are the elements that make the sculpture and art of Florence so meaningful, that artistic magnet that has drawn thousands of visitors to it each year.

Designated a historical museum, the synagogue attracts Jews and non-Jews. Florence remains one of the few cities in Europe where guides point out the local synagogue. It is not that in other cities tour leaders fail to mention Jewish houses of worship because of prejudice; it is because synagogues in Europe are generally not conspicuous. But the synagogue in Florence is considered a beautiful temple and a tourist site.

Unlike other synagogues, this one possesses its own compound and is not located on a congested street; nor is it hidden behind high walls. Standing tall and proud, surrounded by a garden of flowers and palm trees, it can be seen from distant hills. The synagogue, built in 1882, symbolizes the emancipation of the Jews of Italy and freedom from the ghetto. The Jewish community also wanted to contribute to the architecture of Florence. They wanted a building that would show their pride.

What style should they choose for the religious building? In the early nineteenth century, many of the synagogues built in Europe were in the Gothic style. Florentine Jewry felt that Gothic was too much associated with Christianity. Instead, the Jewish community adopted the Moorish style, with a central cupola. Eastern influence is also shown by its polychromatic decoration. They wanted to portray an association with the Golden Age of Spain, although Carol Herselle Krinsky, in *Synagogues of Europe*, says many of its features are found in Ashkenazic synagogues.

Beth Haknesset Firenze, the synagogue of Florence.

The construction is pure Moorish style, completely covered with frescoes on the inside and rich Venetian mosaics in the *Ehal* (area of the Holy Ark) and on the vaulted ceilings. The doors on the Holy Ark are gilded. The bulk of the funds for the temple came from a David Levi, president of the Council of the Jewish University between 1860 and 1870. In his will, dated March 15, 1868, he requested that his assets be utilized for the building of a monumental temple worthy of Florence. At Levi's death on February 16, 1870, it was disclosed that he had left 1,492,255 lire. In 1874, the first stones came from Jerusalem and were laid on October 24, 1882, the date the building opened.

This Sephardic synagogue contains 1,000 pews in a beautiful chandeliered hall. As in many Orthodox synagogues, the women sit upstairs in a balcony. On Saturdays, because of a scarcity of worshippers, prayers are conducted in a special section on the right-hand side of the sanctuary. On holidays, however, it is packed.

The temple has survived wars, barbarism, floods, destruction, and plagues. During World War II, the synagogue was dynamited by the Germans; sections were severely damaged. One can still see the bayonet marks inflicted by the "Nazi Fascists," as the guides refer to them, on the doors of the Holy Ark. The Germans used the temple as a garage where they repaired trucks.

On November 6, 1943, the first group of Jews was deported from the synagogue to the extermination camps. It was from the temple, too, that the Nazis arrested the beloved Rabbi Natan Cassuto and others. The rabbi was the son of Umberto Cassuto, who had abandoned his own career as a physician and had assumed the post of rabbi of the community. Ironically, together with a group of Italian Catholic priests, the rabbi forged documents that permitted Jews to escape to Switzerland or sail to Allied lines. His secret cell was caught in 1943, and its members, rabbis and priests, were sent to Auschwitz. On June 6, 1944, 16 old Jews were taken from the Home for the Aged and sent to Germany. The synagogue was occupied, bombed, and heavily damaged. After the war, Jews held services in a theater until the sanctuary was repaired.

A total of 243 Jews were deported from Florence, of whom only 13 returned. Eight more Jews were shot and 4 out of 22 who had taken part in the underground struggle fell.

During World War II, the prayer books and scrolls were hidden in Catholic churches and even in banks. But it was Alfiero Borghini, the shamash (beadle) who had been a member of the Italian partisans, who told me that they had also been hidden in a garden in a small town nearby. The shamash later joined the Jewish Brigade, the unit from Palestine that fought its way through Italy in World War II.

The destructive flood of November 4, 1966, was another recent traumatic experience for the synagogue and Florentine Jews. The muddy waters of the Arno River inundated the beautiful structure, causing great damage to the sacred objects and the library. More than 90 Sifrei Torahs (Torah scrolls) were lost. Fifteen thousand Jewish books were destroyed.

The building raises funds from the donations of people who take the synagogue tour. In the synagogue, the eternal theme of Judaism greets each visitor: "Bless he that cometh, bless he that goeth."

A **Jewish school** is also located here. The two-story building was named after the chief rabbi of Florence, Natan Cassuto, who was murdered by the Nazis. About 35 children attend this school.

Another attraction of Florence's synagogue is its **Jewish Museum,** a sight certainly worth seeing. It is on the second floor of the synagogue and opened in 1987. Religious articles, such as *rimmonim* and kiddush cups; prayer shawls; and a pictorial display are all here to be absorbed. There are other ritual objects, including silver ornaments and embroidered vestments.

The museum was founded by the Friends of the Jewish Museum of Florence, a nonprofit association whose aim is to contribute to the maintenance of the exhibition and to the enrichment of the historic and artistic collection.

Suggested Reading

Chamberlain, E. R., and the editors of Time-Life Books. *Rome: The Great Cities.* Amsterdam: Time-Life Books, 1976.

Harrison, Barbara G. *Italian Days.* New York: Weidenfeld, 1989.

Hochhuth, Rolf. *The Deputy.* New York: Grove Press, 1964.

Hughes, H. Stuart. *Prisoners of Hope: The Silver Age of Italian Jews, 1924–1974.* Cambridge, Mass.: Harvard University Press, 1983.

Kahler, Erich. *The Jews Among the Nations.* New York: Frederick Ungar, 1967.

Katz, Robert. *Black Sabbath.* New York: Macmillan, 1969.

Lewry, Guenther. *The Catholic Church and Nazi Germany.* New York: McGraw-Hill, 1964.

Mann, Vivian B., ed. *Gardens and Ghettos: The Art of Jewish Life in Italy.* Los Angeles: University of California Press, 1989.

Michaelis, Meir. *Mussolini and the Jews: German-Italian Relations and the Jewish Question in Italy 1922–1945.* Oxford University Press, 1978.

Morton, H. V. *A Traveller in Southern Italy.* New York: Dodd, Mead, 1964.

Roth, Cecil. *The History of the Jews of Italy.* Philadelphia: Jewish Publication Society of America, 1946.

Segre, Dan Vittorio. *Memoirs of a Fortunate Jew.* Bethesda, Md.: Adler and Adler, 1987.

Vogelstein, Herman. *Rome.* Philadelphia: Jewish Publication Society of America, 1940.

Zuccotti, Susan. *The Italians and the Holocaust: Persecution, Rescue and Survival.* New York: Basic Books, 1988.

Spain
Columbus, a Jew?

"O Spain, one-half of thy face is fiesta and the other, misery."
So wrote novelist Perez Galdos of his nineteenth-century
homeland. Spain is the home of Cervantes, El Greco, flamenco and castanets, the bullring, and the conquistadors.

The enchanting cities of Castile and Andalusia are found
here, as well as the Alhambra of Granada and its surrounding
gardens that recall the Arabian Nights. The Moors and the
Jews, the Christians and the Inquisition make up Spain's history. Hemingway and the Civil War, Franco and the Lincoln
Brigade—there is no question that many world-famous events
and figures are linked to this country.

But for the Jewish traveler who arrives in Spain, the nation
has a special meaning—*history*. Coming here is like coming
home, except that no longer is it a "Jewish neighborhood."
Synagogues have become churches. Vanished are the Hebrew
academies and the libraries. We visit Spain to recount our glorious past, when one-third of the population of Iberia once
contained Jewish blood.

A Brief History

The Jewish people still recall their "Golden Age" in Spain.
To this day, Jewish history does not record a similar success
story. Jews have rarely lived anywhere else as "harmoniously or
creatively" as in Spain.

For in Spain, moreover, the people of culture were Jewish. They contributed to the developing societies of both Moslem and Christian Spain. Jews who had been in Spain since the destruction of the First Temple lived peacefully with the Arabs on the Iberian peninsula ever since that wintry night in 711 when Tarik Ibn Ziyad ferried an army across the Strait of Gibraltar and freed the Jews from the barbarious Visigoths.

The Moslems went on to cultivate science, medicine, philosophy, and poetry. The Spanish Jewish communities produced doctors, mathematicians, philosophers, court advisors, diplomats, and military leaders.

Nearly 1,000 years ago, there were cities in Spain where most of the inhabitants were Jewish. Spain contained the largest Jewish community in Europe.

In the Middle Ages, several hundred thousand Jews, one-half of world Jewry, lived in Spain. To this day, we call these Jews "Sephardim," after "Sepharad," the Hebrew word for Spain. Some of the greatest Hebrew scholars in Jewish history, who devoted themselves to studying both the written and the oral law of Judaism, were from Spain, including Maimonides (1135–1204), known as the *Rambam,* which stands for Rabbi Moses ben Maimon. These scholars fostered the study of all branches of Jewish literature. They spoke Arabic and established schools and libraries. They wrote the finest Hebrew poetry ever created. The Zohar, the main work of Jewish mysticism, is said to have been written by Moses Ben Shem Tov de Leon (1240–1305) of Guadalajara. He is thought to have been born in Avila. And the works of the Hebrew poets Yehudah HaLevi, Solomon Ibn Gabirol, and Moses Ibn Ezra move us to this day.

But as often happens, history took a turn for the worse for the Jews. By the 1300s, they became vulnerable, no longer needed. In 1391, terrible anti-Jewish riots occurred throughout the country. About 20,000 Jews simply gave up the fight and converted. These "New Christians" were called "Conversos," but many of them only pretended to be Christians; secretly they practiced Judaism. We know them also as "Marranos," the Spanish word for "swine," or "criptojudíos," "false Jews." They were never trusted by the Spaniards.

Soon one of the most horrible words in the lexicon of the Jewish people was created—the Inquisition. Spain had to be pure Catholic.

Between "4,000 and 8,000 secret Jews and suspects were burnt alive" in the 15 years of Tomas de Torquemada's reign. During the three centuries of its terror in Iberia, nearly 350,000 people were indicted and about 30,000 "Judaizers" were burned at the stake. Another 15,000 were burned in effigy and several hundred thousand were "penanced" because it was thought they were Jews. The burning of New Christians was to be a lesson to the converted: don't dare revert to Judaism.

Tragically, the Inquisition taught many in the world to focus on "pure blood" and "pure race." If you possessed a certificate of *limpieza de sangre* or "certificate of pure blood," you could rise to the top. The others dropped out. In the end, Spain suffered because it excluded too many bright, intellectual persons. It "surrendered itself to the chimera of racial purity," notes Barnet Litvinoff. It never regained the glory it had achieved before it expelled its Jews, who went on to settle in Africa, Turkey, Italy, Portugal, and France. Dr. M. Kayserling maintains, moreover, that the Inquisition and the expulsion had one purpose: to grab the property of secret Jews for the state treasury, even if they had to do it under the guise of religion.

Thus, in 1492, the year Columbus set sail for America, several hundred thousand Jews were expelled, not to return until 1859. The numbers of Jews expelled vary; I have seen estimates from 100,000 to a half-million and upwards. For 400 years, if a Jew was found in Spain, he could be punished by death.

Jews began to trickle into Seville after the Constitution of 1869 decreed liberty for religious faiths. By 1877, there were 406 Jews in Spain. Refugees fleeing from Czarist Russian pogroms reached Madrid in the 1880s. By 1910, a Jewish community had been set up. One of its founders, Ignazio Bauer, was the first Jew elected to the Spanish parliament.

During World War I, many Sephardic Jews of Spanish ancestry moved from Salonika, Greece, and Istanbul, Turkey, to Barcelona and Madrid. Zionist leader Max Nordau, who was an Austrian citizen, was forced to leave France during World War I, and he, too, moved to Spain.

After World War I, Jewish communities existed in Seville, Madrid, and Barcelona. In 1924, Prime Minister Primo de Rivera declared that those who were descendants of the Sephardic exiles of 1492 would be recognized as Spanish citizens.

In 1927, Spain offered citizenship to all Sephardic Jews. Under the new Constitution of 1931, Jews enjoyed "full legal equality." This legislation and the Constitution were later nullified by Franco.

About 4,000 Jews resided in Spain when the Spanish Civil War broke out in 1936. "An inner psychic wound" was the way Barbara Probst Solomon described the conflagration. Figures vary, but some say nearly one million lives were lost in the struggle. Terror reigned; there were excesses on both sides. The overwhelming majority of Jews were on the side of the Republic—10 percent of the 40,000 foreign volunteers who fought for the Republic were Jewish. But Franco and his Fascist generals were victorious. At the start of the Second World War, Spain was closely tied to Nazi Germany but was nonbelligerent. As the war progressed, she quickly became neutral; obviously the Axis powers were losing.

By 1940, Jews were trying to return to Spain and Portugal as Hitler engulfed the Continent. Large numbers of refugees from Nazi-occupied France fled across the Pyrenees into Spain. Although most were interned by the Spanish, they were not deported.

Stanley G. Payne, in his book, *The Franco Regime, 1936–1975,* writes: "Altogether, during the first part of the war, some 30,000 Jews had received safe passage through Spain, and there is no indication of any Jew who reached Spanish soil being turned back to German authorities. Approximately 7,500 more may have passed through between 1942 and 1944, and during the latter phases of the S.S. roundup in Hungary and the Balkans, Spanish consular officials managed to provide protection (through citizenship status) to more than 3,200 additional Jews, many of the latest, Sephardic."

But Spain never exhausted its capabilities in saving Jews

during the Holocaust. At times, it allowed Jews to cross the border from France to safety. In the second half of the war, it saved more than 10,000 Jews, according to Haim Avni in *Spain, the Jews and Franco.*

Post-World War II Jews moved cautiously as Franco continued to tighten his grip over Spain.

A number of people claim that Franco had direct Jewish ancestry that could be traced back to the Inquisition. Perhaps! But many people in Spain, it is said, have "Jewish blood."

After World War II, Spain followed the lead of the Vatican, which failed to recognize Israel as a state in 1948. In 1950, Israel voted against Spain in the U.N. when the world body revoked a resolution condemning Spanish actions during the war. This hardened Franco's position not to recognize Israel.

After the death of Franco in 1975, a new life began for all Spaniards, including Jews. In the 1990s, dynamic, vibrant Spain, with 40 million citizens, is molding itself into a democracy and catapulting itself into the twenty-first century. Spain, a member of the European community, is often called Europe's "moveable feast," with its famous dress designers, rock stars, and chic cafe people.

A decline in religious observance has marked post-Franco Spain. Although the 1492 expulsion edict has never been officially annulled (it is still "on the books"), the Constitution of 1978, which guaranteed non-Catholics "the right of religious freedom and religious equality," abrogated it de facto. On February 21, 1990, the government signed an accord that officially placed Jewish and Protestant faiths on par with Roman Catholicism. In 1992, King Juan Carlos I signed a royal decree officially cancelling the 1492 Edict of Expulsion of the Jews.

After a long and arduous diplomatic effort, Spain and Israel established diplomatic relations in 1986, and, in the same year, Spain became a member of the European Union.

Yes, there are Jews in Spain today. Indeed, a renascence of Jewish life has occurred. A few schools and a half-dozen synagogues serve about 14,000 Jews, who are devoted to leading a full Jewish life. They are building a community.

Andalusia

Fly to Andalusia in the south of Spain. The Moslems called it "Al-Andalus," their appellation for the conquered lands of Iberia. For millions, the image of Spain is Andalusia. In the days of Moslem Spain, the heart of Andalusia was represented by three great cities: Seville, Cordoba, Granada. They are Moorish cities, and even today Moorish traditions remain strong. But they were also Jewish cities with literary salons, Talmudic schools, and synagogues. Visit Andalusia and your eyes will view luscious landscapes, singing birds in olive groves, and fertile valleys.

SEVILLE

Let us begin our journey with Seville—the capital of Andalusia; city of romance, poetry, and art; Spain's fourth-largest urban area; and the largest city in southern Spain.

Seville, with its approximately one and a half-million persons, is the mythical home of Don Juan, Carmen, and Figaro; the Alcazar, the fourteenth-century palace for Christian kings built like the Alhambra; the Columbus Archives of the Indies, a museum; the Torre del Oro, Tower of Gold, and the huge, imposing Seville Cathedral; and the spiritual home of flamenco and bullfights and Gypsies.

Today there are 15 Jewish families in Seville. It used to be that every Friday night—rain or shine—Simon Hassan Benasayaq left his apartment at 17 Monte Carmelo St. here in Seville ("Sevilla" in Spanish) and directed his footsteps to a **synagogue** housed in a rented flat at 10 Peral St. He didn't miss a Friday night. As his son Moises put it, "Someone may need the synagogue." Now, however, the lease on the synagogue-apartment has been lost and new facilities are being sought. Contact the Benasayaq family at 427-5517 for up-to-date details on a new location.

What is remarkable is not only Mr. Hassan's opening the synagogue every Friday night, but that there is a synagogue at all in Seville and that there are Jews here: 70 at the latest count.

Some 600 years ago, there were 23 synagogues (all

destroyed), thousands of Jews, and a Jewish quarter whose remnants we can see today. This Jewish section is called **Barrio de Santa Cruz,** a tourist attraction in this city that Columbus helped to make famous.

Today, in this Santa Cruz section of Seville, you can stroll through the narrow lanes of whitewashed homes and realize that the "Sephardim" (Spanish Jews) lived a full, comfortable life and that members of the Jewish community were even advisors to the vizier.

The Santa Cruz quarter contains the remains of the old Jewish quarter, which may have run as far as the Alcazar. There is indeed a new hotel called **Las Casas de la Juderia** (The Houses of the Jewish Quarter), made up of individual apartments and located in the midst of the labyrinth of the old Jewish quarter. Located near the Plaza Santa Maria la Blanca, near the Murillo Gardens, the address is 7 Callejon de Dos Hermands. Tel: 441-5150. FAX: 442-2170.

Tragedy, of course, came to Seville, in the form of riots, pogroms, conversion of synagogues into churches, and the Inquisition. The Jewish community would never recover.

One legend that came out of that time concerns a street in the Barrio de Santa Cruz called **Calle Susona,** street of Susona. Once it was named Calle de la Muerte, street of death.

Visit it; it has an interesting tale. Don Diego Suson, a Marrano whose ancestors originally had converted to Catholicism in 1391, organized a group of Marranos who were trying to halt the Inquisition. Don Diego's daughter, who was called "beautiful Susanna," may have betrayed a secret meeting of the Marrano group to her Christian lover, who in turn reported it to the authorities. Don Diego and his associates were burned to death as "false Jews." Shocked beyond grief, Susanna placed herself in a convent. But when she was about to die, she repented. She asked that her corpse, and later her skull, be hung in front of the house she had betrayed. The street was known as Calle de la Muerte for many years.

Within a decade, Jews were expelled from Spain. Romantic Seville became a tragic port of embarkation for Jewish refugees from western Andalusia, most of whom left for North Africa.

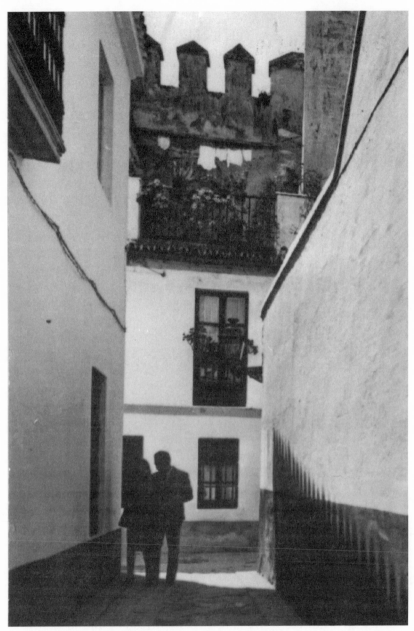

Passageway in the Barrio de Santa Cruz, the old Jewish quarter, in Seville.
(Photo courtesy Tourist Office of Spain)

Today, interestingly, most of the Jews in Spain (and in Seville) are also from North Africa, from cities across the Mediterranean Sea, some of whose exotic names are Ceuta and Melilla, the latter still governed by Spain. These Moroccan Jews, besides having a synagogue, hold a Passover Seder in Seville, celebrate Jewish holidays as best they can, teach their children Hebrew, and bury their dead in a Jewish cemetery. They face the same problems as Jews all over the world: assimilation, intermarriage, and a desire for Jewish education and knowledge.

But they are not that isolated at the end of the twentieth century. The Jews of Seville belong to a National Federation of Spanish Jewish Communities; they visit Jewish communities in nearby Malaga. It is only an hour's flight on Iberia, airline of Spain, to Madrid where there are about 4,500 Jews. And, of course, there is Israel, which most of them have visited. Like Mr. Hassan, who has a daughter in the Jewish State, many have relatives and children in Israel. With Israel and Spain now extending diplomatic recognition to each other, the Israeli Embassy in Madrid helps in providing educational and cultural activities.

Sites in Seville

In the **Seville Cathedral,** Jews of Seville presented a symbolic key to Fernando III when he conquered the city from the Moors in 1248. The key is still located in the cathedral treasury, engraved in Hebrew: "The King of Kings will open, the King of the Lord shall enter." The silver tomb of Fernando III rests in the cathedral, with an epitaph written in Latin, Arabic, and Hebrew.

When the Moslems ruled here the cathedral was the city's main mosque. Today, it stands as one of Christendom's most spectacular houses of worship; only the squares of Rome's St. Peter's and London's St. Paul's are larger.

Interesting to both Jews and non-Jews is **Columbus Archives of the Indies** at 3 Avenida Queipo de Llano, which contains the account books of Luis de Santangel, a descendant of a Marrano family. A supporter of Columbus, he has been called the "Disraeli of Spain." He held the posts of chancellor of the Royal Household and controller general of finance in Aragon. He made a private loan of 17,000 ducats to Columbus, "money out of his own pocket," writes Dr. M. Kayserling. Without Santangel's enthusiastic support, "the first voyage of Christopher Columbus would never have taken place," says Cecil Roth. Incidentally, Columbus's first letter telling of his trip was written to Santangel, who with "his kinsman Gabriel Sanchez were the most zealous patrons of Columbus," according to Dr. Kayserling. Other Marranos may have pitched in to help Columbus, but Abraham Seneor, the crown rabbi of Castile, a go-between in the royal marriage of Ferdinand and Isabella, also supported Columbus, as did Don Isaac Abravanel, formerly of Lisbon, now the Jewish spokesperson in Spain, says Litvinoff. Seneor himself would eventually convert. Santangel, though a devout Catholic and counsel to the king and queen, also tried to alleviate the situation of the Jews.

The 1992 world's fair in Seville celebrated the 500th anniversary of Columbus's discovery of America. Columbus returned often to Seville; they like him here.

Was Columbus descended from a Jewish, or ex-Jewish, family? Was he a Marrano, a secret Jew? We simply do not know. Evidence exists on both sides. He could have been a converted Jew and/or Marrano. The famous writer Blasco Ibanes was convinced that Columbus was indeed a Marrano—i.e., ostensibly a Christian, but actually of Jewish descent. Other Spanish authors have said he was of Iberian Jewish stock.

Did he not begin his account of his famous voyage with a reference to the expulsion of the Jews from Spain? Why did he cite the expulsion, scholars ask. Other scholars say the expulsion of Jews and Columbus's voyage are a coincidence: "In the same month in which their majesties issued the edict that all Jews should be driven out of their kingdom and its territories, in the same month they gave me the order to undertake with sufficient men my expedition of discovery . . . to the Indies."

Finally, other scholars note Columbus was mysterious about his religion. He seemed to have something to conceal. He had a strange affinity for Jewish and Marrano society. He deliberately postponed the day of his sailing until August 3, 1492. Why did he wait one day? Perhaps it was that the previous day, August 2, was the "unpropitious fast day of the Ninth of Av known as *Tisha B'Av,*" which commemorates the destruction of the Second Temple. As Cecil Roth notes in *Responsibilities and Events in Jewish History,* "One who does work on the Ninth of Ab, the rabbis say, will never see a blessing therefrom."

Professor Roth maintains Columbus had an obsession with Jewish matters. He points to the theory that the Colombo family were Spanish Jews who settled in Genoa and who, "following the traditions of their race, had remained faithful to the language of their country of origin." "He indubitably had a curious mystical Jewish obsession and was always referring in his notes to the facts of ancient Jewish history," writes Professor Roth.

Also, letters that Columbus wrote to his son, Diego, have been preserved. In the corners were written the Hebrew letters *Bet Heh,* for "B'ezrat Ha Shem" (with the help of God). According to the *Encyclopedia Judaica,* Columbus "boasted cryptically about his connection with King David."

Columbus may have studied Jewish literature firsthand. But Professor Yosef Yerushalmi is quoted as saying: "There is not a shred of convincing evidence that he was either a Jew, a Marrano, or a proto-Semite, although many *Conversos* helped fund his ventures. After all, it was a business." In part, the voyage can be considered a Jewish enterprise because exploration was a business, and Jews were involved in efforts to find new lands. Those who overwhelmingly supported Columbus were "men of Jewish extraction," such as Luis de Santangel, Gabriel Sanchez, and Alfonso de la Caballeria.

Luis de Torres, a Marrano, was Columbus's interpreter on his historic journey. A linguist, he spoke Hebrew. Luis de Torres may have been baptized just before Columbus set sail. "He was the first European on these expeditions to step upon American soil," says Erich Kahler in *The Jews Among the Nations.* Dr. Kayserling also notes that Luis de Torres was the first European who discovered the use of tobacco and "was the first person of Jewish stock who settled in Cuba." There may have been other Jews among Columbus's crew.

We know that, in his journeys, the explorer used the nautical instruments perfected by Joseph Vecinho, who was Jewish.

Navigation was traditionally a Jewish trade.

Abraham Zacuto compiled the navigational almanac. Zacuto, who had ties to the University of Salamanca, went to Portugal at the time of the expulsion and apparently died in Damascus. One of his major contributions was the invention of the copper astrolabe.

The key mapmakers were all Jews. The most famous, of course, were Abraham and Yehuda Cresques, who established a school of cartography in Palma de Mallorca.

Jewish sites of those days still stand, like the **Plaza de Santa Cruz,** the **Arco de la Juderia,** and the streets with Jewish names: **Calle de Cal** (Kahal)—street of the congregation; **Calle de Cal Major**—street of the large congregation; **Juderia Vieja,** the Old Jewish Quarter; **Calle de dos Tintes**—street of the dyers.

In 1492, there were three events that changed the world. The Moslems were defeated in their last battle with Christianity at Granada and Spain was reunited under the Catholic kings. Then Jews, who were seen as the "traitor burrowing from within," were expelled and would not return for 400 years. And on August 3, 1492, Columbus sailed for America, a day or two after the last Jews left the soil of Spain and one day after *Tisha B'av,* the Jewish holiday that laments the destruction of the Temple.

With 1492 being so important, it is no wonder that the International Jewish Committee Sepharad '92 was formed to commemorate the 500th anniversary of the expulsion of the Jews from Spain, and celebrate the rebirth and subsequent growth of the Sephardic heritage and its place in Jewish history. And so as one walks through Seville, one thinks of Columbus, the Jews, and the Inquisition. But the sounds and sights are of the present. This is a city to tour and absorb. The Moors and the Jews loved Seville. A proverb says, "If one were to ask for bird's milk in Seville, one would be able to get it."

Today Jews enjoy Seville. Mr. Hassan says there is no discrimination. He appears on Spanish TV to discuss Jewish topics. He was welcomed when he settled here, and has a certain pride about this municipality.

Sometimes when he walks in the huge open area in the middle of the city, he recalls that 500 years ago, 700 *Conversos* were burned at the stake and more than 5,000 were reconciled with the Catholic church, all within seven years. Even in 1484, Tomas de Torquemada, a converted Jew himself, chaired a convention of the Inquisition in this city to define the procedures of the torture process used to obtain so-called truth. "They tried to kick us out, but we're still here; we were stronger than they were," Mr. Hassan reflects.

CORDOBA

It is good to visit Cordoba after Seville. About 100 miles separate the two cities. To those Jewish travelers interested in Jewish history and culture, Cordoba evokes memories of a brilliant Jewish intellectual center in the Golden Age of Spain. Today one can visit one of the three existing Jewish synagogues of ancient Spain; gaze at the statue of Maimonides in Tiberias Square; or walk in the narrow alleys of the famous Juderia (Jewish Quarter) near the cathedral and the alcazar, where tourists and students sit in the Plaza de Juda Levi and sip coffee or a drink.

Cordoba, where once lived Averroes, the Arab philosopher who was a contemporary of Maimonides, is a Moorish city with narrow winding streets, gardens, olive and orange groves, and a population of one and a quarter million. The capital of the caliph, it contained 200,000 buildings, 3,000 mosques, 27 free schools, and a university that attracted scholars from throughout the world. In the Middle Ages, Cordoba, a scientific center, possessed a vibrant economy that made it the largest city in the world, and the wealthiest and most civilized city in Western Europe. Stanley G. Payne, professor of history, says: "In size, services, culture and economy, the city was without a peer in Western Europe and was rivaled in the East only by Constantinople."

Famous for its libraries and bookshops, Cordoba was the high-water mark of the Arab civilization in Europe. It once contained a library of 400,000 catalogued volumes.

The past and its rich cultural and religious mix can be seen in the La Mezquita (mosque) building, which shares the same foundation as the cathedral. The combined structure—not far from the Jewish Quarter—boasts a Moslem forest of pillars and white Moorish arches with a domed ceiling, a testimonial to the days when Cordoba was the capital of Islamic Spain. But after the Christian conquest ended in 1492, 60 columns were torn out of the mosque to make room for the cathedral in the mosque's center.

Today, once again, Jews live in Cordoba, which the poet Antonio Machado y Ruiz called "Roman, Moorish and silent." To be sure, there are only a few Jews here in this Andalusian city of about 750,000, the birthplace of the genius scholar, Maimonides. Once, too, it was the temporary home of Yehudah HaLevi, one of the great Hebrew poets. It was the home of Hasdai ibn Shaprut (915–70), physician, diplomat, and advisor to the caliph, who established the first Talmudic school here. This city contained a galaxy of Hebrew scholars, philosophers, and poets who attended the court of Abd-al Rahman III (912–61).

When I was in Cordoba, I talked with an American Jew, Mrs. E. Fereres, who with her husband, Elias, had been living in Cordoba for five years. As she tells it, the Spaniards often confuse the Jews with the Moors. Doesn't Maimonides wear a turban? One thing she did say was that there is a heightened interest in Jews among Spaniards, especially in the Sephardic past. She cited a group of Catholics who organized themselves into a group called Beit Sephardim.

There are a number of people who speak Hebrew here. A Greek Jew, Eli Nachmias, who lives here part of the year, has been instrumental in helping to restore one of the synagogues. Jewish history courses are taught at the Faculty of Philosophy and Letters, a fine college here. In 1985, the 850th anniversary of the birth of Maimonides brought much attention to the Jewish past in Spain, and there were symposia held, bringing about increased Jewish consciousness.

The Jewish Quarter in Cordoba

When you enter the Moorish gateway known as the **Puerta de Almodovar** (it was once called "Bab-al-Yahud"), you are in the **Juderia,** which is located between the Plaza de las Tendillas and the River Guadalquivir. Turn right down the **Calle de los Judios** in the Jewish Quarter. You have to imagine that Cordoba was once the "New York City of Europe," that along these narrow passageways of flower-laced streets and white-washed abodes, of gardens and orange groves, a population of one and one-quarter million thrived and lived in this capital of the caliph. The Jews flourished in Cordoba. Under the Moors, the Talmudic school of Cordoba was famous throughout Europe. Jews served in high positions as ambassadors and advisors. Many of the caliphs hired Jewish physicians.

The Statue of Maimonides, erected in 1964, is located near the synagogue on Calle de los Judios. Actually, it is just down the street from the synagogue in a square named **Plaza Tiberias** to perpetuate the ties between his Spanish birthplace and Tiberias, the city in Israel where he is buried.

Maimonides was one of the greatest Jewish thinkers and scholars of all time, author of the *Guide of the Perplexed,* and a doctor who lived from 1135 to 1204. Barnet Litvinoff says Maimonides "stands as the most significant Jewish intellect and teacher from the time of the Prophets until Spinoza."

Born Maimonides, this remarkable figure in post-biblical Jewish history fled from his native Cordoba because of persecution from the Almohad sect, whose military forces rampaged Andalusia in 1146. He mastered medicine and, through tireless study, absorbed many other fields of knowledge, such as mathematics and astronomy. By 1185, he was already a leading physician at Saladin's court in Egypt and knew Richard Coeur de Lion. In 1180, he compiled the *Mishneh Torah,* "Repetition of the Law." His 13 articles of belief would be incorporated in the creeds of Judaism, and his *Guide of the Perplexed* scrutinized the revelation at Sinai through the lens of reason. It is not hard to imagine Maimonides walking through the old Jewish Quarter in Cordoba, with its narrow streets, white walls, and delicate window grilles.

Statue of Maimonides. (Photo by M. Serels)

The courtyard is small and the statue of Maimonides, sitting in the middle, dominates the area of plain, whitewashed walls. The sage sits on a marble bench atop an attractive cube. He is wearing the robes and twisted turban of the desert. In his lap, he holds a book, his right thumb marking the spot. His face, his posture, and his robes are those of a philosopher and, as you look at the statue, you understand why his admirers said, "From Moses to Moses there was no one like Moses."

Just up the street from the statue of Maimonides is the small, "cubicle-in-shape" **synagogue** built in 1315. On the east wall of the small Moorish-designed building is a vacant niche that once held the Ark of the Law. On the south wall can be seen intricately designed Scripture and prayers in Hebrew. In his book, *Travels in Jewry,* Israel Cohen writes that one of the verses in Hebrew says: "A little sanctuary and a house of testimony which was built by Isaac Mehab, son of the wealthy Ephraim, erected in the year 75 [1315] as a temporary structure. Arise, O Lord and hasten to rebuild Jerusalem." Upstairs, in the upper part of the south wall, you can clearly make out a women's gallery. The building later served as a church, the Church of Saint Crispin.

The spirit of Maimonides is everywhere. Right in the Juderia, not far from the statue of Maimonides, you will find a square called **Plazuela de Maimonides.** This may have been the site where Maimonides lived when he resided in Cordoba. Visualize silversmiths, silk embroiderers, and leather-goods makers who sold their products. Extending from this street is **Calle Rambam Maimonides.**

Walk to 5 Calle de los Judios, along the street that was the main street of the medieval ghetto. This is **Casa Maimonides,** the actual spot (if not house itself) where the great Maimonides was born.

In 1935, the Spanish government sponsored an 800th birthday celebration of Maimonides. Jews came from all over the world. For the first time in 443 years, a Jewish prayer service was held in Cordoba. In the synagogue courtyard, the municipality of Cordoba erected this plaque: "On the occasion of the eight-hundredth anniversary of the birth of Rabbi Moses ben Maimon, the Spanish government, in the name of the entire nation, expresses its recognition of that immortal Jewish spirit. Cordoba, his birth place, honors his memory."

During the Moslem period, the Jewish Quarter was located near the alcazar (fortress) in the northwest section of the city. It continued in existence after the Christian reconquest.

Walk down **Juda Levi Street,** named for the Jewish poet who was born in Tudela in 1075, but who lived for a number of years in Cordoba.

The proprietor of the cafe in the **Plaza de Juda Levi** spoke to me about the poet, philosopher, and physician for whom this historical square is named. Born in Tudela (1085–1140), he traveled south to the literary salons of Andalusia and passed through Cordoba on his way, with the intention of going on to Granada. In Cordoba, HaLevi participated in a poetry writing contest and won the competition for imitating a complicated poem by Moses Ibn Ezra, who invited HaLevi to his home. HaLevi lived in many communities in Spain. When he lived in Toledo, he practiced medicine.

"His was the sweetest and most poignant of all the nightingale voices of that time," writes Chaim Raphael. He gave the Jewish people the electrifying "Ode to Zion"; "Songs of Exile"; and "Poems of Zion," or as we know them, "Zionides." "He was the most beloved poet in post-Biblical Hebrew literature," says Raphael. He dreamed of reaching the Land of Israel and freeing himself of the enslavement of Exile. One of his most famous lines is "My heart is in East, and I in the uttermost West." Finally, he did leave Toledo. According to legend, HaLevi reached Jerusalem, which was occupied by Crusaders. He bowed down and kissed its stones. As he recited the opening words of one of his elegies, "Zion, wilt thou not ask if peace be with the captive," an Arab horseman pierced his heart with a lance.

But the more likely story is that he died six months after reaching Egypt and was buried there. His "Ode to Zion" expresses Israel's yearning for its homeland. He said the ideal existence for the Jew was attainable only in his own homeland. A Spanish writer, Filipe Torroba Bernaldo de Quiros, says that he united "Sefardite nostalgia of Spain with Palestinian Zionism."

The cafe owner, too, decries the decision 500 years ago of the Jewish expulsion. "Spain today is not racist," she says. "It is not possible to have one people; we have to have many peoples."

Today, the Spanish people are still remarkably hospitable. There is a feeling in Spain that the country is moving forward once again toward democracy. It is in the air, on TV, in the press.

Of course, despite progress, Spain possesses many of the same problems prevalent in the world today: drugs, crime, the decline of moral values. Spain, however, has passed through a peaceful transition from repressive dictatorship to parliamentary government.

GRANADA

Once it was called "Gharnata' al-Yahud," "Granada of the Jews." It was also known as "Villa de Judios," the description of the city by the first great poet of Hebrew Spain, Samuel haNagid (Ibn Nagrela). This poet, "the Prince," was also a philosopher-soldier, who lived in Granada.

"Whoever has not seen the splendor of the Jews of Granada, their fortune and their glory, has never seen true glory . . . for they were great with wisdom and piety."

The best place to find Granada's Jews is the **University of Granada,** at the Cartuja Campus. Chances are that, at the university, you will first run into dynamic Dr. Maria Jose Cano, a Catholic who teaches in the Department of Semitic Studies. Dr. Cano, who studied at the Jewish Theological Seminary in New York and who attended the Hebrew University and Tel Aviv University, speaks and reads Hebrew and has written scholarly papers on the poetry of Solomon Ibn Gabirol and Maimonides.

Here is her story. When she was a young girl, at Easter time the children of her village would travel to a nearby village and make papier-mâché targets depicting Jews. They would then throw stones at them.

Her father told her this was wrong, so she never participated in this hatred. Her father explained to her that Jews are people like all people—not the devil as depicted by the children. She believed her father was an upright, honest man and what he said must have been true. So she pursued her interest in this people, the Jews, because her father had shown kindness toward them. She went to Israel and studied Hebrew in a kibbutz ulpan as well as at the Hebrew University in Jerusalem.

"Interest in Jewish studies and Israel is rising in Spain," she said in an interview in her office at the university, "especially with the finalization of diplomatic relations between Spain and Israel in early 1986." For example, the town in which she grew up commissioned her to write a paper on Jewish life in that village as it was centuries ago. Dr. Cano hopes her students will also engage in research into the Sephardic past.

I met a number of Spanish students who were eager to visit Israel. They talked about Israel and the Jewish people.

One problem in the Department of Semitic Studies is a lack of books on Jewish history and Israel. Persons willing to contribute books in English, Spanish, and Hebrew can mail them to Dr. Maria Jose Cano at the University of Granada, Department of Semitic Studies, Faculty of Philosophy and Letters, Cartuja Campus, Granada, Spain. Being interested in Judaism, she is a good source on Jews who live in Granada.

I also met a Jewish family in Granada, Dr. and Mrs. Shaul Belilty Cohen, who are from Spanish-ruled Melilla in North Africa. Dr. Cohen is a urologist. He enjoys Granada and does not hide the fact that he is Jewish—all his friends and colleagues know it. He often travels to Malaga, an hour and a half away, where there is a Jewish community. The Cohens light candles and say kiddush on Friday nights. He has visited Israel several times and has relatives there, as well as in Morocco.

He grew up as a member of Hashomer Hatzair in Morocco and attended the University of Granada. He has two children. While he has a good life in Granada, he worries about raising his children Jewish. He tries to help Dr. Cano expand the Department of Semitic Studies at the university.

People like Dr. Cano and Dr. Cohen, by their work and by their presence, try to tell the story of the past and still keep Judaism alive.

The Alhambra Palace and the Jews

The Alhambra, the palace of paradise, is also of historic significance to Jews. It is the "apex of Moorish design extravagance." All routes led to the Alhambra Palace, which is the most beautiful monument in all Spain. The royal palace—which is a fortress—was constructed on a 35-acre plateau atop a last spur of the Sierra Nevada to express the spirit of the civilization that was Moslem Spain.

It is said that the best time to view Granada is when the colors of the sky are lilac, rose, gray, blue, hazel, aquamarine, red, and dusty-gold. Surrounding the Alhambra are flowering gardens, courtyards, and splashing fountains. The scene brings to mind an idea of what life must have been like under the Arabs. Nightingales sing in the Alhambra Gardens, a wonderful legacy of the Moors, who "designed their gardens not only in the visual sense, but also aimed to catch a visitor's ear, arouse his tastebuds and coax him into touching all that summoned him."

Looking up at the Alhambra, one recalls that the Ibn Nagrela family may have had something to do with building part of the structure. Joseph Ibn Nagrela was the son of the famous Samuel Ibn Nagrela, "The Nagid" (933–1055). Samuel, the vizier of Granada, achieved the highest position as a Jew in medieval Moslem Spain. Joseph, who succeeded his father, built a huge palace. It is believed that this was later destroyed, and the present Alhambra built on that site.

Joseph came to an untimely end as a result of a palace intrigue. He was assassinated on December 30, 1066, and a day after his murder, a Moslem mob stormed through the Jewish Quarter of Granada in what was one of the few recorded pogroms of Moslems against Spanish Jews.

The Moors who conquered Spain in the eighth century believed that the fertile plain of Granada would be heaven, as told in the Koran. They built a grand city here and created the impressive fountains of the Alhambra, whose walls owe their redness to bricks made from ferrous mud. The "Red Fort" is still one of the most admired monuments in Spain.

The guides who take you around the Alhambra cite Jewish influence in the "ruddy hue" of the palace. Some say the famous "Lion Fountain," "Court of the Lions," was a gift of the Jews of Granada. Others say the 12 lions are patterned after 12 oxen of King Solomon's Temple, which Joseph Ibn Nagrela had copied for his palace.

The Alhambra is history. Perhaps that is why two million persons visit here each year. The Alhambra, a symbol of Moorish surrender to the "Catholic kings," still stands as the last bastion of Islam in Spain. It fell on January 2, 1492. But this Moorish architectural gem contains within its silent walls much of Jewish history in Spain.

Let us go first to the **Hall of the Ambassadors.** Under its 60-foot-high domed ceiling, the Catholic kings, on March 31, 1492, signed the document expelling the Jews. The huge square room contains nice large windows from which one can look down to the city of Granada,

In the very same room, Ferdinand and Isabella signed an agreement allowing Columbus to sail west to America.

Here in this hall, Don Isaac Abravanel (1437–1508), Jewish philosopher, statesman, and supporter of Columbus, and Abraham Seneor of Segovia tried to change the minds of their Catholic rulers about the expulsion of the Jews in 1492 by offering a large bribe. They almost succeeded, but as Litvinoff writes: "Tomas de Torquemada, Confessor to the Queen, Inquisitor General of the Inquisition and converted Jew, is said to have taunted Abraham Seneor, a confidant of Isabella, who then converted." Torquemada stopped any wavering on the part of the "Catholic kings," and the Jews were forced out.

After the expulsion decree, incidentally, Don Isaac Abravanel left Spain on May 31, 1492, first to Italy, then to Corfu, and finally to Venice in 1503, where he wrote mystical works and biblical commentaries. He died in 1508 at the age of 71 and was buried in Padua. The expulsion edict was promulgated at the end of April, and the Jewish exodus began in May and continued until August 2, 1492. More than 100,000 Jews went to Portugal, just across the border. They were seeking a haven. Instead, they ran right smack into danger once again. In Portugal, they would soon be forced into baptism and sold into slavery.

Jewish Madrid

It is only about an hour's flight from Granada to Madrid, a city of bullfights and "machismo." Hemingway called it "the most Spanish of all cities, the best place to live in, the finest people . . ."

Madrid symbolizes the New Spain—busy and active, now moving at a fast pace to make up for lost time. The energy is addictive.

Greater Madrid boasts five million *Madrileños* who traverse wide boulevards and bask in the sun at dramatic fountains and statues of heroes. Here Cervantes wrote *Don Quixote*. Here Lope de Vega wrote plays. Here El Greco painted.

Madrid, which became the capital in 1561, lies almost in the center of the Iberian peninsula, the highest capital city in Europe. Situated in the Meseta, this somewhat isolated city rests on an undulating plateau of sand and clay. Because it suffered severe damage in the Civil War, which ended half a century ago, many of its buildings and homes were rebuilt. Rarely seen is a piece of physical damage of the two-and-a-half-year civil war that ended on March 28, 1939, when Franco's troops entered the capital.

SITES IN MADRID

In 1977, a new day school, including a Jewish college, **Collegio Estrella Toledano,** was established on Paseo de la Cobendas in the suburb of Moraleja. It was dedicated by leading dignitaries, including Sephardic Chief Rabbi Ovadia Yosef. The school offers classes in Hebrew and Jewish history.

Arias Montano, Institute of Jewish Studies, 4 Calle del Duque de Medinaclli, in front of the Palace Hotel and American Embassy. Located in the heart of Madrid, this library contains more than 16,000 volumes, manuscripts, and publications about Sephardic Jewish history. It was opened in 1940, during World War II, at a time when Franco was an admirer of Hitler.

University City offers courses in Hebrew and Sephardic studies.

Sefarad Handicrafts, 54 Gran Via, Madrid. Jewish religious articles and Spanish handicrafts can be bought here.

Walk down the **Calle de la Fe,** the "street of the faith." Some say it was once called "Calle de la Synagogue." On this street, Jews once owned stores and real estate. In the riots of 1391, many Jews were massacred here. Others were converted on the spot. A synagogue destroyed during those disturbances stood next to the San Lorenzo Church. Other streets in the old Jewish quarter, called the **Juderia,** are **Calle de Bailen, Plaza de Oriente,** and **Plaza de Lavapies.**

BETH YAAKOV SYNAGOGUE

Beth Yaakov Synagogue and Jewish Community Center, 3 Calle Balmas. Tel: 445-9843. Located near the Plaza Sorolla. Sephardim from Europe and North Africa began settling in Spain after World War II, but it was not until the public dedication of a new synagogue in Madrid on September 17, 1968, that recognition and a new era began for the Jews in Spain. It was 476 years after the Jews were expelled from Spain. Today, laws in Spain grant Jews the legal right to observe their religion. Present at the historic ceremony were the archbishop of Madrid and representatives of the Foreign and Justice ministries. Baruch Garzon Serfaty had the honor of being the first rabbi of the new synagogue.

Actually, the nucleus for this congregation was established after World War II. Later, when many Ashkenazi Jews arrived in Spain, they began to meet in a room at **Calle del Cardinal Cisneros.**

This building on Calle Balmas serves as religious and cultural center and contains a library, a kosher catering facility, a youth lounge, and another small synagogue. Downstairs there is even a letter from President George Washington of the United States of America. Arrangements for kosher meals can be made here, but write and order in advance. There is a kosher kitchen that even dispatches wine and matzah to other Jewish communities at Passover.

Kosher food is available if one calls in advance and makes a reservation. Tel: 446-7847.

The synagogue, which is Orthodox, contains a separate women's gallery, as well as a meeting hall for youth groups.

The community center section of the building also includes a rabbinical office and a Talmud Torah of about 200 children and a Sunday school of 40 also function. Youth activities include summer camps and a growing Maccabi sport movement.

Friday night services at the synagogue are usually at 7:30, 8:30 in summer; on Saturday morning they are held at 9:30. Services are daily and on holidays, but do call to check on times.

When I first went to Spain in 1964, I searched and searched for the synagogue. I had difficulty finding it, for in those days, a Jewish house of worship could not display exterior signs. I remember I walked up a long flight of steps in an apartment building to reach the nearly hidden synagogue.

The synagogue is now not difficult to find. You might easily spot it from a distance because of security. When I visited the congregation, for example, a police car was parked in front of the building.

The Sunday morning I attended services, a small minyan had gathered. They were Moroccan Jews. As we talked about life in the Spanish capital, cake was served. At the synagogue, I also talked to a Lubavitcher Chassid, Rabbi Yitzchak Goldstein. A teacher, he is the brother of a Lubavitch rabbi at the University of Michigan, Rabbi Aaron Goldstein.

The cornerstone of the new synagogue building reads: "This house of prayer is the first ever to be built in Madrid. May it be a symbol and a memorial for the Jewish communities that existed in this land until 1492 and a portent for the revival of Judaism in Spain."

ORGANIZATIONS

Amistad Judea Christiana. The new climate in the Catholic world of Vatican Council II made possible the organization of the Amistad Society, which eliminates textbook passages of material offensive to the Jewish people and religion. Many Jews in Madrid praise this group.

Chabad Center, 9 Calle Jordan, apt. 4D, Madrid, 28010. Tel: 341-445-9629.

MUSEUMS

Museo Sefardito de Madrid, 18 Calle Zorilla, one block from the American Express office. This museum has an interesting display of Jewish historical documents, art replicas, and other objects related to the history of the Jews in Spain.

National Archaeological Museum, 13 Calle de Serrano. This museum contains casting of Hebrew inscriptions from medieval buildings.

The Prado, Paseo del Prado. Madrid is the home of one of the world's outstanding art museums, the Prado, also called the National Museum of Painting and Sculpture. In 1994, it celebrated its 175th birthday and interestingly, one and a half million persons visited it in 1993. Hemingway wrote that if the city "had nothing else than the Prado, it would be worth spending a month in Madrid every spring, if you have money to spend for a month in any European capital." There are about 2,000 paintings by Spanish and foreign masters, including more than 30 works by El Greco, 100 by Francisco Goya, and 50 by Diego Velazquez.

Of special Jewish interest in the Museo del Prado are Titian's famed *Moses Saved from the Waters* and Murillo's painting of *Rebecca and Eliezer,* as well as two works depicting an auto-da-fé of the Inquisition.

Barcelona

Barcelona makes noise and money.

Even in the twelfth century, that world traveler, Benjamin of Tudela, mentioned the prosperity and beauty of Barcelona, according to Dr. Kayserling.

Miguel de Cervantes of Barcelona once wrote that "Barcelona was the fatherland of all valiant men." A beautiful city, it is conveniently situated, and it once welcomed

Columbus home from a long journey to the Americas.

Even at midnight, there is a difference between Madrid and Barcelona. Hardworking and energetic, Barcelonians walk fast as if going somewhere in a hurry. Madrid is slower. The second city in size and 2,000 years old, Barcelona, with its four and a half-million citizens, stands as the great metropolis of the northeast coast. Some say it would make a better capital than Madrid, with its nearly five million persons. As one of the oldest and largest Mediterranean seaports and as the capital of Catalunya, historic Barcelona flaunts itself as an international city and looks across the Mediterranean to Alexandria, Genoa, Pisa, and Venice. Visit the **Ramblas** (long avenue) with its stalls and outdoor cafes; "it's always gay and lively." It was especially so in 1992 when the city was the site of the summer Olympics and the commemoration of the 500th anniversary of the discovery of America and the expulsion of the Jews.

Once a center of Talmudic learning, Barcelona is known for the great disputation between Rabbi Moses ben Nachman, known as Nachmanides, and members of the Dominican and Franciscan orders. (We shall meet Nachmanides in Gerona, where he was born.)

In 1391, Spain's Jewish community was almost destroyed. Barcelona's Jewry never recovered—by 1396, not a single Jew lived in the city. Since Barcelona was a harbor, many of the Jews who were expelled left from this harbor for safer lands. This was the port, too, where Columbus briefed the "Catholic kings" after his first voyage to America.

At the beginning of the twentieth century, a few Jewish peddlers from Morocco and Turkey settled in Barcelona.

The Jewish community was legalized in 1902. After Salonika was taken from the Turks by the Greeks in 1912, more Jews arrived. The Spanish government encouraged settlement of Spanish Jews on its territory, and another wave of Jewish immigration moved in from the Balkans after World War I.

More than 100 Jews lived in Barcelona in 1918. By 1932, the number rose to about 3,000, mostly of Sephardic origin. German Jews, fleeing Hitler, began arriving in 1933, and they brought the figure to more than 5,000 Jews, mostly Ashkenazim.

During the Spanish Civil War of 1936–39, however, many of Barcelona's Jews left for France and Palestine. Some of the city's German Jews emigrated after the defeat of the Republic in 1939. But ironically many, if they had not been able to get to America or England, quickly came back, for Barcelona became a center for refugees fleeing from Hitler. After World War II, the government granted permission to open a synagogue in Barcelona.

In 1965, together with leaders of the Madrid Jewish community, Barcelona's Jewish community officers were received by Franco in the first meeting since 1492 between a Spanish head of state and Jewish leaders.

JEWISH SITES IN BARCELONA

Mountain of the Jews. Much of the Jewish history of Barcelona evolves around two hills called Tibidabo and Montjuich. The latter is on the southern side of the city. Vast amounts of land lie between these two mountains. In Catalan, "Montjuich" means "Mountain of the Jews," where obviously Jews once owned much land. Here again, we meet the old Jewish neighborhood.

In the eleventh and twelfth centuries, Jews helped establish Barcelona's commercial greatness. A Jewish cemetery about 1,000 years old is kept up with a special section still set aside for Jewish graves. Located on Montjuich is the outstanding **Museum of Art,** with its excellent collection of Romanesque art.

Synagogue Maimonides and Community Center, 24 Avenir. Tel: 200-6148 or 200-8513. FAX is also 200-6148. Near the President Hotel, it was established in 1954. From that date one can realize that it was the first synagogue to be built in Spain in almost 500 years. The first floor is the Sephardic prayer hall; the second floor is Ashkenazic, which holds services on Rosh Hashanah and Yom Kippur. The Sephardim hold services every day. The building maintains recreational rooms and classrooms, and many activities are offered.

In the entrance lobby of the five-story edifice, just beyond

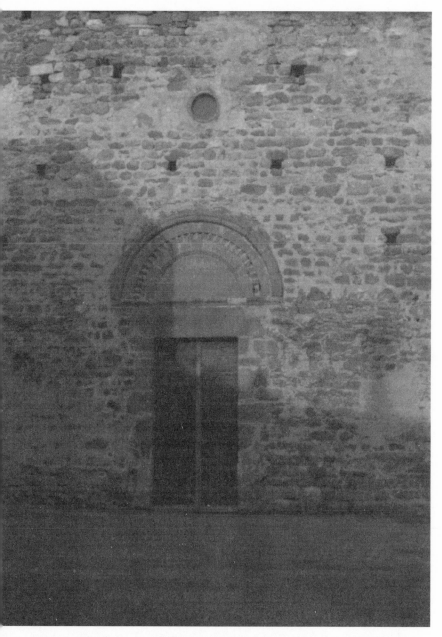

Synagogue of Vilajuiga (Jews' Village) near Barcelona. (Photo by Ruth Serels)

the outside iron gates, is a tablet in Hebrew and Spanish dedicating the building to Maimonides. For kosher food, call or write the center office.

There is also a store at Avenir 29 that sells kosher products. It is open from 10 A.M. to 1 P.M. and 3 P.M. to 7:30 P.M. Friday, 10:00 A.M. to 1 P.M. Closed Saturdays.

Calle del Call. From the end of the eleventh century, the Jews of Barcelona lived in a special quarter in the heart of the old city, near the main gate and not far from the harbor. The main street of the quarter is still called "Calle del Call" or "Carrer del Call," "the quarter of the kahal." In the Catalan language, *call* is the equivalent of the Hebrew *kahal*, community. A part of the old ghetto wall is built into a Gothic house at **No. 5 Calle del Call.**

The University of Barcelona offers courses in Judaism.

Vegetarian restaurant, 41 Calle Canuda.

Gerona

If ever there was a place where the footsteps of Jews still seem to echo in the streets, it is Gerona. This Spanish municipality lies in the province of Catalonia in the northeast corner of Spain between the Pyrenees mountains and the Mediterranean Sea. Just 30 miles from the French border and 60 miles from Barcelona, Gerona is called "the mother of Israel," a name given to but a few sites in the world known to be spiritual resting places for "the wandering Jew." Little known is the fact that this city was one of the most important Jewish communities in the area, and that once it was the first center of Kabbala (mysticism) in Spain. Some people consider the well-preserved and old Jewish Quarter here to be the most representative in Europe after that of Prague.

An interesting area to visit is the **Call** itself, the Jewish district in Gerona, which probably had its origins back in the ninth century. Renovated in the early 1980s, it may, without doubt, be one of the most interesting visits in Jewish Spain. There were about 300 Jews in the area, also known in Arabic as Alsama (or Alsima).

The main artery of the Call is the **Carrer de la Forca.** This urban stretch is the axis around which the whole Jewish quarter formed itself. It was once known as Calle del Call Judaic (the street of the Jewish community).

On Carrer de Sant Llorenc is a restored medieval building called **Isaac the Blind Center** (Isaac el Cec or Blind Isaac), once thought possibly to have been a synagogue with an attached mikveh or a Kabbala school. The name of the institution refers to an important "blind" Kabbalist of the twelfth century who lived in the Call of Gerona. Attached to this building in its courtyard is a well where, when it is sunny, stone slabs can be seen. The stones were once doorposts of houses of Jews and are cut with slots that once contained mezuzoth. A visit to the **Saint Pec de Galligan History Museum** reveals a collection of engraved tombstones from the cemetery on Barcelona's Montjuich.

Perhaps Gerona's best-known citizen is Rabbi Moses ben Nachman (Nachmanides) who was born here and often called the "Rabbi of Gerona." He has been described as the outstanding personality in Jewry during the thirteenth century. Nachmanides' halachic works rank among the masterpieces of rabbinic literature and many of them have become classics. We also know Nachmanides as a philosopher, Kabbalist, biblical exegete, poet, and physician. A street named after him here is **Bonastrug da Porta,** his name in the Catalan language.

Nachmanides was chief rabbi of Catalonia. He is famous for the disputation in Barcelona in July 1263, when at the request of King James I, he debated several Dominicans, including the convert Pablo Christiani. Permitted to speak as he wished, Nachmanides (also known as the Ramban) took full advantage of the opportunity and spoke frankly, for which the king rewarded him. The distinguished historian Yitzhak Baer says of him, "His personality was the product of diverse influences: the Spanish cultural background, French talmudist, German pietism, the mysticism of the Kabbala and an acquaintance with Christian theological writings." He wanted Jewish thought to embrace mystical ideas.

After the Barcelona Disputation, Nachmanides codified his views at the request of the local bishop. Still the Dominicans attempted to put him on trial. Even with the king's help in obtaining his release, Nachmanides barely succeeded in escaping from Spain to Israel.

Toledo

Experts say that if you have only one day to visit Spain, spend it in touring Toledo, once the ancient capital of Spain. Like Florence in Italy, the city is preserved as a museum.

Historic Toledo boasts that it is the most fascinating, aristocratic metropolis in all Spain and among the most interesting cities of Europe. It still stands today just as the great Spanish artist El Greco painted it centuries ago. Indeed, this city of a half-million persons houses his masterpieces, as well as those of artists Goya and Velazquez. Toledo, 40 miles from Madrid, rests on a mountain. A deep-etched gorge caused by the winding Tagus River surrounds it on three sides.

In the Civil War of 1936, the streets of Toledo actually "ran red with blood." The alcazar, which housed an infantry academy, was held by the Fascists. For 72 days, Franco's forces withstood wave after wave of fierce attacks from the Republic's troops and survived.

As the seat of the Spanish primate, Toledo records Catholic history. Its main cathedral, a Gothic masterpiece with paintings by El Greco, stands at the top of the hills of the city. Joseph L. Andrew, Jr., observed in *The Jewish Advocate* of February 23, 1989, "It is apparent even from the city's geography that the Jews had a less lofty status than the Catholics as you must descend from the summit of Toledo's hills with their cathedrals down to the Jewish Quarter, near the bottom, through narrow lanes, past weathered golden-hued limestone buildings."

Toledo is one of the few towns in Spain where remnants of Jewish edifices have been preserved. Jews came to Toledo in the fourth and fifth centuries. By the seventh century, Toledo possessed a large Jewish population that helped the Moors capture the city from the Visigoths. By the eleventh century, 40,000 Jews resided in Toledo; one-third of the city was Jewish and they lived in peace with the Moors and Christians. The name Toledo comes from "Toledoth," the city of "generations." Legend has it that Toledo was founded 4,000 years ago by a direct descendant of Noah. Others say that the first Jewish exiles to Toledo were members of the tribe of Benjamin.

What we do know for certain, however, is that, because of its outstanding Jewish scholarship and community structure during the Middle Ages, Toledo became known as the "second Jerusalem." Perched on a hill and surrounded by walls, it still resembles Jerusalem. Some say it was the "most important Jewish city in Spain."

As a center of Spanish Jewry, Toledo, with its schools and libraries, attracted poets, translators, and writers. Yehudah HaLevi, the great Hebrew poet, resided here.

Surely not all Jews in Toledo were scholars. They served as tailors, felt makers, masons, butchers, farmers, and craftsmen. The Jewish Quarter in Toledo, a spacious area, functioned virtually as a city in itself.

For about 600 years, Jews lived in peace. In the twelfth century, there were 12,000 Jews there. But in 1391, mobs attacked and nearly slaughtered the entire Jewish community of Toledo. In a moment of weakness, many wealthy Jews sought to save their lives by converting; they became New Christians. Expulsion followed. Today, the Cathedral of Toledo, completed in 1477, contains, on an interior wall, a plaque memorializing the Expulsion of the Jews in 1492. Despite its sad history, Toledo has been named the "World Sephardic Capital."

Recent reports indicate there are nine Jewish families in Toledo, but they are not organized. When I visited Toledo, I found a **restaurant** that is run by a Jewish Moroccan. It was not kosher, but it had a Jewish-Israeli atmosphere. Many Israelis came here. The owner said he conducts a Passover Seder for 140 friends and their families every year. The establishment is near the El Transito Synagogue (see below).

He told me he knew a man who lights candles every Friday night and does not eat pork. The man did not know the religious significance of what he did, but he said he was told to do it by a grandparent. Shadows of the Marranos, the secret Jews, over and over again are perceptible in modern democratic Spain.

SYNAGOGUES IN TOLEDO

Once Toledo housed numerous synagogues. Today, there are only two. But these two are famous and a "must" on a tour of Jewish sites in Toledo. They are located in the eastern side of what was once the Jewish Quarter. Indeed, Santa Maria la Blanca and El Transito are considered two great architectural treasures of medieval European Jewry.

Santa Maria la Blanca, with its inspired Almohad art, was founded in 1203—the oldest Jewish monument in Toledo. Like all medieval synagogues, it is unimpressive on the outside. But the inside is a forest of 32 pillars supporting a long vista of horseshoe-shaped arches, surrounded by limestone block walls. The octagonal columns are richly decorated with designs of a Moorish-Jewish motif. There are arched galleries and you can see signs of a separate women's upper gallery. In the fifteenth century, it was converted into a church by Vicente Ferrer, who stirred up many riots against Jews and was responsible for many conversions. The church later became a military barracks, a warehouse, and even a dance hall. Now it is a national museum.

El Transito Synagogue got its name from a church that the building housed after the Inquisition. Samuel Levi Abulafia built the structure in about 1360. He was a finance minister and advisor to Pedro the Cruel, king of Castille, who ruled from 1350 to 1369. He not only managed Pedro's finances but, as a diplomat, defended his interests. His reward was the king's permission to build a new synagogue despite clergy and city opposition. Barnet Litvinoff writes that Abulafia "maintained a style in Toledo almost as regal as the masters." He wanted the building to be a private synagogue for his own house, which still stands and supposedly from which there was an entrance to the synagogue. The artist El Greco lived in this house, which some say is the Casa el Greco (House of El Greco), now known as the **El Greco Museum.**

To build the synagogue, Abulafia, it is said, imported cedars from Lebanon, as did Solomon when he built the Temple in Jerusalem. The graceful Moorish arches, the artistic designs, and the quotations from the Torah that line the entire length of the synagogue walls at ceiling level bring the entire Golden Age back to life. The building boasts alabaster columns, a wall with stone tracery, and 54 elegant windows.

The building of El Transito Synagogue contains the **Sephardic Museum and Library** and is located on the **Calle de Samuel Levi,** an old ghetto lane named after Samuel Levi Abulafia. The museum contains Sephardic relics, documents, other pieces of Judaica, reproductions, and manuscripts. Abulafia hid his wealth here in the house. He had a long tunnel dug out connecting his home in Toledo with the Tagus River so that, in case of a popular uprising, he and other Jews could escape. It did not help him. Pedro the Cruel tortured and executed him.

El Transito served successively as a church, a monastery, a hospital, a military storehouse, and army barracks. But in 1877, it was designated a national monument. The building cannot be restored to its original state because no one knows what it looked like.

In 1964, the El Transito Synagogue became a museum for the history of the Jews in Spain. A synagogue service celebrating the opening of the museum holds the distinction of being one of the first public Jewish meetings in Spain since Jews were expelled.

Suggested Reading

Ashtor, Eliyahu. *The Jews of Moslem Spain.* Philadelphia: Jewish Publication Society of America, 1973.

Avni, Haim. *Spain, the Jews and Franco.* Philadelphia: Jewish Publication Society of America, 1982.

Baer, Yitzhak. *A History of the Jews in Christian Spain.* Philadelphia: Jewish Publication Society of America, 1966.

Cohen, Israel. *Travels in Jewry.* New York: Dutton, 1953.

Kayserling, Dr. M. *Christopher Columbus and the Participation of the Jews in the Spanish and Portuguese Discoveries.* New York: Hermon, 1968.

Lipschitz, Rabbi Chaim U. *Franco, Spain, the Jews and the Holocaust.* New York: Ktav, 1984.

Litvinoff, Barnet. *Fourteen Ninety Two: The Decline of Medievalism and the Rise of the Modern Age.* New York: Charles Scribner's Sons, 1991.

Morris, Jan. *Spain.* Oxford University Press, 1979.

Morton, H. V. *A Stranger in Spain.* New York: Dodd, Mead, 1955.

Netanyahu, Benzion. *The Marranos of Spain.* Millwood, N.Y.: Kraus Reprint Company, 1973.

Payne, Stanley G. *The Franco Regime, 1936–1975.* Madison: University of Wisconsin Press, 1989.

———. *A History of Spain and Portugal.* Madison: University of Wisconsin Press, 1973.

Pritchett, V. S. *Marching Spain.* London: Ernest Benn, 1928.

Raphael, Chaim. *The Road from Babylon: The Story of Sephardic and Oriental Jews.* New York: Harper & Row, 1985.

Roth, Cecil. *A History of the Marranos.* New York: Hermon Press, 1974.

———. *The Spanish Inquisition.* New York: Norton, 1964.

Wiesenthal, Simon. *Sails of Hope: The Secret Mission of Christopher Columbus.* New York: Macmillan, 1973.

Yahil, Leni. *The Holocaust: The Fate of European Jewry, 1932–1945.* New York: Oxford University Press, 1990.

Portugal
Saying the Mourner's Prayer in Rossio Square

Think of Portugal and you think of the sea, explorers and navigators, and weather-beaten faces of fishermen hauling in the day's catch.

Think of Portugal and you can see yourself riding the waves along 500 miles of Atlantic Ocean beachfront, as well as sunbathing in the southern Algarve.

Think of Portugal and you consider driving up to Estoril, the fashionable resort, and Cascais, "the town of fishermen and kings." You see yourself sitting in the coffeehouses, drinking smooth port wine and strong coffee, and listening to moody *fados*, those melancholy songs of the Portuguese fishermen.

Some people label Portugal an anachronism. Long ago, Prince Henry the Navigator, Vasco da Gama, Magellan, and Cabral, who sailed uncharted waters, led Portugal into its golden age as a great power. Few European countries reached such seafaring heights. But then it crumbled and lost its colony, Brazil, and later was ruled by a dictatorship. Finally in our own day, a peaceful revolution, "the Revolution of Flowers" of 1974, would install a democracy.

Portugal is one of the smallest countries in Europe. Containing 35,516 square miles, or one-sixth of the Iberian peninsula, it is located on the far western edge of the peninsula. Because Iberia was isolated from Europe for centuries,

Oporto

PORTUGAL

LISBON

Faro

people said Europe began and ended at the Pyrenees. No longer! A free, democratic atmosphere envelops the country today, bringing tourists to Portugal.

For Jewish travelers, the Jewish connection lies just beneath the surface, more in knowledge of the past than in the sites themselves. Most of the cities and towns contained an area that was assigned to the Jews and known as "Juderia." Today, many of them can be found . . . with difficulty. For starters, ask if there is a "street of the Jews."

A Brief History

Some sources say the Jews migrated to Portugal after the destruction of Jerusalem by Nebuchadnezzar, settling there before the establishment of the first Portuguese kingdom. By the year 900, with the Moslems in control, Jews worked as wine growers. In the reign of Sancho I in the twelfth century, Don Solomon Jachia, a Jew, was a field marshal commanding the Portuguese Army.

For a long time Portugal befriended Jews. Before the sixteenth century, most of the rulers of Portugal considered the Jews a valuable resource, especially their financial and commercial talents. Christian noblemen often married daughters of wealthy Jews.

Until 1497, no profession or occupation was barred to Portuguese Jews. They were active in government, philosophy, botany, finance, medicine, and astronomy. They improved Portuguese typography so that it could compete with Italy and Germany. A Hebrew printing press was set up in Lisbon at the end of the fifteenth century. Vasco da Gama, who discovered the sea route to India, was advised by Jewish scholars and financed by Jewish businessmen. He also followed maps and instruments made by Jewish manufacturers. Jewish physicians were on board his ships. Jews possessed a great reputation in the sciences. Portuguese Jewish doctors rivalled their co-religionists in Spain.

During the thirteenth to fifteenth centuries, Portugal's rulers even allowed a synagogue to develop in Lisbon. By the end of the fifteenth century, Portugal's 200,000 Jews made up one-fifth of the population. Included were many of the several hundred thousand Jewish refugees who had been expelled from Spain in 1492. The reception, while not warm, was tolerant. Jews were forced to pay a poll tax of eight cruzados per adult and agree not to remain longer than eight months.

Romance, intrigue, and expulsion now entered the history of the Portuguese Jewish community in the person of Emanuel I, the Fortunate (1495–1521). He was an unfortunate monarch for the Jews. Ambitious, he soon initiated Machiavellian scenarios. Assuming power in 1495, he hoped to rule all of Iberia. He would do this simply by marrying the Spanish princess Isabella, the daughter of Ferdinand and Isabella. But as a condition for marriage, the Spanish king and queen demanded that Emanuel expel the Jews from Portugal. He had to "purify" his kingdom of the Jews, and then, as Barnet Litvinoff writes, he could "Christianize Portugal."

Emanuel reluctantly banished the Jews and Moslems in December 1496, a month after the royal marriage, but soon changed his edict—because he needed their revenues. He tried to persuade them to convert to Christianity. He then went so far as to strike at the parents through the children. "Be baptized or die," he decreed. On March 19, 1497, all Jewish children between the ages of 4 and 14 were forcibly baptized in one single day in an attempt to keep the parents in Portugal. On another occasion, shortly thereafter, when 20,000 parents were forced to gather in Lisbon, only seven or eight badly beaten persons escaped the forced baptism. But like their Spanish brothers and sisters, these Jews would become Marranos and flee the country. By 1499, however, Marranos were denied emigration and had to revert to subterfuge to leave.

For several decades, Jews in Portugal managed to ward off the Inquisition. However a papal brief on May 23, 1536, ordered Portugal to establish a Holy Office of the Inquisition to be patterned after the Spanish model. An auto-da-fé was held in Lisbon on September 20, 1544. Sebastion Jose de Carvalho e Mello halted the Inquisition in 1821. History knows him as Marqués de Pombal. During the three centuries of the

Inquisition, more than 40,000 persons were indicted, of whom 30,000 were sentenced at autos-da-fé in Portugal. About 1,200 persons were actually burned at the stake.

Sir George Young suggests that had the Jews been left alone, Lisbon might have become the commercial capital of Europe, a position the country was firmly headed toward a hundred years before London.

The Portuguese Jews who left Iberia between 1540 and 1800 would establish communities or join their Sephardic brothers and sisters in such cities as Venice, Hamburg, Amsterdam, London, and Bordeaux in Europe; Recife in Brazil; Surinam in South America; Curaçao, Jamaica, Barbados, Nevis, and St. Thomas in the West Indies; and New York City and Newport, Rhode Island in the New World. Some of them became international Jewish personalities. One son of a Portuguese Marrano whom we know as Baruch Spinoza, the seventeenth-century philosopher, later would be excommunicated by his own people in Holland.

Trade caused the return of Jews to Portugal after 400 years. It is said that an admiral invited two Jews from Gibraltar to come to Portugal to create a commercial outlet. The two merchants, Isaac Aboab and Moses Levi, accepted the offer. Thus began the return of the Jews to Portugal.

By 1820, the city of Faro had a small Jewish community. Jews began to arrive as merchants when foreigners were allowed freedom of worship under the Charter of 1826. In 1868, the Jews were recognized as a colony. At the turn of the century, Eastern European Jews found in Portugal a haven from persecution.

Official recognition permitting religious services was granted to Jews in 1892. A synagogue was erected in 1902. The new Portuguese republic, established by the revolution of 1910, finally gave the Jewish community official status in 1912.

During the Holocaust, neutral Portugal adopted a liberal immigration policy, with about 45,000 Jewish refugees entering the country. Later, Portugal would at times withhold asylum because of its concern that the country would be overrun with refugees, and sailings across the Atlantic were limited. Still, it granted consular protection to Jews in occupied countries. Indeed, Portugal, with other neutral countries in 1944, managed to save many Hungarian Jews.

Ironically, even as late as the Holocaust, some Christians or descendants of Marranos would help Jews. One such person was Aristedes de Sausa Mendes do Amaral e Abranches, a Portuguese consul in Marseilles. He issued 10,000 visas to stranded Jews in defiance of his own government. He did the same thing in Bordeaux. (With a Portuguese visa you could travel through Spain.) Ousted from the diplomatic corps, where he worked around the clock to save Jews, he was never reinstated, according to Rabbi Chaim U. Lipschitz, but was helped by a Jewish organization. He died in 1954, forgotten and impoverished. In 1961, Israel and Yad Vashem planted 20 trees in the Martyrs Forest in his memory, and in 1967, posthumously awarded him a medal in deep appreciation and gratitude.

The story of Portuguese Jewry in the 1990s makes it seem like a miracle that this Jewish community is still alive. After World War II, 12,000 Jews resided in Portugal, which has a population of slightly more than 10 million. Recent figures put the number of Jews at between 500 and 700.

They live mainly in Lisbon, the capital, chief port, and largest metropolis of the country. Strategically, it is "the most splendidly situated capital in Europe," says V. S. Pritchett in *At Home and Abroad: Travel Essays.* Lisbon—called the quintessence of Portugal—is home to nearly two million Portuguese. This city, whose sea aroma wafts from the Atlantic Ocean, may pale next to expansive Paris or London. Yet, there is much for the tourist to see and do, including the Sao Carlos Opera House, Castle of Sao George, Tower of Belem, the Museum of Ancient Art, the city's many public squares, statues of national heroes, tree-lined avenues and small parks, and the 25th of April Bridge, one of the longest suspension bridges in the world. In the past few years, several hundred Jews from foreign lands, such as Israel and South Africa, have moved to Cascais, just outside of Lisbon.

Notable Portuguese Jews

While the Jewish schools of Portugal may not have produced a Maimonides, they could boast of their Abravanels, as well as many others whose names resound among great literati.

Other Jews contributed much to Portugal. Abraham Zacuto, innovator of navigational instruments such as the first astrolabe in copper and astronomical tables, also emigrated from Spain to Portugal at the time of the expulsion and went on to become royal astronomer to advise Vasco da Gama on his voyage to India. In 1497, when King Emanuel forced the Jews to convert, Zacuto left Portugal and went to Spain. Cresques headed the Academy of Navigation founded by Prince Henry the Navigator. Pedro Teixeira explored South American territories in the early seventeenth century. Joseph Vechino was a court physician and advisor to Joao II. The nation's first printing press was set up by Samuel Porteira. And of course Jewish scholar Judah Abravanel served as royal treasurer of Joao I.

Jewish Lisbon

ROSSIO SQUARE

Imagine landing in the middle of Lisbon's main square and reciting "kaddish," the Hebrew prayer for the dead. That is what many a pious Jew would do if he stands in the Plaza Rossio (Rossio Square) in this busy capital of Portugal. Here in the center of the city, not far from the Royal Palace in 1506, between 2,000 and 4,000 New Christians, known as Marranos, were butchered.

In the Plaza Rossio stood the Palace of Estaos, which housed the Inquisition. The building was destroyed by the earthquake of 1755, and the National Theatre of Dona Maria was constructed in its place. During the Inquisition, Jews were forcibly baptized at the Church of Sao Domingo, which is located in the adjacent square. Rossio Square is a good spot to stand and reflect on the world of the Marranos, a world in which no one could trust anyone.

A vast difference existed between Spain and Portugal in terms of the Inquisition. Portuguese Jews had 20 to 30 years longer to adjust to Christianity and practice Judaism secretly before the Inquisition came on the Portuguese scene. This meant that crypto-Judaism in Portugal contained deep roots and enabled these New Christians to revert to their former Jewish faith whenever they managed to escape to free lands.

But Elias H. Lindo writes in *History of the Jews of Spain and Portugal* that the Inquisition of Portugal exercised the same cruelty as that of Spain towards the New Christians. Those who were discovered or suspected of practicing Jewish rites, and under torture confessed their Judaism, suffered death and expired in the flames of the autos-da-fé.

The Inquisition concentrated on rooting out all traces of Judaism. Basically it succeeded. In fact, many of the victims of the Inquisition were not guilty. There are those historians who claim that the purpose of the Inquisition was really to enrich church coffers. But it never completely crushed the Marrano movement, which is important to understand.

The visitor on a trip to Portugal keeps hearing and seeing the word *Marrano*. The term *Marrano* is derived from a Spanish word meaning *swine;* it was an ugly, contemptuous word. Jews prefer to use the Hebrew word *anussim,* meaning those whose change of religion was forced upon them, but "who lived according to the precepts and laws of their ancestral faith," writes Dr. M. Kayserling.

In Portugal and Spain, they were also called New Christians, or "Conversos." The church was suspicious of the Conversos. They suspected that these newcomers had not given up their Judaism. Dr. Kayserling writes that these outward Christians "celebrated the Sabbath and holidays, assembled in subterranean or other secret synagogues, and practiced Jewish rites in their homes." The true-born Christians, the old Christians, "who were free from any taint of Moorish or Jewish blood," frequently participated in riots against the New Christians.

These secret Portuguese Jews, some believe, are considered the first modern Jews of the Diaspora. They set the stage for the center of world trade, moving from southern to northern

Europe. The Marranos were always looking for a home where they could openly proclaim their religion. Many of them, joined by their Spanish and Portuguese brothers and sisters, settled in the West Indies, but especially in Brazil. They also tried to get to Holland, which had turned Protestant and welcomed persons of all religions. Remember, Marranos were valued because European businessmen perceived them as having connections with relatives and friends throughout the world. These Jewish merchants and entrepreneurs knew Spanish and Portuguese. They had helped make Lisbon the commercial center of the continent. They maintained contact with Jews who had settled in North Africa after the 1492 expulsion from Spain. They controlled more than a quarter of the stock of the Dutch East India Company. But even though they were respected traders outside of Portugal, many were still afraid to say openly that they were Jews. So they called themselves Portuguese. Thus, "Portuguese" became synonymous with "Jewish." Others, as soon as they felt secure, openly professed Judaism. To understand the story of the Marranos is to understand Portuguese Jewish history.

KOSHER FOOD IN LISBON

Kosher meals are obtainable, if prior notice is given, from **Mrs. R. Assor,** rua Rodrigo de Fonseca, 38, Tel: 386-0396; **Rev. L. Toledano,** av. Alvares Cabral 5-5, Tel: 640-906; and **Mrs. S. B. Castel,** rua Sociedade Farmaceutica 7-3. But do check ahead.

SYNAGOGUES AND ORGANIZATIONS IN LISBON

Shaare Tikvah Synagogue, a Moorish building, stands at rua Alexandre Herculano 59. Tel: 658-604. The cornerstone bears the Hebrew name, *Kehilla Kedusha Shaare Tikvah,* in Portuguese, *Portas da Esperanca* (Gates of Hope). On the Holy Ark, it says in Hebrew, "Know before whom thou standest. . . ."

The building contains 20-foot wooden gates and high concrete walls that enclose the synagogue. A beautiful courtyard extends behind the building. There are several candelabra, common to Sephardic houses of prayer, in the sanctuary. Services are Friday night at 8 and Saturday morning at 9. The service is Sephardic ritual.

Within walking distance from hotels, the building features a blend of Eastern and North African styles inside. In 1948, the congregation rebuilt sections of the building. The chief rabbi of France, Jacob Kaplan, attended this public dedication ceremony that symbolized the rebirth of the Portuguese Jewish community. "After an interval of 500 years, the inhabitants of Lisbon looked on with curiosity and admiration at the procession of the sacred Jewish scrolls, which their forefathers had outlawed, despoiled and put to flames," wrote one reporter. In 1949, a second balcony and additional seats were added to the synagogue. As you walk into the synagogue, on the left-hand side you will see a memorial room to victims of the Holocaust. Refugees from Nazi-occupied France knew that neutral Portugal was their best hope of fleeing the Germans in World War II.

For information, call 658-604 or 388-1592.

The Headquarters of the Jewish Community is also located in the same building as the synagogue.

Ashkenazic Synagogue, rua Elias Garcia 110, Lisbon. 797-5283. This synagogue is not open at all times. Services are irregular. Call to check on times of services and programs. Members of the Sephardic synagogue, Shaare Tikvah, can also inform you as to services at the Ashkenazic Synagogue.

Jewish Community Center, rua Rosa Araujo 10, Lisbon. The focal point of the Jewish community, this center opened in 1948. It is located three blocks from the Shaare Tikvah Synagogue. Check with the people at the synagogue to learn more about the activities and hours at the center.

Belmonte, Guarda, Covilha

Visit the towns of Belmonte, Guarda, and Covilha. Marranos live here as well as in **Monsanto** and **Castelode Vide.** Samuel Schwartz, the Polish-Jewish mining engineer, discovered these villages in 1919.

Belmonte is a farming and wine area in the northern province of Beira Alta. In 1988, Michael Fink reported a community center of two cramped rooms: "On the walls are a tiny

Israeli flag, a roster of the members of the community and a generic synagogue dedication in Hebrew." Recent reports indicated that there are 200 Marranos in Belmonte, with a rabbi from Israel to lead them.

Schwartz said that Marranos in Belmonte "were completely ignorant of the existence of other Jews with different religious rites." The old Marrano women who acted as "keepers of the faith" did not recognize Schwartz's Hebrew prayers and rejected him. Obviously, these Marranos lived outwardly as Christians—they attended Catholic church services and joined in Catholic sacraments—but kept alive secretly some form of Jewish rites. Observers say their distrust of outsiders made them wary even of fellow Jews. (They seemed to believe that they were the only remaining pure Jews.)

Even today, Belmonte's Jews find it hard to be open about their religion. They still attend Mass with their Catholic neighbors at the village church where, for so many generations, they have been baptized, married, and buried under marble tombstones, writes Paul Ames of the Associated Press in *The Jewish Week* of June 22, 1990. According to Colette Avital, Israel's ambassador to Portugal, "They've lived on the outside like Christians. On the inside, in their houses, they were not Christians, they were Jews, and they have transmitted this from father to son."

Descendants of the original Marranos who still live in and around Belmonte are uncircumcised and baptized, but otherwise practice Judaism in secret, lighting their Sabbath lamps in the cellar. They do not eat pork; they marry amongst themselves and are known by their neighbors as Judeos—Jews. They are not officially recognized by world Jewry. Although they were discovered in 1919, attention was not drawn to them until the neighboring town of **Guarda** was "twinned" with the Israeli town of Safed in 1982.

According to *Time* magazine of April 11, 1977: "The Marranos shun all Saturday work: a telltale sign of their identity. But paradoxically, most of the men have not been circumcised because that could disclose their secret."

Here is a further description in *The Jerusalem Post* of these descendants of Jews who fled from the Inquisition: "They get together for Yom Kippur eve services; they observe the Purim eve Taanit Esther fast, but not the Purim celebration. They observe baking their own matzot, according to a generations old recipe, reciting certain traditional blessings at various stages of the process; they have a short seder meal that includes bitter herbs, but they do not read the haggada. . . ."

When Marrano communities were discovered, Jewish organizations began to raise money to bring them back into the fold. But success has been limited. The Marranos have been difficult to reach.

Anthropologists have found the Marrano communities living in semi-isolation and cut off from most of the developments in the world and from their own religion. The estimate of the number of these Marranos has been revised downward. They seemed to be disappearing. Decades and even centuries of intermarriage were noted in the poor health of community members. Most were poor and earned their livelihoods as wandering tradesmen. Those who had managed to achieve upward mobility had achieved it through marriage outside the group and subsequent departure from Jewish tradition.

Faro

Faro was a famous center of Hebrew printing in the fifteenth century. The first printed book in Portugal, a Hebrew edition of the Pentateuch, was published here in 1487 by Samuel Porteira.

Today in Faro, the Jewish traveler will find a medieval **Jewish cemetery** dating from about the fourteenth century. A new cemetery was started in 1820.

Oporto

There is a handful of Jews in Oporto, a city of contrasts: baroque architecture and a modern commercial center. Oporto is a city of granite and grey—a city of port wine lodges.

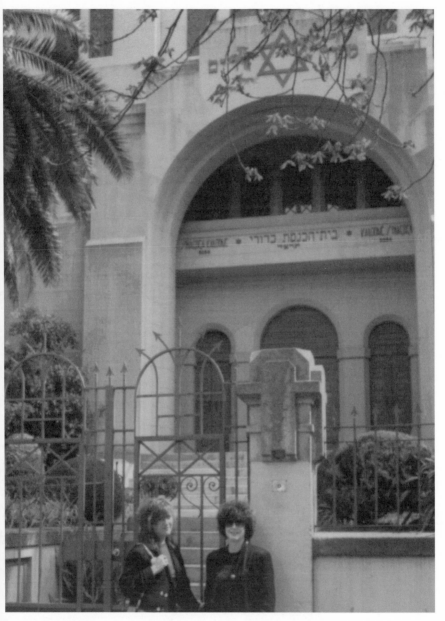

Kahal Kodosh Mekor Haim Synagogue, Oporto. (Photo by Ed Robin)

Kahal Kodosh Mekor Haim Synagogue (Kadoorie Synagogue), rue Guerra Junqueiro 340. Tel: 602-20. This was the first synagogue built by and for native Portuguese Jews in more than 400 years. Opened in 1929 under the initiative of Capt. Burros Bastos, Portuguese hero of Marrano descent, the synagogue received funds from the famous Kadoorie family of Baghdad. For more than 20 years, Bastos led this synagogue. He hoped to bring the Marranos back to Judaism. While the synagogue is still in the building, this house of worship is not often used.

Suggested Reading

Bradford, Sarah. *Portugal.* New York: Walker, 1973.
Mocatta, Frederic David. *The Jews of Spain and the Portugal, and the Inquisition.* New York: Cooper Square, 1973.

Austria
Where Jews Have Memories

"Something out of the dim past . . . when Vienna was a free city, where Herzl lived and worked and created the Zionist movement, where the *Neue Freie Presse* was one of the great liberal newspapers in the world; where Freud developed his ideas; where Yiddish writers . . . could be found . . ." This passage by Joseph Leftwich comes to mind as the car leaves the city of Vienna and heads toward the green forest around the capital. The tourist guide-driver turns on the cassette tape and the music of Strauss's "Tales from the Vienna Woods" bursts forth. You can visualize the majestic, uniformed men and the gowned ladies waltzing in the grand ballroom. All you need is a piece of *sacher torte mit schlag,* cake with whipped cream. But that comes later when you are back in Vienna and after you visit Stadtpark, that pleasant place where the statues of Strauss and Beethoven lure you back to the city's heyday where Haydn, Mozart, Brahms, and Schubert also composed.

Walk to the Ringstrasse, one of the most beautiful streets to be found anywhere. On this main boulevard are situated the university, the town hall, the Parliament buildings, the National Library, the Museum for Natural History and the History of Art, the State Opera House, the famous hotels, and stately offices. Still, "few cities have lost so much cosmopolitan splendor so quickly," writes author Richard Bassett.

In Vienna you practically inhale nostalgia. Where else can you still buy picture postcards of Emperor Franz Joseph or

books on the Hapsburg Empire of 100 years ago?

But like other Jewish communities in Europe, 50 years after the fall of the Nazis, Vienna for some may no longer be a popular place for Jewish settlement. Some feel the Holocaust actually began in this capital. Here lived the art student Hitler, who became insane with the idea that he had to murder Jews; and this city, say some commentators, is "the cradle of modern political anti-Semitism." Says author Judith Miller, "Austria also has become synonymous with the country of Kurt Waldheim, the former United Nations Secretary General [and former] President of Austria who lied about his past for 40 years and who told Austrians that he, and by implication, they had only done their duty in yielding so willingly to the Third Reich." Waldheim, did not run for a second term in 1992, was shunned by virtually every Western European leader after it was disclosed that he had covered up his service in a German Army unit that was accused of atrocities in the Balkans in World War II. His 1986 political campaign was marked by anti-Semitic overtones that obviously affected the small Austrian Jewish community. Throughout Waldheim's presidency, Austrian-Israeli relations remained strained and were reinstated only after Waldheim left office.

In 1993, Austrian Chancellor Franz Vranitzky was the first head of the Austrian government to visit Israel.

Today about 90 percent of the Austrian Jewish community lives in this capital of 1.6 million, although small Jewish communities exist in Salzburg, Linz, Graz, and Innsbruck.

Nine-tenths of what the world celebrated as Viennese in the nineteenth century was "promoted, nourished and created by Viennese Jewry," wrote novelist and thinker Stefan Zweig (1881–1942). Zweig was to take his own life in Brazil because he could not stand the horrible crimes being committed against the Jewish people.

A Brief History

Jews probably arrived in Austria with the Roman legions. By the tenth century, they are mentioned as "paying tolls on merchandise." An early Jewish tombstone dating from 1130 was found near St. Stephan (Carinthia) and the first reliable evidence of a permanent Jewish settlement is 1194.

A synagogue was built in Vienna in 1204. By the thirteenth century, Austria had become a center of Jewish learning, and a ghetto would grow around the Judenplatz square. The ghetto is gone but the square still exists today near the main synagogue.

At the end of the thirteenth century and during the four-teenth century, Vienna was recognized as the leading commu-nity of German Jewry. In 1421, the Jews were expelled from most of Austria, including Vienna. In the fifteenth and six-teenth centuries, only a small number of Jews remained in Vienna; they were restricted to ghettos.

Community life was revived at the beginning of the seven-teenth century, especially in the Leopoldstadt section, named after Leopold I. At one time, about 500 Jewish families occu-pied 136 houses.

During the Turkish War of 1683, the Imperial Armies were financed by court Jews Samuel Oppenheimer and Samson Wertheimer. The latter was called the "Jewish Emperor." They helped stop the Turks at the gates of Vienna. Wertheimer's home in Eisenstadt, capital of the State of Burgenland, 60 miles south of Vienna, where many Jews once resided, became the site of the **Austrian Jewish Museum** in 1982.

By 1753, about 500 Jews lived in Vienna, many in the provinces. The ruler of Austria was Maria Theresa (1740–80), who hated the Jews—unless they converted to Christianity, that is. Maria Theresa once wrote of Jews: I know no worse plague than this nation, therefore, as far as possible they are to be kept away from here and their numbers kept down." But the financial motive was so strong during her reign that she was forced to cultivate wealthy members of the Jewish community. Her son Emperor Joseph II, known as the "lover of mankind," brought about Jewish emancipation. In 1782, this enlightened monarch issued his *Toleranzpatent,* which guaranteed Jews cer-tain rights, such as allowing them to attend general schools and to engage in agriculture and handicrafts.

The Revolution of 1848 altered the course of Jewish and

Hapsburg history when the ghetto walls came down. Modern Austrian Jewish history begins with this period. Jews had been very active in the Revolution, including Adolf Fischer, who was chief of the new police force, and Ignaz Kuranda, the first Jewish parliament member.

Only 197 Jewish families lived in Vienna in 1848. The very next year, thousands arrived from Czech lands, as well as from Galicia. The Austria-Hungary Constitution of 1867 extended basic civil and religious rights to all in the Hapsburg Empire, including Jews.

In the early 1900s, Vienna had the largest Jewish population in Western Europe, 175,318 by 1910 with only Warsaw and Budapest having greater numbers of Jews. Every tenth Viennese was Jewish. Sixty percent of Vienna's physicians were Jews, reminiscent of fifteenth-century Spain. Vienna was said to be a "land-locked version of New York City." Jewish travel from Eastern Europe to Western Europe went via Vienna, still a transfer point.

World War I began the process that led to the destruction of European Jewry. During that war, thousands of Jews died for Austria.

After 1918, the powerful Hapsburg monarchy shrank and Austria became the state no one wanted. The Jews became the scapegoat for its defeat. No matter what they did, even reminding the Austrians of the part they played in the country's development, "they could do nothing to counter the violent hatred against the Jews ingrained in wide sectors of the Austrian population."

Still, Jews there considered themselves Austrians first. Even in 1933, few could foresee that the disaster that would soon crush German Jewry would be repeated in Austria five years later. "The Jews underestimated the danger of persecution by Hitler," says Nazi-hunter Simon Wiesenthal.

Jewish life was doomed by the German annexation of Austria, the Anschluss, in March 1938. But as Stephen Brook says in *Vanished Empire,* "The idea that staunch little Austria was brutally invaded by the Nazi hordes in 1938 is a fiction, for the ground had been prepared ever since 1934 for closer ties with

Germany." The vast majority of Austrians not only welcomed Hitler, but unleashed "a violent explosion of race hatred the like of which even the Jews of Germany, who had already endured five years of Nazi rule, had not experienced," wrote George Clare. Fortunately, about 120,000 frightened Viennese Jews would escape Austria between 1938 and 1941.

World War II soon erupted and engulfed the world. Ironically, the Allies, hoping Austria would resist Nazi occupation, made the mistake of calling Austria "the first victim of the Nazis." It left the Austrians believing they were innocent.

During that war, one-third of Austria's Jewish population, about 60,000 to 65,000 out of approximately 180,000, was killed.

"My Fuehrer, I report to you that Vienna has been cleared of all Jews." Baldur von Schirach, Vienna's Nazi gauleiter, sent that message to Hitler. In 1945, 29 Jewish children remained in Vienna and only a few hundred adults. After the Holocaust, between 250 to 500 persons, the remnants of Vienna's original 180,000 Jews, survived. But it was not the end.

First impressions are crucial, but often misleading. One can easily leave Vienna with the feeling that the Jewish community today is dying. But a community that publishes several Jewish newspapers and maintains about a dozen synagogues, a community center, a day school that includes primary and secondary education, Talmud Torahs, kosher facilities, and a modern senior citizens home is not dormant. And since the Waldheim affair, the Jewish community has become more active. Thousands of Jews joined with a quarter of a million Austrians in 1993, in the same square where a crowd of similar size cheered Adolf Hitler more than 55 years ago. In the infamous Heldenplatz—the same spot where Hitler addressed the Viennese masses after Nazi Germany annexed Austria in the 1938 Anschluss—crowds gathered in 1993 to hear speakers with a different message, such as Rabbi Paul Chaim Eisenberg, Austria's chief rabbi.

The present Jewish population is composed of those who returned from Western countries where they had fled from Hitler or those who emigrated from former Iron Curtain cities, including 3,000 to 4,000 Soviet Jews, Polish and Romanian

Jews, as well as Iranian Jews. Today, about 12,000 Jews live in Austria, of whom only 6,300 are registered with the community. Of all the Austrian Jews today, it is estimated that only about 2,000 of them are from the pre-1938 generation. A large percentage of the community consists of Jews who arrived here during the Hungarian Revolution in 1956. Above all, as Georg Haber, managing director of the new Jewish Museum put it in an interview, "it is a very heterogenous community as far as its origins and today's culture of the people are concerned." This community also participates in the growth of Austria, and a significant event regarding Austria took place in the summer of 1994 when that nation was admitted to the European Union. The Austrians later approved the admission.

Between 1945 and 1952, 400,000 Jews from Eastern Europe passed through Vienna en route to Israel. And between 1968 and 1988, more than 270,000 Soviet and Iranian Jews used Austria as a gateway to freedom.

The Viennese Jewish population is elderly: more than half the population is over 60 years old. More members of Austria's Jewish community are over 85 than are under 5 years of age. The senior citizens are single, or if married, without extended families.

On the whole, however, Austrian Jews live a nice life. Despite all the difficulties of combatting the anti-Semitism that arose as a result of the Waldheim case, Jews will probably remain here. They are active in community events, Rabbi Paul Chaim Eisenberg told the author. However, he noted that there is a generation missing because of the Holocaust. He refers, of course, to those Jews who would have been born between 1938 and 1945 and who now would be in their fifties had they lived.

Notable Austrian Jews

Some prominent Jews of Austrian culture include Gustav Mahler, composer; Arnold Schoenberg, initiator and creator of the Vienna School of Music; Solomon Sulzer in religious music; and Sir Rudolf Bing, general manager of the New York City Metropolitan Opera. In drama, there are the well-known Max Reinhardt, founder of the Salzburg Festival; and Berthold Viertel and Billy Wilder, producers.

Jewish Nobel Prize winners of Austrian origin were Alfred Hermann Fried, Nobel Prize for Peace, 1911; Karl Landsteiner, 1930, and Otto Loewi, 1936, Nobel Prize for Medicine; Robert Barany, Nobel Prize for Physiology, 1914; and Elias Canetti, Nobel Prize for Literature, 1981. Isidor Isaac Rabi won a Nobel Prize for Physics (1944).

Jewish contributions to psychiatry included Sigmund Freud; his daughter, Anna Freud; Alfred Adler; William Reich; and Theodor Reik.

Austrian Jews prominent in journalism and literature were Hugo Bettauer, Martin Buber, Hans Habe, Franz Kafka, Franz Werfel, Stefan Zweig, Arthur Schnitzler, and Hugo von Hofmann. Arthur Koestler, although born in Hungary, was educated at the university in Vienna.

JEWISH SITES IN VIENNA

Community Headquarters, Seitenstettengasse 4, 1010 Vienna 1. Tel: 531-040, FAX: 533-15-77. The Jewish Community of Vienna, the only representative body of Viennese Jewry "recognized by the authorities," naturally comprises all religious and political organizations. The 24 members of its governing board are elected to a four-year term by the members of the community. A newspaper called *Die Gemeinde* is published once a month. In the foyer of the headquarters is an exhibit of Jewish religious items.

Leopoldstadt, now the Second District, is indeed an interesting neighborhood. The area holds 1,500 of Vienna's approximately 12,000 Jews. In 1937, one-third of Vienna's Jews, about 60,000, lived in Leopoldstadt where they were one-half of the district's total population. For Jews, Leopoldstadt meant home, even if it was a ghetto. Even as far back as the seventeenth century, it was known as the Metropolis of Learning. Especially famous were the district's doctors.

Rossauer Cemetery, Seegasse 9, 1090 Vienna. Recently, this first Vienna Jewish cemetery, the oldest Jewish cemetery in the city, was completely renovated and rededicated. The cemetery was restored with funding by the City of Vienna along with the local Jewish community. About a third of the destroyed tombs and headstones have been restored. The oldest tombstone is dated 1582, with the last funeral taking place there in 1783. Later the cemetery became a historical monument.

Buried here is Samuel Oppenheimer, along with other famous eighteenth-century Jewish financiers. Open Sunday through Thursday, 7 A.M. to 5 P.M.; Friday, 7 A.M.to 3 P.M.

The Vienna Central Cemetery, Simmering Hauptstrasse, Vienna XI. Tel: 76-62-52. Graves of famous rabbis, authors, and artists can be found here. Gate 4 is an entrance to the Jewish section; Gate 1 is for an older section. At the Simmering Hauptstrasse entrance, the hours are Sunday through Thursday, 8 A.M. to 5 P.M. and Friday, 8 A.M. to 3 P.M. At the Zentralfriedhof entrance of Gate 1, contact Mr. Pagler, who is coordinator of the restoration of the old part of the cemetery. Tel: 877-1371.

KOSHER DINING IN VIENNA

Arche Noah Kosher Restaurant, Seitenstettengasse 2, 1010 Vienna 1. Tel: 533-13-74. This restaurant next to the synagogue entrance on the Judengasse (the old ghetto) is very attractive and the food is excellent. Strictly kosher and under the supervision of Rabbi David Grunfeld of Agudas Yisroel.

Kosher Bakery, Hollandstrasse 3, (1020 Wien) Vienna 2. Tel. 33-35-65 or 33-46-74.

Kosher Shop, Tempelgasse 8, 1020 Vienna 2. Tel: 24-83-94. This store sells kosher food.

Kosher Supermarket and Kosher Bakery, Hollandstrasse 10, 1020 Vienna 2. Tel: 26-96-75. Also located here is a Jewish bookstore.

SYNAGOGUES IN VIENNA

Stadttempel, Seitenstettengasse 4, 1010 Vienna 1. For a guided tour, telephone the Jewish Community Center, Tel: 531-04-15 or 531-04-16. The chief rabbi is Rabbi Paul Chaim Eisenberg. The synagogue serves as a rallying point for the community, which has maintained and centralized facilities that consist of a community center, and Arche Noah restaurant often frequented by Jewish travelers to Vienna. There are two buildings that compose the complex: The synagogue and the offices of the Jewish community are located at 4 Seitenstetten-gasse and the community center hall and the restaurant, Arche Noah, are situated at 2 Seitenstettengasse.

The Stadttempel, located in one of the oldest sections of the city, opens Monday through Friday at 7 A.M., Sunday at 8 A.M., and Sabbath morning, Saturday, at 9 P.M. Daily services are held in the afternoon for mincha and in the evening for maariv. The pale blue and gold sanctuary is a fitting tribute to a once very large congregation.

Although badly damaged by the Nazis during *Kristallnacht* in 1938, the synagogue remained the only house of worship not destroyed by the Germans. (The Nazis leveled 22 synagogues and 40 small prayer houses.)

This synagogue, the oldest existing Jewish house of prayer in Vienna, was founded on April 9, 1826. The builder was Josef Kornhausel. The structure is also noted as the burial place of the founder of modern political Zionism, Theodor Herzl (1860–1904), who died in Vienna on July 3, 1904. After World War II, Herzl's remains were taken to Jerusalem for final burial. Thousands of Viennese lined the streets. Thus, it is difficult to walk through the streets around the Judenplatz and not think of Herzl, that "black-bearded prophet of the Jewish people who led them back to Zion restored." Vienna was the headquarters of the Zionist movement under Herzl. His book *The Jewish State* called for a sovereign Jewish nation for those who wished to go there.

Herzl, born in Budapest, was a student of law in Vienna from 1878 to 1883. He wrote journals for the Vienna newspaper *Neue Freie Presse* and became Paris correspondent for the paper in 1891. *Neue Freie Presse* was comparable to *The Times* in England or *Le Temps* in France. Writers such as Anatole France, Ibsen, Zola, and Shaw were associated with this journal.

Herzl had earlier experienced a tide of economic anti-Semitism in 1891 and in 1894. He was appalled to see France in an alliance with Russia when pogroms were killing Ukrainian Jews. Witnessing the degradation of Capt. Alfred Dreyfus framed by the French military, Herzl was moved by the need to create a Jewish state. He became the hero of the Jewish world, especially to the East European masses, although the term "Zionism" had been coined in May 1890 by a Vienna-born journalist, Nathan Birnbaum (1864–1937).

Agudas Yeshurun, Riemergasse 9, 1010 Vienna 1. Orthodox.

Bet Hamidrash Torah Etz Chayim, the former Schiffschul, Grosse Schiffgasse 8, Vienna 2. Orthodox.

Mizrachi Synagogue, Judenplatz 8, 1020 Vienna 1. Tel: 535-4153. Open for prayer Monday through Friday, 7 A.M.; Sunday, 8 A.M.; Sabbath, 9:30 A.M. The sanctuary and banquet hall are on the second floor. Here also are the headquarters of the Zionist religious youth, Bnei Akiva. Call for information on activities and lessons.

Nearby is **Judenplatz** or Jews Square, where there are plaques recalling the site of an older synagogue, hospital, and place where Jews lived in medieval times.

Ohel Moshe, Lilienbrunngasse 19, 1020 Vienna 2. Tel: 26-88-64. Orthodox.

Shomre Haddas, Glasergasse 17, 1090 Vienna. Orthodox.

Synagogue Agudas Israel, Grunangergasse 1, 1010 Vienna 1. Tel: 512-83-31. This synagogue opens Monday through Friday at 7 A.M., Sunday at 8 A.M., and Sabbath at 8 P.M.

Synagogue Agudas Israel, Tempelgasse 3, 1020 Vienna 2. Tel: 24-92-62.

Synagogue Machzeke Haddas, Friedmann-Platz 22, Vienna 1. Tel: 512-52-62. Services are held Monday through Friday at 6:30, 7:30, and 8 A.M. in summer; 7, 7:30, and 8 A.M. in winter; Sunday at 7 and 8 A.M.; and on Sabbath at 8:30 A.M. Call to confirm hours.

Hotel: A recommended hotel in the Second District, but a 10-15 minute walk to the main synagogue is **Hotel Stefanie,** Taborstrasse 12, 1020 Vienna, Tel: 21-150-0. FAX: 21-150-160.

ORGANIZATIONS

Jewish Welcome Service, Stephansplatz 10, 1010 Vienna 1. Tel: 533-88-91. FAX: 533-40-98. Dr. Leon Zelman, director, and his staff will be glad to help you contact the Jewish community. This Jewish Welcome Service, a branch of the Austrian Tourist Office, is located at one of the busiest subway stops in

Stephansplatz, in the shadow of the 700-year-old St. Stephan's Cathedral, a landmark that is to Vienna, this very Catholic city, what Notre Dame is to Paris. No matter where you are in Vienna, you can see the cornice of St. Stephan's. When he can find the time, Dr. Zelman stands in front of his office in the square where the station is located and watches hundreds of subway passengers emerge from the underground on an escalator, out into the square where they cannot help seeing the sign: "Jewish Welcome Service—Israel Tourist Information."

Dr. Zelman, a leader of the Vienna Jewish community and a Holocaust survivor, is proud of that sign. It is almost as if it is a reminder to Europe, to the world, that a Jewish community is very much alive in the capital of Austria and under the shadow of St. Stephan's.

Dr. Zelman says no one dreamed that a Jewish community would ever again exist in the land of the Anschluss. Jewish leaders saw no future for the Jews in Austria. Young people emigrated to other lands. But Dr. Zelman is convinced that the Austrian Jewish community will continue as a vital and viable entity. His theory about the Jews of Vienna may be extended to other Jewish communities in Europe. He disagrees with those Jews who say that after World War II, Jews should have abandoned Europe completely, simply left for good. "Many of us who stayed sometimes feel that we have done so because we didn't want to give Hitler his victory." The task, as Dr. Zelman sees it, remains to keep the light of Judaism shining in Vienna.

B'nai B'rith, Taubstummengasse 17, 1040 Vienna 4. Tel: 533-80-54.

Hashomer Hatzair, Desider-Friedmann Platz, 1b, Vienna 1. Tel: 53-74-99.

The Jewish Old Age Home, Bauernfeldgasse 4, Vienna. Tel: 36-16-55.

Jewish Students Organization, Wahringerstrasse 1020 24, 1090 Vienna 9. Tel: 34-54-99.

Jewish Youth Home, Krummbachgasse 8, 1020 Vienna 2.

Lubavitch Organization, Grunentorgasse 26, 1090 Vienna 9. Tel: 319-11-499. FAX: 319-11-498.

WIZO, Desider-Friedmann Platz, 1010 Vienna 1.

Zionist Federation, Poale Zion and the Revisionist Zionists, Seitenstettengasse 2, 1010 Vienna 1.

Zvi Perez-Chajes School, Castellezgasse 35, 1020 Vienna 2. Tel: 216-40-47. Housed in the refurbished building of the old Chajes Gymnasium and located a few steps from the Leopoldstadt section. Opened in 1984. It contains a preschool, a kindergarten, an elementary school, and a high school.

MUSEUMS

Jewish Documentation Center, Salztorgasse 6, 1010 Vienna 1. Tel: 533-91-31. This primary source of information on Nazism is under the direction of Simon Wiesenthal. Obtain an appointment before visiting; permission needed. This building is a stone's throw from the gestapo headquarters.

Fifty years after World War II, there must be many who are afraid of the man whose office and small staff are located in the building at Salztorgasse 6. Simon Wiesenthal has spent more than half his life tracking down evidence against living Nazis. As founder and head of the Jewish Documentation Center, Wiesenthal has acted as the nemesis of the Nazis. He has guided more than 1,000 cases to trial and has been named the head of the Association of Jewish Victims of the Nazi Regime.

Melodramatic but true: no Nazi war criminal can rest in peace with Wiesenthal stalking him. His most famous conquest was Adolf Eichmann. Through the collaborative efforts of Wiesenthal and Israeli agents, Adolf Eichmann was located in Buenos Aires, Argentina, in 1959, where he was living under the alias of Ricardo Klement. Captured and brought to Israel for trial, Eichmann was found guilty of mass murder and executed on May 31, 1961.

Wiesenthal grew up in a small town in Galicia at the easternmost extremity of the Austro-Hungarian Empire. His mother perished in the Holocaust. Most of his wife's relatives did not survive the concentration camps. A total of 89 members of both families perished. He ended up in the Mauthausen concentration camp located near Vienna. Weighing less than 100 pounds and lying helplessly in a barrack where the stench was so strong that even hard-boiled S.S. guards would not enter, Wiesenthal was barely alive when Mauthausen was liberated by an American armored unit on May 4, 1945.

His main point hits home: the trials of ex-Nazis remain an educational experience for the world. Wiesenthal was often at loggerheads with the late Bruno Kreisky, a Jew, who was prime minister of Austria from 1970 to 1983. Kreisky was described as "born a Jew, but he became a hater of Israel and a front-line activist against the Jewish state," according to Edmund Schechter in his *Viennese Vignettes: Personal Recollections.* Obviously, Kreisky's relations with Israel were tense because of his policy of talking with the PLO. In view of the famous "handshake" in Washington, D.C., in 1993 between Prime Minister Yitzhak Rabin of Israel and Yasir Arafat of the PLO, some say they admire "Kreisky's foresight." History will tell.

In 1993, Wiesenthal, who was 85 years old that year, became embroiled in charges that he discovered and concealed evidence of alleged World War II crimes committed by Kurt Waldheim. But Wiesenthal wrote that the accusations being made against him "have no basis in fact." He denied the author's allegations.

Meanwhile, even into 1994, Wiesenthal was often invited to speak to schools and university audiences in Austria, where he is regarded as a leading representative of survivors of the Holocaust and he rarely refuses. Indeed, all of the city's high school students were able to see the movie *Schindler's List* for free, and then the students were given the chance to question Holocaust survivors. The first witness was Weisenthal, according to a report by the Austrian Information Services.

Sigmund Freud Museum, 19 Berggasse, 1090 Vienna 9. Tel: 319-15-96. The apartment building at 19 Berggasse where Dr. Sigmund Freud lived and worked for 47 years looks like any multi-unit building in this section of North Vienna, except it was the home of the man whom author Peter Gay calls the "Columbus of the mind." The Sigmund Freud Museum is open Monday, Wednesday, Friday, 9 A.M. to 12:30 P.M.; Tuesday, 3 to 6 P.M.; Saturday, 10 A.M. to 1 P.M. Closed Thursdays, Sundays, and public holidays. Guided tours by prior arrangement. The house and the study on Berggasse *(berg* means mountain) have been restored and the consulting rooms converted into a museum. The site is sponsored by the Sigmund Freud Society and the Vienna Municipality.

The staircase to the 14 rooms where Freud lived from 1891 to 1938 has not been changed. The rooms contain memorabilia, some 420 items on display in four museum rooms. There are 60 items from Freud's own archeological collection. Much of the museum is devoted to the history of psychoanalysis.

On a visit to Freud's apartment you see his rooms, his desk, his collection of Greek, Roman, and Egyptian antiques, pieces of sculpture, his books, and his Oriental rugs. The traveler will see Freud's waking cane, his hiking flask, his hat, a suitcase, and a travel bag. You will observe his comprehensive library and part of his collection of antiques.

Near his study, the tourist will note that Freud's youngest daughter Anna set up her office dedicated to the psychoanalysis of children in the mid-1920s. The displays in this memorial room, accessible to the public from late 1991 on, show original documents from Anna Freud's psychoanalytic work with children.

Sigmund Freud, the founder of psychoanalysis and the best-known Austrian throughout the world after Johann Strauss, was born to Jewish parents on May 6, 1856, in Freiberg, a small town in Moravia, now the Czech Republic. He attended school in Vienna and entered the university as a medical student where, it is said, he encountered anti-Semitism. Because of his Jewishness, he was sometimes excluded from the academic community of Vienna, the center of world medicine. However, he found a haven in Ernest Brueck's psychological laboratories. The rest is history.

Freud was not a practicing Jew. He wrote that he did not understand Hebrew. Some would accuse him of being estranged from Judaism. But author Amos Elon asserted in the *New York Review of Books* that "Freud was attached to the Jewish world with ties he knew to be indestructible," and is even said to have contemplated briefly, in 1922, settling in Palestine. He remained a steadfast member of the Jewish community and of the Vienna B'nai B'rith lodge, which author George E. Berkley says he had helped found. Freud once wrote: "My parents were Jews, and I remained a Jew myself."

Sigmund Freud Park and Memorial, located in front of Vienna's Votive Church, only steps from the Medical School of the University of Vienna and from Bergasse. Freud lectured at the university. The park was dedicated in 1985. In the park, which adjoins the University on one side, Vienna's Mayor and Governor, Dr. Helmut Zilk, unveiled a memorial to Freud. It is a simple stone facing the university and bearing the Greek letters, psi alpha, and the inscription, "The voice of reason is soft." Freud himself had used the Greek letter combination psi alpha as the logogram of psychoanalysis and it has become worldwide scientific shorthand.

Jewish Museum of the City of Vienna, Dorotheergasse 11, Vienna. It was a cold, partially snowy day on Sunday, November 21, 1994, and yet they stood in the cold waiting to enter, this the first day of the new Jewish Museum. Even more significant was the fact that this inauguration brought out huge crowds, which made it necessary for long lines to go around the building. It was an opening day in which "The Jewish Museum Introduces Itself." Admission was free and a special post office was established for stamp collectors.

Vienna Jewry and the city have made a serious commitment to this museum, which is open to the public Sunday to Friday, 10 A.M. to 6 P.M., except on Thursday, when it's open until 9 P.M.

In addition to general museum work such as exhibitions and collections, the Jewish Museum says it intends to become a place of meeting and contact where Jews and non-Jews can exchange ideas at lectures and presentations, symposia and seminars, film shows and musical events.

The museum also is proud of a lecture hall/cafeteria called "Cafe Teitelbaum," and a book store offering a selection of books and magazines on Jewish history and culture.

A highlight of the museum is the Berger collection, which with its approximate 10,000 items, includes religious and ritual objects, medals, paintings, prints, and archive material. The exhibit covers the entire spectrum of Ashkenazi art. A

Various Jewish museums recently have been set up in Germany and Austria. One example is the Jewish Museum in Hohenems, Austria, which is housed in the historical Villa Heimann-Rosenthal built in 1864. One room is dedicated to the music of Hohenems-born Solomon Sulzer (1804–90), who composed religious music. (Photo by Monica Wollner of New York, great-granddaughter of Malwina Rosenthal, whose family owned the villa, now the Jewish Museum in Hohenems.)

collection on the Jewish community of Vienna contains material from the old Jewish Museum, which was closed in 1938 by the
Nazis. Another important collection is that of Martin Schlass,
which was donated to the Jewish Museum in 1993. This collection contains 5,000 items of anti-Semitic objects such as fig-
urines, household utensils, manuscripts, prints, and postcards.

The first Jewish museum was opened in 1897 and lasted
until the Nazi era. Where were all the objects now housed in
the new museum? After the war, all the Jewish objects found in
different parts of Austria and Vienna itself were handed over
to the Jewish community for keeping.

A municipal Jewish museum was located in the Vienna
Jewish community center-synagogue until the museum opened
in Dorotheergasse. The new museum building was originally a
palace that dates back to the sixteenth century when it was
separated from the adjacent Dorotheestift convent. After frequent changes of ownership over the centuries, it finally
became in this century an art gallery and in the last decades, it
has housed the art department of Vienna's biggest auction
house. In 1993, the auction agency put the palace at the dis-
posal of the Jewish Museum of the City of Vienna.

The museum has made it clear that the Jewish Museum "will
always have to be aware of the fact that the Nationalist Socialist
policy of persecution and annihilation has created a traumatic
counterpoint in the history of Jews and non-Jewish Austrians."
It added, "the memory of the Holocaust will therefore permeate all activities undertaken by the Museum; at the same time,
the Museum also represents a new beginning, by employing
the methods available to a museum of cultural history to
reconstruct and preserve the past."

Georg Haber is the managing director of the new museum.
The director is Professor Julius H. Schoeps from Germany who
is professor of history at the newly created University of
Potsdam and also director of the Moses-Mendelsohn Center
for European Jewish Studies.

If the first day was any example, the exhibits on display were
superbly presented. Travelers to Vienna would do well to visit
this wonderful museum.

MEMORIAL SITES

Gestapo Victims Monument. The monument in Morzinplatz honors hundreds who were murdered here, including many Jews. The gestapo headquarters were located in the Hotel Metropole. Although Austrians accounted for only 8 percent of the population of the Third Reich, about one-third of all people working for the S.S. extermination machinery were Austrian. Almost half of the six million Jewish victims of the Hitler regime were killed by Austrians.

The Mauthausen Concentration Camp, A-4310, Mauthausen-Marbach 38. Tel: 07-238-2269. The Mauthausen memorial site consists of watchtowers, barbed wire, and a gas chamber. Mauthausen is located 17 miles from Linz and 80 miles west of Vienna. About 200,000 persons perished here, and one-third were Jews. Methods of execution included pushing inmates from one of the 186 steps that they had to climb while carrying rocks from the quarry or ordering them to run to the barbed wire and then shooting them as escapees. Often, the mortality rate was three times that of other camps.

The University of Stuttgart concluded its report on Mauthausen with, ". . . deliberate extermination played a more significant role in this camp than in other concentration camps."

According to James E. Young, author of *The Texture of Memory: Holocaust Memorials and Meaning in Europe, Israel, and America,* "Mauthausen has been transformed from a hellish scar on the landscape to a clean, beautifully maintained state memorial."

There are 20 national monuments here, and the Jewish memorial monument is one of them. It consists of a menorah and a stylized Hebrew lettering spelling out *zachor* in Hebrew, "remember."

Young points out that the former Soviet Union's monument to victims of fascism at Mauthausen, "seems inspired partly by Nathan Rapoport's Warsaw Ghetto Monument."

The visitor can see all the buildings of the former concentration camp and its museum with 133 pictures and exhibits. A guide is available or you can obtain a tape as well as a film. Additional exhibits show the fate of Austrians in the concentration camps of Dachau, Buchenwald, Sachsenhausen, Ravensbruch, Auschwitz, and Theresienstadt. Every May 4, ceremonies are held to honor the camp's liberation by the Americans.

Sculpture Monument. A sculptured figure of a Jew forced to scrub political slogans off the street, a common scene during the 1938 Anschluss when Nazi Germany marched into welcoming Austria, can be viewed. This stone ensemble is located on a square behind the Opera and the Sacher Hotel. Alfred Hrdlicka is the sculptor. The sculptural ensemble by Mr. Hrdlicka, one of Austria's most prominent sculptors, was meant to guide the viewer through Austria's suffering under Hitler, through its participation in the German crime, and finally its liberation from the Nazi hell.

Suggested Reading

Bassett, Richard. *A Guide to Central Europe.* New York: Viking, 1987.

Berkley, George E. *Vienna and Its Jews: The Tragedy of Success 1880–1980s.* Lanham, Md.: Madison Books, 1988.

Fraenkel, Joseph, ed. *The Jews of Vienna, Essays on the Life, History and Destruction.* London: Valentine Mitchell, 1967.

Herzstein, Robert Edwin. *Waldheim: The Missing Years.* New York: William Morrow, 1988.

Hofmann, Paul. *The Viennese: Splendor, Twilight, and Exile.* New York: Doubleday, 1988.

Lengyel, Emil. *The Danube.* New York: Random House, 1939.

Magris, Claridio. *Danube: A Journey Through the Landscape, History and Culture of Central Europe.* Farrar, Straus and Giroux.

Miller, Judith. *One, by One, by One: Facing the Holocaust.* New York: Simon & Schuster, 1990.

Schechter, Edmund. *Viennese Vignettes: Personal Recollections.* New York: Vantage Press, 1983.

Wiesenthal, Simon. *Justice Not Vengeance.* New York: Grove Weidenthal, 1989.

Young, James E. *The Texture of Memory: Holocaust Memorials and Meaning in Europe, Israel, and America.* New Haven: Yale University Press, 1993.

Switzerland
Home of the First World Zionist Congress

An Israeli I once met said that the most beautiful place in the world is Switzerland, the country of the Alps, of civilized behavior, famed for cheese, chocolate, clocks, and watches. Many Jewish travelers favor Switzerland because for 700 years it has remained without conflict and seems calm and content. Golda Meir, the former prime minister of Israel, once said that Jews were the most nervous people in the world. So there is Switzerland, a place to soothe their nerves.

Moreover, Orthodox Jews, who encounter problems in countries where there are few kosher restaurants and Jewish institutions, find in Switzerland at least a half-dozen kosher hotels and resorts.

Welcome to Switzerland, one of Europe's most popular tourist destinations.

This "heart of Europe," this "tiny vessel," covers 15,941 square miles or about one-third the area of France. Switzerland's population of 6,510,000 includes about 20,000 Jews, or 0.3 percent of the population, who live mostly in the big cities. Five large cities dominate Switzerland: Zurich has 357,000 citizens; Basel, 178,000; Geneva, 159,000; Bern, the capital, 142,000; and Lausanne, 121,000. Sixty-five percent of the people speak Swiss German; 18 percent speak French; 12 percent speak Italian; and 1 percent speak Romansch.

Switzerland is an independent nation, supporting an economy based on international trade and banking. The Swiss banker is known the world over. It is said that "the responsibility of the Swiss is to prosper."

In World War II, while Europe destroyed itself, neutral Switzerland was untouched. Only the Swiss resisted involvement in two world wars. With a freely convertible currency, Switzerland has served as an international finance and communication center. After New York and London, Swiss banks are rated third in the world.

A traveler to Switzerland will see that its people are both orderly and literary. Zurich, Basel, Bern, Lausanne, and Geneva have more bookstores than other big cities in the world. Two of the world's greatest educators, Jean Jacques Rousseau and Henrich J. Pestalozzi, hail from this land-locked state. Well-known Swiss painters include Alberto Giacometti and Paul Klee.

A Brief History

The Swiss date their origin from 1291. Men from Uri, Unterwalden, and Schwyz gathered to form the nucleus of the Swiss Confederation. To this day, a Swiss's first loyalty is to his or her canton, of which there are 23. In 1315 the Hapsburg invaders were defeated; the cantons were united to form a confederation.

During the sixteenth century, Switzerland was considered the headquarters of the Protestant Reformation.

In 1798, the French occupied Switzerland. The Confederation set up a formal constitution that established the Helvetian Republic. The Congress of Vienna recognized Switzerland's "perpetual neutrality," a condition that has endured to this day. A new confederation was established in 1848, with Bern as its capital. The Swiss have the peculiar distinction of being the only country in the Western Hemisphere to delay the right of women to vote until the 1970s. (Before the modern era, some cantons allowed the vote, while others did not.)

A Jewish presence in Switzerland appears in the thirteenth

century. Jews first settled in Basel in 1213, in Lucerne in 1252, followed by Bern in 1262, and finally in Zurich in 1273. A French expulsion edict in 1306 caused French Jews to move here, only to experience the Black Plague (1348). For allegedly having poisoned the wells, a common medieval anti-Semitic accusation, Jews were tortured.

In 1622, Jews were expelled again. Later, only a handful of Jewish physicians was allowed to remain in some towns, with a few in the canton of Baden.

Until the French Revolution, Jews lived mainly in the canton of Aargau in northern Switzerland. Two Jewish villages, **Endingen and Lengnau,** actually became the cradle of today's Swiss Jewry. If you have a half-day's time in Switzerland, you should definitely visit the two villages and their synagogues, not quite an hour's drive from Zurich. Endingen, by the way, is the only village in Switzerland that has a synagogue and no church, although there are practically no Jews living there anymore. The **Jewish cemetery** located between the two villages, its oldest section romantically secluded in a small forest, is "one of the most touching in Europe," says Willy Guggenheim of the Zurich Jewish community.

But in the 1850s, the United States, England, Holland, and especially France pressed Switzerland to end its discrimination against Jews. Again under French pressure, the Federal Constitution of 1866 was revised to allow Jews to live anywhere in Switzerland. The cantons followed suit and finally, in 1879, Endingen at last granted emancipation to Jews.

In the late 1980s, the canton of Zurich contained 6,713 Jews; Geneva, 4,321; Basel, 2,577; and Lausanne, more than 1,000. The "Schweizerische Israelitische Gemeindebund" (SIG), "Union of Swiss Jewish Communities," is the umbrella organization of Swiss Jewry and has 22 member communities.

The majority of Swiss Jews are Ashkenazic but since 1945, Sephardic Jews from the Mediterranean area have arrived. "The community is largely middle class, its members increasingly employed in the specialized professions, large corporations and the civil service," according to the Institute of Jewish Affairs' book, *The Jewish Communities of the World.*

A silver Torah ornament from Endingen. (Photo courtesy Swiss National Tourist Office)

Notable Swiss

Switzerland has been known to be a refuge to many expatri-ates and to the persecuted. Here are the tombs of Rainer Maria Rilke, Thomas Mann, James Joyce, Robrt Musil, George Kaiser, and E. Weicher. Goethe, Byron, Franz Liszt, Johannes Brahms, Stefan Zweig, Eric Maria Remarque, Albert Einstein, Thomas Mann, and Paul Klee all found peace and a chance to carry on their work in Switzerland after they had been forced to flee their own native countries. Ernest Bloch lived in Switzerland, as did Wolfgang Pauli, physicist, and Tadeus Reichstein, med-ical researcher who won Nobel Prizes in Physiology and Medicine in 1950.

Basel

Basel Stadt Casino, 14 Steinenberg. In the story of Zionism and the State of Israel, Basel looms large. The Basel Program—"to create a publicly recognized secured home for the Jewish people"—was adopted here. Theodor Herzl would later write in his diary: "In Basel I found the Jewish state. If I said this out loud today, I would be answered with universal laughter. Perhaps in 5 years, certainly in 50, everyone will know it."

The First World Zionist Congress began on August 29, 1897. Frankfurt Jewry had refused its city as the site of the Congress, so it was held in the Basel Stadt Casino, which in 1938 was replaced by a new concert hall on Steinenberg Street. Today a plaque commemorates the Congress. The English Jewish writer Israel Zangwill referred to the First World Zionist Congress when he wrote: "By the rivers of Babylon we sat down and wept as we remembered Zion. By the rivers of Basel, we resolved to weep no more."

In this city of museums on the Rhine River, Herzl was elect-ed president of the World Zionist Organization. The year 1997 will be the 100th anniversary of the first Zionist Congress and a festive celebration is being planned.

Centuries ago, Jews were not allowed to live in Basel. They had to live outside the city walls. Indeed, still standing is a city gate where Jews and their animals were required to pay a special

A view of the Basel town hall. (Photo courtesy Swiss National Tourist Office)

fee. Ironically, Basel became a center for Hebrew printing.

People enjoy living in Basel, the second largest Swiss city. It is an academic as well as chemical/pharmaceutical center. An aura of scholarship, history, humanism, publishing, and love of the arts permeates the place. The city likes to be known as the "cultural heart" of Switzerland.

Three Kings Hotel (Hotel Drei Könige/am Rhein), 8 Blumenrain, is only a hotel, but it is a symbol for Jews. Every American tourist is familiar with the claim, "George Washington slept here." Well, Theodor Herzl, the founder of modern Zionism, did sleep here during the First World Zionist Congress in 1897 and several times afterward. Mounted on many a wall throughout the world is the famous photo of him standing on the balcony of his room in the Three Kings Hotel overlooking the Rhine and its bridges in the background.

Another fine hotel is **Hotel Euler Basel,** 14 Centralbahnplatz, 4002, Basel.

The **Hotel Basel Hilton,** Tel: 271-66-22, offers special weekends, including "Herzl Weekend" packages.

The **synagogue,** known as the Israelitische Gemeinde Basel, is located at 24 Leimenstrasse. Daily services are held. A Hebrew school and a day school are housed here.

The Jewish Community Center adjoins the synagogue and houses a **kosher restaurant** known as Topas (Tel: 271-87-00 or 22-87-01). According to Swiss law, ritual slaughtering of animals is forbidden and kosher meats are imported from France.

As for most Jewish residents in Europe, assimilation remains a major problem. New leadership is hard to find and often one leader serves for many years in many roles.

Still, Basel Jewry is active: B'nai B'rith, a local World Zionist Organization, a UJA group, and Bnei Akiva are the main groups. The community sponsors kosher meals on wheels for its senior citizens.

The Jewish Museum, 8 Kornhausgasse. Tel: 25-95-14. This museum is the only Jewish museum in Switzerland and is certainly worth visiting. It reflects the Jewish population of more than 2,000 in Basel and exhibits the history of Swiss Jews, who now number approximately 21,000. Although a small museum, it exhibits some exceptionally rare and remarkable items, such as tiny tefillin and rare books of Esther (the story of Purim), as well as havdalah candles, a Polish-Jewish Hanukkah menorah and other Judaic items, and memorabilia from the First World Zionist Congress of 1897. Open from 10 A.M. to noon and from 2 to 5 P.M., Monday, Wednesday, and Sunday.

The Basel Tourist Board is located at Blumerain 2, CH-4001, Basel, Switzerland.

Lugano

The whole world seems to come to Lugano, a summer resort whose city population is about 30,000. They call it the "Rio de Janeiro of the Old World," because of its subtropical vegetation and the peaks of San Salvatore.

Located on Lake Lugano on the southern edge of the Alps, this town has a distinctive Mediterranean character. It "dances in sunshine and is fringed with palms and mimosa trees," making it one of Switzerland's most popular summer holiday resorts. Most of the tourists walk along the calm, cool lakeside promenade. Others visit the sector known as Castagnola. The Villa Favorita, perched at the town's border, contains one of the finest private art galleries in Europe. Day trips on the lake round out the visitor's trip to this garden city.

About 800 Jews live here; many are black-coated, black-knee-socked, bearded Chassidim who are seen in the city streets. The community boasts Orthodox families, many of them Chassidim, a Talmud Torah (afternoon school), a day school, and a synagogue. About 50 Orthodox families live and work in Lugano.

Hotel Dan, Via Fontana. Tel: 54-10-61. This kosher hotel is an institution in this small Jewish community. Hotel owner Moshe Gefen hails from Keltze, Poland. Mr. Gefen, who settled here after the war, speaks Italian, French, German, Hebrew, Yiddish, Polish, and, of course, a little English. His hotel is efficient, clean, and *heimisch*. The glatt kosher food is tasty and well cooked. Mr. Gefen has owned the hotel for more than 25 years, remarkable for a precarious business such as a kosher hotel. He prides himself on doing much of the cooking.

Many Jewish business persons, he said, stay in the kosher facility, which holds religious services during the morning and evening and draws worshippers from throughout the city. Many of these business people stay in the hotel during the merchandise fairs held in Milan, Italy, about an hour's drive south. Although politically Swiss from 1512, Lugano remains Italian in ambiance and culture.

Many Jewish retirees reside in apartments and in the hotel during the year, some of them receiving reparations from Germany. The air and the life-style help people relax. The hotel is open all year, but sometimes closes "in deep winter," as Mr. Gefen puts it.

If Lugano is an example, Jews in Switzerland today appear to be comfortable, with complete equality and religious freedom. They feel at home.

A **synagogue** is located at 11 Via Maderno. Tel: 23-61-34. The **Conservative synagogue** of the Associazione Ebraica de Canton Ticino is situated at Via E. Bosia 15-17 in the Lugano-Paridiso district.

Geneva

Old-fashioned elegance is one way to describe the setting of Geneva, often called "the city of God" or "the city of Calvin." A "geographic crossroads" and "peace hub of the world," it takes international crises in its stride, although it is the seat of many peace and disarmament conferences and administrative headquarters of the International Committee of the Red Cross and 150 other global organizations.

Here is Geneva, Switzerland's most cosmopolitan city, where the art and jewelry dealings are endless; where one out of three residents is a foreigner. On the banks of a beautiful lake, the sights are attractive, including a new Red Cross Museum and the Opera at the Grand Theatre. Here stands the Palais des Nations, with architecture similar to Versailles. Here sat the League of Nations from 1936 to 1939. And here is the European headquarters of the United Nations.

When Philip Augustus expelled the Jews from French soil in 1182, many businessmen and doctors resettled in Geneva. They were not welcomed with open arms, for, if you were Jewish and passing through the city, you had to pay a poll tax.

Officially recognized in 1853, the Geneva Jewish community founded a synagogue in 1859.

The World Jewish Congress was set up in Geneva in 1936. In August 1939, the last Zionist Congress before World War II took place here. During that war, Geneva served as an important center for information regarding the fate of Jews in Nazi-occupied Europe.

After the war, Eastern European Jews arrived in Geneva. Later came Jews from North Africa and the Middle East. In 1945, the Jewish population was 2,245, by 1968, 2,700. Now it has passed the 4,000 mark.

KOSHER RESTAURANTS IN GENEVA

Restaurant Jardin, 10, rue St-Leger. Tel: 29-63-98. Dairy.

Restaurant Pizzeria Pinto, 50, route de Malagnou, 1208, Geneva. Tel: 36-97-93.

Restaurant Shalom, 78, rue du Rhone. Tel: 28-90-93. This is an attractive, clean restaurant, in the heart of the shopping district, near all the fashionable jewelry stores.

SYNAGOGUES IN GENEVA

The Liberal Synagogue (Bet Gil), Quai du Seujet. Tel: 32-32-45. Services on Friday evening at 6:30 and Saturday morning at 10:30. Beautiful sanctuary. There are Talmud Torah classes, activities, conferences, community dinners, and a sisterhood. Many people here speak English. Established in 1984, the congregation has about 400 family members of Reform or Conservative movement backgrounds. Services are in French and Hebrew; some are in English. During the community seder, prayers are in English. Rabbi François A. Garai, originally from France, speaks excellent English. A friendly atmosphere invites visitors.

The Great Synagogue, Place de la Synagogue. A memorial plaque stands in front of the courtyard at this 100-year-old synagogue honoring the six million Jews who died in the Holocaust.

This would be a good place for the Jewish traveler to consider the Holocaust and the Swiss role in that event.

There are many sides of the debate as to how much Switzerland could or could not have done during the Holocaust. What is true is that by 1942, the situation of the Jews in Europe became extremely dangerous. Yet to understand the problem, we must go back to 1938. On July 6 of that year, in nearby Evian, which is located on the French side of Lake Geneva, an international conference was called to solve the refugee problem. Nobody "lifted a finger." There was only silence. Some even reduced the refugee quota. No one wanted Jews. Switzerland maintained it could only be a transit country for fugitives from Germany. "This was by no means a glorious chapter in Swiss history," says Dr. Guggenheim.

"It was a Swiss—the head of the police administration in the Ministry of Justice—who concluded that 'J' for 'Juden' inscribed in German, in passports held by Jews, would help Hitler control the flight of Jews from Germany." Four years later, in August 1942, Switzerland closed its borders. Leni Yahil says Switzerland "took the position that the right of asylum is the sole prerogative of the State—not that of the refugee." A Swiss official compared Switzerland to a lifeboat, with thousands of drowning people clamoring to get into that only available lifeboat with very limited space and provisions. In August 1942, at about the time of the sealing of the borders, he said that the lifeboat was full.

From 1939 to 1945, a total of 295,381 fugitives received asylum in Switzerland, some for only a short time. But about 10,000 Jews were refused admission. Many did not even hazard an attempt to get across the freedom line. During the war years, about 23,000 Jewish refugees were saved and taken care of in Switzerland, according to Dr. Guggenheim.

Nearly 1,700 Jews from Hungary were brought to Switzerland via Bergen Belsen, 1,200 Jews from Theresienstadt were rescued, as well as the 400 children who came from the Buchenwald concentration camp. After the war, many left for other lands.

The Machsike Hadass Synagogue, 31, boulevard Helvétique or 2, Place des Eaux Vives. Tel: 35-22-98. Services Friday evenings at 6 and Saturday mornings at 9.

Sephardic Synagogue, 10, rue St-Leger, in the Jewish Community Center. Services are Friday evenings at 6 and Saturday mornings at 9.

Hekhal Haness, 54 ter, route de Malagnou. Tel: 736-96-32. Sephardic.

ORGANIZATIONS

Travelers should know that the **U.S. Consulate** is located on rue de Temple.

Many Jewish organizations maintain offices in Geneva:

American Jewish Joint Distribution Committee and HIAS (Hebrew Immigrant Aid Society), 75, rue de Lyon, 1211, Geneva. Tel: 345-93-50. HIAS is the international migration agency of the organized American Jewish community.

The Jewish Community Center, 10, rue St-Leger. Tel: 310-46-86. This building is the center of the Jewish community. There are lectures, Talmud Torah classes, a fine library that also has books in English, and a kosher snack bar that is open Monday to Thursday for lunch.

ORT, 1, rue de Varembe. Tel: 734-14-34.

World Jewish Congress, 1, rue de Varembe. Tel: 734-13-25.

One recommended hotel is Le Warwick, 14 rue de Lausanne, CH-1201, Geneva. Tel: 731-62-50. FAX: 738-99-35. This 169-room hotel is located in the city's new commercial center across from the main Cornavin railway station with a six-minute direct airport connection. It is a short stroll to the lake-front, the pedestrian mall, and the old city.

Israel Mission, 9 chemin Bon Vent, 1206 Geneva/Cointrin. Tel: 798-05-00.

Zurich

"Athens on the Limat River" is how Zurich is described. This is Switzerland's largest city and the commercial and financial

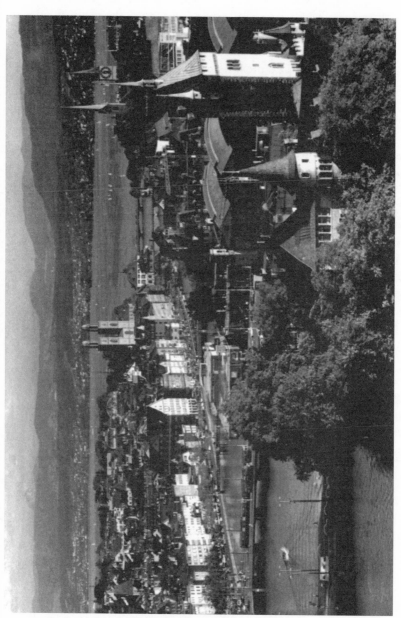

The Zurich skyline. (Photo courtesy Zurich Tourist Office)

capital. It is a Swiss "New York City," known for its efficiency and exactness. This second city of psychoanalysis stands as a prime gateway to Europe.

Even if it is a communications and industrial center, Zurich is still one of Europe's most beautiful cities because of the hills surrounding it, the fresh air blowing down from the mountains, and the red geraniums, roses, and begonias that decorate this urban area.

Zurich is a city for strollers, especially on the luxurious and prosperous Bahnhofstrasse, where one might just by chance meet one of the city's 6,000 Jews.

Jews first arrived in Zurich in 1273 and were mainly money-lenders. But eventually came bad times and bad memories, among them the Black Death of 1348 when Jews were burned at the stake, as well as the expulsion from Switzerland in 1634. After the French Revolution in 1789, a few Jews returned to Zurich. The Swiss waited until 1866 to grant civil and legal equality, and only then did a new Jewish community arise. Swiss Jewry, and especially Zurich's Jews, are very well organized into the 22-member SIG, the umbrella organization of Swiss Jewry.

A must for the first-time or even second-trip visitor is the city's attractive section across the river, "the East Bank." This area is fast becoming a preserved area of guildhalls and medieval houses. These charming Old-World structures are still among the most precious landmarks in the old town.

SITES IN ZURICH

Marc Chagall, France's famed Jewish artist, is also well known in Zurich. His five stained-glass windows are located in the chancel of the **Fraumunster Church.** There is the Prophets Window, Jacob Window, Christ Window, Zion Window, and Law Window.

The Jewish ghetto here was once called the **Judengasse.** You would never know it now; there isn't very much left. We do know, however, that one small street now called **Froschaugasse** was located in the ghetto. Book and antique stores give the street a peaceful shopping appearance. Nearby is the building where Nikolai Lenin lived from February 1916 to April 1917. The sign on the building calls him "the Father of the Russian Revolution."

SYNAGOGUES IN ZURICH

The main address of the Zurich community is the **Cultural and Community Center** at 33 Lavaterstrasse, 8027, Zurich. Tel: 201-1659 or 201-1660. The building contains an extensive library and meeting halls. A synagogue is located here, too, as well as a kosher "cafe-restaurant," called **Schalom.** Tel: 201-14-76. The library is open Monday, 10 A.M. to noon, and 3 to 6 P.M. Closed Tuesday. On Wednesday, 12 noon to 5 P.M.; Thursday, 10 A.M. to noon. Closed Friday. Sunday, 10 A.M. to noon. It is closed the last Sunday of the month.

Placed just off the fashionable Bahnhofstrasse and its designer stores is the oldest **synagogue** in Zurich, at 10 Lowenstrasse, 8001, Zurich. Built in 1883 in a Moorish style, it has two magnificent cupolas and an exterior of brown and whitish stone. While the rabbi is Orthodox and the service is Orthodox, many non-Orthodox Jews attend services here, I was told.

A **prayer room** is situated at 36 Nuschelerstrasse, 8001, Zurich. Tel: 211-68-80.

Beth Chabad Lubavitch is located at 198 Manessestrasse, 8038, Zurich. Tel: 201-16-91.

Bet Chabad Lubavitch Zollikerberg, Forchstrasse 362, 8008 Zurich. Tel: 386-8403.

A traditional **German Orthodox Congregation** stands at 37 Freigutstrasse, 8002, Zurich. Tel: 201-67-46.

Many Ashkenazi Jews from Eastern Europe pray at the **synagogue** at 8 Erikastrasse, 8003, Zurich.

Or Chadasch, a Liberal or Progressive synagogue, is at 13 Fortunagasse, 8001, Zurich. Tel: 221-11-52 or 221-11-53.

Other Kosher Hotels and Restaurants in Switzerland

To sum up for those traveling to beautiful Switzerland, here are just a few other kosher hotels and restaurants to stop at when you visit this country in the Alps.

Arosa: Levin's Hotel Metropol. Tel: 081-31-10-58.
Davos: Ethania Restaurant Home. Tel: 081-46-54-04.
Engelberg: Hotel Marguerite. Tel: 041-94-25-22.
Grindelwald: Wagner-Kahn's Hotel Silberhorn. Tel: 036-53-28-22.
St. Moritz: Hotel Edelweiss. Tel: (082) 3-55-33.

Suggested Reading

Hasler, Alfred A. *The Lifeboat Is Full: Switzerland and the Refugees, 1933–1945*. New York: Funk and Wagnalls, 1969.
Martin, Lawrence and Sylvia. *Switzerland: An Uncommon Guide.* New York: McGraw-Hill, 1965.
Schwarz, Urs. *The Eye of the Hurricane: Switzerland in World War Two.* Boulder, Colo.: Westview Press, 1980.
Sorell, Walter. *The Swiss: A Cultural Panorama of Switzerland.* New York: Bobbs, Merrill, 1972.

Belgium
Diamonds, Rubies, and the Most Luxurious Ghetto in the World

If you cannot tell a book by its cover, you certainly cannot feel the cultural life of a nation by its scenery. As you whiz by train from Holland to Belgium, the contrast before you is remarkable. Whereas Holland flashes tulips and gardens, windmills and canals, Belgium serves up iron and steel, factories and workshops. Rarely do you see a farm on the Belgian side.

And yet, here along the North Sea lies Belgium, a rich nation of 12,000 square miles, the size of Maryland, with outstanding cultural and artistic complexes blanketing the country. And its capital, Brussels, is now considered the capital of the European Union and headquarters for NATO.

As nations go, Belgium is a youngster, becoming an independent entity only in 1830. Its nineteenth-century creators hewed out an "artificial state" that had previously been ruled by Rome, Burgundy, Spain, Austria, France, and the Netherlands. It was also to be overrun by Nazi Germany in the twentieth century.

Belgium is situated at the crossroads of northwestern Europe like a checkpoint: bounded in the north by the Netherlands, northwesterly by the North Sea, west and south by France, and east by Germany and Luxembourg.

Belgium has been a battlefield that saw many turning points in history: Waterloo in 1815, Ypres in World War I, and Bastogne during the World War II Battle of the Bulge. Indeed,

Antwerp

⭐ BRUSSELS

BELGIUM

the hills and forests of the Ardennes and Flanders witnessed the snuffing out of thousands of young lives in both world wars.

Tourists are attracted to Belgium's ubiquitous castles and small beautiful towns. The cities of Bruges, Ghent, Antwerp, and Brussels contain and maintain much art and culture.

Belgium, with its 9.86 million persons, also holds the distinction of being the second most densely populated nation in Europe—after its neighbor, the Netherlands, that is. Belgium is flat—trisected by the Scheldt and Meuse rivers with the hills and forests of the Ardennes in the south.

A Brief History

The area came to be known as Belgium because it was settled by Belgic tribes of Celtic origin who were known as Belgica. Much of Jewish settlement in Europe began with the Roman conquests; Jews followed the path of those Roman legions in Belgium in the years 53 to 57 c.e. A group of Jews may have reached the country just after the destruction of the Second Temple in the year 70 c.e. Even with limited evidence, we know that Jews lived in Belgium from the ninth through the thirteenth centuries.

As in most countries of Europe, Belgian Jews were sometimes tolerated and at other times persecuted, depending on who ruled. Jews who were expelled from England in 1290 and from France in 1306 settled in Belgium and Holland. But in 1309, crusaders rampaged the area. Then came the Black Death of 1348, with its scapegoat, the Jews, who were charged with poisoning the wells and the Christians massacred nearly the entire Jewish community of Belgium. In 1380, Jews were accused of desecrating Christian religious symbols. They were dragged from their homes and burned at the stake.

Belgium remained Catholic; Holland had become Protestant. The Belgians never welcomed the Jews as warmly as did the Dutch. And so, the Jews did not come in any significant number until the sixteenth century. Attracting them to Belgium were the commercial cities of Zeeland and Flanders.

The latter needed skilled newcomers for the lively markets of Antwerp and Bruges.

Enter the Marranos, the "secret Jews" who arrived in the Belgian cities in the early sixteenth century. Antwerp's star was rising and the Marranos were sharp businessmen. Because Antwerp needed them, the city fathers gave these Iberians or "New Christians" safe-conduct passes. The Marranos accepted the offer, settled down, and introduced the flourishing silk trade in 1526.

Marranos could not go directly from Spain or Portugal to southern lands in the Mediterranean, so some would pass through Antwerp en route to, of all places, "hospitable" Turkey. An underground railroad from Spain and Portugal via Antwerp to Holland and Turkey was set up. For example, Joao Miguez, a famous Jewish personality of the day, the future Duke of Naxos, Joseph Nasi, came to Antwerp to reach Turkey. He maintained many important commercial contacts. Antwerp also became the first stop on the long odyssey of the Marranos over the Alps into Italy or the Balkans. The clergy, enforcing the Inquisition, watched every move of these New Christians, many of whom secretly practiced Judaism and sought religious freedom.

Later, with the establishment of a free Jewish community in Amsterdam, the main tide of Marrano settlement from Iberia moved from Antwerp toward Amsterdam, which then became the metropolis of the Marrano Diaspora. Still, because Belgium displayed a high quality of life, it would continue to attract Jews.

But waves of unrest surfaced in the seventeenth and eighteenth centuries. Holland and Belgium were split when the northern provinces under Maurice of Nassau won their independence from Spain in 1609. That division continues to this day.

Belgians have learned that they must get along with each other in order to survive. The country exists as a bicultural, bilingual state. People here speak both Flemish and French and some German.

One group, the Flemings, speak Flemish (a dialect of

Dutch). They outnumber the other group, the Walloons, by about two million. The Flemings live in Flanders, along the North Sea and on the northern plains, in an area rich in agriculture. The Walloons live in Wallonia, which is in the southern plains and in the hills of the Ardennes. Bordering on France and Luxembourg, they speak French.

When Belgium, which had been governed by Spain since 1519, was turned over to Austria in 1713 according to the Treaty of Utrecht, the Jewish community began to live in relative freedom and attracted Eastern European Jews.

In 1794, the French invaded the Netherlands, which then included Belgium, and immediately introduced religious equality for the 800 Jews. In 1808, Napoleon established the Consistoire Central Israelite, which to this very day stands as the representative body of Belgian Jewry.

After Napoleon was defeated in the Battle of Waterloo, the great powers, meeting at the Congress of Vienna in 1815, did not feel France should rule Belgium. The British pushed for a single state for both the Dutch and Belgians. Nobody bothered to ask the people of Holland and Belgium what they thought about a unified state. The union lasted 15 years.

In 1830, Belgium began its revolt against Dutch rule and soon won its independence. In the new state, religion received official recognition and Jewish religious freedom was written into the constitution guaranteed by the Concert of Europe.

Throughout the nineteenth century, the Jewish population in Belgium increased. By 1900, Antwerp contained 8,000 to 10,000 Jews, including many who would soon be on their way to the United States. Others were attracted to the city by the diamond industry. Jewish life, however, was interrupted by World War I, as Belgian neutrality was scrapped by the invading Germans.

Between World Wars I and II, the Jewish population in Belgium continued to grow, reaching about 100,000, a quarter of them refugees from Nazi Germany. After the Nazis' rise to power in 1933, Antwerp counted 55,000 Jews and Brussels, 30,000. When the Germans unleashed their blitzkrieg strike on the Western front on May 10, 1940, many Belgian Jews fled to

France. But they were not safe there, as France, too, was conquered and large numbers of Jews would later be rounded up and returned to Belgium, which itself capitulated to the Germans in May 1940.

By August 1942, the Nazis began transporting Belgian Jews to Auschwitz. Within a year, about one-third of the Jews in Belgium were murdered. By war's end, about 40,000 of the 85,000 Jews who had lived in Belgium perished. After the war, thousands of Jewish refugees from Eastern Europe, many of whom awaited permission to enter the United States and Israel, poured into the country. By the 1960s, both immigration and emigration decreased. The community stabilized.

Today, the majority of Belgian Jews are middle class and are active in the fur, textile, and diamond industries. Total Jewish population is approximately 40,000. About 20,000 Jews live in Brussels, 13,000 in Antwerp. Small Jewish communities exist in Charleroi, Ostend, Ghent, Liege, Mons, Arlon, and Knokke.

Jewish Brussels

A noble marketplace in a huge square, that is what some call the resplendent Grand Place of Brussels. With its gilded seventeenth-century Flemish gables, it is a link to the past. The guildhalls here certainly make the Grand Place an exciting square.

Brussels shows off huge office buildings of glass and steel, crowded little brick shops, and gaily gabled Flemish dwellings. Huge government bureaus take up entire blocks in this European capital. Here, too, are the headquarters of the European Union, Benelux, and NATO. It is no wonder foreigners make up 10 percent of the population. Diplomacy is big business in Brussels, and it helps the city proclaim itself "the administrative capital of Europe."

Some feel this city of about a million citizens vies with Paris as one of Europe's liveliest metropolises. Shopping streets like Avenue Louise attract both tourists and residents. And the people are generally friendly. City parks and the cathedral round out the major attractions of the Belgian capital, with Flemish and French sharing the official language status.

Jews probably arrived here in the mid-thirteenth century. The Black Death nearly wiped out the entire Jewish community in 1348. Further unrest and exclusion kept the Jewish population at a low level.

From time to time, Marranos found their way here, and in 1713 the Treaty of Utrecht brought Austrian rule and the return of some Jews. In 1757, the Jewish community of Brussels consisted of 21 men, 19 women, and 26 children, many of whom had moved here from Holland. But with the French annexation of Belgium in 1794, Jews again began flocking to Brussels in large numbers. Over the next 150 years Jews came from Holland, Germany, and Eastern Europe. By 1939, 10,000 Jews lived in Brussels.

JEWISH SITES IN BRUSSELS

Cercle Ben Gurion, Jewish Student Union, 27 rue des Hellenes, 1050. Brussels. Tel: 649-08-08. This center was opened in 1959, with the aid of funds from the Conference of Jewish Material Claims Against Germany. The center is the headquarters for all Jewish youth organizations. The **Jewish Student Union** and **Maccabi** are situated here, as is **Radio Judaica.** It is closed Friday evenings, Saturdays, holidays, and during student vacation. A monthly French-language review of the Central Organization for Jewish Social Work is published here.

Jewish old age home, 31-35, rue de la Glacière.

An impressive **National Monument to the Jewish Martyrs of Belgium** is at rue Emile Carpentier and rue de Goujons in the district of Anderlecht. The square is called Square of the Jewish Martyrs, and 23,838 names are inscribed on the wall. A small museum is also located here. Office: U.D.J.B. 68 Av. Ducpetiaux. Tel: 538-98-66.

KOSHER DINING IN BRUSSELS

Chez Gilles, 21, rue de la Clinique, 1070 Brussels. Tel: 523-94-22.

Seven Seventy, (dairy). 87 Av. du Roi, 1060 Brussels. Tel: 534-62-93.

SYNAGOGUES AND SCHOOLS

The Great Synagogue, 32, rue de la Régence. Tel: 512-4334. Built in 1878, it was not damaged in the Holocaust. The chief rabbi maintains his offices here. The **Consistoire Central Israelite de Belgique** (Tel: 512-21-90, FAX: 512-35-78) and the **Communauté Israelite de Bruxelles** (Tel: 512-92-37) have their headquarters here, with the entrance to the offices being at 2, rue Joseph Dupont, a side entrance of the building. Eventually, in several years, the **Jewish Museum** will be housed here, too, but now it is located at 74, avenue Stalingrad (Tel: 512-19-63).

The Orthodox Jewish community known as **Machsike Hadass** (Communauté Israelite Orthodoxe de Bruxelles) is located at 67a, rue de la Clinique. Tel: 521-12-89. Here, too is the Orthodox synagogue, the Rabbinat, the Beth Din, and the mikveh.

Sephardic synagogue, 47, rue du Pavillon. Tel: 215-21-38 or 215-05-25. Dedicated in 1964. The Sephardic community headquarters is also here.

Brussels has a **Reform congregation,** which Belgian Jews call "Liberal," located at 96, avenue de Kersbeek. Tel: 332-25-28. The Temple is a member of the Union of Progressive Judaism (see "Organizations" below).

Ahavat Reim, 73, rue de Thy, St-Gilles.

Beth Hamidrash, rue de Chapeau, Anderlecht.

Beth Israel, 74, avenue Stalingrad.

Beth Israel, 13, rue Houzeau de Lehaie, Molenbeek.

Synagogue Maale, 11, avenue Messidor.

Athenee Maimonides, 67 Bd. Poincare, 1070 Brussels. Tel: 523-63-36. This school has a full primary and secondary program. About 400 children attend. It also maintains a kosher lunch program available to tourists, but telephone ahead.

Beth Aviv, 123, avenue Molière. Tel: 347-37-19. A primary school of about 150.

Ecole Ganenou, 3, rue du Melkriek, 1180 Brussels. Tel: 376-11-76. A primary and secondary school of about 560.

Institut d'Etudes du Judaisme—Institut Martin Buber, 17, avenue Franklin Roosevelt, Brussels. Tel: 650-33-48. FAX: 650-

33-47. This is part of the Free University of Brussels. Conducting studies in Judaism at the university level, it is also known as Institue Universitaire d'Etudes du Judaïsme Martin Buber. The **Centre National des Hautes Etudes Juives (the National Center of Higher Jewish Studies)** is also located here. Tel: 648-81-58, ext. 3348.

ORGANIZATIONS

Beth Chabad, 87, avenue du Roi. Tel: 347-08-87.

B'nai B'rith, 68, avenue Ducpetiaux. Tel: 537-39-17.

Fédération Nationale des Anciens Combattants et Résistants Juifs Armés de Belgique, 148, Chaussée d'Ixelles.

HIAS, 42, rue de Livourne.

Jewish Community Center, Centre Communautaire Laïc Juif, 52, rue Hôtel des Monnaies. The **Federation of Jewish Youth** is also here. Tel: 532-82-16.

FAX de Jerusalem, semi-monthly review of the Zionist organization of Belgium, 66-68, avenue Ducpetiaux, Brussels. At 68, avenue Ducpetiaux is **The Zionist Federation** (Tel: 538-56-29) and the **Comité de Coordination des Organizations Juives de Belgique** (Tel: 537-16-91). The Union of Deportees Organization and the World Jewish Congress (Belgian Section) are also here.

Union of Progressive Judaism, 61, rue de la Victoire, 1060 Brussels. Tel: 537-82-45.

The Royal Windsor Hotel, rue Duquesnoy 5, 1000 Brussels. Tel: 02-505-5555. This hotel is located near the Great Synagogue.

Antwerp

A proverb says: "Antwerp owes the Scheldt to God and everything else to the Scheldt River." The latter made Antwerp the business and commercial capital of Northern Europe and the second largest city of Belgium.

Antwerp is proud of its many museums: the Plantin Moretus and the Fine Arts Museum are the best known.

The Jewish traveler to Antwerp, a world port and a mecca

Diamond industry workers in Antwerp. (Photo courtesy Belgian National Tourist Commission)

for art lovers, has no problem whatsoever in finding Jews. Head for the streets called **Pelikaanstraat** or **Hovenierstraat.** You'll find synagogues, bookstores, restaurants, kosher bakeries, and, of course, diamond marts. The area just looks Jewish.

"This is the most luxurious ghetto in the world," said one Jew who lived on **Bieli Street,** where many Jews reside. He quickly added, "It's a free-will ghetto, of course." No doubt the Jews of Antwerp are very tightly knit. They live together and work together. After all, about 90 percent of the Antwerp Jewish population of 13,000 is involved in the diamond industry.

When you speak of diamonds, you speak of Antwerp. You see, when other Jewish emigrants from Eastern Europe found jobs in Antwerp, they often secured them in the diamond industry that burgeoned after being exploited in South Africa in the nineteenth century.

Antwerp always has been a "Jewish" city. As one Jewish leader put it, "The non-Jews of Antwerp are so used to living with Jews, they don't see them as Jews." Non-Jews know that their Jewish friends like to live alone and are not too involved in the political and social life of the city.

Most of the Jews of Antwerp are of Polish origin and Orthodox. They admit they just don't mingle. One must remember that the diamond industry is built on everyone knowing everyone else; reputation and trust are paramount. This breeds a certain amount of introversion, to say the least. They live in a "diamond world." More Chassidim live here than in any other city in Europe, five or six different sects, such as Belz, Gur, Lubavitch, Satmar, Chortkov, and Vizhnitz. In fact, some say the Lubavitch are not that active in Antwerp, because at least 75 percent of the community is Orthodox. "It is another life and another world, a religious world," a Jew in Antwerp told me.

Ninety percent of the Jewish children of Antwerp go to Jewish day schools, which include yeshivot of such sects as Belz, Satmar, and Vizhnitz.

Others point out that, unlike other cities in Europe, intermarriage is not high here because obviously people are religious. "If you are in the diamond business, you don't want people to think of you as one married outside the religion," said one merchant.

A Dutch-language weekly is published in Antwerp, as are various Yiddish publications. The Anti-Defamation League in Antwerp publishes a monthly called *In de Naam Van de Vrijheid (In the Name of Freedom)*.

American Jews, religious or nonreligious, who want to inhale the "shtetl" life of Europe before World War II, can still find a shining example in Antwerp. The signs and the institutions are here.

JEWISH SITES IN ANTWERP

Bernard Kahane's Book Store, Pelikaanstraat 112. Mr. Kahane watches over a collection of 10,000 to 15,000 volumes in French, Dutch, and Hebrew, as well as many artworks. The store, which was opened in 1906 and run by his family, was looted by the Germans during the war and he recalls that when he returned, he had nothing. But his Christian friends, wholesalers themselves, helped him get started again.

The old **Plantin Moretus Museum** in the Virjdagmarkt has examples of Jewish printing, as well as the Polyglot Bible. This was the home of the great sixteenth-century printer Moretus and of his descendants. In 34 years, he published about 1,500 different works, a phenomenal achievement. Included were editions of classical authors, Hebrew Bibles, and liturgical pieces. The press room, foundry, proofreaders' room, and bookshop are still in their original state. The Plantin Moretus Museum also contains an exceptional collection of manuscripts, books, wood blocks, copperplates, and tapestries, as well as paintings by Rubens and others. It is well worth a visit.

The Romi Goldmuntz Center, Nerviersstraat 12-D14. Tel: 239-39-11. Built in 1968, this beautiful, modern structure maintains a library, meeting rooms, a catering hall, sports facilities, and a kosher snack bar.

Tachkemoni School, Lange Leemstraat 313. Tel: 239-04-67. This Jewish day school with about 780 pupils is Zionist oriented.

The courtyard of the Plantin Moretus Museum. (Photo courtesy Belgian National Tourist Office)

292 A TRAVEL GUIDE TO JEWISH EUROPE

Yesodei Hatora Beth Jacob, Lange Van Ruusbroeck Straat. This day school has about 1,100 pupils. Some say about 90 percent of the Jewish children in Antwerp attend this school or the Tachkemoni one. The Jewish day schools of Antwerp are unique in Europe, and the Jewish Board of Education maintains good relations with the government's Bureau of Education.

KOSHER RESTAURANTS IN ANTWERP

Nearly a dozen kosher restaurants and deli restaurants exist in Antwerp. Here are a few.

Blue Lagoon, Applemansstraat 18. Tel: 226-01-14. This is a kosher Chinese restaurant.

Drezsdner, Simonsstraat 10. Tel: 231-60-42.

Fogel, H. Lange Leemstraat 249-51. Tel: 239-16-87.

Gelkop, Van Leriusstraat 28. Tel: 233-07-53.

Hoffman, Lange Kievitstraat 49. Tel: 234-35-35.

Jacob, Lange Kievitstraat 49. Tel: 233-11-24.

Koplovitz, Hovenierstraat 36-38. This is a dairy restaurant.

Moszkowitz, Lange Kievitstraat 47. Tel: 226-04-71.

Sam's, Diamond Exchange, Pelikaanstraat 78. Tel: 233-92-89. This is a kosher restaurant; however, you probably need a member to bring you in.

A **snack bar** is located at the **Romi Goldmuntz Center,** Nerviersstraat 12.

SYNAGOGUES

There are more than 20 synagogues here in Antwerp, plus many "shtieblach" (small prayer halls).

Americans usually pray at the **Romi Goldmuntz Synagogue,** not located at the community center, but at Van den Nestlei 1.

"Hollandse" Synagogue, Bouwmeesterstraat 7.

Moriah Synagogue, Terliststraat 35.

Sephardic synagogue, Hovenierstraat 31.

ORGANIZATIONS

There are many Jewish cultural, political, and youth organizations in Antwerp.

B'nai B'rith, Nervierstraat, 14, Antwerp. Tel: 03/230-17-79.

Fédération Sioniste & Keren Hayesod, Schupstraat 1. Tel: 232-97-74.

Jewish National Fund, Hovenierstraat 12. Tel: 231-26-28.

Maccabi, Nervierstraat, 12, Antwerp. Tel: 03/239-56-73.

Machsike Hadass, Jacob Jacobstraat 22. Tel: 233-55-67. This is the headquarters of the Orthodox community.

WIZO, Gretrystraat 53. Tel: 239-05-71.

Other Jewish organizations include **Agudat Israel** and the very active **Mizrachi Religious Zionists.** Zionist youth organizations such as **Hanoar Hazioni, Benoth Agudat Israel, Betar,** and **Hashomer Hatzair** thrive.

Suggested Reading

Lerman, Anthony, ed. *The Jewish Communities of the World: A Contemporary Guide.* London: Macmillan, 1989.

Pilkington, Roger. *Small Boat through Belgium.* London: 1957.

HOLLAND

Amsterdam

⭐ THE HAGUE
● Rotterdam

Holland
The European Jewish Grandees and Anne Frank

Amsterdam conjures up water, canals, and an active port. Sit and watch the barges ply the canals. Stare at gleaming diamonds in polishing factories. Stroll on streets strewn with leaves as the cool sea breeze bites your face. Then follow the path of nearly 200 canals that were created by the dredging of infected marshes.

Visit the city's museums; Van Gogh and Rembrandt are just two Dutch masters to see. Inhale the spirit that covers the home of the young Anne Frank, whose name will live forever.

A Brief History

This is Amsterdam, the Netherlands, a place that has always welcomed political and religious refugees. For centuries, Jews have carried on a love affair with Holland, a relationship that began in the twelfth century. Called "Little Jerusalem" and "Mokum, the place," Holland has never persecuted Jews.

In this country of harbors, the first large-scale immigration of Jews came here via the sea from Spain and Portugal in 1580. The newcomers were Marranos, secret Jews, who had escaped to Holland and were no longer forced to hide their religion. They could also apply their financial acumen to careers in banking, importing, and exporting in the city that was founded about 700 years ago and which, by the second half of the fifteenth century, was the "emporium of Europe," a commercial

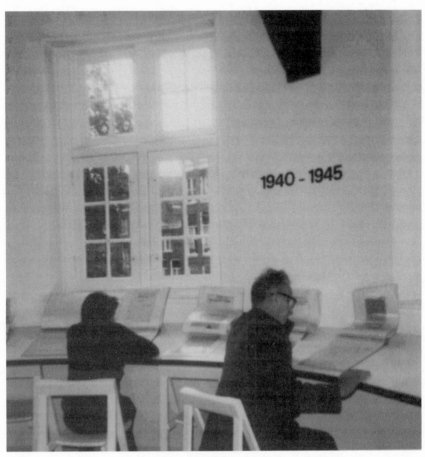

Inside the Anne Frank House. (Photo by Doris B. Gold)

capital, a melting pot. This was the place to be, especially for Jews who thrive in a pluralistic society.

These grandees, the aristocracy of Dutch Jews, came here for economic opportunities, religious freedom, and culture. Their names still resound through Jewish history: Spinoza, Cardozo, Pereira, de Castro, Da Costa, Lopes Mendes, Suasso, Teixerira de Mattos. They worked as silk manufacturers, sugar refiners, printers, book dealers, tobacco merchants, brokers, and doctors.

Legend has it that Uri Ha Levi, a rabbi from Emden, came to Amsterdam about 1600 and met his fellow Jews at a tower that still stands, the **Montel-baanstoren Church.** The first Jewish neighborhood was said to have begun here.

Amsterdam would later become the the the "metropolis of the Marrano Diaspora." With freedom to worship and unrestricted economic choice, most became entrepreneurs. They became involved in the Dutch West and East Indies companies and, as a result, they became plantation owners and merchants in Brazil, Dutch Guiana, Curaçao, and the Dutch East Indies.

Yet, they did not live by bread alone. As heirs of Spanish, Portuguese, and Moorish culture, Dutch Jewry, made up mostly of Sephardim, would become one of the most important "cultural conveyors" of Jewish life in Europe.

In 1601, the Amsterdam Municipal Council approved a law that Jews could live anywhere in the city they desired. Jews held religious services in a home in 1607 and, the very next year, a congregation was established. In 1610, Jews were already living in the Hague, Rotterdam, Haarlem, Amersfoort, and Alaamaar. Two years later, a synagogue was built in Amsterdam.

In 1616, authorities officially sanctioned the community as members of the Hebrew nation, and Rabbi Isaac Uziel writes that the Jews "live peacefully in Amsterdam." A basic law was passed in 1619 declaring that each city in the provinces could adopt its own local policy toward the Jews.

In 1627, the first Hebrew book was printed. Fifty years later came a Spanish-language paper and Yiddish biweekly, the *Kurant,* according to Jules B. Farber in his *Amsterdam, City of the Seventies.*

In some localities, Jews were singled out, excluded from many trades, guilds, and professions. But compared with Jews in Catholic countries, here was "exceptional liberty," granted by liberal-minded Protestants.

And one man who was on particularly good terms with the Christian community was Manasseh Ben Israel (1604–57), alias Manoel Dias Soeiro, a Marrano, born in Madeira. He was one of the most illustrious rabbis of his age and of world Jewry. His parents brought him to Amsterdam in 1605. At age 18, he became rabbi at a synagogue no longer in existence, located at Waterlooplein. He acquired fame for his knowledge of Hebrew and the classical languages, and this enabled him to build contacts with many Christian theologians in Holland and abroad, with whom he discussed religious and philosophical matters. His Hebrew printing press in Amsterdam printed more than 70 books.

In 1650, he wrote *Hope of Israel.* In this volume, he discussed a report dealing with the so-called discovery in South America by Aaron Levi Montezinos of the Lost Ten Tribes. He worked day and night to obtain permission for Jews to live once more in England, an event which he maintained had Messianic implications because it would complete the dispersion of the Jews to *Kezeh ha Arez* (the end of the earth; *Kezeh ha Arez* is the medieval Hebrew term for *Angle Terre* or England). He believed that the Jews would not be redeemed until they were scattered over the four corners of the earth.

His trips to England and his appeals in 1655 to Oliver Cromwell had effect, although Manasseh Ben Israel felt he had failed because neither Cromwell nor the conference had made it official. Even though he had induced Cromwell to admit the Jews to England, he returned to Holland a broken man, and died in 1657.

The year 1648 was a milestone: the Treaty of Westphalia brought an end to 80 years of fighting between the Spaniards and the Dutch. Holland (the United Provinces) was now free, meaning less restrictions on Jews. In 1657, Holland officially recognized the Jews as subjects of the country. Related to independence was the fact that Amsterdam had topped Antwerp as the chief port in northwest Europe and captured the Belgian city's lucrative trade. Jews immediately moved north to their new Dutch home. The Treaty of Westphalia also closed the navigation of the Scheldt River and almost reduced Antwerp to a dormant city, a condition that would last for two centuries. Jews soon realized that Holland was "where the action was."

With their trading contacts in Spain, Portugal, and the Ottoman Empire, Jews also became very useful. They played an important part in Holland's economic growth. They were involved in the East Indies and West Indies companies. Obtaining control of 25 percent of the shares of the East India Company, they brought in capital and established new enterprises.

By 1672, there were 7,500 Jews in Amsterdam, out of a total population of 200,000. In those days, the Jewish quarter resembled a small Lisbon and Madrid. Spanish and Portuguese was spoken on the streets. The city became a center throughout the Jewish world, the mother community of London, New York, and West Indian Jewry. Many of the 10,000 Jews in Amsterdam, at the close of the seventeenth century, served as academicians, teachers, and rabbis in this city of Jewish printing and learning.

By 1780, the Ashkenazim had by far overtaken the Sephardim, so that only 10 percent of Holland's Jews were Sephardim. (By the early twentieth century, it would be only 6 percent Sephardim.)

By the middle of the eighteenth century, Amsterdam possessed the largest Jewish community in Europe, and the French Revolution would dramatically alter Jewish life in Holland. In 1795, the French conquered the Netherlands and its 23,400 Jewish residents. On September 2, 1796, the Batavian National Assembly gave Jews full civil rights. Louis Napoleon, Napoleon's brother, ruled the country until 1815.

Holland became the first country in Europe to elect Jews to its parliament. Here was a precedent, for Holland would become one of the few European nations where Jews would hold many government posts.

Rulers and governments might come and go, but for the Jews

of Holland, "unqualified religious equality was the rule until the Nazis entered in 1940." Like other countries in Europe in the nineteenth century, however, assimilation and discrimination would eat away at the vitality of the Jewish community.

Still, many Jews embraced Zionism and the Eighth Zionist Congress was held at the Hague in 1907. By 1940, 1,500 Dutch Jews had settled in Palestine.

In 1933, many German Jews crossed the border into Holland to escape the Nazis. No one knew that seven years later Hitler would follow them there.

Of all the countries in Western Europe, Dutch Jews in Holland suffered proportionately the most in the Holocaust. Holland, after all, was close to Germany, and the Jews were concentrated in the large cities. From the day the Nazis swallowed up the Netherlands in 1940, until the very end of the war five years later, Jews were hunted down and deported to death camps.

At the beginning of World War II, 156,000 Jews lived in Holland. About 106,000 would perish in the Holocaust. "The Dutch Jewish death rate was the highest in Western Europe. In the East, only Poland had a higher kill ratio," writes Judith Miller, in *One, by One, by One.* By 1943, "about the only way a Jew was seen now, was floating down in a canal," wrote Miep Gies in her *Anne Frank Remembered.* About 22,000 Jews were hidden by friendly Dutch Christians. About 8,000 were discovered and deported. Interestingly, "the percentage of Jews deported from France did not exceed 24 percent in contrast to Holland, whence 76 percent were deported," writes Leni Yahil.

Perhaps because of their naiveté and slavishness to rules, many Dutch Jews obeyed deportation call-ups. Feeling very at home in Holland, they may have been lulled into a false sense of security when the Nazi threat hovered. Some, according to Judith Miller, felt the Dutch Jewish councils "let themselves be used for the liquidation of Dutch Jewry." "They collaborated with the Germans by compiling registers of deportees and in many other ways, all of which facilitated the final murder of the Jews," said a Dutch Commission finding, reported by Ms. Miller in her book.

"Onderduikers" or "divers" was the name given to those hidden underground. They lived in cellars or secret rooms. Often, Jews who became fugitives or resistance fighters were supported by clandestine organizations. About 16,000 Jews of the 25,000 Jews in hiding managed to survive the war, according to Judith Miller. After the war, between 20,000 and 30,000 Jews returned to their former homes. About 30,000 Jews live in Holland today, and two-thirds of them reside in Amsterdam.

The Netherlands survived the war. Most of the Jews did not. Anne Frank, the Jewish proletariat, the rabbis, the Jewish doctors and lawyers, and the diamond cutters did not. But as Jules B. Farber wrote, "Unlike the Dutch, who tallied their war dead, the Jews counted those who were alive."

Jewish Amsterdam

SITES IN AMSTERDAM

The Anne Frank House, 263 Prinsengracht, 1016 GV Amsterdam. Tel: 626-45-33. Open daily 9 to 5 and Sundays 10 to 5, except major Jewish holidays. Trams 13 and 17, buses GVB 21 and 33, or a five-minute walk from Dam Square will take you here. This site is near Westermarkt.

Now an international center against discrimination, this is the four-story house where teenager Anne Frank (1929–45) hid from the Nazis and kept a diary.

A million Jewish children died in the Holocaust. She became their voice and their symbol. The secret annex, consisting of two upper floors and an attic, is the building behind the structure on 263 Prinsengracht. The building would turn out to be a good hiding place, for Mr. Otto Frank sold herbs and spices and the inventory had to be stored in the dark. It looked natural, therefore, when the windows at the back of the building were blacked out and painted over.

Miep Gies would risk her life and bring food to the Frank family and the others. Her husband Jan, helped hide the Frank family. He died in 1993 at the age of 87.

The entrance to the hiding place was hidden behind a

hinged bookcase. The top of the door was hidden by a map. When you pass through, make sure you watch the brief video tape in the first room, after you pay admission.

The first room you see is the room of the Frank family; Mr. and Mrs. Frank and their eldest daughter, Margot, slept here. On the wall, you spy a newspaper map of Normandy. Otto Frank marked the Allied armies' advances with colored pins. Next to the map, you see the pencil marks where the Franks and the Van Daans measured the height of their teenage children.

Anne's room comes next. She shared the room with Mr. Albert Dussel, the dentist. Recently, a collection of letters and photographs belonging to Mr. Dussel were found and are now displayed in the Anne Frank House. Anne cut movie star pictures out of magazines and pasted them on the walls. They can still be seen. As you walk through to the narrow top floor of the house, you think, "What was it like to live in secret?" Privacy was impossible. Emotions had to be contained. Silence was an absolute necessity, even at night and on weekends. Caution was paramount. Garbage had to be burned in the stove.

Visit the next room, the Van Daan family room. The washroom and toilet were next to Anne's room. The facilities could be used only when people were not working downstairs.

A steep stairway leads from the washroom to the room of Mr. and Mrs. Van Daan, which also served as the hideaway's kitchen and living room. There were a kitchen stove and sink. In the evening, all the windows had to be blacked out.

Peter Van Daan's room is preserved, too. Peter's room can be entered by mounting the stairs leading to the attic. The room contained the only window that could be opened safely. A small supply of food was stored here.

Downstairs, you see a photo exhibit on Anne Frank and her diary and the Holocaust. Her dairy has been translated into more than 40 different languages. On the other side of the room, you find panels on current events that show modern examples of prejudice, discrimination, and repression.

The end of the story came on August 4, 1944, when the police raided the secret annex and destroyed and plundered the apartments. Simon Wiesenthal claims a Dutchman gave them away; he was never found. All eight persons were arrested and sent to concentration camps.

Anne's father, Otto, was the only survivor. In March 1945, two months before the liberation of Holland, Anne died in the concentration camp at Bergen Belsen.

According to Mr. Frank, the S.S. man who discovered them flung some papers on the floor. Anne's diary was among those papers. "Had he taken the diary with him, no one would have known anything about my daughter." Among the pile of old books, newspapers, and magazines left lying on the floor, Miep Gies and Elli Vossen later found Anne's diary.

After the war, Otto returned to the annex and was given the diary. The world now knows it as *Anne Frank: The Diary of a Young Girl.*

As you exit, you know and feel that something happened here. Anne Frank gave the sufferers of Nazism a soul.

Antiquariaat Spinoza, 26 Den Texstraat, 1017 2B Amsterdam. Tel: 624-23-73. Bookstore.

Bibliotheca Rosenthaliana, 421 Singel, 1012, WP Amsterdam. Tel: 525-23-66. Known as the Rosenthal Collection of the Amsterdam University Library, it contains 500,000 volumes, including the 5,000 volumes of the Rosenthal Collection of Jewish Literature, one of Europe's greatest collections of Hebraica and Judaica. This library is particularly interesting to those who wish to research some aspect of Jewish history and culture.

Hebrew Day School, Buintenveldet.

Huis de Pinto, 69 St. Antoniebreestraat. Established by Isaac de Pinto, a Portuguese Jew from Marrano ancestry who bought the house in 1651, this house is now used as a public library. This is a wonderful street to walk through, as it has a Jewish past.

Waterlooplein is the old Jewish neighborhood area also known as "Vlooyenburg." Years ago, poor Jews resided around Waterlooplein, which is in the heart of this old section known as "Jodenbuurt" ("Jews' quarter"). By the end of the nineteenth century, the Jodenbuurt had become a slum. It was

Portuguese Synagogue. (Photo courtesy Netherlands Board of Tourism)

destroyed between 1941 and 1943. One of its hundreds of famous residents was Baruch Spinoza (1632–77), who lived at 41 Waterlooplein. At No. 33-39 was the synagogue, now demolished, that banned Spinoza.

Who was Baruch Spinoza? He was a Bible scholar and philosopher. Born here in the Waterlooplein area, he was a descendant of Portuguese Marranos. His questioning of ideas angered the leaders of the Jewish community when he criticized aspects of the Bible and refused to consider it as ultimate truth. In 1656, the Jewish community expelled him for his "heretical views." He left for the Hague, where he died in 1677.

The Waterlooplein Flea Market, now held around the Town Hall and Muziek Theater complex, was once the daily market in the Jewish quarter from 1886. Originally, Jews were barred from owning shops, and so they bought and sold on the street. Actually, the old Waterlooplein Flea Market replaced the old market that used to stand on St. Antoniebreestraat and Jodenbreestraat.

KOSHER RESTAURANTS IN AMSTERDAM

Hatikva, 86 Kastelenstraat, Buitenveldert. Tel: 64-24-299. Kosher vegetarian restaurant.

Mouwes, 261 Kastelenstraat, Buitenveldert. Tel: 66-10-180. Kosher deli.

Sal Meijer (Sal Meyers), 45 Scheldestraat, Amsterdam. Tel: 673-13-13. This is located in the southern part of the city.

Theeboom, 45-47, Bolestein, Buitenveldert. Tel: 642-70-03. Bakery and lunchroom.

The Dutch chief rabbinate can help the visitor with a list of kosher products. Address: 26 Van der Boechorststraat, Amsterdam. Tel: 644-38-68.

SYNAGOGUES IN AMSTERDAM

The Portuguese Synagogue, 3 Mr. L. E. Visserplein, 1011 RD Amsterdam. Tel: 624-5351. It was just as I pictured it. Still I had to use my imagination to envision the existing huge square building in front of me without the present crisscross of highways and cars, but with several handsome synagogues and thousands of worshippers. This area, this inspirational center of Dutch Jewry, is famous and recognized as the largest historical monument to Jewish Holland.

Like many former Jewish communities in Europe, very few Jews now live in this neighborhood, which includes the street called Jodenbreestraat, the heart of the Jewish neighborhood. They perished in the Holocaust or have moved to other neighborhoods in Amsterdam.

Walk along the heavily trafficked road called Mr. L. E. Visserplein. (Mr. Visser, 1871–1942, was a Dutch Jewish burgher who aided Jews at the beginning of the Holocaust.) Here you can see the historic Portuguese Synagogue, the most important building of the old Jewish Quarter. Indeed, it was the first synagogue in Western Europe to be recognized as such and was the model for synagogues in many countries. At one time, it was the largest Jewish house of worship in the world. It is said to be modeled after King Solomon's Temple in Jerusalem, especially the courtyard around the synagogue.

These Sephardic Jews had waited more than 200 years to pray together openly. They wanted the finest synagogue possible and they achieved it. The synagogue was dedicated with such pomp and circumstance that a contemporary witness observed that the people might have been forgiven for thinking they were rededicating the Temple in their homeland.

When it was consecrated in 1675, the mayor and alderman of Amsterdam attended the festivities, which went on for eight days, just as long as the consecration of the Temple in the days of the Maccabees.

The synagogue is always open for services on Saturday mornings at 8:45. It is within walking distance of the major hotels like Krasna Polski, Holiday Inn, the RodeLeeuw, and others. On Sunday mornings at 8:30, and on some Friday nights, services are held, but it is better to telephone ahead to see when services are being conducted, as there are security precautions.

Across the main entrance is a Hebrew text: "For I shall enter your house through your abundant kindness." This is part of the text said upon entering a synagogue.

Enter the hall and you are struck by its size and its spiritual atmosphere. The synagogue itself is one huge room. Twelve stone Ionic columns support the women's galleries and symbolize the 12 Tribes of Israel. Low-hanging brass chandeliers hold 1,000 to 1,500 candles, all of which still have to be lit for services. Seventy-two bow-shaped windows adorn the walls and the light easily shines upon a magnificent ark.

Designed by Elias Bourman in 1675, this house of worship took four years to build and cost 186,000 guilders, an enormous sum in the seventeenth century.

The congregation today consists of 500 to 600 members, but attracts some 25,000 visitors a year. It houses unique works of art, many from the sixteenth and seventeenth centuries, and exquisite antique silver.

In 1993, a major restoration was completed and the building regained much of its original beauty.

Officials still wear traditional dark garb with tall hats. When evening services, bar mitzvahs, and high holiday services are held in the main synagogue, the candles are lit. In the winter, a small attached synagogue is used for prayer when the main hall itself is too cold, as the latter is not heated.

The Ets Haim Library, at the Portuguese Synagogue, is open Sundays from 9 A.M. to 1 P.M. Check visiting hours by telephoning 622-6188. This is the library of the Jewish community, one of the major Jewish libraries in the world. It began in 1616 as the library of the Portuguese-Jewish Seminary, an institute that trained rabbis. Its collection contains many remarkable Jewish books, manuscripts, and drawings. There are also copies of famous editions of Hebrew books, such as the books produced by Rabbi Manasseh Ben Israel, one of Dutch Jewry's earliest leaders.

Today, the active synagogues and Jewish center are in the south of the city. Here is a list.

Ashkenazic Synagogues:

Synagogue, 238 Gerard Doustraat is in Jacob Obrechtplein, Amsterdam.

Synagogue, 61 Lekstraat.

Synagogue, 26 Gerrit Vd. Veenstraat.

Synagogue, 105 Linnaeusstraat.

The above synagogues are not far from the Hilton Hotel.

Liberal Synagogue, 8 Jacob Soetendorpstraat, 1079 RM Amsterdam. Tel: 642-35-62. Services are at 8 on Friday evenings and at 10 A.M. on Saturdays. Phone for correct prayer times.

Synagogue, 26 Van der Boechorststraatm, Buitenveldert.

Synagogue, 10 Straat van Messina, Amstelveen.

ORGANIZATIONS

B'nai Akiva, 665 Amstelveenseweg, 1081 JD Amsterdam. Tel: 646-38-72. FAX: 642-58-72.

Beth Chabad, 85 Havikshorst, TP Amsterdam. Tel: 646-60-17.

The Federation of the Dutch Jewish Communities (N.I.K.), 26 Van der Boechorststraat, 1081 BT Amsterdam. Tel: 644-99-68. FAX: 644-26-06. This is the headquarters of the Dutch Jewish community. Also located here are the Ashkenazic community offices. **N.I.H.S., Jewish Community of Amsterdam,** 26 Van der Bolchorststraat, 1081 BT, Amsterdam. Tel: 646-00-46. Call for information on services.

Mensa Student Youth Groups, 13 de Lairessestraat, 1071 NR Amsterdam. Tel: 676-7622. Kosher facility, but call first for reservation.

Habonim-Dror Zionist Youth, 5 Landskroon, Amsterdam. Tel: 644-14-06.

IJAR Nederland, Student and Youth Movement, 13 de Lairessestraat, Amsterdam. Tel: 676-82-26.

MUSEUMS

The Boas Building, Uilenburgerstraat. This is part diamond museum and part showcase, where diamond cutting is observed by visitors who can view exquisite diamonds and jewelry. Most of the original workers were Jews. In the eighteenth century, observant Jews turned Amsterdam into a fine international diamond center. Many still consider it a "city of diamonds." They became involved in diamond finds in Brazil in 1844.

World War II was the darkest period for these men and women. In 1985, the fortieth anniversary of Holland's liberation from Nazi occupation was observed. Ceremonies were conducted at Westerbork, the deportation site from which more than 100,000 Dutch Jews were sent to the death camps by the Nazis in World War II, including more than 2,000 diamond workers.

Today, only about a third of Holland's diamond workers are Jews.

The Jewish Historical Museum (Joods Historisch Museum), 2-4 Jonas Daniel Meijerplein St., 1011 RH Amsterdam. Tel: 6269-945. Admission can be secured by a $10 museum card, which grants entrance to all of Holland's museums. For tour guides for the museum or the area Jewish sites, contact Educational Department, Jewish Historical Museum, P.O. Box 16737, 1001, R.E., Amsterdam. Tel: 31-20-626-9945.

Here we see that several synagogues have been restored to their pre-1828 state, and are connected by modern steel bridges and a glass-covered courtyard. The entrance is on the side street, Nieuwe Amstelstraat, once also a heavily populated Jewish street. Queen Beatrix attended the opening ceremony on May 3, 1987, as did Austrian Chancellor Franz Vranitzky and Nazi-hunter Simon Wiesenthal. It is hard to believe that this, an area now crisscrossed by highways, was, during the eighteenth century, the heart of the Jewish community and the site of four Ashkenazic synagogues that adjoined one another and faced the great Portuguese Synagogue. All that hustle and bustle over the centuries, particularly on Friday nights and the holidays, must have generated warmth and inspiration.

The new museum is a complex of Ashkenazic synagogues connected by passageways and is now said to be the largest center of Jewish culture in Europe. The street is named after Mr. Jonas Meijerplein, a jurist. He was the first Jew in the Netherlands to be admitted to the bar. He reconciled the differences between conflicting Jewish congregations during the rule of the French king Louis Napoleon.

Standing in the square facing the Jewish Historical Museum, we are reminded, according to Hebrew scholar Naftali Herz Weisel, that it all began in 1671, when the Jewish community borrowed the equivalent of $8,000 from the City of Amsterdam

Inside the New Synagogue of the Jewish Historical Museum. (Photo courtesy Jewish Historical Museum; photo by Jeroen Nooter)

The interior of the Great Synagogue, in the Jewish Historical Museum. (Photo courtesy Jewish Historical Museum; photo by Jeroen Nooter)

Jewish Historical Museum. (Photo courtesy Jewish Historical Museum; photo by Jeroen Nooter)

to build the large and luxurious Grote Shul (Great Synagogue). Facing the museum, this is the synagogue on the right. Adjacent to the *shul* were a mikveh and study rooms. But the community soon outgrew the large synagogue. In 1686, on an adjacent plot, the community built the Obbene Shul (the Upstairs Synagogue), so named because of the kosher butcher hall constructed under it. It is now a kosher coffee shop and bookstore. In 1700, the Dritt Shul (Third Synagogue) was established. This synagogue is now used as administrative offices for the museum. Finally, in 1730, the expensive Neie Shul (New Synagogue), which could seat close to 1,000, was constructed. (This is the synagogue on the left.) These four synagogues functioned separately.

The Jewish Historical Museum has a remarkable history of its own. It was founded in 1932 on a floor of the Historical Museum of the City of Amsterdam, which was in the Waag (Weighing) House, built in 1488. When the Nazis invaded Holland in May 1940, the Waag was closed. In 1943, all the Jewish Historical Museum materials were hauled off to Germany. After the war, however, the majority of the artifacts were recovered. They were not damaged because the Germans wanted to furnish a future Nazi museum for remnants of the "extinguished race."

The museum was reborn in 1955, once again on a floor of the Waag. In 1974, the City Council designated the city-owned synagogue complex, deserted and delapidated since the war, as the future home of the museum. In the last year of the war, after the Germans had looted the synagogue buildings, the Dutch people, cold and starving, scavanged for any speck of wood and literally ripped up planks from the buildings. After the war, the Amsterdam city government granted restoration permits. The $14 million project began with the synagogues being integrated into what we know today as the Jewish Historical Museum.

The Ashkenazic Synagogue complex, now a museum, remains a memorial not only of the past, but also a monument to the future. The information in the Jewish Historical Museum buildings is divided into three headings: Jewish identity, elements, and aspects; Jewish religion and culture, illustrated through the Jewish festivals and daily life; and then history of the Jews in the Netherlands. Included in the collection are Torah scrolls and a selection of seventeenth-century Hebrew books printed in Amsterdam. The most beautiful objects in the collection of the Jewish Historical Museum date from the seventeenth and eighteenth centuries. Glass showcases display ritual silver objects. One item that brings interest to all is a silver candelabrum with three oranges. It was a gift from the monarch of Holland. In 1688, Prince William III of Orange obtained a loan of two million Dutch gold pieces without interest from a Jewish merchant, Francisco Lopez de Suasso. William and Mary thus proceeded to England to be joint rulers.

Seen throughout the museum will be exhibitions and photos showing the "gash" in the history of Amsterdam and the Netherlands caused by the Holocaust. And yet, the museum shows that Jewish life has not died but has been rebuilt and is remembered.

The **Museum Route** for the Jewish Historical Museum begins in the renovated eighteenth-century **New Synagogue.** This synagogue was probably designed by city architect G. F. Maybaum. The most impressive part of this building is its glass-domed roof, beautifully decorated both on the inside and outside. The inventory, as well as the richly ornamented ark dating from 1750, was lost in World War II. In the New Synagogue, the visitor is introduced to the theme of Jewish identity. A Holocaust display is located here.

The new section inside the synagogue, the **Gallery** is used for temporary exhibitions. From here you can reach both the Hans Jaffe room and the extensive "mediatheque" or resource center. The well-stocked **mediatheque** with its 5,000 books, 4,500 photographs and slides, hundreds of video and sound tapes, and 3,000 documents is open to the public on weekdays from 1 to 5.

The **Great Synagogue** is the oldest public synagogue in Western Europe. The plan and elevation resemble the Protestant churches of city architect Daniel Stalpaert. When this synagogue was restored, the original shades of blue and green were used. A striking feature is the marble ark dating from 1671, placed against the eastern wall. Also noteworthy are the galleries for both men and women, which have been restored to their original state. And during restoration work, the original ritual bath, or mikveh, was found and can now be seen.

The objects of the Great Synagogue emphasize Jewish rituals and prayer: Portuguese silver, a prayer book that Manasseh Ben Israel printed in 1654, a magnificent silk and satin curtain that hung in front of the ark during circumcisions. The oldest item is a large thirteenth-century holiday prayer book. In the **galleries** of the Great Synagogue, attention is focused on the social history of the Jews in the Netherlands. The main theme deals with the concept of "tzedakah," the Hebrew word meaning "generosity and righteousness." This gallery has been linked via a bridge to the gallery in the New Synagogue, which is used for temporary exhibitions.

Rembrandt House Museum ("Het Rembrandthuis"), 4-6 Jodenbreestraat, 1011 NK Amsterdam. Tel: 6249-486. This house stands across the street from the home of Manasseh Ben Israel, who lived there from 1639 to 1657. That latter structure is gone today. But this charming Rembrandt museum is located in the house of Rembrandt's family and it contains about 250 of his etchings and paintings. The house is open daily from 10 to 5, Sundays and holidays from 1 to 4. Directions: From the Central Station, ride to the Nieuwmarkt subway stop or take Tram No. 9 to Waterlooplein.

As a friend of the Jews, Rembrandt van Rijn (1606–69) is deeply involved in Dutch Jewish history. A friend of Ephraim Bueno and Manasseh Ben Israel, Rembrandt, who literally lived in a Jewish neighborhood, painted Bueno and Ben Israel's portraits. He rarely painted everyday scenes without biblical allusions and the influence of the Jewish neighborhood clearly can be seen in his work. He was often asked by Jews to do their paintings and he loved their biblical faces. He could even mix Ashkenazim with Sephardim. Rembrandt also studied Jewish law and lore. Biblical prints include *Nebuchadnezzar's Dream* and *The Triumph of Mordecai*. There is

Rembrandt House Museum.

also a sketch, *Jews in the Synagogue.* Some say Jozef Israels, Dutch Jewish painter, saved the house from being torn down.

Resistance Museum, 63 Lekstraat, 1079 EM Amsterdam. Tel: 644-97-97. Tram 4, 25. Housed as part of a synagogue, this museum is open Tuesday to Friday, 10 to 5; Saturday, Sunday, and holidays, 1 to 5. Closed Mondays.

The Rijksmuseum, Stadhouderskade. There are many paintings of Jewish interest here, including a number by Rembrandt, most famous of which is *The Jewish Bride* (room 221) and *Jeremiah's Lamentations* (room 220). Also in room 221 is *A Portuguese Synagogue* by Emmanuel de Witte. *Jewish Wedding* by Jozef Israels is on view in room 148. A highlight in this museum of course is Rembrandt's *Night Watch.*

MEMORIAL SITES

The Dutch Playhouse, 24 Plantage Middenlaan. Once a building of joy, then a place of pain and humiliation, today this is a monument. The Nazis took this 1892 structure, a former Dutch theater, at the time called the Jewish Theater, and used it as a detention center before they shipped the Jews off to a concentration camp. Today, only the facade of the playhouse and part of the jagged stone walls are left. The site has been made into a memorial garden. A Ner Tamid (eternal flame) burns in the foyer, and a mourning chamber is filled with paintings from Israel. A plaque commemorates "our Jewish compatriots who were deported between 1940 and 1945 and did not return." The children taken to the theater were often housed in the kindergarten across the street. Many escaped and a plaque on the school building commemorates the fact. The theater is open Monday to Saturday, 10 to 4; Sundays and holidays, 11 to 4.

The Dockworker Statue ("De Dokwerker"), Jonas Daniel Meijerplein Square. This statue, that of a strong, hefty dockworker, stands between the Portuguese Synagogue and the Jewish Historical Museum. Each year on February 25, Dutch Christians and Jews come out and commemorate the bravery of the Dutch people. In 1941, these dockworkers stood up for the rights of their fellow Jewish citizens. Their bravery began when, on February 22, the Nazis rounded up about 400 young Jews for deportation. The Amsterdam dockworkers staged a protest strike that was brutally put down by the Germans. This is perhaps the only time that the population of a city rose against the Third Reich. The statue was designed by Mari Andriessen, who wrote about Amsterdam's collective protest: "Not in Moscow, not in Warsaw, but in Amsterdam, and that is what Amsterdam should always be remembered by."

Gratitude Monument Memorial, Weeperstraat. Established to commemorate those who helped the Jews during World War II, this monument was designed by the sculptor Johan G. Wertheim and erected in 1947 by the Jews of Amsterdam.

The Hague

Kosher food can be obtained at **Jacobs,** 220 Haverkamp the Hague.

Synagogue and Community Center, 11 Cornelis Houtman-straat, 2593 RD the Hague. Tel: 070-347-3201. The Hague's Jewish community headquarters are situated here.

Synagogue, 44 Harstenhoekweg, 2587 SL the Hague (Scheveningen.)

Rotterdam

Synagogue and Community Center, 4 A. B. N. Davidsplein, 3039 KA Rotterdam. Tel: 4669765.

Suggested Reading

Barnouw, Adrian J. *Pageant of Netherlands History.* New York: Longmans, Green, 1952.

Bloom, Herbert I. *The Economic Activities of the Jews of Amsterdam in the 17th and 18th Centuries.* New York: Kennikat Press, 1969.

Farber, Jules B. *Amsterdam, City of the Seventies.* De Haan/ Bussum, 1975.

Frank, Anne. *Anne Frank: The Diary of a Young Girl.* Garden City, N.Y.: Doubleday, 1952.

Gans, Mozes Heiman. *Memorbook: Pictorial History of Dutch Jewry from the Renaissance to 1940.* Bosch & Keuning, D.V., Baarn, Netherlands, 1977.

Gies, Miep, with Alison L. Gold. *Anne Frank Remembered: The Story of the Woman Who Helped to Hide the Frank Family.* New York: Simon & Schuster, 1987.

Hillesum, Etty. *An Interrupted Life: The Diaries of Etty Hillesum 1941–1943.* Translated by Arnold Pomerans. New York: Pantheon, 1984.

Koning, Hans, et al. *Amsterdam.* Amsterdam: Time-Life Books, 1977.

Presser, Jacob. *Ashes in the Wind: The Destruction of Dutch Jewry.* New York: Dutton, 1969.

Roth, Cecil. *A Life of Menasseh Ben Israel: Rabbi, Printer and Diplomat.* New York: Arno Press, 1975. Originally published by The Jewish Publication Society of America, 1934.

BERLIN ☆

GERMANY

• Dusseldorf

• Frankfurt

• Worms

• Munich

Germany
Jews Do Live There

Jews have a hard time with Germany; it doesn't evoke enthusiasm. Germany is not their number one destination, to say the least. "The Third Reich was a lesson in history that still haunts our collective memory," writes Fritz Stern.

Consider that the rebuilt synagogue of Worms was destroyed seven times by Germans, the last time on *Kristallnacht,* November 9, 1938.

Consider that the "greatest concentration of murderous hatred ever attained on earth came about in our own century in the shape of Hitler's Third Reich," as Conor C. O'Brien puts it. No wonder many people feel the place has been poisoned.

In a dozen years, Germany brought about 29 million deaths; including two out of every three Jews in Europe, and one-third of world Jewry, according to Milton Meltzer in *Never to Forget: The Jews of the Holocaust.*

"Sometimes it is impossible to imagine how 35,000 Jews in 65 communities could continue to live in a country of their murderers," wrote Jack Zipes in *Germans and Jews Since the Holocaust.* At World War II's end, there were fewer than 100 Jews under the age of 20 in Germany. By 1994, the Jewish population in Germany was estimated at 60,000.

Why did Jews return to Munich, Berlin, and Frankfurt after the war? How could they? Many returned to collect German reparations and stayed. Despite war destruction, Germany became an economic haven even by the mid-1950s. Many Jews also fled the then Communist-ruled East Germany. Some even married German spouses and settled in West Germany, where mixed marriages made up a high percentage of the Jewish community.

Many of the parents of Jewish children born in postwar Germany did not tell their offspring of their suffering in the Holocaust. After the war, these children grew up in a Germany where, at least for a few decades, no one dared to express anti-Semitic thoughts.

For the Jewish visitor flying over Germany, it is hard to forget that one's fellow Jews were gassed and burned by Germans. Upon seeing factory smokestacks, the Jewish traveler may "see" the smoke rising from the ovens in the concentration camps. Even if you try to avoid going to a camp, the subconscious visions and symbols haunt you.

For example, if you visit Munich, you keep seeing road signs announcing "Dachau," which reminds most Jews of the name of the concentration camp. But actually Dachau, while it is the name of the death camp, is also the name of a suburban town of Munich where the camp was actually located.

Wherever you are in Germany, if you are Jewish you may start calculating the age of every person you meet. "How old were you between 1939 and 1945?" you usually ask yourself silently. But as the years go by, that too is changing. In the 1990s, a German would have to be in his or her sixties or seventies to have been a Nazi involved in the wartime German armed or police forces. One German told me, "My parents did not know what was going on." Few Jews believe that.

Martha Gellhorn, the wife of Ernest Hemingway, writes in *The Face of War* that, as she traveled through Germany at the war's end, people would tell her that no one was a Nazi, and no one had anything against Jews. Then how did it happen?

William L. Shirer quotes Hans Frank, the wartime governor of Poland, as saying "a thousand years will pass and the guilt of Germany will not be erased."

Still for Jews, as hard as it is, there obviously is a Germany before 1933 and after 1945, as Fritz Stern points out. We should never play down the achievements of German Jewry and the extent to which they were woven into the fabric of German society, he adds. One-quarter of all the Nobel Prizes won by Germans in the first third of this century were won by German Jews, says Otto Friedrich.

A Brief History

It all began when the Romans came to Germany. The Jews tagged along with the centurions as they settled the towns along the Rhine. Jewish traders moved by raft and cart, up and down villages of the Rhine, Rhone, and Danube rivers. By 321, they had settled in Cologne.

In the following centuries, Jewish settlements could be found in Mayence, Metz, Worms, Trier, Speyer, Regensburg, and Wurtzburger.

By the ninth century, the words "merchant" and "Jew" had become synonymous, and later "moneylender" would be added to the vocabulary.

Regarded as a group with initiative and business skills, Jews were given guarantees of rights in various places. For five centuries, the Franks—German pagans who had crossed the Rhine—ruled the Jews but left them alone.

The year 1096 heralded in the First Crusade's murderous wrath against Jews. Jewish communities that lived along the Rhine, however, chose a martyr's death. Rather than allow their children to be baptized, Jewish mothers cut their throats. Jews call that *kiddush hashem* ("the sanctification of the name," loyalty to God).

Disaster and riots plagued Jews in the thirteenth and fourteenth centuries. The Black Plague (1348–50) nearly wiped out one-half of the population of Europe. Jews were accused of having poisoned the wells. By now, Germany was nearly "judenrein," "cleansed of Jews." Still, they would return again and again; they were needed for their financial acumen.

The law forbade usury by Christians so, although excluded from the guilds, Jews served as bankers. "The pecuniary motive explains the continuity of Jewish history in Germany," writes H. G. Adler in *The Jews in Germany*. Emperor Frederick II declared in 1296 that the Jews of Germany were "servants of our treasury."

Not until the seventeenth century, after the disastrous Thirty Years' War, were Jews slowly invited back to help rebuild the devastated north. "Germany could live neither with its Jews, nor without them," according to Marvin Lowenthal.

The institution of "Court Jews," or privileged Jews, began in Germany. They were called "shtadlan" (go-betweens) and were the official representatives of the community, so chosen because they were wealthy and influential. Often they put their financial skill to work for the prince and helped prevent anti-Jewish measures. One such leader was Joseph Oppenheimer (1698–1738), known as "Jew Suess." Another was Samuel Oppenheimer (1635–1703), who financed Vienna's military operations against the Turks who had besieged Vienna.

Later the spirit of the French Revolution would move to Germany. In 1812, Wilhelm von Humboldt and Karl August von Hardenberg liberated the Jews of Prussia. Napoleon created the Confederation of the Rhine. But Jewish rights were soon lost when the Holy Alliance defeated the French emperor.

The first Reform Temple was established in Hamburg in 1818. Abraham Geiger (1810–74) was spiritual father and one of the leaders of the Reform Movement. On the other hand, under the leadership of Rabbi Samson Raphael Hirsch (1808–88), a new Orthodoxy was launched in Germany.

Banking became a Jewish enterprise, with family branches all over Europe. The Mendelssohn family banking house developed the banking firm of Bleichroeder. The House of Rothschild, the Warburg family, including Max, S. G., Paul, and Felix Warburg, the Guggenheims, the Lewisohns, the Kuhns, and the Loebs contributed much to German economic growth.

The Revolution of 1848 helped emancipate the Jews in Central Europe.

After the German victory over Austria in 1866 and the establishment of the North German Confederation, the Reichstag passed a resolution banning religious discrimination. The

Constitution of the North German Federation in 1869 ensured full equality, so much so that many cases of assimilation and conversion soon arose. Only Eastern European Jewish immigration into Germany maintained the population level. But then came the anti-Semites: Georg von Schoenerer and Dr. Karl Lueger, as well as Eugen Duehring, Joseph von Treitschke, Houston Stewart Chamberlin, Wilhelm Marr, Alfred Rosenberg, and Adolf Hitler, all spreading hate and fear.

Yet, until Hitler, cases of violence against Jews, such as pogroms and riots, were rare in both Germany and Austria. During World War I, the Zionist headquarters remained in Germany. Moreover, throughout history, German Jews were always respected and envied by their Diaspora co-religionists.

From 1871 to 1914, German Jews comprised about 1 percent of the German population, hovering between the 500,000 and 600,000 figure.

More than 100,000 of the 550,000 German Jews fought in World War I, and 80,000 of them were in the front lines. At least 12,000 died in the war. About 35,000 were decorated, with more than 2,000 promoted to officers, and 23,000 received German awards for bravery.

But by the 1930s, "millions of Germans began to believe that Adolf Hitler, a semi-literate incompetent, a failure in everything he had ever attempted, somehow had the skill and intelligence to solve all the nation's problems," writes Otto Friedrich in his book, *Before the Deluge: A Portrait of Berlin in the 1920's.* As we look back in history, we note the police could have deported him; they did not. Later the democratic world powers could have stopped him before it was too late; they did not. Many Jews thought Nazism would blow over. People do not just pick up and leave their homes, family businesses, or jobs. They did not foresee the catastrophe of Hitler. As Henry Kissinger noted in *The New York Times* on April 24, 1994, "Hitler's advent to power marked one of the greatest calamities in the history of the world. . . . The orgy of killings . . . that it unleashed was the work of one demonic personality."

Of approximately 500,000 German Jews, about 330,000 would flee between 1933 and 1939. Most of them reached the

United States, the United Kingdom, France, and Palestine; the rest would perish.

After the war, the Zionist movement actually opposed Jews returning to Germany, which it called "accursed land." Jews generally do not return to places of tragedy. About 15,000 Jews resettled in Germany. And of these 15,000, only 8,000 would remain; the rest would emigrate to the United States and Israel. By 1986, close to 30,000 German Jews were registered and gave money to the Jewish community. Today about 8,500 Jews live in Berlin, nearly 5,000 in Frankfurt, 1,400 in Hamburg, 1,300 in Cologne, 5,400 in Bavaria, 3,600 in North Rhine Westphalia, and 2,000 in Baden Wurttemberg.

A law exists in Germany that makes it illegal to spread lies about the Nazi war crimes, lies and crimes that insult the memory of the Jewish dead. Anti-Semitic racism is punishable by law. In *Post-Mortem: The Jews in Germany Today,* Leo Katcher wrote that there are many cities and towns where not a single Jew lives. Millions of Germans under 21 still have never known, seen, or spoken to a Jew. Only about 15 percent of the total Jewish population are native Jews, the majority being Eastern Europeans who came after the war, as well as several thousand Israelis and Soviet Jews. That is why some observers, such as Amity Shlaes, feels that "the truth is this: there may be Jews who live in Germany, but there are no more German Jews."

Jewry here is made up of five groups: those who survived the Holocaust; those who returned after World War II from other countries such as England, Palestine, and China in which they had found refuge; those displaced persons or camp survivors who took temporary refuge in Germany after the war; those emigrants and refugees who were attracted to Germany by its economic prosperity or who fled from persecution; and finally the Soviet Jews of the 1980s and 1990s.

What will the new Germany be like regarding Jews and Israel? John McCloy once said, "The world will carefully watch the new Germany, and one of the tests by which it will be judged will be its attitude toward the Jews and how it treats them."

Jews in Germany appear to be economically well-off. Most

do not feel overt anti-Semitism, but they realize that the neo-Nazi extremism has threatened the stability of Central Europe and that means Germany, too. In Germany, it seems the former terrorists have come in from the cold. The unification has brought difficulties in Germans in the West and Germans in the East in comprehending each other. Jews in the 1990s felt the "hostility and discontent." Since 1990, there have been riots and attacks on foreigners . . . sometimes killing them. Murray Gordon, writing in the March/April 1994 issue of *Congress Monthly,* reports that these incidents "have badly scarred the image built over the past 40 years by the German Federal Republic for tolerance and democracy. They are taking place against a background of an increasingly strident German nationalism." He adds that numerous attacks have been carried out against Jewish institutions, synagogues, and Holocaust monuments. Still, he quotes Ignatz Bubis, the chairman of Central Council of Jews in Germany, as saying, "The Germany of today is not the Germany of Weimar. My belief in democracy in Germany, in democratic Germany is still very strong."

Mr. Gordon notes that "until the early 1990's democracy in Germany was easy. . . . Germany lived smugly under the American security blanket"; and it did not have to deal with the problems of the "failed" East German state. No doubt, as the 1990s progress, the neo-Nazis will have to be watched.

The Jews in Germany praise what they call Christian Jewish societies, which are very active and sponsor various projects. One program invites those who were born or lived in Germany before the war to come and visit their former homes. Some municipalities pay the air fare. Others give the visitors spending money, tickets, and a tour.

Many visitors come from Israel. Indeed, most German Jews have visited Israel; the ties between German Jews and Israel are strong. For example, the Jewish State helps Dusseldorf Jewry with teachers, principals, and even rabbis.

Jews raise funds for Israel's institutions. German Jewry was proud to state that, after Holland, they came in second in collecting monies for Israel.

On September 10, 1952, the reparations agreement was signed by the representatives of West Germany and Israel. Reparations came to about $8 billion or 25 billion German marks to Israel direct, while 15 billion marks were paid to individuals. The two nations established diplomatic relations in 1965. Despite obvious negative feelings among Israelis about Germany, Germany is Israel's number two trading partner (after the United States).

In the book *The Federal Republic of Germany at Forty,* edited by Peter H. Merkl, Lily Gardner Feldman argues that the special relationship with Israel, which John McCloy once said would be the test of German rehabilitation, has flourished and has been strengthened over the years, although it may be severely tested over the next decade.

There are ultraconservatives among the conservatives who deny the existence of gas chambers and the Nazis' extermination of millions of Europeans. While they are a minority, their numbers are growing.

German Jews have called upon their government to take stricter measures against neo-Nazi groups. But in the final analysis, it all depends on whether Germany continues to defend its democratic rights against terrorism and dictatorship. If so, Germans also must be ready to explore the Nazi period more deeply.

But Chancellor Helmut Kohl initiated and pursued the commemoration at Bitburg. Many felt that to count the Waffen-S.S. among the victims of Hitler was "historical travesty."

"For no people can step out of its own history and disown it. It is a legacy which cannot be denied," said former Israeli President Chaim Herzog.

Anson Rabinbach and Jack D. Zipes maintain that ever since the establishment of the Federal Republic in 1949, the policy of the West Germans toward Jews has generally been supportive. The obvious reason for this support was to make clear to the world that Germany wanted to overcome its anti-Semitic past. Still the authors say "de-Nazification" was hollow and ritualistic. War criminals were not actively prosecuted in West Germany until after the Eichmann trial of 1960–61.

In a 1988 speech, former German President Richard von Wiezsacher said: "The German nation cannot make others responsible for what it and its neighbors endured under national socialism. . . . Auschwitz remains unique. It was perpetrated by Germans in the name of Germany. This truth is immutable and will not be forgotten."

According to the German ambassador to the United States in *Near East Report,* July 8, 1991, Germany intended to make good on East German promises to pay reparations to Jews who suffered at the hands of the Nazis.

Yet a generation of Germans who were not even born when the Berlin Wall went up finds it hard to shoulder responsibility for the Germany of fifty years ago. Chancellor Kohl pledged on reunification that Germany would fight anti-Semitism and would work to keep alive the memory of the Holocaust.

Notable German Jews

German Jews "identified with Germany as their homeland," according to Leni Yahil, and contributed much to their country's political, social, and cultural life. Here are some outstanding German Jews.

Ferdinand Lassalle, an adherent of Marx, founded the German labor movement. German shipping magnate Albert Ballin directed the Hamburg American line, and was a close friend and advisor to Kaiser William II. Kurt Eisner was a Jewish socialist who headed a People's Republic in Bavaria at the beginning of November 1918; he was assassinated in 1919. Nobel Prize laureate Albert Einstein (1879–1955), known as one of the world's greatest physicists, discovered the theory of relativity. David Ben-Gurion, first prime minister of Israel, invited Einstein to become president of the Jewish State.

Germany also boasts a great list of Jewish writers: Ernest Toller, Jakob Wasserman, Arnold Zweig, Alfred Doblin, Kurt Tucholsky, and Walter Benjamin. German Jewish musicians include Felix Mendelssohn, Jacques Offenbach, Otto Klemperer, Bruno Walter, Fritz Kreisler, Paul Hindemith, Kurt Weill, and many others.

Jewish Berlin

Berlin is not as I pictured it. As the Jewish community of Germany, it is not as I had understood it to be.

There is a new vitality here, partly, it seems, because Germany is one of the richest countries in the world and partly because as Karl E. Meyer wrote in *The New York Times,* "it boasts world-class art museums, exemplary subways and a pulsating street life reminiscent of Brecht and Weill's 'Three Penny Opera.'" During the past few years, several thousand Russian Jews have come to the Jewish community and are being welcomed by German Jews. Russian Jews, who will probably continue to come here, may help revitalize the Berlin Jewish community, at least in numbers, until they can once again partake in free Jewish expression.

Like it or not, the unification of East and West Germany has affected everyone, even the cantor in the drab surroundings of his synagogue at Rykerstrasse 53, in the eastern section of Berlin. He does not always get a minyan on Saturday mornings, but he tells tour after tour of East Germans that the former government, while it did not exactly suppress religion, was not very enthusiastic about it.

True, about 8,500 Jews live in Berlin, but almost none of them were born here. And with the arrival of Russian Jews, with Germany one of the richest countries in the world, with Berlin once again the nation's official capital, a Jewish community will exist in the future, too. Much obviously depends on the route traveled by a united Germany. Despite the many overall problems of reunification, such as unemployment in the eastern sector of Germany and the need to pour investment money to upgrade the east zone, the economy eventually will improve.

But, as noted, the problem of mass immigration into the country already has caused escalation of neo-Nazi violence. This development has set off an alarm in Germany's Jewish community.

Still, Jews will probably settle down here again for a number of reasons. Berlin is the major city between Moscow and Paris, a bridge between East and West. (Lenin said, "He who has

The Russian Memorial in Berlin, near the Brandenburg Gate. (Photo by Howard Green)

A memorial to Moses Mendelssohn near the cemetery in former East Berlin.

Berlin, has Germany, and he who has Germany, has Europe.")
Berlin has joined Paris, Brussels, and Rome as being "where
the action is." Jews will come to this creative center, mostly for
business, economic, and professional opportunities. How they
will live and how they will withstand the pressure of memory
cannot be foretold. Russian Jews say that they had it so bad in
the former Soviet Union, that the past here does not affect
their functioning in society. Of all the cities in Germany, Berlin
and its landmarks remind you of the Nazis. It is "an open air
museum of the nation's history": Hitler's bunker-grave in the
form of a mound of dirt; the Reichstag; Unter den Linden and
the Brandenburg Gate under which the jackbooted Nazi hooli-
gan army marched singing "Death to the Jews" and "Tomorrow
the World."

Jews who do come here say this city is attractive, scintillating,
and creative. Outwardly, it throbs: the opera, the state library,
the university, and the Kurfürstendamm, that exciting main
boulevard that declares, "Berlin could not be Berlin without
me, the Ku-damm."

Berlin, which once rivalled Paris and London culturally,
inspired the Jews in the nineteenth and early twentieth century, as Paris influenced the world, according to Barnet
Litvinoff. Henry Adams once described the city as a "poor,
keen-witted provincial town, simple, dirty, uncivilized," and
Mark Twain named it "German Chicago." This "European New
York" of 3.5 million people evolved over the years along an
east-west axis centered by the Brandenburg Gate, that gigantic
neo-Grecian portal supported by 12 Doric columns, 65 feet
high, and surmounted by a sculpture of four horses drawing
the chariot of the Goddess of Victory.

"Athens on the Spree," they called it. Now, of course, "there
is one big difference," wrote Frederick Kempe in the *Wall Street
Journal* of June 20, 1991. "Berlin's once-large Jewish community which was at the center of its cultural life, is gone and that
has left Berlin a more provincial and less diverse city."

Jews, who never numbered more than 5 percent in Berlin,
arrived there in the thirteenth century. A cemetery was established in 1543. In 1671, Elector Friedrich Wilhelm admitted 50

Jewish families from Vienna and the community grew. The first synagogue was built in 1714.

Moses Mendelssohn (1729–86), philosopher, settled in Berlin in 1743. With access to the king, his home also became a center for intellectuals of the Enlightenment (Haskalah). The son of a poor Torah scribe, Mendelssohn was born in Dessau. This eighteenth-century scholar and philosopher helped launch the renascence of Jewish culture. Mendelssohn was a friend of the famous German Christian writer, Gotthold Ephraim Lessing, who immortalized him in the play, *Nathan the Wise*. Mendelssohn said that Jews should abandon Yiddish, purify Hebrew, and learn German. In 1768, he published his translation of the Pentateuch for his co-religionists. His follow-ers were called "maskilim" (the Enlightened). They urged Jews "to broaden their minds by studying the culture of those among whom they lived."

The homes of Henriette Herz, Rahel Varnhagen, and Dorothea Schlegel also became centers of the Jewish elite of Berlin.

After the Franco-Prussian War of 1870, Berlin replaced Vienna as the center of the German-speaking world. Jews flocked to Berlin. By the 1930s there were about 150,000 to 180,000 Jews in a city that, before the war, maintained several hundred synagogues and now has seven or eight. About one-third would be murdered in the extermination camps, and the rest would flee. Hitler took power in 1933. Four months later, a boycott of Jewish stores in Germany began; the rest is histo-ry. In 1945, Berlin was 2.6 billion cubic feet of rubble. Now rebuilt, the city covers more than 550 square miles, is bigger than Chicago, five times the size of the District of Columbia, 15 times the size of Bermuda, and about as large as the five bor-oughs of New York City.

One thing about Berlin that the tourist will see is the unprecedented building boom in office towers and retail cen-ters that reunification has brought to Germany's once and future capital. There are 31 major projects under way. In the mid-1990s, Potsdamer Platz was probably the "largest con-struction site in Europe," wrote Stephen Kinzer, on October

13, 1993, in *The New York Times.* For developers, Berlin's attractiveness now comes primarily from the fact that the national government will move here by the year 2000. Berlin is sure to be Germany's leading city and the gateway to expanding markets in Eastern Europe. We must remember Poland is two hours away.

By the mid-1990s, Berlin had about 3.5 million inhabitants and is considered one of the least dense great cities of the world.

And Berlin, considered to be located at the most important crossroads in Central Europe, is vying with Prague as Central Europe's most cosmopolitan city. This point emphasizes the fact that with reunification, Germany has moved from being an Atlantic state to a Central European state and that will be extremely significant by the twenty-first century.

SITES IN BERLIN

Berlin Wall. A 1.3-mile stretch of the Berlin Wall remains. It boasts graffiti and paintings, like an outdoor gallery, with huge, bizarre drawings. By the way, on one of those paintings, there is half a six-pointed Jewish star next to a cracked glass, symbolizing *Kristallnacht.*

Community Center, Oranienburgerstrasse 28. Tel: 282-3327. Located in the eastern part of Berlin, not far from the synagogue on Rykerstrasse 53, the building contains a library and lecture hall. Before unification, the East Berlin Jewish community numbered between 200 and 400 persons.

Day School, Bleibtreustrasse. This day school is the pride of the Jewish community. Hebrew is taught here and spoken as there are several Israeli teachers on staff. Kosher luncheon is given to the children. Holidays are celebrated.

Jewish Cemetery, Herbert Baumstrasse 45, Berlin-Weissensee, in the northeast suburbs of former East Berlin. Tel: 365-3330. These graves evoke the days of the mid-nineteenth century when Berlin's flourishing and gifted Jewish community played an influential role in the cultural life of the city. Baum incidentally was a German Jewish resistance fighter executed by the Nazis in 1943.

The Jewish Center, Fasanenstrasse 79/80, 1000 Berlin 12. Tel: 884-2030. This is the headquarters of the Berlin Jewish community and is located not far from the Kurfürstendamm, near the Kempinski, Bristol, and Steigenberger hotels. This attractive, well-designed Jewish community center was built in 1959 on the Fasanenstrasse site of the Great Synagogue, which seated about 1,700 persons and was completely destroyed on *Kristallnacht* in 1938. As you face the building, you will see, incorporated right into the facade around the front door, the old portal that once stood above the former main synagogue entrance. The new building was also constructed with a column from the old synagogue, thus showing the crack in human relations on the one hand but also hope for the future.

The center is the focal point of many activities in Berlin, as the community center sponsors lectures, concerts, and dances. A synagogue in the building is used for major holidays such as Rosh Hashanah and Yom Kippur.

In the lobby are photos taken on *Kristallnacht,* which still sears the minds of German Jews. On November 7, 1938, Herschel Grynszpan, age 17, an exile from Germany who was living in Paris, shot Ernst vom Rath, the third secretary of the German Embassy in Paris. He said he had avenged his parents, who had been among those dumped on the Polish border, a common Nazi tactic and practice. The Germans knew that the Poles would refuse entry to Jews. When vom Rath died, the Gestapo organized a bloodbath designed as a "spontaneous reaction of the people." The date was November 8-9, 1938. *Kristallnacht,* this "Night of Crystal," derives its name from the shattering of glass, as the Nazis literally went berserk when they broke the stained-glass windows of synagogues throughout Germany. The broken glass littered the streets on the morning of the ninth. Edmond Engelman called it "the glitter of the night's flying glass." About 90 Jews were killed during *Kristallnacht,* and about 7,500 Jewish shops were destroyed. Around 25,000 Jews were thrown into concentration camps. Approximately 200 synagogues were destroyed, shops and offices were looted, and plate-glass windows were smashed. Yet it was the Jews who were fined one billion Reichsmarks.

Along the wall of the Jewish Center stands a map of the concentration camps in Nazi Germany during the war. (Photo by Howard Green)

The center also contains a library and kosher restaurant:

Library. Tel: 884-2035. Nine to 10,000 volumes in all languages, which may be circulated. Most of the 2,000 visitors each year are non-Jewish. Arcady Fried is head librarian and speaks English. He welcomes visitors and the library is open to the public.

Kosher restaurant, second floor. Open every day from 11:30 A.M. to 3:30 P.M. and 6:30 to 11 P.M., on Shabbat from 11:30 A.M. to 2:30 P.M., a buffet on Tuesdays. Those who would like to eat in the restaurant on the Sabbath can order and pay for their meals beforehand. This is the only kosher restaurant in Berlin.

The Reichstag. Above the entrance to the Reichstag, which overlooks the Spree River and the famous park, Tiergarten, are three words: "DEM DEUTSCHEN VOLKE." This neoclassical structure of the past soon will be the seat of Germany's parliament. If you go inside, you will see an exhibition entitled "Questions of German History," which covers the Holocaust period and German efforts to establish democracy. Outside is a plaque listing the names of 97 members of the last all-German parliament who were murdered by the Nazis.

The Reichstag was built in 1894 when Germany was still a monarchy, and it was from a second-floor window there that the German Republic was proclaimed in 1918. In 1933, the building was gutted in a mysterious fire that Adolf Hitler used as an excuse to impose emergency rule. An historic event occurred on May 5, 1945, when Soviet troops raised their flag above the Reichstag, ending the "Thousand-year Reich." After the War, the Reichstag for many years remained an empty shell. The Berlin Wall, which was put up in 1961, ran just behind the eastern facade. Early in the morning on October 3, 1990, hundreds of thousands of ecstatic Germans gathered in front of the Reichstag to celebrate the unification of Germany. Parliament later voted to return from Bonn to its traditional home in Berlin. It has already held several sessions in the Reichstag, and is to move there permanently in 1998. The administrative government will perhaps be in Berlin by the year 2000.

Singles Club, Pasauer 4. Meets Thursday evenings at 8.

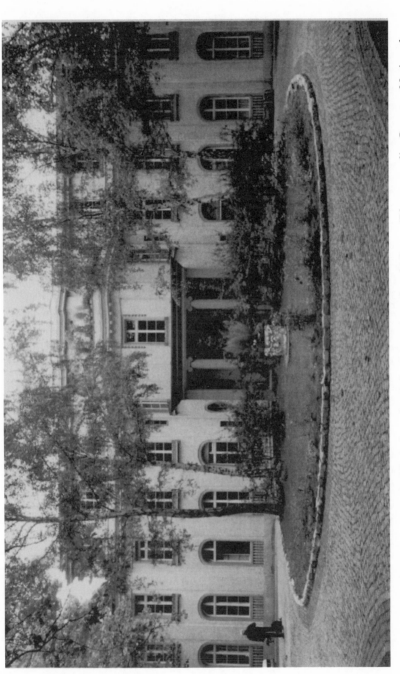

The villa at Wannsee where the Nazis formulated the destruction of world Jewry. (Photo credit: German National Tourist Office)

Walther Rathenau House, Koenigsalle 65. Now a private building containing offices, this was formerly the villa of the noted Jewish industrialist, philanthropist, and statesman. Born in Berlin in 1867, Rathenau managed A.E.G., the electric light complex that was founded by his father. While foreign minister, he negotiated the Rapallo Treaty with the U.S.S.R. in April 1922, which eliminated the political isolation of Germany. He was assassinated by Fascist sympathizers.

Wannsee Memorial—A villa in Wannsee, which is a suburb on the southwestern fringes of Berlin and located at No. 56-58 on the west side of the Wannsee Lake, was the site where members of the Nazi Party, the gestapo, and the German Foreign, Interior, and Justice ministries agreed that Jews in Europe should "fall away," or as Adolf Eichmann, one of the participants said, "we were all happy to be taking part in the final solution of the Jewish question." The meeting was held on January 20, 1942, and was called the Wannsee Conference. *The Economist* magazine wrote on February 1, 1992, that the "Wannsee meeting was not even a conference, but rather a business-like 'workshop' on how best to implement Hitler's Final Solution of the Jewish Question. Reinhard Heydrich, the security chief, was at pains to impress upon the assembled bureaucrats that he was in charge of the whole operation." The villa was probably the first permanent memorial in Germany to the six million Jews who died in the Holocaust, according to Stephen Kinzer in *The New York Times,* January 20, 1992. A permanent exhibit, entitled "Reminder for the Future," exists in the building and the exhibition is from 10 A.M. to 6 P.M. and Sunday, 2 to 6 P.M. Visiting the villa, one can see the handsome salon where the conference itself was held. On the second floor of the building is a library that contains thousands of books about Nazism, anti-Semitism, the genocide, and related topics. There is also a collection of videos, microfilm texts, and documents from the Nazi era.

SYNAGOGUES IN BERLIN

Synagogue, Joachimstalerstrasse 13. This Orthodox synagogue, originally built as a Masonic lodge in 1902 and

A TRAVEL GUIDE TO JEWISH EUROPE

converted into a synagogue after World War II, is the popular
house of worship. Also located here are offices of Jewish organizations such as the Jewish Agency, the Jewish National Fund,
the Keren Hayesod, and offices to help Soviet Jews. Services
are at 6 Friday evening and 9:30 Saturday morning. The synagogue holds many activities, including a Passover seder. Out-of-
town visitors are welcomed at services. In the synagogue you
often see Russian Jews coming for help and aid. They are welcomed. Right now, I am told, Russian Jews probably repress the
German past. They feel they have suffered so much that nothing can stop them from adjusting in this well-off, free country
that also hands out local and federal subsidies to them.

Synagogue, Pestalozzistrasse 14. This is a famous synagogue.
An organ is used during services. Open only at prayer times.

Synagogue, Frankelufer 10-12.

Synagogue, Dernburgstrasse 26.

Synagogue, Rykerstrasse 53. This red brick Moorish structure, built in 1903, is located in former East Berlin. Services
may not take place according to schedule, for this congregation is not always able to obtain a minyan (quorum of 10 men
needed for a service), even on a Saturday morning. By the way,
the reason the building was not destroyed during *Kristallnacht*
was that the Germans were afraid the apartment buildings next
door would catch fire if they torched the synagogue. Visiting
this area now, you notice the grime and the run-down buildings—a few peppered with shrapnel from the war, a symbol of
East Berlin under communism. What will it be like in five
years? Many believe that the West Germans will succeed in
rebuilding the homes and lives of their Eastern brothers and
sisters. According to Paul Goldberger in *The New York Times
Magazine* on February 5, 1995, during the Nazi era, the
Rykerstrasse synagogue "was only a couple of miles from the
headquarters of the Gestapo."

Synagogue, Oranienburgerstrasse 30. This great synagogue
with its Moorish style was set ablaze in 1938 and further gutted
during the war by the Allied bombing of the city in 1943. This
was once the heart of Jewish life in Berlin. It is intended to be
used as a museum and research center. According to Carol

Herselle Krinsky, writing in *Synagogues of Europe,* it was the largest synagogue in the world when completed in 1866. "The fact that the Jews could build a synagogue that was as visually impressive as a church, located in central Berlin and on a street rather than a lane, marked a significant victory," she says, adding, "the synagogue, representing the achievements of modern technology and civilization, remained as a skeletal presence besides the Jewish community office building in the former East Berlin." The reworked facade was completed in 1991, the 125th anniversary of the original dedication. The synagogue's exotic dome, topped by a gilded Star of David, was restored. Over the main entrance of the structure is an inscription in Hebrew, "Open ye the gates, that the righteous nation which keepeth the truth may enter in" (Isaiah 26:2). The building was still under construction in 1992 but is expected to have opened by 1995. A modern museum of Jewish life in Berlin will occupy part of the former vestibule. The synagogue is near the S-1 and S-2 underground lines. Next door are a kosher restaurant and cafe.

Jewish Community House, Oranienburgerstrasse 31, Berlin. Tel: (30) 280-1305, next door to the synagogue. Located here are historical exhibits on Jewish life in the capital and memorabilia.

Further information on the synagogue and community house can be obtained by calling the New Synagogue Foundation, (30) 280-1250.

MUSEUMS

Checkpoint Charley Museum. For 40 years, the world experienced the "cold war" and no two words better describe the memory of those four decades in Berlin than "Checkpoint Charley." The sentry point that separated East and West Berlin is today a noteworthy museum. It shows how the famous Berlin Wall went up in August 1961, and came down in late 1989 and early 1990.

The Jewish Museum for now is housed in the Berlin Museum, Lindenstrasse 79. It contains a Judaica room and is open from 11 A.M. to 6 P.M., Tuesday to Sunday. But the bulk of the collection is in the Martin Gropius-Bau. Plans have been drawn up for the Jewish Museum to be an extension of the Berlin Museum. "It will contain religious artifacts, a panoply of art, from paintings to fashion to furniture, and a section devoted to the achievements of Jews who spent time in German concentration camps," according to Paul Goldberger in *The New York Times Magazine* on February 5, 1995.

Martin Gropius-Bau Museum, Stresemannstrasse, Berlin. A fine exhibit of Judaica. On display, there are more than 2,500 objects of ancient tablets, illuminated prayer books, Zionist posters, and portraits of Jewish heroes. Facing the Museum is a desolate plot of land that was Hitler's bunker.

MEMORIAL SITES

German Resistance Memorial Center, Stauffenbergstrasse 13. Also known as the Bendeerblock. The victims were those generals who rose against Hitler on July 20, 1944. At the wall in the courtyard, a number of generals were shot. A memorial is located at the spot. On the second floor of the former Army High Command building is a museum devoted to the entire range of the German resistance, including the White Rose movement. The White Rose movement was founded by two Munich students, a brother and sister, who were arrested and executed. Each of the 26 rooms has an exhibit dedicated to a different aspect of the Third Reich and its opponents. Also on display is a section devoted to resistance by Jews.

A **Rosa Luxemburg plaque** stands alongside the Landwehr Canal in Berlin, not far from the zoo garden area. There is also a square and a street in former East Berlin named after Rosa Luxemburg, who was born on March 5, 1871, in Russian Poland and who emigrated to Germany in 1888. Imprisoned during World War I, she and Karl Liebknecht formed the Spartacus Union.

In October 1918, two German battleships mutinied and hundreds of thousands of Berliners, joining the sailors, poured into the streets calling for a revolution. Liebknecht, who led radical left-wing Spartacus Union, which became the Communist party at the end of 1918, prepared to proclaim a

Soviet Republic, with Rosa as a co-founder. Near civil war atmosphere existed; some called it the German Revolution of 1918. But the Free Corps Army crushed the workers and the army picked up Luxemburg and Liebknecht.

The case against them was shaky. Both had moderated their stand and neither seemed to be murderous Bolshevik types, it is said. "Red Rosa," who had taken part in the 1905 Russian uprising, had urged an end to violence. But the army, while moving them to a prison, shot them and dumped their bodies into the Landwehr Canal. A stamp was issued by the East German government in 1955 that depicted Luxemburg as "leader of the German Workers Movement."

"Some of the older men and women in the Communist Party in East Berlin were Jewish. Their ties to the Party and its orthodoxies had to do with the 1930s and with an anti-Nazi movement that found a home and a raison d'etre in the Communist underground," writes Jane Kaplan. Until the Communist regime fell over the winter-spring of 1989–90, the East Germans never apologized for the Holocaust. On April 12, 1990, the East German Parliament admitted "joint responsibility on behalf of the people for the humiliation, expulsion and murder of Jewish women, men and children. We feel sad and ashamed and acknowledge the burden of German history. We ask the Jews of the world to forgive us. . . . We ask the people of Israel to forgive us for the hypocrisy and hostility of official East German policies toward Israel and for the persecution and degradation of Jewish citizens also after 1945 in our country. . . ." Yet since unification occurred, Jews have begun to worry about the fact that the new freedom has brought out into the open popular anti-Semitism, which had been nurtured, but kept under wraps, by the former East German Communist leaders who also were very hostile toward Israel.

Dusseldorf

Dusseldorf includes an "old town" section: tourist pubs, boutiques, art galleries, an area where one can hear languages from all over the world.

The "desk of heavy industry," Dusseldorf is home to many large corporate headquarters. The region is a very highly industrialized part of Germany, which now has one of the highest standards of living in the world.

Jews have gone back to this urban, vibrant, cosmopolitan, and charming Rhine River city. There are about 2,000 Jews in Dusseldorf out of a total population of 600,000. This metropolis contains the fourth largest Jewish community in Germany, following Berlin, Frankfurt, and Munich.

What strikes one immediately about the community is that 90 percent of the Jewish population is not made up of German Jews, but mainly of Jews who emigrated from Eastern Europe. In recent years, too, a number of Israelis also took up residence in Dusseldorf.

Jews are attracted to Dusseldorf because it is an artistic and cultural center. It is known as the Paris of Germany because of its fashion industry and famous boulevard of designer shops called the Koenigsallee, which is the heart and showplace of the city. The chic avenue is called the "Ko." Dusseldorf has been described as a "brash town flush with new money and the financial center for the industrial Ruhr."

Here are a few places to visit in Dusseldorf.

Heine Statue, in a small park at Schwanmarkt (a square and park) on Haroldstrasse. Heinrich Heine (1797–1856), the famous Jewish writer and poet who lived in both Germany and France, once wrote that his birthplace, Dusseldorf, "is very beautiful. When you are far away from it, you think of it and you get a strange feeling that says, 'I was born there and I feel as if I would have to go back there immediately.'" Heine was one of Dusseldorf's distinguished citizens.

Heinrich Heine Institute, Bilkerstrasse 14. Original manuscripts of "The Lorelei" and "The Rabbi of Bachrach" are housed in this museum. A great poet, Heine accepted baptism, the "entree card into European culture." Still, he wrote, "I make no bones about my Jewishness to which I have not returned because I never left it." Heine was born in Dusseldorf. In 1831, he emigrated to Paris, where he died in 1856.

In "The Lorelei," he wrote, "When I think of Germany in the night, I am robbed of my sleep. . . ." Heine also said, "What we now call the hatred of the proletariat against the rich was formerly called Jew hatred." Except for the French Jewish writer Marcel Proust, there was no Jew who could hold a candle to Heine. He feared grave developments in the near future: "Germany is still a little child—but the sun is its nurse. The sun does not suckle it with soothing milk, it suckles it with wild flames."

Synagogue, Zietenstrasse 50. Tel: 480-312 or 480-313. Before the war, there was only one synagogue in Dusseldorf, which then had a population of about 5,000 Jews. The synagogue, then located on Kasernenstrasse, was destroyed in 1938 and it is now the site of the *Handelsblatt,* the *Wall Street Journal* of Germany. A stone monument recalls the synagogue.

The synagogue in Dusseldorf calls itself Liberal, meaning it closely resembles the Conservative Movement of Judaism in the United States. Friday evening services are at 6 in the winter, Shabbat morning services are at 9:15, and morning services during the week are at 7:30. There is no kosher restaurant in Dusseldorf, but a kosher kitchen exists at the synagogue's community center and arrangements can be made for kosher meals.

Dusseldorf Memorial Center, Muhlenstrasse, 29, Dusseldorf. Open Tuesday through Sunday. Exhibits and memorials focus on how the Nazi era affected the city. Opened in 1987, it shows the visitor how the Germans themselves remember. There is a memorial book of 2,213 names, the names of Dusseldorf Jews who were deported. Exhibits are in German.

Frankfurt

Located at the center of Western Europe is Frankfurt-am-Main, the financial capital of Germany. Just gaze at the modern all-glass high-rise offices and you can see why Germany is the economic colossus that it is. Although Frankfurt has only 627,000 people, this Rhine-Main industrial area takes in nearly 400 banking concerns. But then, Frankfurt always has been a center of trade and commerce. Just stand on one of the bridges over the Main River and you can see why trade flourished here.

Frankfurt is also the home of Goethe. His home, **Goethehaus,** is open to the public at Grosser Hirschgraben 23. He lived in this house—now a wonderful museum—from his birth until the age of 26.

Some of the famous Jewish native sons of Frankfurt include, of course, the Rothschilds, as well as the artist Moritz Oppenheim, Erik Erikson, Nahum Goldmann, and Daniel Cohn-Bendit. Martin Buber was a professor at Frankfurt University during the Weimar Republic years. Buber, who later emigrated to Israel, sought to resurrect the heritage of Chassidism for the modern Jew and offered his mystical view of the Jewish people. Leopold Sonnemann was the Jewish founder of one of Germany's most prestigious newspapers, *Die Frankfurter Zeitung.*

The book fairs of Frankfurt were always attended by Jewish printers and booksellers. Jewish book people from the United States and Israel still come to the Frankfurt Book Fair, which attracts nearly 250,000 persons. In fact, Sohar, the kosher restaurant here in Frankfurt, is usually the scene of a dinner of Jewish book dealers sponsored by the city's Jewish community.

Jews probably already traded in this flourishing city in the twelfth century. We know that a massacre occurred in 1241. But to Jews, Frankfurt meant the Rothschilds and the ghetto.

JEWISH SITES IN FRANKFURT

The Ghetto. In 1462, the Jews of Frankfurt were transferred to a specially constructed street, known as the Judengasse. It was a ghetto that was enclosed within walls and gates. The Jews possessed their own quarters, but the area could not be enlarged.

The Rothschilds once lived in the ghetto. In the 1560s, Isaac Elchanan, the first Rothschild, obtained a house here that displayed a red sign on the board of a shield, "rot schild" meaning "red sign." While those descendants might have moved, the name Rothschild stuck. On February 23, 1743, Mayer Amschel Rothschild was born. He later established a relationship with

William of Hanau, who loved coin collecting. Mayer Amschel would offer him coins and William in return offered a patronage that eventually blossomed into the Rothschild financial empire.

By 1750, there were 3,000 men, women, and children in the Frankfurt ghetto—all crammed into 200 houses. The building regulations made it impossible to see into the houses of Christians. The side windows of the Jews were walled in and pasted over. The Jews were restricted to the Judengasse, afterwards known as the Bornestrasse; the street still exists. The Jews were locked in after sunset on weekdays and as early as 4 o'clock on Sundays. On certain holidays and festive public occasions, they were forced to remain indoors during the day and were let out only in the evening.

The Bornestrasse is near the Zeil, a pedestrian mall. To get to the Judengasse (Bornestrasse) from the Zeil, head south on Fahrgasse and make a quick left to Ander Staufenmauer. You'll pass through the arch of what was the city wall in the twelfth century and became the ghetto wall in the fifteenth century.

In 1796, the French Revolutionary Army liberated the Jews of Frankfurt, and in 1798, the prohibition on leaving the ghetto on Sundays and holidays was abolished.

Frankfurt became a center of Reform Judaism. In 1845, a conference of rabbis sympathizing with the Reform movement was held there. A leading member was theologian Abraham Geiger, an early German Reform rabbi, first in Frankfurt and then Berlin. Emancipation of the Jews of Frankfurt came in 1864.

Before the Nazis came to power, Frankfurt had a higher percentage of Jewish citizens than any other German city, including Berlin; and Jewish patronage was responsible for the establishment of many of the city's internationally known institutions, including its university and its paper, *Die Frankfurter Zeitung*.

The Bornestrasse Synagogue occupied the same site as the ghetto synagogue until it was destroyed on *Kristallnacht*. A plaque on the building that now houses a city statistical office identifies the site.

The configuration of the street was changed by the Allied bombings of World War II—it now comes to a dead end at a parking lot. Just past the synagogue plaque, the street now curves in the opposite direction from the old Judengasse. The Rothschild home probably stood in a place that is now one block over, near the Canon Copier store on Kurt Schumacherstrasse.

The Frankfurt Municipal Library contains the largest collection of Judaica in Germany, about 25,000 volumes and 325 manuscripts.

The Jewish Community Center in Frankfurt (Judische Gemeinde Frankfurt), Westendstrasse 43, 6000 Frankfurt-am-Main. Tel: 740-7215. The first time the visitor sees this massive structure, he should go to the other side of the building on Savignystrasse 66. On this impressive side, one sees a menorah set high above the entrance. But to the left is a single, blank tablet of law with cracks to symbolize the break between the Germans and the Jewish people. There are about 5,000 Jews in Frankfurt and most make this their center of activity. They sponsor a day school that goes up to the seventh grade. Lectures, movies, senior citizen clubs, and talks by Israeli leaders all add to the program mix offered by this facility. It also contains a gym.

Sohar Kosher Restaurant is located in the Jewish Community Center. Tel: 75-2341. The proprietors are Israelis. The Sohar serves kosher and Israeli-style dishes; Shabbat meals can be ordered in advance.

Jewish Museum, Untermainkai 14-15, 6000 Frankfurt. Tel: 212-8805 or 212-5000. Open Tuesday to Sunday, 10 A.M. to 5 P.M.; Wednesday until 8 P.M. Closed Monday. Significantly, the museum was opened on November 9, 1988, in the former Rothschild Palais on the occasion of the fiftieth anniversary of *Kristallnacht.* The Jewish Museum is the largest of its kind in the German-speaking world. It features a history of Jews in Germany from the Middle Ages to the present with the Jewish community as the main example. The building was the home of Baron Carl von Rothschild and housed a vast library now in the Municipal and University Library. In the words of Georg Heuberger, the director, "the aim of the Jewish Museum is to provide the knowledge relating to the history, culture and religion of the Jewish people necessary for a dialogue between Jews and non Jews." The museum, one of the finest in Europe, includes exhibits on Jewish life, rituals, festivals and holidays, a 1731 Haggadah, and portraits of Gotthold Ephraim Lessing and Moses Mendelssohn.

A video tape shows the history of the Jews of Frankfurt.

The exhibit on the Holocaust is outstanding. A memorial wall bears the names of 11,000 Jews of Frankfurt who lost their lives. It is quite moving!

The museum contains a wooden scale model of the Frankfurt ghetto. The model of both sides of the Judengasse (street) shows Jewish life in the Middle Ages, and was made from plans drawn in 1711. There is an exhibition on the architecture of the synagogue, as well as on Jewish holidays and religious items. Other exhibits are about achievements in the area of civil rights, the development and social structure of the Jewish community, integration (a superb exhibit), assimilation, and anti-Semitism. There is a well-documented section on the Nazi era. Many non-Jews visit this building; it is in effect a learning center.

Book-Cafe is a very popular institution in the Jewish Museum in Frankfurt. Hanna Solomon manages this book store where one can find German-Jewish and Israeli newspapers and magazines on the racks.

In a room whose theme is the struggle for the Jewish State, Americans will be pleased to see the American flag flown high in a photo exhibit of the liberation of the concentration camp at Dachau. A poster in the display says, "Freedom can only be with the realization of a Jewish National Home in Palestine."

An electronic encyclopedia on Jewish subjects and a bookshop and cafeteria are included in this impressive building.

The Jewish Museum is not the only museum on what is called the Museum Row, Museum Mile, or Museum Embankment. In recent years, Frankfurt, which in 1994 celebrated its 1,200-year anniversary, embarked on much museum construction and it now also is considered a city of art. It has established a Museum Embankment containing a number of museums on Schaumainkai, the tree-lined avenue along the left bank of the Main River. The Jewish Museum is always mentioned as part of this museum complex, although technically, it is located across the river, on Untermainkai, 14-15. Included in the museums that are in the area are the Museum of Applied Arts, Museum of the City of Frankfurt, German Film Museum, German Architecture Museum, Stadel Art Institute, Liebreghaus, an extensive collection of sculpture, and the Jewish Museum. It is also not far from the excellent Frankfurter Hof hotel, Bethmannstrasse 33.

Rothschild Park. The affluent Jews of Frankfurt lived in the Westend and this is still the home of many Jews, and their cultural and religious center. The park once housed the mansion of the Goldschmidt-Rothschild family and was located behind the Opernplatz.

Senior Citizen Center, Bornheimer Landwehr 79b. Tel: 43-96-02. The Atereth-Zvi Synagogue is also located here.

SYNAGOGUES IN FRANKFURT

Synagogue Baumweg, Baumweg 5-7.

Synagogue, Roderbergweg 29.

Synagogue, Henry and Emma Budge-Stiftung, Wilhelmshoherstrasse 279. Tel: 47-87-10.

Westend Synagogue, Freiherr-vom-Stein-strasse. This is the only Frankfurt synagogue to have survived *Kristallnacht*. The grey stone building features vaulting stone arches on four sides under a massive cupola, with Star of David stained-glass windows in blue and white. Although a Liberal synagogue before the war, it is now Orthodox, as are all the Frankfurt synagogues.

Munich

About 4,000 Jews now live in the Bavarian capital. One thing is certain: they want, and work for, an active Jewish community. And they don't like to be asked, "How can Jews live in Germany?" To them, and to the other 35,000 Jews in Germany, this is their home. Most of the young people are professionals and of the middle class. Only one-third of Munich's Jews are native-born; Israelis and Polish and Russian Jews make up the rest. Many of the Russian Jews who emigrated from the U.S.S.R. did not go on to Israel.

Following Berlin and Hamburg, Munich is Germany's third largest industrial city. This warmhearted metropolis is famous for its art collections, its theater, the largest museum of science and technology in the world, and the largest university. Over a million people reside here in Germany's "secret capital." It is said that 60 percent of all Germans would like to live in this area. Surrounded by green valleys and dark green forests, the Muncheners are not poor in nature or wealth; on the contrary, they are probably the richest in all of Germany.

This city of Old-World elegance is a center of art and culture. Alongside its art galleries and museums are open-air beer gardens and the Hofbrauhaus. The Oktoberfest was once described as a Teutonic drunk scene. Fine buildings of every period, grand boulevards and squares, and the Marienplatz all highlight this city. Theodor Herzl, father of modern Zionism, wanted Munich as the seat of the First World Zionist Congress. But the local Jewish community protested because its German patriotism might be questioned. And that is how Basel, Switzerland, came to be the site of the Congress.

In the Schwabing district, the center of European intellectual life, lived Brecht, Mann, Klee, Kandinsky, Trotsky, and Spengler. Munich was the site of the Red Commune in 1919, as well as the birthplace and center of the Nazi movement. In 1923, it was the scene of Hitler's Beer Hall Putsch. In spite of this failed attempt to overthrow the government, Hitler made Munich the headquarters of the Nazi party. In the spring of 1913, Hitler had arrived in this city as a "young artist and German nationalist," according to Stephen Kinzer in *The New York Times*, January 4, 1994. Then, and after World War I, Munich was the scene of great political upheaval. To this day, the area around Munich—the capital of the state of Bavaria—remains one of Germany's most conservative regions.

Munich also has become synonymous with appeasement. In 1938, British Prime Minister Neville Chamberlain signed the Munich Pact with Hitler at the then Fuhrer Ban (headquarters). "Peace in our time," it was called, but it was clear, outright appeasement, the sellout of Czechoslovakia, and the tragic forerunner of Hitlerian victories.

JEWISH SITES IN MUNICH

Judisches Museum Munchen, Maximilianstrasse 36. This new museum was dedicated in 1989. Open from Thursdays and Fridays, 2 to 6 P.M.; and Saturdays, 10 A.M. to 2 P.M. Check on hours.

Literatur Hundlung, Furstenstrasse 17. The owner of this only Jewish bookstore in Germany is Rachel Salamander. She once told *Jewish Week* reporter Toby Axelrod that she had "the biggest collection of Yiddish music and lyrics in Europe." Here are found books on the Middle East, Israel, children's books, and Yiddish records. She is also considered an "unofficial Jewish cultural director" and arranges films, lectures, exhibitions, and readings in Munich.

SYNAGOGUES IN MUNICH

Main synagogue, Jewish Community Center, Reichenbachstrasse 27. Tel: 201-4960. Located here is a synagogue, mikveh, restaurant, and various Jewish community organization offices, such as WIZO and United Israel Appeal. The synagogue occupies the site of the old synagogue. Call for information on prayer times, kosher food, and community activities.

Lubavitch Beth Chabad, Ishamingerstrasse 62, 8000 Munich.

Synagogue, Georgenstrasse 71, Schwabing, near the university.

Synagogue, Possarstrasse 15, in Mittersendling.

Synagogue, Schulstrasse 30, in Neuhavsen.

DACHAU

Dachau, the site of the infamous Nazi death camp, is the fourth most visited site in Germany, with one million visitors in a year, and not all foreigners or school groups.

A visitor to Dachau who knows something about the Holocaust wonders. He thinks; he is nonplussed. Suddenly, he sees a sentence in the booklet distributed at Dachau today in the 1990s that reassures him and reminds him why he came:

"Those who cannot remember the past are condemned to repeat it. . . ." (George Santayana).

Robert St. John described Dachau as "an ugly little word." Dachau was opened on March 21, 1933, in what had been a World War I munitions factory. Between 1933 and 1941, the camp was finished and actually had a reputation among inmates as "relatively luxurious," according to James E. Young in his book, *The Texture of Memory: Holocaust Memorials and Meaning in Europe, Israel, and America.* He writes that while several thousand Soviet Army officers were executed here, and Jews were killed at Buchenwald, "the only extermination centers on German territory were Mauthausen and Hartheim Castle in Austria, with their operational gas chambers." But as the war ended and the Soviet troops moved in from the East, "the Germans evacuated masses of starved, diseased ravaged Jews from the death camps in Poland to Germany," according to Young. Dachau became a death camp. "It was inundated with open cattle cars of dead and dying prisoners." Today, there are memorials in Dachau—the sculpture by Nandor Glid of "a 45 ft. long, black bronze grid of human forms enmeshed in barbed wire," is well-known throughout the world. There is also a Jewish monument of a stone vault. A path descends downward to the vault and on both sides of the path is a barbed iron gate with Stars of David on either side. Inside, one gets the feeling of being in the pit of a furnace looking up through the chimney—it "mirrors the shape of crematorium ovens."

Officials say that Americans are among the most numerous of the foreign visitors to Dachau. Many of the visitors wear yarmulkes. There are German youth from the schools, as well as students arriving on tour buses from Italy. There are English men and women on holiday. They all come to Dachau. An excellent historical museum that traces the brutal rise of Nazism and tells what went on here in the first death camp occupies the premises. Some of the camp's original structures still stand, and two of the barracks have been reconstructed.

What goes on in the visitors' minds? While they say Dachau is not as gruesome in its preservation as, say, Auschwitz, they get the message. Perhaps they hope that the world will be better, that there were righteous Christians even in Germany who saved Jews.

Several miles away from the camp in the town of Dachau itself, I met Johann Waltenberger, principal in the Josef Effner High School, whose student body numbers 1,500. It seems that Waltenberger, who is not Jewish, was moved by the television film *Holocaust*. He immediately set out on his own to bring two peoples, Germans and Israelis, together "to remember the past."

Waltenberger is a religious man. He always has been interested in the Bible and in the Holy Land. He has visited Israel several times and is fond of it. He talks like a Zionist. A number of years ago, with some help from the Jewish community of Munich, he wrote a long letter to a number of Israeli schools and asked them if they would be interested in an exchange program of students and teachers.

The Israelis answered back politely, in effect, "Thank you, but no thank you." Waltenberger said the Israelis wrote that he should teach the Holocaust in his class and drop the matter.

Waltenberger says he understood their reaction but was not deterred. On his next trip to Israel, he visited several of the Israeli educators and personally talked to them about the program.

He was persistent. He says he had to try. After a year of negotiations, six Israeli teachers were scheduled to come to Dachau for a week to exchange ideas, discussions, and methods regarding teaching the Holocaust.

In Waltenberger's school, of course, the Holocaust is taught. Unbelievable though it seems to many, there is one Jewish family in the town of Dachau. This family has lived there since the end of the war, and their children went to Waltenberger's school. His pupils visit the camp, which contains a museum, a sample barracks, several memorials, as well as a synagogue and two churches.

"Emotions," Waltenberger says, "are not enough; dialogue is important. We must do these things." He set up the whole program himself. All of this could be brushed aside as infinitesimal compared to the thousands upon thousands who perished at Dachau. But there are those in the American Jewish community and the German Jewish community who believe that Jews should never cease to remind the world about the Holocaust. As emotionally trying as a visit to Dachau becomes, homage should continue to be paid to the six million Jews on the soil where they died. The world must remember!

Worms

A number of Jewish scholars lived in Worms.

Jewish cemetery. Located just beyond the southwest corner of the city wall is this Jewish cemetery, one of the oldest in Europe. Comprised of 2,000 tombstones, it was probably founded in 1076. Many great scholars are buried in Worms. A section of the cemetery designated as the "Valley of the Rabbis" has directional signs in Hebrew to guide visitors. The municipality tends to the grounds.

Rashi Haus. This is a Jewish museum as well as the city archives and is located next to the synagogue. It was opened in 1982 on the site of a yeshiva where once stood a hospital and an old age home. And just to remind us where we are, there was once on this very site an assembly of Jews, half of which were dispatched to the concentration camp.

Rashi Synagogue. This is one of the most significant Jewish historical sites in Germany. Built first in 1034 and destroyed several times thereafter, it is one of the oldest Jewish houses of worship in Europe. The mikveh (1186) and the Rashi Chapel (1624) were destroyed by the Nazis in 1938, but they have been reconstructed. Although Rashi lived here for only five years, his disciples still come to inhale the atmosphere in which he lived and thrived. The Rashi Chapel has a chair that may have been used by the venerable scholar. A large room to the left of the bimah was a separate women's synagogue built in the thirteenth century. The wall between the two buildings was removed in the nineteenth century and the room now stands empty, except for a memorial marker for the 500 Worms Jews who died in the Holocaust. The Jewish community has never been re-established in Worms.

Synagogueplatz. This is the square just off the Judengasse that runs parallel to the remnants of the city's north wall.

Suggested Reading

Adler, H. G. *The Jews in Germany: From the Enlightenment to National Socialism.* Notre Dame, Ind.: University of Notre Dame Press, 1969.

Berenbaum, Michael. *The World Must Know: The History of the Holocaust As Told in the United States Holocaust Museum.* Boston: Little, Brown, 1993.

Bolitho, Hector, ed. *Twelve Jews.* Freeport, N.Y.: Books for Libraries Press, 1934.

Fest, Joachim C. *Hitler.* New York: Vintage, 1973.

Friedrich, Otto. *Before the Deluge: A Portrait of Berlin in the 1920's.* New York: Harper & Row, 1972.

German National Tourist Office. "Germany for the Jewish Traveler." New York.

Herz, Emil. *Before the Fury: Jews and Germany Before Hitler.* Philosophical Library, 1966.

Katcher, Leo. *Post-Mortem: The Jews of Germany Today.* New York: Delacorte, 1968.

Kramer, Jane. *Europeans.* New York: Farrar, Straus & Giroux, 1988.

Krinsky, Carol Herselle. *Synagogues of Europe: Architecture, History, Meaning.* Cambridge, Mass.: MIT Press, 1985.

Lowenthal, Marvin. *The Jews of Germany: A Story of Sixteen Centuries.* New York: Longmans, Green, 1936.

Meltzer, Milton. *Never to Forget: The Jews of the Holocaust.* New York: Harper & Row, 1976.

Nelson, Walter Henry. *The Berliners, Their Saga and Their City.* New York: David McKay, 1966.

Rabinbach, Anson, and Jack D. Zipes, eds. *Germans and Jews Since the Holocaust: The Changing Situation in West Germany.* New York: Holmes & Meier, 1986.

Ryan, Cornelius. *The Last Battle.* New York: Simon & Schuster, 1966.

Schalk, Adolph. *The Germans.* Englewood Cliffs, N.J.: Prentice-Hall, 1971.

Shirer, William L. *The Rise and Fall of the Third Reich.* New York: Fawcett Crest, 1959.

Shlaes, Amity. *Germany, the Empire Within.* New York: Farrar, Straus & Giroux, 1991.

Sichrovsky, Peter. *Strangers in Their Own Land: Young Jews in Germany and Austria Today.* New York: Basic Books, 1986.

Young, James E. *The Texture of Memory: Holocaust Memorials and Meaning in Europe, Israel, and America.* New Haven and London: Yale University Press, 1993.

Zweig, Stefan. *The World of Yesterday: An Autobiography.* New York: Viking, 1943.

Salonika

GREECE

ATHENS

Greece

Grandeur at
the Jewish Museum

Nikos Stavroulakis, founder of Athens' Jewish Museum, sits back reflectively and says, "You know, there always have been Greek-Jewish tensions since the days of the Maccabees. The Greeks have always felt and maintained a strong identity about themselves."

Nikos is right. There was a clash 2,000 years ago between Jewish and Greek culture. Often, Greek merchants envied their Jewish rivals and sought to restrict their progress.

Today tension is not felt in the ancient city of Athens, whose majestic Acropolis looks down on you. Jews still live here. They go to the synagogue and they visit the community center. They come and go as they please to Israel. And above all, they keep Judaism alive.

The Jewish traveler can experience Greek Judaism in Athens. He or she will find Athens to be friendly, warm, and quiet—almost like a little peaceful village—despite the rush hour traffic around Constitution Square and the congestion in the city. The past permeates the air as tourists descend in the millions on this capital that many say you either love or hate.

Athens prides itself on being located at the crossroads of Europe, the Middle East, and Africa. About four million people live in the Athens area, out of a total population of nearly 10 million Greek citizens. This city contains an old Jewish community that originated probably in the first century before the

common era. It is small, but united. About 10 to 15 bar mitzvahs and 17 weddings occur each year. Of course, the death
knell of the Jewish community in days to come could be the
low birthrate. Unfortunately, there are more funerals than
births.

This is a wonderful Jewish community: appealing, warm,
welcoming. Greek Jewry has a high rate of intermarriage due
to the isolation of young Jews in small communities. But
because there is no civil marriage in Greece, the intermarriage
rate is probably less than in other countries. Greek Jews are
said to be extremely loyal to their Greece—"passionately," was
the way one writer put it.

Israel has always helped the Greek Jewish community with
shlichim (messengers, helpers). Many Greek Jewish youth
spend their summers in Israel; it is nearby.

A Brief History

Actually, the first Jews to arrive here came from the Holy
Land. Archeological discoveries tell of the existence of
colonies of Palestinian Jews on the Greek islands a century
after the destruction of the First Temple in Jerusalem in 586
B.C.E. But they may have been slaves, for as Raphael Patai notes,
"the history of the Jews in Greece begins with scattered reference to Jewish slaves." Some centuries later, prisoners from the
Maccabean Wars (170–140 B.C.E.) were brought here and were
later freed.

In the first century B.C.E., when the apostle Paul traveled
through Greece, active Jewish communities existed in Corinth,
Thessaloniki (the ancient name of Salonika), and Patras, as
well as on the islands of Rhodes, Somos, and Delos. The original Greek Jews were called Romaniots. Influenced by Greek
culture and language, their family names were Greek and their
synagogues were known by their Greek names.

Under the Christian rulers of the Byzantine Empire, Jewish
rights became limited when Jews were expected to convert to
Christianity. Crusaders on their way to the Holy Land would
kill Jews living in Greece.

As Christianity spread, substantial legal and economic restrictions were placed on Jews, but they continued to exist. They developed their own variant of Jewish rituals and customs, which came to be known as the Romaniot rite.

Benjamin of Tudela found large numbers of Jews in Greece in 1170 when he toured Jewish communities. He found them in Corfu, Patras, Thebes, Salonika, and other cities, including the Greek islands. They worked in dyeing, weaving, and the making of silk garments. Jews were well off, he reported.

The Turkish conquest in the fifteenth century (Athens was conquered in 1456) ushered in a "Golden Age" for Greek Jewry when the Sephardic migration from Spain and Turkey overwhelmed and absorbed the older Byzantine Jewish communities. The newcomers revived the Sephardic way of life, including the Ladino language.

When Jews were expelled from Iberia, many Spanish and Portuguese Jews settled in Salonika, so much so that by 1553, 20,000 Jews lived in Salonika.

The sultan, Bayazid II, had welcomed tens of thousands of Iberian Jews to Istanbul in Turkey and to Salonika, now in Greece but then ruled by the Ottoman Turks, who were to remain in Greece until 1822.

In the sixteenth century, prominent rabbis lived in Salonika. One was Sh'lomo Alqabetz, who wrote the stirring, romantic Shabbat Hebrew song, "L'cha Dodi."

In the seventeenth century "Jewish" Salonika radiated power as the center of rabbinic and Kabbalistic studies and the seat of leading halachic authorities.

Meanwhile, between 1453 and 1821, Greece as a nation-state vanished from history. And it was in 1821–22 that Jews obtained equal and legal rights, even though many Jews lost their lives for backing the Turks.

By 1920 Greek Jews were organized into 24 religious communities with stable institutions and numerous activities. Salonika itself boasted 40 synagogues, which were named after the once-famous Jewish communities in Spain. Two newspapers were published in Ladino. After population exchanges between Greece and Turkey in 1923, and the arrival of 100,000

Synagogue of Corfu. (Photo courtesy Jewish Museum of Greece; photo by Timothy DeVinney)

Greeks from Anatolia, the Jewish communities declined some-what. In 1940, there were 77,000 Jews in Greece. At war's end, only about 10,000 to 15,000 Jews survived the Holocaust. Between 1945 and 1955, 3,500 Greek Jews, mostly Sephardim, settled in Israel, and about 1,200 journeyed to the United States. After the war, Greece promulgated a law that makes racism and anti-Semitism a criminal act. Still, it was one of the few European countries to vote against the 1947 U.N. Partition Plan creating a Jewish state.

Greeks themselves, it appears, are "not indisposed" to the Jews, writes Arnold Sherman in the Jerusalem *Post,* April 6, 1990, though anti-Israel propaganda at times appears in the press and on television. There are monuments and memorials dedicated to the Jewish victims of Nazism throughout the country that were paid for by either municipal or private, non-Jewish funds. Sherman said while Andreas Papandreou inveighed against Israel, more Greek business persons made deals with Israel than ever before. Prime Minister Constantine Mitsotakis changed the policy finally, it appears, with full diplomatic relations between Greece and Israel in 1990.

In 1994, Andreas Papandreou returned to power—Greece at this time promised to reform its economy and it appeared that if tensions could be kept at bay with the former Yugoslavia and the Republic of Macedonia, Greece could move toward a bright future.

Jewish Athens

JEWISH SITES IN ATHENS

Beth Shalom Synagogue, 5 Odos Melidoni. Tel: 325-2773. An attractive white building, with ample seating.

Jewish Community Center, Vissarionis Street and Sina Street. Activities abound at the Jewish youth and community center: lectures, a seder, Purim, holiday celebrations, Israel Independence Day, Tu B'Shvat.

Jewish Community Headquarters and Center, 8 Odos Melidoni, Athens. Tel: 325-2823. Almost the whole Jewish

Beth Shalom Synagogue. (Photo courtesy Jewish Museum of Greece; photo by Timothy DeVinney)

The Holocaust Exhibit in the Jewish Museum. (Photo courtesy Jewish Museum of Greece; photo by Timothy DeVinney)

community turns out for high holiday services. Jews in Athens are merchants and industrialists in the textile, garment, and jewelry industries. The offices here can tell the traveler about organizations such as WIZO; the Zionist Federation, which organizes summer trips to Israel for teenagers and young adults; and the Pan-Hellenic Jewish Youth movement. A most successful project is the Athens Youth Club. Also at 8 Odos Melidoni is the **Romaniot Synagogue,** which is open primarily on high holidays.

Jewish Community Center, Sina and Vissarionos streets, Athens. Tel: 36-37-092.

Jewish Youth Square. This area commemorates Jewish youth who perished in the Holocaust. Pafous Square in the Patissia area.

The Jewish Museum, 36 Amalias Ave. Tel: 323-1577. Open Sunday through Friday, 9 A.M. to 1 P.M.. Perhaps the history of Greek Jewry haunts the community. Perhaps it plagued the artist, educator, and historian Nikos Stavroulakis so much that he almost single-handedly created one of the finest Jewish museums in Europe. If you are nearby, it is worth a special visit to Greece to see this wonderful museum.

The Jewish Museum is located smack in the heart of Athens, convenient to the city's major hotels. It is a good place to begin a visit to the Jewish community of Greece. With much to see and study, it is not unusual to spend a good half-day here. Nikos began his museum project by collecting "war leftovers." He obtained 15 cloth bags from the Bulgarian government. The sacks contained 2,800 items that had been confiscated from Greek Jews during the war. Included were watches, rings, and amulets. You can now look at them in this museum: silver from Rhodes, furniture from the Patras Synagogue, and gravestones from Hania in Crete.

He saved and collected and recorded, and today we benefit from his work. Ancient Hebrew books have been preserved. Displayed are Timothy DeVinney's photographs, which he took in his travels around the country and from which you can appreciate the remnant of Greek Jewry.

Visitors come from all over the world: Long Island,

Philadelphia, Winnipeg, Oslo, and Israel. They come to identify with their people. Rarely does anyone write a nasty or anti-
Semitic comment in the guest book. But someone did just that
in the museum's welcome volume. And the next entry was "Am
Yisrael Chai" ("The Jewish people lives").

The Holocaust is remembered and portrayed in the museum. Nearly all of Greek Jewry perished in it, about 80 percent,
one of the highest in the Holocaust, according to historian
Leni Yahil. The Nazis killed more Jews in Greece proportionately than in any other country except Poland. In the museum,
you stare at the pictures of the mass roundups. I remember
looking at the identity cards, some real, some fake. I focus on
the card of a woman I had talked to that very day. An eerie feeling results. By all demonic logic, she should have been dead.
But she lives and bears witness to the tragedy that befell the
Greek Jewish community.

During the war, almost all of the synagogues had been
destroyed or severely damaged.

A U.S. Embassy report once singled out the Greeks as one of
the few European peoples who not only helped its Jews, but
sheltered them at the risk of being killed if they were discovered.

The Jewish Museum houses the culture of Greek Jewry that
was part of the birth and rebirth of Greece. Fittingly, when you
walk out of the modern building to the sounds of the busy traffic on Amalias Avenue, you observe the ancient monument
Pillars of Zeus across the street.

Those interested in helping or finding out more informa-
tion about the museum can contact American Friends of the
Greek Jewish Museum, P.O. Box 2010, New York, NY 10185.
Or, write to the museum directly in Athens.

ORGANIZATIONS

B'nai B'rith, 15 Paparigopoulou.
The Central Board of Jewish Communities in Greece, 2
Sourmeli St. Tel: 88-39-951. The umbrella organization for all
Greek Jewry. Athens, thus, is the home to the Central Board of
Jewish Communities in Greece—the governing body of the

6,000-member Greek Jewish community. The council is composed of representatives of the Jewish communities in Athens and other areas of Greece. More than two-thirds of Greek Jewry reside in Athens.

Jewish National Fund, 2 Nikis St.

Thessaloniki (Salonika)

An Oriental air hovers over Salonika, Greece's second city, located on the Aegean Sea. It is a gateway to the Balkans, and right on the road between Athens and Istanbul. Thessaloniki is named for the sister of Alexander the Great. It is a short drive from Pella where excavations have revealed Alexander's capital city of Macedonia and from Veria, another city where Jews flourished. Alexander's brother-in-law, Kassandros, who built Thessaloniki, apparently asked the king of Egypt to send him Jewish artisans. This is supposed to have marked the start of the Jewish community of Thessaloniki (Salonika). By the end of the fifteenth century, Salonika became a melting pot for European Jewish communities. Each brought their own exotic-sounding names to the city. Calabria, Majorca, and Lisbon were among its thirty separate Jewish communities. Eventually, all the groups embraced Ladino. Also settling here was a large group of Marranos from Portugal.

In the sixteenth and seventeenth centuries, the city of Salonika, then part of Turkey, became a great center of Sephardic Jewry. "Salonika in 17th century terms was as Jewish a city as is New York in the 20th century," says Barnet Litvinoff. This Greek metropolis was known throughout the world for its famous rabbinical scholars and seminaries, Hebrew printing presses, and Jewish libraries. Actually, until the mid-twentieth century, Salonika was "a Jewish city." Shabbetai Zevi, the false messiah born in Smyrna, tried to make Salonika his base of operations. But in 1657, he was expelled from the city.

By the end of the nineteenth century, 80,000 of Salonika's 120,000 citizens were Jews who spoke Ladino. In 1900, 90,000 Jews made up more than half of the city's population. The community supported hospitals, orphanages, schools, daily newspapers, and rabbinical seminaries where Hebrew, Ladino, and French were spoken. Despite hardships, it remained a center of Jewish learning and culture.

In 1912, Greece conquered Turkish-held Salonika and proceeded to Hellenize the city by settling Greeks within it. According to Israel Cohen, a fire in 1917 leveled the Jewish quarter, destroying 20,000 homes, 30 synagogues, 8 schools, and residential and commercial buildings. Nearly two thousand years of history went up in smoke.

While many people emigrated to the then Palestine, the most interesting group who picked themselves up and went to the Land of Israel seems to have been Greek fishermen, relates Cohen. As far as we know, they were the only organized body of Jewish fishermen in the world, descendants of the exiles from medieval Spain. They continued their family occupation and established their own synagogue. For centuries they had been the only fishermen in Salonika. But their monopoly was brought to an end with the Greeks taking over. Some 16 families were transported with all their boats and fishing tackle to a stretch between Atlit and Acre in Palestine.

There are no words to describe the brutal death of Salonika Jewry during World War II. We know 56,000 Jews lived there before the Nazis invaded, with about 85 percent being deported to the death camps, according to Israel Cohen.

Simon Wiesenthal estimates that it took 11 or 12 days to transfer these wonderful, stoic, hardworking Jews from Salonika to Auschwitz, where about 60,000 out of 77,000 Greek Jews were murdered. Of that group, 46,000 were from Salonika.

About 13,000 Jews fought for the Greek army when Germany and Italy attacked.

Today, approximately 1,200 Jews live in Thessaloniki (Salonika), out of a total population of about 6,000 Greek Jews.

Jewish Thessaloniki (Salonika)

Monastirioton Synagogue, 35 Sygrou St., Thessaloniki. Tel: 031-524-968.

Synagogue and Center for Historical Studies, 24 Odos Tsimiski, Thessaloniki. Tel: 031-223-231. The Jewish Community Center is located in the same building, 24 Odos Tsimiski, Thessaloniki. Tel: 031-277-803.

Cemetery and Memorial to Holocaust Victims. Located in the suburb of Stavroupolis, Thessaloniki.

Square of the Jewish Martyrs of the Holocaust. Located between the streets of Papanastasiou, Karakassi, and Priamou, Thessaloniki.

Jewish Elementary School, 17 Fleming St., Thessaloniki.

Suggested Reading

Brinn, Herb. *Ich Bin Ein Jude.* Middle Village, N.Y.: Jonathan David, 1983.

Cohen, Israel. *Contemporary Jewry.* London: Methuen, 1950.

———. *The Journal of a Jewish Traveler.* New York: Dodd, Mead, 1925.

Elazar, Daniel J., and Harriet P. Friedenreich. *The Balkan Jewish Communities: Yugoslavia, Bulgaria, Greece, and Turkey.* Lanham, N.Y.: University Press of America, 1984.

Patai, Raphael. *The Vanished Worlds of Jewry.* New York: Macmillan.

Turkey
Jewish History from Constantinople to Istanbul

Istanbul, on the edge of Europe, is one of the great cities of the world, infused with religious shrines, historical structures, and ear-piercing calls of the muezzin from the minaret five times a day. Minarets, mosques, and palaces with pencil-like turrets; commuter ferryboats in the Golden Horn; the Galata Bridge and Galata Tower; the belly dancers; the streets where you can hear a dozen languages, including Hebrew; and the Grand Bazaar of 4,000 shops within 50 acres all remind you this is also a gateway to Asia.

A Brief History

Benjamin of Tudela, of Spain, who visited Jewish communities in the mid-twelfth century, said of Istanbul (called Constantinople until 1930): "It is a bustling city, with business coming to her from all foreign lands on land and on sea. There is no other city like her except Baghdad. There are the Church of Sophia, and the Pope of the Greeks . . . and as many churches as there are days in the year, and in them, incalculable wealth . . . more than in all the churches of the rest of the world [together]. And there is a Hippodrome where the king organizes great games on the birthday of Jesus of Nazareth, and in that place are drawn pictures of all kinds of men in the world before the king and queen with all types of sorcery. . . ."

That was eight centuries ago and once upon a time, Istanbul

was one of the most important Jewish centers of the world, replete with Jewish schools and scholars. It was even called the Jewish "mother city." Although Jews lived here in Byzantine times, it was not until the Ottoman conquest in 1453 that Muhammad II welcomed Jews. He wanted them to develop business and trade and help Turkey's growth.

Jews found a haven in this city in 1492 when Sultan Bayazid II, hearing that Ferdinand and Isabella of Spain had expelled the Jewish people, is reported to have said: "You call Fernando of Spain a wise king—he who has impoverished his country and enriched ours. . . ."

Granted asylum, the Jews who came to Turkey were treated extremely well, especially under Suleiman the Magnificent. They called him "King Solomon," not only because of his name, but also because of his wisdom and legislative programs. During his rule, the Jews of the Ottoman Empire made great cultural and economic strides. Jewish intellectual life rose to new heights. They devoted themselves to secular science, physics, astronomy, math, and medicine.

By the sixteenth century, Istanbul, with 40,000 Jews, had the largest Jewish population in the world. The Jews became a protected minority, although sometimes subject to discriminatory legislation that included dress, taxes, and housing. During this time, the Turkish Jewish community was the home of some wonderful personalities, such as Gracia Nasi and Joseph Nasi.

Gracia Nasi (1510–69) was a Portuguese Marrano who openly returned to Judaism. As a stateswoman and patron, she helped Marranos flee Portugal. In 1537, after her husband's death, she left Portugal and went to Istanbul, where she was joined by Joseph Nasi. Nasi, a Portuguese Marrano, married her only child, Reyna.

When Nasi arrived in Istanbul in 1543, she brought with her large amounts of capital. In addition to her banking and economic activities, she founded yeshivot (religious schools) and synagogues and continued her efforts on behalf of persecuted Marranos and Jews.

Meanwhile Joseph Nasi (1524–79), who became one of the most influential figures in the Ottoman Empire, had been named duke of the island of Naxos and surrounding isles. Gracia Nasi had obtained a grant to set up a yeshiva in the ruined city of Tiberias, Israel. In 1561, Joseph Nasi extended the grant and began the rebuilding of the ruined walls of Tiberias. This whole enterprise turned out to be one of the practical attempts to establish a Jewish political center in Palestine between the fourth and nineteenth centuries.

In Turkey, too, Joseph Karo (1488–1575) wrote the "Shulhan Arukh," the code of Jewish law. Indeed, Turkey became a great center for the study of Kabbala and was the birthplace of a number of prophetic and messianic movements. Here grew the legend of Shabbetai Zevi. Actually, we cannot visit Turkish Jewry without recalling Shabbetai Zevi, the Kabbalistic mystic who attracted thousands to his following (see Achrida Synagogue below).

The visitor to Turkey will also learn about the Karaites and the Dönmeh.

During the eighteenth and nineteenth centuries, Jews began moving westward from Turkey as world trade was shifting from the Mediterranean to the Atlantic coast of Europe. Seeking greater opportunity, Jews now would relocate to Holland, England, and the states along the Danube River.

At the turn of the twentieth century, about 100,000 Jews lived in Turkey. Before World War I, Theodor Herzl approached Istanbul leaders, but could not persuade them to grant a national home to the Jewish people in Palestine. During the reign of the Sultan Abdul Hamid II (1876–1909) the attitude of the Sublime Porte toward Jews was positive. Jews were involved in the economic and political life of the empire. In 1908, the Young Turks overthrew the sultan and Jews actively participated in the Young Turk movement. During World War I, in which the Turks sided with the Germans, the Jews of Istanbul prospered greatly. But after the war, Jews suffered anti-Semitism in former Turkish lands taken over by the Greeks.

Between the wars, Turkey was not fundamentally hostile to Jews; it was anti-foreign and anti-traditional. In 1927, about 82,000 Jews lived in Turkey—46,000 in Istanbul, over 16,000 in Izmir, 5,700 in Edirne, and the rest in 14 other communities.

During World War II, however, Turkey was neutral. Many refugees from Nazism found their way here and continued on to Palestine. After the 1948 Israel Declaration of Independence, Jews began to leave Turkey. Nehemiah Robinson wrote that between 1948 and 1956, about 43,000 Jews emigrated from Turkey. Today, approximately 22,000 Jews reside in Turkey, which has a population of about 50 million.

Although Turkey and Israel have had diplomatic relations since 1949, when Turkey became the first Moslem state to recognize Israel, relations between the two have experienced frequent ups and downs. The two countries elevated their diplomatic relations to the ambassadorial level in March 1992. In November 1993, Turkish Foreign Minister Hikmet Cetin arrived in Israel. His was the first official visit by a Turkish foreign minister. In January 1994, Israel President Ezer Weizman became the first Israeli head of state to visit Turkey. But by mid-1994, Turkey's Islamic fundamentalists won an election in Istanbul and observers were watching this important nation to see if its days as a secular state were numbered. Still, Turkey and Israel had opened a new era of cooperation and new economic ties were discussed.

Undoubtedly some anti-Semitism exists. Still, the Jewish community of Turkey "is fighting for survival," writes Mios Liberles. "Moreover, Turkish law forbids Turkish citizens to have any formal links or even contact with foreign countries or international organizations." This policy applies to all groups.

Many Jews live in suburbs, such as Beyoglu, Sisli, Ortakoy, Kuzguncuk, Kadikoy, Sirkeci, Galata, Tunel, Taksim, Nisantas, Macka, and others.

There are large summer communities on three of the islands off of the Bosporus in the Sea of Marmara. The largest communities are located in Buyukada and Heybeli Ada.

JEWISH SITES IN ISTANBUL

Headquarters of Chief Rabbi David Asseo, Yemenici Sokak 23, Beyoglu District. Tel: 144-0472 or 144-5327. This is the headquarters of the Turkish Jewish community and tourists and visitors would do well to stop off here for information on the Jewish community. His staff is friendly and will help tourists.

As you walk to the office, you are apt to recall that as recently as World War II, Turkey contained one of the most creative and distinguished Sephardic communities in the Diaspora. This may be Turkey, but 500 years after their arrival from Iberia, Jews still speak Spanish here. Once Arabic, Armenian, Greek, French, Italian, and yes, even Ladino, was spoken here. Ladino, an archaic form of Spanish, absorbed a considerable vocabulary from the local language, primarily Turkish and Greek, as well as a Hebraic and Talmudic component. This Judeo-Spanish was commonly used in Turkey and some of the Balkan countries ruled by Turkey, according to Bernard Lewis. Under the Ottomans Jews did not normally speak Turkish— only Ladino, which remains the language of the older generation. Ladino still is spoken and read here, as witnessed by the Jewish weekly, *Salom*. That newspaper contains seven pages in Turkish and one in Ladino and is helping keep alive the language of the Sephardim that younger Jews here are increasingly unable to speak. Young people now speak Turkish as their first language. Today, Jews are trying to keep Ladino alive here in Turkey.

Here at the chief rabbi's headquarters, I met the Jewish poet and artist Joseph Habib Gerez, a leader of the Jewish community. He writes in Turkish and describes the glories of Istanbul. He is a man who has traveled the world yet still loves his city, which commands a central position in maritime communications between the Black Sea and the Mediterranean and where you see Russian freighters and cruise ships sailing down the Bosporus. His paintings reflect Jewish life in Istanbul.

The suburb of Galata. Even today, Jews live in Pera and Galata, which is on the heights above the Golden Horn. In Byzantine days, it was a colony of European merchants. The hills north of Galata were favorite places for foreign envoys. The Europeans called that area Pera, from a Greek word meaning "beyond" or "across," i.e., across the Golden Horn from Old Istanbul or beyond the Galata Tower. Many Jews moved to these popular new neighborhoods; at the end of the nineteenth century, half of Istanbul Jewry was living in the Galata and Pera sections. However, the Jews in each quarter maintained their own communal institutions, rabbinical courts, schools, budgets, and councils. According to Hilary Sumner-Boyd and John Freely, the area in front of the Galata Bridge was once a Jewish quarter inhabited by Karaites, a sect that denies Talmudic rabbinical tradition. The Karaites broke off from the main body of Orthodox Jewry in the eighth century.

The Topkapi Palace. The Palace of the Sultans "is the most extensive and fascinating monument of Ottoman civil architecture in existence," according to Sumner-Boyd and Freely. Many Jewish women occupied the palace harem. When you tour the palace and see the harem, remember Esther Kyra. She was a Jewish broker, only she did not deal in stocks and bonds. Her exchange was the royal harem. She had free access to it, where she sold jewels, cosmetics, and rich fabrics and generally made herself indispensable to the ladies. She won the favor of Sultan Murad III's mother, Nur Banu, and of his preferred concubine, the Venetian, Safya Baffo, both of whom had enormous influence. Through them, Esther, in turn, exercised considerable influence in imperial appointments and became involved in political affairs. Her power and wealth spawned jealousy and she was murdered. In 1593, her fortune was confiscated.

The Jewish women in the palace bribed the eunuchs who kept the doors, ruled over the women, and bought and sold for them. The Jewish women became rich. Bernard Lewis tells us that when Sultan Murad III learned that Sephardi girls were wearing choice garments and ornaments with precious stones, he issued a decree to exterminate all Jews throughout all the provinces of his empire. Through the influence of the sultan's mother, the decree was revoked, but an order was given that Jews must wear, in place of the yellow turban, a strange tall hat, pointed above and wide below, like those of the Spaniards.

SYNAGOGUES IN ISTANBUL

There are about 15 synagogues, a Jewish school, a hospital, and a home for the elderly here in Istanbul.

Achrida Synagogue, Kurtci Cesmi Sokak 15, Balat section. In

1992, in honor of the 500th anniversary of the Iberian Jews' arrival here, the Achrida Synagogue was restored. Many festivities, concerts, the opening of a new Jewish Museum, and major ceremonies highlighted the 1992 celebration of 500 years of Jewish history in Turkey. Built in 1412, it existed when the city was in Byzantine hands. Shabbetai Zevi preached here. Born in Smyrna, July 1626, his birthday occurred on the Ninth of Av, the day in which the First and Second Temples had been destroyed. At age 18, he was honored by the rabbis of his town.

According to Barnet Litvinoff, he was the son of a merchant who traded with England. While bathing in the waters of the Aegean Sea, the idea dawned on him that he was the Messiah, the one appointed by God to save the Jews and lead them back to the Holy Land. Late in 1648, during the synagogue service, he stood at the Holy Ark and pronounced the full name of God, an act which only the priest had the right to perform. He proclaimed himself as the Messiah.

Shabbetai Zevi met Raphael Joseph Chelebi in Cairo, who was known as the "prince of the Jews of Egypt and head of that country's treasury." In Gaza, Nathan Benjamin Levi helped Shabbetai, who sojourned for a while in the Holy Land and attracted followers. In 1665, he returned to an ecstatic reception in Smyrna. There he prophesied the impending defeat and abdication of the sultan. The Jews would usurp his empire, said Shabbetai Zevi, reestablishing the Lord's rule in Jerusalem. He, Shabbetai Zevi, would be the king of kings. The Sultan naturally had to get rid of Shabbetai Zevi—either convert him to Islam or put him to death. To save his skin, Shabbetai converted to Islam. So, he was appointed as chamberlain in the royal palace and received a salary. Later he was banished to a small town in Albania, where he died in 1676. It was a severe blow to world Jewry—a betrayal, demoralizing a great part of the Sephardic world.

Ashkenazi Synagogue, Yuksek Kaldirim 37.

Italian Synagogue, Okcu Musa Caddesi 29.

Neve Shalom Synagogue, Buyuk Hendek Caddesi 67. On September 12, 1986, more than 20 people were killed in a terrorist attack on the Neve Shalom Synagogue. The incident shattered the peaceful existence of 500 years, but life goes on. Today, one or two policemen stand guard and a strong security check, including television cameras, is maintained in a bulletproof glass enclosure just inside the door. You can still see the clock that on that Sabbath Saturday stopped at 9:17 A.M., the time the terrorists attacked the house of prayer. Near the bimah, you can see the patched-up bullet holes.

The synagogue also serves as a community center.

Neve Shalom, probably the most modern synagogue in Istanbul, is close to the Pera Palas Hotel, the last of the old-school grand hotels on the Galata Hill, the section of Galata where the Jews live. Located very near the American Consulate, this hotel sports "Old World charm."

The Sisli Synagogue, Efe St. 4, Osmanbey. Tel: 140-6599. Near the Galata Tower. This was the quarter overlooking the Golden Horn where the Jews lived. Sisli Synagogue is close to the Hilton Hotel.

Suggested Reading

Freid, Jacob. *Jews in the Modern World*. New York: Twayne, 1962.

Lewis, Bernard. *The Emergence of Modern Turkey*. London: Oxford University Press, 1961.

———. *Istanbul and the Civilization of the Ottoman Empire*. Norman, Okla.: University of Oklahoma Press, 1972.

———. *Semites and Anti-Semites*. New York: Norton, 1986.

Mann, Vivian B. *A Tale of Two Cities: Jewish Life in Frankfurt and Istanbul, 1750–1870*. New York: The Jewish Museum, 1982.

Settle, Mary Lee. *Turkish Reflections*. New York: Prentice-Hall, 1991.

Simon, Joseph. *The Itinerary of Benjamin of Tudela, Travels in the Middle Ages*. Malibu, Calif.: Pangloss Press.

Sumner-Boyd, Hilary, and John Freely. *Strolling Through Istanbul: A Guide to the City*. Istanbul: Redhouse, 1972.

Scandinavia
Something for Everyone

"Scandinavia!" exclaimed a Jewish travel agent. "Why, there are only four Jews there."

Not true; probably more than 25,000 is the accurate figure. It may be small in numbers, but Scandinavian Jewry is alive and well and a visit to four capitals—Helsinki, Stockholm, Copenhagen, and Oslo—will show how that old, dire prediction that Jews will disappear here through intermarriage and assimilation still remains somewhat premature. True, extremely high intermarriage ratios exist; some have put it at 80 percent in Denmark, for example. But having said that, there are valiant efforts being made to stem the tide.

Approximately 18,000 Jews reside in Sweden, about 8,000 in Denmark, 1,000 in Norway, and about 1,300 in Finland. Truly, these numbers are miniscule. In fact, as it was once aptly put, there are more Jews in Minnesota than in all of Scandinavia. And Jews settled in New York City (1654) before their co-religionists moved into Scandinavia.

For the founders of the Scandinavian Jewish community, these vast northern lands, where anti-Semitism rarely rears its ugly head, were not their first choice. They needed a place of refuge. And one of the places they came to was Denmark and its "fun city," Copenhagen, where, as the travel brochures declare, "there is something for everybody."

Trondheim

SWEDEN

FINLAND

NORWAY

HELSINKI

Turku

OSLO ☆

STOCKHOLM

☆

Gothenberg

COPENHAGEN Malmo

☆

DENMARK

Jewish Copenhagen

On my "city tour" in Copenhagen, our very vocal guide made his passengers memorize the years of the reign of Christian IV who did so much for Copenhagen, in the way of institutions, fortifications, and palaces. The years, 1588 to 1648, were welded into our minds. In fact, we often were instructed to bellow out the dates in hearty unison.

The guide, however, never mentioned that in 1622, Christian IV invited Portuguese Jews from Amsterdam, probably Marranos, to settle in Gluckstadt. Although now in Schleswig-Holstein in North Germany, it was once an area ruled by Denmark.

Most tourists do not, of course, come to Denmark to learn about Christian IV. They come to see the environment immortalized by the Hans Christian Anderson stories and recounted by the late actor-comedian Danny Kaye; to gaze at the Little Mermaid—and she is indeed little—sitting in the harbor; and to inhale and experience Tivoli, the granddaddy of all amusement parks and one of the tourist wonders of Europe.

Denmark is a good land for Jews. Following King Christian IV was King Frederick III (1657–59), who allowed Sephardic Jews to settle in Denmark. Israel David, a goldsmith, and his partner, Meir Goldschmidt, settled in Copenhagen in 1684. Seven merchants and craftsmen followed. They, too, were Marranos who had obtained permission to leave their country. At first, they all prayed behind closed doors. But soon, not only would the government decree punishment for anyone who harassed those of another religious faith, it also voided its ban on Jewish employment of Christian servants. By 1766, the first synagogue in Copenhagen was erected.

Nearly 2,000 Jews—merchants, craftsmen, and entrepreneurs—lived in Copenhagen in 1782.

In 1834, more than 4,000 Jews inhabited the country. Chief Rabbi Dr. Abraham Alexander Wolff (1801–91) served as rabbi for 62 years and kept the community united. In 1837, Jews were allowed to hold municipal office. Jews achieved full emancipation when Denmark abolished the absolute monarchy in 1849 and adopted a constitution.

Jews administered their own affairs with little or no anti-Semitism holding them back from assimilation into the country's economic and intellectual life. Prominent Jews have included Mendel Levin Nathanson, father of Danish journalism; Georg Brandes, literary critic and historian; Gen. C. I. de Meza, commander of the Danish Army; Victor Borge, the entertainer who still comes home to his native Tivoli in Copenhagen to entertain; and Niels Bohr (1885–1962), a Danish physicist and Nobel laureate who also escaped the Nazis by going to Sweden in a fishing boat in 1943. His mother was from a prominent Jewish banking family.

Following the Kishinev pogrom in 1905, several thousand Jews entered Denmark. By the end of World War I, 96.7 percent of the Danish Jewish community lived in Copenhagen. In the 1930s, many Jewish refugees from Germany poured into Denmark, and then went on to Palestine and the United States. The Jews believed that King Christian X would stand by them. As events would prove, they were correct. They remembered that in 1933, Christian X attended services in Copenhagen's synagogue. This was the year when Hitler took over Germany. Denmark and its ruler, however, were one in protecting their Jewish citizens. A "bone" in his throat, was the way Hitler described Jewish freedom in Denmark. Adolf Eichmann himself, the S.S. officer who put into operation the execution of Europe's Jews, admitted that in Denmark he could not do as he wished. Not only did the Danes resist the ill treatment of Jews; they saved their Jews (as we shall soon see) in one of the most remarkable rescue operations in history, certainly in recent Jewish history.

After the war, between 1966 and 1967, about 2,500 Polish Jews arrived in Denmark. Poland had unleashed another of one of its waves of anti-Semitism; this time aimed at Jewish members of its Communist party. Not all Polish Jews wanted to go to Israel; Denmark was among the few nations to welcome them. On the other hand, in the last two decades alone, 700 to 800 Danish Jews (close to 10 percent) have emigrated to Israel.

Many Jews visiting Copenhagen head for **Israelsplads** (Israel Square), where they find a large memorial stone from Israel. A ceremony took place here in 1968. During the event, the name of "Gronttorvet" (the Vegetable Market Place) was changed to "Israel Square." And at the same time, the Beth Hakerem Park in Jerusalem was renamed "Kikar Daniah" (Denmark Square). On weekends, Israel Square turns into a flea market.

In October 1943, the Danish people and the resistance movement defied Nazi occupation of their country to rescue their fellow citizens. During a period of 10 nights, almost all of the Danish Jews were carried across the body of water known as Oresund Strait, in fishing boats and other small craft, to safe Sweden. Israel and Jews all over the world will never forget the rescue. If we were editing the Bible in the 1990s, the saving of the Jews from the Nazis in October 1943 would be told in the Scriptures, similar to the Book of Esther. In the latter biblical event, a wicked Haman wanted to kill the Jews, but the Jewish people were spared. Thus, too, were the Jews of Denmark saved. "This modern-day legend will be commemorated for generations to come," writes Aage Bertelsen in his book, *October, 1943*.

Some headline the events of October 1943 a "Jewish Dunkirk." The Danes rescued virtually the entire Jewish community from the Germans and brought it safely to Sweden. The Nazis had planned to deport the Jews on the night of the Jewish New Year, October 1–2, 1943. But at a religious service on September 29, the acting chief rabbi of Denmark, Dr. Marcus Melchior, rushed into the Great Synagogue on Krystalgade street in Copenhagen and warned his congregants to hide. But where could they find shelter? Where could they flee? Where could they find friends? But they managed: they hid in small groups until their turn came to board the small fishing boats to nearby Sweden.

The Danish police had set up a sea escape route and turned a blind eye to the boats leaving the shore. Some Germans even accepted bribes and allowed trucks of refugees to pass, but it has been conjectured that they did this because they knew if they stopped the vehicles, they might incur the wrath of the Danes. About 7,900 Jews escaped, including 686 non-Jews who were married to Jews. About 30 were lost at sea or committed suicide. On the day of the action, the Germans managed to capture 284 Jews and in the next few weeks, 190 Jews were arrested while trying to escape. Thus, 474 were picked up, of which 101 were non-Danish refugees. Fifty-one of the deported persons died in the concentration camp Terezin (Theresienstadt), in the Czech Republic, while the rest returned safely home in 1945.

A shipping expert in the German Embassy tipped off the Jewish community. He was George Ferdinand Duckwitz (1904–73), according to the book *The Rescue of the Danish Jews.* After the war, he served as West Germany's ambassador to Denmark (1955 to 1958).

But not only did the Danes physically help the Jews escape, they never forgot their Jewish brothers and sisters who were arrested by the Nazis and imprisoned in Theresienstadt. Between October 1943 and April 1945, the Danes pressured the Germans to release all those deported and to allow food parcels to get through. These Danes prevented Denmark's Jews from being transferred from Theresienstadt to the death camp at Auschwitz, and those food packages probably saved the Jews from starvation.

Historian Leni Yahil offers five reasons for the success of the sea evacuation: First, the number of Jews was small. Second, Sweden was nearby. Third, conditions in Denmark were different than in other countries in Nazi-occupied Europe. Fourth, the Germans were reeling after their defeats at El Alamein and Stalingrad. The final reason is "the special character and moral stature of the Danish people and their love of democracy and freedom."

Rabbi Bent Melchior also told me in an interview in 1991 that the organized church in Denmark was very active in helping to save Jews. To the Danes, he asserted, the treatment of its Jewish citizens was "every citizen's business," not just that of a few leaders or "good souls."

During "Little Dunkirk," Acting Chief Rabbi Marcus Melchior was rescued. Today, his two sons, Rabbi Bent and Arne, are prominent in Denmark.

Rabbi Bent Melchior is chief rabbi of Denmark. He is the

eighth generation of his family in Denmark, the Melchiors having lived there, it is said, for 300 years. A number of streets in Copenhagen are named after this illustrious family. Rabbi Melchior, who fought in Israel's War of Independence, once told an interviewer, "We have a mission in Denmark. We were saved by the Danes and must continue the community." In 1983, Rabbi Bent Melchior received Denmark's Order of Knighthood.

Arne Melchior holds a high position in the Jewish community of Denmark and in the government. Having served as a cabinet member and a member of Parliament, he also was in the Haganah in Israel's War of Independence. He is a cantor and has flown to Oslo to lead holiday services. Now his nephew, Michael, son of brother Bent, leads the prayers in Norway's capital. Another of Rabbi Marcus Melchior's grandsons, Rabbi Uri Schwartz, served in Finland and now is in Israel. Rabbi Michael Melchior's son, Eitan, often leads the synagogue service in Oslo in his father's absence.

Religiously, Danish Jews belong to the "Mosaic Community," which is governed by a 20-member board of delegates selected every two years.

JEWISH SITES IN COPENHAGEN

Caroline Skoline, 18 Bomhusvej. Tel: 29-95-00. This is a Jewish, co-ed day school founded in 1805. At one time, half of the Jewish children in Copenhagen attended this school. Today about 300 pupils are enrolled. If you want to visit this school, you should telephone ahead for an appointment.

Jewish Community Center, 6 Ny Kongensgade, 1472 K. Copenhagen. Tel: 33-12-88-68. Kosher meals are offered in the cafe, but check when the facility is open. Also located here are Bnei Akiva youth group, Hakoah Sports Club, and the Jewish Youth Club. Adults are active in Keren Kayemet (JNF), WIZO, and the Danish Zionist Federation. A museum and library display Judaica.

Resistance Museum, Esplanade in Churchill Park. Tel: 33-13-17-14. This building should head every tourist's must-see list. Its many exhibits tell the story of the Danish fight for freedom in 1940–45 and there are sections devoted to the rescue of Danish Jews. You will know you have arrived at your destination when you see a tank on the pavement in front of a brown wooden building with the words, "Frit Danmark" ("Free Denmark"). The entrance gives the appearance of a ship; you quickly remember how the Danes rescued the Jews in fishing boats. From May 6 to September 15, the museum is open Tuesday through Saturday, 10 A.M. to 4 P.M.; and on Sunday, 10 A.M. to 5 P.M. From September 16 to April 30, the museum is open Tuesday through Saturday, 11 A.M. to 3 P.M.; and on Sundays, 11 A.M. to 4 P.M. Closed on Mondays. Admission is free.

Exhibition cases 40-42 tell the story of the rescue operation of October 1943, when nearly all of Denmark's Jews were smuggled out on small fishing schooners and ferried to Sweden. Many thank-you letters and plaques grace exhibition cases 83-85 (off to the side and down the steps). Ask the guard if you cannot find these cases.

You will see greetings from many synagogues and Jewish community centers, such as Beth Sholom Mens' Club of Pittsburgh, Adath Jeshurun Congregation in Minneapolis, and other congregations in Spring Valley, New York; Jersey City; and the Boro Park section in Brooklyn. National organizations also have dispatched their thanks, including a large impressive plaque from the Rabbinical Council of America, the largest Orthodox rabbinic group in the world. All voice the sentiment that Israel and Jews everywhere will never forget the rescue of Danish Jews from the Nazis to neutral Sweden. In the courtyard of the museum is a sculpture made by Knud Nellemose; it commemorates those who gave their lives to Danish resistance to the Nazis.

The Royal Danish Library (Bibliotheca Judaica Simonseniana), 8 Christians Brygge. 1219 Copenhagen. This library houses one of the largest Jewish book collections in the world. About 80,000 volumes and manuscripts in Hebrew, Latin, Arabic, Aramaic, Ladino, Yiddish, Ethiopian, Persian, and many other languages occupy the shelves. Because it relates history, the library stands as a magnet for scholars from throughout the world. It holds the only illuminated copy of Maimonides' *Guide of the Perplexed*, penned in Barcelona in 1148.

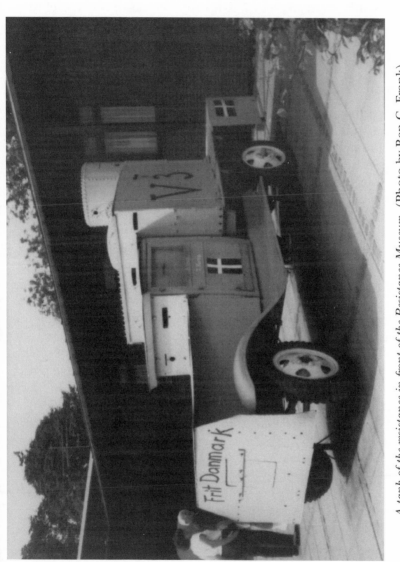

A tank of the resistance in front of the Resistance Museum. (Photo by Ben G. Frank)

KOSHER DINING IN COPENHAGEN

I. A. Samson, 3 Rorholmsgade. Kosher groceries and provisions. **Kosher Delikatesse,** 87 Lynbyvej. Tel: 33-18-57-77. Delivers kosher meals to hotels, airlines; or pick-up.

LODGING

The Hotel Villa Strand, Kystvej 12, Hornbaek. This glatt-kosher hotel-pension, located just 45 minutes from Copenhagen, stands on a beautiful North Sea coast of Hornbaek. It features newly furbished rooms and full board, including Jewish and Danish cuisine; a synagogue stands just around the corner. The hotel overlooks inviting sandy beaches. April through August, call or FAX: 49-70-00-88. The rest of the year, Tel: 43-96-94-00. FAX: 43-96-91-37.

SYNAGOGUES IN COPENHAGEN

Krystalgade Synagogue, 12 Krystalgade, is the main synagogue. Most community events occur in this Orthodox house of worship, including weddings and bar mitzvahs. Services are held Friday evenings in the summer at 8 and at 3:45 in the winter; Saturday mornings at 8. There is no mixed seating in the synagogue—women sit in an upstairs gallery. Erected in 1833, this beautifully designed building features inside walls painted white and decorated with gold. The prayer hall seats 650 persons, with standing room for about 100 people. The synagogue is near the main shopping area and the pedestrian street, Frederiksberggade, as well as close to major hotels, such as the SAS Royal.

Machsike Hadas, 12 Ole Suhrs Gade, 1354 K. Copenhagen. This synagogue maintains ties to Agudath Israel. It sponsors daily Orthodox services in addition to Sabbath services. In the summer, services also are held at 6 Granvaenget, Hornbaek, N. Seeland. About 20 families belong to this congregation.

ORGANIZATIONS

Association of Polish Jews, 74 Norre Farinagsgade. Tel: 14-30-92 or contact the Jewish Community Center. The members came here in 1969 and are now integrated into the community.

Entrance to the main synagogue in Copenhagen, the Krystalgade Synagogue.
(Photo by Ben G. Frank)

Sweden

Sweden is peaceful. This country has not fought a war since 1814. Once for a brief moment, it wielded great power. Its large towns by and large were peopled by Hanseatic merchants who settled in a long and narrow country that today is bordered on the west by Norway, on the north by Norway and Finland, and on the east and south by the Baltic Sea.

Peaceful Sweden remains the envy of the Continent. With a higher living standard than even the United States, it sponsors one of the most extensive social-welfare systems in the world. This program takes up more than 70 percent of the national budget. Perhaps that is why the socialist economy is now in financial difficulty, if you listen to the Swedes who complain of a 25 percent V.A.T. tax. But you rarely see poverty or shabbiness.

Sweden encompasses an area of 179,896 square miles of forests and dark lakes. The 1990 population was put at 8,340,000, 94 percent of which is Evangelical Lutheran. Although religious observance is on the wane, the stern Lutheran ethic places high value on discipline, hard work, and achievement.

A BRIEF HISTORY

The story of Jewish settlement begins in 1774. A gem-carver, Aaron Isak, of Mecklenburg, Germany, became the first Jew granted the right to live in Sweden; he was invited by King Gustav III. A year later, his brother arrived. Aaron brought a minyan of 10 Jewish men and their families, so he could hold services. Eight years later, the Swedish Parliament passed a law, the so-called Jew Regulations of 1782, authorizing the settlement of Jews, but only in Stockholm, Gothenburg, and Norrköping.

The Jews who arrived at the end of the eighteenth century and first half of the nineteenth century came from Germany. In 1838, the king repealed restrictions that had been passed in 1782 and incorporated the Jews into the Swedish state. After several revisions, all limitations to full citizenship were removed by Parliament in 1870.

Jews were now entitled to hold political office and were emancipated. (The Law of Freedom of Religion in 1951 abolished the regulation of 1838 requiring that citizens affiliate with a religious organization.)

In 1880, the Jewish population reached 3,000; in 1910, 6,112. In 1930, nearly 8,000 Jews resided in the country, with nearly half in Stockholm.

During World War II, Sweden sought and won complete neutrality as she had done in World War I. In 1940, the Swedes managed to stay out of the Soviet-Finnish War.

In the decade preceding the outbreak of World War II, Sweden's immigration policy was a restrictive one, according to *News & Views*, published by the World Jewish Congress. While there were Nazi sympathizers and while Sweden did maintain diplomatic relations with Germany, Jews were not persecuted. As the War went on, Swedish public opinion switched and Jews were admitted into the country. In fact, the Jews of Sweden were directly or indirectly involved in several important life-saving efforts during World War II, including the rescue of about 7,000 Danish Jews. A booklet put out by the Great Synagogue in Stockholm cites the name of Gilel Storch. The pamphlet says he "is relatively unknown, although he was the driving force behind many projects, the most successful being the supplying of some 170,000 food packages to name given persons in Nazi death and work camps. Numerous testimonies prove the value of these packages, which were sent from Sweden directly or by way of Portugal." When the Nazis invaded Norway in 1940 and began to round up Jews, about 700 escaped to Sweden, which offered them asylum. Swedish Count Folke Bernadotte and Raoul Wallenberg later saved thousands of Jews from concentration camps.

The largest and most important Jewish immigration to Sweden occurred immediately after World War II, when thousands of survivors were brought from the death camps. About 7,000 remained in Sweden, although the majority soon left for the United States, Canada, and Israel. After the upheavals in Communist Eastern Europe, 550 Jewish refugees arrived here in 1956 from Hungary. In the 1960s, 3,000 Jews emigrated from Poland. By 1970, Sweden had a Jewish population figure of 13,500; it is currently about 18,000, more than double the combined Jewish populations of Norway, Finland, and Denmark. Jews play a major role in the cultural life of Sweden, out of proportion to their numbers, especially in the fields of music, painting, and literary criticism.

Half of the Jews who inhabit Sweden today were victimized by the Nazis or emigrated from Eastern Europe after the war. Today, about 8,000 Jews live in Stockholm (5,000 are members of the community), approximately 2,500 in Gothenburg, and 2,500 in Malmö; the remainder have settled throughout the country.

Swedish-Israel relations were somewhat tense because the former had offered long-term and hearty support for the PLO. The Swedes worked to have the Palestine Liberation Organization (PLO) Chief Yasir Arafat enunciate so-called moderate positions toward Israel and renounce terror in December 1988, a declaration that brought about the off-again, on-again, now off-again contact between the United States and PLO; and by the fall of 1993, Israel and the PLO had begun direct, face-to-face negotiations.

JEWISH STOCKHOLM

Summer light stands for Stockholm—a city of islands, canals, and museums. Stockholm proclaims itself as the most beautiful and cosmopolitan of the Scandinavian capitals, replete with outstanding architecture and charm. Often called the "Venice of the North," the capital is the largest city of Sweden, with a metro population of 1,377,560. With water, water everywhere, you soon discover the city is built on 14 islands connected by about 50 bridges, under and around which ply more than 100,000 boats.

From downtown Stockholm with its modern business area to the Old Town (Gamla Stan) and its pedestrian streets; to the City Hall and its beautiful surrounding calm waves of water to boat rides in the canals alongside Renaissance buildings, you inhale this relaxing city. Visit the new Vasa Museum featuring the 1628 warship that was raised in 1961 from its water grave after sinking, or the 75-acre Skansen Outdoor Museum of Swedish Life, a great tourist attraction of 150 rebuilt old buildings spotlighting traditional handicrafts and domestic life.

This is Stockholm—clean, pure air and a wonderful traffic pattern. Much of Stockholm can be explored by foot. I immediately took a liking to the area around Nybroplan; the Number 47 bus goes there. Here is the Strand Hotel and its park areas; the Royal Dramatic Theater; the ferryboat to the Skansen Outdoor Museum; the Raoul Wallenberg Park; Judaica House, which is the headquarters of the Jewish community; and the famous Great Synagogue.

Jewish Sites in Stockholm

The Jewish Museum, Halsingegatan 2. Stockholm. Tel: 667-56-08. Open Wednesdays and Sundays, noon to 5 P.M.

Judaica House, Nybrogatan 19. Tel: 662-6686 or 663-6566. This is the Jewish Community Center of Stockholm, the center of Jewish cultural and social activity. Located in the fashionable Ostermalm section of Stockholm, the center sponsors many programs, such as Israeli folk dancing and sports clubs. A kosher dining facility (dairy) functions in Judaica House, but check to see if it is open; a gymnasium and Jewish student club meeting rooms are part of the complex. Built in 1963, with a grant from the JDC (Joint Distribution Committee), the center also encompasses a meetinghouse for such groups as Bnei Akiva, Habonim, Maccabi, Keren Kayemet (Jewish National Home), WIZO (Women's International Zionist Organization), and other organizations. Most of the time, at least one *shaliach* (advisor and teacher from Israel) resides in Stockholm and maintains his or her office here. Offices, a mikveh, as well as a gift and book shop round out the facilities in the building. But above all, there are many cultural, social, and recreational activities. Please contact the center in advance to see if the cafeteria is open. Take the Number 47 bus to Nybroplan and you can walk a few short blocks to Nybrogatan 19. Two sightseeing guides have been recommended. They are David Fischer, Tel: 886-4521, and Birgit Blideman, Tel: 612-9494.

Next door to Judaica House is a **Jewish day school.** But one

Rabbi Narrowe in the courtyard of the Great Synagogue in Stockholm. (Photo by Ben G. Frank)

The Holy Ark in the Great Synagogue of Stockholm. (Photo by Ben G. Frank)

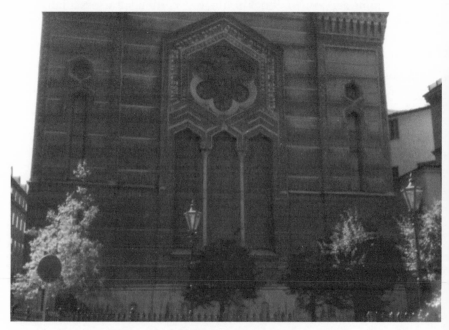

The Great Synagogue. (Photo by Ben G. Frank)

should inquire at the Jewish center for permission to visit. Kosher food may be available here.

Raoul Wallenberg Park. During the six months between July 1944 and January 1945, tens of thousands of Hungarian Jews were saved from the Nazis by a 32-year-old non-Jewish Swede, Raoul Wallenberg. In desperation and fear of certain deportation, the Jews of Budapest appealed for help to neutral embassies. In response, the understaffed Swedish Embassy asked Stockholm to send extra personnel to help them cope with the large number of Jews in need. At the same time, arrangements were being made by the Swedish Foreign Department, the American War Refugee Board, and the World Jewish Congress to initiate a last-minute operation to save Hungarian Jews.

Wallenberg, who was unmarried and a skillful organizer and negotiator, volunteered for the job. He was able to save Jews by giving them the famous "schutzpass," a type of protective passport stating that they were under Swedish jurisdiction. After the Russian liberation of Budapest in January 1945, Wallenberg was picked up by Russian soldiers and taken to the Soviet Union, never to be heard from again. The Soviet government told Sweden in 1957 that Wallenberg had died in a Moscow prison in 1947, but witnesses claim to have seen him in prison as late as the 1980s. In 1996, he would have been 84 years old.

Synagogues in Stockholm

The present head rabbi of the Stockholm community is dynamic Rabbi Morton H. Narrowe, who has been chief rabbi of Sweden since 1965 and can be reached at the Great Synagogue. Born in Philadelphia, he is a graduate of the Jewish Theological Seminary of America. His son is a rabbinical student in the United States. I would agree with a colleague who said Rabbi Narrowe "radiates warmth and bursts with enthusiasm."

The Great Synagogue, Wahrendorffsgatan 3. Tel: 679-5160. This brick building is one of the most beautiful synagogues in Europe and was designed by Fredrik Wilhelm Scholander. The seating capacity is 830 persons. Carol Herselle Krinsky, in her book *Synagogues of Europe: Architecture, History, Meaning,* claims this house of worship possesses "an Eastern identity."

In September 1870, Rabbi Ludwig Lewysohn dedicated the synagogue by kindling the gas-burning eternal light (Ner Tamid) over the Holy Ark *(aron ha-kodesh).* This date is confirmed by the Hebrew inscription over the main entrance to the synagogue. While the lamp is from that time, the cloth decorations around it are traditionally attributed to the time of King Gustav III, although no one is really certain of the truth of this claim. On the other hand, the eight-branched Hanukkah menorah is definitely a gift, according to the Hebrew text on which it stands, that was donated in 1792 after approval by King Gustav III. The legs of the menorah are in the shape of the royal *G,* which certainly stands for "Gustav." Those of the base upon which the menorah stands are formed in the shape of an *S.* The queen's name was Sofia Magdalena and the donor was Strelitz, so the meaning behind this letter is unclear.

The Raoul Wallenberg Room in the Great Synagogue is dedicated to Raoul Wallenberg, the Swedish diplomat who saved thousands of Hungarian Jews from the Nazis by issuing them diplomatic passports.

Most Jews here in the synagogue follow what probably is close to the Conservative movement of Judaism in the United States. Rabbi Narrowe describes the synagogue as Ashkenazic, Liberal, and Conservative—with an organ and mixed seating in one section.

Saturday morning services are at 9:15. Shabbat mornings are an exciting time to be in the synagogue, as the service is rewarding and the kiddush that follows gives travelers a chance to meet the Jews of Stockholm. Rabbi Narrowe gives the sermon in Swedish. The kiddush is held in the lecture hall, which features paintings of the past leadership of Swedish Jewry.

Winter brings darkness. Shabbat can begin as early as 2:30 on a Friday afternoon. A Monday and Thursday morning minyan is scheduled for 8, but check these times by calling the synagogue.

Tourists should note that few activities are scheduled in the summer, as most Swedes go on vacation, especially in July. The synagogue sponsors a popular Jewish summer camp that includes not only several hundred children, but senior citizens, too. Often, both a grandparent and grandchild will meet on the campgrounds.

The SAS Strand, Grand, and Diplomat hotels are near the synagogue. The Royal Viking Hotel, Vasagaten 1, near the central railroad station, is a little farther, but it is an excellent place to stop in the Swedish capital.

Two small Orthodox synagogues function in Stockholm: **Adas Yeshurun** and **Adath Israel.** Rabbi A. Katz is spiritual leader at both congregations, which in outlook are close to the Agudas Israel Orthodox group. About 200 families belong to the two congregations.

Adas Yeshurun is located in the school building next door to Judaica House, at Nybrogatan 19. The address is Riddergatan 5. Tel: 661-82-82. The synagogue is furnished with benches, Holy Ark, pulpit, and table that were in a small synagogue in Hamburg and miraculously survived *Kristallnacht.* These religious objects were sent to Stockholm's Orthodox Jews by the Orthodox Jewish community in Hamburg. "This synagogue and its furniture have great emotional value for all of Stockholm's Jewry. They express symbolically the faith that Judaism is eternal and that it lives throughout the world and in all ages," says a synagogue brochure.

The other Orthodox house of worship, **Adath Israel**, is located at St. Paulsgarten 13. Tel: 44-19-95.

GOTHENBURG

Jewish Community Center, Ostra Larmgatan 12, 41107, Gothenburg. Tel: 17-72-45.

MALMÖ

Jewish Community Center, Kamregatan 11, 21156, Malmö. Tel: 11-84-60 or 11-88-60.

Synagogue, Foreningsgatan, Malmö.

Norway

Norwegian Jewry is unique. For example:

- One rabbi is in residence only about half of the year and lives in Israel the other half.
- An Arab runs the kosher provision store, which is stocked with kosher meat and food packages from Israel and Europe.
- The last name of the synagogue president is Rothschild but he is no relation, he believes, to the illustrious family.
- The year 1992 was the 100th anniversary of Norwegian Jewry as a congregation, according to Norwegian Jewish leader Herman Kahan.

Kahan has written a book, part of which explains Judaism to this "caring," and "friendly" Norwegian society and another section on the history of this young Jewish community, a community that Kahan came to after the war, when he realized his sister was alive and living here. He fell in love with the people and country, which is attractive, clean, and very environmentally conscious. Although Norway can be expensive, it still offers some travel bargains.

There is a Jewish community here and it is alive. Except for the **kosher provisions store,** which is located at Stensberggate 19, Oslo, you need only one address when you are visiting the city—Bergstien St. 13, 15, 17—which is the Community Center and synagogue (see below).

Nearly 1,000 Jews live in Norway, most in Oslo and its suburbs, with about 120 to 150 in Trondheim. A few Jews reside in Bergen. Actually, because less than 4 percent of its land is livable, most of Norway's 4 million-plus citizens inhabit Oslo, Trondheim, and Bergen.

Today, Norway welcomes tourists to its attractive, picturesque villages and spectacular scenery of fiords, cliffs, rugged uplands, and forests that once were the paths and sealanes of Viking warriors. They were those hearty warriors who sailed to North America between the ninth and eleventh centuries. Norway covers 125,057 square miles, with a 2,125-mile jagged coastline along the North, Norwegian, and Baltic seas. Norway lies back to back with Sweden along a peaceful 1,000-

mile border. Actually, from 1814 until 1905, the country was held by Sweden. In the north, it shares a boundary with Finland and the former U.S.S.R.

Norway boasts the fifth largest merchant fleet in the world—more than 200 shipping companies. So one can see why the sea and the fishing industry remain paramount in Norway. The fiords, which are deep inlets of the sea extending back into the mountains sometimes for more than 100 twisting miles, complete the beautiful picture of this fine nation. Despite latitudes equal to Alaska, Norway's climate remains mild because of warm ocean breezes. A welfare state and the discovery of oil and gas have helped give the country a high standard of living.

A BRIEF HISTORY

For many years the history of Norwegian Jews was linked to Denmark's Jewish community since Norway was ruled by Denmark for 400 years until 1814, when Sweden took over. Norway may have been one of the last countries in Europe to admit Jews. The first Jews arrived here about 300 years ago, but 1851 seems to be the date they settled down. Immigration really got under way after 1881, with an influx of Jews from Eastern Europe. In 1890, 214 Jews lived in Norway, most of them in Oslo.

Norwegian Jews erected their first synagogue in 1920, when there were about 1,500 Jewish inhabitants.

Nazi Germany invaded Norway on April 9, 1940. Hitler needed this peace-loving land to secure the transports of iron ore from northern Sweden along the Norwegian coast in the winter when the Baltic Sea is iced. Norway could be exploited as a base to attack northern Great Britain. About 1,800 Jews inhabited the country, including several hundred Jewish refugees. Vidkun Quisling (who gave us the word *quisling*—traitor) was "minister president" of a puppet regime. He became dictator and turned Jews over to the Nazis. He was executed after the war.

In late 1942, 770 Jews were rounded up and shipped to Nazi death camps. Only 12 survived. Twenty additional Jews were murdered in Norway.

With the help of the Norwegian underground, some 930 Jews escaped to Sweden. This action was carried out with the aid of a group called the Norwegian Lifeboat Society.

After World War II, about 800 Norwegian Jews returned from Sweden. The Norwegian government, however, allowed several hundred Jews to enter from displaced persons (D.P.) camps, under the category of "war casualties." By the mid-1950s, about 1,000 Jews resided in Norway, of whom 700 settled in Oslo, and 150 in Trondheim.

A democratic state, Norway fights anti-Semitism and is proud that the first secretary-general of the United Nations was Norwegian Trygve Lee, who helped gain passage of the 1947 U.N. Partition Plan Resolution creating the State of Israel. To fight a 50 percent mixed-marriage rate, many young Jews are sent to Stockholm, Copenhagen, London, and, of course, Israel to find a Jewish spouse. But the rate of mixed marriages here is believed to be lower than in Sweden and Denmark because many Norwegian Jews are newcomers from Eastern Europe and have not as yet assimilated fully.

Norwegian Jewry lauds its religious freedom, the absence of anti-Semitism, as well as government and public support for the Jewish community. The Jewish community here lives in a prosperous environment, so well off that the assimilation process may be accelerated.

JEWISH OSLO

Oslo, this bright, busy capital city of slightly less than a half-million, situated on 175 square miles and founded nine centuries ago in 1050, is a friendly city. From the new, modern Oslo Plaza Hotel to the comfortable, calm harbor area, the City Hall, the museums and restaurants, Oslo has many sites for the visitor. One of the most fascinating European tourist attractions is the open-air Vigeland Sculpture Park in Frogner Park. There, more than 200 bronze, granite, and wrought-iron statues of men, women, and children, reflecting the relationship between the sexes, draw tourists. Anyone visiting the Norwegian capital should pay a visit to Vigeland's present to the city of Oslo.

Informal Oslo proudly advertises that nearly everyone speaks English in this land of sailors and ships and merchant marines. The museums reflect the sea, especially the Kon-Tiki Museum on the Bygdoy Peninsula, which contains the raft of the anthropologist and adventurer, Thor Heyerdahl. Other museums include the Norwegian Folk Museum, also on the Bygdoy Peninsula. Oslo was also the site of the negotiations that led to Israel and the PLO signing "protocols" in Washington, D.C., in September 1993.

Jewish Sites in Oslo

Community Center and Synagogue, Bergstien St. 13, 15, 17. Three attached buildings—a senior citizen home, a synagogue, and a community center—make up the Jewish community complex on Bergstien Street. Friday evening and Sabbath morning services are scheduled.

The prayer times obviously depend on the season in these northern lands. For instance, in July, the Sabbath could begin at 8:20 P.M. and not end until 1:05 A.M. early Sunday morning. On Saturday mornings, after the services, a kiddush takes place. Tel: 19-21-22. The telephone number of the office at the Community Center is 606-826. Leon Rothschild is gabai of the synagogue. His phone number is 22-59-48-74. Herman Kahan is a leader of the community. His telephone number is 603-190; FAX: 461-394. Kai Feinberg, P.O. Box 740, Oslo, 0105. Tel: 22-30-29-29, is also a leader of the community.

The synagogue was founded in 1892 and the present structure built in 1920. After World War II, King Olav V, then Crown Prince, attended the reconstruction ceremony. The building had been miraculously spared by the Nazis in the war. In 1992, the 100th anniversary of the synagogue was celebrated.

Michael Melchior, of the Danish Melchior family, is rabbi and has served since 1978. He was educated at Yeshivat HaKotel in Jerusalem and in the late 1980s, he settled in Israel. His father is the chief rabbi of Denmark, a position once held by his late grandfather, Rabbi Marcus Melchior. Rabbi Michael Melchior can be found at the synagogue at Bergstien 15, 0172, Oslo. Tel: 47-29-26-12. The synagogue is difficult to find as it is

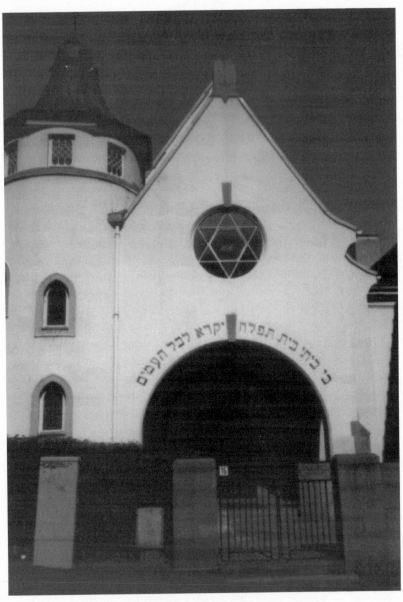

The Oslo synagogue. (Photo by Ben G. Frank)

located in a residential community. The synagogue is situated on the east side of St. Hans Haugen Park. If you are walking, follow Ullevalsveien to Knud Knudsens Plass and follow the east side of the park to Bergstien Street.

The Jewish community is active. Zionist groups, B'nai B'rith, and WIZO meet at the Community Center, which is next door to the synagogue.

HJM—Help the Jews Home, Colletsgatge 43, 0456, Oslo. Tel: 69-23-70. Mrs. Jackie Feinberg, the group's secretary, can be reached at 14-11-13. An active Russian Jewry Committee has been on the scene in Oslo. Mrs. Feinberg reported that the group called "Help the Jews Home" was raising funds for Russian Jews. This group was established in 1990 by eight Christian, secular, and Jewish organizations.

Jewish War Victims Memorial, Stroensveten 105, in the Jewish cemetery, an enclave in the municipal cemetery. A large Magen David is engraved on the memorial's panels and it includes the names of 620 Norwegian Jewish men and women who perished in the Holocaust. From the center of the star rises a column in the shape of a truncated tree trunk, on which a memorial plaque is affixed. King Olav V and the Royal Family attended the unveiling ceremony.

The Jewish Memorial Park in the suburb of Hurum, on the Kjerrlgrav Hill, overlooking the Oslo Fjord. A planeload of Tunisian Jewish children crashed on this spot in 1949.

The Resistance Museum. Part of Oslo's Akershus Castle, the medieval stone fortress of the Viking king Harkon, this museum is close to the monument to heroes who lost their lives in World War II. Described as "informative," "interesting," and "stirring," Norway's Resistance Museum deals with Norwegian resistance against the German occupation, 1940–45. The building is known as the Double Battery and The Frame House. The basement consists of two stone vaults built in about 1650 to accommodate six cannons and an adjacent powder magazine. Later, a battery was positioned on top of the vaults, hence the name. The frame building above, erected in the mid-eighteenth century, was used mainly as a military storehouse right down to 1862, when the building was made available for use as a museum. The museum was opened to the public by the then Crown Prince, now King Harald, on May 8, 1970, 25 years to the day after the end of the war in Europe.

The Wergeland Monument. Each year on May 17, which is "Constitution Day" in Norway, Jews, especially Jewish youth, come together at the Wergeland Monument in the Var Frilser's Cemetery to honor Henrik Wergeland (1808–45), the national poet. They lay bouquets of red and white carnations at the foot of the statue of Henrik Wergeland. Wergeland was instrumental in having the ban against Jewish immigration lifted. Creating a welcome climate for Jews, he wrote a book entitled *Jodinden, The Jewess.* He did not live to see the ban against Jewish immigration lifted, as he died in 1845. Donated by Swedish Jews, the inscription reads: "To the indefatigable fighter for freedom and the rights of man and citizens." On the other side of the monument it says: "Grateful Jews outside the frontiers of Norway erected this monument to him."

Another monument to Wergeland stands in Studenter-luden, a park on Karl Johansgate Street, which is the main pedestrian avenue, replete with shops and restaurants.

For further information on sight-seeing in Oslo, contact the Oslo tourist office: Tel: 83-00-50.

Vegetarian Restaurant. Vegeta Vertshus, 3-B, Munked-amsvei, Oslo.

TRONDHEIM

The northernmost **synagogue** in the world stands in Trondheim, Norway. Originally a railroad station, this imposing structure is located at Arkitekt Christiesgate 1B, near Nidaros Cathedral. The building—used by the Nazis as a warehouse in the war—was enlarged in 1955 by adding a Jewish community center that also includes a Hebrew school. More than 100 Jews live in the city. The sanctuary can seat 150 people, including a women's gallery. The telephone number of the synagogue is 47-29-434.

The Jewish War Victims Memorial in Trondheim is located in the Jewish cemetery. The monument consists of three granite slabs on which are inscribed the names of the 60 Trondheim Jews murdered by the Nazis.

Finland

Welcome to Finland, land of a thousand lakes, land of the "sauna." Five million people inhabit 130,119 square miles, in some places one person per square mile.

Bounded on the north by Norway, on the east by Russia, on the south by the Baltic Sea, and on the west by the Gulf of Bothnia and Sweden, Finland is as beautiful as a picture post-card, with 187,888 lakes—one lake for every 26 persons.

Much of the Finnish population lives in the south and that means they reside in and around the capital, Helsinki, a large industrial city, cultural center, and Baltic port.

This "white city of the North," with its numerous white buildings, rose in the 1550s and was built to be inhabited by humans. Helsinki grows on you. You cannot take in this city in one day. It must be observed and returned to in order to get the feel of it. Even with the end of the cold war, it still remains a bridge between the West and the vast expanse of Russia to its east. For those flying back from Russia or Baltic countries, Helsinki still positions itself as a welcome stopping-off spot.

Walk around Market Square and watch the people. Look out to the water buses in the south harbor. Stroll along Esplanade Park surrounded by shopping streets and hear the concerts at the bandstand. Buy some fruit in the market near the water.

The Jean Sibelius Memorial in Sibelius Park and Finlandia Hall are sights not to be missed.

The passenger ships of the Silja Line to Stockholm await you. A good way to arrive here from New York is on the daily Finnair jet flights.

A BRIEF HISTORY

In the Middle Ages, Finland was joined to Sweden. But in the eighteenth century, sections of southeastern Finland were ceded to the czar. Moreover, in the Peace Treaty of Hamina in 1809, Finland was formally ceded to the czar, but kept its status of an autonomous grand duchy that retained its previous law and institutions. In 1812, the country's capital was transferred from Turku to Helsinki (Helsingfors). While the Russian

Revolution raged in 1917, Finland declared its independence on December 6. An ensuing civil war between Finnish Whites and Reds nearly devastated the country, with the Whites winning the conflict. Peace was signed in 1920.

Until Russia grabbed up Finland in 1809, Jewish settlement in Sweden was forbidden. When the Russians took over the country, a few Jews who served in the army were permitted to reside here. We call these ex-Jewish soldiers "cantonists." These "cantonists" were Jewish boys torn from their parents at a very young age and kept in the czar's military service for 25 years. But after that long quarter of a century of service, these veterans were permitted to settle anywhere in the czar's dominions, including Finland.

The edict of 1858 has been regarded by the Jews of Finland as a "Magna Carta," granting them precious rights and privileges, but still not complete emancipation. By 1880, about 1,000 Jews lived in Finland, but they had to stay in only a few cities, including Turku and Vyborg.

When independence was achieved in 1917, Jews were granted full civil rights. After the Russian Revolution, many Russian Jews found a haven in Finland. By 1930, the Jewish population of Finland was about 1,700.

Zionism had a strong hold on Finland's Jewish population. In May 1939, Ze'ev Vladimir Jabotinsky, the leader of the Revisionist group in the Jewish State, visited Helsinki. Twenty years earlier, he had addressed the Jews of Finland. Only this time, with war beckoning, he desperately called on Jews to leave Sweden, Finland, Estonia, and Latvia and settle in the Jewish State. Jabotinsky called for a "clear nationalist feeling and a battle for liberation," according to Hannu Rautkallio. Nobody listened.

A few months later, the Russians attacked Finland in what became the Russo-Finnish Winter War, and Jewish lives were again lost as they rallied to the blue and white flag of Finland. The Finns fought the Soviets with "religious fervor." The Finns drew the admiration of the world as they mounted a desperate defense of their country. Many Jews served in the Finnish Army in that war of 1939–40 as well as during the Continuation War of 1941–44. The losses suffered by Finnish Jews were substantial; of the country's Jewish population, no less than one-fifth had served in the Finnish armed forces (more than 300 men, of whom 26 had been killed or reported missing—nearly 8 percent of the total number of Jews who served).

But even more unbelievable was the fact that Jewish soldiers fought in units that were alongside German soldiers in World War II. They actually did, and they did it on the Finnish-Russian border. In fact, during the war, the Finnish Jewish soldiers built a field synagogue by the River Suir, "no doubt, a very exceptional event in an Army fighting on the German's side during the war," writes Tapani Harviainen, a professor at the University of Helsinki.

Finnish Jews serving with Germans? How did it happen? The Finns say they were on the side of the Germans because in this case, the enemy of both nations was the then U.S.S.R. This unique situation actually began on August 23, 1939, with the signing of the infamous Molotov-Ribbintrop pact. Nine days later, on September 1, 1939, Hitler invaded Poland and Russia gobbled up the eastern part of Poland. The Soviets soon made harsh demands on Finland and the Russo-Finnish Winter War broke out on November 30, 1939, with the bombing of Helsinki. "It was naked, unprovoked, inexcusable aggression," wrote William L. Shirer. The war lasted 105 days and Finland, in 1940, ceded much territory to the U.S.S.R. But the fighting between Russia and Finland would start again a year later, in what became known as the "Continuation War."

The way the Finns tell it, Finland joined in the Continuation War in 1941 after it was attacked by Russia during the same time that the Germans launched their June 1941 invasion of the U.S.S.R. Thus, the Finns maintain, the Russians attacked first in 1941, and this was a "separate war." The Finns, continues the argument, were not "allied" to Germany, but merely a "co-belligerent." Therefore, "the Finnish campaign was a defensive struggle separate from the war of the great powers," says Eino Jutikkala.

However, in reality, one must also remember that as the Nazi blitzkrieg swept across Russia in 1941, the Soviet Union seemed doomed and the Finns saw it as an opportunity to regain their land lost in the 1939–40 war. They did so briefly, but by 1943, the Russians hurled back the German invaders and broke through the Axis lines to assault Finland. Britain had declared war against Finland. The latter was obliged to make peace, once again ceding land and reparations to the U.S.S.R. At the same time, the Germans in their retreat through Finland ravaged Finnish land and killed many civilians.

The Finnish government withstood German pressure to harm Jews. By 1939, the Jewish population had grown to 2,000, and Finland gave temporary sanctuary to fleeing Jews and saved its Jewish residents. It gave shelter to a substantially larger number of westward-bound Jewish refugees than official statistics indicate, Rautkallio says. In 1944, 200 stateless refugees came to Sweden from Finland. Rautkallio states that Finland refused to hand over Finnish Jews to the Germans. The record shows that perhaps less than 20 non-Finnish Jews were surrendered to the Germans, the *Encyclopedia Judaica* puts the figure at 50 Jewish refugees from Austria and the Baltic countries, and Finnish Jewish publications and leaders today say 8. But it is clear that the Jews of Finland escaped being drawn into the Nazi net. As Raul Hilberg has affirmed, the process of the destruction of Jewry never extended as far as Finland. Finland was the only nation fighting on Germany's side against a common enemy that was never pressured to hand over the Jews, according to Rautkallio. He notes that the Germans were quite aware of the public outcry that would have been raised in Finland if there was so much as a hint of any coercive action against Jews. Persecution or anti-Semitism could hardly be discerned in Finland. Although quite late in the war, on Finland's Independence Day in 1944, Marshall Mannerheim attended a ceremony in the Helsinki synagogue.

Commenting on Rautkallio's book, Irving Abrahamson, in *Reform Judaism* magazine, said, "If, on the one hand, Rautkallio's book shows that the Finns took no part in the Final Solution, on the other it shows that the Nazis made no effort to impose the Final Solution on them."

In the end, Finland suffered many casualties. She lost 11

percent of her territory to the Russians. As Aini Rajanen points out, the Finns are "people who fought 42 wars with Russia and lost every one of them."

In World War II, there may have been up to 2,300 Jews in Finland, refugees and descendants of the cantonists; by 1949 there were 1,700 Jews in Finland.

Finland was the third nation, after the United States and the U.S.S.R., to recognize the State of Israel in 1948. Twenty-nine Finnish Jewish youths fought in Israel's War of Independence, proportionately the highest number in the Diaspora. More than 100 emigrated to Israel. Today, the Finns display strong support for Israel.

About 1,300 Jews live in Finland, 1,000 of them in and around Helsinki. Several hundred Jews reside in Turku, the oldest city in Finland, and 50 in Tampere. Those Finnish Jews, recognized as Jews according to halacha or through halachic conversions, are members of the community, which is Ashkenazic and mostly upper middle and middle class. The three Finnish Jewish communities of Helsinki, Tampere, and Turku are united under the Central Council of Jewish Communities in Finland. Its executive board includes nine members, six from Helsinki and three from Turku. The Central Council represents the Jews of Finland, both nationally and internationally. This council is a member of the World Jewish Congress and the World Zionist Organization.

Some assert that at least half the Jewish population intermarries, and that rate is rising. "A marriage of two Finnish Jews has long been a rare exception," wrote Harviainen. Still, Jewish leaders note that many non-Jewish partners convert and the majority of the mixed couples prefer to send their children to the Jewish kindergarten and the Jewish school.

Jews voice their happiness with living in Finland. Why not? Finland's economy generally is good. There are no international problems, and no anti-Semitism hovers over the Jewish community. A very homogeneous society, Finland has no minority problems. Finns don't bother Jews, Jewish leaders told me. And while the people are reserved and not as gregarious as their neighbors, the Swedes, they love their country and their land and are trying to keep their national identity.

As for Finnish Jews, most of the older generations are independent business persons or shopkeepers, while the younger generation enters the professions.

Jews are active in all professions and walks of life. Max Jakobson was former Finnish ambassador to the United Nations and actually ran against Kurt Waldheim of Austria for the post of secretary-general of the United Nations. Jakobson lost when the Soviets vetoed his candidacy. Dr. Simon Parmet is a noted composer and conductor. Sam Vanni is a famous painter, a member of the Finnish Academy and the European Academy of Science, Art and Literature. In 1979, Ben Zyskowicz was the first Finnish Jew to be elected a member of Parliament.

Still active is a Finnish Jewish War Veterans League that was founded in 1979, with a membership in 1991 of 86 members, 70 of whom live in Finland, according to Gideon Bolotowsky.

JEWISH HELSINKI

Kosher Dining in Helsinki

Jewish Community Center. Malminkantu 26, next to the synagogue. Tel: 694-1296. Kosher meals are available at the center if you phone in your order ahead of time. At the Community Center and in the synagogue one is likely to meet Russian Jews, many of whom wait here in Helsinki for their connecting flight to Israel.

Kosher butcher and delicatessen, Ritus, Uudenmaankatu 28. Tel: 644-951.

Jewish Sites in Helsinki

Synagogue and Jewish Community Center, Malminkatu 26. Tel: 692-1297 and 694-1302. All organizations meet here. The congregation is one of the few in Scandinavia holding daily services, which are scheduled Monday to Friday mornings at 7:45. Friday evening services are at 6:45 and Saturday morning services are at 9. The synagogue was built in 1906. Renovated and enlarged in 1926, this house of worship added a library to the

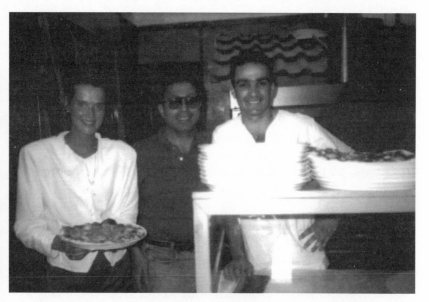

Rafael Maimon of Helsinki, center, originally from Israel, with two of his employees in his restaurant in the Forum. Many Israelis gather in the restaurant section of the Forum, a huge shopping complex in downtown Helsinki. (Photo by Ben G. Frank)

The synagogue in Helsinki. (Photo by Ben G. Frank)

building that same year. Unlike many synagogues in Europe, this synagogue is very visible. Services in the synagogue follow Orthodox Lithuanian ritual. Rabbi Lazar Kleinman is the spiritual leader of the congregation.

The Jewish Community Center, next to the synagogue, was dedicated in 1962. Facilities include a senior citizens home and an auditorium, lounges, meeting rooms, and a mikveh. Here the Helsinki Jewish community sponsors a day school. At one point, 80 percent of the Jewish children in Helsinki attended the school, founded in 1918. Enrollment has gone up because the Israelis send their offspring to the school.

Jewish organizations that meet at the Community Center include the 125-year-old Chevra Kadisha, the Chevra Bikur Cholim, WIZO Finland, which has several hundred members, as well as branches of the JNF and Keren Hayesod. Cultural activities are promoted by the Jewish Choral Society, the Club Judaica, and the Hebrew language club, the Chug Ivrit.

Makkabi Sports Club, also located at the Community Center, is the oldest existing Maccabi sports club in Europe. Pictures of its famous athletes adorn the walls of its club room in the Jewish Center section of the complex.

The community publishes a bi-monthly magazine called *Ha' Kehila.*

Preserved in the synagogue is a wreath presented by Field Marshall Carl G. Mannerheim when he made a visit to synagogue services in 1944. The wreath memorialized the 23 Jewish soldiers who had died in the Russo-Finnish War. Mannerheim was president of Finland from 1944 to 1946. His statue stands tall in several places, including near the Parliament Building in Helsinki. His former home is a museum now.

The Mannerheim Museum, Kalliolinnantie 14, 00140, Helsinki. Tel: 635-443. The guides at this museum are excellent. To the Finns, Mannerheim is George Washington, Abraham Lincoln, and Winston Churchill all rolled into one. Jewish senior citizens maintain it was Mannerheim who saved the Jews.

TURKU

With a population of slightly more than 150,000, this seaport and one-time capital is one of Finland's oldest cities. Often called the "cradle of Finnish culture," for much of the country's early history occurred here, it is surrounded by great forests.

Synagogue and Community Center, Brahenkatu 17. Tel: 312-557. This brick building, located on a corner site, also has a distinctive cupola that can be seen from a distance. The structure was built in 1912, with an adjoining community center erected in 1956. Several hundred Jews support the center. The community maintains a Burial Society, a Bikur Cholim society, and a Makkabi Sports Club. Also, Talmud Torah classes are held here.

Suggested Reading

Bertelsen, Aage. *October, 1943.* New York: Putnam, 1954.

Bradley, David. *Lion Among Roses: A Memoir of Finland.* New York: Holt, Rinehart & Winston, 1965.

Goldberger, Leo, ed. *The Rescue of the Danish Jews: Moral Courage under Stress.* New York: New York University Press, 1987.

Jutikkala, Eino, with Pirinen, Kauko. *A History of Finland.* Translated by Paul Sjoblom. Helsinki: Weilin and Goos, 1984.

Krinsky, Carol Herselle. *Synagogues of Europe: Architecture, History, Meaning.* Cambridge, Mass.: MIT Press, 1985.

Rajanen, Aini. *Of Finnish Ways.* Minneapolis: Dillon Press, 1981.

Rautkallio, Hannu. *Finland and the Holocaust: The Finnish Experience.* New York: Holocaust Publications, 1987.

Shirer, William L. *The Challenge of Scandinavia, Norway, Sweden, Denmark and Finland in Our Time.* Boston: Little, Brown, 1955.

Yahil, Leni. *The Rescue of Danish Jewry.* Philadelphia: Jewish Publication Society, 1969.

The Czech Republic
The Spotlight Shines on Prague

I stand on the banks of the Vltava River—in German, it is called the Moldau. Being in Prague, I naturally start humming Smetna's wonderful symphonic poem, "The Moldau," which salutes Bohemia's noble past and rich culture. Many Jews and non-Jews know that the yearning anthem of Zionism and later the National Anthem of the State of Israel, "Hatikvah," was adapted from the same Czech folk song on which Smetna based his famous E minor melody.

Cities often take on characteristics of their rivers or harbors as the case may be. Prague is such a city. It imitates the embracing calm and serene flow of the Moldau. The tourist wants to hug this Bohemian capital, Prague. Mention Prague and we feel good. Jews have a kind word for this Czech capital. It was, and can be again, a shining light of Jewish scholarship. It remains one of the few cities in Europe where Jewish sites have been preserved.

And yet for all our fondness, in our memory there is another side of the ledger that comes to mind:

In a speech to the British people in 1938, that archappeaser, Prime Minister Neville Chamberlain, said:

"how 'horrible, fantastic, incredible, it was that we should be digging ditches and trying on gas masks here because of a quarrel in a faraway country between people with whom we know nothing.'"

413

A Czech Airlines (CSA) flight from New York, nonstop to Prague. (Photo courtesy Czech Airlines)

The "faraway" country was Czechoslovakia and the people were the Czechs and Slovaks. Because the French and British sought to appease Hitler, the Munich agreement sacrificed Czechoslovakia to the Nazis. It would take fifty years for this wonderful country to begin to emerge from the consequences of Fascist and Communist totalitarianism.

In coming to Prague, you journey to the heart of Europe. Photograph Prague as you would a perfectly cut diamond, because Prague is the jewel of Central Europe. And as you travel through this city, remember history. History will tell you that Prague has always vied with Warsaw and Berlin for the title the "heart of Europe."

Prague is in the limelight now because Americans are flocking there for its beauty, charm, and vibrancy. Young people love it, just as they love Paris, only Prague is less expensive. Once, Paris, too, was the home of the American expatriates: Hemingway, Stein, Crowley, Fitzgerald, and Ford Maddox Ford. Today the spotlight shines on Prague, the "Left Bank of the 1990s," the new Paris of American expatriates with writers, tourists, and students arriving here by the thousands to observe its Bohemian culture and patronize its cafes. They crowd Wenceslas Square—the downtown center of shopping and sight-seeing. And they rent apartments in the Old Town, if they can get them or if they can afford them.

A young Jewish man who lives in the new nation of Slovakia told me that while he is a Slovak citizen, whenever he sees the flag of the Czech Republic, he cries. He has good reason: "For 10 centuries, Prague (Praha) and the areas of Bohemia and Moravia ignited the torch of liberty in Central Europe. Sometimes it was the only light in a vast darkness." When it was independent, Czechoslovakia was one of the most progressive countries in the world. Timothy Garton Ash writes in his book, *The Magic Lantern,* "historically, Czechoslovakia was much the most democratic state in the region before the War." He believes culturally that "Prague is *the* Central European city."

But, like the former U.S.S.R., Czechoslovakia as a united state no longer exists. The year 1993 was a momentous one in the history of the former Czechoslovakia: the divorce between

the Czech lands and Slovakia became official. When it was united (between 1918 and 1939, and 1945 and 1993), Czechoslovakia was the size of New York state. Now the Czech
Republic has 10.2 million people in 30,000 square miles with
1.2 million persons living in Prague.

The Czech Republic and Slovakia still stand at the major
crossroads of Europe. "Not a single major European conflict
has left the area untouched in its thousand year history," wrote
Czech President Vaclav Havel in the October 17, 1993, *New
York Times*. He added that "wars have started or ended in our
territory, and the main threads of history have sometimes been
wound together and unraveled here."

Bounded in the west by Germany, in the north by Poland, in
the east by Slovakia, and in the south by Austria, the Czech
Republic takes pride in its economic progress, with a budget
surplus and a healthy export market to the West. By 1994, sixty
percent of production came from privatized companies, and
unemployment was low. The Czech Republic is waiting to enter
the European Union, as well as NATO, without reservation.
But in the mid-1990s, the West seemed to be keeping the
Czechs at arm's length, although by the end of the century
admittance will probably occur.

For the traveler's purpose, Czech history starts when Slavic
tribes pushed down from the north, perhaps as early as the first
century A.D. Then came the Roman legionnaires, who were followed by waves of fierce Avars and Magyars and then Tartars and
Turks—all of whom spilled rivers of blood through these lands.

A Slavic empire flourished until the tenth century. While the
Slovaks chafed for a thousand years under Hungarian rule, the
Czechs briefly enjoyed their own kingdom. Bohemia existed
for several centuries. But then came the Hapsburgs who ruled
for three hundred years, until 1918. Freedom lasted only twenty years until the flames of Hitlerism raged across this democratic nation. Following the war, Czechoslovakia was stifled by
communism for forty years. In 1989, the Czech Communist
world collapsed in the wake of the "Velvet Revolution," a
peaceful mass revolt in which not one person died. The
prognosis looks good. "The Czech Republic has a real chance of

making the larger transition from planned to market economy, with relatively less economic pain than its neighbors: although I stress the word, 'relatively,'" writes Timothy Garton Ash.

A Brief History

Jews have lived in Czechoslovakia—always an important Jewish cultural center—for at least a thousand years. For much of the time, it was one of the richest and most advanced nations in Europe, with a high degree of religious freedom and cultural development. Jews flocked there. As Jewish merchants moved eastward from the Rhineland in the West to the Fertile Crescent in the East, they plied the trade routes of Central Europe and probably arrived at the end of the tenth century in what we now call the Czech Republic.

Until the twelfth century, Jews lived under favorable conditions. With the Third and Fourth Lateran Councils (1179 and 1215), the Catholic church cracked down on Jews and Jews lost many of the rights they had enjoyed. By the thirteenth century, sixteen Jewish communities existed in Bohemia and Moravia, all actively seeking religious freedom. It is no wonder that Jews by the thousands poured into these provinces. There they could live in peace and practice their religion. They became moneylenders, and because they also paid higher taxes than most people, they were somewhat protected by the king. But the king often turned against them and cancelled all debts to Jews. At other times, the Jews had the backing of the king and the nobles. During these periods, they were particularly creative: they established the first Hebrew printing house in Prague; they designed and published the Prague Haggadah. Prague took on cultural and economic importance, especially when Ferdinand I declared that Jews could not live in other towns. Jews owned land and they even farmed. They traded, practiced medicine, and served the court. They excelled in crafts. They contributed to Jewish learning and literature.

A momentous event occurred in Czech history in 1402. That year, the preacher Jan Hus reached the masses with the idea of Church reform. For his criticisms of Church practices, he was burned at the stake on July 6, 1415. The Hussite Reformation shook Europe a hundred years before Martin Luther emerged.

In 1522, 600 Jews resided in Prague. By 1541, the number had risen to 1,200.

A milestone in Czech history was the Battle of Mohacs on August 29, 1526. In that conflict, Louis II of Hungary was defeated and killed, leaving the throne vacant for the ascension of Ferdinand I of Hapsburg as ruler of the Bohemian lands and Hungary. The Golden Age of Prague Jewry appeared on the horizon in that century and early in the next as Jews began to prosper economically. They gained privileges, economic freedom, and the right to live anywhere.

The Battle of White Mountain in 1620 saw the defeat of the Czechs at the hands of the Austrians. In one fell swoop, the Austrians overwhelmed the Czech people and their noblemen, executing 27 members of the Czech aristocracy and exiling 150,000 Protestants. Geoffrey Moorhouse in *Prague* writes: "The story of Prague since 1620 is essentially the story of alien domination. Unless the outsider can guess this fact, he or she will not understand this city, nor appreciate the wary, stoic temper of its people."

The Counter-Reformation, which was the response of the Catholic church to the Protestant Reformation of the sixteenth and seventeenth centuries, "helped destroy religious freedom, national independence, and the educated classes of Czechoslovakia. In the Thirty Years' War, the Counter-Reformation was imposed on the Czechs, and they in effect lost their national independence." On the heels of the good life came oppressive laws, plagues, death, and pogroms. The Jewish quarter was burned to the ground and Maria Theresa (1740–80) banished the Jews from Bohemia and Moravia for three years. They were allowed to resettle, however, despite the anti-Semitism of this Holy Roman empress.

Joseph II of Austria (1780–90), who issued the *Toleranzpatent* of 1782 ("patents of toleration"), improved the quality of life of the Jewish community. Yet he wanted the Jews to be totally assimilated and to be useful to the state as participants in a modern economic system. Jews took advantage of Joseph's reforms and expanded economic activities. They established factories and even worked in agriculture. Prague joined with Berlin and Vienna to become an important center of Jewish Enlightenment.

By 1848, the number of Jews in Prague reached the 10,000 mark, compared to Vienna, with only 4,000. Just as Jews began to achieve equal rights, the Jewish community of Prague dwindled as new Jewish centers arose in Berlin and Vienna. Yet by the 1900s half of the Jews of Bohemia resided in Prague. Those Jews were active in the politics and cultural life of the city, which once again became a major center of European Jewry.

After Czechoslovakia gained its independence in 1918, more and more Jews began to speak Czech. In Slovakia and Carpathian-Russia, they spoke Yiddish and Hungarian. Before 1918, the history of the Jews in Bohemia, Moravia, and Silesia was an integral part of the history of Austrian Jews, whereas the Jews of Slovakia and Carpathian-Russia shared their history with Hungarian and Transylvanian Jews.

Jews played an important role in the Czech economy during the years of independence, notably in textiles, food, and paper industries. Estimates vary, but at least thirty to forty percent of the total capital invested in Czech industry in the 1930s was initiated by Jews.

But the independence and the relatively good life would not last. An event took place in Bavaria in 1938 that began the countdown to World War II, although much of the world thought it was a reprieve. In Munich, the British and French appeased Hitler and sold out the Czech people, who then really had little choice but to cave in. But who cared? The world knew little of Czechoslovakia. Hitler gained the "rich rim of Czechoslovakia for nothing," writes John Lukacs, in *The Last European War.* "The ignorance of the Western democracies regarding Eastern Europe was and remains inexcusable."

At Munich on September 29, 1938, 20,000 Jews were literally handed over to Nazi Germany. Another 25,000 fled to the unoccupied part of the country, only to be caught in the Nazi trap within the next few years. The fate of the Jews would be in the hands of the Reich security main office in Berlin and that meant the hands of the notorious Adolf Eichmann, who would organize the deportation of Jews to death camps.

As for Slovakia in the east, it became Hitler's lackey after the Nazi dictator told them on March 13, 1939, to proclaim Slovak independence or to suffer occupation. On March 15, 1939, the Nazis seized and incorporated western Czech lands into the Reich as the "Protectorate of Bohemia and Moravia." Slovakia went on its way to fascism under clergyman Jozef Tiso. A government-in-exile was later set up under Dr. Eduard Benes. During World War II, a high percentage of Czech military units consisted of Jews. Almost fifty percent of Czech soldiers abroad were Jews.

When Czech independence ended in 1939, only the Czech Jews out of all the Jews of Europe could "look back warmly on the period between 1918 and 1939," says Charles Hoffman in his book *Gray Dawn: The Jews of Eastern Europe in the Post-Communist Era*. That indeed says a great deal for the people and nation of Czechoslovakia.

After the war and the Holocaust and the Communist coup of February 1948, the surviving Jews greeted the establishment of the State of Israel in May of that year. Between 1948 and 1950, 18,879 Jews left Czechoslovakia for Israel. More than 7,000 departed for other countries. In 1950, the Communist rulers barred Jewish emigration. Only about 18,000 Jews remained. Some 5,500 of them waited for a chance to settle in Israel. Few were allowed to go. And the Jews became fearful of this harsh Communist regime, which they suspected would inflict upon them suspicion and humiliation. The blow would come soon.

RUDOLF SLANSKY TRIAL

In 1951, Rudolf Slansky, the Secretary-General of the Czech Communist Party, and thirteen co-defendants were purged in a trial that was a signal that scapegoats were being sought for the crimes and shortcomings of the regime, which Slansky himself helped create. It was the morning alarm clock ringing and calling for an intensive anti-Semitic campaign. Peter Meyer calls it "the great anti-Semitic show trial."

The 1951–52 Prague show trials were watched with horror

and revulsion throughout the free world. The purge even embraced a Nazi type of anti-Semitism. The Czechs actually followed the pattern of Soviet political trials. Staged by the Russians, these shows could easily have played at home to U.S.S.R. audiences.

Many of the accused were branded Zionists. Eleven of the 14 defendants were Jews. Eventually 11 were executed, 8 of them Jews. Paul Lendvai maintains that Slansky "was undoubtedly an innocent victim of the Soviet-sponsored purge since the specific charges against him were patently untrue."

So, after the trial, Czechoslovakia would be ruled as a closed society—except for the fresh air of the "Prague Spring" of 1968, and until communism was dissolved in 1989 and Prague once again basked in freedom.

Notable Czech Jews

Jewish contributions to Czech literature and culture were out of all proportion to the small minority of Jews in the country's population. Achieving international recognition were Franz Kafka, Max Brod, Franz Werfel, Oskar Baum, Ludwig Winder, Leo Purutz, and Egon Erwin Kisch.

Eduard Goldstuechker served as president of the Czech Writers' Union during the Prague Spring days of 1968 when the Czechs tried to release the severe grip of the Communist police state. Albert Einstein taught in Prague for a year in 1911. The composer, Gustav Mahler, a native of Bohemia, spent several years in Prague.

Most of these artists spoke German. Often they were middle class, secularized, and assimilated into the larger society.

Jewish Prague

Mother of cities, this elegant city is a chronicle in stone. It is a museum and an art gallery. As a tourist site, Prague is "in." And it is less expensive than Paris. Perhaps travelers flock here now because the Communist regime kept it isolated for four decades; it probably was the most closed of the large Eastern European capitals.

Above all, civilized Prague remains a delight, charmingly laid out on hills and slopes. Not damaged by the war, it remains "Europe's most ravishing city, a perfectly preserved confection of Gothic, Renaissance, baroque and rococo and decorated with an icing of art nouveau," writes one observer. People who visit the city are still charmed by the capital's beauty and location, and its architectural gems, cultural traditions, and extraordinary millennium-long history. Prague is a highly recommended tourist destination because many believe it is the soul of Europe. It truly rewards the Jewish visitor.

For centuries, this city has been proclaimed and acclaimed as "Golden Prague," where Jews have lived for at least a thousand years. Indeed, a thousand years ago, a Jewish Arab merchant, Ibrahim Ibn Jacob said this about Prague:

> The town . . . is built of stone and limestone and it is the biggest town as regards trade. Russians and Slavs come here from the royal town with goods. And Muslims. Jews and Turks from the lands of the Turks also come here with goods and trade coins.

Destined to become an important trade route along a major commercial river, Prague attracted Jewish leaders in 995. Rewarded for the aid they rendered to Christians in their fight against the pagans, they set up their own residential area. They built a school in what is now the "Mala Strana," the Little Quarter or Lesser Town, as it is sometimes called.

These Jewish pioneers settled around the area of what is now Dusni Street. Their next move was to the area known as the Old Jewish Town that for the last hundred years or so has been called Josefov, after the Hapsburg Emperor, Joseph II.

Here is what Alois Jirasik said in an old Czech legend:

> Six gates marked the division. And beyond those gates, every-thing was different. Strange buildings which excluded an air of poverty and neglect. Architecturally, there was all manner of weird additions, balconies, protrusions, dark dilapidated court-yards. The streets were very different, too. They were short and narrow, meandering, seedy and unpaved. And Jews at every turn, people of different customs and manners.

But Prague is not a stagnant city-state. This old city in the 1990s is studded with new retail shops, computer companies, banks, and a visual explosion of restaurants and bars. Alongside these establishments move a well-educated and cohesive population. And Prague trades extensively with its neighbor and one-time bitter foe, Germany.

Today, in Prague, there are only about 1,200 "registered" Jews, out of approximately 3,000 Jews in the Czech Republic, although the latter figure could be much higher. The figures do not tell the complete story. Notice the word *registered*. There could be at least 10,000 Jews residing in the Czech Republic. Since being Jewish no longer carries political stigmas as it did under the Communist regime, the "unregistered" Jews may some day participate in community activities. Still, due to a high degree of assimilation, which existed even in pre-war Czechoslovakia, many are simply not aware they are Jews and many of those that are aware do not identify with Judaism in any way.

So, cross the crooked medieval span of the Charles Bridge and look down onto the gentle Vltava River, which flows from the Bohemian hills and splits the capital Prague. Then enter into the Jewish Town.

You can stroll through Wenceslas Square, through the Old Town, past medieval architecture, past the big square in front of the city hall, down Pariska Street to the Jewish quarter, and then down the narrow cobblestone streets, through the old Jewish quarter. When you come to the banks of the Vltava River, set back your imagination ten centuries and visualize Jewish merchants traveling the trade routes and arriving at the very spot where you now stand. The Vltava still inspires romantic artists, writers, and historians.

Make sure you visit the Altneuschul. Then go on to the Klaus Synagogue, the Pinkas Synagogue, and the High Synagogue (also called the Town Hall Synagogue), which was built in the second half of the sixteenth century next door to the Jewish Town Hall. The latter is now the head-quarters of the Prague Jewish community. Stand in the Maisel Synagogue reconstructed in 1885–1913. And be sure you take some time to wander through the Old Jewish Cemetery.

From November to April, most of the synagogues and sites are open from 9 A.M. to 5 P.M., Sunday to Thursday. On Shabbat, the museums and offices are closed. On Friday, these institutions usually stay open until 1 P.M. In the summer, the hours are from 9 A.M. to 6 P.M. To obtain a guide, one can call the Jewish community at 2481-0099. The admission to the museum buildings is 80 kroners for all objects. For groups, admission is half-price. The admission to the Altneuschul (Old-New Synagogue) is separate and amounts to 30 kroners and is also half-price for groups.

THE JEWISH TOWN

Prague may have existed as a settlement for six thousand years, but for the modern traveler, it is the Old Town that draws and inspires the tourist. A living museum of medieval architecture, it contains nearly two thousand historic buildings. Few are more popular with tourists than the synagogues, the Jewish Town Hall, and the cemetery of *Josefov*—the Old Jewish Town. Actually, these sites still remain central to Prague Jewry and will probably be so for as long as Jews live in this city by the Vltava River. More than 500,000 tourists, predominantly non-Jewish, visit the Jewish quarter or Jewish Town, as it is called, each year. During the peak tourist season, thousands daily stroll through the narrow streets.

Hear the words of Franz Kafka describe this ghetto, which he knew in his childhood:

> Living within us are still those dark corners, mysterious corridors, blind windows, dirty backyards, noisy pubs, and closed inns. We walk down broad streets of the newly built towns. But our steps and looks are uncertain.

In 1896, a city-wide development project demolished the Jewish quarter, except for the Altneuschul, the Pinkas, Maisel, and the High (Hoch) synagogues. Many Jews moved out of the Old Quarter to new city areas. In 1870, more than half of Prague Jewry still lived in the Old Quarter. By 1900, less than one-fourth remained. Still, the Jewish ghetto has played an important role in Prague's history.

The Jewish Museum. The "exotic museum of an extinct race"—that is what the Nazis had in mind when they spoke of a Jewish museum. In Czechoslovakia, Jewish religious objects were saved because the Germans in their skewed insanity wanted to transform these museums into "museums of hate"—after all the Jews were annihilated by Nazi killer squads, of course.

Two notorious Nazis, Reinhard Heydrich and Adolf Eichmann, sadistically added items to the Czechoslovakia Jewish community's pre-war collection of Judaica by seizing Jewish books, manuscripts, and religious and art objects in Germany and other countries in Europe and bringing them to Prague for storage. This insane behavior saved an immeasurable wealth of Jewish cultural objects. At the end of the war, 8 buildings in the Jewish quarter and 50 warehouses throughout Prague were packed with Torah scrolls, ritual objects, musical instruments, paintings, furniture, and other stolen items. The Nazis seized these items from Czech and Slovak homes and from at least 168 synagogues that they destroyed in Bohemia, Moravia, and Slovakia.

Today, the Jewish Museum, founded in 1906, is housed in the surviving Prague synagogues that were not leveled by the Nazis. These former houses of worship possess a great collection of religious and secular Judaica, much of it from other European nations—a unique treasury of Jewish history. Actually, it may even be the richest Judaica collection in the world. One estimate is that there are more than 30,000 religious and artistic objects and a library of 100,000 volumes, most of which the Nazis had stolen from synagogues and from the homes of 92,000 Czech Jews who were deported to concentration camps, where 77,297 died.

The **Altneuschul,** or **Old-New Synagogue (Staronova Synagoga),** corner of Cervena and Maislova streets, Prague. If you have time to visit only one site in Jewish Prague, this world-famous early Gothic synagogue should be it. Services are held every day at 8 A.M. Shabbat morning services are at 9 A.M. (The building is closed to sightseers on Shabbat.) Erected around

Inside the Altneuschul, "the Old-New Synagogue," in Prague. (Photo by Ed Robin)

1270, the "Altneuschul" stands in the ancient Jewish Town. Today, architects, artists, and scholars fix their sights on this and other buildings that were not touched by the Holocaust. The traveler should do likewise. Lest we forget, this is the oldest monument of Prague's ghetto and the oldest functioning synagogue in Europe. This synagogue of synagogues is among the most impressive of early European Gothic style. And during the summer tourist season up to 2,500 persons may visit the synagogue in a single day.

Located in this city of Gothic, neo-Renaissance architecture, the Altneuschul comes upon you very quickly. Its portrait looks better in photos. When you look closely you may see the marks of age. You realize it contains within its walls seven hundred years of Jewish history and the will to survive. Stories have been told and legends have been created. Thousands of people from all over the world have come to see this synagogue, one of the most important early Gothic brick buildings in Europe, and one of the world's oldest Jewish architectural monuments.

In the past, some sentimental visitors reported that the history of the Jews of Prague flashed on the walls before them. The blood of *pogroms* became visible to them on its whitewashed walls, they said. Jews were murdered in this building and the bloodstains, they were told, have never been whitewashed off the walls out of respect for the martyrs, according to Carol Herselle Krinsky in *Synagogues of Europe: Architecture, History, Meaning*. However, the stains have apparently faded away.

In 1254, Premysl Ottokar II granted certain Jews "privileges," which meant he would protect their houses, cemeteries, and organizations. Following up on this, Prague Jewry obtained permission to build a new synagogue and to hire masonry workers who were constructing nearby St. Agnes Church, which still stands.

Even the synagogue's name can be considered mythical. Interwoven into the history of how it obtained its name, the "Alneuschul"—the Old-New Synagogue—are numerous legends.

Construction of the synagogue was completed between 1270 and 1290. To differentiate it from another older synagogue, it was named "new." At the end of the sixteenth century, or at the beginning of the seventeenth century, another "new" synagogue was built and the former "new" synagogue came to be known in German as the "Alte Neu Schul," or "the Old-New School," a name that was later written in one word, "Altneuschul." Thus we see that the Altneuschul's original name was the New or Great Synagogue (schul). The name, "Old-New" (*Altneu* in German), came into use only after other synagogues in the ghetto were erected in the late sixteenth century.

Another explanation is given by Jan Lukas, who recounts in *The Prague Ghetto* that "some experts maintain that the name 'Old New' developed precisely from the fact that the new part of the building was built on top of the old one which had been uncovered by the children at play."

Yet another source attributes the unique name to a vague expression that arose from the translation of the German word, *alt-neu*. The correct term, they say, is the Hebrew *al-tnai,* "on condition" or "temporarily"; that in fact, Jewish legend says the foundation stones for the construction of the Altneuschul were brought by angels from the destroyed Holy Temple in Jerusalem "on condition" (*al-tenai* in Hebrew) that the stones would be returned when the Temple was restored.

Still another legend maintains that the Jews were not permitted to change or to repair anything in the Altneuschul. When something had to be fixed or built onto the synagogue, the builder was always punished by misfortune or even death. For this and other reasons, the synagogue remained unchanged for many centuries.

At one time, according to yet another Altneuschul legend, the synagogue was protected against fire in the ghetto by angels who changed into doves.

A different folktale relates that the remains of the *golem,* the artificial creature made of clay and brought to life by the famous scholar, Rabbi Loew, are deposited in the synagogue—perhaps hidden away in the attic. Even today, it is said, no one dares to go up to the attic and the author was even told that during the Nazi occupation, two German soldiers climbed up to the attic to seek jewels and were never seen again. We shall discuss the rabbi and golem again when we visit the Old Jewish Cemetery.

Today, this oldest preserved synagogue in Europe still serves the needs of Prague's Jews. In the middle of the synagogue waves a historic banner of the Prague Jewish community. The right to have a banner of their own as a symbol of independence was first granted to the Jews of Prague by Charles IV in 1357. Attached to the western pillar of the main nave, the banner was altered to its present form in 1716 on the occasion of the birth of a son to Emperor Charles VI. The center of the banner bears the Star of David and contains a pointed Jewish hat that for centuries was the sign of Prague Jewry. The hat was also one of the traditional items of clothing of Prague's Jews. In certain periods Jews were not allowed to leave the ghetto without the mark of their religion.

There were times when conflict followed conflict. Historically, hatemongers—often incited by the Church itself—blamed the Jews for the Black Death in the fourteenth century, for example, and accused them of poisoning the wells "in order to destroy the whole of Christendom." The largest pogrom in the history of the Prague ghetto took place during Easter 1389. The killing was so onerous that this horrible event is still remembered in a special prayer that is read on Yom Kippur in today's Old-New Synagogue. Rabbi Avigdor Kara is the author of this elegy commemorating the pogrom that overwhelmed the Jews in 1389.

The synagogue's structure is in the shape of a reticulated nave. Its gateway is a portal with plant ornamentation. This original portal with a tympanum is decorated with stylized vine leaves. The hall-type double nave has a five-part rib vaulting supported by two octagonal pillars. The purpose of the fifth rib was to avoid giving a "cross" form to the vault, writes Rachel Wischnitzer in *The Architecture of the European Synagogue*. At the eastern wall stands the *aron ha-kodesh* (cabinet containing the scrolls of the Torah). The prized bronze chandeliers are from the sixteenth and seventeenth centuries.

"The synagogue is a grayish stone structure composed of a double-naved main room for men." The hall of worship is 49 x 29 feet. On three sides the main building is surrounded by low annexes that serve as a vestibule and a nave for the women. The latter section is connected with the synagogue's main room only by slit openings in the wall to enable the women to hear a service. The floor of the main nave is somewhat lower.

Statue of Moses. Near the Altneuschul is a statue of Moses by sculptor Frantisek Bilek. It is Moses on his knees in despair after his descent from Mount Sinai. When he sees the results of his anger: the fragments of the shattered tablets of the Law, he despairs. He broke the tablets out of anger when he found that his co-religionists had been worshipping idols.

Sculpted at the turn of the century by Bilek, the statue was "meant to be the first of an unfinished series of numerous biblical characters and prophets to demonstrate the spiritual development of mankind." The original sculpture that was placed in the small park next to the Altneuschul in 1935 was destroyed by the Nazis. A copy was unveiled in the same spot in 1948.

Jubilee Synagogue, u. Jeruzalemska, 7, Prague. Located in the Nove Mesto or New Town. This and the Old-New Synagogue still serve the existing Jewish community. Services are held Friday evenings and Saturday mornings. The organ is sometimes used and men and women can at times sit together. The community calls it modern Orthodox. The Jewish community decided to erect this synagogue "at the time of the Silver Jubilee of Franz Joseph I's ascension to the Austrian throne, which is why it is called the Jubilee Synagogue in his honor."

The Jewish Town Hall, 18 u. Maislova, Prague. This impressive building is the heart of the Jewish community. This Jewish Town Hall with its distinctive Hebrew clock, with Hebrew numerals moving counterclockwise, serves as the community center and boasts a kosher restaurant (see below). The present rococo appearance of the Town Hall dates from 1763.

The kehila offices, rabbi's study, community archives, and dining hall are all contained here in this early seventeenth century building located just up the street from the Old-New Synagogue.

Karol Sidon is the new rabbi in Prague. He left Czecho-slovakia in 1983 and studied Judaism in Heidelberg, Germany, and Israel. A writer and friend of Vaclav Havel, he was one of the dissidents who had gathered around President Havel. He became rabbi in Prague in 1992. A remarkable man, born of a Jewish father and a Christian mother, he underwent formal conversion. In 1992, he succeeded Rabbi Daniel Mayer, who had resigned.

Federation of Jewish Communities, 18 u. Maislova, P.O. Box 297, 11001, Prague. Tel: 0042-2-2481-0130, or 2481-1090. FAX: 0042-2-2481-0912.

A **kosher restaurant** is located in the Jewish Town Hall, at 18 u. Maislova, Prague. It is open for lunch daily from 11 A.M. to 2 P.M. except Saturday night and Jewish holidays. In the tourist season, about 250 persons eat here each day. It is strictly kosher.

A **drug store,** at the corner of Maislova and Siroka streets, was set up recently by Charles Benibghi, who likes to help tourists find their way to Jewish sites.

Hotel Inter-Continental, Prague. Tel: 0042-2-2488-1111. FAX Reservation: 0042-2-2481-0071. This modern, luxury hotel is practically in the Old Jewish Town and is a fine stopping place for those who wish to visit the Jewish sites extensively.

Park Hotel, Prague. This is a more modest hotel than the Inter-Continental. On an outside wall of the hotel is a memorial to the Holocaust.

Mosaic Tours and Travel offers an opportunity to experience Jewish life in Prague in a service offered by Travel Judaica. Reservations in the U.S. for this tour, which includes a stay in a Prague hotel, and information about the tour to the Czech Republic are available from 1-800-Shalom-94. Mosaic Tours and Travel is located at 420 Lincoln Rd., Suite 448, Miami Beach, Florida 33139.

CEDOK

Cedok Czechoslovak Travel—In Prague, one of the many Cedok branches is located at Bilkova 6, directly across from the

Hotel Inter-Continental. In New York City, Cedok Czechoslovak Travel is located at 10 East 40th St., New York, New York 10016. Tel: (212) 689-9720.

Charles Bridge

Of the fifteen bridges linking the two halves of Prague, the oldest and best loved is the Charles Bridge. After making Prague his capital in 1346, this Holy Roman Emperor and King of Bohemia, Charles IV (1346–78) built the bridge on the site of an old Slavic fort. Thirty stone saints line the bridge, the oldest stone bridge in Central Europe. Most of the stone saints were carved in the eighteenth and nineteenth centuries. Under Charles IV, a Czech national hero, Prague became an important medieval capital with the first university in Central Europe.

Another important figure in Czechoslovakian history and Jewish history in Bohemia and Moravia is that of Rudolf II (1552–1612), Holy Roman Emperor and King of Bohemia from the year 1576. In 1583, Rudolf transferred his court to Prague. This move improved the position of the Jews, and Jewish culture flourished. Rudolf was in constant touch with Marcus Mordecai Maisel, who served him as a banker and supplier of art objects for his art collection. He received Rabbi Judah Loew ben Bezalel (the *Maharal*—the Hebrew acronym for "most venerated teacher and rabbi") in an audience, it is said. Rudolf created the category of the *Hofbefreiter Jude* (1582): Jews who were attached to the court and enjoyed such privileges as exemption from taxes and from wearing the Jewish badge. From them the institution of "Court Jew" developed.

But how King Randolph and Rabbi Judah Loew ben Bezalel met on the Charles Bridge comes from another legend. The Marahal, according to Elie Wiesel's account of the meeting in his book *The Golem*, was standing in the middle of the bridge waiting for King Rudolf. Onlookers argued that the rabbi might be run over because the king might not stop because "his horses run faster than the wind." "'Not this time,'" said the Maharal. People sneered. Soon, the horses came running

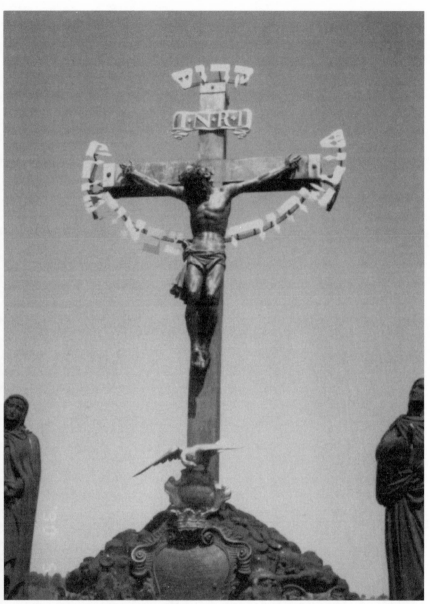

On the Charles Bridge, the crucifix surrounded by huge guilded Hebrew letters that spell the traditional Hebrew sanctification: "Holy, holy, holy is the Lord of Hosts." (Photo by Sam Urman)

as though they would trample the rabbi under their feet . . .
"and then, suddenly they stopped." The king wanted to know
why the Maharal risked his life. "'I had to,'" said the Maharal.
"'My people's lives are in jeopardy. Have you not signed a
decree ordering them to go into exile?'" The king invited the
Maharal to the castle and they became friends. The Maharal
became a frequent visitor in the role of intercessor and
defender.

Although Jews were persecuted in Prague, during his life-
time Emperor Charles IV protected the Jews. He was a statesman, writer, scholar, linguist, and builder.

At the end of the bridge named for him, you pass into the
"Mala Strana," the Little Quarter—one of the three ancient
areas of historical Prague.

On the Charles Bridge, the visitor will observe a great crucifix surrounded by huge gilded Hebrew letters that spell the
traditional Hebrew sanctification, *Kadosh, Kadosh, Kadosh
Adonai Tzvaot,* "Holy, Holy, Holy is the Lord of Hosts."
According to various commentators, this piece, degrading to
Jews, came about because in 1609 a Jew was accused of desecrating the crucifix. The Jewish community was forced to pay
for putting up the Hebrew words in gold letters. The Nazis
removed the gold.

Another explanation is that a Jew spit at the cross and for
this he was to be put to death as punishment. When this man
begged for his life, the king, seeking to have good relations
with the Jews, said the Jewish community had to rectify the
offense, and the Jewish man would have to put up a cross. A
Jew is not allowed to put up a cross, but the man was forced to
do so. By adding the words, *Kadosh, Kadosh, Kadosh,* the Jew felt
exonerated from wrongdoing to his religion because the sanctification contains the words, *Adonai Tzvaot,* so that the man
was in effect saying his god is *Adonai Tzvaot.*

High Synagogue, also known as the **Town Hall Synagogue,
Vysoka (Radnicni) Synagoga,** u. Cervena, Prague. This syna-
gogue is located across the street from the entrance to the
"Old-New Synagogue," or the "Altneuschul." The High
Synagogue, or "Hoch Synagogue," was built in 1565. The name

High Synagogue probably comes from its unusual location on the first floor, which suggested its then exclusive and nonpublic character. Originally, it was accessible from a room on the first floor of the Jewish Town Hall. It was used as a prayer house by leaders of the Jewish community.

The High Synagogue and the Maisel Synagogue were financed and built by Mordechai Maisel (1528–1601), the so-called mayor of the Jewish Town Hall. The architect was Panacius Roder. In 1907, the High Synagogue's entrances on the eastern facade were removed and the existing entrance opposite the Altneuschul was constructed.

Like the other synagogues, the High Synagogue today is a museum. Exhibition cases and wall displays will mesmerize the visitor. Significantly, the High Synagogue contains several thousand synagogue curtains, draperies, Torah mantles, and binders that were seized by the Nazis from Czech Jews and from Jewish families throughout Europe.

The Prague Jewish community was especially known for its embroidery workshops. There is an exhibit showing the continuous development of synagogue textiles from the sixteenth to the twentieth centuries. An early baroque stone Holy Ark with combined columns on the sides, a symbol of the Torah crown, and an inscribed cartouche distinguish this synagogue.

When you leave the Old-New Synagogue or the High Synagogue, cross Maislova Street and walk down Stareho Hrbitova Street. On the left side of the street and to the left of the entrance to the Old Jewish Cemetery is the Klausen Synagogue.

Klausen Synagogue (Klausova Synagoga), u. Stareho Hrbitova, Prague. Located to the left of the cemetery entrance on u. Stareho Hrbitova, this synagogue, which stands as a museum, is especially noted for its permanent exhibition of Hebrew manuscripts and prints. The exhibits here contain examples of Jewish cultural and religious items.

Three small buildings that comprised the then-synagogue were destroyed by fire on June 21, 1689. That fire ravaged all of the 316 houses in the ghetto and most of the synagogues and public buildings.

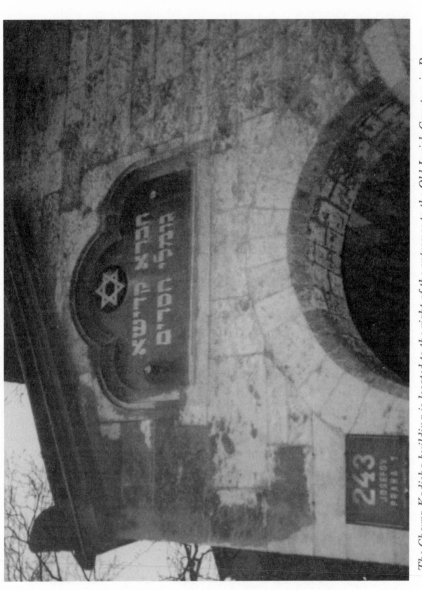

The Chevra Kadisha building is located to the right of the entrance to the Old Jewish Cemetery in Prague. (Photo by Ben G. Frank)

The Klausen Synagogue was completed in 1694, thanks to Shlomo Kohen, a printer. The name "Klausen" may be derived from the Latin *claustrum*. Another source says the name Klausen comes from those small buildings, which were called "klauses." That is why some call this the Klaus Synagogue. The building was enlarged in 1883–84 and partly rebuilt in 1910, according to Carol Herselle Krinsky.

Interestingly, for lack of open space, the Klausen Synagogue was built on its location even though it faced the Old Jewish Cemetery. Shown in the synagogue is an exquisite baroque Torah Ark consisting of three sections. The vaulted ceiling of the synagogue is decorated with a rococo stucco from the eighteenth century.

By the way, the works of Kohen the printer are highly artistic. Well known are the Prague editions of the Pentateuch of 1518 and 1530 and the so-called "Prague Haggadah" of 1526. Kohen also printed selections from the writings of Rabbi Loew.

Chevra Kadisha Building, u. Stareho Hrbitova, Prague. The Chevra Kadisha building, to the right of the entrance to the Old Jewish Cemetery, once served as a mortuary. Today, it contains a heartbreaking display of poems, drawings, and letters from the children of the Terezin concentration camp. The majority of the Terezin children's material was created under the supervision of an established painter, Friedl Dicker-Brandejsova, to whom the children went to for lessons. Altogether 4,000 drawings survived, along with excerpts from illegal magazines published by the children in the camp. The present building, a Romanesque structure, was built in 1906.

Maisel Synagogue (Maislova Synagogue) u. Maislova, Prague. Originally built in 1592, this is now a neo-Gothic, triple-nave building designed by architect Alfred Grotte and remodeled between 1893 and 1905. It is named after Marcus Mordechai Maisel (1528–1601), who commissioned a number of buildings in the sixteenth-century Prague ghetto, including the High Synagogue (Town Hall) on Cervena Street. However, this synagogue was almost completely destroyed by the fire of 1689. Within two years (1691), it was rebuilt in baroque style.

This synagogue remains one of the most spectacular buildings in the Prague ghetto. A permanent exposition of silver and other synagogue objects from the collections of the Jewish Museum draws thousands of tourists. Here one observes synagogue crowns, shields, spice boxes, kiddush cups, and 8,000 silver pieces. The exhibit here is one of the largest collections of silver artifacts in the Czech Republic, with the oldest silver objects dating from the late sixteenth century. The largest part of the collection consists of silver Torah ornaments. The visitor can view Sabbath lamps, pairs of silver candlesticks, and silver kiddush cups for benediction over wine. Most interesting, however, are silver spice boxes of various forms. They are used for the "Havdalah ceremony," which concludes the Sabbath.

Marcus Mordechai Maisel was a remarkable man. A Prague financier, philanthropist, and head of the Jewish community, he was known as the "Maecenas of Science" and "the benefactor hero." A generous and fabulously rich merchant, his clients included the Imperial Court. He has been called the "first Jewish capitalist in Germany." Maisel helped finance Rudolf II, who appointed him counselor during the Turkish wars. He had the streets of the ghetto paved. He bought a garden so that he could extend the area of the cemetery. He also built an infirmary and public baths. Above all, he organized the construction of the two synagogues—the High Synagogue and the Maisel Synagogue—upon which he lavished grand gifts and generous donations. Toward the end of his life in 1590, Maisel, who had so far been engaged in building public structures, bought a piece of land at the southern end of the ghetto on which to build a synagogue for his own use. In 1591, he obtained a special tax immunity privilege from Emperor Rudolf II to do so. A year later, during the holiday, Simchat Torah, the synagogue was dedicated. Architect Judah Tsoref Goldschmied de Herz designed the original building and Joseph Wald built it.

Historian David Gans, Maisel's contemporary, says in his chronicle that the building was unusually impressive. Supported by twenty pillars, its main, vast nave has been acclaimed by architects. Maisel and his wife donated a rich treasure of synagogal textiles, mantles, and curtains to the synagogue. This house of worship also served as the repository for a special banner that Maisel had made for himself on the basis of the privilege granted by Rudolf II in 1592 and kept in the Altneuschul.

During the Renaissance period, the Maisel Synagogue was the largest and most impressive house of worship in the Jewish Town.

Spanish Synagogue (Spanelska synagoga), u. Dusni, and Vezenska ulice, Prague. The building exhibits the distinctive Moorish style that flourished in the 1880s. The exterior's design, which corresponds to the interior's Oriental decoration, gave the synagogue its name. Today, this synagogue, which is located opposite the presbytery of the Church of the Holy Spirit, is closed.

This Jewish house of worship is still called by some the "Old Schul," because it was built in the place of the original synagogue and was erected before the pogrom of 1389. The Portuguese rite had been followed there for many years. In 1868, the synagogue was demolished. The rebuilding was undertaken by Prague architect Vojtech Ignats Ullmann. The interior was designed by architect Joseph Niklas and is entirely Moorish.

The synagogue has a square, central ground plan and a large dome over the middle section. On three sides are balconies of metal construction that open into the main room. The interior was decorated between 1882 and 1893, according to a design by A. Baum and B. Munzberger. It includes a low stucco arabesque of stylized Islamic motifs that is richly gilded and polychromed in green, blue, and red. The same decorative elements are used in the carved decoration on the door around the organ, balcony railing, and wall lining with the ground floor. The windows were filled with painted glass in 1882–83.

During World War II, the Germans used the Spanish Synagogue as a warehouse. It was handed over to the State Jewish Museum after it had been partly restored.

In 1960, the first permanent exhibition of synagogal textiles was opened, and it ran until 1982.

The Old Jewish Cemetery, u. Stareho Hrbitova, Prague. Can you imagine a cemetery that some guidebooks call one of the ten most interesting sights in the world? U.S. President Bill Clinton visited the Old Jewish Cemetery on his visit to Prague in January 1994. And thousands of tourists come here each day.

Called a garden, it "evokes the spirit of the ghetto some feel . . . and . . . defies the passage of time." The Old Jewish Cemetery is one of Europe's oldest and best preserved Jewish burial grounds. About 500 years old, the cemetery contains between 12,000 and 20,000 gravestones. All are crowded into a very tight space and teeter at different angles. Slabs and tombstones date to the mid-fifteenth century. These tombstones are a chronicle of the Prague ghetto.

Actual burials took place here until 1787. The oldest-known tombstone—from 1439—is that of the Kabbalist and poet, Rabbi Avigdor Kara.

Because the tiny cemetery was not large enough to contain all the dead, it was necessary to gradually cover older graves with earth to provide a new burial layer. The result was that an uneven area appeared, and in some places it forms twelve burial layers. Parts of the tombstones from the older layers were raised to higher layers, which created the pile of tombstones that is typical of this cemetery.

All the tombstones carry Hebrew inscriptions giving the date of death and in some cases the name of the deceased and the date of burial. Poetic texts recall the merits of the individual and express the sadness of the relatives. On some stones you can see the biblical tribe, family name, and profession of the deceased. Hands outstretched in blessing represent a person from the priestly tribe of Aaron; a jug signifies the tribe of Levi; scissors are for tailors; a book identifies scribes; a violin is for musicians; and a tweezer marks a doctor.

The most significant tombstones are the large tombs confined by two oblique and two vertical stone slabs; most of these

The Old Jewish Cemetery in Prague. (Photo by Sam Urman)

are in the central part of the cemetery opposite the main entrance.

The visitor really stands in awe here. Beneath the gravestones lie rabbis and scholars. Every human being is precious and significant. Yet we search for the tombs of the so-called mayor of the Prague Jewish Town, Mordechai Maisel, who died in 1661; the grave of Rabbi Loew; as well as the tomb of Hindel, the wife of Jacob Bashevi of Truenburg who died in 1628.

Rabbi Loew

One cannot really discuss the Old Jewish Cemetery and the Altneuschul or the Prague Town Hall without commenting on the legendary, and some say miraculous, Rabbi Judah Loew ben Bezalel. In the cemetery you will see the gravestone of Rabbi Judah Loew ben Bezalel, creator of the *golem*. His tomb, located in the rear of the cemetery, resembles a sarcophagus. This famous rabbi is supposed to have invented an artificial man we have come to regard as the golem, considered by Elie Wiesel to be "the most fascinating creature in Jewish lore and fantasy." As the story goes, Rabbi Loew is said to have constructed a clay figure that he brought to life in the Altneuschul with the help of God.

Owing to his profound knowledge, including the Kabbala, he thus entered popular lore as the miracle worker who could secretly give life and breath to the golem, which became a robot figure serving the rabbi as a reward for his good works. "Without the Maharal and the golem, the Jewish community of Prague might not have survived," Elie Wiesel maintains.

The golem, constructed to represent a human being, was to be the Rabbi's servant and defend the Jews from their persecutors, notably ritual-murder accusers. But it ran amok. Finally, legend has it, the rabbi was forced to destroy his creation by removing the magic name from underneath its tongue. He left the body of the golem in the attic and forbade any access to the attic in the Altneuschul. To this day, no one is to go up to the attic.

Rabbi Loew, who was also known as Der Hohe Rabbi Loew because of his great height, was a rabbi, Talmudist, moralist, mathematician, and philosopher. And he was a philosopher of great originality. His profound wisdom and wide-ranging scholarship influenced not only Jewish religious philosophy, but also ethics and pedagogy. He was the spiritual head of the Jewish community from the end of the sixteenth century until the early seventeenth century.

He was known as the Maharal. Maharal is the Hebrew acronym for "most venerated teacher and rabbi." Some people call him a wondrous magician who vanquished the angel of death. Known throughout the Jewish world as one of the greatest Talmudic scholars, he was acclaimed as the celebrated "Wonder Rebbe of Prague."

Born circa 1525, Rabbi Loew resided in Prague from 1573 to 1584, then from 1588 to 1592, and then again in 1597, until his death in 1609. When he died, he was serving as a rabbi and head of the yeshiva in Prague.

We think he was named after the Kabbalist Reb Yehuda Loew, also of Prague. His tombstone states that he belonged to the royal line of David. We know he left Worms to study in Prague. He later married Pearl, the daughter of Rabbi Shmelke Reich, when he was thirty-two and she was twenty-eight. They had a daughter and one son.

He lived during the reign of Rudolf II, a time supposedly of the supernatural, which gave rise, obviously, to many of the legends surrounding him.

He is best known as the author of commentaries, essays on ethics, and mystically oriented writings. In his scholarly works he emphasized a logical progression from the simple biblical texts and postbiblical religious and legal writings called the Mishnah to the more difficult Talmud.

Rabbi Loew died at the age of ninety-seven, leaving behind a legacy of works covering every aspect of Jewish religious life and a legend that "consoles the hunted, the persecuted," according to Elie Wiesel.

Prague Town Hall. An impressive statue of Rabbi Loew adorns the entrance of the Prague Town Hall. It portrays a tall, severe figure with a high cylindrical hat and a long flowing beard fending off a naked woman who appears to be holding him.

This statue was sculpted by Ladislav Saloun, a non-Jew who also designed Jan Hus's monument in the Old Town Square.

While working on the statue when the town hall was created in 1910, Saloun was inspired by a legend of Rabbi Loew's death: "Unable to approach the almost century-year-old scholar who was always absorbed in the study of holy books, death hid in a rose that was offered to the rabbi by his unsuspecting granddaughter."

After you walk through the cemetery, you can visit the Pinkas Synagogue, where a further treasure awaits you.

Pinkas Synagogue (Pinkasova Synagoga), u. Siroka, Prague. At the other end of the cemetery in the heart of the old Jewish quarter is the Pinkas Synagogue. It was originally set up on the site of a Jewish house of prayer that existed before 1492. At that time, the house belonged to the Horowitz family. A descendant of the family, Zalman Munka Horovic, also known as Aaron Meshullam, financed the construction of the synagogue. Built in 1535, it was modeled after a late-Gothic, partly Renaissance synagogue built in 1479. One of the oldest and most valuable houses of worship in Prague, it was founded by Rabbi Pinkas and enlarged in 1535 by his grandson, Aron Meshule. The construction contains rib vaulting on Renaissance supports. The women's section was added in 1625 by Judah Tsoref Goldschmied de Herz.

Between 1954 and 1959, the interior of the Pinkas Synagogue was turned into the memorial for the 77,297 Bohemian and Moravian victims of the Holocaust, about 85 percent of the community. The names, and family names arranged according to communities, were inscribed on the walls of the main nave, balcony, and anteroom.

Today when you enter the Pinkas Synagogue, you see craftsmen painstakingly inscribing the names of the 77,297 murdered Czech Jews. The engraved names had been inscribed previously, but the Communists allowed the Jewish names to fade away. The memorial to the victims of the Nazi persecution under the Communists, it was closed to the public for more than twenty years. The names have to be inscribed again so they can live in memory.

Although the location of a synagogue near a cemetery is quite unusual, the Pinkas Synagogue was built close to the Old Jewish Cemetery because there was not enough space in the ghetto.

A memorial to Franz Kafka, the great Czech Jewish writer of universal fame, is located at his native house, No. 5, u. Radnice, Old Town of Prague. Kafka (1883–1924) attained worldwide respect and readership. He was born in the Old Town of Prague, in a house at that time located in Jachymova Street. This corner house next to the St. Nicholas Church was destroyed by a fire in 1897 and rebuilt in 1902. Only the portal of the old house was preserved. On July 3, 1966, a memorial tablet by academic sculptor Karel Hladik was unveiled on the house standing at the corner of Kaprova, Maiselova, and Uradnice streets. A Kafka museum is located at this site of his birth.

Nearby is the Golz Kinsky Palace, a large, pink and white rococo structure that played an important role in Kafka's life. There, he attended school in the Palace and often visited his father's dry-goods store located on the ground floor. Kafka studied law at the German university and worked first in a law office and then for an insurance company. He wrote only in his spare time.

Because he was sensitive to noise, Kafka stayed and worked for some time in a small house on the Golden Lane in the area of the Prague Castle. The building was rented from its owner, Mrs. Michlova, by Kafka's youngest sister, Ottla. In the winter of 1916–17, Kafka wrote during the evenings and nights a number of shorter prose works and stories that he published in 1919.

Kafka did not live to bear the pain of the Holocaust. His works were suppressed by the Communists as "subjective and pessimistic." Now, of course, his writings are in great demand.

Kafka is buried in the New Olsany Cemetery alongside his parents. A stone marks their burial spot. A plaque also remembers his three sisters who died in the Holocaust. Located in Nad Vodovodem Street, this new Jewish cemetery includes prominent Jewish community leaders, such as the founder of the Jewish Museum, Dr. Salomon Hugo Lieben.

Hradcany Castle (Castle Hill) or Prague Castle—Look up to Prague Castle. Below the castle wall are hanging gardens and ancient roofs descending to the water's edge. Built by Bohemian kings, the castle was also the residence of Czech kings of old as well as of modern Czech leaders, such as Thomas Garrigue Masaryk and Eduard Benes. The Jews who came to Prague probably lived around the marketplaces in what is now Hradcany, a popular tourist attraction and a must-see on any visit to the Czech capital. It is a labyrinth of castles, churches, and museums perched on one of the seven hills on which Prague is built. Head for the sprawling edifice that dominates the city, the Hradcany or Prague Castle. Everyone looks to the castle for leadership as a symbol of strength.

After the Jews settled near the castle, they ran up against difficulties from the community and invaders torched the oldest Prague synagogue as well as the Jewish quarter that was located just below the castle. As a result, the Jews moved to the right bank of the Vltava River, which became the Jewish quarter we know today.

One occupant of the castle, Thomas Garrigue Masaryk (1850–1937), a profound writer and thinker, was certainly a friend to the Jews and to men of goodwill everywhere. Without Masaryk, "there would have been no Czechoslovakia," according to Josef Korbel in *Twentieth Century Czechoslovakia: The Meanings of Its History.*

By 1918, Masaryk and Czech leaders had convinced the French, the British, and U.S. President Woodrow Wilson that the Austro-Hungarian monarchy must be dismembered and that an independent Czech-Slovak state be set up. A declaration proclaiming the new nation of Czechoslovakia was signed in 1918 by Czech and Slovak émigré politicians in Pittsburgh, Pennsylvania.

Throughout his life, Masaryk fought anti-Semitism. Emil Ludwig writes that Masaryk had "a life-long sympathy for the Jews. As a Czech, he himself knew what it meant to be a member" of a downtrodden people. After World War I, anti-Semitism existed in most parts of Eastern Europe; it was much less of a problem in Czech lands.

During the Hilsner affair—a blood libel case occurring at the turn of the century—Masyrk wrote pamphlets declaring anti-Semitism an uncivilized and slanderous attitude. The Hilsner case involved trumped-up anti-Semitic charges against a young Czech Jew, Leopold Hilsner, who was arrested for the murder of a seamstress. Masaryk intervened; he did not have to do this. His pamphlets won the day and Hilsner's sentence was commuted to life imprisonment, and he was pardoned in 1916.

But Masaryk and Eduard Benes, who succeeded Masaryk, were not the only ones to occupy Prague Castle.

Even the hated Nazi invaders walked up the carpet-lined stairways of the castle. Hitler proclaimed from the castle that Czechoslovakia no longer existed. And it was the home of hard-line Communist rulers who leaned hard on the people of this country for forty years. The popular playwright and intellectual, Vaclav Havel, a true dissident against the Communist regime and now Czech president, comes to work here every day, although he does not live here. In February 1990, in one of his first acts as president of Czechoslovakia, Havel re-established full diplomatic relations with Israel, ties that had been broken in 1967. Havel became the first head of state in modern Eastern Europe to visit Jerusalem in 1990. The next year, he hosted the then-Israeli President, Chaim Herzog, in Prague. He called Communist rule "20 years of timelessness."

WENCESLAS SQUARE

Most visitors will tell you that the first place they visit in Prague is Wenceslas Square, an 800-yard-long avenue of shops and restaurants. This is a great place for a leisurely stroll. Not only does stately Wenceslas Square cleave the heart of Prague, not only is it the "Main Street" of this wonderful metropolis, but it is also the symbol of Czech freedom and of a people's desire for liberty.

The square is named after Prince Wenceslas, later the "Good King" of the Christmas carol who lived more than a thousand years ago. His equestrian statue looks down on the square that bears his name. They say that today flowers are placed at its base in memory of those who died or committed suicide in Prague Spring. The statue was a symbol of good during the Velvet Revolution. Here in the middle of the square, President Vaclav Havel addressed the Czech and Slovak people. Here is where the hated Nazi troops entered in 1939. Here in Prague Spring 1968, Czech students hurled rocks at the Soviet armored tanks that creeped into Wenceslas Square. And here in 1989, thousands gathered to celebrate the end of communism in what the world knows as the Velvet Revolution.

The 1968 Prague Spring was a symbol of hope and opportunity. The people of Czechoslovakia wanted to ease the toughness of Communist rule. But on the night of August 20–21, 1968, troops of the Warsaw Pact invaded Czechoslovakia. Soviet airborne forces, including tank and artillery units, were landed in Prague and Bratislava. The invasion, said the Soviets, was a domestic affair. But the world did not buy it and was outraged. Telephone lines were cut and soldiers armed with machine guns took over Hradcany Castle. The invasion even then was a testimony to the failure of Marxism-Leninism.

But the Czechs fought back in their own way. They painted swastikas on the Russian tanks. They spat at the Russians. They turned street signs in the wrong direction to confuse the Soviets. They practiced passive resistance. Indeed, the tanks in 1968 were wholly inadequate weapons because in Czechoslovakia, they fired at "ideas with no hope of hitting the target."

The late Alexander Dubcek and other Prague Spring leaders were taken to Moscow, where behind closed doors in the Kremlin, Leonid Brezhnev forced Dubcek's government to surrender to undemocratic experiments. Among the Czechs was Frantisek Kriegel. A dedicated reformer, Kriegel, who had been called "that Galician Jew" by one of the Soviet leaders, was an abstainer to the Communist proposal to stop the reforms. The Russians kept him hidden and claimed that he was sick. The Czechs who were at the airport ready to depart for Prague said they would not leave until the Russians produced Kriegel. The Russians, who had every intention of keeping him, finally freed him and he took off with the delegation, according to Patrick Brogan in his book *The Captive Nations: Eastern Europe, 1945–90*.

But Prague still remained the "city of Kafka and Soviet tanks." Wenceslas Square had the submerged, slow motion quality of a nightmare. As Havel is said to have remarked, "The clocks had stopped." In the 1980s, however, Czechs kept alive the desire for freedom. At this time, 12,000 Jews remained in Czechoslovakia. Their average age was 60; it would stay that way for several decades, for there were only about 1,000 young people between the ages of 15 and 20. Some of these young Jewish persons would be among the those who brought about the Velvet Revolution in 1989. In those 21 autumn days, without a drop of blood spilled, the people of Czechoslovakia broke the power of their Communist rulers. "It was a glorious, gentle revolution."

TEREZIN (THERESIENSTADT)

It is not easy to get to Terezin, forty minutes northwest of Prague. And yet they come day after day after day. On the bleak, rainy day I was there, I saw members of a teenage Canadian hockey team, a Danish college student, and an American university professor—all who spent one hour by bus to reach this city in Bohemia, this death station of the Nazis. Horrible things happened here in Terezin, especially to children.

To get there, you travel north from Prague. The fields at first are flat and neatly plowed. Farmland and sweeping highways spotlight a rich farm area that turns hilly as you approach the town of Terezin. The scenery actually gives little idea of the gruesome fortress town of Terezin, the star-shaped garrison town named for the Austria Empress Maria Theresa, who perhaps was a harbinger of the horrible inflictions hurled at the Jewish people there. In German, the town is called *Theresienstadt*. In the late 1700s, Terezin was a bulwark against the Prussians, who often would barrel their way down from the north. The name will probably send shudders down the spines of men and women of goodwill everywhere for hundreds of years to come, those who know the story of Terezin and the Holocaust.

About 277,000 Jews who had resided within the pre-Munich boundaries of Czechoslovakia lost their lives in the Holocaust. Approximately 25,000 escaped from Bohemia and Moravia before the war broke out, which left a Jewish population of about 90,000 in those two provinces. Only 10,000 of these Jews would survive.

In 1938, about 135,000 Jews resided in Slovakia, of whom 40,000 lived in the territory ceded to Hungary (Ruthenia and Sub-Carpathia). About 5,000 Jews emigrated voluntarily before the war, leaving about 90,000 Jews in Slovakia itself. According to Lucy S. Dawidowicz in *The War Against the Jews: 1933–1945,* a total of 110,000 Slovak Jews were murdered.

In 1941, the Nazis occupied this walled municipality; they emptied out its inhabitants and turned a citadel into a transit camp for Jews on their way to the death camps.

It was as if a whole town had been cleared to become a ghost town as well as a transport center to transfer Jews to the gas chambers in Poland and beyond. Today, it still maintains a drab look, especially in the fall or winter.

Officially, Terezin was a self-governing ghetto. But in reality, it was a concentration camp, probably without the gas chambers, although bodies of people who had died of typhus there were sent to the crematorium nearby, which the visitor can still see today. About 150,000 men, women, and children passed through this ghetto for Jewish prisoners between 1941 and 1945. At least 117,000 were tortured to death and murdered elsewhere. Of 15,000 children under the age of 15 who passed through the camp, fewer than 100 survived.

Nazis Reinhard Heydrich and Adolf Eichmann met on October 4, 1941. The Germans decided on the establishment of the Theresienstadt Ghetto on October 10, 1941, in a secret meeting at the Prague Castle chaired by Reich Protector Heydrich. The Nazis planned that from Terezin (in German, Theresienstadt), the Jews were to be deported to the East. Adolf Eichmann's plan was to evacuate the Jews from Terezin and transfer them to the concentration camps in Poland and beyond and then turn the whole area into a model German settlement. But Terezin took on an atmosphere that was worse than an "animal-like holding pen." At one point, nearly 60,000 persons lived in barracks designed to house 7,000 combat troops.

As a young child, the Czech author and one of the best-known Czech writers in the West, Ivan Klima, was packed off to Terezin. He writes about seeing the constant presence of death. "People died in the room where I lived. They died by the dozens," he wrote, adding, "the constant threat of the transports hung over the inhabitants."

Terezin also served as a "showplace," a facade for the International Red Cross monitors. The Nazis spruced up the camp to make the inspectors believe the Jews were being treated well. It was trickery par excellence—even in the midst of fake cultural activities, such as an orchestra concert given by the prisoners, transports from Terezin were continuously leaving for Auschwitz and Birkenau camps.

Several hundred Danish Jews were sent to Terezin because not all the Jews of Denmark escaped to Sweden. But the Danish government never gave up on their Jewish citizens and representatives from Denmark did visit the camp. And the government in Copenhagen sent food supplies to the Jewish Terezin. On April 14, 1945, the Danish prisoners left Terezin in Swedish Red Cross buses that were bound for freedom.

The Small Fortress at Terezin

A sign above the entrance of the Small Fortress declares: *Arbeit Macht Frei*. "Work Makes You Free," is the literal translation, but its real meaning was death. We know that now; the six million did not.

The first stop at Terezin might be the Small Fortress on the outskirts of town. This fort was built as part of the fortification system near the confluence of the Elbe and Ohre rivers. From the beginning, it was used as a prison. Jailed here, for example, were many nationalist leaders who wanted to overthrow Austrian rule. The 1914 assassins of Franz Ferdinand d'Este— archduke of Austria—were imprisoned here.

When Bohemia and Moravia were occupied by the Nazis in 1940, the Small Fortress became the prison of the Prague gestapo. The first prisoners were brought there on June 14, 1940, and some 32,000 inmates, including 5,000 women,

A sign above the entrance of the Small Fortress at Terezin declares, Arbeit Macht Frei. *"Work Makes You Free" is the actual translation, but its real meaning was death.* (Photo by Riva Frank)

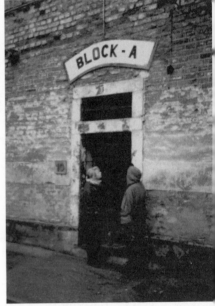

A cell block at the Small Fortress at Terezin. (Photo by Ben G. Frank)

passed through the fortress during the war. The life of imprisoned Jews in this fortress was especially difficult, because it was a way station to Nazi trials, jails, prisons, and the concentration camps.

At the end of the war a typhoid epidemic killed many prisoners. On May 8, 1945, the first Soviet armored vehicles arrived in Terezin.

Between 1945 and 1948, the Small Fortress served as a detention camp for the Germans expelled from Czechoslovakia. During your visit, you will see the guards' office; the prison commander's office; the courtyards; the prison block cells, as well as 20 solitary confinement cells; the hospital block; the mortuary; places of execution; the S.S. barracks; and the national cemetery.

A documentary film is shown and there are special exhibits. It is also possible to purchase brochures, literature, and videotapes.

The Ghetto Museum at Terezin

After you visit the Small Fortress, turn right on the main road into the town of Terezin and you will come to the Ghetto Museum. On the front door are the Hebrew letters forming the word, *Yizkor,* "Remember." The museum was opened on October 17, 1991, fifty years after the beginning of the deportation of Jews from Czech lands.

Only after the 1989 Velvet Revolution could the building be handed over to serve as a memorial. Before the war, the museum building housed a school. During the ghetto period, it became, "L-417," and served as a home for boys 10 to 15 years old. Ironically, a "museum of Czechoslovakian police and revolutionary traditions of the Northern Bohemian region," was later set up in this former home of Jewish prisoners.

The exhibits are in good taste, well done, and include photographs, videotapes, and newspaper clippings of other materials in several languages. The exhibition is organized chronologically and begins with the Nazi take-over in Germany and ends with the liberation of Terezin.

In the Ghetto Museum, besides a tour of the permanent exhibition, there is an art gallery where you can see works of art created at the Terezin Ghetto. Guides are available.

Operating hours of the Small Fortress and Ghetto Museum, open throughout the year:

Winter: October 1 to March 31, 8 A.M. to 4:30 P.M.
Spring: April 1 to April 30, 8 A.M. to 5:30 P.M.
Summer: May 1 to September 30, 8 A.M. to 6:30 P.M.

The museum is closed December 24–26 and January 1.

The Crematorium at Terezin

While the Communists controlled the country, local Terezin residents and guides often would not even tell you about the crematorium. While there were no gas chambers at Terezin, Jews and others were shot, tortured, or died from starvation or disease. The dead were disposed of in the crematorium, an old laundry building that usually is the third stop of a visit to Terezin. One can see the ovens.

A large Jewish cemetery is located near the crematorium. The site was visited by former Israeli President Chaim Herzog, who was on a state visit in 1991.

Between November 1 and February 28, the crematorium is accessible only with an official guide from the Ghetto Museum; otherwise, it is open every day, except Sunday, from 10 A.M.to 5 P.M.

Many travel agencies have tours to Terezin. The Federation of Jewish Communities, at 18 Maislova, Prague, Tel: 24-81-01-30, can advise you and is a good source for all of your questions.

The traveler can also go by bus from the Prague bus terminal to Terezin. Take the line to Litomerice and Usti Teplice. Check the terminal bus timetable.

Suggested Reading

Ash, Timothy G. *The Magic Lantern: The Revolution of '89 Witnessed in Warsaw, Budapest, Berlin & Prague.* New York: Random House, 1990.

———. *The Uses of Adversity: Essays on the Fate of Central Europe.* New York: Random House, 1989.

Brogan, Patrick. *The Captive Nations: Eastern Europe, 1945–1990.* New York: Avon, 1990.

Dawidowicz, Lucy S. *The War Against the Jews: 1933–1945.* New York: Bantam, 1986.

Hoffman, Charles. *Gray Dawn: The Jews of Eastern Europe in the Post-Communist Era.* New York: HarperCollins, 1992.

Hoffman, Eva. *Exit into History: A Journey Through the New Eastern Europe.* New York: Viking, 1993.

Korbel, Josef. *Twentieth Century Czechoslovakia: The Meanings of Its History.* New York: Columbia University Press, 1977.

Krinsky, Carol Herselle. *Synagogues of Europe: Architecture, History, Meaning.* Cambridge, Mass.: MIT Press, 1985.

Kurlansky, Mark. *A Chosen Few: The Resurrection of European Jewry.* Reading, Mass.: Addison-Wesley, 1995.

Lendvai, Paul. *Anti-Semitism Without Jews: Communist Eastern Europe.* Garden City, N.Y.: Doubleday, 1971.

Meyer, Peter, Bernard D. Weinryb, Eugene Duschinsky, and Nicolas Sylvain, eds. *The Jews in the Soviet Satellites.* Syracuse, New York: Syracuse University Press, 1953.

Moorhouse, Geoffrey, and the editors of Time-Life Books. *Prague.* Amsterdam: Time-Life Books, 1980.

Wechsberg, Joseph. *Prague: The Mystical City.* New York: Macmillan, 1971.

Weinberg, Gerhard L. *A World at Arms: A Global History of World War II.* New York: Cambridge University Press, 1994.

Weisel, Elie, ed. *The Golem: The Story of a Legend.* New York: Summit Books, 1983.

Wischnitzer, Rachel. *The Architecture of the European Synagogue.* Philadelphia: Jewish Publication Society of America, 1964.

Yahil, Leni. *The Holocaust: The Fate of European Jewry, 1932–1945.* Oxford: Oxford University Press, 1990.

Hungary
The Largest Jewish Community in Eastern Europe

This is Hungary, the sixteenth largest country in Europe, roughly the size of the state of Indiana. We now call this nation the "Republic of Hungary." But from 1949 to 1989, it was known as the Hungarian People's Republic and it was Communist.

When it was a kingdom, Hungary was a major national geographical unit, with three-fourths of its frontiers bounded by the Carpathians. But looking at a map, one can see that the area lies in an exposed crossroad of Europe. It is easy to understand why it has expanded and contracted over the centuries.

Today's borders of Hungary were established after World War I—a war the Central Powers of Austria, Hungary, and Germany initiated and lost. In 1920, the Treaty of Trianon sliced nearly three-quarters of the land off the Kingdom of Hungary and bisected out of the country 58.5 percent of its population. After being carved up, Hungary tried to regain lost lands and repeatedly failed. Encompassing 35,919 square miles, Hungary contains 10 million citizens. Gypsies, Germans, Jews, Slovaks, Serbs, Slovenes, Croats, Romanians, and Greeks make up a diverse population. Of these, nearly 70 percent are Catholic.

Seven nations hug Hungary's landlocked borders: Austria to the west; the former lands of a united Yugoslavia, Slovenia, Croatia, and Serbia to the south and southwest; Slovakia to the north; and the Ukraine to the northeast.

Hungary is situated in the western marches of what was once the great pale of Jewish settlement, where the majority of the Jews there lived in abject poverty. That great area had the unfortunate distinction of being the anti-Semitic center of the world. Here anti-Semitism was "endemic and occasionally violent." Pogroms were common. The pressure on them mounted and a large number of Hungarian Jews, like other Eastern Europeans, migrated to the United States at the end of the nineteenth and beginning of the twentieth centuries. The Jews who remained would face the "between-the-war years" of depression, fascism, and the Holocaust. If they survived the last of these, forty years of Communist tyranny awaited them.

The Hungarian people are known ethnically as Magyars. The language of 98.5 percent of the people is Hungarian, a language belonging to the Finno-Ugric linguistic group of the Ugric family. Among the Magyar languages of Europe, it is related to Finnish and Estonian. A most difficult language, the Magyar language is an orphan European tongue, belonging to neither Latin nor Germanic nor Slavic languages.

Where did this language and people originate?

In 895, the Magyars—a tough, pagan, Mongol tribe from Central Russia—swept into the area we know as Hungary. This pagan band fought across the steppes from the Ural Mountains to the Carpathians. Once settled in the Great Hungarian Plains, they abandoned their nomadic life and organized themselves into a state. They stubbornly held their land against invaders from all sides.

The Magyar clan chiefs had chosen a chieftain named Arpad to lead them in their migration. Under his leadership, the Magyars went on to ravage Central Europe until they were defeated by Otto I in 955. Twenty years later, Arpad's grandson, Geza, accepted Christianity and his son, Stephen I, was crowned Hungary's first king on Christmas Day in the year 1000. Stephen continued Hungary's Christianization and development.

The Danube basin offers invaders a hallway to Europe and so in 1241, the Mongols, moving through the basin, invaded Hungary. After pillaging half the population, they withdrew.

The native Arpad dynasty died out in 1301. From that date until 1918, Hungary was ruled almost continuously by foreign powers.

Without fail, the Hungarian people placed their faith in the losers of every war since the sixteenth century, including World War II. And after that bloodbath Joseph Stalin made sure the U.S.S.R. dominated Hungary. Before 1989, Hungary's total experience of democracy was about thirty months—in 1918 for two and a half years; and in 1956, the Hungarian Revolution raged for ten days. All of this history tells us a great deal about the nation we shall be visiting.

A Brief History

Jewish historical tradition mentions Jews in Hungary from the second half of the eleventh century. From that time, the pace of Jewish immigration quickly picked up, with Jews arriving from Germany, Bohemia, and Moravia. By the twelfth century, Jews had settled in Bratislava, which was then ruled by Hungary.

We also know that Jews settled in Buda after the Mongol invasion in the 1250s; they had been granted that privilege by King Bela IV in 1251. This sovereign also gave Jews the "right" to maintain a synagogue and he guaranteed them legal status.

Jews came to occupy important positions in the economic field, so much so that the nobles, feeling threatened, sought to curb Jewish advancement. Thus, the Golden Bill of 1222 included prohibitions directed at Jews.

In the reign of Anjou Louis the Great (1342–82), Jews were expected to convert to Christianity. When they refused, they were expelled—but as it usually turned out, not for long.

The Magyars were followed by the Ottoman Turks, who conquered Buda and defeated the Hungarians in 1526. The Hungarian defeat paved the way for the country's occupation by foreigners. The Turks seized central Hungary and the eastern part of the country, which they called Transylvania. The Austrian Hapsburgs seized the western and northern sections, and by the 1600s the Austrians drove the Turks out of most of

Hungary and gained complete control of the country in the
early 1700s. After central Hungary was incorporated into the
Ottoman Empire, the status of the Jewish people was stabilized.

Buda would become one of the most important communities of the Ottoman Empire before the Ottomans were chased
out of all of Hungary.

Although the Hapsburgs ruled autocratically, it was
Emperor Joseph II, the son of Maria Teresa, who eased the lot
of the Jews with his *Toleranzpatent* of 1782 ("patents of toleration"). By the mid 1850s, the Jews, often protected by owners
of large estates and local administrators, made considerable
advances in business and the professions. They enhanced their
adoptive Magyar culture.

In the 1848 revolution, the Hapsburg ruler called on the
Russians to help quell the rebellion. Because the revolution
was in full swing, Jews were granted equal rights along with
other religious denominations in Hungary. But it did not matter. The victorious Austrian government did not permit Jewish
emancipation, until 1868, that is.

The Emperor Franz Joseph ruled for two decades before he
changed the character of the relationship between the two
countries. In the second half of the nineteenth century,
Hungarian leaders realized that to build a liberal Hungarian
nation under Magyar leadership they had to eliminate all religious discrimination, including that against the Jews. First, the
Compromise of 1867 created the Dual Monarchy. Under that
act, the Hungarian Government would take control of its own
domestic affairs while the Austrians managed foreign affairs.

Secondly, the Emancipation Act of 1868 granted the Jews
equality before the law. No longer were they excluded from
owning property or holding public office. Some barriers still
kept them out of politics and public life, but they certainly
would play a large part in creating the Hungarian economy.
The anti-Semitic mayor of *fin de siècle* Vienna, Karl Leuger, even
referred to Budapest as "Judapest," suggesting that Jews dominated the city.

Because the Magyars ruled and dominated society, "considerable advantages were to be gained if one acknowledged

one's Hungarianess, including the ability to speak Hungarian," writes Jorg Hoensch in his book, *A History of Modern Hungary, 1867–1986*. By 1889, 700,000 Jews who already had obtained equal rights considered themselves Hungarian.

A century later, the Jewish population numbered 932,000, representing 7.2 percent of the population. Jews made up 23 percent of Budapest's citizens, and 75 percent spoke Hungarian, their first language. Jews accounted for 54 percent of commercial business owners; they comprised 85 percent of financial institution directors and owners and 62 percent of commercial employers.

As a capitalist economy grew, so did the Jewish population in Budapest. In the half-century before World War I, Jews prospered and made significant achievements in science and in the arts. Pest itself became a center of Jewish life. The period 1867–1918 was indeed Hungarian Jewry's "Golden Age."

Large numbers of Jews entered the professions: Before World War I, 45.3 percent of all lawyers were Jewish and 78.9 of all physicians. Jews also played prime roles in government. Between 1867 and 1918, 17 Jews were members of the Upper Chamber of the Imperial Diet, 103 Jewish deputies were in the Lower Chamber.

The Jewish economic role in Hungary was disproportionately large, represented by industrialists, bankers, and tradespersons. Jews were needed to fill a gap. Hungary was being industrialized and trade and banking flourished. The Jews helped build up Hungary's banking and industry. Jews started concerns in sugar refining, flower milling, textiles, and metallurgy, according to William O. McCagg in *Jewish Nobles and Geniuses in Modern Hungary*. "Still, most of Hungary's Jews would spend their lives tediously eking out pennies to survive," adds McCagg.

More than anywhere else in Central and Eastern Europe, Hungarian Jews were not only fully assimilated, they were "the only middle class between a large landowning aristocracy and an impoverished gentry on the one hand, and millions of landless peasants on the other," writes Paul Lendvai in *Anti-Semitism Without Jews: Communist Eastern Europe*.

On June 28, 1914, a Bosnian Serb assassinated the heir to the Austrian throne, Archduke Franz Ferdinand. The world shook; the course of history changed. Within days, Austria and Hungary presented Serbia with an ultimatum that made war inevitable. For Hungary, the war was a tragedy: about 3.6 million Hungarian soldiers became casualties. The end was near. The Hapsburg Empire collapsed.

Austria-Hungary signed an armistice with the Allies on November 3, 1918, and a few weeks later was declared a republic. The new state of Czechoslovakia also raised its flag.

In the truncated state, Hungarian Jews would suffer. All the problems of Hungary after the Great War, including an unstable economy, and the Communist dictatorship of Bela Kun were vented on the Jews. A quota system was introduced in Hungarian colleges and universities that limited Jews to five percent of the student body. Beyond the student population, many middle-class, assimilated Jews were targeted. Hungarian Jews would "become the victim of rampant anti-Semitism and terroristic outrages," writes Paul Lendvai. Hungarian Jews would face a worldwide depression, dictatorship, the Nazis, the Holocaust, and communism. The last of these, communism, collapsed in 1989 and a new Hungary arose. However, already in 1994, ex-Communists who called themselves Socialists appeared to be making a comeback because of an electorate soured by its first taste of a market economy.

Notable Hungarian Jews

Hungary owes much to its Jewish scientists, musicians, writers, artists, and journalists, who have been vital to the country's intellectual and cultural development. While the list of contributors is endless, let us name some of the luminaries.

In the area of science, there are Leo Szilard and Edward Teller, who helped father the atom and hydrogen bombs. Albert Szent-Gyorgy, the biologist, was from Hungary. Theodore von Karman, John von Neumann, George Polya, Georg de Hevesy, and Jeno Wigner were major figures in the history of modern mathematics, chemistry, and physics—and all were sons of Jewish nobles. The most surprising aspect of this galaxy of Hungarian "geniuses" is that many were related to each other and even attended the same schools.

The noted sociologists, Karl Mannheim and Oszkar Jaszi, and Sandor Ferenczi and Franz Alexander were at the forefront of psychology. Georg Lukacs was a well-known contributor to philosophical studies.

Theodor Herzl and Max Nordau were the early leaders of modern Zionism. Herzl, the founder of modern Zionism, was born May 2, 1860, in Budapest in a house that stood on the site now occupied by the Jewish Museum on Dohany Street. His bar mitzvah was in the Liberal synagogue in Tabakgasse and he went to school in Pest. In 1878, after the death of his only sister, Pauline, who was one year older, the family moved to Vienna. After watching anti-Semitic outbursts in the streets of Paris during the sentencing of Capt. Alfred Dreyfus on trumped-up charges of espionage, Herzl wrote *The Jewish State.* And in 1897, he organized the first World Zionist Congress, which met in Basel, Switzerland. To Jews throughout the world, he is considered the father of Zionism and founder of the World Zionist Organization.

Arthur Koestler, a well-known author, was the son of an unsuccessful Jewish business person. He left Budapest in the early 1920s and lived in Vienna, Palestine, Berlin, Moscow, Paris, and London. More influenced by Weimar Germany and certain German thinkers, Koestler did not write in Hungarian or identify with Hungarian causes.

Karl Polanyi and his brother, Michael, gave much to the study of political economy.

Bela Kun, part-lawyer and part-journalist, seized control of the Hungarian government; and in October 1918, he established a Hungarian Soviet Republic. A number of intellectuals, including many Jews, marched under his banner. His dictatorship lasted only 133 days. After the failure of a Hungarian Army counteroffensive in a battle with Romania, Bela Kun fled first to Vienna and then to Soviet Russia. He was ultimately executed by Stalin.

Jewish Budapest

Buda and Pest, once two separate cities, joined together to become Budapest in 1873, one of the world's most beautiful urban centers. Its growth was phenomenal and was surpassed in Europe only by Berlin. The growth rate was two-and-a-half times that of London in the first 90 years of the last century. In 1841, the population was 107,240. By 1939, it had risen to 1,115,877.

Today, two million persons live in this capital, which, Emil Lengyel says lies in the heart of Hungary but belongs to a different world—"a world of rich culture on the threshold of Asia." It is often called "the meeting place of Europe and the Balkans," with incidentally three English newspapers and an English radio station in a multicultural atmosphere.

Budapest still remains "Europe's most seductive capital," according to many of its visitors. The setting of Budapest is exceptionally beautiful and it costs no money to climb the hills on a Sunday afternoon and gaze out over the city spread out on the banks of the Danube. Anyone who has lived in a city alongside a river, such as Pittsburgh, Pennsylvania, knows the feeling when seeing the city below from on high. Actually, in Budapest, the Danube runs swifter than it does in Vienna. But it is not blue. As one Hungarian guide told me, the "blue" in Johann Strauss's "Blue Danube" was a figment of his wonderful imagination.

Although 850 miles from the Black Sea, Budapest enjoys the status of a harbor, thanks to the Danube; and without the Danube, Hungary could not have existed, writes Emil Lengyel. Budapest is the only large city that the majestic Danube flows through the middle of; in fact, the river evenly divides the city. It is, John Lukacs writes in *Budapest, Nineteen Hundred: A Historical Portrait of a City and Its Culture,* "as if the Danube has been invented for the esthetic purposes of the city." And if you go to an observation post high up on the Buda side, you realize Lukacs is correct.

Buda was named after Buda, brother of Attila the Hun, according to *World Book Encyclopedia.* "Pest is derived from a Russian word meaning oven, the name was given to the town probably on account of its great lime kilns," says *World Book.*

Most visitors are confused as to which side is Buda and which side is Pest. But it is really very simple. Buda rides the hills and slopes of the west bank, "garnished by gardens, crowned by castles, church spires and forts." Buda is characterized by medieval cobblestone streets and neo-Gothic buildings.

Pest, on the other hand, lies wide and flat, a tabular city, neat as a ledger, with wide massive streets, boulevards, and buildings. Crowded with shops and government buildings, Pest is the "busy corner" of Hungary.

But it does not really matter on which side of the city you stand. "Nature made Budapest one of the leading cities of the Danube," writes Emil Lengyl in *The Danube*. Budapest has become a city of museums and its architecture possesses a definite Austrian influence. One observes the embracing scene of the Buda Castle complex of buildings together with the Chain Bridge, both built in neoclassic style. Fitting in alongside the vistas are wonderful evenings at theater festivals, the opera, or ballet, and, of course, fashion and food—always part of this lovely East European metropolis.

Old and new blend well here. Visit the domed Royal Palace. It positions itself as an outstanding museum of art, sculpture, and history and it dominates Castle Hill. Today, the Royal Palace is a cultural center, including the National Szechenyi Library and the Hungarian National Gallery. And everywhere the views are magnificent.

Transportation here is good and remember that while London was the first city to build an underground train system, Budapest boasts the oldest subway system on the European continent.

Indeed, we must mention **Imre Steindle's Parliament Building** completed in 1902. This is the largest parliament building in the entire world. Its architecture combines Magyar medieval, French Renaissance, Westminsterian, and Gothic styles, with a neo-baroque ground plan and an interior filled with polychrome. Eighty-four pounds of 22-carat gold were used in its decoration, according to John Lukacs.

Throughout their history, each of the towns of Buda, Pest, and Obuda maintained active Jewish communities.

The **Buda-Pest Tunnel,** according to the *Encyclopaedia Judaica,* marks the area where a Jewish community was established by the end of the eleventh century. A cemetery was located near the Buda end of what is now the Pest-Buda Tunnel. We know that Jews moved here in 1250 after the Mongol invasion. In 1348 and 1360 the Jews were expelled from Buda, but they returned after a short interval.

From 1364, the Jewish quarter was located in Buda on the north and southwest side of what is today Tancsics Mihaly street. This is where Jews lived until the Turks left Hungary in 1686. Here, they built two synagogues. The site of **Medieval Syna-gogue,** part of the historical section along Tancsics Mihaly street, is located at Tancsics Mihaly 26. Open May to October, from 10 A.M. to 2 P.M., Tuesday to Friday and until 6 P.M. on weekends.

Whether they lived in the then-separate cities of Pest or Buda, Jews built community institutions. Actually, Jews are first mentioned as being in Pest in 1406. Often these Jews welcomed merchants who between the thirteenth and fifteenth centuries brought various goods to Hungary from the Rhine district. At this time, too, Polish and Lithuanian Jews participated in trade relations with Hungary and Bohemia-Moravia, according to *A History of the Jewish People,* edited by Haim H. Ben-Sasson. By 1504, Jews owned houses. In 1547 there were 75 Jewish residents in Buda and 25 newcomers. After the Austrian conquest in 1686, Jewish residence in the city was prohibited. As for Obuda, it possessed a Jewish community in the fifteenth century. An old synagogue here was demolished in 1817. An imposing new one, still in existence, was consecrated in 1820. By the mid-nineteenth century, nearly 1,500 Jewish families resided in Pest. In the 1848 revolution, a revolution that swept over much of Europe, many Jewish youths enlisted in Hungary's revolutionary cause.

The Pest Jews contributed much to the 1848 revolution, which turned into a war against Austrian oppression. But the fight for Hungarian freedom was quickly and firmly suppressed by Austria. Emancipation for Jews went out the window. After Austria granted joint rule with Hungary in 1867, the Jewish community of Hungary was emancipated in 1868. Hungarian Jewish families helped transform Budapest from a provincial bourgeois town into a large and cosmopolitan capital.

In 1869, there were 44,890 Jews living in Budapest; in 1890, 102,000; in 1920, 215,512; and by 1930, 204,371. In Hungary, as in other nations, Jews in ever-increasing numbers moved to larger towns and capital cities. After World War I, about 46 percent of all Hungarian Jews lived in Budapest, according to *A History of the Jewish People.*

The Hungarian Jewish community today stands as the largest Jewish community in Central and Eastern Europe. Estimates of its numbers vary. Usually the figure given is 80,000, although it could be 100,000. Some people say there are up to 150,000 Jews in Hungary if you include the many Jews who are not registered as Jews, as well as those who are considered "half-Jews" (those with one Jewish parent), according to Charles Hoffman in *Gray Dawn: The Jews of Eastern Europe in the Post-Communist Era.* Interestingly, many dedicated Jewish Communists were never told by their parents that they were Jewish.

Hungary and France are now the only European countries in which Jews represent as much as one percent of the population. Before World War I, Jews made up five or six percent of the population in some parts of Europe. In pre-World War II Poland, the Jewish population was ten percent.

Today, about eight out of every ten Jews in Hungary live in Budapest. Unbelievable as it may be, anti-Semitism may be more pervasive in the provinces where there are no Jews than in cosmopolitan Budapest. Anti-Semitism is less evident now than it was in prior years, "despite the periodic charges and countercharges" in the political debate of the country. Many would like to blame the Communist fiasco on the Jews. It is true that in the beginning many totally assimilated Jews, Jews in name only—were in the top leadership of the Communist party, including Bela Kun, Malyas Rakosi, and Erno Gero. In the 1990s, one can find a latent anti-Semitism. Some Hungarians see Jews, including Christians of Jewish descent, as a non-Magyar minority. But others are quick to point out that this is not so, because many Jews are from families that have lived in Hungary for more than a century.

JEWISH SITES IN BUDAPEST

Your first visit of a Jewish site can be to what one might call a complex of Jewish institutions and monuments around the Jewish Community Center and headquarters of the Federation of Jewish Communities of Hungary, at 12 Sip utca, Budapest. This complex includes the beautiful Dohany Street Synagogue, the Jewish Museum, a Holocaust memorial in a nearby court-yard, and a memorial chapel known as the Heroes Synagogue at Wesselenyi utca, 5, 7, Budapest, which was dedicated to Hungarian Jewish soldiers who were killed in World War I. Services are held every day. During the war, the MIOK build-ing, at 12 Sip utca, was marked off as a ghetto; and Jews were herded into this area.

Federation of Jewish Communities of Hungary, located at Sip utca 12, Budapest. Tel 122-64-78 or 122-18-13. This federa-tion, also known as MIOK (Magyar Orszagos Kepviseleteor National Representation of Hungarian Israelites), is close in ideology and practice to what American Jews know as the Conservative movement of Judaism. But some say that the type of Judaism that Hungarian Jews practiced in the nineteenth and twentieth centuries and known as neology was similar to a form of Reform Judaism. Office hours are Monday through Thursday, 8 A.M. to 4 P.M.; on Friday, 8 A.M. to 2 P.M. The American Joint Distribution Committee and the World Jewish Congress also have their offices here. The Jewish Center build-ing (MIOK) was built around 1860. Through its courtyard one can also reach the Dohany Street Synagogue.

The Dohany Street Synagogue (also called the Great Syna-gogue), Dohany utca 4-6, Budapest. Established in 1859, it is probably the longest and largest synagogue in Europe and one of the largest in the world. Its length reaches 180 feet; it is 84 feet wide and 65 feet high; and it seats a congregation of 3,000. The synagogue was designed by the architect Lajos Forster between 1854 and 1859. The interior was done by Frigyes Feszl. At one time it was known as Tabaktempel because the original street name was Tabak street. A complete renovation project was under way in the 1990s, so the synagogue may be closed if you visit Budapest in 1996. If it is closed, and you wish to attend Sabbath eve services or Sabbath morning services, you can go to **Heroes Synagogue,** Weselenyi utca 5-7, Budapest, where there are services every day. Friday night services are at 6 P.M. Saturday morning services are at 9 A.M. Daily services include a morning service at 7 A.M., Sunday service at 8 A.M., and evening service at 6:30 P.M. Call Jewish Center headquarters at Sip utca 12, to check on the service schedule, Tel: 122-64-78.

The Dohany Street Synagogue boasts two very tall, minaret-like towers crowned with bulbous cupolas. It seats about 3,400 persons and has an organ of 5,000 pipes. Franz Liszt and Camille Saint-Saens played their compositions on it. Once the Nazis surrounded the synagogue with a wooden fence to create the Budapest Ghetto.

In the courtyard is a memorial plaque to Channa Szenes (1921–44). This heroine grew up in Budapest and went to Palestine. She trained as a British commando and parachuted into Eastern Europe to locate downed Allied pilots and help the Jews. She remained with Tito's partisans in Yugoslavia. Szenes was captured shortly after she infiltrated Hungary to organize Jewish resistance in that country. She was executed in 1944; she was twenty-three years old. Szenes' remains were taken to Israel in 1950 and interned on Mt. Herzl. Before her death, she wrote the famous poem, "Blessed is the Match." In Israel and in the Zionist movement, her name became "a symbol of devotion and self-sacrifice."

According to Carol Herselle Krinsky in *Synagogues of Europe: Architecture, History, Meaning,* the Great Synagogue was constructed in a mode that was soon to become part of the architecture of monuments in Budapest. Besides gilded cupolas, the structure contains stone and terra-cotta trim and wrought and cast iron. The two octagonal banners are more than 41 meters high.

Krinsky says the Dohany Street Synagogue shows the "greater self confidence of Jews in the 1850's." During that period Jews were able to commission buildings with conspicuous street fronts in a supposedly Jewish style.

Mass Grave Cemetery. Just outside the synagogue and behind the museum is a mass grave cemetery. When the Jewish ghetto was liberated at the end of the war, thousands of Jewish bodies were buried here because they could not be taken elsewhere. The plaques do not mark individual graves; they are only markers put up by families and friends of the victims. Between 3,000 to 5,000 Jews, murdered by the Hungarian Arrow Cross Fascists and the Nazis, were buried in this courtyard.

Weeping Willow Memorial Tree. This Holocaust memorial, at the corner of Rumbach Sebestyen and Wesselenyi, Budapest, is a sculptured weeping willow tree. Cast in steel, its leaves are engraved on each side with the names of Holocaust victims as remembered by loved ones. Designed by the sculptor Imre Varga, it was first dedicated in 1988. Simcha Dinitz, then chairman of the Jewish Agency, was on hand, as was the famous American movie star, artist, and author, Tony Curtis, whose parents came from Hungary. A plaque says the Memorial Tree was "dedicated to the 600,000 Hungarian Jews who perished in the Holocaust and to the many valiant heroes of all faiths who risked their lives to save untold members of Jewish men and women from certain death."

For further information on the Weeping Willow Memorial Tree Sculpture, in New York contact the Emanuel Foundation at 97-45 Queens Blvd., Rego Park, Queens, Tel: (718) 896-8300. In Budapest, contact the foundation at the Jewish Community Center, Sip utca 12. Hours are Monday through Friday, 9 A.M. to noon and 2 P.M. to 4 P.M. Tel: 121-5227. People who would like to make memorial gifts or have names listed on a leaf may contact the Emanuel Foundation.

Planned for 1995–96 is a **Raoul Wallenberg Park for Righteous Hungarians.** According to Rabbi Andor Weiss, executive director of the Emanuel Foundation, a park will be established in the area of the Weeping Willow Memorial Tree and a marble monument will be set up to cite the more than 250 righteous Hungarians who helped save Jews during the Holocaust. There will be a sitting area for contemplation and

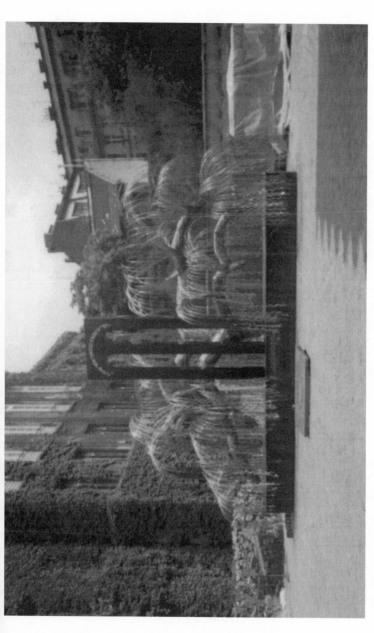

The Weeping Willow Memorial Tree. This Holocaust memorial in Budapest is a sculptured weeping willow tree. (Photo by Sylvia Ackerman)

the area will be designed as a memorial park. For further information, call the Emanuel Foundation in the U.S., (718) 896-8300, or in Budapest, 121-5227.

Monument to the Swedish Diplomat Raoul Wallenberg. This monument is located on a grassy expanse on the Buda side on Szilagyi Erszebet fasov, at the corner of Lupeny utca. Take metro train line 2 from Moszkva Terrace. Continue from there on the bus to Szilagyi Erszebet fasov.

During the war, the United States asked Sweden, who was neutral, to open a special section of its legation in Budapest to help rescue Hungarian Jewry. Raoul Wallenberg was then thirty-two years old and a distinguished Swedish diplomat who had studied architecture at the University of Michigan. Risking his life daily, he issued so-called "letters of protection" and even Swedish passports. He hoped against hope that those who possessed these documents would be spared. Wallenberg saved between 50,000 and 100,000 Hungarian Jews from the Nazis by his dedication, determination, ingenuity, and skill, according to Harvey Rosenfeld in *Raoul Wallenberg, Angel of Rescue: Heroism and Torment in the Gulag.* He even got hold of advance copies of the daily lists of Jews to be deported so he could provide them with protection passports. Reportedly, he was shot at and even chased by cars and trucks. He continually used his daring and resourcefulness to save Jews.

But still terror reigned in Budapest. Wallenberg tried, but his protection could not reach everywhere. Bands of Arrow Cross Fascists drove Jews to the banks of the Danube, murdered them, and dumped their bodies into the river. About 200,000 Budapest Jews were crammed into the ghetto (yellow star section). Then came the gestapo-led marches on foot to the concentration camps. Many Jews starved along the way. Those who were too weak to walk were shot by Fascist guards. "The road to Vienna was lined with corpses," wrote Dr. Ilona Benoschofsky in *The History of Jews in Hungary.*

Wallenberg was arrested by the Soviets on January 17, 1945, imprisoned as a spy, and died, the Russians say, somewhere in the former U.S.S.R. January 17, 1995, marked the fiftieth year of Raoul Wallenberg's disappearance. The Wallenberg

Monument to the Swedish diplomat Raoul Wallenberg, who has been called the "Swedish angel of rescue." He saved thousands of Jews from the Nazis during World War II. (Photo by Riva Frank)

committees throughout the world insist that his fate is unre-
solved and they continue the search. This "Swedish Angel of
Rescue" will always be a hero to the Jewish people and men
and women of goodwill everywhere.

Also active in Budapest during the terrible days of late
1944 was Charles Lutz of Switzerland, who helped Jews find
shelter in safe homes or in neutral legations. "Wallenberg is
the better known of the two because of the tragic conclusion
of his mission, but Lutz was no less actively involved in the
rescue operation," writes Leni Yahil in *The Holocaust: The Fate
of European Jewry, 1932–1945.* In 1944, Lutz, a professional
diplomat, not only represented his Swiss legation, but also
other countries when he dealt with Jewish emigration from
Hungary. Like Wallenberg, he had visited Palestine. He often
was in touch with pioneering Zionist youth movements,
according to Leni Yahil.

It is fitting, when standing near the Holocaust Memorial
and here in the cemetery area where thousands of Jewish victims were buried, to recall the tragedy and nightmare of
Hungarian Jewry. Remember that Hungary fought alongside
the Axis powers, although halfway through the conflict it tried
to "disentangle" itself from Germany.

According to various Hungarian racial laws of 1938, 1939,
and 1941, Jews were removed from professional and intellectual positions. Adm. Miklos Horthy was in power. Appointed
originally only as a regent, he had transformed Hungary
between the wars into a "Fascist dictatorship." His goal was to
recapture lost lands.

In August 1941, 12,000 Jews were deported from Hungary
and murdered because of so-called "uncertainties" concerning
their citizenship. Thus began the nightmare that was to last
until Hungary was freed by Russian soldiers early in 1945.

Some Hungarians do not like to talk about their role in
World War II. Or they answer lamely, "What could we do? We
were surrounded by enemies." A Protestant cleric and historian, Jozsef Elias told *The New York Times* on April 18, 1994, "the
fact is most Hungarians didn't reject Nazism, they accepted it."
Hungary participated in the German invasion of the Soviet

Union in June 1941. Hungarian troops fought beside the Nazis in the Ukraine. The Hungarians suffered 200,000 casualties, including 130,000 dead, at the battle of Stalingrad in Russia during the winter of 1942–43. It is no wonder that Hungarian public opinion turned against the war.

When Hungary allied itself with Germany, Hungarian Jews received a reprieve from deportation. But many were pressed into labor battalions. The Nazis distrusted Horthy; they believed he might make a deal with the Allies. On March 19, 1944, Germany occupied Hungary and on that very day, Adolf Eichmann was dispatched to Budapest to "solve Hungary's Jewish problem." The Jews now numbered 800,000, but Hungarian Jewry was doomed, according to Charles Hoffman in *Gray Dawn: The Jews of Eastern Europe in the Post-Communist Era.* Within four months, between April and July, most Hungarian Jews were stripped of their remaining property, forced into ghettos, and deported to Auschwitz.

When the deportations were stopped in July due to international pressure on the Horthy government, the Nazis had managed to deport virtually all Jews from outlying areas, but only one half of Budapest Jewry. About 25,000 had found safety under the protection of the Swiss and Swedish embassies.

In the fall of 1944, Horthy—the Hungarian leader who had collaborated with Hitler and who had promoted the idea of Hungarian expansion—was forced to resign. Realizing the Russians were near, Horthy had tried to get an armistice. The Germans, however, organized a coup, neutralized Horthy, and appointed Arrow Cross leader Ferenc Szalasi as prime minister.

The Arrow Cross Fascists took over and hunted down Jews. Jews picked up in the streets were tortured and killed, as were those caught in hiding. A series of pogroms reigned; the Jews were being decimated. But historian Jozef Elias said that "whatever is said now about Horthy saving Jews is not true."

Many people see Adm. Miklos Horthy as the man who presided over the deportation to Auschwitz alone of 438,000 Hungarian Jews, mostly from rural areas. Of this number, about 250,000 to 300,000 were exterminated. To others, he is seen as a leader who tried to resist German demands for the mass exportation of Budapest's middle-class Jews and who was finally pushed aside by Hitler in late 1944. After the German coup in Budapest in October 1944, Horthy was sent to Bavaria, where the Americans wanted to arrest him for trial at Nuremberg. A Hungarian historian of the period, Francois Fejto, said Stalin intervened and exile in Portugal was arranged for Horthy. He died in 1957 in Portugal at the age of eighty-nine.

In 1930, 445,000 Jews resided in Hungary. After the infamous Munich Pact, Hungary added another several hundred thousand Jews to its population from Slovakia, Yugoslavia, and Transylvania for a total of about 650,000 Jews in Greater Hungary, according to Lucy S. Dawidowicz. She added in her book, *The War Against the Jews: 1933–1945,* that more than 450,000 Jews, 70 percent of the Jews of Greater Hungary, were deported or murdered under the occupation of the Nazis. Other researchers put that toll at approximately 600,000 Jews.

Dr. Ilona Benoschofsky, writing in *The History of Jewry in Hungary,* indicates that there were 700,000 Jews in Greater Hungary before the Holocaust. She says there were even 100,000 more who did not profess Judaism; still, the anti-Jewish laws applied to them.

Despite the rescue efforts of Charles Lutz and Raoul Wallenberg, by 1945, about three out of four Jews who lived in Hungary before World War II were dead. And Jews amounted to three-fourths of wartime Hungarian losses in life, according to Paul Lendvai. He added, "There is peculiar tragedy in the fate of Hungarian Jewry: it survived intact until the middle of 1944 and was then annihilated in less than eight weeks, when even the perpetrators knew that the war was lost." Almost 50 percent of Budapest's residents of Jewish origin died during the Holocaust period.

Approximately 85,000 Jews remained in Budapest by the end of World War II. According to Peter Meyer, the Russian soldiers who captured the capital in January 1945 acted beastly. Cashing in on their rigged election, the Communist party followed a negative policy and the Jews who were persecuted were often shoved into camps and treated as aliens. "Eastern

Europe was not livable for Jews," wrote Meyer. According to Charles Hoffman, Jews were allowed to emigrate to Israel until 1951. "After that time, Soviet hostility toward Israel greatly increased, restrictions on Jewish life grew more severe, and harsh measures were taken to prevent contacts between Israeli diplomats and local Jews," he wrote.

Hungarian Jewry, until the late 1980s, was on the one hand cut off from Jewry and on the other hand seemed more or less "content with their Goulash Communism and Goulash Judaism," wrote Hoffman.

The Jewish Museum in Budapest, Dohaney utca 2, Budapest.
It is not difficult to locate this museum in Budapest. Adjacent to the Dohaney Street Synagogue and opened in 1932, the founders of the Jewish Museum wanted an institution that would, "awaken and maintain Jewish historical self-respect because that is tied up with the Jewish-life ambition and is more important than the collection of treasures with absolute artistic values." During the war, the museum was a hiding place for Jews and many were saved.

The museum is usually open only from late spring and through the summer because it cannot be heated and is also often closed for repairs. Officially it opens on May 1 and may be visited on Tuesday and Thursday afternoons from 2 P.M. to 6 P.M. and on Sunday from 10 A.M. to 1 P.M.

Through original documents, manuscripts, and photographs, museum exhibits present the history of Hungarian Jews. Here are Judaic cups, rimonim, Torah crowns, candlesticks, spice boxes, and textiles along with an important collection of manuscripts. Especially meaningful are documents about Jewish participation in the Hungarian War of Independence (1848–49), as is the material introducing the Hungarian struggle for emancipation. Modern paintings, sculptures, and medals by twentieth-century Jewish artists are displayed. Some pieces of this collection were stolen in the early 1990s, according to *The New York Times,* April 12, 1994.

As mentioned earlier, Theodor Herzl, the founder of modern Zionism, was born in 1860, in a house on this site. There is a memorial plaque marking the birthplace.

Aided by the American Joint Distribution Committee, the rebuilding of the museum started in 1947. But little money was available for its upkeep during the Communist era, and for decades, only two permanent exhibits were on display: Highlights of Hungarian Jewish life during World War II and an anti-Fascist exhibit. Today, the museum presents the full Hungarian Jewish tragedy through documents, photographs, and newspaper articles.

Rabbinical Seminary, Josef Korut 27, Budapest. During the Iron Curtain period, it was the only rabbinical seminary in Eastern Europe. Founded in 1877, it is now old and dusty, a corner building not in very good physical shape. But its library and its history are fascinating. One can see the bullet holes in the books themselves—bullets fired during World War II. When the Russians were retaking Budapest at the end of that war, the Fascists used the roof as an army outpost against the Red Army. The building also served as a detention center during the war. The library contains 100,000 to 150,000 books. This author saw the dust on the books, dust that had accumulated during more than 40 years of Communist rule. But even in those dark days, there was hope for Jews.

Jews participated in the Hungarian Revolution in 1956 and in the events of 1989. "For 12 days in 1956, Budapest lived through one of the great dramas of the 20th century Europe," writes Patrick Brogan in his book, *The Captive Nations: Eastern Europe, 1945–1990.* It probably is hindsight, but now we know that the Revolution was in effect a rejection of communism throughout the Eastern bloc. "Hungary cried, but no one heard," a former East European told this author. As Henry Kissinger wrote in his book, *Diplomacy,* America and its allies, "acted as if they were bystanders with no direct stake in the outcome." Soviet tanks crushed the revolt and 2,000 persons were executed, including Imre Nagy, who had formed an obviously liberal government. About 200,000 Hungarians escaped to the West, including about 20,000 Jews, according to Mark Kurlansky in his book, *A Chosen Few: The Resurrection of European Jewry.*

A little more than thirty years later, thousands of East Germans would flee communism, also headed westward via Hungary.

Again, one sees Hungary playing a large part in the final "knock down" of communism as it allowed the East Germans entry onto their soil and opened the floodgates to them. The Berlin Wall soon came down and East European communism also crumbled because everyone knew that in 1989 the Soviets, under Mikhail Gorbachev, would not send in their tanks.

Anne Frank High School for Boys and Girls, 26 Somogyi Bela utca, Budapest. Tel: 114-3806. This school, which receives strong input from Israel, enrolls 135 students in grades 8 through 12. The Anne Frank school, which existed under communism, is a coeducational secondary school. Even during the Communist regime, religious education was provided.

New Orthodox School, funded by the Reichman family, Wesseleny 44, Budapest.

The Lauder Yavneh School, Lendvai utca 17, 1062, Budapest. Tel: 361-131-6160. Located in a building that once housed the Communist party's force, this new school began its innovative program in the fall of 1990. According to the school, it provides a foundation of Jewish scholarship and heritage along with high academic standards. The Ronald S. Lauder Foundation is committed to rekindling Jewish life in Eastern Europe. The Lauder Foundation is located in Vaci utca 19/21, Suite 607, 1052, Budapest. Tel: 011-361-266-9168/9169. FAX: 011-361-251-4237.

Orthodox Center, Dob utca 35 and Kazinczy utca, 27, Budapest. This Orthodox complex contains a Talmud Torah, prayer centers, and offices. Services are held every day. The kosher restaurant, Hannah, which is supervised by the Orthodox rabbinate, is also situated in this center.

Main Orthodox Synagogue. The main synagogue entrance is Kazinczy 27, Budapest. The synagogue certainly is well worth a visit, although it is closed in the winter. During that season, access to a smaller synagogue as well as access to the kosher restaurant can also be from Dob utca 35. The smaller synagogue conducts services every day.

Synagogue, Dessewffy utca, 23, Budapest. Services each day.

Lubavitch of Hungary, Wesselenyi utca, 4 1/1, Budapest, 1075. Tel: 361-268-0183.

480 A TRAVEL GUIDE TO JEWISH EUROPE

RESTAURANTS IN BUDAPEST

Hannah Restaurant, Dob utca 35, Budapest. Tel:1-421-072. This establishment is under Orthodox supervision. In the winter, lunch is from 12 noon to 3 P.M. But phone ahead to make arrangements. Dinner is served on Friday nights. Again, phone in your reservations.

Kosher Bakery, Kazinczy utca 28, Budapest.

Shalom Kosher Restaurant, Klauzal ter 1-2, Budapest. Tel: 141-3369 or 122-1454 or 173-2467. This restaurant is under MIOK supervision, which is Conservative. Open at noon. Food can be obtained until 11 P.M. But call ahead to find out arrangements.

Carmel Restaurant. This restaurant is not kosher, but many Jewish-style dishes are served. It is next door to the Orthodox synagogue.

Gundel Restaurant, Allatkerti utca 2, Budapest. It is not kosher, but it is a first-class, expensive restaurant frequented by tourists. Excellent food and entertainment, including Hungarian folk music via the violin.

Besides the first-class hotels on the Buda side of the city, such as the Hilton, there is a moderate business persons' hotel in the center of the city, known as the **Korona,** Kecskemeti utca, Budapest, 1053.

Suggested Reading

Bierman, John. *Righteous Gentile: The Story of Raoul Wallenberg, Missing Hero of the Holocaust.* New York: Viking, 1981.

Brogan, Patrick. *The Captive Nations: Eastern Europe, 1945–1990.* New York: Avon, 1990.

Burant, Stephen R., ed. *Hungary: A Country Study.* Washington, D.C.: Library of Congress, 1990.

Dawidowicz, Lucy S. *The War Against the Jews: 1933–1945.* New York: Bantam, 1986.

Hoensch, Jorg. *A History of Modern Hungary, 1867–1986.* text ed. New York: Longman, 1984.

Kissinger, Henry, *Diplomacy.* New York: Simon & Schuster, 1994.

Krinsky, Carol Herselle. *Synagogues of Europe: Architecture, History, Meaning.* Cambridge, Mass.: MIT Press, 1985.

Kurlansky, Mark. *A Chosen Few: The Resurrection of European Jewry.* Reading, Mass.: Addison-Wesley, 1995.

Lendvai, Paul. *Anti-Semitism Without Jews: Communist Eastern Europe.* Garden City, N.Y.: Doubleday, 1971.

Lengyel, Emil. *1,000 Years of Hungary.* New York: John Day, 1958.

———. *The Danube.* New York: Random House, 1939.

Lukacs, John. *Budapest, Nineteen Hundred: A Historical Portrait of a City and Its Culture.* New York: Grove/Atlantic, 1990.

McCagg, William O. *Jewish Nobles and Geniuses in Modern Hungary.* text ed. Boulder, Colo.: East European Quarterly, 1972.

MacLean, Rory. *Stalin's Nose: Travels Around the Bloc.* New York: Little, Brown, 1993.

Meyer, Peter, Bernard D. Weinryb, Eugene Duschinsky, and Nicolas Sylvain, eds. *The Jews in the Soviet Satellites.* Syracuse, N.Y.: Syracuse University Press, 1953.

Rosenfeld, Harvey. *Raoul Wallenberg, Angel of Rescue: Heroism and Torment in the Gulag.* rev. ed. New York: Holmes & Meier, 1995.

Sugar, Peter F., et al, eds. *A History of Hungary.* Bloomington and Indianapolis: Indiana University Press, 1990.

Yahil, Leni. *The Holocaust: The Fate of European Jewry, 1932–1945.* Oxford: Oxford University Press, 1990.

Young, James E. *The Texture of Memory: Holocaust Memorials and Meaning in Europe, Israel, and America.* New Haven: Yale University Press, 1993.

Slovakia
Jews Are Here to Stay

At Hanukkah in 1993, a significant event took place in the history of the Slovak Jewish community: a Hanukkah torch relay lighting ceremony—the first of its kind—was held in the city of Bratislava, the capital of the new nation of Slovakia. An escort of about twenty young Jewish runners accompanied the torch from the burial place of the great Orthodox scholar, Hatam Sofer, to the old Jewish section and the site of a former synagogue that stood in the path of the newly constructed bridge now spanning the Danube. The president of Slovakia, Michal Kovach, was on hand and Chief Rabbi Baruch Myers spoke.

Ceremonies in Eastern Europe are symbolic. This Hanukkah torch parade, similar to the carrying of the freedom torch by the Maccabees of old and run every year in Israel to the ancient town of Miron, signaled to the Slovak people that the Jews are in Slovakia to stay. This is crucial to the future of the Jews in Slovakia, for like in Russia and other countries in Eastern Europe, the Jewish community here appears to be uneasy.

Indeed, "anti-Semitism today [in Slovakia] is also a heritage of the war-time Slovak state, a vassal republic controlled by Hitler which expelled its Jewish citizens to German extermination camps and paid the Nazis set fees for each person deported," wrote Olga S. Hruby in *The New York Times*, November 11, 1991.

This is one Jewish community in Europe where American Jewish visitors, for instance, can make a difference in a people-to-people relationship. Slovak Jews need to know that there is also a bridge between the largest Jewish community from the Diaspora, the United States, and one of the smallest, Slovakia. If you really want to know how a small Jewish community exists in Eastern Europe, visit Slovakia.

Slovakia (Slovenska Republic)

Near the center of Europe, in the great Danubian valley, live the Slovaks. Today, most reside in a country called "Slovenska Republic," which covers 18,933 square miles and counts 5.3 million persons. Bordering the Czech Republic, Poland, Ukraine, Austria, and Hungary, it was once considered a "rural backwater" in the Austro-Hungarian Empire. But it is considered that no longer, because today it is strategically located between Ukraine and Hungary.

We know that Slovaks settled in Central Europe before A.D. 500. In the 800s, they were part of the Great Moravian Empire and around the year 900 they were conquered by the Magyars. Yet, throughout their long history, the Slovak people kept their own language, always "harboring nationalist feelings," longing for independence.

As Eva Hoffman writes in *Exit into History: A Journey Through the New Eastern Europe,* Slovakia's "brief moment of grandeur came in the 9th century when the Slovaks were united with the Moravians for the first time." The Great Moravian Empire was short lived and by the tenth century the Slovaks were conquered by Hungary, she adds. In fact, the Slovaks would endure Hungarian rule for most of their history. The Czechs at least enjoyed power and influence before bending to Austrian Hapsburg control.

Hungarians like to call the period between 1867 and World War I (1914) a particularly creative and productive era in Hungarian history; but for the Slovaks, it brought "relentless magyarization," including the increasing promulgation of Hungarian as the official language. As a result, the Slovaks faced cultural extinction.

By 1918, powerful support existed among the Slovaks to unify with the Czechs, with the country to be called Czechoslovakia. So after World War I, much of the nation of Czechoslovakia was literally "cobbled together" from provinces of the defeated Austro-Hungarian Empire. Slovaks always felt the Czechs overpowered them intellectually and they resented Czech power. Constitutionally, there was no discrimination, according to author Josef Korbel. Czechs and Slovaks had common ties through ethnic identity. But over and over again the thousand-year history of separation had created two dissimilar societies and different cultural experiences. It soon became clear that the Czechs and Slovaks were "mismated," as Emil Lengyel puts it in *The Danube.*

Despite the assurances of the Czech patriot Thomas Garrigue Masaryk, who concluded what is called "the Pittsburgh Pact" in 1918 with Slovak Americans to win their support for a common state, Slovak self-rule never really occurred. During World War II Slovakia was a Nazi puppet state. The Slovaks "never had an opportunity to establish their own identity," it was said.

With the crumbling of the Communist states, the Czechs and Slovaks parted ways on January 1, 1993, a day the Slovaks waited a thousand years for. The Slovaks once again stand on their own two feet. But the terrain of independence is rocky, especially economically. "In contrast to the Czech Republic where inflation and unemployment have been kept under control, Slovakia has suffered from economic and political gyrations," wrote Jane Perlez in *The New York Times* on October 3, 1994. It must be recalled that it was the Slovaks who pushed for separation and the Czechs went along with it; many Czechs perhaps believed they were "carrying" the Slovak sections of the country and could do better on their own. The country is remote from Western Europe both geographically and culturally; and its relations with Hungary, a strong neighbor to the south, are tense. Unemployment stands at approximately fourteen percent. The economies of the Czechs, Poles, and Hungarians seem to be pulling ahead. It is hoped that Slovakia can catch up.

As time goes on, experts seem to agree that the Czech Republic got the better deal from the separation, certainly from an economic point of view. The economic news from Slovakia is not promising. Some even say the Czechs all along wanted to go it alone. They probably were correct to do so.

Remember as you travel through this part of Eastern Europe that a dominant sentiment is suspicion: Where once there was one country—Czechoslovakia—there now are two separate states, including separate armies, separate borders and passport control, and separate trade policies. The Czechs and Slovaks are glad they divorced. Many Slovaks do not like the Hungarians. The Hungarians say the Slovaks are causing trouble by trying to divert the Danube River. Remember, the Slovaks were under the thumb of Hungary for a thousand years. Noteworthy is the fact that 600,000 Hungarians live in southern Slovakia. Also, both countries were under the rule of the Austrian Hapsburgs for several hundred years, a fact one must always recall when considering Slovakia.

A Brief History

Who are the Jews of Slovakia? Once they were called "Highland Jews."

The history of Slovakia was often identified with Hungarian history—Slovakia was even called at various times Upper Hungary and Northern Hungary.

Slovak Jewish communities have flourished in the area since the thirteenth century.

By the fourteenth century, 800 Jews lived in Bratislava. Sometimes, they lived in an autonomous political unit headed by a communal leader. Generally, they were moneylenders engaged in commerce and finance.

After the Battle of Mohacs (1526), which began the rule of the Hapsburgs with Ferdinand I, Jews were expelled from the Slovak area towns and did not return until the beginning of the eighteenth century. From time to time, nobles granted them protection and some liberty.

The Austrian Emperor Joseph II (1780–90) granted Jews

some limited civic rights, which made wider spheres of livelihood possible. This area in Northern Hungary became so popular for Jews that it was called "Magyar Israel." Many Moravian Jews arrived and created new areas of Jewish learning, especially in Bratislava itself. There, a yeshiva was established in 1700. The city became particularly prominent with the spread of the influence of Rabbi Moses Sofer, the Hatam Sofer, whose descendants for generations became rabbis of Bratislava and surrounding towns.

With the establishment of the dual monarchy of Austria and Hungary in 1867, the Hungarian Parliament passed an emancipation law the following year. The Jews of Slovakia became free men and women. The increased "magyarization" of the population, however, took its toll in the form of Jewish assimilation.

After the new nation of Czechoslovakia was established in 1918, Zionist activity emerged. For the first time, Jews had the right to declare themselves members of a Jewish nationality.

In the 1920s and 1930s, about 135,000 Jews, representing 4.5 percent of the Slovak population, lived in the Slovak region of Czechoslovakia. Political stability in the late 1920s brought prosperity for many Jews. Cultural and social life thrived around Zionist organizations and youth movements. The study of the Hebrew national culture and the increased focus on the Hebrew language led to close ties with the nascent Jewish community in Palestine. Jewish writers and journalists wrote in both German and Hungarian. However, in the late 1930s, as fascism spread over Europe, the position of the Jewish population deteriorated. The Munich Pact sellout resulted in the dismantlement of Czechoslovakia. Slovakia became a German satellite and agreed to set up a Nazi regime. Disaster lay ahead for the Jews. Jewish businesses became aryanized. Jews were fired from their jobs and were rounded up; they were shipped to the killing camps.

Thus began the Holocaust in Slovakia. By 1944, three-fourths of the Jewish community had been exterminated, and more than ninety percent of Jewish youth had been deported. Less zeal on the part of the Slovaks would have saved many Jewish lives. As early as 1941, Slovak leaders Tuka, Tiso, and

488   A TRAVEL GUIDE TO JEWISH EUROPE

Mach negotiated the question of deporting the Jews. Documents attest that in 1941, "Slovakia was the first state whose Jews the German Reich was prepared to take over." Adolf Eichmann gave Slovakia five hundred marks for each Jew as a guarantee that the Jews would not be returned.

The irony of it all: the first deportations from West Europe to the concentration camp Belzec took place on March 24, 1942. Two days later, the first Jews were deported to Auschwitz. They came first from Slovakia. On the following day, other Jews arrived from France. In her book, *The Holocaust: The Fate of European Jews, 1932–1945*, Leni Yahil writes that between March and November 1942, nearly 60,000 Jews were deported to Auschwitz and other concentration camps.

According to the book, *Tragedy of Slovak Jewry*, prepared by the Documentation Center of CUJCR, in Bratislava, and published in 1949, Slovak Jews "were exterminated so thoroughly and mercilessly during the years 1939–1945, that not one of the once happy and prosperous community has lived through the murderous storm without the irreplaceable loss of part or all of his family, without severe mental shock, or gravely impaired health."

Slovak Jewry lost about 110,000, including those deported in the spring of 1944 from territories that had been annexed by Hungary, according to Leni Yahil.

Bratislava

Welcome to Bratislava, the old city by the Danube—the capital of Europe's newest small nation, the Slovak Republic, and the country's largest city. Walk through Slovak National Uprising Square. Drive through this hilly metropolis, now trying quickly to shake off the forty-year Communist drabness, although it is succeeding somewhat. However, it will take time to undo the poor city planning of the Communists.

Even today—as in books—you cannot tell a city by its cover. There are some wonderful sites to see. Visit the gardens of Bratislava Castle. From there, you can see the splendid new bridge over the Danube. There is also the cathedral where 10

Hungarian kings and 8 Hungarian queens were crowned. Stop at the Baroque Old Town Hall courtyard and the Primatial Palace, which has its own art gallery and English tapestries based on Greek myths. And the Jewish community here is hospitable and will welcome the traveler.

With a population of 441,500 persons, Bratislava is crucial to Central Europe Jewish history. At the beginning of the nineteenth century, the noted Rabbi scholar Moses Sofer, the Hatam Sofer, made Bratislava the spiritual center of Hungarian Orthodox Judaism. The yeshiva in Bratislava once was the most important in Central Europe.

Throughout its history, the city was called, in Hungarian, "Pozsony"; in German, "Pressburg." The name Bratislava was coined by the Slovak archeologist P. G. Safarik in 1837. Some say the city was never a citadel of the Slovaks, for when it was separated from Hungary by the Versailles Treaty, its Slovak population was less than twenty percent. We must remember that Bratislava was the seat of the Hungarian Parliament for three centuries during the Turkish wars, and Hungarian kings were crowned in its cathedral. Actually, this old city on the Danube was the capital of Hungary from 1536 to 1683. It once stood as the second largest city in Czechoslovakia. Only thirty-five miles east of Vienna, it is now a center of rail and boat transport. Its factories churn out chemicals, textile machinery, and petroleum products. It is a working man's city, a factory town.

In the nineteenth and early-twentieth centuries, "a trip to Bratislava was considered a chic Sunday outing for Viennese noblemen."

Bratislava was the site in 1903 of the first Zionist convention in Hungary. Thirty-five years later, this metropolis, as capital of the German vassal state, lives in memory for the tragedy of the Jews' mass deportation to the death camps. That forced, deadly expulsion was set in motion and organized by one man, the late dictator Monsignor Jozef Tiso. Not only was he a puppet of the Nazis, but he headed Slovak fascism and even had his troops commit anti-Semitic atrocities.

After the war, Slovak history became Czech history. Under communism, Slovak Jew and Christian would suffer alike.

The entrance to the Hatam Sofer Mausoleum in Bratislava. (Photo by Riva Frank)

The postwar Jewish community was re-established on April 15, 1945, a few days after the country was liberated from the Germans.

By 1947, 7,000 Jews lived in Bratislava and a second synagogue opened. Jews had a difficult time reclaiming their property, however. Anti-Jewish riots erupted, and about 4,000 Jews emigrated to Israel just before the Communists took over. More left during "Prague Spring" in 1968, when Czechoslovakia launched fresh reforms, a new era of "socialism with a human face." This meant more civil rights, minority protection, and a possiblity to emigrate.

Under the Communists, Jews could not easily or openly practice their religious or cultural customs. Jewish organizational property was turned over to government ownership and control. Any attempts to revitalize Jewish life were cut short and threats were made constantly. For example, in January 1952, the Communist newspaper, *Bratislava Pravda* warned that the country's "Jewish citizens are in the service of the American imperialists who are trying to undermine Slovak life."

Only several thousand Jews resided in Slovakia during the forty years of Communist rule. They lived under the threat of dismissal from employment, compulsory manual work, evacuation to different places of residence, and long prison terms.

Prague Spring 1968 brought relaxation of the strictures, but the reforms did not last long. With backing from the Russians, a new Communist political leadership in the country cracked down even harder. A year later, the Jewish population of Bratislava in 1969 was estimated at about 1,500.

Because of the strong tradition of Jewish scholarship in this city, it is fitting that we visit first the burial place of Hatam Sofer.

JEWISH SITE IN BRATISLAVA

Hatam Sofer Mausoleum. The Hatam Sofer Mausoleum is a rarity among the sites of Slovakia. You would never know it is one of the most revered sights of Jewish Central Europe. It is located in what is called "Vajanskeho Nabrezie." It looks like a bus stop shelter. In a way it is, because people actually stand there while waiting for a bus. There are no Jewish monuments or memorials around it. But here rests perhaps the greatest Jewish scholar of the nineteenth century. He is Rabbi Moses Sofer, known as Hatam Sofer, rabbi, halachic authority, and leader of Orthodox Jewry. He was indeed the leader of pre-modern Orthodox Jewry "in its battle against the initial manifestation of the Reform Movement of Judaism," writes Jacob Katz in *From East to West: Jews in a Changing Europe 1750-1870*. His coffin, it is said, was made from the slabs of his lecture desk.

Twenty-three graves and 41 separate tombstones are in the mausoleum today; once they were on the hillside of the cemetery behind the mausoleum. Visitors even leave notes just as they do at the Western Wall in Jerusalem. The mausoleum itself is part of the former Jewish cemetery that dates back to the years 1670 to 1847.

A "man of letters," the Hatam Sofer was the rabbi of rabbis. Rabbis came from all over Europe to Bratislava. He and his yeshiva—the largest since the Babylonian yeshivot—influenced the development of Orthodox Jews in western and central Hungary. Torah study became widespread among large sections of Orthodox Jewry. Yeshivot were established.

Hatam Sofer was born on September 24, 1762, in Frankfurt-am-Main. A brilliant scholar, he was offered many positions. But he accepted the offer of the Bratislava Jewish community and on October 13, 1806, he became Chief Rabbi. In 1809, when Bratislava was besieged by Napoleon's army, he fled and organized a charitable activity.

He was a voluminous writer. His works comprise volumes of responsa, sermons, commentaries, letters, poems, and a diary— all bearing the imprint of his Orthodoxy. Hatam Sofer fought for the usage of the Hebrew language and for the idea of a return to Zion. He died on October 3, 1839. He educated many hundreds of rabbis who became spiritual leaders all over the world. He had devoted his life to religious judicial activity.

The mausoleum is visited by Jews from throughout the world who come here to say their prayers and pay tribute to Hatam Sofer. The key to the mausoleum may be obtained from the Jewish Community Center. Arrangements for a visit should be made in advance.

KOSHER RESTAURANT AND HOTEL

Chez David Kosher Restaurant and Hotel, Zamocka 3, 81101, Bratislava, Tel: 42-07-316-943 or 313-824. FAX: 42-7-312-642. This attractive establishment is clean as well as reasonably priced. The food is excellent. Among the many items on the menu are steak, cholent, and vegetable pâté. Rooms in the hotel are comfortable. This is a good place to meet the Jews of Bratislava, as well as Americans and Europeans working in the city and countryside.

SYNAGOGUES

Synagogue, Heydukova St., 11-13, Bratislava. During the forty years of communism, as an act of defiance, many brave Jews, upon entering this synagogue, would wave at the hidden cameras of the secret police. Before 1989, it was difficult to be Jewish, but not any longer. Many young people are coming forward and declaring that they are Jews, even admitting that they have one Jewish parent. This attractive synagogue schedules services on Monday and Thursday mornings, Friday nights, and Saturday mornings. The time of services depends on the season.

Today, nearly 3,000 Jews are registered in the Slovak Republic, of whom 1,000 live in the capital city of Bratislava. Between 500 to 1,000 Jews live in the city of Kosice. The rest are found in in small communities scattered throughout the country. But the Jews are uneasy when they read that opinion polls indicated that more than half of the Slovak population fear Jewish influence. Czech Jewish leader Thomas Kraus told author Andrew Nagorski (in *Birth of Freedom*), "The Jewish community is nervous about the new state. . . . After independence, the standard of living will quickly drop and people will look for someone to blame." He predicted in May 1992, "At that point, we would have a revival of anti-Semitism."

Here again, we see the phenomenon of "anti-Semitism without Jews."

Community Center and Offices, Kozia St. 18, Bratislava. This building serves as the community activities center for the Jewish community, which now, according to Rabbi Baruch

Myers, is composed of close to 1,000 Jews. For thirty years, the community was without a spiritual leader. Rabbi Myers, who became the first post-Communist rabbi in Bratislava, studied under the Lubavitch Rebbe in Brooklyn, New York. He told this author that not too many Jews are totally observant, but he had managed to set up the synagogue, a kosher kitchen, and study groups. An active Chabad movement holds meetings several times a week; there are activities for Jewish youth; a *shali-ach* (adviser-educator) from Israel works with the community; bar mitzvahs are being celebrated. In 1990, a Jewish forum began holding meetings with several hundred in attendance.

Rabbi Myers was the subject of international headlines in 1993. Two teenage skinheads hurled the epithet "yuden raus"—"Jews, out"—at the rabbi. The Nazis had used that expression when rounding up Jews in the ghettos of Europe for deportation to the death camps. Myers was kicked and suffered minor injuries. He told this author he had been shaken up psychologically, but he indicated he would not be driven away.

Chabad Center, 22 Augusta No. 19, Bratislava, 81107. Tel: 011-427-323-246.

The Headquarters of the Union of Jewish Communities in Slovakia. Kozia Street, 21, Bratislava. Although small in size, Bratislava Jewry sponsors a B'nai B'rith group with 55 members. Dr. Prof. Pavel Traubner, who heads the Jewish community in the mid-1990s, also told the author that 60 to 70 percent of the people in the Jewish community are 80 years old or more. And many in the Jewish community help older parents. Dr. Traubner said his dream "is a revival of Jewish life." He declared, "For now, we will help keep alive our survival. We will stay here."

Suggested Reading

Brogan, Patrick. *The Captive Nations: Eastern Europe 1945–1990.* New York: Avon, 1990.

Hoffman, Charles. *Gray Dawn: The Jews of Eastern Europe in the Post-Communist Era.* New York: HarperCollins, 1992.

Hoffman, Eva. *Exit into History: A Journey Through the New Eastern Europe.* New York: Viking, 1993.

Korbel, Josef. *Twentieth Century Czechoslovakia: The Meanings of Its History.* New York: Columbia University Press, 1977.

Lengyel, Emil. *The Danube.* New York: Random House, 1939.

MacLean Rory. *Stalin's Nose: Travels Around the Bloc.* Boston: Little, Brown, 1993.

Malino, Frances, and David Sorkin, eds. *From East to West, Jews in a Changing Europe, 1750–1870.* Cambridge, Mass.: Basil Blackwell, 1990.

Nagorski, Andrew. *Birth of Freedom.* New York: Simon & Schuster, 1993.

Tragedy of Slovak Jewry. Bratislava Documentation Center of CUJCR, 1949.

Yahil, Leni. *The Holocaust: The Fate of European Jews, 1932–1945.* New York: Oxford University Press, 1990.

Poland

Someplace Along the Polish Road, You Will Shed a Tear

"I realized I didn't know any Jews. . . . So, I asked myself and I asked others: Where do Jews exist? I was told: Poland. And so I went to Poland."

—Alfred Doblin

Someplace along the line, dear reader, if you travel to Poland today, you will shed a tear.

This implies, of course, that not everyone will want to visit this rapidly advancing, modern country, a nation in no way displaying the poverty one sees in Russia, a nation quickly moving along the fast track of market reform and free enterprise. Yes, it is free at last from forty years of the drabness and darkness of communism imposed by the former U.S.S.R. You will find no Third-World country here. Actually, there are fine restaurants and extremely modern hotels, such as the Marriott in Warsaw, and a high-speed train from Warsaw to Cracow. People are even friendly and extremely polite.

Logistics make Poland a launching pad to the former Soviet republics, as well as a distribution center to Scandinavian nations and others in the European Union. Its dynamic economy exhibits "dramatic recovery with sustained growth." Despite inflation, the country is moving fast, privatizing, and reforming. So welcome to Poland.

• In no other country since ancient Israel have Jews lived continuously for as many centuries in as large numbers and with as much autonomy as in Poland. Eighty percent of the Jews in the world during the Middle Ages lived in Poland. In the seventeenth century, three-quarters of the world's Jews resided in this land. In 1897, despite the effects of large-scale Jewish emigration, 14 out of every 100 Polish citizens were Jews. The tourist knows from history that in the 1920s, 1 out of every 5 Jews in the world still lived in Poland, about 10 percent of that country's total population. Nowhere else in the world did Jews form such a high percentage of the total population: 3,351,000 Jews made Poland the second largest Jewish community after the United States in 1939. Its capital, Warsaw, ranked as the second largest urban Jewish center with 350,000 people, or approximately 30 percent of the city's residents. By 1939, two-thirds of the world's Jews lived in Europe and three-quarters of them, half of all world Jewry, were concentrated in Eastern Europe. Remember, if you are a Jew residing in the United States or in the State of Israel, chances are your ancestors are from Poland, Czarist "Pale of Settlement," which included parts of partitioned Poland, or from Russia itself.

• Jews played a key role in laying the foundations of trade and industry in Poland. They created a vast network of religious, political, and social institutions. Artistic and cultural activity reigned: Yiddish literature, Kabbala, the mysticism that lasts to this very day, and Talmudic rationality. More than three-quarters of Polish Jews settled in cities and town, constituting 27 percent of Poland's urban population. About 40 percent were engaged in industry and handicrafts, more than 33 percent in trade and commerce, and about 6 percent in the professions. All came from this wonderful Jewish community.

• Poland was the spiritual and religious heart of the Jewish Diaspora, which for 1,000 years followed in the footsteps of matching the achievements of the Babylonian Exile or the Golden Age of Spain and produced one of the greatest world centers of Talmudic study.

• Poland's yeshivot and Talmudic libraries were the envy of world Jewry.

• Poland is a country with a long and serious history of anti-Semitism that often erupted and still does, but now is labeled "anti-Semitism without Jews." Indeed, Polish "skinheads" and other extremists use the term *Jew* as a label for any of their targets, Jewish or not.

• Poland's Jewish community in 1930 could boast 180 publications, including 20 daily newspapers, most of them in Yiddish but a few in Hebrew and Polish. By 1937, the number had grown to nearly 300. One newspaper, *Haint* (*Today*) employed 1,000 correspondents and was read by millions of Jews throughout the world. Contributors included David Ben-Gurion, the first prime minister of the State of Israel, and Sholem Asch, the noted Yiddish writer.

What hurts about visiting Poland? Three million Jews were murdered in the killing fields of this country. This is where the Germans erected their death camps, a half-dozen in Poland alone, including Auschwitz, a name that still sends shivers down the spines of people throughout the world. The Nazis made Poland the center for the extermination of all European Jews.

With all that pain, why go?

Some Jewish tourists visit Poland to seek their roots, to see the town their parents and grandparents called home, to physically observe and touch the "remnants," even a single surviving Warsaw Ghetto wall. Some place a pebble on a gravestone in the famous Jewish cemetery in Warsaw or stand in awe in front of the monument to the Warsaw Ghetto Uprising, which depicts the Jewish heroes and martyrs and marks the first armed, large-scale civilian resistance against the Nazis in occupied Europe.

Some recite psalms or a special prayer on the ground of the death camps or at the railroad platforms at Birkenau, where evil incarnate Dr. Joseph Mengele stood. Some journey here to make a statement that the Jewish people live, that "we are here." They walk with the young people who participate in the "March of the Living," where every two years, about 6,000 Jewish teenagers from 40 countries march from Auschwitz to Birkenau.

Jewish tourists do go and they do meet Jews. At least

5,000–6,000 Jews reside here. There are probably thousands more who have not declared that they are Jews, although every day more and more do so. A Jewish community still exists in Poland, and in the opinion of many, it should be visited and helped despite the pain of the past.

"Willingly or unwillingly, Poland will never be able to forget the Jews," writes Aleksander Hertz in *The Jews in Polish Culture.* Certainly, the Jewish chapter as it was is closed. While we will never forget the three million Jews who perished, there is "no obituary yet for Polish Jewry and there is no place for an obituary."

Jews don't visit Poland dispassionately. Sholem Asch once said that the broad shallow river, the Vistula, the queen of Polish rivers, spoke to him in Yiddish. No matter what language you speak, the Vistula—"on whose bank the Jews dwelt for centuries"—will speak to you about the Jewish past in Poland, a past that must be remembered. Our roots are too deep in Polish soil to die. As long as Jews live there and Jews visit there, they will not wither away.

Location

"God wanted to place Poland at the heart of Europe. But, as with man, he missed. Our heart lies off-center on the wrong side of the Germany," says the author of *Stalin's Nose: Travels Around the Bloc.* Poland should "nestle" next to France, "not lie trapped, as it is, on the open plains between two hungry autocracies, Russia and Germany." Poland lies astride the invasion corridor from Berlin to Moscow; it is too important geographically for its status to be left to chance. This frequently partitioned nation was swallowed up first by Prussia, Russia, and Austria, and later by Germany and the Soviet Union. "In the course of its history, Poland has taken a large number of different forms. Almost every century has witnessed its territory modified and the political lines that bounded it changed." But Bernard D. Weinryb, author of *The Jews of Poland: A Social and Economic History of the Jewish Community in Poland from 1100 to 1800,* says Poland has always remained hemmed in. For much of the past 300 years Poland did not exist as an independent state. It possessed an "unusual talent" to lose its independence for such a long time. Only after World War I, did Poland win freedom. And then after World War II, its borders were shifted from east to west by 150 to 200 miles, meaning that a big swatch of Polish territory was absorbed by the former Soviet Union.

This large, Central European nation, which covers an area of 120,725 square miles, is only about 60 miles from Berlin, and from east to west, it extends about 430 miles. With a population of about thirty-nine million, Poland is named for the Polane, a Slavic tribe that lived more than a thousand years ago in the land we now call Poland. The name *Polane* comes from a Slavic word that means, "plain," or "field." Postwar Poland's population is more than 90 percent Catholic and more than 98 percent ethnically Polish.

A Brief History

And to think that it all began probably as far back as the tenth century, even though the first official documents attest to the Jews being in Poland in the twelfth century. After the Mongols overran Poland in 1240–41, many German Jews crossed the border into Poland, where they received a special invitation, also known as charters or privileges, from King Boleslav V the Pious, Duke of Kalisz, in 1264. These charters were called the "Kalisz Statutes," and they became the legal basis for the settlement of these German Jews. These privileges, too, were extended several times by King Casimir III.

To Jews, Casimir III, later known as Casimir the Great, looms large. In 1334, a year after he ascended the throne of Poland, King Casimir, who ruled from 1333 to 1370, issued a proclamation that substantially broadened those privileges originally granted to Jews. It is recorded in legend that Casimir had a Jewish mistress, Esther, and that their daughters were raised as Jews.

A crowning point, obviously affecting Jews, was the 1385 Polish Lithuanian Union. The Lithuanians wanted to rely on the Poles to stop the always present German threat. Pagan

Lithuania sought a union with Christian Poland. They needed each other. In 1385, Jagiello, Grand Duke of Lithuania, "promised to convert his people to Christianity, to bind his armies to Poland's armies," writes Anne Applebaum, author of *Between East and West Across the Borderlands of Europe*. Jagiello became a Christian, married the Polish Princess Jawiga, and was named King of Poland. The Lithuanians converted to Christianity, too, and together, the Poles and Lithuanians defeated the Teutonic Guard Master at the Battle of Grunwald (Tannenberg) in 1410. This victory gave the Poles 200 years of growth and consolidation.

"The Jews are seen, accepted and defended as a group whose main business is money lending against pledges," according to the *Encyclopedia Judaica*. Jews are "protected moneylenders." The pledges were protected and ratified by King Casimir IV Jagiello in 1453, and later by other Polish kings.

Certainly not lacking in the case of Poland are the facts as well as legends concerning how Jews arrived in this nation. One legend connects the Jews with the 1492 Spanish expulsion. According to this tale, when Jews were dispatched from Spain by that country's king and queen, they wandered eastward. When they finally rested, they declared, "Poh Lin," which in Hebrew means, "Here, stay overnight." Also, Rabbi Moses ben Israel Isserles coined a pun on the Hebrew form of Poland and explained that it derived from two Hebrew words: "Poh Lin": "Here he shall rest." And again we have the same Rabbi Isserles who said: "It is preferable to live on dry bread and in peace in Poland, than in other dangerous lands."

A proverb began circulating that went something like this: "Poland, the heaven of the aristocracy, the paradise of the Jews, the hell of the peasants," according to Alfred Doblin.

THE FIRST JEWISH SETTLERS

Who were these Jews, these first Jewish settlers? While there were Sephardic Jews from Iberia and the Mediterranean basin, the bulk of the first settlers were Ashkenazim and they came from the west and southwest. In the Dark Ages in Western Europe, the Jews repeatedly had been accused of causing the

Black Plague, of practicing witchcraft, and of committing ritual murder. So they fled from Bohemia to the "emerging kingdom of Poland." They were welcomed, and this was the beginning, some say, of Poland itself. Many of those merchants and their co-religionists were fleeing from the Crusades. Driven from Germany, they brought with them skills in various crafts and experience in trade. Other newcomers hailed from the Ukraine and from Khazar. Early Polish rulers encouraged them to establish shops and develop industry, wrote S. L. Schneiderman in *The River Remembers*. Jews were needed in the backward economy of Poland. They became innkeepers, artisans, and traders. They plied the overland route through Poland, which linked the Ottoman Empire with Central and Western Europe. No middle class existed between the landed gentry and the peasants. So the Jews brought with them their arts, crafts, trades, professions, and ability as merchants and financial agents. International trade and banking flourished.

Moreover, during the Middle Ages, Jews were not segregated. According to the privileges granted them between the thirteenth and fifteenth centuries, they could live anywhere. By the end of the fifteenth century, 10,000 Jews resided in Poland. Already it was believed by Jews in Germany that "Poland was the safest place for Jews."

Remember that after the 1492 expulsion from Spain, the only country in which Jews were permitted to engage freely in trade and crafts was Poland. By the end of the sixteenth century, therefore, Poland still was being hailed as "the new golden land of the Jews," writes Norman F. Cantor in *The Sacred Chain: The History of the Jews.*

In the sixteenth century, a Jewish parliamentary body, the Council of Four Lands (Vaad Arba Artzot), with headquarters in Lublin, was established and became an independent representative government of Polish and Lithuanian Jewry. It distributed the tax load among the various Jewish communities. Described as the highest institution of Jewish autonomy, it also concerned itself with matters of security and morals.

Between the end of the fifteenth century and the partitions of Poland in 1772, 1793, and 1795, Poland had expanded and reached its highest peak. Territorially it was the second largest state in Europe and ranked sixth in population. By the sixteenth century, Polish rule stretched from the Baltic Sea in the north to the Black Sea in the south and eastward to the gates of Moscow. Poland then was second only to France in size and population.

Polish nobility became the dominant political force, mainly because Polish farming was "primitive and feudal." The nobles realized that greater profits could be had if the lands produced more efficiently. So they turned to the Jews, according to Abba Eban in *Heritage: Civilization and the Jews*. Jews soon became active and valued partners to the nobility in many enterprises.

Jews who leased the land from the nobles were called *rendars,* and they enlisted other Jews to help them administer vast domains. Thus, the interests of Jews and Polish magnates coincided and complemented each other between the huge estates of the nobles and the private towns organized by the Jews. Jews "were made estate agents sent out to the outlying properties of the nobility to govern the serfs and produce revenue for the lords," writes Norman F. Cantor. He adds that Jews obtained the monopoly of the liquor trade in the countryside in the Ukraine. Polish peasants had to buy from Jewish tavern owners, often creating friction and hatred. It was part of the age-old Jewish problem—as tax collectors, managers of estates, or distributors of wine and liquor, you don't exactly make friends. An old Polish proverb, "What the peasant earns, the noble spends, and the Jews profit by," reflects the true sentiments of the masses.

The nobles opened up huge regions of the Ukraine wilderness and brought them under Polish rule. But this also brought difficulties: the Ukrainians were Eastern Orthodox, and they hated the Roman Catholic Poles, as well as their Jewish rendars.

THE CHMIELNICKI POGROM

To Ukrainians, he is a hero. To Jews, Ukrainian officer Bogdan Chmielnicki (1595–1657) is anathema. Chmielnicki hated Poles and Jews, and after an argument with a Polish nobleman, he fled across the Dnieper River to Zaporozh'ye, a Cossack stronghold. There, he roused the Cossacks to rebellion. And in 1648, he changed the history of the Ukraine and Poland because his revolt altered the balance of power in all of Eastern and Central Europe. The Cossacks now swore allegiance to the Russian Czar and thus, the Russians would go on to become a world power.

Poles and Jews suffered horrible deaths at the hands of the Cossacks. Jews were buried alive, sold as slaves, skinned alive, burned in towns. They suffered through several years of massacres. Thousands were killed. Thousands were forced to convert to Christianity. Their homes were destroyed and their imposing wooden synagogues burned to the ground. From that moment on, Polish Jews began emigrating westward. The upheaval inaugurated Jewish poverty, especially in the villages of Eastern Europe.

By 1655, Poland began to decline for the Polish people and for the country's 1.5 million Jews. By the end of the eighteenth century, Poland disappeared from the map of Europe. Major changes occurred in the Jewish community in the seventeenth century. Jews tried to move out of money lending into other occupations, even agriculture and other branches of trade. But even during this decline, Poland stood strong as a reservoir of Jewish spirit and manpower that resisted assimilation and apostasy.

In the eighteenth century, Poland was partitioned out of existence; it became the "plaything of its neighbors and its political system was the laughing stock of Europe," says Robert I. Frost in his book, *After the Deluge: Poland and the Second Northern War, 1655–1660*.

Out of the wars and the Cossack uprisings grew the great messianic movements of Eastern European Judaism. And as the eighteenth century drew near, messianic claims of Shabbetai Zevi stirred the masses.

The Shabbetai Zevi messianic movement of the seventeenth century did not originate and develop in Poland, but it had an impact upon Polish Jewry. Zevi was born in 1626 in Smyrna, Izmir. Interested in Jewish mysticism, Kabbala, in 1648 he began to believe that he was destined to be the "savior of the Jews." Abba Eban says that "never before had one man united the Jewish people of all lands in a movement so inspired with enthusiasm and hope."

Zevi met and acquired a so-called "prophet," Nathan of Gaza. As the two wandered the Mediterranean area, the Turks, fearing an insurrection, arrested Shabbetai Zevi in 1666. Facing execution or conversion, he renounced Judaism and adopted Islam.

The impact of Jacob Frank was also great. Alfred Doblin says Frank was a Jewish sectarian. "He fantasized the Jews, got them to convert to Christianity." Incredibly successful, he was supported by the Polish king.

Polish-born Frank, who lived 1726–91, spent twenty-five years in Turkey before he came back to his homeland and founded the cult named after him. Like Shabbetai Zevi, whom he admired, he said people should seek the joy of life and communion with God through "ecstasy." Thousands of fanatical adherents followed him. He first became a Moslem and then a Christian. Several thousand of his followers converted to Christianity.

Jews felt they had been spiritually deserted by these false messiahs. But now a new movement came on the scene: *Chassidism.* Abba Eban defines Chassidism as "a special enchanting world, rich with stories, homilies, and endless wonders about the rabbinical court and dynasties that are the heart and center of the Chassidic vision."

Chassidism's founder was Israel ben Eliezer (1700–1760), who was of humble origin. We know him as the Ba'al Shem-Tov, literally, "the Master of the Good Name." After years of wandering and taking on various jobs, for example, as a beadle in a synagogue, teacher, herbal healer, and hermit—in 1735, he appeared as a pious miracle worker, according to Maurycy Horn in *Polish Jewry History and Culture.* His main power lay in the "force of his personality"; he offered hope to the Jews of Poland. Estimates state that half of Polish Jewry flocked to Chassidism. They believed he was a prophet; they found refuge in his wishful vision.

The 1648 *pogroms* and the closing of the Council of Four Lands in 1734 had sharply curtailed the once vibrant spirit of Polish Talmudic Judaism. The masses yearned for comfort; Chassidism filled the vacuum and became the greatest religious revival in the long history of the Jewish people.

In the nineteenth century, Poland became the seedbed for the intellectual movements that were to transform the Jewish world: Zionism, secularism, socialism, and neo-orthodoxy.

The Russians ruled Poland with an iron fist and again, after the 1863 Polish uprising, imprisoned thousands and exiled many of the Poles to Siberia. The czars, who had annexed large chunks of Polish territory, treated Poland as if it were nothing more than a "Province of Russia." They called it "Russification." These rulers of Russia kept the Jews as downtrodden as they could by confining them to a massive ghetto area of Russian Poland, called the "Pale of Settlement."

Before World War I, relations between Poles and Jew became strained. Jews were promised their own schools, that never happened. Jews were promised status as a minority rights, that never happened. Jews were promised financial aid and support for schools, that never happened. All of these broken promises were symptomatic of Poland's difficulties, created bitterness, and lead even to deaths. Gerald Stillman reports in the publication *Jewish Currents,* April 1993, that between 1935 and 1939, some 500 Jews were killed and 5,000 injured in various pogroms throughout the country.

In 1936, Ze'ev Vladimir Jabotinsky, leader of the Zionist Revisionist Party and founder of Betar, its youth movement, pleaded with Jews to leave. They did not; many could not, and often those who wanted to were barred by highly restrictive immigration policies of Western nations, including the United States. Between the wars, as we shall see, Zionism, the national rebirth of the Jewish people, was one of the most important Jewish organizations in Poland. So, too, was the BUND, the acronym for the "General Jewish Workers Union in Lithuania, Poland, and Russa."

The BUND demanded cultural and national autonomy for national minorities, especially for the Jews. The BUND perceived the necessity of organizing Jewish workers into one national party. Generally, this group opposed political conservatives and Orthodox Jewish religion. The BUND saw that the only chance of solving the Jewish question in Poland was the building of a socialist society.

Despite the pogroms after the First World War, despite discrimination in Poland's universities, despite the increasingly hostile atmosphere, despite poverty and economic boycotts, a vast network of religious, educational, philanthropic, social, and cultural institutions flourished in Poland "without comparison elsewhere in Europe," according to Lucy S. Dawidowicz in *The War Against the Jews: 1933–1945*. Jews had political parties of all views and delegates and senators in the Polish parliament. She adds that the rise of Nazi Germany, the death of Marshal Jozef Pilsudski in 1935, and Poland's accelerating Fascist course all brought near-disaster to the Jewish community. A torrent of anti-Semitic legislation, brutal pogroms, and an official government policy of "evacuating" the Jews from Poland overwhelmed them. By 1939, more Jews had left Poland than Germany, well over 400,000, and they went mainly to France, Belgium, and Palestine. To add insult to injury, the Polish government even studied the feasibility of settling Polish Jews on the island of Madagascar. In 1938, laws were enacted to revoke the citizenship of Polish Jews residing abroad.

The year 1938 will always be remembered as the year of Munich. On September 1, 1939, Hitler unleashed the German army and sent it into Poland. The long chapter on Polish Jewry was closed. A new disastrous chapter would begin. We know, of course, that after World War II, only about 200,000 Jews out of 3.5 million survived. Fifty years later, there would be only about 5,000 to 6,000 "registered" Jews in Poland. An even newer chapter would start.

Notable Polish Jews

Many Jews served as court physicians to Polish princes and magnates. Tobias Cohn (1652–1729) may have been the first physician to provide a detailed description of the disease known as *plica polonica,* a skin disease affecting the scalp.

A large number of Jewish moneylenders became involved in trade and helped establish villages on large tracts of land.

By far, some of the greatest Jewish scholars, luminaries of Talmudic scholarship, hailed from Poland. Among these rabbis were Yom Tov Lippmann Heller; Solomon Luria; Moses Isserles; Isaiah b. Abraham ha Levi Horowitz; Meir b. Gedaliah of Lublin; Mordechai b. Abraham Jaffe of Lublin; and the Chassidic masters, including Israel b. Eliezer Ba'al Shem Tov, the founder of Chassidism, to name a few.

Thirteen Jewish representatives sat in the first Polish Parliament in 1919. Noted among these was Professor Mojzesz Schorr, historian and Zionist, as well as being a member of the Polish Parliament.

Other important figures include Dr. Zygmunt Bychowski (1865–1934), prominent neurologist; Vladimir Medem (1879–1923), writer and leader of the BUND, which was founded in Vilna in 1897; Majer Balaben (1877–1942), historian, professor at Warsaw University, and once head of the Institute for Jewish Studies.

Polish Jewish musicians included Ignaz Friedman and Arthur Rubinstein, the singer Marya Freund, and harpsichordist Wanda Landowska.

Lazar Rundsztein was flyweight boxing champion of Poland in 1937.

Many of the leading Zionists and leaders of Israel came from Poland, the prime example being David Ben-Gurion, the first prime minister of Israel. Another noted Polish and later Zionist leader in Israel ws Yitzhak Gruenbaum. A large part of the Israeli population had been born in Poland, and many were the organizers of the Jewish self-defense units in Palestine, known as the Haganah, which came out of Jewish defense movements in Poland, wrote Mark Kurlansky, author of *A Chosen Few: The Resurrection of European Jewry.* After the death of Theodor Herzl, the founder of modern Zionism, the leadership of the Zionism movement passed to Polish and Russian Jews, who carried on the idealistic work and vision. Poland once stood as one of the most important centers of the

Zionist movement, with Polish Zionists playing an important role in World Zionist affairs. Various Zionist parties, like Hechalutz (a pioneering youth movement), were founded in Poland, as were groups such as the Revisionist Zionists. Unlike their German co-religionists, many of whom leaned toward assimilation, the Jews of Poland responded "wholeheartedly to the movement for a national revival." The first conference of the *Hoveve Zion,* "Lovers of Zion," movement was held in Katowice. Nahum Sokolow, who headed the Zionist movement in Poland, became a member of the World Zionist executive committee. A tremendous increase in membership in the Zionist movement occurred in Poland between the wars. According to the *Encyclopedia of Zionism and Israel,* "no other country with the exception of Palestine and, to a degree, Lithuania, experienced so encompassing a Zionist impact on Jewish life." The encyclopedia also notes that the Polish government in the 1930s did not place obstacles before the Zionist movement "on the assumption that this would increase the stream of emigrants from Poland to Palestine." We will see that the Zionist youth groups in particular played a crucial role during World War II in the Jewish underground and the Warsaw Ghetto Uprising. In 1965, of the 17 cabinet members of Israel, 8 were of Polish extraction; of the 120 Knesset members, about 30 percent had come to Israel from Poland.

Rosa Luxemburg (1870–1919) was swept up in the radical currents of the time. Born in the area of Russian Poland, she helped found the Spartacists, the forerunner of the German Communist Party. She was murdered by German rightwing soldiers in Berlin.

Julian Tuwim (1894–1953) wrote in Polish and is considered one of Poland's greatest modern poets.

Yiddish writers Solomon Rabinowitz, known as Sholem Aleichem (1859–1916); Shalom Abramovitsch, known as Mendele Mokher Soforim (1835–1917); and Isaac L. Peretz (1851–1915) immortalized the *shtetlekh* (Yiddish word for those Jewish rural communities of Russia and Poland). I. J. Singer (1893–1944) and Isaac Bashevis Singer (1904–91) were Yiddish novelists and short-story writers. The Singer brothers were born in Poland. I. J. Singer achieved fame for such novels as *Yoshe Kalb, The Brothers Ashkenazi, East of Eden,* and *The Family Carnovsky.* Isaac Bashevis Singer won the Nobel Prize for Literature in 1979. The books he is known for include *The Family Moskat, Gimpel the Fool, The Magician of Lublin,* and *The Manor.* Simon An-sky (1863–1920), folklorist and author of the famous play *The Dybbuk,* and Isaac Manger (1901–69) are also noted Jewish writers. To understand the life of Jews in Poland, the works of these authors make impressionable reading.

Sholem Asch (1880–1957), Polish-born, was the foremost Yiddish novelist of the early twentieth century. Also a dramatist, short-story writer, and journalist, Asch lived in Warsaw under the influence of Isaac Leib Peretz. Asch began writing in Yiddish in order to reach a worldwide Jewish audience. He lived and worked in several European countries as well as the United States and Israel. Some charged him with "becoming an apostate" and inciting further hatred of Jews, but he denied these accusations. He wrote *The Nazarene, The Apostle, Mary, Moses, Three Cities, The Mother,* and *East River.*

Polish Jewry Today

A Polish woman in her late forties recalls that as far back as thirty-five years ago the Polish Jewry community had only 5,000 members and was dying. "Thirty-five years later, I hear the same thing," she relates.

Never write off a Jewish community. The pundits said the same thing about the Jews of Vienna in the 1970s; that it was a dying community. Today, the Austrian Jewish community is a vibrant congregation. True, the history of Polish Jewry may be close to coming to an end, but it has not yet. Can organized communal life continue? Polish Jewry has received strong support from the American Jewish Joint Distribution Committee and from the Ronald S. Lauder Foundation. Other groups also have appeared on the scene. Things must be picking up because recent newspaper reports now indicate there may even be intergroup tension among the various units aiding Polish Jewry.

Rabbi Haskell Besser, director of the Ronald S. Lauder Foundation, recounted that in a meeting with the late Lubavitch Rebbe, the Rebbe told Rabbi Besser that he should get involved "with the living in Poland," and not the dead. According to various sources, Lubavitch itself is not involved in activities in Poland.

Before the fall of communism, many Jewish parents masked or at least downplayed their Jewish identity because memories of the Holocaust were too painful and to be Jewish was not to their advantage. But now tens of thousands of full Jews, half-Jews, quarter-Jews, as well as non-Jewish spouses and in-laws are declaring their Judaism. In 1989, according to Rabbi Michael Schudrich, director of the Lauder Foundation in Poland, thousands of young Poles began seeking their Jewish roots.

Now, Jews and other minorities feel comfortable in practicing Judaism. The restrictive policy of a Communist police state toward religion, toward Zionism, toward Israel, has been lifted.

Many of the young people tell of having one Jewish parent. During the Communist regime, these youths never thought of asking their mother if she was Jewish. As the story goes, that would have been like asking one's mother if she was a virgin when she got married. These people were one step past total assimilation. One young man knew so little, he did not even recognize he was Jewish when one day his mother blurted out, "By the way, my mother's mother was Jewish." According to Jewish law, that made the young man Jewish—Orthodox Judaism states that if your mother is Jewish, you are Jewish.

Because Rabbi Besser, the Lauder Foundation, the American Jewish Joint Distribution Committee, and other groups have been there tending to Jews who live in Warsaw, Cracow, Lodz, Lublin, Katowice, Wroclaw, Gdansk, and other cities, Polish Jewry can survive. "The Sabbath Candles Have Gone Out" is the title of the first chapter of Alexander Hertz's book, *The Jews in Polish Culture*. The lights may have been flickering, but they still can be seen.

"The eternal spark of the Jewish soul is never extinguished. We should not try to extinguish sparks that the Nazis and Communists failed to extinguish," declares Rabbi Schudrich.

Jewish Warsaw

If Warsaw is the heart of Poland and it is, then despite all, Warsaw is still the heart of Jewish Poland. But from 1939 to almost the year 2000, is like the difference between night and day. The Warsaw Jews knew and loved is gone. And indeed for Jews, "the city, its people and its life will never be the same again." Once, one out of every three Warsavians was Jewish, today nobody even knows the exact figure, more than a thousand Jews, less than a thousand Jews.

The largest city of Poland, Warsaw lies on both banks of the Vistula River. The center of Warsaw and most residential areas are on the left bank.

In the years of the 900s, a small Slavic sect lived here. From the 1200s to the 1500s, Warsaw was the home of the dukes of Mazovia, a state that entered the Polish kingdom in the 1500s. In 1596, King Sigismund III moved the capital from Cracow to Warsaw. During the partitions, Prussia controlled Warsaw in the late 1700s; then the city became the capital of the Duchy of Warsaw from 1807 to 1813. In the next phase, the Russians controlled Poland until 1914 and after the German occupation in World War I in 1918, Warsaw became the capital of an independent Poland.

Today, Warsaw is bustling. In the Old Town square, we find the most elegant area in Warsaw and one of the most exciting in Poland. On an early Sunday morning, all is quiet except for the ringing of the church bells. This is what parts of Warsaw must have been like before World War II. The Old Town was reconstructed from utter ruin. All is recent creation. A "cultural hub," "stimulating city," and "surging metropolis," are all good descriptions of Warsaw.

Today Warsaw covers 170 square miles and has a population of about 1,700,000.

In 1781, 2,609 Jews lived in Warsaw, including several hundred in fashionable Praga, a suburb of the city on the east bank of the Vistula River.

In 1867, the Jewish Warsavian population reached 219,128.

Warsaw for the Jews symbolized study and cultural activities;

Warsaw even had six full-time Yiddish theaters and a hundred Jewish troupes toured the country. Two major centers of Hebrew literary activity from 1880 to 1914 existed in Eastern Europe; Warsaw was one, Odessa in the Crimea, the other. Eventually, entire neighborhoods in the Warsaw suburbs were inhabited mainly by Jews, many of whom attended *shtibels,* Chassidic houses of prayer.

But between the world wars, the depression, the anti-Semitic policies of the Polish government, and the fall of Marshal Pilsudski, all "combined to keep the economic level of the Jewish community low," declared Lucy S. Dawidowicz. In his *Journey to Poland,* author Alfred Doblin was shocked by the poverty of the Jews. He described Jews in medieval garb with their own language, religion, and culture. He saw black-bearded Jews as vendors; he saw elderly Jewish women, Jews in caftans and skull caps. They were not an "exotic tribe." They were lower middle-class workers, small businessmen, and laborers. By the 1930s, close to thirty percent of Polish Jews were receiving some form of financial assistance from Jewish communal funds.

There were renunciations of minority rights. There were pogroms. There were killings. There was anti-Semitism. There were numerous restrictive clauses. But there was not mass murder.

Warsaw remains a symbol of the tragedy of World War II. Without doubt, it had the distinction of being the "capital of the war," the first city to be bombed and the first to be turned into a battlefield.

Try to picture Stalingrad after that famous, devastating battle. Soviet officers who fought there maintain that Warsaw was the most destroyed city in Europe. Already ruined, Warsaw was burned to the ground during the German retreat. Early on, Hitler had decided to make Warsaw a "second Carthage," and in the 1944 Polish Uprising, the Germans bombarded the city, "literally to rubble," writes Eva Hoffman in *Exit into History: A Journey Through the New Eastern Europe.*

"Wartime in Poland lasted longer than for any other country, except Germany. In proportion to its size, Poland incurred far more damage and casualties than any other country on earth," according to Norman Davies in *Heart of Europe: A Short History of Poland.*

JEWISH SITES IN WARSAW

Because the Jewish community today is small, the tourist realizes that the major Jewish sites are pretty much within walking distance, so for our first visit we should head for Twarda Street and the Nozyk Synagogue.

Nozyk Synagogue, Twarda Street, Warsaw. A Thursday is a good day to visit Nozyk Synagogue since it is an officially designated historic monument and is open that day. Actually, any day is good to see this house of worship, since, if you are a male, you just may be the tenth Jewish man needed for a *minyan* (Orthodox quorum) in this stately Orthodox synagogue founded in 1900 and named after the founders, Zalman and Rywioka Nozyk, who died in the early part of this century.

Rectangular in shape, the synagogue is more than 19 meters long, more than 15 meters wide, and almost 12 meters high. It has a "galleried basilica," according Carol Herselle Krinsky in *Synagogues of Europe: Architecture, History, Meaning.*

The entrance to the women's gallery section is at the south end of the structure. The *aron ha-kodesh* (Holy Ark) is located in the main hall and covered by the curtain (Parokhet) with a inscription of the prayer "Shema Yisrael." A member of the congregation led the prayers when I attended and his stand was on the right side facing the *aron ha-kodesh* and the chair of Rabbi Joskowitz. Services were delayed as the rabbi waited; he wanted to be sure of a minyan of Jewish men.

How this synagogue, with alternating square piers and columns supporting the galleries, survived the Holocaust is a miracle. The Nazis used it as a stable. The dedication of the renovated synagogue, which is mainly Romanesque, took place on April 18, 1983, a day before the fortieth anniversary of the Warsaw Ghetto Uprising.

Jewish Religious Union in Poland, ul. Twarda 6, Warsaw. Tel: 206-234, 200-676, and 201-037. This organization coordinates activities for more than fifteen synagogues in Poland and looks after Jewish cemeteries.

The Nozyk Synagogue at 6 Twarda St., Warsaw, is the only functioning synagogue in the Polish capital. (Photo by Ben G. Frank)

Ronald S. Lauder Foundation, ul. Twarda 6, 00-104 Warsaw. Tel: 203-496. One might call this the eyes and ears of the Polish Jewish community. Here one finds a group of dedicated men and women. The director of the foundation in Poland is Rabbi Michael Schudrich, whose office is located here. His telephone number is 203-496.

Ronald S. Lauder Foundation, Youth Club, ul. Twarda 6, Warsaw.

Ida Kaminska's Jewish Theater in Warsaw, Pl. Grzybowski, 16/18, Warsaw. Named after Esther Rachel Kaminska, this 400-seat theater was opened in 1970 at a cost of more than $1 million. Its founder and star performer, Ida Kaminska fled Poland after the anti-Semitic outburst of 1968.

It has been said that Yiddish and the Hebrew language and culture, as well as the Yiddish theater, springs from Poland and it exists because the people and the community want to keep it alive and the government and the American Jewish Joint Distribution Committee support it. Productions are attended mainly by Poles.

In Warsaw, the first attempt to create a Jewish theater was recorded in 1837. In the 1890s, Yiddish productions were stimulated by Abraham Goldfaden, considered father of the Yiddish theater. Drama circles began to flourish in Warsaw and Cracow. The dramatists included such literary celebrities as Shalom Abramovitsch, known as Mendele Mokher Soforim, and Solomon Rabinowitz, whose pseudonym was Sholem Aleichem. The latter's plays still thrill the world, including *Tevye the Dairyman.* We know that play as *Fiddler on the Roof.*

We also recognize the Yiddish and Hebrew poet, Isaac Leib Peretz (1852–1915), and Ossip Dymov (1878–1942). Ossip Dymov, born in Bialystok, had been a publicist before he began writing for the theater. Only at the turn of the century did the Jewish theater start to develop "vigorously."

In 1892, Esther Rachel Kaminska (1870–1925) made her appearance in Warsaw's Eldorado Theater. Kaminska, who would later found the theater in Obozna Street, won fame as an actress and performed in the first Jewish films. By her side, the great talent of her daughter, Ida Kaminska (1899–1978), grew.

The Jewish theater in Poland—chiefly in Warsaw and Vilna—gave premiers of plays, which were often dramatic adaptations by Sholem Aleichem. The audience also had the opportunity to acquaint themselves with Jacob Gordon's vast repertoire. The most creative period of the Jewish theater occurred in the 1920s and 1930s, when Yiddish theater companies were quite active in Poland, according to Lucjan Dobroszycki and Barbara Kirshenblatt-Gimblett in *Image Before My Eyes: A Photographic History of Jewish Life in Poland, 1864–1939.*

Even in the Warsaw Ghetto, the world's largest concentration camp, the Nazis permitted several theaters to operate. Between December 1940 and July 1942, five such theaters functioned. "The theatrical interlude in the Warsaw Ghetto was only one more element of the perfidious tactic of showing victims already doomed to death, a flicker of hope which would soon vanish on the way to the gas chambers," writes Zygmunt Hoffman in *Polish Jewry History and Culture.* After the war Jewish theater commenced production.

It was not until 1955 that the State Theatre, named after Esther Rachel Kaminska, found a permanent home in Warsaw.

TSKZ Club, Pl. Grzybowski, 12-16, Warsaw. These are the letters for the Polish words meaning, "Social Cultural Society of Jews in Poland." This organization deals with cultural activities in Poland and is a lay organization organized in Jewish communities in the country. It publishes the only Jewish newspaper in Poland, *Dos Yiddishe Vort.*

Restaurant Menora. Pl. Grzybowski 2, Warsaw. Tel: 20-37-54. Telephone of the *mashgiach,* 24-13-60. It is open from 10 A.M. to 9 P.M. We live in a strange world indeed. Much of the joy of travel is meeting people you know or who should know someone you know, very often a loved one. For forty years now, I've been traveling the world and when I tell people along the way, in Israel, France, Italy that I hail from New York City, they would say, "perhaps you know my cousin in Brooklyn, or my aunt in Queens, or my friend on Long Island." But in 1995, in Warsaw, I met Shimon Heustein, the *mashgiach* of the restaurant. He knew my late father-in-law, Rabbi Solomon Spitz, not in Poland where both he and Rabbi Spitz were born, but in Omaha, Nebraska, and Sioux City, Iowa, where both men worked as ritual slaughterers and kosher inspectors. He told me the Menora Restaurant serves 110 meals a day. The food, strictly kosher, is good.

Cafe Eilat, al Ujazdowskie 47, 00-536 Warsaw. A cafe near the U.S. Embassy where many young Polish intellectuals, Jewish and non-Jewish, gather. Actually, it is the mailing address of the Polish Council of Christians and Jews, according to Stanislaw Krajewski, who is a leader in the Warsaw Jewish community. The Polish Council of Christians and Jews was established in 1991 to enhance mutual understanding between both Christians and Jews. Such an organization did not exist before 1989, the year communism dissolved in Eastern Europe.

WARSAW GHETTO AREA

Those who know the tragedy that befell the Jewish people know this visit to the former Warsaw Ghetto area is not your usual simple walk-through, even though part of it is a nice, quiet area. It sports a beautiful green park and apartment buildings, children play, and shoppers hover about picking out bargains. Tourists bustle from place to place and melt into the busy scene. When the knowledgable traveler visits the area of the former Warsaw Ghetto and its monument, he or she remembers that between November 1940 and June–July 1943, "along this path of suffering and death," about 450,000 Jews were either driven away from the city to the gas chambers housed in the Nazi death camps or were buried underneath these fine apartment houses.

The Jews, who accounted for thirty percent of the Warsaw population, were jammed into 2.4 percent of the city's area. We call that a *ghetto,*—in this case, a "concentration of Jews defined by racist criteria," points out Yisrael Gutman in *The Jews of Warsaw, 1939–1943: Ghetto, Underground, Revolt.* The section that you walk in—there are memorial stones in parts of it—was known as the Central Ghetto, including the streets of Wolynska, Szczeszluva, Ostrovska, Niska, Stawki, Nalewki,

Gesia, Dzika (Zamenhofa), Mila, and Maranowska. We shall visit the "Memorial Route" soon.

Actually, as best as we can tell, the Holiday Inn hotel was the southern border of the Warsaw Ghetto. Near the Holiday Inn is 60-62 Zlota (gold) Street and in the courtyard there is a remnant of the wall of the ghetto. Also at 55 Sienna Street is another wall remnant; a plaque was placed there by the United States Historical Memorial Museum.

"The sidewalks were filled with masses of people whose threadbare clothing reeked with the smell of rotting foodstuffs, and human sweat," writes Gutman. "Dead bodies rolled in the street." People dropped like poisoned flies. The ghetto was swarming with Jews brought from outlying villages. The smell of death was everywhere. Out of a half-million Jews, fewer than 50,000 remained by mid-1943.

The story of the Warsaw Ghetto actually begins with the victory of the Nazis over Poland. The Germans divided up Poland with the Russians, then later they established what they called the Generalgouvernment—an area of 39,000 square miles, composed of four districts: Cracow, Lublin, Warsaw, and Radom. This area became a dumping ground for Jews and Poles who had been expelled from Germany and parts of Poland. Now penniless and near starvation, these people were placed under German civil administration. Hans Frank served as Governor General. He was appointed on November 8, 1939, and set up his headquarters in Wawel Castle in Cracow.

With about 450,000 Jews jammed into the Warsaw Ghetto, the Nazis turned the area into a human stockyard. Isolated, they were forced into close, squalid conditions with dwindling food, fear, intimidation. No hope for the future existed in their depressed minds.

Penned in on all sides, the sentence was death by starvation and disease. People became skeletons almost overnight. They were forbidden to teach or to learn. They starved. Some even sold their bodies for bread. No library, no school, nothing reached them. Escape from the ghetto was almost impossible. Marek Edelman, a survivor of the Warsaw Ghetto Uprising, said once that only one out of thousands was able to escape.

You needed money to bribe the guards, including at times Polish police. Even before their scheduled final journey to the Treblinka concentration camp, many had died of disease and hunger. Others thought they could hide in the ghetto and somehow survive.

The Nazi goal was to isolate Jews, plunder their property, force them into slave labor, and actually starve them gradually to death, according to Israel Gutman in *Resistance: The Warsaw Ghetto Uprising.*

The Germans knew that by giving Jewish spoils to the Poles, the Nazis "gained ardent supporters. There is no doubt that Polish satisfaction with the fate of the Jews under the Nazis stemmed from economic considerations," wrote Joseph Kermisz in *The Warsaw Diary of Adam Czerniakow: Prelude to Doom.* But above all, was the dynamism shown by the Jews of Warsaw, "their tenacious resolve to hold onto life in spite of everything." With the intensification of German attempts to destroy the ghetto, resistance increased.

The Nazis concentrated Jews in cities at railway junctions and in the words of Martin Gilbert, author of *The Holocaust: A History of the Jews of Europe During the Second World War,* "into ghettos such as had not existed in Europe since the Middle Ages." The ghetto which was "shaped like a hammer head," covered 840 acres of slums and housed about 450,000, a figure that included Jews from the suburbs as well as towns, villages, and cities of Poland.

In the beginning of the Nazi occupation, Jews had no idea of the death that awaited them. The Germans used every possible ruse to deceive the Jews, including even telling them in the death camp that the gas chambers were merely showers.

You could walk through the ghetto in forty minutes. Dan Kurzman, in *The Bravest Battle: The Twenty-Eight Days of the Warsaw Ghetto Uprising,* describes the ghetto as a "pressure cooker surrounded by a brick wall 10 feet high and 11 miles long." Glass splinters "embedded in plaster" were on top of the wall. The houses at that time were nineteenth-century, slope-roofed tenements, two to six stories high. The wall had twenty-two gates, reduced in the course of time to thirteen. At the final stage of the ghetto's existence, there were only four gates. At the gates stood the guards of three police forces, German, Polish, and Jewish. Every person, every wagon, and every vehicle that approached was thoroughly searched. Crowded in the narrow streets of the ghetto existed ("lived" is not the word) a population equal to that of a city in other parts of the world. Twenty-six thousand Jews "lived" in Pawia Street; 20,000 in Mila Street, and 20,000 in Gesia Street. They were for all intents and purposes at the mercy of the Nazis and the "representative of the regime," the Judenrat, which in effect was "the sole channel between hundreds of Jews and the authorities and the outside world at large," according to Yisrael Gutman. But they were handpicked by the Germans and some like Adam Czerniakow of Warsaw tried to mediate with the Germans, but to no avail. He later committed suicide. Others used their position to save themselves and their families. The Judenrat "was infiltrated by men who were controlled by the Germans and had been hired by express order of the authorities." A Jewish police force was established within the ghetto and "of all the frameworks and services for which the Judenrat assumed responsibility, the police force was the institution most remote from and alien to the traditions of Jewish communal life in the Diaspora."

Probably in 1940, the Germans decided to establish a ghetto to systematically segregate the Jews and by the fall of that year began to relocate them. On November 16, 1940, the Nazis sealed off the ghetto area. From that date until July 22, 1942, the isolated ghetto existed in its "normal format," according to Yisrael Gutman, but from July 22, the Germans initiated the mass deportation of Jews and in the following seven weeks of deportation of Jews, "about 75 percent of the Jews were driven out of their homes and transported to the Treblinka death camp."

WARSAW GHETTO UPRISING

The Warsaw Ghetto Uprising was the largest single act of armed civilian resistance until the outbreak of the Polish Warsaw Uprising fifteen months later, as well as the most famous armed Jewish insurrection against the Nazis. The uprising came as a result of the German cold-blooded, organized, calculated, and deliberate act to destroy Jews.

A rabble army, without a decent weapon, held at bay the mightiest military power the world had ever known for 42 days and 42 nights; all of Poland in 1939 held the Germans off for less than a month.

Furthermore, Dan Kurzman maintains that the military encounter was one of "the most stirring, impossible and important battles in history." As for Jews, they had rebelled previously. But the uprising, "more than any other event, symbolically ended two thousand years of Jewish submission to discriminate oppression and finally genocide." The Jew became a young warrior.

During the uprising, small episodes terrorized the Germans. Before the uprising, according to Yitzhak Zuckerman, whose code name was Antek, "all a German had to do was yell *'Raus,'* and the Jews would come out. This time, no Jew came out. This time, the Germans came up to us and we killed them."

No longer did Jews feel they were going to their death like cattle. Armed resistance gained mass support only when people understood that the Nazis planned to kill all Jews and that there was no way out of the ghetto, according to Israel Gutman. He asks why the Jews did not revolt sooner. They did not, he points out, because of extreme starvation and weakness. They were reduced to "utter impotence." They did not know death awaited them.

By January 1943, the Jews were expecting another action. Called "the second action" *(aktion),* it came by surprise on Monday, January 18, 1943, and lasted until January 22. Before that, Mordechai Anielewicz, who had been engaged in underground work, began to organize. He came back to the ghetto in October 1942. He was among the organizers of the Jewish Fighting Organization (Z.O.B.), whose definition was a "broad merger of political and ideological factions that bridged various and often antagonistic philosophies."

January 18, 1943, marked a turning point in the existence of the Jewish Fighting Organization. On that date, in the "second action," the Germans surrounded the ghetto. Until January 18,

Jews were "passive prey." But then they fought back and those acts of resistance were very important. On January 18, with Anielewicz in command, a number of Jewish ghetto fighters attached themselves to the lines of the deportees being led to concentration camp-bound trains. Armed with pistols, and at a given signal, the freedom fighters opened fire; they shot a few German soldiers; they hurled some hand grenades and scattered the surprised Germans at the corner of Zamenhofa and Niska streets. "It was baptism under fire." The Jewish civilians ran and escaped.

After that day, the interval between January 22 and April 19, 1943, a space of 87 days, was used to train and prepare resistance. In April 1943, when the Germans once more moved to liquidate the Warsaw Ghetto, they again encountered armed resistance from the Jews.

The Nazis wanted the ghetto *judenrein* (free of Jews). And they wanted the job to be completed by April 20, Hitler's birthday. A year before, in April and May 1942, the ghetto contained about 350,000 Jews. The mass deportation or *aktion* of Warsaw Jews began on July 22, 1942, and continued until September 12, 1942. During those seven weeks, about 265,000 Jews were uprooted from Warsaw, transported to the Treblinka death camp, and murdered in the gas chambers, wrote Yisrael Gutman in *The Jews of Warsaw, 1939–1943: Ghetto, Underground, Revolt.*

The Germans entered the ghetto armed to the teeth on the morning of April 19, 1943; that night would be the first night of the Passover Seder. To this day, many Jewish families throughout the world pause during the Seder to recall the heroes of the Warsaw Ghetto. In that engagement thousands of German soldiers fought against a maximum of 1,200 Jewish fighters: "13 heavy machine guns against which the Jews had no equivalent armament; 69 hand-held machine guns, against which the Jews had none; a total of 135 submachine guns against which the Jews had two; several howitzers and other artillery pieces of which the Jews had none; a total of 1,358 rifles, as against only 17 rifles among the Jews," according to Martin Gilbert. The number of Jewish fighters varies. In *Admitting the Holocaust: Collected Essays,* Lawrence L. Langer says estimates of the Jewish Fighting Organization range from 250 to 800 out of 50,000 to 60,000 Jews who were still alive in the Warsaw Ghetto.

Author Ber Mark describes the Jews "as poorly equipped, inexperienced, minuscule and starving bands of ghetto warriors, with organized forces comprised of 600 members from the Jewish Fighting Organization," and about 400 from Farband and other groups. Thousands of these surviors participated spontaneously. The Jewish fighting units greeted the Germans "with a hail of grenades, bottles, bombs and rifle shots." The fighters trapped the invading Germans in a crossfire. The Jews fought from the rooftops and bunkers of the ruins. Their key element was surprise. They hid in cellars, bunkers, and sewers in the ghetto.

It is impossible to list all the names of the heroes of the Warsaw Ghetto Uprising. There was Yitzhak Zuckerman, Z.O.B. second in command, known as "Antek." He survived. There was Zivia Lubetkin, a Z.O.B. commander who, like others, escaped through the sewer system. She later became Zuckerman's wife. She and her husband and other ghetto fighters settled at Kibbutz Lohamei ha Gettaot in Israel. Marek Edelman, another commander, survived and still lives in Lodz, where he is a physician.

Of course, heading the list was Mordechai Anielewicz, the twenty-four-year-old commander who was born in Warsaw, attended Warsaw Hebrew High School, and was a member of Hashomer Hatzair, a pioneering socialist Zionist youth movement. At the beginning of the war, he escaped from the Nazis and helped organize Zionist activities in Russia-occupied Poland. According to Israel Gutman, writing in the *Encyclopedia of Zionism and Israel*, Mordechai Anielewicz was arrested by Soviet government troops as he tried to get to Palestine and was released after he volunteered to return to German-occupied Poland to help in the illegal activities of Hashomer Hatzair. He became head of Hashomer Hatzair in the ghetto and commander of the Z.O.B. and organized the remnants of the ghetto for the final battle in which he perished at MILA 18. He was "the handsome commander loved by all." In his last message sent to his deputy, Yitzhak Zuckerman, he wrote: "The dream of my life has been fulfilled. I have lived to see Jewish defense in all its greatness and glory."

Today, besides his reproduction in the statue of the Memorial to the Victims of the Warsaw Ghetto Uprising, another statue of Mordechai Anielewicz stands at Kibbutz Yad Mordechai, in Israel, in front of a bombed water tower damaged by Egyptian armed forces in the Israel War of Independence.

On May 16, 1943, Nazi commander Jurgen Stroop reported to his superiors that the Warsaw Ghetto "is no longer in existence." The action ended at 8:15 P.M. To celebrate, the Germans blew up the Great Synagogue.

But it would take months to end Jewish resistance. Jews defended building after building, bunker after bunker, street after street. They fought. Soon, however, starvation, exhaustion, and sickness took their toll. The skirmishes lasted in the ruins of the ghetto into July 1943. According to author Ber Mark, Polish sources cited evidence of armed groups of Jews fighting on "in the razed ghetto area in 1944!" Thousands of Jews were killed, thousands were burned in their hideouts, and 56,000 who had survived the fighting were shipped off to the death camps. But the legends of the Warsaw Ghetto will grow.

Memorial to the Victims of the Warsaw Ghetto Uprising. at the corner of Anielewicza and Zamenhofa streets, Warsaw. As a journalist and editor, I had seen pictures for forty-five years of that magnificent monument of the fighters of the Warsaw Ghetto and Jewish resistance. Its dedication in Hebrew, Yiddish, and Polish moves the viewer: "To the Jewish People— its Heroes and Martyrs."

I visited the monument, located in a park square, on a quiet Sunday afternoon in February. People walk slowly. They put their pet dogs through hoops; the apartment buildings look well kept. I found it to be a nice neighborhood. One would never believe what went on here between 1939 and 1945. One has to remember this area in 1945 was all rubble. You could not tell in that year where a certain street was located or where a house stood.

In December 1970, Willy Brandt, world Socialist leader, former mayor of West Berlin, chancellor of West Germany, was in Warsaw for negotiations for the new treaty between Poland and the Federal Republic of Germany. He visited the Memorial and he fell to his knees before it. "This gesture . . . was not planned. Oppressed by the memories of Germany's recent history, I simply did what people do when words fail them," wrote Brandt, according to *The New York Review of Books,* July 14, 1994. Over the years, the world's leading figures have come to the site of the memorial for the heroes of the ghetto uprising, including Presidents Jimmy Carter and Bill Clinton, as well as Pope John Paul II, who in 1978, then a Polish cardinal, became pope of the Roman Catholic Church. Solidarity also held demonstrations here.

The traveler should stand at the corner of Anielewicza and Zamenhofa. Now called Anielewicza, it is the former Gesia Street where the historic Jewish community was located. It has been renamed for the heroic commander of the Warsaw Ghetto Uprising, Mordechai Anielewicz. The streetcar, with the sign Anielewicza, today motors through the new section of the city. It covers concrete streets probably laid right on top of the ruins of the Jewish ghetto and the tram ends its route at the Jewish cemetery. Also at Anielewicza Street and Zamenhofa, a stone tells us the Dr. Ludwig Zamenhof, creator of Esperanto, the International language, lived on this street at no. 5.

"Of all the thousands of memorials created after the war to commemorate aspects of the Holocaust, Nathan Rapoport's Warsaw Ghetto Monument emerges as possibly the most widely known, celebrated and controversial," according to James E. Young in *The Texture of Memory: Holocaust Memorials and Meaning in Europe, Israel, and America.* A copy of the monument stands at the Yad Vashem Museum in Jerusalem, Israel. Interestingly, the memorial's granite blocks were originally cut and stacked for the Germans to use them in a Nazi victory monument in Berlin.

The thirty-six-foot monument was unveiled on April 19, 1948, five years after the Warsaw Ghetto Uprising, before 12,000 survivors, military personnel, and government dignitaries.

As I stood before this wall of granite, it came alive for me and I agreed with Young's description of the seven persons on the front wall that represents the burning side of the underground bunker. "A muscular prophet figure on one knee picks up a rock, a young boy at the left, clutches a dagger, a young woman at the right cradles a Kalashnikov rifle, the leader Anielewicz clenches a homemade grenade. Even the mother engulfed by flames raises her right arm defensively as does the baby in her other arm." The ghetto is being swallowed by flames, but the men, women, and children in tattered clothes are led into battle by Anielewicz.

On the back of the wall, one sees twelve stooped and huddled figures, showing fear and despair—depicting the contrasting scene of Jews hopelessly on their way to the death camps. One sees only three Nazi helmets and two bayonets barely visible in the background. There is a rabbi holding a Torah scroll in one arm. He "looks up and reaches to heaven as if to beseech God." Two huge menorahs, symbolic of Judaism and the State of Israel, flank the main part of the monument.

As you walk in the area, you will note black memorial stones. The route is called "A Memorial Route to the Struggle and Martyrdom of the Jews 1940–1943." Some call it Memory Lane. People come by here every day. But April 19 is special. This is the day to commemorate the Warsaw Ghetto Uprising. People march along Zamenhofa and Dubois streets to Stawki Street and then to the Umschlagplatz Wall Memorial. The groups lay flowers, light candles, and say prayers. You, the traveler, can do the same.

The memorial route begins at the Monument to the Heroes of the Ghetto, runs down Zamenhofa Street past Samuel Zygielbojm Square and the mound and stone on the corner of Mila Street dedicated to Mordechai Anielewicz and the Jewish Fighting Organization, then down Stawki Street past the S.S. Unit Command and past the former school and Jewish transit hospital, and it ends at the entrance to the Umschlagplatz.

Starting at the monument, we see the first monument built right after the war, in 1946, in the shape of a sewer top, to signify escape hatches—the only way out of the flaming ghetto. There are four memorial stones around the monument area. Nearby is the Tree of Shared Remembrance, an oak planted on April 19, 1988, to commemorate the murder of Polish Jews and Poles who perished saving Jewish lives.

To the left of the monument is a memorial stone dedicated to Emmanuel Ringelblum (1900–1944), historian and founder of the Underground Ghetto Archives.

At the corner of Lewartowski (Joseph) and Zamenhofa stand stones to Joseph Lewartowski and Michael Klepfisz. The former was a leader of the Communist party, and the latter was an activist in the BUND.

Then we leave Zamenhofa and come to Samuel Zygielbojm Square, where we observe a stone dedicated to Zygielbojm, the man from London who tried to alert the world to the murder of the Jews in Nazi-occupied Europe. But he felt he failed in his attempt to arouse the international community. As a protest against the atmosphere of indifference to the tragedy of the Jewish people, he committed suicide on May 12, 1943.

The visitor should now head back to Zamenhofa Street toward Mila Street. There on the corner are two stones dedicated to Arie Wilner and Mordechai Anielewicz, both members of Hashomer Hatzair, the Zionist youth movement. Both died in the bunker, Mila 18.

MILA 18

Mila 18, on Mila Street, commemorates the site of the last bunker of the Warsaw Ghetto Uprising. Today a monument for all to see is mounted on top of what would have been Number 18.

Mila 18 was the central bunker of the Z.O.B., the Jewish Fighting Organization. At times, it housed about 350 persons, including 80 military personnel, according to Ber Mark. Zivia Lubetkin, fighter and Dror activist, fought here. The Germans sought out this bunker. Probably tipped off as to its location, the German troops on May 8 surrounded the area, fired grenades, and injected gas into the bunker. The victims began choking, some committed suicide, others were killed by

Memorial to the heroes of Mila 18, the central bunker of the Jewish Fighting Organization in the Warsaw Ghetto Uprising. (Photo by Ben G. Frank)

The Umschlagplatz Wall Monument, dedicated to the hundreds of thousands of Jews who were deported by train from this railroad depot to the death camps. (Photo by Ben. G. Frank)

German gunfire. It is clear that almost all the fighters perished.

"Thus fell Mordechai Anielewicz, one of the finest and noblest warriors, who from the beginning put his life at the service of his people," according to Emmanuel Ringelblum, the noted Jewish writer who chronicled the events in the Warsaw Ghetto. After the war, those who came to Warsaw did not find a city, a house, or a relative. They climbed onto the heaps of ruins. Nothing was recognizable. One could not tell where a certain street had been or where a house had stood. However, they discovered the spot, the hole, where the house on Mila 18 had stood. They took a great black stone, a mass of dull rock, stone, and dirt, and placed it there. In simple lettering in three languages, the following was etched on the stone: "Here on the 8th day of May, 1943, Mordechai Anielewicz, the commander of the Warsaw Ghetto Uprising, together with the staff of the Jewish Fighting Organization and dozens of fighters fell in the campaign against the Nazi enemy."

After visiting the bunker at Mila 18, we continue our walk down Dubois Street, which is a continuation of Zamenhofa. We come across memorial stones to Pawel Frenkiel, commander of the Jewish Military Union (ZZW), and Frumka Plotnicka, liaison-officer of the Jewish Fighting Organization. Still on Dubois Street, there are memorial stones to the leader of the Religious Zionist party, Rabbi Yitzhak Nissenbaum, a noted Zionist, and a stone dedicated to Janusz Korczak (Henryk Goldszmidt), educator and writer who accompanied his children (orphans) on their last journey from the Umschlagplatz to Treblinka.

We then turn left on Stawki Street and observe a memorial stone dedicated to Itzhak Katznelson, a poet-author who wrote "Poem of the Murdered Jewish Nation." He fought in the ghetto, but since he had a Honduran passport, he was sent to the Vittel concentration camp in France and later to Auschwitz, where he perished. The poem is one of the greatest literary expressions of the tragedy of the Holocaust.

Another stone cites the building at 5/7 Stawki Street, the headquarters of the S.S. And another stone at 6/8 Stawki cites a building in which the Jews were held before being transported to Treblinka. A stone to the left of the Umschlagplatz Wall

Monument cites the 450,000 Jews packed into the ghetto and murdered by the Nazis.

Umshlagplatz. Today it is a busy road. The cars speed by. Watch how you cross the street. The wall in front of you is a fitting monument to the victims of the Holocaust and it lists some first names of Jews who perished in the Holocaust and in the Warsaw Ghetto. In the early 1940s it was a large square at the northern edge of a ghetto: a railway siding, a "railhead for resettlement" to the German death camp. When the ghetto was established, food supplies were brought in to this railroad siding, which is located exactly at the foot of the ghetto. But from July 22, 1942, this loading dock became a one-way ticket to Treblinka. About 6,000 Jews were loaded into boxcars that first day the deportation began and then it was 10,000 every day after, until the ghetto was completely destroyed and no Jew could be found. In fact, whenever the Germans could not meet their daily 10,000 quota, they and their henchmen, the Ukrainians and the Latvians, even Jewish police, would guard and round up people right off the street. Chaos and hysteria ruled, thousands of men, women, and children were jammed into boxcars. Day after day, the "grisly caravans departed for the gas chambers with their loads of human flesh." Sometimes two trains would come at once. Everyone could carry only a single bundle; a three-kilogram bag. Some—very few—escaped through the hospital, only to be picked up the next day.

As I stood on the Umschlagplatz, I recalled one of the saddest events that occurred there. Janusz Korczak (1878–1942), physician, children's writer, educator, and head of an orphanage, on August 5, 1942, accompanied his two hundred orphan children to the Umschlagplatz and from there to the gas chambers at Treblinka even though he was not scheduled for deportation at that time. Korczak was a Jew who had been born Hersh Goldszmidt. However, he made Polish—not Yiddish—his mother tongue and he used his Polish name, Henryk. In other lands, he became known as Janusz Korczak, which he used as a pen name. When the Germans came for his two hundred children from the orphanage he headed, he brushed and polished the children and dressed them in their best clothes.

He told them to take their schoolbooks so they could study when they weren't "working in the forest." Holding one child by the hand, he calmly signaled to the others, who were silently lined up behind him in neat rows, and they began marching toward the boxcars.

As we walk around the Umschlagplatz Wall Monument, we notice that the wall of the monument has white marble with a black band like a tallis (prayer shawl). The wall skirts a small rectangular area, one side of which is the outer wall of a school, the former Jewish hospital. The area inside the wall is symbolic. In the wall opposite the entrance from Stawki Street is a narrow opening that looks out onto a tree, a symbol of hope. Over the entrance is a black slab in the shape of a Jewish tombstone. Besides inscriptions dedicated to the Jews who were driven from the ghetto, there is a wall of four hundred first names in Hebrew, Yiddish, and Polish. Original paving stones have been preserved on the site of the former Umschlagplatz entrance, next to the former hospital and school building. On the other side wall of the school, next to the Wall Monument, is a white marble band with a verse inscribed from the book of Job (16:18): "O Earth, cover not my blood, and let my cry for justice find no rest."

Korczak Orphanage, 8 Jalikosowska St., Warsaw. This is a children's home and a statue of Janusz Korczak stands tall in front of this building. He is considered a hero of Poland. A moving statue of Janusz Korczak is located in the Jewish Cemetery, which we shall visit next. Here, the statue shows Korczak holding a child in his arms and leading other children who are behind him.

Jewish Cemetery, ul. Okopowa 49/51, corner of Gesia Street, 01-043, Warsaw. Tel: 382-622. The "Pantheon of modern Polish Jewry, a forest of the dead." Open every day except Saturday, of course, from 10 A.M. to 3 P.M. This huge historic cemetery is not kept in the best of condition, but sincere efforts are made to keep it up. The cemetery's stone wall has gaping holes that were made by thieves who vandalized the marble tombstones and by plunderers who were still searching for gold teeth as in Auschwitz, according to S. L. Schneiderman. Here, despite the weeds, broken tombstones, and blurred engravings, lie the leaders, the writers, the doctors, and the men, women, and children of the last 150 years. You can inhale Polish Jewish history from the stories recounted on the tombstones.

Dr. Zamenhof, creator of the international language, Esperanto, is buried here, as is Esther Rachel Kaminska, world-renowned Yiddish actress. Also, Rabbi Osjasz Thon, leader of Polish Jewry and noted Zionist, lies here.

In a special pantheon lie I. L. Peretz (1851–1915), Yiddish writer; Jacob Dinesohn (1858–1919), Yiddish novelist; and S. An-sky (1863–1920), author, who wrote the famous play, *The Dybbuk.*

Here is the grave of the head of the Warsaw Ghetto Judenrat, the engineer, Adam Czerniakow (1880–1942), who committed suicide on July 23, 1942, rather than living and doing the bidding of the Germans who were on a path toward total annihilation of the Jews. Born in Warsaw, Czerniakow served as the head of the Warsaw Judenrat during the "Great Action." Realizing that the Jews were being taken for extermination, he wrote many of his thoughts in the now-published *The Warsaw Diary of Adam Czerniakow: Prelude to Doom,* an important source of information on the ghetto.

Jewish Historical Institute, Tlomackie 3/5, Warsaw. Tel: 27-83-72. Often, in Europe, and very often in Poland, you end up talking about a synagogue that was. In the case of the destroyed Great Synagogue in Warsaw, part of it survives in what is now the Jewish Historical Institute. The Institute was once a wing of Warsaw's Great Synagogue at Plac Tlomacki. This classical prayer building contained a large dome and on top rested the Star of David. This was the synagogue of the middle class, the enlightened, and the emancipated. The assimilated came here, wrote Alfred Doblin. The Synagogue, which recessed from Tlomacka Street, could seat 1,100 persons. The buildings boasted a porticoed central section, domed receding wings, and projecting terminal elements. "It looked remarkably secular, usually an indication that the Jews wished to avoid imitating a church or looking exotic," says Carol Herselle Krinsky in her book, *Synagogues of Europe.* It was erected in 1877, in German neo-Renaissance style. The Italian architect, Leonardo Marconi, drew the plans.

Heinrich Himmler, head of the gestapo, ordered the synagogue destroyed at the so-called official end of the ghetto uprising. "A Wehrmacht sapper team under Stroop's supervision placed huge charges of dynamite under the building: the noise of the explosion shook all of Warsaw," wrote Ber Mark.

The Jewish Historical Institute contains one of the most outstanding collections of Judaica in the world, including manuscripts and the complete archives of Emmanuel Ringelblum, whose diary was found after the war hidden in sealed milk cans in the Warsaw Ghetto; it is one of the best records of the Warsaw Ghetto and is displayed for public viewing. Entitled *Notes from the Warsaw Ghetto,* it was not only Ringelblum's life work; it was also his death work. He did have an opportunity after the uprising in 1943 to be smuggled out of the country by the Polish underground, but he refused. He survived until March 1944, when he was discovered and shot by the gestapo.

The Institute was once the magnificent library attached to the former Great Synagogue. Today, the library contains about 50,000 to 60,000 books and periodicals gathered from all over Poland after the war. Many important manuscripts are here as well as documents from the Warsaw, Lodz, and other ghettos during the war, as well as from theological seminaries. Paintings, sculptures, Judaica art objects, and other items, many from World War II, complete the vast holdings of this building, which survived the war and the restrictions of the Communist regime. Situated here, too, is a martyrs' museum devoted to the Warsaw Ghetto Uprising.

In 1995, the Institute was headed by Dr. Grazyna S. Pawlak, executive director. She told this writer that she had presented plans to create a Jewish history museum in the park in front of the monument to the Warsaw Ghetto Uprising located at Zamenhofa and Anielewicz streets. This proposed building would contain archives, a library, a museum, and educational departments.

At the Jewish Historical Institute, Yale Reisner, who is on the staff of the Ronald S. Lauder Foundation, is working on a

Sculpture in the Jewish Historical Institute in Warsaw. (Photo by Ben G. Frank)

genealogical project to assist people in researching their family history. For further information on this project, call the Jewish Historical Institute, Tel: 27-92-21. Mr. Reisner related that there are hundreds of wartime diaries in the archives, as well as at least 7,000 testimonials regarding the war.

Dr. Pawlak, like her colleagues at the Jewish Historical Institute, does not accept the description of Polish Jewry as "one big cemetery." She and her staff are dedicated to preserving Jewish history and culture in this land.

A twenty-minute walk from, let us say, the Marriott Hotel brings you to the Jewish Historical Institute. Your landmark is a tall, white skyscraper structure with the word Sony on top. It stands on the very soil where the Great Synagogue once stood. Next door is the only surviving remnant, the Jewish Historical Institute.

The Jewish Historical Institute survived the war. East European Jewry, a reservoir of world Jewry, came to an abrupt end, and a chapter closed. After the war, the Zionist youth organization, Hashomer Hatzair, for instance, maintained that Jews should not live on the "cursed ground of Poland." "We have to leave Poland, we have to get up and go," they said. "To most Polish Jews, it was unthinkable to renew their life on the Polish soil, soaked with the blood of millions of Jews," where Nazis found "thousands of collaborators among the local population eager to cooperate in the extermination of the Jews," states the *Encyclopedia Judaica*. Now began a mass migration of Jews from Poland and Eastern Europe, in 1945 to 1950.

The Polish attitude was disbelief that any Jew was alive. "You're still alive?" one Pole told a survivor, Harry Joskowitz, my wife's uncle. "You survived the war and you want your apartment, your houses back?" was the common attitude. The Poles indeed had expropriated businesses and real estate abandoned by the Jews.

This must be clearly stated. Many Poles experienced the annihilation of Polish Jewry as a colossal shock to their psyches. Many, however, found that "Hitler did the dirty work for us." Some did not think the work was so very dirty. The Poles considered Jews to be social outcasts and the Polish response to the Jewish plight fits in with the toothache theory of Yitzhak Zuckerman, "Antek."

Antek explains that they thought that once the world was aware of what was happening to the Jews, someone would come to their rescue—certainly the Poles on the other side of the wall. "After the war, when I began reading memoirs of members of the Polish government in London, I was stunned by the extent of their alienation from and indifference to the Jewish issue, which was about as important to them as a toothache."

Jewish historians and leaders generally agree that the "Polish underground's supply of arms to the Jewish uprising leaders was scanty and inappropriate. . . . They provided pistols when the Jews needed rifles and machine guns for the street fighting," writes Lawrence L. Langer in *Admitting the Holocaust: Collected Essays.*

And yet no matter how we view Polish anti-Semitism, we must remember the Poles did not start World War II. The Poles did not destroy Warsaw. The Poles did not order or build the death camps. The Poles did not serve as executioners; six million Poles, half of them Jews, died in the war. The Poles suffered great losses during the fighting and bombardments in 1939 and then in 1944. Approximately 2.5 million Poles were sent to Germany as forced laborers.

A recent poll showed forty percent of the Polish respondents said that both Poles and Jews suffered equally from Nazi persecution. Opinion polls, according to Jane Perlez, writing in *The New York Times* on January, 27, 1995, indicate that Poles today do not recognize the magnitude of the losses of Poland's Jews. An American Jewish Committee survey, by the Polish firm, Demoskop, discovered only 13 percent of 1,145 respondents knew that more than 80 percent of the Jews in Poland were killed by the Nazis during World War II. And more than half the persons questioned grossly overestimated the minute Jewish population in Poland today.

"Everywhere in the Nazi New Order when faced with the plans to deport and murder local Jews, a proportion of the population attempted to aid and succor the Jews, a proportion assisted the Nazis and the majority remained inactive some-where in between," say the editors of *The Jews in Polish Culture.* There was no question about Polish complicity in a large segment of the population.

In discussing the Nazi policy towards Poles and Jews, a Polish underground hero who helped Jews and who tried to warn the world's leaders of the Holocaust, Jan Kozielewski, known as Karski during the war, told President Franklin Delano Roosevelt, "the Germans want to ruin the Polish state as a state, they want to rule over a Polish people deprived of its elites. With regard to the Jews, they want to devastate the biological substance of the Jewish nation." This underground leader went from world figure to world figure. Most of the people he appealed to did not believe him. Many did not want to believe the reports of the murder of Jews as early as the fall of 1942 or early 1943. Or, if they did believe, they did not want to do anything about it.

Elie Wiesel has written, "It is true that not all victims were Jews. But all Jews were victims." He said on the fiftieth anniversary of the liberation of Auschwitz: "The Jewish people—singled out for destruction during the Holocaust—have shouldered history's heaviest burden."

Although one-third of Jews managed to survive, says Lucy S. Dawidowicz, although the Jewish people and Judaism have out-lived the Third Reich, the "Germans nevertheless succeeded in irrevocably destroying the life and culture of East European Jews." The thousand-year-old culture of Ashkenazic Jews that originated in the Rhine basin came to an end, she adds. But in *Tales of My People,* Sholem Asch maintains that "the terrible flame could destroy only the physical substance, not the spiritual essence of the Jew."

Estimates vary; however, at war's end only between 50,000 to 80,000 Polish Jews survived. An additional 180,000 were repatriated from the Soviet Union, which brought the total to somewhat over 200,000 survivors. A Jewish leader told me that every single Jew who survived had to have been saved by Poles. After the war, some Jews who remained in Poland saw communism as an answer to their problems. "For a Jew in Poland, at last, there was an answer to the Jewish question: No religion at all, for anyone," according to Mark Kurlansky. But in the 1968 anti-Semitic campaign, that belief would be meaningless.

Because this building also is a historical institute, we should recall the date of September 1, 1939, when "night" fell on Poland, the night the Nazi cancer continued its unchecked spread through the body politic of Europe. On paper, the September 1 invasion was labeled "Operation White"; we know it as *blitzkrieg*.

Nearly two million German troops invaded Poland on that day. Poland was butchered; it never had a chance. The Jews of Poland were trapped. Martin Gilbert informs us that on the evening of September 1, the Great Synagogue in Tlomackie St. was "full to overflowing. Large crowds also stood outside and prayed."

On September 17, 1939, Russia—who had betrayed Poland and free men and women everywhere by signing the infamous Molotov-Ribbentrop Pact of August 23, 1939, by which Hitler and Stalin agreed to divide Poland between the two of them—invaded Polish soil. Ten days later, Poland capitulated. The partition and occupation of Poland gave Hitler the opportunity to put his racial policies into effect.

After Stalin took over, in the late 1940s, only about 70,000–80,000 Jews remained in the country. By the mid-1950s, many Poles began to express discontent with government policies and resentment of Soviet domination and its Stalinist regime. In 1956, after worker unrest, Wladyslaw Gomulka, who had been imprisoned in 1951, was freed from prison and again became head of the Communist party.

Stalin's crimes were made public. Yiddish papers blasted Soviet anti-Semitism. Approximately 2,500 repatriated Jews came back from Russia. The JDC and ORT were allowed to reopen. But many Jews moved out: 50,000 left in 1958 and 1959. At that time, approximately 30,000 Jews remained in Poland. As a result of the Six Day War and the anti-Israel stance of the former U.S.S.R., Poland, still a Communist satellite, broke relations with Israel in 1967.

Under the Communist regime, Polish media would now invent a new target for Polish hatred. The new enemy became the "Jewish conspiracy" and the State of Israel. The Polish government campaigned against Jews and intellectuals. It initiated and sponsored in 1968 a sweeping virulent anti-Semitic campaign, according to Eva Hoffman in *Exit into History: A Journey Through the New Eastern Europe.*

After the Six Day War, in 1967, Gomulka went along with Mieczyslaw Moczar, the interior minister. Student demonstrations were the pretext for the government's anti-Semitic campaign. Gomulka labeled the Jews "rootless cosmopolitans." He said the Jews were a "fifth column." Gomulka gave the Jews permission to go; large numbers did. Jews were dismissed from jobs. Organizations such as JDC and ORT were closed down. The Polish government in effect "liquidated" all organized Jewish life. Anti-Semitism "purged" Poland of nearly all its Jewish population. In 1968, it was "a matter of mental terror, of frightening Jews out of Poland," according to author Kazimierz Brandys in his book, *A Warsaw Diary: 1978–1981.* Mark Kurlansky states that Jews "could forfeit their homes and whatever property they might have and emigrate to Israel." He adds, "Only Jews were allowed to emigrate and Israel was the only acceptable destination."

"Not even in the heyday of Stalinism did the world see anything like the virulent, open and institutionalized racial discrimination practiced in the spring and summer of 1968 in 'People's Poland,'" Paul Lendvai says in his *Anti-Semitism Without Jews: Communist Eastern Europe.* While no one was killed, at least forty persons from Jewish and non-Jewish families were known suicides. One thing was certain, if you wanted to be Jewish, you left Poland in 1968; or if you stayed, you opted out of Jewish life.

The Lauder Morasha School. The Lauder Morasha School, which had 15 students in the first grade, was reported to be the first Jewish school established in Poland in a quarter-century, the first to open in Warsaw in forty-five years.

Ronald S. Lauder Foundation Kindergarten, Bagatela 13 m 14, Warsaw.

Ronald S. Lauder Morasha School, a kindergarten, 78 Krolowej Marysienki, Warsaw.

PALACE OF CULTURE AND SCIENCE

The Palace of Culture is truly a bizarre sight.

In any book on Jewish travel and Jewish communities in Europe, certain national monuments and sites we visit invoke memory of past events. In Poland, moreover, international events—especially those between Russia and Poland—deeply affected Jews. Examples quickly come to mind: the 1939 Molotov-Ribbentrop Pact, the outbreak of World War II, and the 1989 collapse of communism. While not a monument, the Palace of Culture and Science building stands in the center of the city as a symbol. It was, after all, a Soviet gift to the Poles. Built in the early 1950s in the traditional Russian-Soviet architectural style, it was immediately labeled the "wedding cake." This massive structure contains 3,288 rooms, a Congress Hall for 3,000 people, three theaters, a swimming pool, and a museum. A view from the thirtieth floor gives the tourist a bird's-eye view of Warsaw. A Jewish leader told me he and his wife took courses there. It should have reminded them of the "looming specter of Russia."

Speaking of the Russians, some of the ire of the Poles and many other people today is the Molotov-Ribbentrop Pact, which many believe helped cause the outbreak of the war because of the secret protocol signed in Moscow by Nazi Ribbentrop and Communist Molotov on August 23, 1939. The two countries would carry out a joint attack on Poland and divvy up the area. Without the assurance of Soviet collusion, the Germany army could not have launched a unilateral attack on Poland. "Suddenly it became clear that if Hitler were to invade Poland, the Soviet Union would stand aside," writes Martin Gilbert in his book *The Holocaust: A History of the Jews of Europe During the Second World War.* That was "ominous news" for the Jews of Poland. Hitler invaded, two years later betrayed his Russian ally, and on June 21, 1941, stabbed the Soviet Union and unleashed a destructive war that would include the death of about twenty-five million Russians alone.

Survivors from Poland did fight. I heard about the Polish army unit, a certain group in Gen. Wladyslaw Anders' division, from my father-in-law, the late Rabbi Solomon Spitz. In 1941, the Soviets permitted a Polish army group to form under General Anders. Polish prisoners of war held by the Russians were allowed to join General Anders to fight with the allies. In March 1942, the new Polish unit crossed into British-controlled Iran. When the group arrived in Palestine, many Polish Jews left the unit and opted to stay in Palestine. Many, too, like my late father-in-law, joined the Jewish Brigade of the British Army in order to fight the Germans.

In 1944, the Soviet Army entered Poland and Stalin installed his Communist Poles as the new government in Lublin. On August 1, after the Red Army had reached the Vistula River, the Home Army of the London Poles launched an insurrection to liberate Warsaw before the Soviet troops arrived.

The Polish Uprising was an armed insurrection against the Germans, but, politically and more clearly, it was an uprising against the Russians. The Poles wanted to avoid a "Red Warsaw." The Soviet Army stood by and let the Germans slaughter the insurgents and utterly destroy the capital.

To this day, Poles also believe the Allies betrayed and sacrificed Poland at the February 1945 Yalta Conference held at that Crimean seaside resort. Here, the Western Allies accepted the new status quo in Poland and agreed to recognize the Stalin-backed Lublin government. Stalin would settle for nothing less than a Polish government controlled by Communists. He "scorned" his promises for a free election.

TREBLINKA

"Before the War, on the Siedlec-Malkinia Railways, not far from the great axis running from Warsaw to Bialystok, there was a forgotten little station with the strange and beautiful name of Treblinka. It rose unexpectedly in a damp, sandy plain dotted with little pine woods and marshes," wrote Jean-François Steiner in his book, *Treblinka*. Here between 800,000 and 850,000 Jews were murdered by the Nazis, but here as in other camps, a revolt occurred on August 2, 1943; it was brutally suppressed and the camp destroyed.

This is one camp that has an unusual monument, to say the least. At least 17,000 huge stone slabs make up a symbolic cemetery. Engraved on the stones are the names of cities and villages from which the Jews were rounded up and brought here. The densely packed stones surround a huge 26-foot high obelisk-type stone sculpture shaped like a mausoleum and topped by a large menorah. It appears that the menorah is "carved into the cap" of the obelisk and is "jumbled" together. It protrudes in all directions. At the bottom of the obelisk, where there is a great crack, a stone plaque reads from top to bottom in Yiddish, Russian, English, French, German, and Polish, "Never Again."

Today, you can see that the railway, which once was abandoned, has been re-created symbolically with concrete sleepers to commemorate this railway that conveyed Jews to their deaths.

Martin Gilbert in his book, *The Holocaust: A History of the Jews of Europe During the Second World War,* says that in 1959, he ran his hand through the soil of Treblinka: "The earth beneath my feet was coarse and sharp; filled with the fragments of human bone."

At Treblinka, we again meet Janusz Korczak. In 1978, the hundredth anniversary of his birth, a stone was inscribed with his name and put with the thousands of others. It is the only stone dedicated to an individual, and Korczak is a Polish hero, too.

Treblinka itself is located in Sokolow Podlaski province near Warsaw. Jews in the Warsaw Ghetto between 1940 and 1943 who were deported to death camps probably died at Treblinka.

The Death Camps

- Auschwitz and Birkenau—Approximately an hour's drive from Cracow.
- Majdanek—Set up in the Lublin suburb of Majdan Tartarski.
- Sobibor—The camp was located in the small village of Sobibor on the Chem-Wlodawa railway line, almost 5 miles south of Wloadawa.
- Belzec—A small town in the southeast of the Lublin district. Located on the Lublin-Zamosc-Rava-Russkaya-Lvov railway

line. The death camp was located about a third of a mile from the Belzec railway station.

- Treblinka—Located 62 miles northeast of Warsaw.
- Chelmno—Situated on the Ner River, 37 miles from Lodz.

LUBLIN

If someone asked me how I feel about Lublin, it would be that my late father-in-law, Rabbi Solomon Spitz, was born there and went to the famous Lublin Yeshiva. The one scene in my mind that he did not see (apparently he was living in Warsaw at the time or had escaped to the East) keeps haunting me. The Germans in all their sadism took all the thousands of holy books out of the famous yeshiva library and threw them down on the ground and loaded them into vehicles and, according to Earl Vinecour, they burned the books in the marketplace. The fire lasted twenty hours. And the Jews of Lublin watched this nightmare. They cried so that their voices rose above those of the Nazis. The Germans had to bring in their army band to drown out the agonizing shouts of protest.

Lives are more important than books. The Germans murdered most of the Jews of Lublin. Destroying human beings and books will end civilization. Records, incidentally, say that the Germans confiscated 22,000 volumes and about 10,000 periodicals.

The city of Lublin, wrote a Chassid, "is the land of Israel." Yes, Lublin ranks as a special metropolis in the galaxy of Jewish life in Poland. In the 1920s, Doblin described Lublin as "not sleepy" like a small town in Germany, because the poverty suffered by the Jews kept them moving. Before the war, 97 percent of all the city's tailors were Jews; it is doubtful if there is a Jewish tailor today. Lublin in 1939 contained a Jewish population of about 40,000 Jews. It was literally "a Jewish Oxford," famous for its yeshiva throughout Europe, famous for Talmudic and Kabbalist learning. Lublin, a center of Hebrew printing, was known for its fairs and marketdays. Annexed by Austria in 1795, and later incorporated into Russia-Poland in 1815, Lublin served as "the spiritual heart of Polish Jewry."

Jews arrived here in 1316. At first, they were denied rights, but King Casimir III permitted them to settle nearby in 1336. In 1602, 2,000 Jews made their home in Lublin. They were expelled in 1780. By 1806, 2,973 Jews resided here and by 1897 the figure jumped to 23,586.

Synagogue, 10 Lubartowska, Lublin. This synagogue is not used frequently. There are no daily services scheduled, rarely a minyan. Part of the building is also used as a museum.

Yeshivat Hachmei Lublin, 85-83 Lubartowska St., Lublin, at the corner of Unicka Street. Today it is a medical college, but many Jews close their eyes and see before them youthful yeshiva students studying Torah, chanting afternoon prayers, or walking along the streets of this once great center of Judaism.

Today the medical college displays only by a modest plaque commemorating the yeshiva. Built with funds raised from all over the world, the yeshiva was opened in 1930. The building was designed by Agenor Senduchowski.

For centuries, the king of Poland appointed the rector of the yeshiva of Lubin. In 1935, 50,000 people, including high-ranking government officials, attended the ceremonies dedicating the new headquarters for the yeshiva. It consisted of 6 stories, 120 rooms, a huge auditorium, and even a scale model of the Temple of Jerusalem. In 1939, 500 students attended.

Lublin is renowned for its scholars and sages, one of them so great that he was referred to as the "Seer of Lublin." He was Rabbi Jacob Isaac ha-Hozeh. And living in Lublin were other great rabbis: Jacob b. Joseph Pollak, Jacob b. Samuel Bunim Koppelman, and Mordechai b. Abraham Jaffe.

At the densely wooded Grodzisk Hill, near the yeshiva, is the Old Cemetery. A great stone wall shields this sixteenth-century Jewish burial ground. The entrance to the cemetery is on Kalinowszcyna Street. Here rests another great Talmudic scholar, Rabbi Solomon Luria (1510–74), known by the acronym, Maharshal (Morenu ha-Rav Shelomo Luria).

Another great rabbi of Lublin buried in the cemetery is Meir b. Gedaliah (1558–1660), known as the Maharam of Lublin. The Maharam is an acronym for Moreinu-Ha-Rav Meir, "Our Teacher, the Rabbi Meir." This great halachic authority became head of the Yeshiva of Lublin at the age of twenty-four.

In Lublin, also, sat the Council of the Four Lands, which became an independent Jewish parliament and supreme court. It coordinated a system of autonomous Jewish institutions. The Council settled disputes between Jewish communities and appeals made by individuals against decisions rendered by other rabbis and courts. The Council existed from 1580 to 1764.

Majdanek

"If Auschwitz was hell on earth, then Majdanek was the morgue. Auschwitz could be smelled from afar, but Majdanek was in your living room," wrote Professor Eric Epstein in *Martyrdom and Resistance,* January–February 1994.

The city of Lublin rises over Majdanek. The Nazis felt no need to conceal the camp from the local populace. In the summer of 1942, construction of the Majdanek concentration camp near Lublin, in the quarter, Majdan Tartarski, was completed. It, too, was part of Operation Reinhard, named after S.S. General Reinhard Heydrich, who was assassinated by two Czech patriots on May 27, 1942, in the Czech town of Lidice. After his death, the Nazis began preparations for Operation Reinhard, the deportation of Jews to Treblinka, Belzec, and Sobibor. In Majdanek, more than eighty percent of the 350,000 murdered victims were Jews. It is pretty much preserved as it was. The visitor can see guard towers, barbed wire, barracks, and crematoria. Everything is still intact. In the back of one hall, there are empty canisters of Zykon-B gas. There is a prisoners' clothing display. There are prisoners' shoes piled in the barracks.

Wiktor Tolkin's monument at Majdanek conveys impending danger because the top part of it is the "great weight of memory," which stands on a proportionately undersized base that creates a sense of top heaviness, even danger, for those standing beneath it. As you walk out from the base of the monument, you can see in the distance the dome covering a mausoleum of human ash and bones and to its right, a building with a tall chimney, which was the crematorium and gas chamber complex—the whole area symbolizes a valley of death.

KIELCE

The name of this town in southeast Poland will certainly live in Polish-Jewish history. Just one year after the Holocaust, the Jews of Poland woke up to a good, old-fashioned pogrom. "Jews were even taken off trains and murdered," said Yitzhak Zuckerman. He believed the event may have been instigated by the police or government, a well-organized plot. Forty-two Jews were murdered. The pogrom occurred on July 4, 1946. A monument was erected in the Kielce Jewish cemetery to perpetuate the memory of the pogrom's victims. The pogrom induced a major shock for the Jews—as if they needed one. The price of remaining in Poland, legally and illegally, increased greatly. That is why a mass emigration out of the country took place. Between 100,000 to 150,000 persons departed, including the Polish Jews who had been returning from Russia.

A synagogue is located at Rewolucji Pazdziernikowej but is now used as an archives. A monument to the memory of the pogrom's victims is located at 7 Planty Street.

CRACOW

And everyone crowds into the narrow little streets of the Jewish city and rushes for his place in the synagogue and Kazimierz is full of people and the old temples of Israel reflect the spell of the past.

—Majer Balaben, Polish Jewish historian

There in Eastern Europe, the Jewish people came into its own. It did not live like a guest in somebody else's house, who must constantly keep in mind the ways and customs of the host. There Jews lived without reservation and without disguise, outside their homes no less than within them.

—Abraham Joshua Heschel

Friday night: *"Shabbos."* I use the Ashkenazic pronunciation because that is what was said on Friday nights by Polish Jews. They still say the *Shabbos* now. But now the younger ones pronounce it: *"Shabbat."* The square is empty. I fantasize it was as if you were watching a movie, a large, oblong square, bustling with people, full of people, men in their black gabardines and round hats, milling about the marketplace. Nearby are stone houses, colored blue, white, purple, and green. Then suddenly the film script changes. The same square, but there are no people. The buildings are there, but there are no Jews. You are ready to leave. But wait, faint at first are the sounds of the song, "Peace Be With You," *"Shalom Alecihem."*

You follow the sounds. You go in and there before you are almost fifty young people. This is the headquarters of the Ronald S. Lauder Foundation Youth Center on Kupa Street. Every Friday night, there is a Shabbat dinner where young people are invited to attend. Sometimes, American college students come to services and then to the program dinner. Kiddush is recited. We sing Hebrew songs. We talk about Jews in nearby Ukraine where we are told people are starving. I realize a number of these young people are not Jewish, they are themselves from mixed marriages. Many will convert to Judaism. But these young adults, if they become Jews, are the future of Poland. For further information on youth groups in Poland, contact the Ronald S. Lauder Foundation in Warsaw, or in New York. In Cracow, contact Domick Dybek, Tel: 011-48-12-22-6855.

Jews once lived in the main square of the city. Today, there are very few signs of their one-time residence in the city center.

In 1335, King Casimir the Great founded this once rival city to Cracow on the southern side of town and called it Kazimierz. The Jews settled there soon after its establishment. In 1495, King Jan Olbracht expelled the Jews from Cracow. The Jews moved to nearby Kazimierz, where they settled in a relatively small prescribed area northwest of the Christian quarter and were separated from the non-Jews by a wall. Cut off from the Poles, it would take the Jews four hundred years to get back to the environs of the Main Square in Cracow. Jews arrived in the fourteenth century.

But German and Bohemian Jews came to Cracow in the sixteenth and seventeenth centuries. Here they could live in peace. Those German Jews spoke Yiddish, similar to what the prosperous Cracovians spoke, which was mainly German. In the fifteenth century, Cracow Jews developed trade with Breslau, Danzig, Lvov, and Constantinople.

"Over the course of history," writes Henryk Halkowski, noted writer and historic guide of Cracow, "Jewish Kazimierz joined with Polish Cracow and together they became 'Ir-va-em be-Israel,' (The Mother City of Israel)." Kazimierz was a predominantly Jewish quarter. By the end of the fifteenth century, Kazimierz consisted of a "quadrangle with a few streets enclosed on one side by the city walls and on the other by a wall with three gates leading to the non-Jewish city," says Bernard D. Weinryb.

By the 1570s, about two thousand people lived in Kazimierz, the Jewish section on the other side of town. Here in Kazimierz the famous Talmudic scholar and philosopher Rabbi Moses Isserles, known as Remuh, maintained his academy. Today his grave and synagogue remain places of pilgrimage. That sixteenth-century Cracow became the world famous center of Talmud education was due to Isserles, who is famous for his commentary to the treatise, *Shulhan Arukh,* the code of Jewish law. We shall learn more about him when we visit the only functioning synagogue in Cracow.

For more than four centuries, until emancipation in 1868, Jews of Kazimierz fought for rights to trade and work in Cracow. From the second half of the sixteenth century, a number of yeshivot were founded in Kazimierz, whose fame made Cracow a most important center of Judaism. By 1644, the community maintained seven synagogues, a main synagogue, the Old Synagogue, and Remuh Synagogue. Hebrew printing was introduced in Cracow in 1534. "This suburb was an independent town with its own municipal council until the partition of Poland in the eighteenth century," writes Rachel Wishnitzer in *The Architecture of the European Synagogue.* Until the beginning of World War II, Kazimierz remained the traditional residential quarter of Cracow's Jews. After the war, the section decayed.

A beautiful, ancient city, there is only one Cracow, the residence of the leading Polish princes and a center of Polish cultural life. Cracow is one of the most magnificent cities in all of Poland. In the sixteenth century, this Renaissance city flourished. Until 1609, this was the old capital of Poland with straight and winding narrow streets, renovated monuments, and townhouses. History has been especially kind to this city on the Vistula. Alfred

Doblin described it as the cleanest and most beautiful city he found in Poland in the early 1920s. It still is proud of its university and intellectual look. Who has not heard of Jagiellonian University; Wawel Hill, the seat of Polish kings, including Casimir; or the Cracow Marketplace? Cracow is virtually the only large Polish city that has preserved its old architecture.

The Vistulans or Wislanie lived here. Cracow dates from 465 when traveler Ibrahim ibn Yaqub from Cordova visited the town and mentioned it as a trade center.

Even after World War I, Cracow still retained its cultural center status. In 1921, 45,000 Jews lived here; in 1931, 56,800. By the outbreak of World War II, the city counted 260,000 inhabitants, between 60,000 and 70,000 of whom were Jews.

After World War II, 780,000 persons resided in this third largest city after Warsaw and Lodz. Huge steel works, Howa Huta, were built a few kilometers from the historical center. An ecological disaster, the Communists had attempted to break the traditionally intellectual and religious ties of the city.

In Cracow you can still see a street called St. Anne's Lane. Documents going back to 1304 called it Jews Lane. Jewish merchants held important positions in the city's economic life. At the end of the fifteenth century, a fire destroyed Cracow's Jews Lane and the Christian citizens succeeded in having the Jews expelled from the city. The Jews settled at neighboring Kazimierz, where they were assigned a self-contained area that later was to become the ghetto.

In the early twentieth century, the Zionists and the Socialists gained influence in Cracow and the city became a major stronghold of the Labor Zionists and the Revisionist Zionists.

Before World War II, 70,000 Jews lived in Cracow, about twenty-five percent of the population. When the Nazis entered, they were moved to the ghetto in the Podgorze section. In the ghetto, the "Eagle Pharmacy" was located at 18 Bohaterow Getta and was owned by the Pole, Tadeusz Pankiewicz, one of the leaders of the Resistance who succeeded in saving the lives of several Jews. In March 1943, the Nazis liquidated the ghetto and the last residents were sent to the concentration camps, among them the Yiddish poet and singer, Mordechai Gebirtig.

Sites in Cracow

Old Synagogue-Jewish Museum, 24 Szeroka, Warsaw. It was built in the late fifteenth century on what was Broad Lane in the middle of the Jewish quarter, now called 24 Szeroka. At the far end of Szeroka Street, as you come out of the Remuh Synagogue, look to your right and at the end of the square stands the Alte Synagogue, today functioning as the Jewish Museum. Displayed here are some excellent exhibits, especially on the second floor—an exhibit of photos and drawings, the faces of Kazimierz Jews. The museum is open Wednesday and Thursday, 9 A.M. to 3:30 P.M.; Friday, 11 A.M. to 6 P.M.; and Saturday and Sunday, 9 A.M. to 3 P.M. However it is closed the first Saturday and Sunday of every month and when that occurs, the museum opens the following Monday and Tuesday. It has impressive collections of Jewish ceremonial art and paintings by Jewish painters. The original Gothic structure was destroyed by a fire; the Italian architect Matteo Gucci rebuilt it in Renaissance style in 1557–70. Some say the Old Synagogue housed the library of King Casimir the Great. Since 1958 the building has become a seat of the Judaic Museum, a branch of the Historical Museum of the City of Cracow.

In the room of the museum, on the second floor, such World War II photos with signs such as Jews Are Forbidden to Enter the Park are displayed. This room contains the history of the Jewish community of Cracow of 1939–45. The Old Synagogue probably is the most important synagogue of the medieval period in Poland. After the war the building was not used and was allowed to go into disrepair. During the war, its massive bronze chandeliers were used to decorate the house of the Nazi governor general, Hans Frank. It is not known when the Old Synagogue, or Stara, was built in the former heart of this Jewish community, but it is believed to have been in the fourteenth or fifteenth centuries. Erected by Jewish refugees from Bohemia, it was patterned after the Altneuschul in Prague, wrote Earl Vinecour, "with its two naves and ribbed cross-vault supported on two slim pillars. The Holy Ark reflects a late renaissance influence." The Old Synagogue of Kazimierz measures 17.70 by 12.40 meters, approximately 58 by 40 feet, is larger than the synagogues at Worms and Prague, and taller than the synagogue of Prague. Its two columns are slimmer than the piers of the latter synagogue, and its walls are thinner, too. "The parapet of bricks and stone, decorated with blind arcades, shows the influence of style of the medieval castles of the Cracow nobility," according to Earl Vinecour. This probably is the oldest synagogue in Poland. It contains a doubled-naved, two-pillared edifice. The bimah [the Torah reader's platform] is not only slightly elevated between the two pillars, but is also enclosed in a canopied wrought-iron cage. From time to time, the Communists closed the building. During various insurrections against foreigners, patriotic speeches were given here urging Jews and Poles to unite in defense of their common homeland.

Popper Synagogue, 16 Szeroka St. Donated by the merchant Wolf Popper in 1620, it was rebuilt after World War II and is currently being used by the city of Cracow as a cultural center. Next door is the Ariel Cafe.

The High Synagogue, 38 Jozefa St., Cracow.

Kupa Synagogue, 8 Jonatan Warszauer. Built during the building boom of the sixteenth and seventeenth centuries, it is not owned by the Jewish community.

Temple Synagogue, 24 Miodowa St., Cracow. It survived the war almost unscathed. It was built in 1860 to 1862, thanks to the efforts of the Association of Progressive Jews in Cracow. Also known as a Reform Movement of Judaism synagogue, it is rarely open for services. There is a women's section in a balcony. It is only used when needed, such as on holidays.

Community Offices, also known as TSKZ Club, 2 Slawkowska St., Tel: 561-758, 562-349/22-98-41.

Ariel Jewish Artistic Cafe, 17 Szeroka St., Cracow. Tel: 21-38-70. There is folk music and concerts of Hebrew, Yiddish, Russian, and gypsy music. Heard above the din of the coffee shop are tapes in Hebrew. You may find that many local Polish Jews and, from time to time, many Americans stop here for coffee, cake, and sandwiches, especially on the weekend.

Ronald S. Lauder Foundation, Jewish Youth Group, 18 Kupa St., Cracow. On Friday nights, between 5:30 P.M. and 6 A.M., an

The historic, mid-sixteenth century Remuh Synagogue in the Kazimierz section of Cracow, Poland. (Photo by Ben G. Frank)

oneg shabbat takes place. Young people, students, sit and say Kiddush. They sing Sabbath zemiros, they say the blessing over bread, they enjoy dinner and friendship. A college student wanders in; some people speak English. This is a Jewish youth club and education center opened in Cracow and, in early 1995, the fourth center established by the Ronald S. Lauder Foundation since the Communist government fell in 1989.

Synagogue, also known as the **Congregation of the Mosaic Faith,** located at Skawinska Street. It is now empty and not used.

Remuh Synagogue, 40 Szeroka St., Cracow. If you are in Cracow on a Friday evening or Saturday morning, you can pray at this mid-sixteenth-century synagogue. The synagogue was built by influential members of the Jewish community. Because they were well-off, they were likely to obtain the necessary permits from the authorities, the king, and the clergy; "or the nobility if the town was privately owned," writes Rachel Wischnitzer. Saturday service is at 9 A.M. Friday evening service's time depends on sunset. This is the famous, spacious, Remuh Synagogue, whose name goes back to Israel Isserles, father of Rabbi Moses ben Israel Isserles, who is buried with his family in the cemetery, adjacent to the synagogue. In 1553, Israel Isserles, as a wealthy merchant, obtained a permit from King Sigismund August, son of Sigismund I, to build a synagogue in Kazimierz. He did not erect a new building; he merely adapted a timber structure, which he owned, for synagogue use. A 1557 fire leveled the house of worship, so he rebuilt the structure in masonry.

Remuh—Known as the Remuh Synagogue, after the founder's son, the codifier Rabbi Moses ben Israel Isserles (ca. 1525–72). He was one of Judaism's great scholars. Remuh is the acronym of **R**abbi **M**oses **I**sserles, a great halachic authority. To this day, Isserles, born in Cracow, is venerated by Jews throughout the world. He is known as the "Maimonides of Polish Jewry." He was the outstanding Ashkenazic codifier of religious law. In those days, Rabbi Joseph Karo codified the *Shulhan Arukh,* but that was intended for the Sephardim, according to writer, historian, and guide Henryk Halkowski. "Moses Isserles adapted [those laws] for the use of the Ashkenazim and in this form, as a collaboration of Joseph Karo and Moses Isserles, they became the oracle of Jewish life." He adds, "Even today the Orthodox regard the codex of Joseph Karo and Moses Isserles as defining the principles of their behavior."

Religious Jews undertake pilgrimages to Rabbi Moses Isserles' grave on the Lag B'Omer holiday, the anniversary of his death. He is buried in the Remuh Synagogue's cemetery. His tombstone was not damaged during the war, it was reported.

The synagogue contains a single-nave hall, with round-headed windows set high up in the walls, and a Roman barrel vault. "Tucked away" in a courtyard off the street, next to the ancient Remuh cemetery, it is a plain rectilinear building. The bimah is surrounded by a wrought-iron cage and the ark is similar to that of Old Synagogue. Before the Second World War, the synagogue was led by Rabbi Ozjasz Thon, who was also a member of Polish Parliament and a leading Zionist.

The Cemetery at Remuh Synagogue. Other graves besides that of Rabbi Moses Isserles, who is buried with his family, include Rabbi Joel Sirkes (1561–1640), head of the Cracow yeshiva and one of the greatest Talmudic scholars of Poland, and the famous Polish Kabbalist, Nathan Spira (1585–1633). Also buried here is Yom Tov Lippmann Heller (1579–1633), who also had been the rabbi of Vienna. The latter is most famous for his *Tosefot Yom Tov,* a commentary on the Mishnah. The Nazis razed all tombstones. This cemetery was restored in part by the American Jewish Joint Distribution Committee. At the cemetery is a wall made out of tombstone fragments—a fitting symbol of the Holocaust and, then again, also a sign for the future existence of this building as long as Jews use it and visit it. It is, after all, one of the best examples of a Jewish cemetery from the Renaissance.

Kosher Restaurant—In the summer of 1995, a kosher restaurant opened next door to the Remuh Synagogue on Szeroka Street in Cracow.

The Ajzyk Synagogue, at 16 Kupa, Cracow. Also known as

The Rabbi Isaac Synagogue founded by Isaac Jakubowicz and his wife, Brindla Jakubowicz. He was a banker and elder of the Jewish community and obtained a permit to build a synagogue from King Wladislaw IV in 1638. The opening of the building, however, was delayed by litigation brought against the Jewish community by the priests of the Corpus Christi Church, who objected to passing a synagogue when they were bearing the sacraments, according to Wischnitzer. Still, despite the objection, building went forward and the 55-x-39-foot hall was constructed, and although the exterior has paid a toll because of weather, the portal facing Isaac Street is still beautiful.

New Jewish Cemetery. Buried in their tombs in this cemetery are the famous leaders of Cracow Chassidim, the Epstein brothers and Raphael Landau. The cemetery was laid out in the nineteenth century and contains the graves of important Jews of the nineteenth and twentieth centuries, such as the painters Mauricy Gottleib and Arthur Markowicz, the Zionist leader and representative in the Polish Parliament Rabbi Ojasz Thon, the structural engineer Jozef Sare, the physicians Aaron Kirschner and Jonathan Warszauer, and many others. It is still used today for burial rites.

The Center for Jewish Culture in Kazimierz, Cracow, of the Judaica Foundation, Rabbi Meiselsa St., 17, Cracow. The Center for Jewish Culture in Kazimierz, Cracow, is one result of the revival of interest in Jewish history and culture in Poland that Joachim S. Russek, director of the Jagiellonian University Research Center on Jewish History and Culture in Poland, helped get underway in the mid-1980s. According to Professor Russek, also director of the Judaica Foundation, the goal of the center is to "help both physically preserve the Jewish heritage and to make it more accessible to all." This center provides cultural events; it runs a library; it prepares and distributes publications; it promotes research on Kazimierz; it supports restoration efforts. A recipient of a U.S. Congressional grant, the center possesses a wonderful lecture hall, a great coffee bar, and a fine place for American students to visit. Russek says the "Jewish landscape was an integral part of the Polish landscape, and he believes Poles have an obligation to take care of the

The Center for Jewish Culture in Kazimierz is located at 17 Rabbi Meiselsa St., Cracow. (Photo courtesy The Center for Jewish Culture)

The cafe at The Center for Jewish Culture in Kazimierz is a gathering place for students and visitors. (Photo courtesy The Center for Jewish Culture)

entire history of Poland. Research students often come here.

The Center for Jewish Culture is housed in the former B'nai Emunah prayer house located at 17 Meiselsa, named after rabbi and Polish patriot, Dov Berush Meisels, who was in the Senate of independent Cracow and who rallied Jewish support in the 1863 rebellion against Russia. This former house of prayer was built in 1886 by a worship society, on a site where there had been a smelting facility of the Cracow goldsmith's guild until the seventeenth century. It was the work of the well-known Cracow architect and builder, Jacek Matusinski. The style of the building refers to the trends of the time, with Oriental elements. Inside, the most interesting elements were the *aron ha-kodesh,* the Holy Ark, as well as an iron column in the passageway separating the men's and the women's sections. A large memorial plaque for the founders and others who were connected with the prayer house was part of the synagogue. At the end of the nineteenth century the whole interior was covered with interesting polychromy. The building consists of a library, archives, and reading and study rooms. The center opened at the end of 1993 and operates under the auspices of the Judaica Foundation.

Schindler's List **Tour.**—As I read the brochure citing the sites that would be seen on the tour of the places involved in the filming of *Schindler's List,* I could not but help recall that heart-tearing scene when the gestapo is about to raid the Jewish Ghetto, which in the film version was right here on Szeroka Street in the Kazimierz section of Cracow. A proclamation is read, which paraphrased said that King Casimir the Great invited the Jews to Cracow; they helped Poland prosper; they lived wonderful lives; they contributed to the community. But the Nazis made sure that that life would end. As the next film scenes go on, the anger builds up in any human being at what the Germans did to the Jews then living in the inhuman conditions of the ghetto. The Germans almost succeeded; they killed most of the Jews of Cracow. But as I walked along Szeroka Street, I realized Jews are still here; perhaps not in numbers, but something more spiritual. Evil did not win the day. You may feel the same. And as you take the tour of

Schindler's List sites, if you do, you will recall the film and what it portrayed; and the history of the Jewish people will become more realistic for you, the traveler. Viewers of the film *Schindler's List* certainly know some of the history and sights surrounding Cracow. The **Jordan Company and Jordan Book Store,** located right on Szeroka 2–Miodowa 41, Cracow, conducts two-hour daily tours every day to the sights from the film. Participants can travel in a car or van. But it is wise to make reservations beforehand, Tel: 011-48-12-21-71-66. Steven Spielberg did not film the ghetto scene in the Cracow Ghetto set up by the Germans. The film was actually made in the Kazimierz section along streets that are traversed in the tour: Szeroka, Ciemna, Jozefa, Meiselsa.

The Cracow Ghetto was located across the Vistula in Podgorze. The ghetto took up the area bounded by the Vistula, Krzemionki and Lwowska streets, and Podgorski Square. A **Museum of the Ghetto** stands at Zgoda Square, now called Pl Bohaterow Getta. From this spot, Jews were sent to the death camp. A drug store called "Pod Orlem" was here, and because it was on the edge of the ghetto, the pharmacy owners were able to save some Jews through a concealed passage, it is said. The Cracow Ghetto was "liquidated" in March 1943. A huge labor camp was set up and the tombstones of a Jewish cemetery were used in the construction of the camp buildings.

But before we see the site of the camp, the reader will note that Oscar Schindler's factory building still stands, only now it is used as an electronic parts firm. The Schindler plant is located at 4 Lipowa Street.

The camp itself, now destroyed, was situated on the site of the former Jewish cemetery in Jerozolimska Street and was known as **Plaszow.** It consisted of 34 barracks and 11 watch towers. Inmates there included about 6,000 Jews who survived the deportations from the ghetto. At certain periods, the total number of inmates exceeded 20,000. From the film, we know about S.S. officer Amnon Goeth, commander and chief hangman of the camp who was sentenced to death and hung in 1946. We can still see the house where the Nazi Goeth resided.

Located on Jerozolimska Street, it still contains the balcony from which he shot innocent people during his so-called target practice. On the hill site of the Plaszow camp stands a gargantuan stone sculpture of sharply etched human figures who stand there mourning. There is a huge horizontal gash across their bodies at lapel level.

Guide. A highly recommended guide and historian, one whom foreign tourists would be wise to engage if they so wish, is Henryk Halkowski, Slowackiego 11 A, apt. 6, 31-159, Cracow. Tel: 011-48-12-33-15-64. Please call Mr. Halkowski in the morning or evening. Mr. Halkowski is also executive director of the **Jewish Club,** Slawkowska 14, Cracow. Tel: 011-48-12-22-98-41.

Jordan Company also has a wonderful Jewish book shop at ul. Szeroka 2–Miodowa 41, Cracow. Tel: 21-71-66. It displays books and souvenirs on Jewish culture; it has maps, postcards, cassettes with Jewish music and information, and guides.

Wawel Castle, Cracow. Built in the eleventh century, the town grew around Wawel Hill. In 1241, Tatars set fire to the city and burned Cracow to the ground. This was the seat of Polish kings for more than five hundred years and was of symbolic importance. Buried here is Jozef Pilsudski, who in the 1930s set up a dictatorship in the country. Pilsudski (1867–1935), originally a Socialist, gained fame as a military leader and organizer of armed opposition to Russia. As chief of state at the end of War World I, he led the 1920 victory of the Poles over the Soviet army outside Warsaw. Fed up with public life and corruption, he retired from public life in 1923. Three years later, he returned to power after leading an armed coup. Sanacja (purification) was the name bestowed upon the military regime installed by Marshal Pilsudski. Most Jews felt that Pilsudski, although he remained a dictator, spoke out against violence toward the Jewish people. When he died, the constraints were lifted; a period of greater violence was ushered in. Also buried here is King Kazimierz Willki. He founded Cracow Academy, later renamed Jagiellonian University, "the second in Central Europe after the one in Prague." Nicolaus Copernicus (1473–1543), who would later develop his heliocentric theory, studied in Cracow in 1490–91.

OSWIECIM

On the marshes of the River Sola, a tributary of the Vistula, lies the town of Oswiecim. Ironically, Jews settled there as early as the thirteenth century, when the town served as the capital of a Slavic duchy, all of which bore the same name.

More than a century later, in 1563, King Sigismund August II confirmed the "privilege for Jews" to live in Oswiecim. He denied them the right to own houses in the market square or to build a synagogue. He also barred a further influx of Jewish settlers. The Jews fought vigorously against such restrictions and stressed their contribution to the development of the city. The restrictions were finally lifted and in 1588 the Jews were permitted to build a synagogue and to acquire ground for a new cemetery. Thus in those days, Oswiecim became the spiritual center of the surrounding Jewish communities. In 1939, about 6,000 Jews lived in Oswiecim.

After the liberation of Poland, Oswiecim developed into an important industrial center with a population of more than 30,000—for many years, without a single Jew, according to S. L. Schneiderman. In 1995, I was told a Jewish person resided in Oswiecim but he was not very talkative.

AUSCHWITZ–BIRKENAU

This is Auschwitz-Birkenau, the "epicenter of the Holocaust."

Please Behave Appropriately, says the sign on the entrance to Birkenau. Respect the Memories of Those Who Suffered and Died Here.

I went to the Birkenau concentration camp before I went to Auschwitz. The two camps are located next door to each other, separated only by a 2½-mile "death march road."

They say that if you are somewhat knowledgeable regarding the Holocaust, you should go to Birkenau first. Still, you must bring your history, your knowledge, your religious values, your soul to Birkenau. As you walk through the camp, the experience may be more valuable if you can personalize it, if you can recall relatives who did not survive the Holocaust or someone you know of who died there.

If you have no one relative, then think of the two adults and

young child who were hanged in front of thousands of specta-
tors in an outdoor line-up of all camp inhabitants. During the
hanging, someone behind Elie Wiesel, the author of the book,
Night, said "Where is God? Where is He?" to which Elie replied,
"Where is He? Here He is—He is hanging here on the gallows."

This is not your usual sight-seeing tour because you always
ask: How could all this happen? How could human beings do
this to one another? How could anyone survive here?

Actually, Birkenau is named after "birch tree woods."
Birkenau was built after Auschwitz I, which was the first camp
in the area. Auschwitz was originally intended as an intermit-
tent camp for Polish political prisoners and then Russian
POWs. As for Birkenau, it was built as an expansion to
Auschwitz I and was to serve as a killing camp.

The Germans "razed" the Polish village of Brezezinka, three
kilometers from Auschwitz. Here they built this gigantic complex of barracks, gas chambers, crematoria, and burning pits—
all fed by a rail spur diverted from the main line.

"Over the next four years, some 1.6 million people, 90 percent Jews, were murdered and burned at Birkenau, their ashes
plowed into the soil, dumped into small ponds and scattered
into the nearby Vistula River," writes James E. Young.

This huge, flat, grassy field is still the site of the barren, desolate shacks located here; the public, inhuman "latrines" are
still here; the wreckage is still here. This last built camp had
the honor of housing the largest crematorium.

This is as close as you are bound to get to reality. As Rabbi
A. James Rudin, national inter-religious affairs director of the
American Jewish Committee, and others say that weather is
playing havoc with the facility. Future generations may not be
able to see the grisly horrors of Nazism firsthand. But the
concensus seems to be not to rebuild the camp, otherwise it
could become a "Holocaust theme park," complete with
high-tech displays.

In this "human slaughter house," the crematorium could
burn 3,000 bodies a day. Disease was rampart in all the camps,
Russian POWs, for example, also died by the thousands as did
20,000 gypsies.

Memorial stones at the Birkenau death camp. (Photo by Ben G. Frank)

The author at one of the barracks at Birkenau. (Photo by Riva Frank)

Here was the technology of genocide. It was the poison gas and the crematorium technology that combined to create mass murder. Fifteen furnaces in every crematorium. It took only twenty minutes between the arrival of a trainload to be undressed and the arrival of the special detachment to strip the corpses of hair, gold fillings, and personal jewelry at the entrance of the crematorium, according to Norman Davies in *Heart of Europe: A Short History of Poland.*

There were four crematoria at Auschwitz: II, III, IV, and V.

You will realize, as you study the maps and the organization of this and other camps, that this was a large-scale, organized operation as only the Germans could do it. It evolved quickly.

They knew exactly what to do, what type of facility to build, and how to run death factories. The only way out of Birkenau was through the chimney, as one Nazi said. It was mass murder with one purpose, to eradicate the Jews.

I walked from the main gate at Birkenau along the railway track that brought the prisoners into the camp. The tourist should do the same. When the boxcars opened, an unbelievable stench enveloped the area, the floors had been covered with only lime and straw, and the journey could be several days and nights. When the prisoners stood at the platform, they were groggy, to say the least. Life had oozed from them in the hours spent in unsanitary boxcars. Like cattle, they had been shipped. They were weak. Night clouded their reality. The kapos shouted; the general selection was about to take place. New arrivals had no idea what was going on. They were confused, anxious, frightened.

I passed the spot where Dr. Josef Mengele is supposed to have stood selecting victims as they stumbled off the transports. They were directed to the left for the gas chambers, or to the right for slave labor.

Yes, usually it was Mengele on the selection train station platform. He waved his glove one way to work, the other way to death, but the victims did not know it. They were the old, the young, and those with children, many of them already separated from a spouse, a father, a mother. They had only had a few

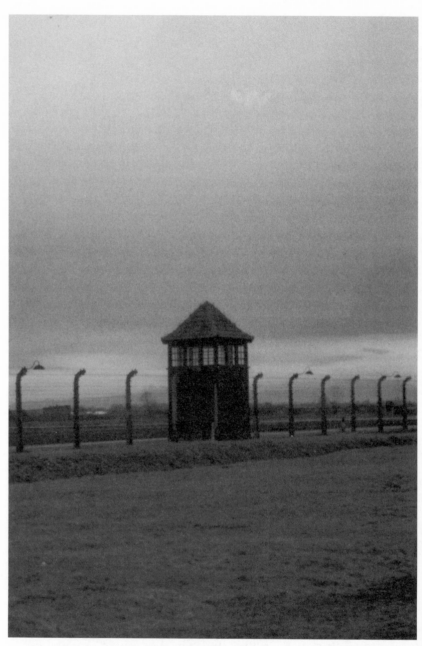

A prison guard tower at Birkenau. (Photo by Ben G. Frank)

minutes to line up. Evil Mengele had looked into the faces of the strong; the healthy he separated from the weak and very young. When you see the vast piles of hair, glasses, and suitcases on display in Auschwitz, you know the people who were there were turned to dust.

The "survivors" then passed by the remains of the pylon fencing. You can still see the fences. The Jews were stopped at the gas chambers. After undressing, hundreds of Jews were shoved into the gas chambers, furnished with showers and water pipes to give a realistic impression of a bathhouse. A Zykon-B pellet was dropped from above. They died instantly.

Today the gas chambers are steel wrecks; the retreating Nazis tried to blow up the camp, to cover up their crime. You can still see the barbed wire. You know many Jews committed suicide by running right smack into the barbed wire.

I then went to Auschwitz or Camp I, the main camp, and there is the cynical sign at the main gate, Arbeit Macht Frei, translated by some, "Work Brings Freedom." The prisoners passed this sign each day on their way to work. On the small square by the kitchen, the camp orchestra would play marches to muster the thousands of prisoners so that they could be counted more efficient by the S.S.

After the war, the "blocks at Auschwitz I were converted into national pavilions, each with an exposition devoted to the national memory of a different country's citizens at Auschwitz," according to James E. Young.

Each person who stops at Auschwitz can observe great bins of victims' suitcases, left behind before the victims died. Their names and birthdates are inscribed on the luggage. I saw the suitcase of M. Frank (not a relative), born 12-4-15. Displayed, too, are children's clothes and infants' booties.

In Block II, you see a model of the furnace, cans of Zykon-B gas, victims' hair.

In Block V, there are victims' glasses, prayer shawls, prostheses, canes, and crutches.

Block VII holds a swimming pool for the S.S.

Block X is where Jewish women were sterilized. There are descriptions of the sterilization process.

The author at the entrance to Auschwitz concentration camp. (Photo by Riva Frank)

Each nation had its block. Block XXI tells the story of the Jews of Holland. You see a film of a train from Westerbork to Auschwitz and then back from Auschwitz to Westerbork to pick up more Jews.

What do we understand of the killers and victims through their remains? Young says that these remains "force us to recall the victims as the Germans have remembered them to us: in the collected debris of a destroyed civilization."

In Block XXVII, the Jewish prison blocks or exhibitions in Auschwitz I, you will hear on tape the chanting of "El Mole Rachamim," a Hebrew memorial prayer for the dead. I said a memorial prayer for the Joskowitz and Spitz families and as I did so, I remembered what Rabbi Besser told me. Holocaust survivors have very few relatives. How could they? For example, my wife's father lost all of his thirteen brothers and sisters and his parents somewhere in Poland, and my wife's mother lost six of her nine brothers and sisters and her parents somewhere in Poland. And to think that my wife's father did not have even one family picture or a single picture of any of his brothers and sisters to pass down to his children or grandchildren. That is what the Germans did to Jewish families—multiplied by six million dead—that is what you learn, recall, and feel at Auschwitz-Birkenau.

"The concentration camps are monuments to bestiality," writes Abba Eban in *Heritage: Civilization and the Jews*. He feels the camps are "kept as places of commemoration by governments and peoples who do not want to forget. Nothing like this violent bestial hatred had ever occurred in history," he continues. "If it had, the Jews would have known about it," he declares, adding, "had not they stood before in anguish, suffering and martyrdom."

This is the killing grounds, the killing fields, and the cemetery of the Jewish people. This was the "Auschwitz Moloch." The greatest mass murder ever committed in human history took place in this twenty-five-square-mile area. Neal Pease, writing in *Poland, A Country Study*, maintains that between 1939 and 1945, six million people, more than fifteen percent of Poland's population, perished in the war, including three million Jews murdered in the death camps of Poland. One out of every two Poles was either killed, wounded, or enslaved during the war. The loss of more than 6 million Polish citizens, half of them Jews, from a total 1939 population of 35 million "represented a casualty rate of 18 percent compared with 0.2 percent in the U.S., 0.9 percent in Great Britain, 2.5 percent in Japan, 7.4 percent in Germany, 11.1 percent in Yugoslavia and 11.2 percent in the former U.S.S.R.," according to Norman Davies.

While estimates range as high as 4.5 million and as low as 1.1 million killed at Auschwitz, more human beings were murdered at Auschwitz than at any other place in history. Historians agree that between 1.1 million to 1.5 million were killed at Auschwitz, 90 percent of them were Jews. "When the Red Army arrived at Auschwitz," according to A. James Rudin, "no one knew exactly how many people had been killed there and no one knows today." Auschwitz's first commandant, Rudolf Hoss, who was executed after the war for crimes against humanity, acknowledged he "personally arranged the gassing of two million persons between June–July, 1941 and the end of 1943." The Russians at one time said the death toll reached four million. And Poles still view Auschwitz as a place of national martyrdom. Most of the Jews killed at Auschwitz were not from Poland. Murdered here were Jews from Hungary, Greece, France, and other nations. Only ten to fifteen percent were Polish. Both Poles and Jews are extremely vulnerable when it comes to discussing the war. Both have experienced "national suffering."

Auschwitz was liberated by Russians who arrived at the camp at 3 P.M. January 27, 1945. One report says the camp was liberated by one Col. Grigori Davidowich Elishavetzki, a Jew. They found 648 corpses and 7,600 survivors: 1,200 survivors in the Auschwitz main camp, and 5,800 at Birkenau, including 4,000 women. There were also 650 survivors at Monowitz, the I. G. Farber Chemical Camp, according to Martin Gilbert in *Auschwitz and the Allies*. Most were deathly sick.

Tens of thousands of others had been forced to move out

westwardly on death marches. Elie Wiesel, the writer and Nobel Laureate, as a teenager, was one of the 58,000 inmates marched out of the camp by the fleeing Nazis. Seven thousand skeletal and sick prisoners were left behind by the retreating Nazis to wait for the advancing Soviet army.

One of the Russians, Gen. Vasili Petrenko, then a colonel of the First Ukrainian Front, tells of finding the remains of four crematoria, one still intact, which the Germans did not have time to blow up when they fled. He said that he found the gas chambers where prisoners had been killed with Zykon-B gas and twenty-nine warehouses filled with the personal belongings of the camp's prisoners. Still horrified by those images today, Petrenko recounted his discovery of thousands of suitcases arranged in rows, and shoes and clothing methodically organized according to age and size. What shocked him the most, however, was seeing the eyeglasses, the masses of false teeth, and seven tons of women's hair packed in boxes. "It is unimaginable how many women had to be destroyed to produce seven tons of hair," he says.

The March of the Living. Every two years, 6,000 Jewish teenagers from 40 countries visit Jewish sights in Warsaw, Cracow, and Lublin as well as the camps of Auschwitz, Majdanek, and Treblinka.

On *Yom Ha'Shoa* (Heroes and Martyrs Remembrance Day), these young people march six abreast from Auschwitz I to Birkenau, a route that some call the death march. After their visit in Poland, they go on to Israel.

At Auschwitz, the material presented by the Communist Party and regime seldom mentioned the Jews killed there; now the signs on the monuments are changing. Slowly, the post-Communist Polish government officially has started to acknowledge that the overwhelming majority of those murdered at Auschwitz and Birkenau were Jews.

Convent. In the mid-1980s, a painful controversy broke out when one of Auschwitz's original buildings, the "warehouse where the Nazis stored the poison gas used to murder their victims," was converted into a Carmelite Convent. Catholic nuns used the building to pray for those murdered at Auschwitz.

The change, in Rabbi Rudin's words, "created an international furor that lasted almost ten years. I was personally involved in the convent crisis, and the deep anger and suspicion on both sides saddened and stunned me," he wrote.

According to Rabbi Rudin, Jews felt the establishment of a convent at Auschwitz was an attempt to "Christianize" the Holocaust, to erase the particularity of Jewish suffering, and to deny that Jews were the principal target of Nazi genocide. Catholics were perplexed and often offended that anybody would object to a few nuns praying at the scene of mass murder. After all, Catholic priests died at Auschwitz.

In 1987, some European Jewish and Catholic leaders, including four cardinals, agreed the Carmelite nuns should move to a new convent to be constructed outside the camp, Rabbi Rudin pointed out, adding, "sadly, the convent imbroglio dragged on for six long years, nearly wrecking many positive achievements of the Catholic Jewish dialogue."

The nuns vacated the Auschwitz building, but only after Pope John Paul II intervened to resolve the controversy. The twenty-four-foot cross was still there in early 1995.

An **Inter-Religious Conference and Research Center** that attracts participants from throughout the world is near the convent, and is located at u.l. s.w. M. Kolbego 1, 32-600, Oswiecim. Tel: (0-381) 310-00. FAX: (0-381) 310-01.

All the pictures in the world cannot bring home the reality of the place. The Monowitz chemical plant was bombed but sadly not Auschwitz. Rabbi Robert L. Wolkoff, writing in *The Hartford Jewish Ledger* on February 17, 1995, says that the Nazis "arranged the extermination as efficiently as they possibly could." He opines that "the only reasonable way to resist was to 'gum up the works,' in any and every possible way." One revolt occurred October 6–7. About six hundred inmates were murdered by the Germans and only three S.S. guards killed. Many have argued that Auschwitz, or at least the railroad tracks, should have been bombed; in 1944, they could have been.

So when you leave Auschwitz or Birkenau, look back at the dust of the men, women, and children who were gassed here. Look back at the wooden huts and the railroad tracks. Whether you are Jewish, Christian, Moslem, or whatever, you can say to yourself, I've been there. And even if you haven't been there to Auschwitz, you actually have, for as Kitty Hart wrote in *Return to Auschwitz, The Remarkable Story of a Girl Who Survived the Holocaust,* you have an obligation to "tell your children what I've told you and shown you, so that it will never be completely erased from history."

Remember!

Never again!

Wroclaw

Synagogue, 9 Wlodkowica St., Wroclaw. Tel: 364-01. The Ronald S. Lauder Foundation Youth Club is also located here.

TSKZ-Club, 28 Swidnicka St., Wroclaw.

Katowice

Synagogue, as well as the community, is located at 13 Mlynska St., Katowice.

Gdansk

The contact person in this city, according to the Ronald S. Lauder Foundation, is Jakub Szadaj, 8/7 Arctowskiego St., Tel. (home): (58) 47-98-02.

How to Get There. Lot Polish Airlines offers twenty weekly nonstop flights from New York City (JFK), Newark, and Chicago, to Warsaw on modern, wide-bodied 767 aircraft.

Suggested Reading

Applebaum, Anne. *Between East and West Across the Borderlands of Europe.* New York: Pantheon, 1994.

Arad, Yitzhak. *Belzec, Sobibor, Treblinka: The Operation Reinhard Death Camps*. Bloomington: Indiana University Press, 1987.

Asch, Sholem. *Tales of My People*. New York: Putnam, 1948.

Brandys, Kazimierz. *A Warsaw Diary: 1978–1981*. New York: Random House, 1983.

Cantor, Norman F. *The Sacred Chain: The History of the Jews*. New York: HarperCollins, 1994.

Curtis, Glenn C, ed. *Poland, A Country Study*. Washington, D.C.: Federal Research Division, Library of Congress, 1994.

Davies, Norman. *Heart of Europe: A Short History of Poland*. Oxford: Oxford University Press, 1986.

Dawidowicz, Lucy S. *The War Against the Jews: 1933–1945*. New York: Bantam, 1986.

Doblin, Alfred. *Journey to Poland*. Translated by Joachim Neugroschel. New York: Paragon House, 1991.

Dubroszycki, Lucjan, and Barbara Kirshenblatt-Gimblett. *Image Before My Eyes: A Photographic History of Jewish Life in Poland, 1864–1939*. New York: Schocken Books, 1987.

Dubnow, S. M. *History of the Jews in Russia and Poland: From the Earliest Times Until the Present Day*. Philadelphia: Jewish Publication Society of America, 1918.

Eban, Abba. *Heritage: Civilization and the Jews*. New York: Summit Books, 1984.

Encyclopedia of Zionism and Israel. Edited by Raphael Patai. New York: Herzl Press/McGraw-Hill, 1971.

Engel, David. *In the Shadow of Auschwitz: The Polish Government in Exile and the Jews, 1939–1942*. Chapel Hill, N.C.: University of North Carolina Press, 1987.

Frost, Robert I. *After the Deluge: Poland and the Second Northern War, 1655–1660*. New York: Cambridge University Press, 1993.

Fuks, Marian, Zygmunt Hoffman, Maurycy Horn, and Jerzy Tomaszewski. *Polish Jewry History and Culture*. Warsaw: Interpress Publishers, 1982.

Gilbert, Martin. *The Holocaust: A History of the Jews of Europe During the Second World War*. New York: Henry Holt, 1987.

————. *Auschwitz and the Allies.* New York: Holt, Rinehart and Winston, 1981.

Gutman, Israel. *Resistance: The Warsaw Ghetto Uprising.* Boston: Houghton Mifflin, 1994.

Gutman, Yisrael. *The Jews of Warsaw, 1939–1943: Ghetto, Underground, Revolt.* Translated by Ina Friedman. Bloomington: Indiana University Press, 1989.

Halkowski, Henryk. "Cracow—City and Mother of Israel." In *Cracow: Dialogue of Traditions.* Cracow: Znak Publishers, 1991.

Hart, Kitty. *Return to Auschwitz, The Remarkable Story of a Girl Who Survived the Holocaust.* New York: Athenum, 1982.

Hertz, Aleksander. *The Jews in Polish Culture.* Translated by Richard Lourie. Evanston, Ill.: Northwestern University Press, 1988.

Hoffman, Eva. *Exit into History: A Journey Through the New Eastern Europe.* New York: Viking, 1993.

Korczak, Janusz. *Ghetto Diary.* New York: Holocaust Library, 1978.

Krinsky, Carol Herselle. *Synagogues of Europe: Architecture, History, Meaning.* Cambridge, Mass.: MIT Press, 1985.

Kurlansky, Mark. *A Chosen Few: The Resurrection of European Jewry.* Reading, Mass.: Addison-Wesley, 1995.

Kurzman, Dan. *The Bravest Battle: The Twenty-Eight Days of the Warsaw Ghetto Uprising.* New York: Da Capo Press, 1993.

Langer, Lawrence L. *Admitting the Holocaust: Collected Essays.* New York: Oxford University Press, 1995.

Lendvai, Paul. *Anti-Semitism Without Jews: Communist Eastern Europe.* Garden City, N.Y.: Doubleday, 1971.

Levi, Primo. *Survival in Auschwitz.* New York: Macmillan, 1987.

MacLean, Rory. *Stalin's Nose: Travels Around the Bloc.* New York: Little, Brown, 1993.

Mark, Ber. *Uprising in the Warsaw Ghetto.* New York: Schocken Books, 1975.

Meyer, Peter, Bernard D. Weinryb, Eugene Duschinsky, and Nicolas Sylvain, eds. *The Jews in the Soviet Satellites.* Syracuse, N.Y.: Syracuse University Press, 1953.

Nagorski, Andrew. *The Birth of Freedom*. New York: Simon & Schuster, 1993.

Polansky, Antony, Chimeri Abramsky, and Maciej Jachimezyk, eds. *The Jews in Poland*. Oxford: Basil Blackwell, 1986.

Read, Anthony. *The Deadly Embrace: Hitler, Stalin and the Nazi Soviet Pact, 1939–1941*. New York: Norton, 1989.

Ringelblum, Emmanuel. *Notes from the Warsaw Ghetto*. New York: McGraw-Hill, 1958.

Schneiderman, S. L. *The River Remembers*. New York: Horizon Press, 1978.

Singer, Isaac Bashevis. *The Magician of Lublin*. New York: Fawcett, 1985.

Steiner, Jean-Francois. *Treblinka*. New York: Simon & Schuster, 1968.

Suhl, Yuri. *They Fought Back: The Story of the Jewish Resistance in Nazi Europe*. New York: Schocken Books, 1975.

Swiebocka, Teresa, comp. *Auschwitz: A History in Photographs*. Bloomington: Indiana University Press, 1993.

Vinecour, Earl. *Polish Jews: The Final Chapter*. New York: McGraw-Hill, 1977.

The Warsaw Diary of Adam Czerniakow: Prelude to Doom. Edited by Raul Hilberg, Stanislaw Staron, and Joseph Kermisz. New York: Stein and Day, 1968.

The Warsaw Diary of Chaim A. Kaplan. Edited by A. L. Katsh. New York: Macmillan, 1973.

Watt, Richard M. *Bitter Glory: Poland and Its Fate, 1918 to 1939*. New York: Simon & Schuster, 1979.

Weinryb, Bernard D. *The Jews of Poland: A Social and Economic History of the Jewish Community in Poland from 1100 to 1800*. Philadelphia: Jewish Publication Society of America, 1973.

Wiesel, Elie. *Night*. New York: Bantam, 1982.

Wischnitzer, Rachel. *The Architecture of the European Synagogue*. Philadelphia: Jewish Publication Society of America, 1964.

Wood, E. Thomas and Stanislaw M. Jankowski. *Karski: How One Man Tried to Stop the Holocaust*. New York: Wiley, 1994.

Young, James E. *The Texture of Memory: Holocaust Memorials and Meaning in Europe, Israel, and America*. New Haven: Yale University Press, 1993.

Zuckerman, Yitzhak ("Antek"). *A Surplus of Memory: Warsaw Ghetto Uprising: Memoirs of a Resistance Leader.* Translated and edited by Barbara and Benjamin Harshav. Berkeley: University of California Press, 1993.

Index

Aargau, Switzerland, 265

Abravanel, Don Isaac, 200, 212, 233

Abravanel, Judah, 233

Adler, Alfred, 243

Aimee, Anouk, 25

Air France Airlines, 25

Aix-en-Provence, France, 55, 86, 104-5

Aleichem, Sholem, 510, 517-18

Alhambra Palace, Granada, 191, 196, 211-13

Allenby, Gen. Edmund, 142

Alliance Israelite Universelle Library, Paris, 56

Alps, 85-86, 91, 263, 277, 282

Alsace, 23-24, 73-75, 98, 109

Altneuschul, Prague, 423-31, 434-35, 442, 552

America, 117, 153, 177, 193, 200-201, 212, 217

American Jewish Committee, 538, 563

American Jewish Joint Distribution Committee (JDC), 53, 274, 468, 478, 511-12, 517, 540-41, 556

Amsterdam: 108, 119, 125, 131, 274, 281, 295-99; Anne Frank House, 301-3; memorials, 315-16; museums, 308-15; organizations, 308; sites, 301-16; synagogues, 305-8

Andalusia, Spain, 191, 196, 197, 199, 208

Anders, Gen. Wladyslaw, 542-43

Anderson, Hans Christian, 379

Angers, France, 23, 70-71

Anglet, France, 80

Anielewicz, Mordechai, 523-25

Anne Frank House, Amsterdam, 296, 301-3

Anschluss, 245-46, 252, 260

An-sky, Simon, 511, 534

Antibes, France, 91, 97-99

Anti-Semitism: Austria, 243-47; Czech Republic, 418, 420-21, 446-47; England, 144; France, 22, 27, 58, 102, 246; Germany, 320, 323-47; Greece, 361; Hungary, 458, 460, 461, 463, 467; Ireland, 155; Italy, 162-63, 172, 181; Poland, 498-99, 508, 514, 517, 538, 540-41; Scandinavia, 377, 380, 398; Slovakia, 483, 489, 493; Switzerland, 265; Turkey, 372-73

Antwerp, Belgium, 281, 282, 283, 284, 287-93, 298-99; organizations, 292-93; restaurants, 292; sites, 290-93; synagogues, 292

Arabs, 28, 99-100, 203
Ardeatine Caves, Rome, 166, 169
Arles, France, 22, 55, 86, 89
Aron, Raymond, 25
Aron, Robert, 25
Arromanches, France, 105
Asch, Sholem, 499, 500, 511, 539
Ashkenazic Jews: Austria, 247-48; England, 119; France, 21-22, 28; Italy, 159, 174; Poland, 502, 539, 548, 555-56; Spain, 217, 218; Switzerland, 265
Attali, Bernard, 25
Aumont, Jean-Pierre, 25
Auschwitz, Poland, 60, 65, 164, 187, 260, 284, 327, 351, 361, 382, 475, 488, 499, 531, 533, 539, 544, 562-73
Austria, 241-61, 283, 322, 416, 457, 460, 465, 466, 484, 500, 545
Austria-Hungary, 245, 418, 485-86
Austrian Jews, 241-249, 251-52
Austro-Hungarian Empire, 485
Avignon, France, 22-24, 55, 68, 85-89, 90
Avignonnais Jews, 57, 80

B'nai B'rith, 21, 53, 102, 176, 183, 269, 364, 401, 494
Ba'al Shem Tov (Israel ben Eliezer), 506, 509
Badinter, Robert, 27
Balaben, Majer, 509, 548
Balfour, Arthur, 122, 139-40
Balfour Declaration, 121, 139-40
Baltic Sea, 396-97, 403, 504
Barbie, Klaus, 61, 78
Barcelona: 194, 216-20; sites,

218; synagogue, 218, 384
Basel, Switzerland: 263-65, 267-70, 349, 463; museums, 269-70; sites, 267-71; synagogue, 269
Basques, 81
Bassani, Giorgio, 164
Bavaria, 327, 348-49, 476
Bayazid II, 359, 370
Bayonne, France, 23, 58, 80-82
Beame, Abraham, 120
Belgium, 23, 117, 279-93
Belmonte, Portugal, 236-38
Belzec concentration camp, Poland, 488, 544, 547
Ben Israel, Manasseh, 119, 125-26, 143, 298, 303, 307, 313
Ben-Gurion, David, 327, 499, 509
Ben Shem Tov de Leon, Moses, 192
Benasayaq, Simon Hassan, 196, 202-3
Benes, Eduard, 420, 446-47
Benjamin, Walter, 327
Bergson, Henri, 25, 72
Berlin: 319, 328-41, 415, 419, 464, 500, 527; community center, 333-35; memorial sites, 340-41; museums, 339-40; restaurant, 335; sites, 332-41; synagogues, 337-39
Berlin, Sir Isaiah, 148
Berlin Wall, 327, 332, 335, 479
Bern, Switzerland, 263-65
Bernadotte, Count Folke, 389
Bernhardt, Sarah, 25, 67
Besser, Rabbi Haskell, 512, 569
Betar, Revisionist Zionist youth movement, 507
Bevin, Ernest, 121
Bevis Marks Synagogue, London, 119, 131-34

Bialystok, Belarus, 543
Biarritz, France, 68, 81-82
Bibliotheque Nationale, Paris, 59-60
Bibliotheque Rosenthaliana, Amsterdam, 303
Bilek, Frantisek, 430
Birkenau concentration camp, Poland, 451, 499, 544, 562-67, 569, 571, 573
Black Plague (Black Death): Belgium, 281, 285; Czech Republic, 429; France, 23; Germany, 321; Poland, 503; Switzerland, 265, 276;
Black Sea, 504
Blitzkrieg, 117, 283, 405, 540
Blood Libel: France, 22; England, 118
Bloom's Restaurant, London, 123, 128-29
Blum, Leon, 27, 72
Board of Deputies, London, 119, 124
Boas (Diamond) Building, Amsterdam, 308-9
Bodleian Library, Oxford, England, 148
Bohemia, 413, 415-21, 425, 432, 444, 449, 451, 453, 459, 466, 503, 552
Boleslav V, the Pious, Duke of Kalisz, 501
Bonaparte, Napoleon, 58, 127, 161, 180, 184, 283, 299, 322, 492
Bonheur, Rosa, 67
Bordeaux, France, 23-24, 68, 79-80, 85, 109, 232
Bornestrasse section, Frankfurt, 345-46

Bousquet, Rene, 61
Brandt, Willy, 527
Bratislava, Slovakia (Pozsony, Pressburg), 459, 483, 486-94; organizations, 493-94; sites, 491-94; synagogues, 493-94
Brighton-Hove, England, 145-46
Briscoe, Benjamin, 156
Briscoe, Robert, 153, 155-56
Brittany, France, 22, 109-11
Brussels: 279-81, 283, 284-87; organizations, 287, 330; restaurants, 285; schools, 286-87; sites, 285-87; synagogues, 286-87
Buchenwald concentration camp, Germany, 260, 273, 351
Buda, Hungary, 459-60, 464-66
Budapest, Hungary, 106, 245, 250, 393, 460-61, 463, 464-480; museums, 463, 468, 477-78; organizations, 468, 479; Rabbinical seminary, 478; restaurants, 480; sites, 465-66, 468-480; synagogues, 468-69, 479
Buda-Pest Tunnel, Budapest, 466
BUND, 507-9, 529
Burgundy, France, 76
Bychowski, Zygmunt, 509

Caballeria, Alfonso de la, 201
Caen, France, 108-9
Canetti, Elias, 248
Cannes, France, 68, 91, 95
Cano, Dr. Maria Jose, 209-10
Cap Ferat, France, 91
Carmelite Convent, Oswiecim, Poland, 511
Carpathian-Russia, 419
Carpentras, France, 23, 86, 90-91

Carter, Jimmy, 527
Casimir the Great, King, 501, 546, 549, 552
Cassin, Rene, 25
Cassuto, Rabbi Natan, 187-88
Catalonia, Spain, 220-21
Catholic church, 23, 58-59, 86, 160-61, 188, 191-93, 195, 197, 199-20, 212-13, 215-16, 237, 417-18, 527, 571-72
Cavaillon, France, 23, 86, 90
CEDOK (Czech-Slovak Travel Agency), 431-32
Cemeteries, Paris, 67
Central Europe, 322, 325, 332, 415, 417, 432, 458, 461, 484, 489, 501, 503-5, 561
Centre National d'Art et de Culture Georges Pompidou, 56
Cervantes, 191, 216
Ceuta, Spain, 199
Cezanne, Paul, 59, 86, 104
Chagall, Marc, 25, 56, 93-94, 276
Chamberlain, Neville, 349, 413
Charles IV, King, Holy Roman Emperor, 429, 432, 434
Charles VI, 429
Chassidim, 270, 289, 344, 506-8, 514, 557
Check Point Charley Museum, Berlin, Germany, 339
Chelmno concentration camp, Poland, 545
Chirac, Jacques, 65-66
Chmielnicki massacres, 24, 504-5
Christianity, 22, 118, 120, 125, 127, 160-61, 178, 184-85, 191-93, 199-202, 203-4, 221, 229-30, 234, 244, 281, 298, 321-22, 325, 358-59

Christians, 191-92, 223, 232, 321, 325, 358
Churchill, Winston, 119, 143-44, 410
Circle Ben Gurion, Brussels, 285
Clifford's Tower of York Castle, York, England, 149
Clinton, Bill, 440, 527
Cohn, Tobias, 508
Colbo bookstore, Paris, 44
Collegio Estrella Toledano, Madrid, 213
Cologne, Germany, 324, 327
Colosseum, Rome, 159-60, 171-72
Columbus Archives of the Indies, Seville, Spain, 199-202
Columbus, Christopher, 193, 196, 199-203, 216
Common Market, 279, 284
Communist Party: Germany, 340-41; Poland, 380, 512, 529, 540, 551, 553, 571
Communists: Czech Republic, 431, 444; Hungary, 462; Slovakia, 491; Poland, 512, 519, 551, 553, 555
Comtat Venaissin, France, 23, 86, 89
Conservative Movement of Judaism, 51, 122, 137-38, 343, 394
Conversos. See New Christians
Copenhagen: 377, 379-88; lodging, 386; organizations, 386; restaurants, 386; sites, 383-85; synagogues, 386
Copernicus, Nicolaus, 561
Cordoba, Spain, 196, 203-9
Corfu, Greece, 177, 212, 359-60
Cossacks, 505
Council of Four Lands, 503, 547

Court Jew(s), 322, 432
Covilha, Portugal, 236-38
Cracow, 497, 512, 417, 520, 544, 548-61
Cremieux Decree, 87, 101
Cremieux, Isaac-Adolphe, 27, 87
Crete, 363
Cromwell, Oliver, 119, 142-43, 152, 298
Crusades, 109, 208, 281, 321, 358
Curtis, Tony, 470
Czech Airlines, 414
Czech Jews,
Czech Republic, 255, 382, 413-55, 484, 586; synagogues, 423, 425-31
Czechoslovakia, 121, 137, 350, 415-21, 423, 425, 431, 446-49, 453, 462, 485, 486, 487, 489, 491
Czerniakow, Adam, 522, 534

D-day beaches, France, 105-6, 108
Dachau concentration camp, Dachau, Germany, 260, 320, 347, 350-53
Danube River, 321, 371, 464-65, 472, 483, 486, 488-89
Danzig (Gdansk) Poland, 549
Dark Ages, 502
Dassin, Jules, 25
David, Israel, 379
Dayan, Moshe, 73
Deauville, France, 109
De Gaulle, Gen. Charles, 73, 97-98
Denmark, 377-87
DeVinney, Timothy, 363
Diaspora, 323, 522, 529
Dijon, France, 23, 76
Dinesohn, Jacob, 534

Disraeli, Benjamin, 122, 134, 141-42
Dnieper River, 50
Doblin, Alfred, 327, 534, 551
Dockworker Statue, Amsterdam, 315-16
Dohany Street Synagogue, Budapest, 468-69, 475
Drancy, France, 63
Drancy Memorial, Drancy, France, 60
Dreyfus, Capt. Alfred, 66-67, 87, 111, 250, 463
Dror Zionist youth movement, 529
Dubcek, Alexander, 448
Dublin: 151-56; sites, 154-56; synagogues, 156
Duckwitz, George, 382
Duehring, Eugen, 323
Dukas, Paul, 25
Dumas, Alexander, 100
Dusseldorf, Germany: 325, 341-43; synagogues, 343
Dutch East Indies Company, 297, 299
Dutch Playhouse, Amsterdam, 315
Dutch West Indies Company, 297, 299
Dymov, Ossip, 517

East Germany, 325, 328, 338, 341, 478-79
Eastern Europe, 22, 38, 58, 120, 245, 284-85, 289-90, 322, 332, 342, 419-21, 446-47, 458, 461, 465, 483-84, 486, 498, 505, 518-19, 537
Eastern European Jews, 27, 231, 245, 247, 272, 277, 284-85, 289, 323-24, 390, 398

Edelman, Marek, 520, 525
Eichmann, Adolf, 253, 380, 420, 425, 450, 488
Einstein, Albert, 267, 327
Eisenberg, Rabbi Paul Chaim, 246-47, 249
Eisenhower, Gen. Dwight D., 73, 108
Eisner, Kurt, 327
El Greco, 191, 213, 222, 224
El Greco Museum, Toledo, Spain, 224
El Transito Synagogue, Toledo, Spain, 224-25
Emanuel Foundation, 470, 472
Endingen, Switzerland, 265
England, 117-49, 218, 265
Ets Haim Library, Amsterdam, 307
European Union, 113, 195, 247, 279, 284, 416, 497

Fabius, Laurent, 27
Farband, Labor Zionist order, 525
Faro, Portugal, 231, 238
Ferdinand I, 417-18, 486
Ferdinand d'Este, Archduke Franz, 451, 462
Ferdinand, King of Spain, 212, 230, 370
Finkelkraut, Alain, 25
Finland, 377, 383, 388, 402-11
Finlandia Hall, Helsinki, Finland, 403
Finnair (Airlines), 403
Finnish, 458
Finno-Ugric, 458
Fischer, Adolf, 245
Fleg, Edmond, 25
Florence, Italy: 164, 183-88; sites, 185-88

France, 21-115, 117, 162, 175, 194-95, 218, 250, 279, 276, 299, 466, 488, 500, 519, 531
France, Anatole, 250
Franco, Francisco, 191, 194-95, 213, 222
Frank, Anne, 71, 295, 301-3, 479
Frank, Anne, House, Amsterdam, 301-3
Frank, Hans, 320, 520, 552
Frank, Jacob, 506
Frankfurt, Germany: 267, 319, 343-48; sites, 344-48; synagogues, 348
French Resistance, 60, 78, 111
French Revolution, 24, 31, 57-59, 80, 87, 89, 91, 109-10, 161, 264-65, 276, 322
Freud Museum, London, 126
Freud Museum, Vienna, 254-56
Freud, Sigmund, 126, 241, 248, 254-56
Freund, Marya, 509
Fried, Alfred Hermann, 248
Friedman, Georges, 25
Friedman, Ignaz, 509

Galata Bridge, Istanbul, 368, 374
Galata Suburb, Istanbul, 372, 373-74, 376
Galata Tower, Istanbul, 368, 373, 375
Gallo-Roman Art Museum, Lyon, France, 78
Gama, Vasco da, 227, 229, 233
Gary, Romain, 25
Gdansk (Danzig), Poland, 512, 573
Gebirtig, Mordechai, 551
Gedaliah, Rabbi Meir ben, 546
Gefen, Moshe, 270-71

Geiger, Rabbi Abraham, 322, 345

Geneva: 263, 264, 265, 271-74; organizations, 274; restaurants, 272; sites, 271-74; synagogues, 272-74

Gerez, Joseph Habib, 373

German Jews, 152, 244, 300, 319-22, 329, 333, 337-39

German Reparations, 326

Germans, 40, 63, 98, 108, 162, 187, 405-7

Germany, 118, 229, 273, 285, 319-55, 416, 423, 438-39, 453, 457, 474-75, 500, 502-3, 514, 520-21, 527, 538, 545, 570

Gero, Erno, 467

Gerona, Spain, 217, 220-22

Gestapo, 162, 166, 253, 259-60, 337, 338, 472, 535, 559

Gestapo Victims Monument, Vienna, 259

Gibraltar, 231

Ginzburg, Natalia, 164

Goeth, Amnon, 560

Goethe, 267, 344

Goethe House, Frankfurt, 344

Golb, Prof. Norman, 106-7

Golden Age of Spain, 191-92, 203

Goldenberg, Jo, 38, 40

Goldenberg's restaurant, Paris, 38, 40

Golders Green, London, 121

Goldfaden, Abraham, 517

Goldmann, Rabbi Alain, 51

Goldschmidt, Meir, 379

Goldsmith family, 120

Golem, 428, 432, 442

Gomulka, Wladyslaw, 540-41

Gonzales, Felipe, 195

Gorbachev, Mikahil, 479

Gordon, Jacob, 518

Gothenburg, Sweden, 388, 390, 395

Granada, Spain, 191, 196, 202, 209-13

Grand Bazaar, Istanbul, 369

Gratitude Monument, Amsterdam, 316

Graz, Austria, 243

Great Britain, 117, 119-27, 127-28, 397, 406, 570

Great Synagogue, Warsaw, 531-35, 537, 540

Greece, 161, 177, 357-67

Greek Jews, 357-61

Gropius Bau, Martin, Berlin, 340

Gruenbaum, Yitzhak, 509

Grunwald, (Battle of Tannenburg) 502

Grynszpan, Herschel, 333

Guarda, Portugal, 236-38

Guggenheim, Dr. Willy, 265, 273

Guggenheim family, 322

Guimard, Hector, 48

Ha Levi, Rabbi Uri, 297

Ha Levi, Yehudah, 192, 204, 208, 223

Habe, Hans, 248

Haber, Georg, 247, 258

Habonim, Labor Zionist youth, 390

Hague, The, Holland: 297, 300, 316; synagogues, 316

Ha-Hozeh, Rabbi Jacob Isaac (Seer of Lublin), 546

Haint (Today), 499

Halkowski, Henryk, 556, 561

Halpern, Bernard, 25

Halter, Marek, 25, 29, 111

Hamburg, Germany, 322
Hamid, Sultan Abdul II, 371
Hapsburgs, 245, 416, 459-60,
    462, 484
Hashomer Hatzair, Zionist youth
    group, 170, 210, 525, 529,
    537
Hatam Sofer, 483, 487, 489-92
Hatam Sofer Mausoleum, 491-92
Hatikvah National Anthem, 413
Havel, Vaclav, 416, 431, 447-48
Hebrew language, 22, 32, 40, 42,
    56, 85, 106-7, 126, 128, 148,
    192, 199, 204, 207, 210, 213,
    255, 270, 272, 290, 339, 384,
    434, 499, 514, 533, 553
Hebrew University, 210
Hechalutz youth movement, 510
Heine, Heinrich, 342-43
Heine Institute, 342-43
Helsinki, Finland: 377, 408-10;
    restaurants, 408; sites, 408,
    410; synagogues, 408, 410
Hemingway, Ernest, 191, 213,
    320, 415
Henry the Navigator, Prince,
    227, 233
Heroes Synagogue, Budapest,
    468
Herzl, Theodor, 66, 67, 123,
    250-51, 267, 269, 349, 371,
    463, 477, 509
Herzog, Chaim, 55, 153-54, 160,
    447, 454
Herzog, Rabbi Isaac, 153-54, 160
Heschel, Rabbi Abraham
    Joshua, 548
Heustein, Shimon, 518
Heydrich, Reinhard, 337, 425,
    450, 547
Hilsner, Leopold, 447

Himmler, Heinrich, 535
Hindemith, Paul, 327
Hirsch, Rabbi Samson Raphael,
    322
Hitler, Adolf, 213, 217, 218, 243,
    246, 252, 260, 319, 323, 326,
    330, 335, 350, 380, 397, 405,
    419, 420, 447, 507-8, 514,
    524, 540, 542
Hohenems, Austria, 257
Holiday Inn, Warsaw, 520
Holland, 231, 279, 281-83, 285,
    295-317, 569
Holocaust: Austria, 243, 252;
    Belgium, 284; Czech
    Republic, 444-47, 449-51, 453-
    54; Denmark, 381-83; France,
    63-66, 74-75, 78, 98, 100-101;
    Germany, 319, 323-24, 330-37,
    341, 345-47, 352-53; Greece,
    361-64, 366; Holland, 300-303;
    Hungary, 462, 470-79; Italy,
    162-63, 166, 169-70, 172, 180,
    187-88; Norway, 397-98, 401;
    Poland, 512, 519-41, 556, 562-
    73; Portugal, 231-32; Slovakia,
    487-89; Switzerland, 273
Honfleur, France, 105
Horowitz, Rabbi Isaiah ben
    Abraham ha Levi, 509
Horthy, Adm. Miklos, 474-76
Hotel Basel Hilton, Basel,
    Switzerland, 269
Hotel Dan, Lugano,
    Switzerland, 270
Hotel de Castille, Paris, 66
Hotel Diplomat, Stockholm, 395
Hotel du Cap, Antibes-Juans-les-
    Pins, France, 97
Hotel du Palais, Biarritz, France,
    81

Hotel Euler Basel, Basel,
    Switzerland, 269
Hotel Grand, Stockholm, 395
Hotel Hilton, Istanbul, 376
Hotel Juana, Antibes-Juans-les-
    Pins, France, 97
Hotel Las Casas de la Juderia,
    Seville, Spain, 197
Hotel Meridien, Nice, France,
    93
Hotel Negresco, Nice, France, 93
Hotel Pera Palas, Istanbul, 376
Hotel Plaza, Nice, France, 93
Hotel Royal Viking, Stockholm,
    395
Hotel Sofitel Splendid, Nice,
    France, 93
Hotel Stefanie, Vienna, 251
Hotel Strand, Stockholm, 391
Hotel Three Kings, Basel,
    Switzerland, 269
Hotel Villa Strand, Hornbaek,
    Denmark, 386
Hove, England: 145-46; lodging,
    146; synagogues, 145
Hradcany Castle, (Prague
    Castle) Prague, 445-48, 450
Hugo, Victor, 49
Hungarian Jews, 232, 393-94,
    458-63
Hungarian Revolution, 247, 459,
    478
Hungarians, 457-61
Hungary, 163, 194, 248, 273,
    389, 418, 450, 457-80, 484-89,
    492
Hus, Jan, 417, 444
Hymans, Max, 25

Iberia, 191, 199, 227, 359, 375,
    502

Ibn Ezra, Moses, 192, 208
Ibn Gabirol, Solomon, 192, 209
Ibn Nagrela, Joseph, 211-12
Ibn Nagrela, Samuel, 209, 211
Ibn Ziyad, Tarik, 192
Ikor, Roger, 25
Innsbruck, Austria, 243
Inquisition: Italy, 160; Portugal,
    230-31, 233-35; Spain, 191,
    192-93, 195, 197, 202
Inter-Continental Hotel, Paris,
    68; Prague, 432
Ionesco, Eugene, 25
Iran, 543
Ireland: 151-56; sites, 154-56;
    synagogues, 156
Isaac the Blind Center, Gerona,
    Spain, 221
Isabella of Spain, 212, 230, 370
Isak, Aaron, 388
Islam, 506
Israel, 59, 60, 67, 153, 171, 195,
    199, 228-29, 231, 247, 267,
    325-26, 358, 361, 371, 372,
    381, 390, 398, 407, 413, 420,
    431, 469, 475, 483, 491, 497-
    98, 511, 518, 526, 528, 540-41
Israelsplads, Copenhagen, 380-81
Isserles, Rabbi Moses ben Israel,
    502, 509, 550, 555
Istanbul: 193, 369-76;
    Constantinople, 549; syna-
    gogues, 374-76
Italy, 23, 86-87, 159-88, 193, 229,
    282, 519

Jabotinsky, Vladimir Ze'ev, 155,
    404, 507
Jacob, François, 25
Jaffe, Rabbi Mordechai ben
    Abraham, 509, 546

Jagiello, Casimir IV, King, 502
Jagiello, Grand Duke of Lithuania, 502
Jagiellonian University, Cracow, 561
Jakobson, Max, 408
Janner, Grenville, 123
Japan, 570
Jawiga, Princess, 502
Jerusalem, 22, 142, 171, 187, 207-8, 210, 306, 381, 399, 428, 492, 527
Jessel, Sir George, 122
Jewish Art Museum, Paris, 56
Jewish Brigade, 144, 171, 188, 543
Jewish cemetery, Warsaw, 533-34
Jewish Chronicle, London, 122
Jewish community centers, Paris, 53-55
Jewish Documentation Center, Vienna, 253-54
Jewish Fighting Organization (Z.O.B.), 523, 525, 529, 531
Jewish Historical Institute, 534-41
Jewish Military Union (ZZW), 531
Jewish museums: Amsterdam, 301-3, 309-15; Athens, 363-64; Basel, 269-70; Berlin, 333, 339-40; Brussels, 286; Budapest, 463, 468; Dublin, 154-56; Frankfurt, 346-47; London, 124-26; Munich, 350; Paris, 56; Prague, 425, 430-31, 434-39, 444-45; Rome, 169-70; Stockholm, 391, 393; Vienna, 253-54, 256-58; Warsaw, 552
Jewish police force, 522, 532
Jewish Prague, 421-45

Jewish Renewal, France, 28
Jewish Town Hall, Prague, 423-24, 430-31, 435, 437
Jewish Town, Prague (Old Jewish Town, Josefov, Prague Ghetto), 422-32, 434-40, 442, 444, 446
Jewish War Victims Memorial, Oslo, Norway, 401
Jewish War Victims Memorial, Trondheim, Norway, 402
Jewish Welcome Service, Vienna, 251-52
Jews, Algeria, 28, 87, 97, 101-2, 110-11
Jews, Morocco, 199
Jews, North Africa, 54, 99, 101, 105
Joan of Arc, 71-73, 106
Jodenbuurt section, Amsterdam, 303-5
John Paul II, Pope, 169-70, 527, 572
Joseph II of Austria, Emperor, 244, 418, 421, 486
Joseph, Franz, Emperor, 241, 460
Joskowitz, Harry, 537
Joskowitz, Rabbi, 515
Joyce, James, 151, 155, 267
Juans-les-Pins, France, 86, 91, 97
Judaica House, Stockholm, 391
Judenrat, 522, 534
Juiverie, Paris, 36

Kabbala, 221, 359, 371, 442, 498, 505
Kadoorie family, 240
Kadoorie Synagogue, Oporto, Portugal, 240
Kafka, Franz, 248, 421, 445, 449
Kahan, Herman, 396, 399

Kahane's Book Store, Bernard, 290
Kahn, Claude, 25
Kalisz Statutes, 501
Kaminska, Esther Rachel, 517-18, 534
Kaminska, Ida, 517
Kara, Rabbi Avigdor, 429, 440
Karo, Rabbi Joseph, 358, 371, 555, 556
Katowice, Poland, 510, 512, 573
Katznelson, Itzhak, 531
Kazimierz section, Cracow, 548-61
Kessel, Joseph, 25
Kibbutz Lohamei ha Gettaot, Israel, 525
Kibbutz Yad Mordechai, Israel, 526
Kielce, Poland, 548
Klausfield, Beate, 78
Klee, Paul, 264, 267, 349
Klemperer, Otto, 327
Klepfisz, Michael, 529
Klima, Ivan, 451
Koestler, Arthur, 248, 463
Kohl, Helmut, 326-27
Koppelman, Rabbi Jacob ben Samuel Bunim, 546
Korczak, Janusz (Henryk Goldszmidt), 531-33, 544
Korona Hotel, Budapest, 480
Kozielewski, Jan ("Karski"), 539
Krajewski, Stanislaw, 519
Kreisky, Bruno, 254
Kreisler, Fritz, 327
Kriegel, Frantisek, 448
Kristallnacht, 250, 332, 333, 345, 346, 395
Kun, Bela, 462-63, 467
Kurfürstendamm, Berlin, 330, 333
Kyra, Esther, 374

L'Isle-sur-la-Sorges, 23, 86
La Rochelle, France, 24
La Scala Opera House, Milan, 174
Labor Zionists, 551, 555
Ladino language, 359, 365, 373, 384
Lake Lugano, 270
Landowska, Wanda, 509
Landwehr Canal, Berlin, 340-41
Lang, Jack, 27
Lanzmann, Claude, 25
Lauder Foundation, Ronald S., 479, 511-12, 517, 535, 541, 549, 553, 555, 573
Lausanne, Switzerland, 263-64, 265
Lazare, Bernard, 87
Le Grand Hotel, Paris, 68
Le Havre, France, 23, 108, 109
Le Warwick Hotel, Paris, 68
League of Nations, 121, 271
Lebron Hotel, Paris, 44
Lee, Trygve, 398
Lelouch, Claude, 25
Lenin, Nikolai, 277, 328
Lessing, Gotthold Ephraim, 331, 347
Levi, Bernard-Henri, 25
Levi, Carlo, 164
Levi, David, 187
Levi, Primo, 164
Levi-Strauss, Claude, 25
Lewisohn family, 321
Liberal synagogues: Amsterdam, 308; Brussels, 286; Geneva, 272; London, 135-38; Marseilles, 103; Nice, 94; Paris, 49-51; Stockholm, 393; Zurich, 277
Libya, 174

Libyan Jews, 174
Lidice, Czech Republic, 547
Liebknecht, Karl, 340-41
limpieza de sangre, 193
Lincoln Brigade, 191
Linz, Austria, 243
Lippman, Gabriel, 25
Lippmann Heller, Rabbi Yom Tov, 509, 556
Lisbon: 232, 233-36; organizations, 235-36; restaurants, 235; synagogues, 235-36
Lithuania, 501-2, 510
Lithuanian Jews, 503
Lithuanian Union, 501-2
Little Dunkirk, Copenhagen, 381-82
Lodz, Poland, 512, 525, 535, 545, 551
Loew, Rabbi Judah ben Bezalel, 428, 432, 437, 442-44
Loewi, Otto, 248
Loire, France, 22, 70, 72
London: 117-24, 145, 147, 463, 465, 529, 538; museums and libraries, 139-41; organizations, 139; other sites, 141-45; restaurants, 128-31; sites, 124-28; synagogues, 131-38
London Museum of Jewish Life, 128
Longfus, Anna, 25
Lorient, France, 111
Lorraine, France, 23-24, 73, 74, 75, 109
Lubavitch: Belgium, 287, 289; England, 139, 148; France, 44, 52, 53, 75, 79, 84, 93, 94; Germany, 350; Holland, 308; Italy, 170, 176; Poland, 512; Slovakia, 494; Spain, 215-16;

Switzerland, 277
Lublin, Poland, 503, 512, 520, 543, 544, 545-47
Lublin yeshiva, 545-46
Lucerne, Switzerland, 265
Lueger, Dr. Karl, 323, 460
Lugano, Switzerland: 270-71; lodging, 270; synagogues, 271
Lurel, Armand, 25
Luria, Rabbi Solomon, Maharshal, 509, 546
Luther, Martin, 418
Lutz, Charles, 474, 476
Luxemburg, Rosa, 340-41, 510
Luzzatti, Luigi, 164
Lvov, Ukraine, 549
Lwoff, Andre, 25
Lyon, France, 68, 76-77; restaurants, 78-79; sites, 78; synagogues, 79, 102, 110

Maccabee, Judah, 160, 386
McCloy, John, 324, 326
Madagascar, 508
Madeira, Spain, 125
Madrid: 193, 194, 213-16; museums, 216; organizations, 215-16; sites, 213-14; synagogues, 214-15
Maeght Foundation, 94
Magyar Israel, 487
Magyars, 416, 458-60, 465, 467
Mahler, Gustav, 421
Maimon, Rabbi Moses ben. *See* Maimonides
Maimonides, 54, 182, 192, 205, 207-208, 209, 220, 384
Maimonides Synagogue, Barcelona, 218-20
Mainz, Germany, 49

Maisel, Marcus Mordechai, 432, 435, 437-39, 442
Maison France Israel, Paris, 55
Majdanek concentration camp, Poland, 544, 547
Mala Strana, Prague, 422
Malaga, Spain, 199, 210
Malka, Victor, 25, 111
Malmö, Sweden, 390, 395
Malraux, Clara, 25
Manchester, England, 146-47
Mandel, Georges, 25
Manger, Isaac, 511
Manin, Daniele, 161
Mann, Thomas, 267, 349
Mannerheim, Marshall Carl G., 406, 410
Mannerheim Museum, 410
Manor House, London, 128
Marais section, Paris, 38, 42, 56
Marceaux, Marcel, 25
March of the Living, 499, 571
Marmertine Prison, Rome, 166
Marr, Wilhelm, 323
Marranos, 23-24, 79-81, 143, 152, 161, 192, 197-99, 200-201, 230-35, 236-40, 237-38, 240, 282, 285, 295, 297, 298, 379
Marriott Hotel, Warsaw, 497, 537
Marseilles, France: 22-23, 86, 99-104; sites, 102-4; synagogues, 102-4
Masaryk, Thomas Garrigue, 446-47, 485
Masliah, Leon, 51
Masorati synagogues, 51
Maurois, Andre, 25
Mausoleo della Fosse Ardeatine Fine, Rome, 166

Mauthausen concentration camp, Mauthausen-Marbach, Austria, 253, 259-60
Mayer, Daniel, 27
Mayer, Rene, 27
Mazovia, Poland, 513
Medem, Vladimir, 509
Medici, 184
Mediterranean Sea, 85-86, 97, 99, 100, 174, 199, 217, 220
Meir, Golda, 73, 263
Meisels, Rabbi Dov Berush, 559
Melchior, Arne, 383
Melchior, Dr. Marcus, 381, 383, 399
Melchior, Rabbi Bent, 382-83
Melchior, Rabbi Michael, 383, 399
Memmi, Albert, 25
Memorial sites, Paris, 63
Mendelssohn family, 322
Mendelssohn, Moses, 331, 347
Mendes-France, Pierre, 27, 71
Mengele, Dr. Joseph, 499, 565, 567
Menton, France, 91,
Metz, France, 22, 321
Michelangelo, 183
Middle Ages, 106-7, 192, 223, 498, 521
Mila 18, Warsaw, 525, 529-31
Milan, Italy: 161, 173-77, 271; organizations, 176, 271; restaurants, 176; synagogues and day schools, 176
Milhaud, Darius, 25, 104
Mitterrand, François, 40, 55, 100
Mocatta, Abraham, 140-41
Mocatta Library and Museum, London, 140-41

Moczar, Mieczyslaw, 541
Modigliani, Amedeo, 25, 55-56, 59, 164
Mohacs, Hungary, 418, 486
Moldau, 413
Molotov-Ribbentrop Pact, 405, 540, 542
Mongols, 458, 501
Monte Carlo, 91-92, 95
Montefiore, Sir Moses, 122, 127, 142
Montpellier, 82-84, 85
Moors, 191, 199, 202, 204, 205, 211, 222, 297
Moravia, Alberto, 164
Moravia, Czech Republic, 255, 415, 418-20, 425, 432, 444, 449, 451, 459, 466, 487
Morocco, 54, 99, 101, 199, 210, 215
Moscow, Russia, 316, 328, 393, 463, 500, 504, 542
Moslems, 191-93, 203-4, 211-13, 230-31
Moulon, Jean, 78
Mountain of the Jews, Barcelona, 218
Moyne, Lord, 121
Mulhouse, France, 23
Munich, Germany: 319, 348-53; Dachau concentration camp, 350-53; sites, 350; synagogues, 350
Munich Pact, 349, 415, 419, 476, 487, 508
Murad, Sultan III, 374
Musée Arlaten, Arles, France, 89
Musée Basque de Bayonne, France, 81
Musée Carnavalet, Paris, 56-57
Musée Cluny, Paris, 59

Musée d'Orsay, Paris, 59
Musée de Bretagne, Rennes, France, 109
Musée de la Resistance, Lyon, France, 78
Musée des Beaux Arts, Rennes, France, 109
Musée des Beaux Arts, Tours, France, 72
Musée du Louvre, Paris, 59
Musée Fabre, Montpellier, France, 82, 84
Musée Judéo-Contadin, Cavaillon, France, 90
Musée Picasso, Antibes, France, 97
Museum of the Jewish East End, London, 141
Museums, Florence, 188
Museums, Paris, 56-60
Mussolini, Benito, 162, 164, 180
Myers, Rabbi Baruch, 483, 493-94

Nachmanides, 217, 221-22
Nagy, Imre, 478
Nantes, France, 24, 71, 109-11
Narbonne, France, 22, 85
Narrowe, Rabbi Morton H., 393, 394
Nathan, Ernesto, 164
Nathanson, Mendel Levin, 380
National Museum Biblical Message of Marc Chagall, 93-94
NATO, 279, 284, 416
Natzweiler-Struthof concentration camp, 74-75
Nazis, 27, 63, 65, 66, 74, 78, 97-98, 126, 144, 162, 166, 169, 172, 180, 187, 194, 243, 245-

46, 250, 252, 253-55, 258-60,
273, 283-84, 300-301, 311,
315, 320, 323-25, 327, 340-41,
345, 347-48, 364, 366, 380-82,
384, 389, 390, 397, 405-6,
415, 425, 429, 434-35, 448-54,
469-77, 483, 485, 487, 499,
508, 512, 515, 518-24, 527,
538-40, 545-47, 551, 559, 563,
571-72

Neo-Nazi, 325-26, 328

New Christians, 192-93, 203,
223-25, 234-35, 282

New York, 106, 231, 264, 276,
299, 331, 377, 519, 549

Newport, Rhode Island, 231

Nice, France: 68, 93-95; sites, 94-
95; synagogues, 91, 102

Nimes, France, 85, 87

Nissenbaum, Rabbi Yitzhak, 531

Nordau, Max, 193, 463

Normandy, France, 105-9

North Africa, 21, 54, 101, 110,
161, 214, 235-36, 272

Norway, 377, 388, 389, 396-402

Norwich, England, 22

Nozyk Synagogue, Warsaw, 515,
517

Obuda, Hungary, 465-66

Odessa, Crimea, 514

Offenbach, Jacques, 25, 327

Oktoberfest, Munich, Germany,
349

Olbracht, King Jan, 549

Old Jewish Cemetery, Prague,
424, 429, 435, 437

Old Jewry Street, London, 118

Old Town, Prague, 415, 423, 445

Olivetti, Camillo, 164

Operation Reinhard, 547

Oporto, Portugal, 238-40

Oppenheimer, Joseph, 322

Oppenheimer, Samuel, 244,
322

Orleans, France, 71

Oslo, Norway: 364, 377, 383,
398-402; memorials, 401-2;
sites, 399-402; synagogue,
399-401

Ostia Antica, Italy, 173

Oswiecim, Poland, 562

Ottokar, II, Premysl, 427

Ottoman Empire, 359, 370, 373,
374, 459-60

Oxford, England: 147-48; synagogues, 148

Oxford Center for Post-
Graduate Hebrew Studies,
147-48

Palace of Culture and Science,
Warsaw, 542-43

Palace of Justice, Rouen,
France, 106

Pale of Settlement, Poland-
Russia, 498, 507

Palestine, 28, 100, 126, 144, 162,
324, 366, 368, 487, 508, 510,
524

Papon, Maurice, 61

Paris: 22, 24, 29-36, 415, 421,
463; cemeteries, 67, 77; community centers, 53-55; lodging, 44; memorial sites, 60-66;
museums, 56-60; officials and
organizations, 51-55; restaurants, 36-44; sites, 32-36, 63-
67; synagogues, 44-51, 82

Parmet, Dr. Simon, 408

Patterson, Dr. David, 148

Patton, Gen. George, 108

Pau, France, 82
Pawlak, Dr. Grazyna, 535, 537
Pera section, Istanbul, 373-74
Père Lechaise cemetery, 67
Peretz, Isaac L., 510-11, 534
Pest, Hungary, 461
Petticoat Lane, London, 122-23
Piazza Navona, 171-72
Picasso, Pablo, 91-93
Pilsudski, Marshal Jozef, 508, 561
Pissarro, Camille, 25, 56, 59
Pittsburgh Pact, 446, 485
Pittsburgh, Pennsylvania, 464
Pius XII, Pope, 162, 172
Plantin Moretus Museum,
    Antwerp, Belgium, 290-91
Pletzel section of Paris, 32-42, 56
Pogroms: Czech Republic, 427,
    429; Hungary, 458, 475, 508
Poitiers, France, 23
Poland, 24, 121, 146, 270, 332,
    352, 364, 390, 416, 450, 467,
    484-85, 497-573
Polane, 501
Poles, 485, 505, 522, 529, 538-
    39, 542-43, 553, 563, 570
Polish Council of Christians and
    Jews, 519
Polish Jews, 246, 289, 348, 380,
    386, 389-90, 497-500, 501-12,
    513-15, 515-19, 541, 545-61,
    573
Polish language, 499, 533, 544
Polish Uprising, 514, 522, 542
Pollak, Rabbi Jacob ben Joseph,
    546
Pope(s), 23, 86-87, 162, 172, 175
"Pope's Jews," 23, 86
Portugal: 21, 79-81, 193-94, 212,
    227-40, 389; Inquisition, 230-
    31, 229-31, 378

Portuguese, 229-32, 234-35
Portuguese Jews, 23, 57, 79-81,
    152, 229-35, 359
"Portuguese Nation," 23, 80-81,
    235
Portuguese Synagogue,
    Amsterdam, 304-7, 309
Prado Museum, Madrid, 216
Praga, Warsaw, 513
Prague: Czech Republic, 137,
    220, 332, 413-51, 552-53, 561;
    cemeteries, 424, 429, 435-37,
    440-43, 445; community cen-
    ters, 423-24, 430-31, 435, 437;
    memorial sites, 445; muse-
    ums, 137, 425, 430-31, 434-39,
    444-45; officials and organiza-
    tions, 423-24, 430-31; restau-
    rants, 431; sites, 423-49; syna-
    gogues, 425-30, 434-39, 443-45
Prague Haggadah, 417
Prague Show Trials, 420-21
Prague Spring, 421, 448-49, 491
Proust, Marcel, 25, 57, 67, 343
Provence, 85-86, 104
Prussia, 127, 322, 500, 513
Pyrenees, 23, 85, 194

Quai d'Orsay, Paris, 100
Quebec, Canada, 105
Quisling, Vidkun, 397

Rabbinical Council of America,
    384
Rabin, Yitzhak, 254
Rachel, 25, 57, 67
Radom, Poland, 520
Rakosi, Malyas, 467
Rambam. See Maimonides
Rapoport, Nathan, 259, 527
Rashi, 22, 49, 86, 353

Rashi Chapel, Worms, Germany, 353

Rashi House, Worms, Germany, 353

Rashi Synagogue, Worms, Germany, 353

Rath, Ernest vom, 333

Rathenau House, 337

Rathenau, Walter, 337

Reform Movement of Judaism, 128, 135, 138, 286, 322, 345, 492

Regine, 25

Reichstag, Berlin, 322, 335

Reik, Theodor, 248

Reims, France, 73

Reinhardt, Max, 247

Reisner, Yale, 535-36

Religious Zionists, 531

Remarque, Eric Maria, 267

Rembrandt, 295, 313-15

Rembrandt House Museum, Amsterdam, 313-15

Remuh Synagogue, Cracow, 550, 552, 554-56

Rennes, France, 109-11

Recife, Brazil, 231

Resistance Museum, Amsterdam, 315

Resistance Museum, Copenhagen, 383-84

Resistance Museum, Oslo, Norway, 401-2

Reuveni, David, 179

Revisionist Zionist Party, 155, 507, 510, 551

Rhine River, 321, 342

Rhineland, 417

Rhodes, 358, 363

Rhone River, 321

Richer, rue, Paris, 33, 42-43

Rijksmuseum, Amsterdam, 315

Ringelblum, Emmanuel, 529, 531, 535

Risorgimento, 161

Riviera, France, 91-99

Rocard, Michel, 40

Rome: 164-73; ghetto, 164-66; museums, 169-71; organizations, 167-70, 330; restaurants, 166-67; sites, 164-71; synagogues, 167-70

Roosevelt, Franklin D., 144, 539

Rosiers, rue de, 32, 36, 38, 40, 42

Rossio Square, Lisbon, 233

Rothschild, Alain, 46

Rothschild, Amschel, 46

Rothschild, David, 46

Rothschild, Elie, 48

Rothschild, Guy, 46

Rothschild, James Jacob, 46, 48, 127

Rothschild, Karl Mayer, 46

Rothschild, Leon, 399

Rothschild, Lionel Nathan, 120, 127, 153

Rothschild, Mayer Amschel, 46, 127, 345

Rothschild, N. M., office of, 127-28

Rothschild, Nathan Mayer, 46

Rothschild, Nathaniel Mayer, 127

Rothschild, Solomon Mayer, 46

Rothschilds, 44, 46, 48, 67, 120, 126, 127-28, 142, 322, 344-45

Rotterdam, Holland, 297, 316

Rouen, France, 23, 106-8

Rubinstein, Arthur, 509

Rudin, Rabbi A. James, 563, 570-71

Rudolf, II, King, Holy Roman Emporer, 432, 438-39, 442
Rundsztein, Lazar, 509
Russek, Joachim, 557
Russia, 127, 146, 250, 403-7, 458, 463, 475, 491, 497-98, 500, 507, 510, 513, 520, 540, 542, 545, 548, 559, 561
Russo-Finnish Continuation War, 405-6
Russo-Finnish Winter War, 404-6, 410

St-Etienne, France, 85
St-Jean-de-Luz, France, 68, 82
St-Lô, France, 108
St-Malo, France, 68, 111
St-Nazare, France, 111
St-Tropez, France, 68, 91, 95
Salomons, Sir David, 122
Salonika, Greece: 193, 358, 359, 365-67; synagogues, 367
Salzburg, Austria, 243
Samuel, Herbert, 122
Sanchez, Gabriel, 200, 201
Sanhedrin, 58
Santa Cruz section, Seville, Spain, 197-98
Santa Maria la Blanca, Toledo, Spain, 224
Santangel, Luis de, 199-201
Sassoon, Siegfried, 122
Saumur, France, 70
Scandinavia, 377-411
Schechter, Solomon, 122
Scheldt River, 287, 299
Schindler's List, 254, 559-60
Schlegel, Dorothea, 331
Schoenerer, Georg Von, 323
Schorr, Prof. Mojzesz, 509
Schudrich, Rabbi Michael, 512

Schwartz, Rabbi Uri, 383
Schwartz, Samuel, 237-38
Schwarz-Bart, Andre, 25
Seneor, Abraham, 200, 212
Sepharad (Spain), 192
Sephardic cemetery, Paris, 67
Sephardic Jews, 21, 24, 28, 52-55, 57, 67, 70, 79, 85, 89, 93, 97, 99-102, 107, 119, 124, 152, 159, 187, 191-93, 202-3, 213-16, 217, 223-25, 235-36, 265, 297, 305, 359, 361, 363, 365-66
Sephardic Museum and Library, Toledo, Spain, 225
Seville, Spain: 193, 196-203; sites, 199-203
Shaare Tikvah Synagogue, Lisbon, 235-36
Shulhan Arukh, 371
Sibelius, Jean Memorial, Helsinki, Finland, 403
Siberia, 507
Sidon, Rabbi Karol, 431
Sigismund III, King,
Singer, Isaac Bashevis, 510
Singer, I. J., 510
Sistine Chapel, Rome, 173
Sitruk, Joseph, Chief Rabbi of France, 51
Six Day War, 540
Skansen Outdoor Museum, Stockholm, 391
Slansky, Rudolf, 420-21
Slovak Jews, 450, 483-89, 491-94
Slovakia, 415-16, 419-20, 425, 450, 457, 476, 483-94
Slovaks, 415, 425, 446, 457, 484-86, 489
Smetna, 413
Sobibor concentration camp, 544, 547

Socialists, 164, 462, 551; under Spain, expulsion, 161, 193, 195, 197, 199-203, 212-15, 217-18, 223, 226, 235, 295, 503

Soforim, Mendele Mokher, 510, 517

Sohar Kosher Restaurant, Frankfurt, 344, 346

Sokolow, Nahum, 510

Solidarity, 527

Soviet Army (Red Army) 335, 393, 404, 448, 474, 476, 514, 543, 561, 563, 570-71

Soviet Jews, 153, 324, 328, 330, 338

Soviet Union, 393, 405-6, 474-75, 500-1, 539-40, 542-43

Spain: 21, 79, 80, 81, 82, 161, 191-226, 232, 502-3; civil war, 191, 194, 213, 222; Golden Age, 191-92, 203; Inquisition, 191, 197, 201-3, 359, 365

Spanish Civil War, 213, 218, 222

Spanish Inquisition, 23, 80, 191, 193, 197, 202

Spinoza, Baruch, 205, 231, 297, 305

Spitz, Rabbi Solomon, 518-19, 542-43, 545

Stadttempel synagogue, Vienna, 249-50

Stalin, Joseph, 459, 463, 476, 540, 543

Stalingrad, 475, 514

Stalinism, 541

Stavroulakis, Nikos, 354, 363-64

Stein, Gertrude, 67

Sternberg Centre for Judaism, 128

Stockholm, 377, 388, 389-94, 398

Stoleru, Lionel, 27, 55

Strait of Gibraltar, 192

Strasbourg, 23, 68, 73-76, 110

Stroop, Jurgen, 526, 535

Sulzer, Solomon, 247, 257

Susona Street, Seville, Spain, 197

Sweden, 377, 382, 388-95, 397-98, 404, 406

Switzerland: 175, 263-78; restaurants, 277-78

Synagogues: Austria, 249-51; Belgium, 286-87, 292; Denmark, 386; England, 131-38, 140; Finland, 408-10; France, 44-51, 70-76, 79-85, 87, 94, 95, 97-99, 102, 104, 112; Germany, 337-39, 343, 348, 350; Greece, 361-63, 367; Holland, 305-8, 316; Italy, 167-69, 170, 176, 181-83, 185; Norway, 398-401; Portugal, 235-36, 240; Spain, 214-15, 218-20; Sweden, 393-95; Switzerland, 269, 271, 272-74, 277; Turkey, 374-76

Szenes, Channa, 469

Szilard, Leo, 462

T.G.V. train, 86, 110

Talmud, 21, 49, 54-55, 84, 169, 204-5, 221

Tartars, 416

Teller, Edward, 462

Temple Victoire, Paris, 44, 46, 48

Theresa, Maria, 244, 418, 449, 460

Theresienstadt (Terezin) concentration camp, 260, 382, 437, 449-54

Third Reich, 243, 259, 316, 319, 340

Thon, Rabbi Osjasz, 534, 556, 557
Three Kings Hotel, Basel,
    Switzerland, 269
Tiberias, Israel, 371
Tiberias Square, Cordoba,
    Spain, 203, 205
Tiso, Monsignor Jozef, 420, 487,
    489
Titus, 171
Titus, Arch of, Rome, 171
Tivoli, Copenhagen, 379
Toaff, Rabbi Elio, 163, 170
Toledo, Spain: 208, 222-25; syna-
    gogues, 224-25
Toleranzpatent: Austria, 244;
    Czech Republic, 418-19;
    Hungary, 460
Tolkin, Wiktor, 547
Toller, Ernest, 327
Topas restaurant, Basel,
    Switzerland, 269
Torah, 97, 169
Torquemada, Tomas de, 193,
    203, 212
Torres, Luis de, 201
Toulon, France, 91
Toulouse, France, 23, 84-85
Touraine, France, 70
Tours, France, 72
Touvier, Paul, 61
Town Hall, Prague, 442-43
Trastevere section, Rome, 165
Treblinka concentration camp,
    Poland, 460, 521-22, 524, 531-
    32, 543-45, 547
Treitschke, Joseph von, 323
Trondheim, Norway, 396, 398, 402
Troyes, France, 49
Tucholsky, Kurt, 327
Tudela, Benjamin of, 13, 86, 89,
    359, 367

Tunisia, 99-100
Turkey, 161, 177, 193, 217, 281,
    359, 365, 369-76
Turks, 244, 322, 361-72, 506
Turku, Finland, 403, 404, 407,
    411
Tuwim, Julian, 510

Ukraine, 24, 457, 475, 503-5, 549
Umschlagplatz, Warsaw, 528,
    531-33
United Nations, 171, 408
United States, 24, 30, 48, 102,
    123, 324, 389, 390, 458, 484,
    498, 507, 511
United Synagogue, England,
    120, 135
U.S.S.R., 145, 337, 349, 397, 405-
    7, 415, 421, 459, 463, 472,
    474, 497, 540, 570
Uziel, Rabbi Isaac, 125-26, 297

Van Gogh, Vincent, 59, 86, 89,
    295
Vanni, Sam, 408
Vargas, Imre, 470
Varnhagen, Rahel, 331
Vatican, 154, 158, 162, 170, 172,
    173, 195, 215
Vatican Library, 106
Veil, Simone, 27, 40
Velodrome d'Hiver Stadium,
    Paris, 65-66
Velvet Revolution, 416, 448-49,
    453
Venice, Italy: 161, 164, 177-83;
    ghetto, 171-77; synagogues,
    181-83, 212, 231
Vichy French government, 27,
    61-63, 65-66
Vienna: 126, 241, 243-60, 419,

460, 463, 464, 472, 489, 511, 556; cemeteries, 248-49; memorial sites, 259-60; museums, 253-58; organizations, 251-53; restaurants, 249; sites, 248-60; synagogues, 249-51
Vigeland Sculpture Park, Oslo, Norway, 398
Vilna, Lithuania, 509, 518
Vistula River, Poland, 500, 513, 560, 563
Vittel concentration camp, France, 531
Vltava River, Poland, 413, 423, 446
Vyborg, Finland, 404

Wagg House, Amsterdam, 311
Waldheim, Kurt, 243, 247, 254, 408
Wallenberg Monument, Budapest, 472
Wallenberg Park for Righteous Hungarians, Budapest, 470
Wallenberg Park, Stockholm, 393
Wallenberg, Raoul, 389, 391, 393, 394, 470-74
Wallenberg Room, Stockholm, 394
Waltenberger, Johann, 352-53
Walter, Bruno, 327
Wannsee Memorial, 336-37
Warburg family, 322
Warsaw Ghetto, 65, 499, 518, 519-39, 544
Warsaw Ghetto Memorial to the Victims of the Warsaw Ghetto Uprising, 259, 526-29, 559
Warsaw Ghetto Uprising, 499, 510, 515, 520, 522-535, 538

Warsaw Jews, 513
Warsaw, Old Town, 513
Warsaw Pact, 448-49
Warsaw, Poland, 316, 415, 497-99, 512, 513-545, 549, 561
Wasserman, Jakob, 327
Waterloo, Belgium, 127, 161, 279, 283
Waterlooplein section, Amsterdam, 303
Wawel Castle, Cracow, 520, 561
Weeping Willow Memorial Tree, Budapest, 470
Weill, Kurt, 327
Weimar Republic of Germany, 344
Weiss, Rabbi Andor, 470
Weizmann, Chaim, 139-40, 146
Wenceslas Square, Prague, 415, 423, 447-49
Werfel, Franz, 248
Wergeland Monument, Oslo, Norway, 402
Wertenschlag, Rabbi Richard, 79
Wertheimer, Samson, 244
Westerbork camp, Holland, 309, 569
Western Europe, 160, 243, 245, 312, 485, 488, 502-3
Westminster Abbey, 117, 141
Westminster Hotel, Paris, 68
White Mountain, Czech Republic, 418
White Paper, 144
White Rose Movement, 340
Wiesel, Elie, 25, 432, 442-43, 539, 563, 571
Wiesenthal, Simon, 245, 253-55, 303, 309, 366
Wilder, Billy, 247
Wilner, Arie, 529

Wingate and Chindit Memorial, London, 144
Wingate, Maj. Gen. Orde, 144
Woburn House, London, 124-26
World Jewish Congress, 271, 468
World War I, 120, 142, 167, 194, 217, 279, 283, 319, 371, 389, 484, 501, 507, 513, 561
World War II, 64-65, 84, 100-101, 106, 111, 117, 120-21, 144, 169-70, 174, 180, 183, 187-88, 195, 213-14, 232, 246, 254, 264, 272, 279, 283, 290, 300, 308, 312, 319, 389, 459, 474-78, 484, 502, 508-10, 513, 535, 538, 542, 550-52, 556
World Zionist Congress, 267, 300, 349
World Zionist Organization, 267, 272, 407, 463
Worms, Germany, 49, 321, 353, 443, 553
Wroclaw, Poland, 512, 573

Yad Vashem Museum, Israel, 527
Yalta Conference, 543
Yarnton Manor, England, 147-48
Yiddish language, 22, 28-29, 32, 36, 40, 56, 85, 120, 123, 128, 159, 270, 297, 350, 384, 419, 499-500, 533, 544, 549, 553

Yiddish Theater, Warsaw, 514, 517-18
York, England, 149
Yosef, Ovadia, Sephardic Chief Rabbi, 213
Young Turks, 371
Ypres, Belgium, 279
Yugoslavia, 361, 570

Zacuto, Abraham, 202, 233
Zamenhof, Dr. Ludwig, 527
Zangwill, Israel, 267
Zehrfuss, Bernard, 78
Zelman, Dr. Leon, 251-52
Zevi, Shabbetai, 365, 371, 375, 505-6
Zionism, 66, 67, 139, 151, 250, 267, 300, 323, 413, 421, 469, 487, 489, 507, 509-10
Zionist, 52, 67, 140, 144, 323, 351
Zohar, 192
Zola, Emile, 66-67, 104, 111, 250
Zuckerman, Yitzhak, "Antek," 523, 538
Zurich, 263-65, 274-77; restaurants, 277; sites, 276-77; synagogues, 277
Zweig, Arnold, 327
Zweig, Stefan, 67, 243, 248, 267
Zygielbojm, Samuel, 528-29
Zykon-B gas, 547, 567, 571
Zyskowicz, Ben, 408